Data Engineering with AWS

A practical guide to building scalable and secure enterprise data platforms

Sanjiv Kumar Jha

bpb

www.bpbonline.com

First Edition 2025

Copyright © BPB Publications, India

ISBN: 978-93-65890-969

To View Complete
BPB Publications Catalogue
Scan the QR Code:

Dedicated to

My beloved parents:

Sh. Hit Narayan Jha

Smt. Premlata Jha

and

My wife Madhulika and my son Pratulya

About the Author

Sanjiv Kumar Jha is a distinguished technology leader and data science expert with over 25 years of experience architecting and implementing large-scale data solutions. Currently serving as principal solution architect at **Amazon Web Services (AWS)**, he specializes in guiding enterprise clients through complex cloud transformations with a focus on data science, AI/ML, IoT, and geospatial technologies. His career spans pivotal roles including chief data scientist and CXO at Quantela, where he led the company's AI transformation and secured Series A funding, and leadership positions at major technology companies including Symantec, Yahoo, and PubMatic.

At AWS, Sanjiv has architected several landmark projects, including DigiYatra, India's digital travel credential initiative, processing over 1 billion records, demonstrating his expertise in designing massive-scale, mission-critical architectures. He built AWS's geospatial vertical from the ground up, achieving multi-million dollar annual revenue, and has guided numerous Fortune 500 companies in oil and gas, energy, and smart cities sectors through their data transformation journeys. A recognized thought leader, Sanjiv was awarded Top Chief Architect in India 2015 and led Quantela to be recognized as a WEF Technology Pioneer. His unique combination of hands-on technical expertise, strategic vision, and deep understanding of AWS services, from real-time streaming to machine learning at scale, makes him uniquely qualified to guide readers through the complexities of building modern, enterprise-grade data platforms on AWS.

About the Reviewers

❖ **Abhik Sengupta** is a seasoned technology leader and principal solution architect with over 18 years of experience in data, cloud architecture, and enterprise transformation. He is recognized as a respected thought leader and mentor in the data ecosystem, known for his visionary approach to solving complex technical challenges through innovative cloud-native architectures.

Abhik specializes in lakehouse design, Apache Iceberg, Snowflake optimization, and DataOps automation, and has led global initiatives to modernize enterprise data platforms. His hands-on expertise includes building secure, scalable cloud solutions across AWS, integrating Snowflake with enterprise identity systems, and enabling seamless data migration from on-premise systems. His architectural leadership spans ERP, CRM, and field service management landscapes, aligning technical solutions with business impact.

In addition to his technical leadership, Abhik actively contributes to the community as a top 1% mentor on Topmate, advisor to startups via Startupbootcamp, and judge for prestigious global recognitions, including the Globee Awards, Claro Awards, and Business Intelligence Group. He is passionate about enabling high-performing teams, guiding enterprise cloud journeys, and driving technological innovation through strategic foresight and industry collaboration.

❖ **Navneet Kumar Tyagi** is a seasoned IT professional with over 18 years of experience in software architecture, data engineering, and cloud-native development. He has contributed to technology solutions across the healthcare, energy, and finance sectors, with a strong focus on scalable system design and enterprise data platforms. Navneet specializes in building modern data ecosystems using AWS services.

As a technical architect, Navneet brings deep expertise in full-stack development, system integration, and governance-focused data solutions. He is passionate about enabling intelligent data sharing and has led initiatives that transformed legacy data workflows into secure, high-performance analytics platforms.

When he is not architecting cloud solutions, Navneet enjoys mentoring emerging developers and exploring advancements in AI-driven data engineering.

He is currently working with Finance of America and is part of the enterprise integration team working on the latest AWS services integration with the company's financial products.

Acknowledgement

There are many people I want to thank for their continued and unwavering support throughout the journey of writing this book. Without their encouragement, expertise, and patience, Data Engineering with AWS would not have been possible. First and foremost, I am profoundly grateful to my father-in-law, Dr. Y. P. Viyogi, whose wisdom and encouragement motivated me to embark on this writing journey. His belief in the importance of sharing knowledge has been a constant source of inspiration.

My heartfelt appreciation goes to my colleagues at Amazon Web Services, customers, and the broader AWS community, who have given me countless opportunities to learn and grow in the fascinating field of data engineering. Working alongside some of the brightest minds in cloud computing has enriched my understanding and provided real-world perspectives that are woven throughout this book. Every challenging project and innovative solution implemented has contributed to the practical knowledge shared in these pages.

Special recognition goes to my brothers, Rajeev and Ranjeev, for their frequent technical discussions and knowledge sharing sessions. Our countless conversations about data architecture, cloud technologies, and engineering best practices have significantly shaped the content and approach of this book. I also want to thank the editorial team, technical reviewers, and the broader data engineering community whose contributions, feedback, and collaborative spirit have made this comprehensive resource possible.

Preface

This book covers the fundamental concepts of data engineering and demonstrates how these principles can be effectively implemented on cloud platforms, with **Amazon Web Services** (**AWS**) serving as the primary implementation example. The book emphasizes the importance of understanding core data engineering concepts before diving into cloud-specific implementations, ensuring readers develop a solid foundation that transcends any particular technology stack. Many of the concepts, patterns, and best practices discussed are cloud-independent and can be adapted to other platforms, making this a comprehensive handbook for data engineering professionals.

This comprehensive guide serves as a handbook for professionals who want to master data engineering fundamentals and understand how these concepts translate to cloud environments. The book bridges the gap between theoretical data engineering principles and practical cloud implementations, demonstrating how traditional data processing paradigms evolve in cloud-native architectures. It addresses core concepts such as data modeling, ETL/ELT patterns, data quality, governance, and architecture design, while showing how these principles are realized using modern cloud services.

This book is structured into 15 comprehensive chapters plus appendices, progressing from foundational data engineering concepts to advanced cloud implementation patterns. The content builds systematically, first establishing theoretical understanding and then demonstrating practical application on AWS. Each chapter explores universal data engineering principles before showing specific cloud implementations, ensuring readers understand both the 'why' and the 'how' of modern data platforms.

Chapter 1: Modern Data Engineering Landscape – The chapter establishes the foundational concepts of data engineering, exploring the evolution from traditional architectures to cloud-native paradigms and introducing the core principles that underpin modern data platforms.

Chapter 2: Building Data Lake Foundations - This chapter covers fundamental data lake concepts, including storage architectures, data organization principles, and governance frameworks, with practical implementation using Amazon S3 as the storage foundation.

Chapter 3: Data Formats and Storage Optimization - The chapter examines data format theory and storage optimization principles, exploring various formats for different data types and demonstrating selection criteria that apply across cloud platforms.

Chapter 4: Real-time Data Ingestion and Streaming - The chapter introduces streaming data concepts, architectural patterns like Lambda and Kappa architectures, and demonstrates implementation using cloud-native streaming services.

Chapter 5: Batch Data Processing - The chapter explores batch processing fundamentals, ETL design patterns, and orchestration concepts, showing how these principles are implemented using cloud-based processing engines.

Chapter 6: Data Transformation and Quality - The chapter covers data quality frameworks, transformation patterns, and validation techniques that form the backbone of reliable data platforms, regardless of the underlying technology.

Chapter 7: Data Warehouse Engineering with Redshift - The chapter examines data warehousing concepts, dimensional modeling principles, and performance optimization strategies, demonstrating modern cloud-based implementations.

Chapter 8: Modern Data Architecture Patterns - The chapter explores advanced architectural concepts including data mesh, transactional data lakes, and polyglot persistence strategies that represent the evolution of data platform design.

Chapter 9: Data Governance and Security - The chapter addresses governance frameworks, security principles, and compliance strategies that are essential for enterprise data platforms across all environments.

Chapter 10: Cross-boundary Data Sharing and Collaborations - The chapter covers data sharing patterns, collaborative analytics concepts, and the architectural considerations for multi-party data exchange in modern organizations.

Chapter 11: Analytics and Visualization - The chapter introduces analytics architecture principles, visualization strategies, and the integration of business intelligence capabilities into modern data platforms.

Chapter 12: Machine Learning Integration - The chapter explores the intersection of data engineering and machine learning, covering MLOps principles, feature engineering concepts, and the architectural patterns for ML-enabled data platforms.

Chapter 13: DataOps and Automation - The chapter addresses operational excellence in data engineering, covering automation principles, monitoring strategies, and the practices that ensure reliable, scalable data operations.

Chapter 14: GenAI Revolution in Data Engineering - The chapter examines the transformation from human-centric to AI-native data platforms, covering enhanced medallion architectures, probabilistic data processing, and the implementation patterns for serving both traditional analytics and generative AI workloads.

Chapter 15: Future-Proofing Data Platforms - The chapter examines emerging trends, architectural evolution, and the principles for building adaptable data platforms that can evolve with changing technology landscapes.

Each chapter balances conceptual understanding with practical implementation, ensuring readers develop both theoretical knowledge and practical skills. The book serves as both a learning resource for those new to data engineering and a reference guide for experienced professionals transitioning to cloud-native architectures.

This handbook empowers data professionals to understand the fundamental principles of data engineering while providing the knowledge needed to implement these concepts effectively on modern cloud platforms, with skills and insights that extend beyond any single technology provider.

Code Bundle and Coloured Images

Please follow the link to download the
Code Bundle and the *Coloured Images* of the book:

https://rebrand.ly/8tatfu7

The code bundle for the book is also hosted on GitHub at
https://github.com/bpbpublications/Data-Engineering-with-AWS.
In case there's an update to the code, it will be updated on the existing GitHub repository.
We have code bundles from our rich catalogue of books and videos available at
https://github.com/bpbpublications. Check them out!

Errata

We take immense pride in our work at BPB Publications and follow best practices to ensure the accuracy of our content to provide with an indulging reading experience to our subscribers. Our readers are our mirrors, and we use their inputs to reflect and improve upon human errors, if any, that may have occurred during the publishing processes involved. To let us maintain the quality and help us reach out to any readers who might be having difficulties due to any unforeseen errors, please write to us at :

errata@bpbonline.com

Your support, suggestions and feedbacks are highly appreciated by the BPB Publications' Family.

Piracy

If you come across any illegal copies of our works in any form on the internet, we would be grateful if you would provide us with the location address or website name. Please contact us at business@bpbonline.com with a link to the material.

If you are interested in becoming an author

If there is a topic that you have expertise in, and you are interested in either writing or contributing to a book, please visit www.bpbonline.com. We have worked with thousands of developers and tech professionals, just like you, to help them share their insights with the global tech community. You can make a general application, apply for a specific hot topic that we are recruiting an author for, or submit your own idea.

Reviews

Please leave a review. Once you have read and used this book, why not leave a review on the site that you purchased it from? Potential readers can then see and use your unbiased opinion to make purchase decisions. We at BPB can understand what you think about our products, and our authors can see your feedback on their book. Thank you!

For more information about BPB, please visit www.bpbonline.com.

Join our Discord space

Join our Discord workspace for latest updates, offers, tech happenings around the world, new releases, and sessions with the authors:

https://discord.bpbonline.com

Table of Contents

CHAPTER 1
Modern Data Engineering Landscape

Introduction

The modern enterprise runs on data. From real-time analytics driving customer experiences to **machine learning** (**ML**) models optimizing operations, data has become the lifeblood of business innovation. At the heart of this data-driven transformation lies data engineering, the discipline of designing, building, and maintaining the systems that make data useful. This chapter explores the evolving landscape of data engineering, with a particular focus on modern architecture and cloud-native implementations on AWS.

Structure

This chapter covers the following topics:

- Evolution of data engineering
- Cloud-native data engineering
- AWS data services overview
- Data engineering design patterns
- Case study on enterprise data platform evolution
- Looking forward

Objectives

This chapter serves as your comprehensive guide to understanding the modern data engineering landscape. As you progress through this material, you will gain deep insights into how data engineering has transformed from its traditional ETL roots to today's sophisticated data platforms. You will develop a thorough understanding of the fundamental principles and practices that shape modern data engineering, particularly in cloud environments.

The chapter will explore the extensive ecosystem of AWS data services, demonstrating their practical applications in real-world scenarios. You will explore essential design patterns that form the backbone of scalable data platforms, learning how to apply these patterns effectively in your own implementations. Through detailed case studies, you will see how these concepts come together in actual enterprise environments, providing you with practical insights you can apply to your own projects.

By the end of this chapter, you will be equipped with both theoretical knowledge and practical understanding of modern data engineering concepts, preparing you for the detailed technical discussions that follow in subsequent chapters.

Evolution of data engineering

The journey of data engineering mirrors the broader evolution of enterprise computing, marked by distinct phases that reflect changing business needs and technological capabilities. The following figure illustrates the chronological progression of data processing paradigms over the past three decades, highlighting four major technological eras and their defining characteristics from the 1990s to the present day:

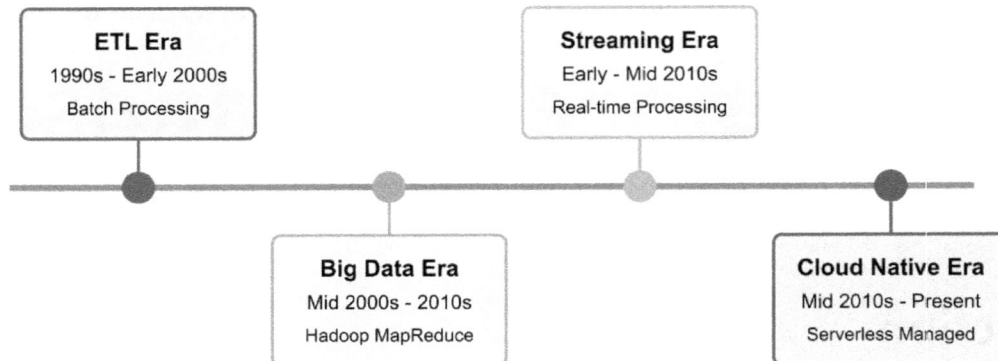

Figure 1.1: Evolution through key eras

ETL era 1990s to early 2000s

Data engineering began with a simple premise: businesses needed to consolidate data from various operational systems into a central repository for analysis. This gave birth to the **extract, transform, load** (**ETL**) paradigm. During this period, data engineers (though they were not called that yet) focused primarily on moving data between relational databases and data warehouses. The following code demonstrates a typical ETL process from the early 2000s with the three distinct steps: extraction of recent orders, transformation of currency values, and loading into a data warehouse fact table. This pattern, while simple, formed the foundation of data integration practices as shown in the code:

```
1.  -- Extract from source system
2.  SELECT order_id, customer_id, order_date, total_amount
3.  FROM orders
4.  WHERE order_date >= DATEADD(day, -1, GETDATE());
5.  -- Transform
6.  UPDATE staging.orders
7.  SET total_amount = total_amount * exchange_rate
8.  WHERE currency <> 'USD';
9.  -- Load into data warehouse
10. INSERT INTO dwh.fact_orders
11. SELECT * FROM staging.orders;
```

Big data revolution mid-2000s to early 2010s

The explosion of web-scale data and the emergence of social media platforms pushed traditional ETL systems to their limits. Companies like *Google*, *Yahoo*, and *Facebook* pioneered new approaches to handling data at unprecedented scale. This era introduced transformative technologies like Hadoop and MapReduce, fundamentally changing how we process and store data.

The following MapReduce code showcases the distributed processing paradigm. The mapper processes log entries in parallel across a cluster, counting events by type:

```
1.  public class LogAnalyzer extends Mapper {
2.      @Override
3.      public void map(LongWritable key, Text value, Context context)
4.          throws IOException, InterruptedException {
5.          String[] fields = value.toString().split("\t");
6.          String eventType = fields[2];
7.          context.write(new Text(eventType), new IntWritable(1));
8.      }
9.  }
```

This approach enabled the processing of petabyte-scale datasets across commodity hardware clusters:

Streaming revolution early 2010s to mid-2010s

As businesses sought more immediate insights, real-time data processing became crucial. This period saw the rise of streaming platforms like Apache Kafka and Apache Storm, enabling real-time data pipelines. Data engineers now had to think about processing data in motion, not just data at rest.

The following streaming code illustrates real-time processing of purchase events. It continuously processes user purchase events, aggregating totals in five-minute windows, enabling real-time monitoring and alerting of customer behavior.

```
1.  StreamsBuilder builder = new StreamsBuilder();
2.  builder.stream("user-events")
3.      .filter((key, value) -> value.getEventType().equals("purchase"))
4.      .map((key, value) -> KeyValue.pair(
5.          value.getUserId(),
6.          value.getAmount()))
7.      .groupByKey()
8.      .windowedBy(TimeWindows.of(Duration.ofMinutes(5)))
9.      .aggregate(
10.         () -> 0.0,
11.         (userId, amount, total) -> total + amount,
12.         Materialized.as("purchase-totals")
13.     );
14.
15.     }
16. }
```

Cloud-native era (mid-2010s to present)

The widespread adoption of cloud computing has ushered in the current era of data engineering. Cloud platforms like AWS provide managed services that handle much of the operational complexity, allowing data engineers to focus on architecture and business value. Modern data engineering embraces serverless computing, managed services, and automation.

The following AWS Lambda function code demonstrates modern cloud-native data processing. It automatically scales to handle incoming data streams, enriches the data, and routes it to appropriate destinations while updating real-time metrics:

```
1. def process_data_event(event, context):
2.     records = event['Records']
3.     for record in records:
4.         # Parse Kinesis record
5.         payload = base64.b64decode(record['kinesis']['data'])
6.         data = json.loads(payload)
7.         # Enrich data
8.         enriched_data = enrich_with_metadata(data)
9.         # Write to different destinations based on data type
10.        if data['type'] == 'transaction':
11.            write_to_firehose(enriched_data, 'transactions-stream')
12.        elif data['type'] == 'user_event':
13.            write_to_firehose(enriched_data, 'events-stream')
14.        # Update real-time metrics
15.        update_cloudwatch_metrics(data)
```

This evolution continues as new technologies and patterns emerge. Edge computing, AI/ML automation, and data mesh architectures are pushing the boundaries of what's possible with data engineering. In the following sections, we will explore the modern data engineering landscape in detail, focusing on practical implementations using AWS services.

Cloud-native data engineering

Cloud-native data engineering represents a fundamental shift in how we design, build, and operate data platforms. Rather than starting with infrastructure and working up, cloud-native approaches begin with services and work down. This paradigm shift enables organizations to build more scalable, resilient, and cost-effective data platforms while reducing operational overhead.

Cloud-native data engineering represents a fundamental shift in how we design, build, and operate data platforms. Rather than starting with infrastructure and working up, cloud-native approaches begin with services and work down. It combines four key principles: serverless-first operations, infrastructure as code, event-driven architecture, and container-native approaches, creating a framework that is both repeatable and highly scalable. This modern architectural approach emphasizes auto-scaling, version control, asynchronous processing, and portability as fundamental characteristics. The following figure depicts the core principles of *Cloud-Native Data Engineering*, showcasing how *Serverless First, Infrastructure as Code, Event-Driven Architecture*, and *Container Native* approaches interconnect as essential components in modern data engineering frameworks:

Cloud-Native Data Engineering Principles

Key components and their relationships

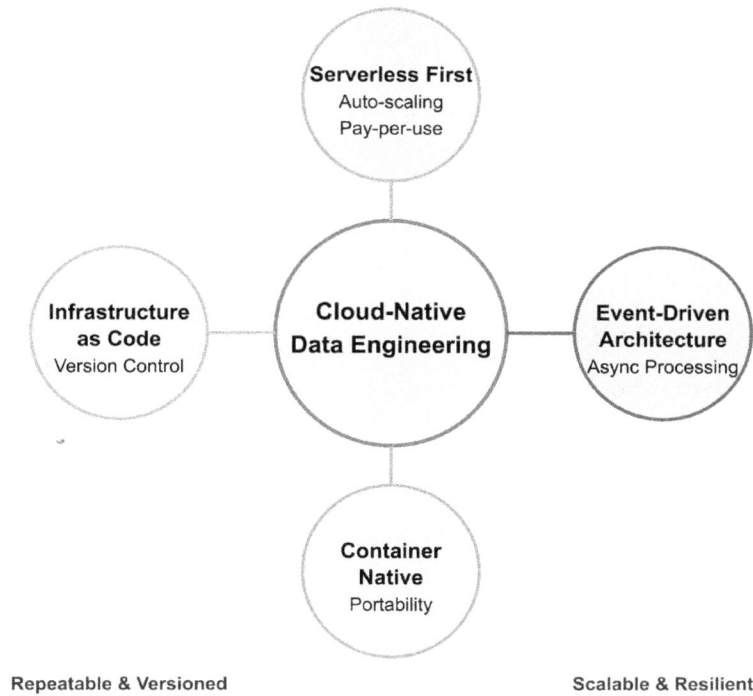

Figure 1.2: Cloud-native data engineering

Serverless first architecture

The serverless paradigm fundamentally changes how we approach data engineering. Instead of provisioning and managing servers, we focus on composing services and writing business logic. Consider this practical example code of a serverless data pipeline:

```
1. from aws_cdk import (
2.     aws_lambda as lambda_,
3.     aws_kinesis as kinesis,
4.     aws_dynamodb as dynamodb
5. )
6.
7. class DataPipeline(Stack):
8.     def __init__(self, scope: Construct, id: str, **kwargs):
9.         super().__init__(scope, id, **kwargs)
10.
11.         # Create Kinesis stream for data ingestion
12.         stream = kinesis.Stream(self, "DataStream",
13.             stream_mode=kinesis.StreamMode.ON_DEMAND
14.         )
15.
16.         # Create Lambda for processing
17.         processor = lambda_.Function(self, "DataProcessor",
18.             runtime=lambda_.Runtime.PYTHON_3_9,
19.             handler="processor.handler",
```

```
20.              code=lambda_.Code.from_asset("lambda")
21.          )
22.
23.          # Create DynamoDB table for results
24.          table = dynamodb.Table(self, "ResultsTable",
25.              partition_key={"name": "id", "type": dynamodb.AttributeType.STRING},
26.              billing_mode=dynamodb.BillingMode.PAY_PER_REQUEST
27.          )
```

This code demonstrates infrastructure as code for a serverless pipeline. It creates a self-scaling Kinesis stream, a Lambda processor, and a pay-per-request DynamoDB table, all without managing any servers.

Event-driven processing

Cloud-native data platforms embrace event-driven architectures, where data flows through the system as discrete events. This approach enables real-time processing and loose coupling between components. The following Lambda function code showcases event-driven processing patterns: event-based routing, error handling with dead letter queues, and metric emission for monitoring:

```
1.  def process_data_event(event, context):
2.      try:
3.          for record in event['Records']:
4.              # Extract data from Kinesis
5.              payload = base64.b64decode(record['kinesis']['data'])
6.              data = json.loads(payload)
7.
8.              # Process based on event type
9.              if data['type'] == 'user_activity':
10.                 process_user_activity(data)
11.                 emit_metric('user_activity_processed')
12.             elif data['type'] == 'system_event':
13.                 process_system_event(data)
14.                 emit_metric('system_event_processed')
15.
16.             # Emit events for downstream consumers
17.             notify_subscribers(data)
18.
19.     except Exception as e:
20.         handle_dead_letter_queue(record, e)
21.         raise
```

Data quality as code

Cloud-native platforms treat data quality as a first-class concern, embedding validation and testing directly into the pipeline. The following code snippet presents a **DataQualityCheck** class that validates streaming data by applying customizable validators to ensure completeness of required fields and proper formatting of values:

```
1.  class DataQualityCheck:
2.      def __init__(self, input_stream):
3.          self.input_stream = input_stream
4.          self.quality_metrics = []
```

```
5.
6.     def check_completeness(self, required_fields):
7.         def validator(data):
8.             missing_fields = [f for f in required_fields if f not in data]
9.             if missing_fields:
10.                emit_quality_metric('missing_fields', len(missing_fields))
11.                raise DataQualityException(f"Missing required fields: {missing_fields}")
12.        return validator
13.
14.    def check_format(self, field, pattern):
15.        def validator(data):
16.            if not re.match(pattern, data.get(field, '')):
17.                emit_quality_metric('format_error', 1)
18.                raise DataQualityException(f"Invalid format for field: {field}")
19.        return validator
20.
21.    def apply_checks(self, data):
22.        for check in self.quality_metrics:
23.            check(data)
```

Infrastructure as code

Cloud-native data engineering treats **infrastructure as code (IaC)**, using tools like AWS CDK to define and deploy resources. The following code demonstrates infrastructure as code principles, defining a complete data lake environment with S3 buckets, Glue Catalog, and crawlers:

```
1.  class DataLakeStack(Stack):
2.      def __init__(self, scope: Construct, id: str, **kwargs):
3.          super().__init__(scope, id, **kwargs)
4.
5.          # Create raw data bucket with lifecycle rules
6.          raw_bucket = s3.Bucket(self, "RawDataBucket",
7.              versioned=True,
8.              lifecycle_rules=[
9.                  s3.LifecycleRule(
10.                     transitions=[
11.                         s3.Transition(
12.                             storage_class=s3.StorageClass.INFREQUENT_ACCESS,
13.                             transition_after=Duration.days(30)
14.                         ),
15.                         s3.Transition(
16.                             storage_class=s3.StorageClass.GLACIER,
17.                             transition_after=Duration.days(90)
18.                         )
19.                     ]
20.                 )
21.             ]
22.         )
23.
```

```
24.          # Create catalog database
25.          catalog_db = glue.Database(self, "DataCatalog",
26.              database_name="data_lake_catalog"
27.          )
28.
29.          # Create crawler
30.          crawler = glue.CfnCrawler(self, "DataCrawler",
31.              role=crawler_role.role_arn,
32.              targets={"s3Targets": [{"path": raw_bucket.bucket_name}]},
33.              database_name=catalog_db.database_name,
34.              schedule={"scheduleExpression": "cron(0 */6 * * ? *)"}
35.          )
```

Monitoring and observability

Cloud-native data platforms require comprehensive monitoring. The following monitoring code shows how to implement comprehensive observability in a cloud-native data platform:

```
1.  def emit_metric(name, value, dimensions=None):
2.      try:
3.          cloudwatch.put_metric_data(
4.              Namespace='DataPipeline',
5.              MetricData=[{
6.                  'MetricName': name,
7.                  'Value': value,
8.                  'Unit': 'Count',
9.                  'Dimensions': dimensions or []
10.             }]
11.         )
12.     except Exception as e:
13.         logger.error(f"Failed to emit metric {name}: {e}")
14.
15. def monitor_pipeline_health():
16.     metrics = {
17.         'RecordsProcessed': get_processed_count(),
18.         'ProcessingLatency': get_processing_latency(),
19.         'ErrorRate': calculate_error_rate(),
20.         'DataQualityScore': calculate_quality_score()
21.     }
22.     for name, value in metrics.items():
23.         emit_metric(name, value)
```

The cloud-native approach to data engineering enables organizations to build more scalable, reliable, and cost-effective data platforms. By embracing serverless architectures, event-driven processing, and IaC, teams can focus on delivering business value rather than managing infrastructure. In the next section, we will explore how these principles are implemented using specific AWS services.

AWS data services overview

AWS provides a comprehensive ecosystem of services for building modern data platforms. The AWS data engineering stack can be organized into four main categories: storage, processing, analytics, and streaming services. The following figure illustrates how these services work together, which is crucial for designing effective data solutions:

AWS Data Services Ecosystem

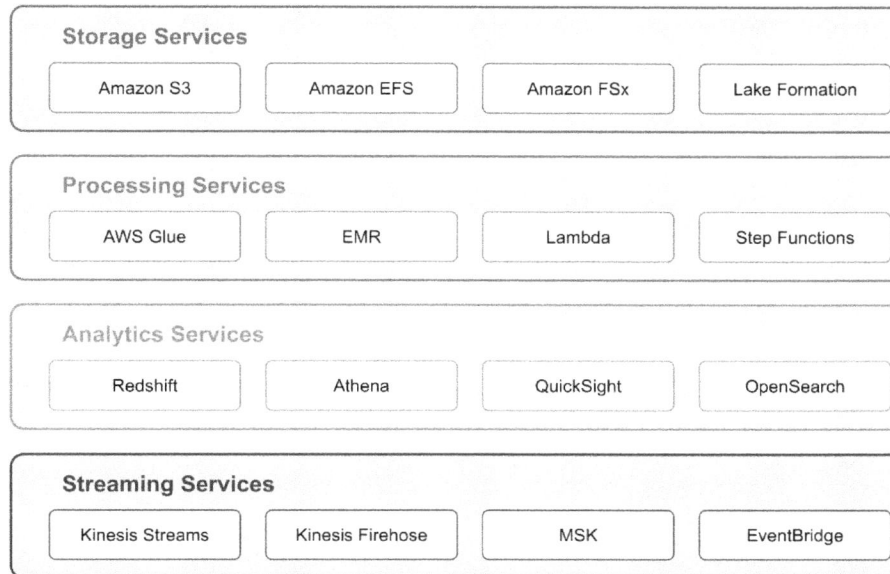

Figure 1.3: AWS data services for data engineering

Foundation of storage services

At the foundation of any data platform lies the storage layer. AWS offers several storage services, each optimized for different use cases. Amazon S3 serves as the cornerstone of most data lake implementations, providing virtually unlimited storage with sophisticated features. The following code demonstrates the creation of an S3-based data lake with versioning enabled and intelligent storage tiering, data older than 90 days automatically transitions to cost-effective storage classes while maintaining accessibility:

```
1.  s3_bucket = aws_s3.Bucket(self, "DataLakeBucket",
2.      versioned=True,
3.      encryption=aws_s3.BucketEncryption.S3_MANAGED,
4.      lifecycle_rules=[{
5.          'transitions': [{
6.              'storageClass': aws_s3.StorageClass.INTELLIGENT_TIERING,
7.              'transitionAfter': Duration.days(90)
8.          }]
9.      }]
10. )
```

The following code shows how Lake Formation implements fine-grained access control for data lake resources, granting analysts read-only access to specific databases while maintaining security boundaries:

```
1.  lf.CfnPermissions(self, "AnalystAccess",
2.      data_lake_principal={'data_lake_principal_identifier': analyst_role.role_arn},
3.      resource={
4.          'database_name': data_catalog.database_name,
5.          'table_wildcard': {}
6.      },
```

```
7.    permissions=['SELECT', 'DESCRIBE']
8. )
```

Processing services of the workhorses

Processing services handle the transformation and computation of data. AWS Glue provides serverless ETL capabilities, while EMR offers managed big data processing. The following code shows the configuration of a Glue ETL job with auto-scaling capabilities. This code creates a job that uses Python 3 and allocates 10 workers for parallel processing, automatically handling resource management:

```
1.  glue.CfnJob(self, "DataTransformation",
2.      command={
3.          'name': 'glueetl',
4.          'script_location': f's3://{script_bucket.bucket_name}/transform.py',
5.          'python_version': '3'
6.      },
7.      role=glue_role.role_arn,
8.      execution_property={'max_concurrent_runs': 2},
9.      glue_version='3.0',
10.     worker_type='G.1X',
11.     number_of_workers=10
12. )
```

The following configuration sets up an EMR cluster with automatic scaling between 3 and 10 nodes based on workload. The cluster is optimized for memory-intensive Spark jobs with **r5.2xlarge** instances:

```
1.  emr.CfnCluster(self, "SparkCluster",
2.      instances={
3.          'master_instance_group': {
4.              'instance_type': 'm5.xlarge',
5.              'instance_count': 1
6.          },
7.          'core_instance_group': {
8.              'instance_type': 'r5.2xlarge',
9.              'instance_count': 3,
10.             'auto_scaling_policy': {
11.                 'constraints': {
12.                     'min_capacity': 3,
13.                     'max_capacity': 10
14.                 },
15.                 'rules': [...auto_scaling_rules...]
16.             }
17.         }
18.     },
19.     applications=[{'name': 'Spark'}, {'name': 'Hive'}]
20. )
```

Deriving insights from analytics services

Analytics services enable data exploration and visualization. Redshift provides data warehousing capabilities, while Athena offers serverless SQL querying. The following code shows a Redshift cluster configuration optimized for query performance, which enables **Advanced Query Accelerator** (**AQUA**) and sets up automated maintenance and backup policies:

```
1. redshift.CfnCluster(self, "AnalyticsWarehouse",
2.     cluster_type='ra3.4xlarge',
3.     number_of_nodes=4,
4.     aqua_configuration_status='enabled',
5.     maintenance_track_name='current',
6.     preferred_maintenance_window='sat:20:00-sat:21:00',
7.     automated_snapshot_retention_period=7
8. )
```

The following code configures and establishes an Athena workgroup with query result management and performance optimizations using the latest engine version:

```
1.  athena.CfnWorkGroup(self, "AnalyticsWorkgroup",
2.      name="data_analytics",
3.      work_group_configuration={
4.          'enforce_work_group_configuration': True,
5.          'result_configuration': {
6.              'output_location': f's3://{query_results_bucket.bucket_name}/results/',
7.              'expected_bucket_owner': account_id
8.          },
9.          'engine_version': {
10.             'selected_engine_version': 'Athena engine version 3'
11.         }
12.     }
13. )
```

Real-time data processing of streaming services

Streaming services handle real-time data ingestion and processing. Kinesis and Amazon **Managed Streaming for Apache Kafka** (**MSK**) provide different approaches to stream processing. The following code creates a Kinesis stream optimized for high-throughput scenarios with enhanced fan-out capabilities, enabling multiple consumers to read at full throughput:

```
1. kinesis.Stream(self, "DataStream",
2.     stream_mode=kinesis.StreamMode.ON_DEMAND,
3.     encryption=kinesis.StreamEncryption.MANAGED,
4.     enhanced_monitoring=True,
5.     stream_name="high-velocity-stream"
6. )
```

The following code configures and establishes a highly available MSK cluster with encryption and performance optimizations. The three-broker setup ensures fault tolerance, while **Elastic Block Store** (**EBS**)-provisioned **input/output operations per second** (**IOPS**) provides consistent performance:

```
1. msk.CfnCluster(self, "StreamingCluster",
2.     kafka_version='2.8.1',
3.     number_of_broker_nodes=3,
4.     broker_node_group_info={
5.         'instance_type': 'kafka.m5.large',
6.         'client_subnets': vpc.private_subnets,
```

```
7.          'storage_info': {
8.              'ebs_storage_info': {
9.                  'volume_size': 100,
10.                 'provisioned_throughput': 250
11.             }
12.         }
13.     },
14.     encryption_info={
15.         'encryption_in_transit': {'client_broker': 'TLS'},
16.         'encryption_at_rest': {'data_volume_kms_key_id': kms_key.key_id}
17.     }
18. )
```

Each of these services is designed to work seamlessly together, enabling you to build sophisticated data platforms. The key to success lies in choosing the right combination of services based on your specific requirements for data volume, velocity, variety, and processing needs.

Data engineering design patterns

In modern data engineering, design patterns serve as proven templates for solving recurring architectural challenges. These patterns have emerged from real-world experiences across industries, offering structured approaches to building scalable, maintainable, and efficient data platforms. Understanding these patterns helps architects and engineers make informed decisions about their data architecture strategy. The following figure outlines the five core components of modern data engineering design patterns, categorizing essential methodologies across data ingestion, processing, storage, serving, and governance domains with their respective implementation techniques:

Modern Data Engineering Design Patterns

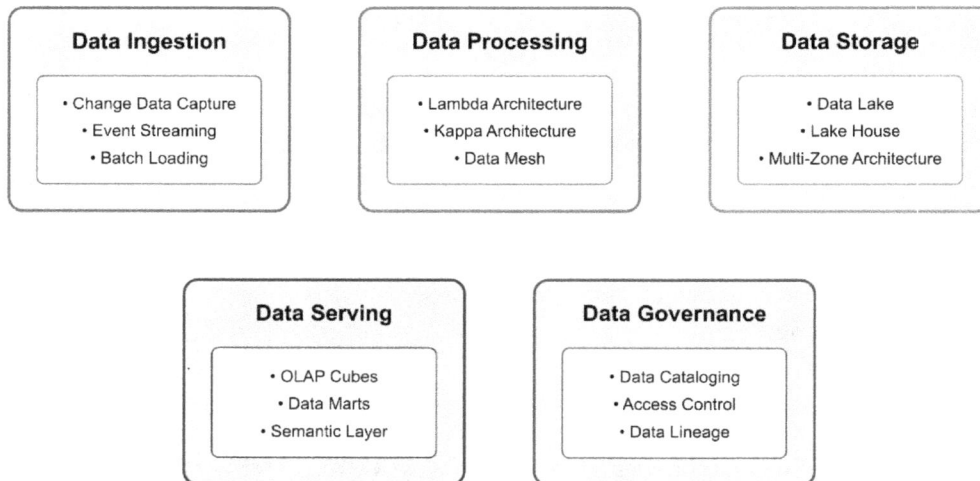

Data Ingestion
- Change Data Capture
- Event Streaming
- Batch Loading

Data Processing
- Lambda Architecture
- Kappa Architecture
- Data Mesh

Data Storage
- Data Lake
- Lake House
- Multi-Zone Architecture

Data Serving
- OLAP Cubes
- Data Marts
- Semantic Layer

Data Governance
- Data Cataloging
- Access Control
- Data Lineage

Figure 1.4: Modern data engineering design patterns

Data ingestion patterns

Data ingestion is a critical component of modern data architectures, serving as the foundation for collecting, importing, and processing data from various sources into target systems. As organizations deal with increasing data volumes and diverse data sources, implementing the right ingestion strategy becomes paramount for successful data operations.

Choosing the right data ingestion pattern is crucial for building efficient and scalable data processing systems. Here are three key patterns to consider:

Change data capture

Change data capture (**CDC**) patterns enable efficient data synchronization by capturing and tracking changes in source systems. Rather than performing full data loads, CDC identifies and processes only modified data. This approach minimizes system load and enables near real-time data replication. Financial institutions frequently employ CDC to maintain synchronized copies of transaction databases while ensuring minimal impact on operational systems.

Event streaming

Event streaming treats data as a continuous flow of events rather than discrete batches. This pattern excels in scenarios requiring real-time processing and immediate insights. For example, e-commerce platforms use event streaming to process customer interactions, update recommendations, and adjust inventory in real-time.

Batch loading

Despite the trend toward real-time processing, batch loading remains essential for many scenarios. This pattern efficiently handles large volumes of data where real-time processing is not critical. Common applications include daily sales reports, monthly financial reconciliations, and periodic data warehouse loads.

Processing patterns

Data processing patterns form the architectural backbone of modern data platforms, defining how organizations transform raw data into actionable insights. These battle-tested approaches offer different strategies for handling data transformation, each optimized for specific business needs and technical requirements.

Lambda architecture

Lambda architecture addresses the dual needs of real-time and batch processing. By maintaining separate paths for speed and accuracy, organizations can serve both immediate insights and comprehensive analysis. This pattern particularly suits scenarios where both low latency and high accuracy are required, such as in fraud detection systems that need both immediate alerts and thorough historical analysis.

Kappa architecture

Kappa architecture simplifies the Lambda approach by treating all data as streams. Instead of maintaining separate batch and stream processing paths, Kappa uses a single technology stack for both real-time and historical processing. This simplification reduces operational complexity but requires careful consideration of processing technologies.

Data mesh

Data mesh represents a paradigm shift from centralized to distributed data ownership, treating data as a product managed by domain teams who understand it best. This architectural pattern addresses the scalability challenges of centralized data platforms by implementing four key principles:

- **Domain-oriented data ownership**: Business domains own and manage their data products, ensuring a deep understanding of data context and quality requirements.

- **Data as a product**: Each domain treats its data as a product with clear interfaces, documentation, and quality guarantees, similar to software APIs.

- **Self-serve data infrastructure**: A shared platform provides common capabilities (storage, compute, monitoring) while domains maintain autonomy over their data products.
- **Federated computational governance**: Governance policies are implemented through code and automation rather than centralized control, ensuring consistency while enabling domain autonomy.

  Implementation typically involves:

  o Domain-specific data products with standardized interfaces

  o Automated quality checks and data contracts

  o Self-service data access through catalogs and APIs

  o Federated governance through policy-as-code

This pattern particularly suits large organizations with distinct business domains and diverse data needs, though success heavily depends on organizational readiness and strong governance frameworks

Storage patterns

Modern data architectures require sophisticated storage strategies that balance accessibility, performance, and cost-effectiveness. These patterns have evolved beyond traditional databases to accommodate the diverse needs of today's data-driven organizations, from handling raw unstructured data to serving highly optimized analytical workloads.

Data lake

Data lakes store vast amounts of raw data in their native format. This pattern provides maximum flexibility for future use cases while deferring schema decisions until data is needed. Modern data lakes often implement a multi-zone approach to manage data quality and access patterns.

Lakehouse

The lakehouse pattern bridges the gap between data lakes and warehouses. It combines the flexibility of data lakes with the performance and reliability of traditional warehouses. This hybrid approach is gaining traction as organizations seek to consolidate their analytical infrastructure while maintaining flexibility.

Multi-zone data lake

This pattern organizes data lakes into distinct zones (typically raw, trusted, and curated) to manage data quality and access patterns. Each zone serves specific purposes and users, from data scientists working with raw data to business analysts requiring curated datasets.

Serving patterns

Data serving patterns define how processed information is made available to end users, focusing on optimizing accessibility, performance, and usability for different consumer needs. These patterns bridge the gap between complex data storage systems and business users, ensuring that insights are delivered in the most effective and efficient manner possible.

Online analytical processing cubes

While traditional **online analytical processing (OLAP)** cubes are less common in cloud environments, the pattern of pre-aggregation for analytical performance remains relevant. Modern implementations often use in-memory technologies or columnar storage to achieve similar benefits with greater flexibility.

Data marts

Data marts provide focused, department-specific views of enterprise data. This pattern simplifies access to relevant data while maintaining a connection to the broader data ecosystem. It is particularly valuable in large organizations where different departments have distinct analytical needs.

Semantic layer

The semantic layer pattern abstracts technical complexity and presents data in business terms. It enables self-service analytics while ensuring consistency in business definitions and calculations across the organization.

Governance patterns

Data governance patterns establish the framework for managing data as a strategic asset, ensuring its quality, security, and compliance throughout its lifecycle. These patterns provide the guardrails and controls necessary for organizations to maintain data integrity while enabling appropriate access and usage across the enterprise.

Data cataloging

Cataloging patterns help organizations discover, understand, and invent their data assets. These patterns become increasingly critical as data volumes and variety grow, enabling users to find and understand available data resources.

Access control

Modern access control patterns go beyond simple role-based access to include attribute-based access control and dynamic data masking. These sophisticated approaches enable fine-grained security while facilitating data sharing and collaboration.

Data lineage

Lineage patterns track data's journey through various transformations and systems. They are crucial for regulatory compliance, impact analysis, and data quality management. Financial and healthcare organizations particularly benefit from strong lineage tracking for audit and compliance purposes.

Pattern selection and combination

Most successful data platforms combine multiple patterns to address different requirements. The key lies in understanding how patterns complement each other and managing the trade-offs each introduces. Consider these common combinations.

Real-time analytics platform

Real-time platform leverages modern event-driven architecture to deliver the instance insight:

- Event streaming for data ingestion
- Kappa architecture for processing
- Lakehouse for storage
- Semantic layer for serving

Enterprise data platform

Enterprise data platform orchestrates end-to-end data management with robust integration, processing, and governance capabilities:

- CDC for operational data sync

- Lambda architecture for processing
- Multi-zone data lake for storage
- Data marts for serving
- Data mesh principles for domain ownership (see *Processing patterns* section)
- Comprehensive governance patterns

Data science platform

Data science platform provides a flexible, scalable environment for advanced analytics and machine learning workflows:

- Batch and stream ingestion
- Data lake for storage
- Flexible processing patterns
- Strong cataloguing and lineage

When selecting patterns, organizations should consider:

- Current and future business requirements
- Data characteristics (volume, velocity, variety)
- Team capabilities and technical expertise
- Existing technological investments
- Regulatory and compliance requirements
- Operational overhead and maintenance costs

The patterns discussed here provide a foundation for building modern data platforms. In subsequent chapters, we will explore detailed implementations of these patterns using AWS services, examining how to translate these conceptual models into practical solutions.

Case study on enterprise data platform evolution

To demonstrate the practical application of modern data engineering patterns, let us examine a hypothetical transformation journey of Global Finance, a fictional financial services organization. This case study illustrates how organizations can evolve from traditional data warehousing to modern, cloud-native data platforms.

Initial architecture

Global Finance's initial data architecture represented a classic enterprise data warehouse approach:

- **Architecture components:**
  o Three Oracle RAC clusters hosting data warehouses (total 50TB)
  o ETL processes using Informatica PowerCenter
  o Business intelligence through Oracle OBIEE
  o File-based data exchange between systems
  o Static resource allocation for computing and storage
- **Key technical challenges:**
  o Nightly ETL window exceeding 8 hours
  o Query performance degradation during peak hours

o   Complex stored procedures for business logic

o   Manual schema management and versioning

o   No support for unstructured data

o   Limited disaster recovery capabilities

Technical evolution

The transformation unfolded across three distinct phases, each introducing new architectural patterns and capabilities.

- **Phase 1: Foundation building:**

  The initial phase focused on establishing core cloud infrastructure and migration patterns:

  o   **Data lake implementation:**
    - Three-zone data lake architecture in S3 (raw, processed, consumed)
    - Automated data ingestion using AWS DMS for database replication
    - Implementation of data partitioning strategy using Hive-style partitioning
    - Data catalogue creation using AWS Glue Data Catalogue
    - Basic data governance using Lake Formation

  o   **Integration architecture:**
    - Hybrid connectivity through Direct Connect
    - Initial data pipelines using AWS Glue for ETL
    - S3 event-driven processing for file uploads
    - Basic monitoring through CloudWatch
    - Security controls using IAM and bucket policies

  o   **This phase has been achieved:**
    - Reduction in storage costs by 40%
    - Improved data availability across regions
    - Foundation for self-service analytics
    - Basic data lineage tracking

- **Phase 2: Pattern implementation:**

  The second phase introduced modern data engineering patterns and real-time capabilities:

  o   **Real-time processing architecture:**
    - Event-driven pipeline using Kinesis Data Streams
    - Stream processing using Kinesis Analytics
    - Real-time data integration using Lambda
    - CDC for operational databases
    - Push notifications through SNS

  o   **Analytics modernization:**
    - Migration from OBIEE to QuickSight
    - Implementation of Redshift for data warehousing
    - Athena for ad-hoc SQL queries

- Integration with SageMaker for ML workloads
- Automated schema evolution handling

o **Key technical achievements:**
- Real-time data latency reduced to seconds
- Query performance improved by 300%
- Automated scaling during peak loads
- Enhanced data quality monitoring
- Comprehensive audit logging

- **Phase 3: Advanced implementation:**

The final phase focused on sophisticated patterns and optimization:

o **Data mesh implementation:**
- Applied the data mesh pattern (detailed in the *Design patterns* section) with domain-oriented data products
- Implemented standardized data product interfaces across business domains
- Established automated quality checks and data contracts
- Enabled self-service data access through enhanced cataloging
- Deployed federated governance model using policy-as-code

Technical architecture evolution

The transformation represented a shift from monolithic to distributed architecture, as shown in the following figure:

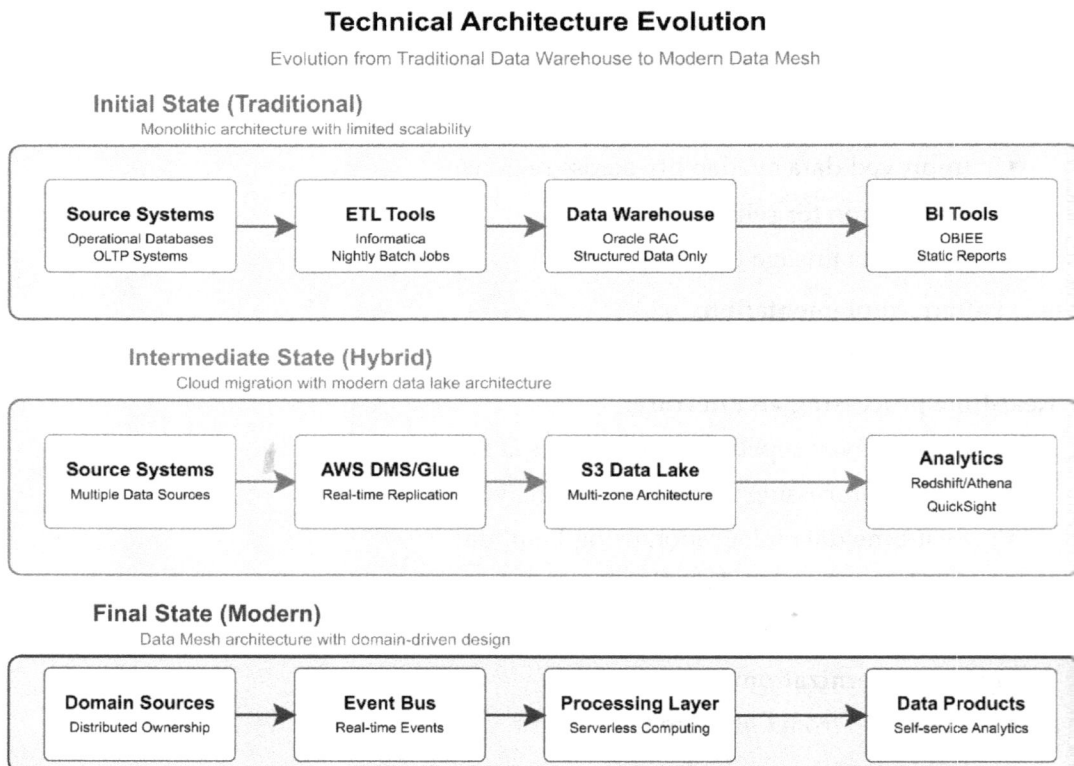

Figure 1.5: Technical architecture evolution

Key technical decisions

Critical architectural decisions that shaped the transformation:

- **Data lake design**:
  - o Choice of S3 for primary storage
  - o Implementation of zone-based architecture
  - o Selection of file formats (Parquet for analytics, JSON for raw data)
- **Processing architecture**:
  - o Adoption of serverless where possible
  - o Mix of batch and streaming processes
  - o Implementation of retry mechanisms
  - o Error handling strategies
- **Data governance**:
  - o Centralized policy management
  - o Automated compliance checking
  - o Comprehensive data cataloging
  - o Fine-grained access control

Roadmap

The platform continues to evolve with emerging requirements:

- **Planned enhancements:**
  - o Implementation of data quality monitoring using deequ
  - o Enhanced ML capabilities through feature stores
  - o Advanced data mesh patterns
  - o Enhanced cost optimization
  - o Expanded edge processing capabilities

This case study, while hypothetical, demonstrates how modern data engineering patterns can be practically applied to transform enterprise data platforms. In the following chapters, we will explore implementing specific components of such a transformation using AWS services.

Conclusion

This chapter has provided a comprehensive foundation in modern data engineering, tracing its evolution from traditional ETL processes to sophisticated cloud-native implementations. We explored how data engineering has transformed through various eras, from the ETL era through the big data revolution to today's cloud-native paradigm. The chapter detailed essential AWS services that form the backbone of modern data platforms and examined crucial design patterns that guide successful implementations. Through the Global Finance case study, we saw how these concepts apply in real-world scenarios, demonstrating the practical implementation of modern data engineering principles.

The next chapter will explore building data lake foundations, a crucial component of modern data architecture. We will explore how to design and implement robust data lakes using Amazon S3, focusing on advanced strategies for data organization, security frameworks, and cost optimization techniques. *Chapter 2, Building Data Lake Foundations,* will provide hands-on guidance for implementing these concepts, helping you translate theoretical knowledge into practical solutions for your organization's data needs.

Join our Discord space

Join our Discord workspace for latest updates, offers, tech happenings around the world, new releases, and sessions with the authors:

https://discord.bpbonline.com

CHAPTER 2
Building Data Lake Foundations

Introduction

The exponential growth of data in modern enterprises presents a unique set of challenges in storage, processing, and analysis. Traditional systems, built for structured data and predefined analytics, often struggle with the volume, variety, and velocity of today's data landscape. Data lakes emerged as an architectural solution to these challenges, offering a flexible and scalable approach to enterprise data management. This chapter explores how to build robust data lake foundations using AWS services, with particular focus on architectural patterns and implementation strategies.

Structure

This chapter will cover the following topics:

- Understanding data lakes
- Common challenges and anti-patterns
- Business drivers and use cases
- Amazon S3 as a data lake foundation
- Understanding and leveraging storage classes
- Architectural considerations for data organization
- Data organization and partitioning strategies
- Evolution and query optimization
- Data lake security and governance
- Comprehensive audit and compliance framework
- Cost optimization techniques
- Implementing data cataloguing
- Building a scalable data lake architecture

Objectives

The chapter aims to provide a comprehensive understanding of data lake architectures and their implementation using AWS services, with particular emphasis on Amazon S3 as the foundation. It focuses on teaching readers how to design and implement scalable data lakes, including advanced strategies for data organization and partitioning. The objectives encompass mastering core concepts of data lake architectures, implementing robust security and governance frameworks, and learning practical approaches to data discovery and cataloging while optimizing costs and performance. Through exploring these aspects, readers will gain the knowledge needed to build efficient data lakes using Amazon S3, understand how to effectively organize and partition data, establish strong security measures, implement governance frameworks, optimize both costs and performance, and develop practical methods for data discovery and cataloging within their data lake environments.

Understanding data lakes

The understanding of data lakes is fundamental to building effective enterprise data management solutions. As organizations grapple with increasing data volumes and variety, traditional data storage approaches often fall short of meeting modern analytical needs. This section explores the core concepts of data lakes, their characteristics, and how they differ from conventional data storage solutions. By understanding these foundational elements, organizations can better architect solutions that address their current needs while remaining flexible enough to accommodate future requirements.

Data lake

A data lake is a centralized repository that enables you to store all your structured and unstructured data at any scale. Unlike traditional databases or data warehouses that store data in files or tables, a data lake stores data in its raw form. Think of it as a large natural lake, where water flows in from various sources in its natural state, and various processing methods can be applied when consuming the water.

Consider a global retail organization with diverse data sources: point-of-sale systems generating structured transaction records, website logs producing semi-structured clickstream data, security cameras creating unstructured video feeds, and social media platforms providing JSON data. Traditional approaches would require separate specialized systems for each data type, creating silos and complexity. A data lake, however, provides a unified platform for storing and processing all these data types, enabling comprehensive analytics and insights.

Consider these key characteristics:

- **Store everything**: A data lake accepts all types of data, structured data like database tables, semi-structured data like JSON logs, and unstructured data like images, videos, and documents Each piece of data is stored in its native format, preserving all original information.

- **Schema on read**: Instead of defining how data should be structured before storage (schema on write), data lakes allow structure to be defined when the data is read (schema on read). This fundamental shift enables multiple interpretations of the same data for different use cases.

- **Unlimited scale**: Data lakes can grow from terabytes to petabytes while maintaining consistent access patterns and management capabilities.

To understand this better, let us compare traditional and data lake approaches:

```
1.    -- Traditional Data Warehouse Approach
2.    -- Must define structure before storing data
3.    CREATE TABLE customer_interactions (
4.        timestamp DATETIME,
```

```
5.        customer_id VARCHAR(50),
6.        interaction_type VARCHAR(20),
7.        channel VARCHAR(20),
8.        -- Schema must anticipate all possible fields
9.        metadata JSON
10.  );
11.
12.  -- Data must conform to this structure
13.  INSERT INTO customer_interactions VALUES (
14.      '2024-02-06 10:30:00',
15.      'CUST123',
16.      'PURCHASE',
17.      'MOBILE',
18.      '{"app_version": "2.1.0"}'
19.  );
```

In contrast, a data lake stores raw data directly:

```
1.  # Data Lake Approach
2.  # Store raw data as-is
3.  store_in_lake('customer/mobile/2024/02/06/', {
4.      'timestamp': '2024-02-06T10:30:00Z',
5.      'customer': {
6.          'id': 'CUST123',
7.          'device': 'iPhone 13',
8.          'location': {'lat': 40.7128, 'lon': -74.0060},
9.          'app_version': '2.1.0'
10.     },
11.     'session': {
12.         'duration': 300,
13.         'pages_viewed': ['home', 'product', 'cart'],
14.         'cart_items': [
15.             {'id': 'PROD456', 'quantity': 1, 'price': 99.99}
16.         ]
17.     }
18. })
19.
20. # Structure is applied when reading, based on specific needs
21. def analyze_for_marketing(raw_data):
22.     return {
23.         'customer_id': raw_data['customer']['id'],
24.         'browsing_pattern': raw_data['session']['pages_viewed'],
25.         'location': raw_data['customer']['location']
26.     }
27.
28. def analyze_for_mobile_team(raw_data):
29.     return {
30.         'app_version': raw_data['customer']['app_version'],
31.         'device_type': raw_data['customer']['device'],
```

```
32.        'session_duration': raw_data['session']['duration']
33.    }
```

Ingesting data schemeless gives the speed of ingestion, and schema on read gives flexibility for unknown use cases.

Advantages of data lakes

Organizations adopt data lakes to address several critical challenges, such as:

- **Data variety**: Modern enterprises generate and collect data in numerous formats from structured database records to semi-structured logs and unstructured documents. Traditional systems handle structured data well, but struggle with other formats.

- **Evolving analytics**: Business requirements change rapidly, requiring new ways to analyze existing data. Data lakes preserve all raw data, enabling new analytics without data migration or transformation.

- **Machine learning**: ML models often require access to large volumes of historical data in its rawest form. Data lakes provide ideal storage for training data while enabling feature engineering.

- **Cost efficiency**: By separating storage from compute and enabling fit-for-purpose processing, data lakes can significantly reduce data management costs.

Data lake architecture patterns

Data lake architectures have evolved to address the complex challenges of managing large-scale data operations while maintaining data quality and accessibility. The choice of architectural pattern significantly impacts the success of a data lake implementation, influencing everything from data quality to query performance and maintenance overhead. Understanding these patterns is crucial for organizations looking to build scalable, maintainable, and efficient data lake solutions. In particular, the medallion architecture and data lakehouse patterns have emerged as leading approaches, each offering distinct advantages for different use cases and organizational needs.

Medallion architecture

The effectiveness of a data lake depends heavily on its architectural design. The most widely adopted pattern is the medallion architecture, which organizes data into different zones based on their processing state and quality. Refer to the following figure:

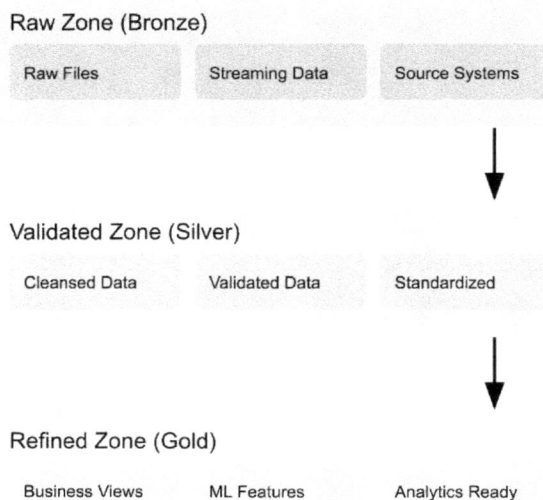

Raw Zone (Bronze)

Raw Files   Streaming Data   Source Systems

↓

Validated Zone (Silver)

Cleansed Data   Validated Data   Standardized

↓

Refined Zone (Gold)

Business Views   ML Features   Analytics Ready

Figure 2.1: Medallion architecture pattern in data lakes

The bronze zone serves as the initial landing area for raw data. Here, data is stored exactly as received from source systems, preserving its original fidelity. This immutable storage proves invaluable for historical analysis, audit requirements, and reprocessing needs.

The silver zone introduces the first level of refinement, where data undergoes standardization and validation. Common transformations include:

- Cleansing and validation

- Schema enforcement and evolution handling

- Data quality checks

- Basic aggregations and enrichments

The gold zone contains highly curated, business-ready datasets optimized for specific use cases. These might include:

- Aggregated analytical views

- Machine learning feature sets

- Regulatory reporting datasets

Bridging lakes and warehouses

Data lakehouses emerged as an architectural pattern that combines the flexibility of data lakes with the reliability and performance of data warehouses. This architecture introduces a transactional layer atop the data lake that enables **atomicity, consistency, isolation, durability (ACID)** compliance through table formats like Apache Iceberg, Delta Lake, or Apache Hudi.

Key characteristics of data lakehouses include:

- **Table formats**: Open-source formats like Delta Lake provide versioning, ACID transactions, and schema enforcement while maintaining files in cloud storage. These formats use optimized file layouts and metadata management to deliver warehouse-like performance.

- **ACID properties**: Achieved through atomic commits and optimistic concurrency control. Multiple users can simultaneously read and write without conflicts, while maintaining data consistency through versioned metadata.

- **Schema evolution**: Supports both schema enforcement and evolution, allowing teams to add, modify, or delete columns without disrupting existing queries or requiring data copies.

- **Time travel**: Enables access to historical versions of data through snapshot isolation, simplifying audit requirements and enabling rollback capabilities.

- **Performance optimization**: Implements techniques like data skipping, z-ordering, and bloom filters to accelerate queries. File compaction and indexing further enhance read performance.

Data organization and contextual indexing

Effective data organization in a data lake requires careful consideration of both logical and physical structuring. The most effective approach combines hierarchical organization with contextual indexing to enable efficient data discovery and access. The following directory structure represents a well-organized data lake, designed to efficiently store and manage data from ingestion through various stages of processing. This hierarchical approach facilitates easy data discovery, access control, and lifecycle management:

```
data-lake/
├── raw/
│   ├── source=iot-sensors/
│   │   ├── year=2024/
│   │   │   ├── month=02/
│   │   │   │   ├── day=06/
│   │   │   │   │   ├── hour=00/
│   │   │   │   │   │   ├── sensor_data_000.json
│   │   │   │   │   │   └── sensor_data_001.json
├── validated/
│   ├── domain=operations/
│   │   ├── entity=sensor-metrics/
│   │   │   ├── year=2024/
│   │   │   │   ├── month=02/
├── refined/
    ├── usecase=predictive-maintenance/
        ├── model=equipment-health/
            ├── version=v1/
                ├── year=2024/
```

This organization implements contextual indexing through:

- Source-based partitioning in the raw zone
- Domain-based organization in the validated zone
- Use-case orientation in the refined zone
- Temporal partitioning across all zones

Contextual indexing helps access just the amount of data needed for any processing context and faster access to relevant data.

Common challenges and anti-patterns

Successfully implementing a data lake requires understanding and avoiding common pitfalls that can undermine its effectiveness. Organizations often face numerous challenges that can transform their carefully planned data lakes into unmanageable data swamps if not properly addressed. By recognizing these challenges early and understanding the anti-patterns that lead to them, organizations can take proactive steps to ensure their data lakes remain valuable, accessible, and maintainable assets. This section examines key challenges and how to address them, focusing particularly on data swamp prevention, governance issues, and access control complexities.

Data swamps and ways to avoid them

The flexibility of data lakes can lead to their deterioration into data swamps, repositories where data becomes difficult to find and use effectively. This typically occurs when organizations prioritize data ingestion without adequate attention to organization and governance. Preventing data swamps requires implementing clear data organization strategies, maintaining comprehensive metadata, and establishing data quality standards from the outset.

Governance challenges

Data governance in lake environments presents unique challenges. Organizations must balance the flexibility that makes data lakes valuable with the control necessary for effective data management. This includes establishing clear ownership policies, implementing data quality frameworks, and maintaining data lineage throughout the data lifecycle.

Access control complexity

Managing access in data lakes requires sophisticated approaches beyond traditional role-based controls. Organizations must implement fine-grained access policies that consider data sensitivity, user roles, and regulatory requirements. This complexity increases when dealing with data sharing across organizational boundaries or implementing column-level security.

Business drivers and use cases

The adoption of data lakes is driven by compelling business needs and diverse use cases across industries. As organizations seek to derive greater value from their data assets, data lakes have emerged as a critical infrastructure component, enabling everything from advanced analytics to regulatory compliance. Understanding these business drivers and use cases is essential for organizations to align their data lake implementation with strategic objectives and ensure maximum return on investment. The versatility of data lakes makes them particularly valuable across multiple business scenarios, from supporting traditional business intelligence to enabling cutting-edge machine learning applications and ensuring regulatory compliance.

Analytics and BI

Data lakes serve as powerful platforms for analytics and **business intelligence** (**BI**). They enable organizations to perform complex analyses across diverse data types, supporting everything from traditional reporting to advanced analytical workflows. The ability to store detailed historical data alongside current data enables rich trend analysis and pattern discovery.

Machine learning

The machine learning capabilities of data lakes prove particularly valuable in modern enterprises. Data scientists can access raw, unprocessed data for model training, while automated pipelines can continuously update models with new data. The ability to store and process unstructured data makes data lakes essential for applications in computer vision, natural language processing, and other AI domains.

Data science

Data lakes provide an ideal environment for data science experimentation and discovery. They enable data scientists to access raw data, perform exploratory analysis, and iterate on different approaches without the constraints of predefined schemas. This flexibility proves invaluable for hypothesis testing and developing new analytical approaches.

Regulatory compliance

Modern data lakes include sophisticated features for meeting regulatory requirements. They support data lineage tracking, audit logging, and fine-grained access controls. Organizations can implement data retention policies, manage **personally identifiable information** (**PII**), and demonstrate compliance with various regulatory frameworks.

Amazon S3 as a data lake foundation

The foundation of any data lake requires careful consideration of storage infrastructure that can handle diverse data types, varying access patterns, and evolving business needs while maintaining cost-effectiveness.

Amazon S3 has emerged as the de facto standard for data lake storage, offering a unique combination of scalability, durability, and flexibility that addresses these fundamental requirements.

Core capabilities for data lake implementation

Amazon S3 implements object storage, a fundamentally different approach from traditional storage systems. In object storage, data is managed as objects rather than as files in a hierarchy (like traditional file systems) or as blocks on a disk (like block storage). Each object consists of the data itself, a unique identifier (key), and metadata describing the object. This approach eliminates the constraints of traditional hierarchical file systems while enabling powerful metadata-driven operations.

Consider the differences:

- **Traditional file system**: Organizes files in directories with path-based access (`/home/user/documents/file.txt`)

- **Block storage**: Breaks data into fixed-size blocks, managed by the operating system

- **Object storage**: Stores complete objects with unique identifiers in a flat address space (`my-bucket/unique-key/data.txt`)

This architectural foundation proves particularly valuable for data lakes. A single S3 bucket can store billions of objects of any size (from a few bytes to five terabytes), making it ideal for housing diverse data types from small JSON configuration files to massive Parquet datasets containing millions of records.

S3 implements strong read-after-write consistency, a critical feature for data lake operations. In distributed systems, consistency models define how and when data updates become visible to different readers. Strong read-after-write consistency means that as soon as data is written to S3, any subsequent read request will immediately see the latest version of that data.

For example:

```
1. # Write operation completes
2. s3_client.put_object(Bucket='data-lake', Key='sensors/latest.json',
   Body=json_data)
3.
4. # Immediate read will see the new data
5. response = s3_client.get_object(Bucket='data-lake',
   Key='sensors/latest.json')
6. # No need for delays or retries - the latest data is
   guaranteed to be available
```

This consistency model eliminates the need for complex application-level handling that would otherwise be required to ensure data freshness, such as implementing delay mechanisms or retry loops. In a data lake context, where multiple applications might be simultaneously ingesting and analysing data, this guarantee is invaluable for maintaining data integrity and simplifying application design.

S3 also provides multiple storage classes, each optimized for different access patterns and cost requirements.

These storage classes retain the same durability and consistency features but differ in availability, retrieval times, and cost structures as given in the following list:

- **S3 Standard**: The default class offering millisecond access with no minimum storage curation or lower retrieval fees. Ideal for actively accessed data lake zones.

- **S3 Intelligent-Tiering**: Automatically moves objects between access tiers based on usage patterns. Well-suited for data with changing access patterns.

- **S3 Standard-IA (Infrequent access)**: Lower storage costs but includes retrieval fees. Good for less frequently accessed validated data.

- **S3 One Zone-IA**: Like Standard-IA, but stores data in a single availability zone for additional cost savings.

- **S3 Glacier Instant Retrieval**: Lowest cost for long-lived data (90+ days) that needs millisecond retrieval.

- **S3 Glacier Flexible Retrieval**: Very low-cost storage with retrieval times from minutes to hours.

- **S3 Glacier Deep Archive**: Lowest cost storage designed for long-term retention, with retrieval times of hours.

This variety of storage classes enables sophisticated cost optimization strategies. Organizations can align storage costs with data value by transitioning objects between classes based on access patterns and business requirements. For instance, raw data might initially land in S3 Standard for active processing, then move to S3 Standard-IA once validated, and finally to Glacier for long-term retention.

Understanding and leveraging storage classes

Amazon S3 provides different storage classes, each designed to offer a specific combination of durability, availability, performance, and cost characteristics. These storage classes are essentially different ways to store objects in S3, each optimized for different access patterns and retention requirements. Understanding these classes is crucial before we explore their strategic application in data lakes.

S3 Standard, the default storage class, provides high durability (99.999999999%) and availability (99.99%) with millisecond access times and no minimum storage duration requirements. It manages data across multiple devices and facilities, protecting against hardware failures and entire availability zone outages. This robust foundation makes it particularly relevant for data lake implementations.

The journey of data through a data lake typically involves varying access patterns at different stages of its lifecycle. These S3 storage classes can be strategically employed to optimize this journey. The Standard storage class, with its high availability and low latency characteristics, serves as the ideal landing zone for raw data ingestion. As data moves through the validation and transformation stages, access patterns often become more predictable, opening opportunities for cost optimization.

Consider a typical IoT data lake scenario. Fresh sensor data requires immediate availability for real-time analytics and anomaly detection, making S3 Standard the obvious choice. However, after initial processing, the data's access pattern changes dramatically. Historical sensor data might only be accessed for quarterly trend analysis or annual reporting. In such cases, transitioning to S3 Standard-IA or even Glacier Instant Retrieval can significantly reduce storage costs while maintaining necessary accessibility.

The introduction of Intelligent-Tiering has particularly transformed storage optimization strategies. Instead of implementing complex lifecycle rules based on predicted access patterns, organizations can let S3 automatically optimize storage costs based on actual usage patterns. This proves especially valuable in data lake environments where access patterns can be difficult to predict and vary across different data categories.

S3 data organization strategy

The organization of data within S3 requires careful consideration of both logical and physical structures. While S3 presents a flat object structure, the effective use of prefixes and naming conventions creates a hierarchical organization that supports efficient data lake operations. Also, check the naming convention to create a contextual index for data organization.

A well-designed bucket strategy forms the foundation of a data lake organization. Rather than treating buckets as simple containers, they should be viewed as strategic boundaries for access control, lifecycle management, and replication policies. For instance, separating raw data ingestion buckets from refined data buckets not only simplifies security management but also enables different optimization strategies for each data stage.

```
1.  # Example of strategic bucket organization
2.  raw_bucket = «enterprise-datalake-raw-{account}-{region}"
3.  refined_bucket = "enterprise-datalake-refined-{account}-{region}"
```

This separation allows for implementing different security policies, lifecycle rules, and access patterns optimized for each data processing stage. Raw data buckets might prioritize write performance and implement strict access controls, while refined data buckets could optimize for read performance and implement more permissive access patterns for data consumers.

Lifecycle management for data evolution

S3 lifecycle management is a feature that allows you to set rules to automatically transition objects between storage classes or delete them after specified time periods. These rules can be based on object age, prefixes (folder paths), tags, or object size. When a lifecycle rule is triggered, S3 automatically performs the specified action, whether it is transitioning data to a different storage class or deleting it.

The dynamic nature of data lakes requires sophisticated lifecycle management strategies. These lifecycle capabilities enable automated data movement and expiration based on various criteria, supporting both cost optimization and data governance requirements. By automating the movement of data between storage classes and managing object deletion, organizations can implement complex data retention policies without manual intervention.

Consider a financial data lake where regulatory requirements mandate the retention of certain datasets for seven years. A comprehensive lifecycle strategy might look like this:

```
1.  {
2.      "Rules": [
3.          {
4.              "ID": "Financial Data Lifecycle",
5.              "Status": "Enabled",
6.              "Filter": {
7.                  "Prefix": "finance/transactions/"
8.              },
9.              "Transitions": [
10.                 {
11.                     "Days": 90,
12.                     "StorageClass": "STANDARD_IA"
13.                 },
14.                 {
15.                     "Days": 365,
16.                     "StorageClass": "GLACIER_IR"
17.                 }
18.             ],
19.             "NoncurrentVersionTransitions": [
20.                 {
21.                     "NoncurrentDays": 30,
22.                     "StorageClass": "GLACIER"
23.                 }
24.             ],
25.             "Expiration": {
26.                 "Days": 2555
27.             }
```

```
28.          }
29.     ]
30. }
```

This configuration automatically manages the entire data lifecycle, from active use through long-term retention to eventual expiration, while maintaining compliance requirements and optimizing costs.

Performance optimization through advanced features

S3 offers several advanced features designed to enhance data transfer speeds and optimize access patterns. These features go beyond basic storage functionality to address specific performance challenges in large-scale data operations.

Let us examine two key features that are particularly relevant for data lake implementations:

- **Multipart upload**: It is a feature that allows you to upload large objects in parts, with each part being a contiguous portion of the object's data. These parts can be uploaded independently, in parallel, and in any order. If transmission of any part fails, you can retransmit just that part rather than the entire object. Objects can be anywhere from 5 MB to 5 TB in size.

- **Transfer acceleration**: It is a performance enhancement feature that enables fast, secure file transfers over long distances between your client and an S3 bucket. It works by utilizing Amazon CloudFront's globally distributed edge locations, routing data through AWS's optimized network path.

The performance requirements of a data lake vary significantly across different use cases and access patterns. These S3 features can be strategically leveraged to optimize performance for specific scenarios.

Multipart uploads prove essential when dealing with large datasets, particularly in data ingestion scenarios. By breaking large objects into smaller parts that can be uploaded in parallel, organizations can achieve higher throughput and better resilience. This becomes particularly important when ingesting large data files from diverse sources:

```python
1. def initiate_multipart_upload(bucket, key, chunk_size=100_000_000):
2.     """Initialize multipart upload with optimal chunk size for data
   lake ingestion"""
3.     mpu = s3_client.create_multipart_upload(Bucket=bucket, Key=key)
4.     return {
5.         'UploadId': mpu['UploadId'],
6.         'Parts': [],
7.         'ChunkSize': chunk_size
8.     }
```

Transfer acceleration, leveraging AWS's global edge network, becomes particularly valuable when ingesting data from geographically distributed sources. This feature can significantly reduce upload times for remote data sources, enabling more efficient global data lake operations.

Access patterns and performance optimization

Understanding and optimizing access patterns is crucial for data lake performance. S3 Select enables server-side filtering of data, reducing data transfer and processing requirements for analytical queries. This becomes particularly valuable when dealing with large datasets where only a subset of data is needed:

```python
1. # Example of using S3 Select for efficient data filtering
2. response = s3_client.select_object_content(
3.     Bucket='my-data-lake',
4.     Key='large-dataset.parquet',
5.     ExpressionType='SQL',
```

```
6.      Expression="SELECT * FROM s3object s WHERE s.year = ‹2024›»,
7.      InputSerialization={'Parquet': {}},
8.      OutputSerialization={'JSON': {}}
9.  )
```

The implementation of request rate optimization becomes crucial as data lake usage scales. While S3 provides virtually unlimited scale, understanding and optimizing request patterns ensures consistent performance. This includes implementing appropriate prefix naming strategies for high-request-rate scenarios and utilizing parallel processing for large-scale data operations.

In essence, S3's capabilities provide the building blocks for implementing robust, scalable data lakes. The key lies not just in understanding these features but in strategically applying them to meet specific organizational needs while maintaining optimal performance and cost-effectiveness. As data lakes continue to evolve, S3's regular feature enhancements ensure that organizations can adapt to changing requirements while maintaining a solid foundation for their data infrastructure.

Data organization and partitioning strategies

The organization of data within a lake represents one of the most crucial architectural decisions that can significantly impact both operational efficiency and analytical capabilities. Unlike traditional databases, where structure is enforced through schemas and indexes, data lakes require careful consideration of organization patterns that can accommodate diverse data types while enabling efficient processing and evolution over time.

Zone architecture paradigm

Building upon our earlier discussion of the medallion architecture pattern, the implementation of data zones requires careful consideration of specific organizational patterns and processing workflows. While we covered the conceptual framework in our previous section, here we will focus on the practical implementation aspects and organizational strategies within each zone.

The raw zone, often termed the bronze zone, serves as the initial landing area for all incoming data. The fundamental principle here is the preservation of source data in its original form. This approach might seem counterintuitive because the data is stored in potentially inefficient formats. It is because of the ability to reprocess data when needed. Consider scenarios where:

- A bug is discovered in the processing pipeline
- New fields in source data become relevant for analysis
- Compliance requirements demand an audit of original records

This is how raw zone implementation might look:

```
1.  def ingest_to_raw_zone(data_stream, source_system):
2.      """
3.      Preserves incoming data exactly as received with robust metadata
4.      «»"
5.      raw_storage_path = generate_raw_path(
6.          source_system,
7.          data_stream.timestamp,
8.          data_stream.type
9.      )
10.
11.     # Store original data with extensive metadata
```

```
12.     store_raw_data(
13.         data=data_stream.content,
14.         path=raw_storage_path,
15.         metadata={
16.             'source_system': source_system,
17.             'ingestion_timestamp': datetime.now().isoformat(),
18.             'original_format': data_stream.format,
19.             'content_hash': calculate_hash(data_stream.content),
20.             'schema_version': data_stream.schema_version
21.         }
22.     )
```

The trusted zone (silver) represents the first level of refinement. Here, we make deliberate choices about data structure and quality. The key considerations include the following questions:

- What constitutes trusted data for your organization?
- Which quality checks must all data pass?
- What level of standardization should be applied?

A typical trusted zone process illustrates these decisions:

```
1.  def promote_to_trusted(raw_data_path):
2.      """
3.      Implements organizational standards for trusted data
4.      """
5.      # Read raw data with full lineage tracking
6.      raw_data = read_with_lineage(raw_data_path)
7.
8.      # Apply organizational data standards
9.      standardized = apply_data_standards(raw_data)
10.
11.     # Validate against quality rules
12.     quality_results = validate_quality(standardized)
13.     if not quality_results.passed:
14.         handle_quality_failure(quality_results)
15.         return
16.
17.     # Convert to optimized format
18.     trusted_data = convert_to_optimized_format(
19.         standardized,
20.         target_format='parquet',
21.         optimization_config={
22.             'compression': 'snappy',
23.             'row_group_size': optimal_row_group_size(standardized)
24.         }
25.     )
26.
27.     # Store with quality metadata
28.     store_trusted_data(
29.         trusted_data,
```

```
30.        quality_results=quality_results,
31.        lineage=raw_data.lineage
32.    )
```

The curated zone (gold) focuses on business value and user accessibility. This zone requires a deep understanding of the following:

- Who are the data consumers?
- What are their typical access patterns?
- What level of data abstraction is appropriate?

Thoughtful partition design

Partitioning strategy represents a critical decision point where physical storage organization meets query optimization. The choice of partition keys directly impacts:

- Query performance and cost
- Data lifecycle management
- Processing parallelism
- Storage optimization

Let us analyse common partitioning approaches and their implications:

Time-based partitioning

Time-based partitioning is fundamental to data lake organization, but determining the right granularity requires careful consideration of several factors. Let us explore these through a practical example of a retail company's sales data lake.

Consider a retail chain with 1,000 stores. Their point-of-sale system generates transaction data that needs to be stored and analyzed efficiently. The choice between daily, weekly, or monthly partitions significantly impacts both operational efficiency and query performance.

The first consideration is data volume. If a store generates relatively small amounts of data—say, 100KB of transaction data per day, daily partitioning would result in thousands of tiny files, creating unnecessary overhead in both storage and processing. In this scenario, monthly partitioning would be more efficient, consolidating the small daily files into more manageable monthly chunks.

Query patterns form the second critical factor. If the business analysts typically run monthly sales reports and quarter-over-quarter comparisons, having data partitioned by month aligns perfectly with these access patterns. However, if the operations team needs daily sales figures for inventory management, monthly partitions would force them to scan entire months of data for daily statistics.

For example:

- **Daily partitioning**:
  1. `sales/2024/02/01/store_transactions.parquet`
  2. `sales/2024/02/02/store_transactions.parquet`

  Ideal for: Daily reporting, real-time analytics, point-in-time recovery.

- **Monthly partitioning**:
  1. `sales/2024/02/store_transactions.parquet`
  2. `sales/2024/03/store_transactions.parquet`

  Ideal for: Monthly reporting, trend analysis, and reduced management overhead.

Data retention requirements also influence this decision. For data that must be retained for several years (like financial records), monthly partitioning reduces the number of objects to manage. A retail chain keeping seven years of transaction data would have:

- **Daily partitioning**: 2,555 partitions (7 years × 365 days)
- **Monthly partitioning**: 84 partitions (7 years × 12 months)

The monthly approach significantly simplifies lifecycle management and reduces metadata overhead.

A hybrid approach might best serve diverse needs. Critical operational data from the past 30 days could use daily partitions for granular access, while older data gets consolidated into monthly partitions for long-term storage and analytical queries. This provides an optimal balance between operational efficiency and analytical flexibility.

The key is to make this decision based on concrete metrics rather than assumptions:

- **Data volume**: If daily data is less than 100MB, favor monthly partitioning.
- **Query patterns**: If most queries span more than 30 days, monthly partitioning typically performs better.
- **Retention period**: For long-term retention (more than one year), monthly partitioning reduces management complexity.
- **Processing requirements**: For real-time or near-real-time processing, daily or even hourly partitioning might be necessary.

This decision is not permanent, as data volumes and access patterns evolve, the partitioning strategy can be adjusted through data migration and partition consolidation processes.

Business domain partitioning

Business domain partitioning reflects organizational structure in data organization, requiring a deep understanding of your organization's operational model. This approach goes beyond simple technical considerations to address business-level concerns and organizational dynamics.

Consider a global retail organization with multiple brands and regional operations. Their domain partitioning strategy might reflect their organizational hierarchy: global divisions, regional operations, and local markets. Each level requires different access patterns and security considerations. For instance, financial data might be partitioned as:

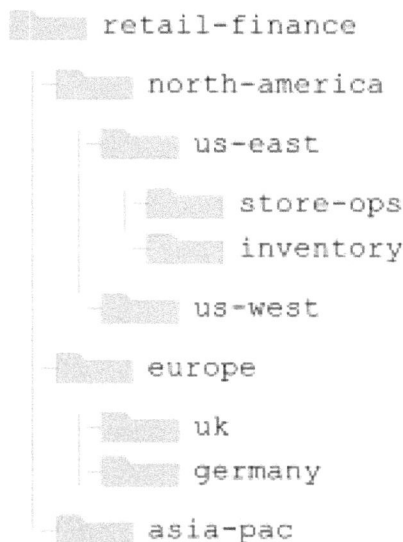

Figure 2.2: S3 folder structure

This structure enables precise access control and data governance. Regional teams can access their specific data while global analytics teams can traverse the entire hierarchy. The partitioning strategy also facilitates data sovereignty compliance, allowing data to be physically segregated based on regional requirements.

When implementing domain partitioning, consider these key factors:

- **Team autonomy requirements**: Different business units may need independent control over their data assets.

- **Cross-domain analytics needs**: Some analyses may need to span multiple domains.

- **Security and compliance boundaries**: Regulatory requirements may dictate specific data segregation.

- **Organizational change management**: The structure should be flexible enough to accommodate organizational evolution.

Multi-dimensional partitioning

Multi-dimensional partitioning represents the most sophisticated approach to data organization, combining multiple attributes to optimize data access and management. This strategy requires careful balancing of various factors to achieve optimal performance without creating excessive complexity.

Let us consider a practical example from the telecommunications industry. A telecom provider manages customer interaction data with the following characteristics:

- Millions of daily customer interactions

- Multiple service types (voice, data, SMS)

- Geographic distribution across regions

- Various customer segments

- Different interaction channels (app, web, call center)

Their partitioning strategy might look like the following figure:

```
service_type=voice
    region=northeast
        segment=enterprise
            year=2024
                month=02
                month=03
        segment=consumer
    region=southwest
```

Figure 2.3: S3 partitioning hierarchy for telecom voice data

The effectiveness of this structure depends on careful analysis of:

- **Query patterns**: Understanding how data is typically accessed helps prioritize partition dimensions. In our telecom example, if most queries filter by service type and region first, these dimensions should appear higher in the hierarchy.

- **Partition cardinality**: Each dimension adds complexity to the partition structure. A dimension with very high cardinality (like individual customer IDs) might create too many small partitions, while one with very low cardinality (like binary flags) might not provide meaningful filtering benefits.

- **Data distribution**: Analyze how evenly data is distributed across partition keys. In our example, if 90% of interactions are voice calls, using service type as the top-level partition might create skewed access patterns.

For instance, consider an analysis requirement for enterprise customer satisfaction across regions. With this partition structure, analysts can efficiently access relevant data by traversing only the enterprise segment partitions across regions, avoiding unnecessary scans of consumer data.

File format selection

The selection of file formats in a data lake represents a strategic decision that impacts everything from storage efficiency to query performance and operational flexibility. Each format offers distinct advantages and trade-offs that must be evaluated against your specific use cases and requirements.

Let us examine this through the lens of a real-world example: a retail analytics platform processing **point-of-sale (POS)** data. This system needs to handle:

- Real-time transaction ingestion from stores
- Daily aggregation for inventory management
- Complex analytical queries for business intelligence
- Long-term storage for compliance

For the initial data ingestion, JSON lines format with Gzip compression might be the optimal choice. This format allows for:

- Schema flexibility to handle varying POS systems
- Record-level processing for streaming ingestion
- Reasonable compression for storage efficiency
- Human-readable format for debugging

However, once data passes validation and enters the trusted zone, converting to Apache Parquet becomes advantageous:

- Column-based storage optimizes analytical queries
- Efficient compression reduces storage costs
- Predicate pushdown improves query performance
- Schema evolution support maintains flexibility

The choice becomes more nuanced for specific use cases. For instance, store operations teams running frequent queries on recent transaction data might benefit from a hybrid approach:

- Keep recent data (last 7 days) in optimized Parquet
- Convert older data to **Optimized Row Columnar (ORC)** with better compression
- Archive historical data to a highly compressed Parquet with optional encryption

Understanding access patterns is crucial. If analysts typically query specific columns (like sales amount and date) across large date ranges, columnar formats like Parquet or ORC significantly outperform row-based formats. However, if applications need to read complete records (like retrieving full transaction details), row-based formats might perform better.

Evolution and query optimization

As data lakes grow, they must evolve to accommodate changing business requirements while maintaining performance.

This evolution manifests in several key areas:

- **Schema evolution**: Business changes inevitably require schema modifications. A retail company expanding internationally might need to add currency and tax fields to their transaction records. The data lake must handle these changes while maintaining access to historical data:

```
transactions/
    ├── schema_version=1/
    │     └── 2023/              # Original schema
    └── schema_version=2/
          └── 2024/              # Enhanced schema with international fields
```

- **Query optimization**: Partition design must evolve with query patterns. Analysis of query logs might reveal that certain time periods or categories are accessed more frequently. This insight can drive partition optimization:

```
product_analytics/
    ├── hot_categories/        # Frequently accessed categories
    │     └── daily_partitions/
    └── standard_categories/   # Normal access patterns
          └── monthly_partitions/
```

This organization allows for different optimization strategies based on access patterns. Frequently accessed data might use finer-grained partitioning and higher-performance storage tiers, while less frequently accessed data uses broader partitioning and cost-optimized storage.

The key to successful data organization lies in balancing immediate needs with future flexibility. While initial implementations might focus on simple patterns, the structure should accommodate growth in data volume, variety, and velocity. Regular monitoring of access patterns, query performance, and storage costs provides the insights needed to evolve the organization's strategy effectively.

Data lake security and governance

Security and governance form the cornerstone of enterprise data lake implementations. While data lakes offer unprecedented flexibility in storing and processing data, this flexibility must be balanced with robust security controls and comprehensive governance frameworks. Let us explore how to implement a complete security and governance strategy using AWS services.

Implementing identity and access management

The foundation of data lake security begins with identity and access management. Think of IAM as your data lake's security guard, checking credentials and enforcing permissions at every access point. In AWS, this is implemented through a combination of IAM roles, policies, and resource-based permissions.

Consider a financial services organization managing sensitive customer transaction data. Their security requirements might include:

- Restricting access based on job functions
- Enforcing time-based data access
- Implementing attribute-based access control
- Ensuring encryption of sensitive data

Here is how this translates into an IAM policy for data analysts:

```
1.  {
2.      "Version": "2012-10-17",
```

```
3.        "Statement": [
4.            {
5.                "Effect": "Allow",
6.                "Action": [
7.                    "s3:GetObject",          // Read-only access to objects
8.                    "s3:ListBucket"          // Ability to list contents
9.                ],
10.               "Resource": [
11.                   "arn:aws:s3:::financial-datalake/processed/transactions/*"
12.               ],
13.               "Condition": {
14.                   "StringEquals": {
15.                       "aws:PrincipalTag/Department": "risk-analytics",
16.                       "s3:prefix": ["2024/"]
17.                   }
18.               }
19.           }
20.       ]
21. }
```

To implement this policy, follow these steps:

1. Create it in the IAM console under Policies.
2. Attach it to relevant IAM roles.
3. Tag your IAM users appropriately (e.g., Department=risk-analytics).
4. Test access through the AWS console or CLI.

Data encryption and network security

Data encryption and network security work together to create multiple layers of protection. Think of encryption as your safe box, and network security as the secure room housing that safe. AWS provides several encryption options and network security controls that can be combined for comprehensive protection.

For encryption at rest, you have two primary choices:

- **SSE-S3**: Managed by AWS, ideal for standard security needs
- **SSE-KMS**: Enhanced control and audit capabilities, perfect for regulatory requirements

This bucket policy enforces encryption in transit and restricts access to specific network paths:

```
1.  {
2.      "Version": "2012-10-17",
3.      "Statement": [
4.          {
5.              "Sid": "EnforceEncryptionInTransit",
6.              "Effect": "Deny",
7.              "Principal": "*",
8.              "Action": "s3:*",
9.              "Resource": "arn:aws:s3:::financial-datalake/*",
10.             "Condition": {
11.                 "Bool": {
```

```
12.                        "aws:SecureTransport": "false"    // Forces HTTPS
     usage
13.                    }
14.                }
15.            },
16.            {
17.                "Sid": "RestrictToVPCEndpoint",
18.                "Effect": "Deny",
19.                "Principal": "*",
20.                "Action": "s3:*",
21.                "Resource": "arn:aws:s3:::financial-datalake/*",
22.                "Condition": {
23.                    "StringNotEquals": {
24.                        "aws:SourceVpce": "vpce-1a2b3c4d"
25.                    }
26.                }
27.            }
28.        ]
29. }
```

Implementation steps:

1. Create your VPC endpoint for S3 access.

2. Configure the bucket policy through S3 console.

3. Set up KMS keys if using SSE-KMS.

4. Update application configurations to use the VPC endpoint.

Cross-account access and collaboration

Modern enterprises often need to share data across different AWS accounts while maintaining security. This might involve:

- Development and production environments
- Different business units
- External partners or vendors

Here is a bucket policy enabling secure cross-account access:

```
1.  {
2.      "Version": "2012-10-17",
3.      "Statement": [
4.          {
5.              "Effect": "Allow",
6.              "Principal": {
7.                  "AWS": "arn:aws:iam::ACCOUNT-B:role/DataLakeAccess"
8.              },
9.              "Action": [
10.                 "s3:GetObject",
11.                 "s3:ListBucket"
12.             ],
```

```
13.              "Resource": [
14.                  "arn:aws:s3:::shared-datalake/*"
15.              ],
16.              "Condition": {
17.                  "StringEquals": {
18.                      "aws:PrincipalOrgID": "o-xxxxxxxxxxx"
19.                  }
20.              }
21.          }
22.      ]
23. }
```

The implementation requires configuration in both accounts:

- **Resource account**:
  - Apply the bucket policy
  - Configure resource permissions
- **Accessing account**:
  - Create appropriate IAM roles
  - Set up trust relationships

Comprehensive audit and compliance framework

Audit logging and compliance monitoring form the final piece of the security puzzle. Think of this as your security camera system, recording all activities for review and compliance purposes.

CloudTrail configuration for comprehensive logging:

```
1.  {
2.      "Name": "DataLakeTrail",
3.      "IncludeGlobalServiceEvents": true,
4.      "IsMultiRegionTrail": true,
5.      "EventSelectors": [
6.          {
7.              "ReadWriteType": "All",
8.              "IncludeManagementEvents": true,
9.              "DataResources": [
10.                 {
11.                     "Type": "AWS::S3::Object",
12.                     "Values": ["arn:aws:s3:::financial-datalake/"]
13.                 }
14.             ]
15.         }
16.     ]
17. }
```

This setup provides:

- Detailed access logging
- Audit trail for compliance

- Security incident investigation capabilities
- Usage pattern analysis

Implementation steps:

1. Set up CloudTrail in the AWS Console.

2. Configure log storage location.

3. Enable log file validation.

4. Set up CloudWatch alerts.

5. Create compliance reports using Athena.

Monitoring and compliance automation

The final layer involves automated monitoring and compliance checking. Configure CloudWatch alerts for security-relevant events:

```
1.  {
2.      "Rules": [
3.          {
4.              "Name": "sensitive-data-access",
5.              "Description": "Monitor access to sensitive data",
6.              "EventPattern": {
7.                  "source": ["aws.s3"],
8.                  "detail-type": ["AWS API Call via CloudTrail"],
9.                  "detail": {
10.                     "eventSource": ["s3.amazonaws.com"],
11.                     "eventName": ["GetObject", "PutObject"],
12.                     "requestParameters": {
13.                         "bucketName": ["financial-datalake"],
14.                         "key": [{"prefix": "sensitive/"}]
15.                     }
16.                 }
17.             }
18.         }
19.     ]
20. }
```

Implementation involves:

- Creating CloudWatch rules
- Setting up SNS notifications
- Configuring automated responses
- Establishing review procedures

This comprehensive security and governance framework ensures your data lake remains both secure and compliant while enabling appropriate access and collaboration. Regular reviews and updates of these controls ensure continued effectiveness as your organization's needs evolve.

Cost optimization techniques

Cost optimization in data lakes requires a thoughtful balance of storage efficiency, query performance, and operational costs. Each component of the optimization strategy plays a crucial role in managing expenses while maintaining performance.

Storage class selection and lifecycle management

Storage class selection forms the foundation of cost optimization. As data ages, its value and access patterns typically change. Fresh data might require immediate access through S3 Standard, while historical data accessed quarterly could move to Glacier Instant Retrieval, potentially reducing storage costs by up to 70%.

To implement lifecycle rules, begin at the AWS Management Console. Navigate through Services | S3 | Your Bucket Name | Management | Create Lifecycle Rule. When creating the rule, you will configure transitions like this:

```
1.  {
2.      "Rules": [{
3.          "ID": "Cost-Optimized-Lifecycle",
4.          "Filter": {"Prefix": "data/"},
5.          "Transitions": [
6.              {"Days": 30, "StorageClass": "STANDARD_IA"},
7.              {"Days": 90, "StorageClass": "GLACIER"}
8.          ],
9.          "Status": "Enabled"
10.     }]
11. }
```

This configuration automatically moves data through storage tiers based on age. The system monitors object age and handles transitions automatically. When setting up these rules, consider your access patterns carefully. For instance, financial data might need quick access for the current quarter but can move to Standard-IA afterward, with annual data shifting to Glacier for long-term retention.

Intelligent-Tiering configuration

When access patterns are unpredictable, Intelligent-Tiering provides automated cost optimization. To enable this feature, access your S3 bucket through the AWS Console, then navigate to Properties | Intelligent-Tiering Archive Configurations | Create Configuration. Here is a typical setup:

```
1.  {
2.      "Id": "AutoTiering",
3.      "Status": "Enabled",
4.      "Tierings": [
5.          {"Days": 90, "AccessTier": "ARCHIVE_ACCESS"},
6.          {"Days": 180, "AccessTier": "DEEP_ARCHIVE"}
7.      ]
8.  }
```

The system will now automatically monitor object access patterns and move data between tiers accordingly. While there is a small monitoring fee per object (about $0.0025 per 1,000 objects), this cost is typically offset by storage savings.

Query optimization and cost control

Query optimization starts with effective data organization. Consider a retail analytics system where data is organized hierarchically by region, date, and product category. This organization enables partition pruning, a powerful cost-saving technique that reduces the amount of data scanned during queries.

For example, when data is organized like this:

```
data_lake/
    └── year=2024/
        └── month=02/
            └── day=07/
                └── region=us-east/
                    └── data.parquet
```

A query filtering by specific dates and regions will scan only relevant partitions, significantly reducing costs. To set up workgroup controls that enforce these optimizations, navigate to Amazon Athena | Workgroups | Create Workgroup and configure settings:

```
1. {
2.     "WorkgroupConfig": {
3.         "BytesScannedCutoffPerQuery": 1073741824,
4.         "RequesterPaysEnabled": true,
5.         "ResultReuseEnabled": true,
6.         "EnforceWorkGroupConfiguration": true
7.     }
8. }
```

Cost monitoring and control

Effective cost control begins with proper tagging. Access the AWS Billing Console through Services | Billing | Cost Allocation Tag. Here you will activate cost allocation tags that enable detailed cost tracking. A comprehensive tagging strategy might include project identifiers, cost centers, environments, and data classifications.

For budget monitoring, navigate to AWS Billing | Budgets | Create Budget. Set up your budget with appropriate thresholds and notifications:

```
1. {
       "Budget": {
2.         "Amount": "10000",
3.         "Period": "Monthly",
4.         "Alerts": [
5.             {
6.                 "Threshold": 80,
7.                 "Type": "ACTUAL",
8.                 "Actions": [
9.                     {
10.                         "Type": "NOTIFY",
11.                         "Recipients": ["team@company.com"]
12.                     }
13.                 ]
14.             }
15.         ]
```

```
16.     }
17. }
```

Monitor your cost optimization efforts through AWS Cost Explorer, accessible via Services | Cost Management | Cost Explorer. Here you can analyse spending patterns, identify optimization opportunities, and track the effectiveness of your cost-saving measures.

Regular review and optimization

A successful cost optimization strategy requires regular review and adjustment. Access S3 Storage Lens through S3 | Storage Lens | Create Dashboard to gain insights into storage patterns and optimization opportunities. Monthly reviews should examine query patterns through Athena's query history, storage class distribution through S3 analytics, and overall cost trends through Cost Explorer.

Remember that cost optimization is an ongoing process. As your data lake grows and usage patterns evolve, your optimization strategies should adapt accordingly. Regular monitoring and adjustments ensure that your data lake remains cost-effective while meeting performance requirements.

Implementing data cataloguing

Data catalogues serve as the central nervous system of a data lake, enabling data discovery, governance, and analysis. AWS Glue Data Catalogue provides a unified metadata repository that makes data discoverable and queryable. Let us explore how to implement a comprehensive cataloguing strategy.

AWS Glue Data Catalogue architecture

The Glue Data Catalogue functions as a persistent metadata store for all your data assets. Think of it as a library card catalogue for your data lake, where each entry contains information about where data resides, its schema, and how to access it. To get started with the Glue Data Catalogue, navigate to AWS Glue | Settings in the AWS Console and configure the catalogue settings:

```
1.  {
2.      "DatabaseSettings": {
3.          "DefaultSecurity": {
4.              "EnableEncryption": true,
5.              "EncryptionType": "SSE-KMS",
6.              "KmsKeyId": "arn:aws:kms:region:account:key/key-id"
7.          }
8.      },
9.      "CrawlerSettings": {
10.         "EnableCloudWatch": true,
11.         "RetentionPeriod": 30
12.     }
13. }
14. {
15.     "DatabaseSettings": {
16.         "DefaultSecurity": {
17.             "EnableEncryption": true,
18.             "EncryptionType": "SSE-KMS",
19.             "KmsKeyId": "arn:aws:kms:region:account:key/key-id"
20.         }
21.     },
22.     "CrawlerSettings": {
```

```
23.            "EnableCloudWatch": true,
24.            "RetentionPeriod": 30
25.        }
26. }
```

Data crawlers automatically discover new data, infer schemas, and update the catalogue. For an e-commerce data lake, you might set up crawlers for different data zones:

```
1.  {
2.      "CrawlerConfiguration": {
3.          "Name": "retail-raw-data-crawler",
4.          "Role": "arn:aws:iam::account:role/GlueCrawlerRole",
5.          "DatabaseName": "retail_raw_catalog",
6.          "Targets": {
7.              "S3Targets": [{
8.                  "Path": "s3://retail-datalake/raw/",
9.                  "Exclusions": ["*.tmp", "*.temp", "_SUCCESS"]
10.             }]
11.         },
12.         "Schedule": "cron(0 0/6 * * ? *)",  // Run every 6 hours
13.         "SchemaChangePolicy": {
14.             "UpdateBehavior": "UPDATE_IN_DATABASE",
15.             "DeleteBehavior": "LOG"
16.         }
17.     }
18. }
```

Create this crawler through AWS Glue | Crawlers | Add Crawler. The crawler will scan your S3 locations, detect file formats, infer schemas, and create or update table definitions in the catalogue.

Metadata management and evolution

As data evolves, so must your metadata management strategy. Access AWS Glue | Tables to manage table definitions. Here is how to handle schema changes through the AWS Glue API:

```
1.  {
2.      "TableInput": {
3.          "Name": "customer_transactions",
4.          "StorageDescriptor": {
5.              "Columns": [
6.                  {"Name": "transaction_id", "Type": "string"},
7.                  {"Name": "customer_id", "Type": "string"},
8.                  {"Name": "transaction_date", "Type": "timestamp"},
9.                  {"Name": "amount", "Type": "decimal(10,2)"}
10.             ],
11.             "Location": "s3://retail-datalake/processed/transactions/",
12.             "InputFormat": "org.apache.hadoop.hive.ql.io.parquet.
    MapredParquetInputFormat",
13.             "OutputFormat": "org.apache.hadoop.hive.ql.io.parquet.
    MapredParquetOutputFormat",
14.             "SerdeInfo": {
15.                 "SerializationLibrary": "org.apache.hadoop.hive.ql.io.parquet.serde.
```

```
ParquetHiveSerDe"
16.              }
17.          },
18.          "VersionId": "1",
19.          "TableType": "EXTERNAL_TABLE"
20.      }
21. }
```

Search and discovery implementation

Enable powerful search capabilities by implementing Lake Formation tags and search indexes. Navigate to Lake Formation | Tables to add business metadata:

```
1.  {
2.      "TagConfiguration": {
3.          "Tags": [
4.              {
5.                  "TagKey": "data_domain",
6.                  "TagValue": "retail_transactions"
7.              },
8.              {
9.                  "TagKey": "data_owner",
10.                 "TagValue": "finance_team"
11.             },
12.             {
13.                 "TagKey": "sensitivity",
14.                 "TagValue": "confidential"
15.             }
16.         ]
17.     }
18. }
```

AWS service integration

The Glue Data Catalogue integrates seamlessly with various AWS services. To enable Athena integration, navigate to Athena | Data Source | Connect Data Source:

```
1.  {
2.      "DataSourceConfiguration": {
3.          "Type": "GlueCatalog",
4.          "DatabaseName": "retail_catalog",
5.          "TablePattern": "transactions_*"
6.      }
7.  }
```

For Amazon **Elastic MapReduce(EMR)** integration, specify the catalogue in your cluster configuration:

```
1.  {
2.      "Classifications": [{
3.          "Classification": "hive-site",
4.          "Properties": {
```

```
5.              "hive.metastore.client.factory.class": "com.amazonaws.glue.catalog.
  metastore.AWSGlueDataCatalogHiveClientFactory"
6.          }
7.      }]
8.  }
```

Monitoring and maintenance

Set up CloudWatch monitoring for your catalogue operations. Create a dashboard through CloudWatch | Dashboards | Create Dashboard:

```
1.  {
2.      "MetricWidgets": [
3.          {
4.              "MetricName": "CrawlerSucceeded",
5.              "Namespace": "AWS/Glue",
6.              "Period": 300,
7.              "Statistic": "Sum"
8.          },
9.          {
10.             "MetricName": "TableVersionsCreated",
11.             "Namespace": "AWS/Glue",
12.             "Period": 300,
13.             "Statistic": "Sum"
14.         }
15.     ]
16. }
```

Regular maintenance ensures your catalogue remains accurate and useful. Schedule monthly reviews of crawler logs, schema versions, and search effectiveness. Update metadata and classifications as your data lake evolves to maintain the discoverability and usability of your data assets.

Building a scalable data lake architecture

This guide demonstrates how to build a production-ready data lake using AWS CDK with Python. The architecture implements a three-zone data lake (raw, trusted, and curated) with security, data cataloging, and monitoring capabilities. For the complete source code and detailed implementation, visit the book's accompanying GitHub repository.

Project structure

The project follows a modular design pattern where each component is separated into its own stack for better maintainability:

```
retail-data-lake-python/
├── retail_data_lake/
│   ├── data_lake_stack.py        # Core storage infrastructure
│   ├── catalog_stack.py          # Data cataloging configuration
│   └── monitoring_stack.py       # Monitoring setup
├── scripts/
│   └── generate_test_data.py     # Test data generation
├── app.py                        # Main CDK app
```

Critical components

This implementation demonstrates a comprehensive AWS data lake setup using the AWS **Cloud Development Kit (CDK)**. The architecture is organized into three main components, each handling distinct aspects of the data lake infrastructure. Below is a detailed breakdown of each component and its implementation:

1. **Core storage infrastructure (data_lake_stack.py):** The data lake stack creates the foundation of our data lake by setting up three S3 buckets for different data zones. Each bucket is encrypted using KMS and versioned for data protection. The following are the steps on how it works:

    a. Creates a KMS key for encrypting all data lake buckets.

    b. Defines common security configurations, including versioning and encryption.

    c. Creates three separate buckets for raw, trusted, and curated data zones.

```python
1. from aws_cdk import Stack, aws_s3 as s3, aws_kms as kms, RemovalPolicy, Duration
2. from constructs import Construct
3.
4. class DataLakeStack(Stack):
5.     def __init__(self, scope: Construct, construct_id: str, **kwargs) -> None:
6.         super().__init__(scope, construct_id, **kwargs)
7.
8.         # KMS key for encryption
9.         encryption_key = kms.Key(self, "DataLakeKey",
10.            enable_key_rotation=True,
11.            alias="retail-data-lake-key"
12.        )
13.
14.        # Common bucket configuration
15.        bucket_config = {
16.            "encryption": s3.BucketEncryption.KMS,
17.            "encryption_key": encryption_key,
18.            "versioned": True,
19.            "removal_policy": RemovalPolicy.RETAIN
20.        }
21.
22.        # Create zones
23.        self.raw_bucket = s3.Bucket(self, "RawZone", **bucket_config)
24.        self.trusted_bucket = s3.Bucket(self, "TrustedZone", **bucket_config)
25.        self.curated_bucket = s3.Bucket(self, "CuratedZone", **bucket_config)
```

2. **Data Catalog configuration (catalog_stack.py):** The catalog stack handles metadata management using AWS Glue. It accomplishes three main tasks; follow these steps:

    a. Creates a Glue Data Catalog database to store metadata.

    b. Sets up IAM roles with necessary permissions for Glue crawlers.

    c. Configures crawlers for each data zone to automatically discover and catalog data.

```python
1. from aws_cdk import Stack, aws_glue as glue, aws_iam as iam
2. from constructs import Construct
3.
4. class CatalogStack(Stack):
```

```
5.      def __init__(self, scope: Construct, construct_id: str,
6.                   raw_bucket, trusted_bucket, curated_bucket, **kwargs) -> None:
7.          super().__init__(scope, construct_id, **kwargs)
8.
9.          # Create Glue Database
10.         database = glue.CfnDatabase(self, "RetailDataLakeDB",
11.             catalog_id=self.account,
12.             database_input=glue.CfnDatabase.DatabaseInputProperty(
13.                 name="retail_analytics"
14.             )
15.         )
16.
17.         # Set up crawlers for each zone
18.         crawler_role = iam.Role(self, "GlueCrawlerRole",
19.             assumed_by=iam.ServicePrincipal("glue.amazonaws.com")
20.         )
21.
22.         # Grant permissions and create crawlers
23.         for zone, bucket in [("raw", raw_bucket),
24.                              ("trusted", trusted_bucket),
25.                              ("curated", curated_bucket)]:
26.             bucket.grant_read(crawler_role)
27.             self._create_crawler(zone, bucket, database, crawler_role)
```

- **Main application (app.py):** The **app.py** file serves as the entry point for deploying our data lake infrastructure. It coordinates three essential stack components that work together to create a fully functional data lake environment:

1. Instantiates the core data lake storage stack.

2. Creates the catalogue stack and links it to the storage buckets.

3. Sets up monitoring with references to all data zones.

```
1. from aws_cdk import App
2. from retail_data_lake.data_lake_stack import DataLakeStack
3. from retail_data_lake.catalog_stack import CatalogStack
4. from retail_data_lake.monitoring_stack import MonitoringStack
5.
6. app = App()
7.
8. # Create and connect stacks
9. data_lake = DataLakeStack(app, "RetailDataLakeStack")
10. CatalogStack(app, "RetailDataLakeCatalog",
11.     raw_bucket=data_lake.raw_bucket,
12.     trusted_bucket=data_lake.trusted_bucket,
13.     curated_bucket=data_lake.curated_bucket
14. )
15. MonitoringStack(app, "RetailDataLakeMonitoring",
16.     raw_bucket=data_lake.raw_bucket,
17.     trusted_bucket=data_lake.trusted_bucket,
```

```
18.    curated_bucket=data_lake.curated_bucket
19. )
20.
21. app.synth()
```

Deployment

Before proceeding with deployment, ensure all AWS credentials are properly configured and you have the necessary permissions. The deployment process involves two main steps:

```
# Deploy infrastructure
1. cdk deploy --all
2.
3. # Generate test data
4. python scripts/generate_test_data.py
```

Sample analytics query

After deployment, you can analyze your data using Amazon Athena. Here is a sample query that shows transaction statistics by month:

```
1. SELECT
2.     year,
3.     month,
4.     COUNT(*) as transaction_count,
5.     ROUND(AVG(amount), 2) as avg_amount
6. FROM transactions
7. GROUP BY year, month
8. ORDER BY year, month;
```

For detailed implementation, including monitoring setup, test data generation, cleanup scripts, and comprehensive deployment instructions, please refer to the complete source code in the GitHub repository.

Conclusion

This chapter has laid the groundwork for building robust data lake architectures, demonstrating how AWS services can be orchestrated to create scalable, secure, and cost-effective data storage solutions through the medallion architecture pattern, comprehensive security frameworks, and automated data cataloguing. The hands-on implementation using AWS CDK has provided practical insights into creating production-ready data lakes with modular design and automated deployment, setting the stage for the next chapter, which explores data formats and storage optimization.

The next chapter will expand upon these foundations by exploring various data formats across structured, semi-structured, and unstructured data, with particular attention to specialized formats like Delta Lake and Apache Hudi, compression strategies, and the technical nuances of row-based versus columnar storage. Readers will gain practical knowledge about format selection guidelines, S3 storage optimization techniques, and hands-on experience with data format migration, enabling them to make informed decisions about data storage that complement the robust data lake infrastructure established in this chapter.

Join our Discord space

Join our Discord workspace for latest updates, offers, tech happenings around the world, new releases, and sessions with the authors:

https://discord.bpbonline.com

CHAPTER 3
Data Formats and Storage Optimization

Introduction

In modern data engineering, the choice of data formats and storage optimization strategies can mean the difference between a highly efficient, cost-effective data platform and one that struggles with performance and cost overruns. Building upon our previous discussions of data lake foundations and cloud-native architectures, this chapter explores the critical decisions and implementations surrounding data formats and storage optimization in AWS environments.

Consider a global retail organization handling millions of daily transactions across various channels, from point-of-sale systems generating structured data to mobile applications producing semi-structured JSON, to security cameras creating unstructured video streams. Each data type presents unique challenges in storage, processing, and analysis. The organization's success depends not just on collecting this data, but on storing it in formats that enable efficient processing while optimizing storage costs.

Having established the critical role of data formats in modern data platforms, let us outline the specific skills and knowledge you will gain from this chapter.

Structure

This chapter will cover the following topics:

- Understanding data format requirements
- Schema evolution
- Performance and cost optimization
- Specialized data formats
- Row-based formats
- Columnar formats
- Binary and compression formats
- Specialized table formats
- Hands-on: Data format migration and optimization

Objectives

In this chapter, we will understand how the strategic selection of data formats and storage optimization techniques serves as a critical foundation for modern data engineering. We will examine various data formats from structured to unstructured, row-based to columnar, and binary to specialized table formats, analyzing how each addresses specific use cases and performance requirements. By understanding these formats and their appropriate applications, you will learn to make informed decisions that significantly impact storage costs, processing efficiency, and query performance. Through practical implementation examples, we will demonstrate how to migrate between formats, optimize compression strategies, and leverage advanced table formats like Delta Lake and Apache Hudi to solve complex data management challenges in cloud environments. The knowledge gained will enable you to design data platforms that efficiently balance performance needs with cost considerations while providing the flexibility required for evolving business requirements.

Understanding data format requirements

Data format requirements form the foundation of any data engineering initiative. The choice of data format impacts every aspect of a data platform, from storage costs and processing efficiency to query performance and data accessibility. Modern enterprises handle an intricate mix of data types, each with its own characteristics and requirements.

Spectrum of data structure

Data exists on a continuous spectrum of structure, ranging from highly organized to completely unstructured. At one end, we find structured data with rigid organization like financial transactions or inventory records. In the middle, semi-structured data offers flexibility while maintaining some organization, such as JSON logs from web applications. At the other end, unstructured data like videos or documents requires specialized processing approaches.

Structured data

Structured data follows predefined models and schemas, typically stored in traditional databases or data warehouses. As the bedrock of enterprise data management, structured data provides the essential foundation for reliable business operations, enabling consistent processing, efficient querying, and accurate reporting. Financial transactions serve as a perfect example. Each transaction record contains specific fields like date, amount, account numbers, and transaction type. This rigid structure enables efficient querying and analysis but can be inflexible when business requirements change.

Banking systems illustrate this well. A transaction record might contain:

```
1.  CREATE TABLE transactions (
2.      transaction_id UUID PRIMARY KEY,
3.      account_number VARCHAR(20),
4.      transaction_type VARCHAR(10),
5.      amount DECIMAL(15,2),
6.      transaction_date TIMESTAMP,
7.      status VARCHAR(10)
8.  );
```

This structure allows for efficient processing but presents challenges when new requirements emerge, such as adding cryptocurrency transactions or new payment methods.

Semi-structured data

Semi-structured data maintains a balance between flexibility and organization. Web applications generate vast amounts of such data. A single user session might capture dozens of interactions, each with varying fields depending on the user's actions. While this data has some structure, it is not as rigid as traditional database tables.

Consider a web analytics event:

```
1.  {
2.      "session_id": "sess_123",
3.      "timestamp": "2024-02-08T10:15:30Z",
4.      "user_agent": {
5.          "browser": "Chrome",
6.          "version": "120.0",
7.          "platform": "Windows"
8.      },
9.      "events": [
10.         {
11.             "type": "page_view",
12.             "page": "/products",
13.             "duration": 45
14.         },
15.         {
16.             "type": "click",
17.             "element": "add_to_cart",
18.             "product_id": "prod_789"
19.         }
20.     ]
21. }
```

This format accommodates varying event types and properties while maintaining enough structure for meaningful analysis.

Unstructured data

Unstructured data encompasses everything from email messages to video files. Healthcare organizations, for instance, deal with a variety of unstructured data: medical imaging files (**Digital Imaging and Communication in Medicine** (**DICOM**) format), physician notes (text), and patient recordings. This data requires specialized processing pipelines to extract meaningful information. For example:

A medical imaging system must handle:

- Image data in DICOM format containing patient scans
- Embedded metadata about the imaging equipment and settings
- Associated physician annotations and notes
- Patient identification information

Having established the fundamental requirements for different data formats, we must consider how these formats evolve over time. As we saw in *Chapter 2, Building Data Lake Foundations,* data structures rarely remain static. Organizations like Global Finance from our earlier case study frequently need to adapt their data models to accommodate new business requirements. This brings us to our next crucial topic: schema evolution.

Schema evolution

Schema evolution represents one of the most critical aspects of data format management to manage growth and change. As business requirements change and new data sources emerge, data formats must adapt while maintaining compatibility with existing systems. This evolution occurs through several mechanisms.

Versioning strategies

Schema versioning enables controlled evolution of data formats. Each schema version represents a specific point in time, with clear documentation of changes and compatibility requirements. For instance, a customer profile schema might evolve:

- **Version 1**:

```
1. {
2.      "customer_id": "cust_123",
3.      "name": "John Smith",
4.      "email": "john@example.com"
5. }
```

- **Version 2**:

```
1.  {
2.       "customer_id": "cust_123",
3.       "name": {
4.           "first": "John",
5.           "last": "Smith"
6.       },
7.       "email": "john@example.com",
8.       "preferences": {
9.           "marketing_emails": true,
10.          "notification_method": "email"
11.      }
12. }
```

This evolution provides enhanced functionality while maintaining backward compatibility.

Compatibility patterns

Successful schema evolution requires careful attention to compatibility:

- **Forward compatibility**: Ensuring old code can read new data formats.
- **Backward compatibility**: Ensuring new code can read old data formats.
- **Full compatibility**: Maintaining both forward and backward compatibility.

These patterns are implemented through:

- Default values for new fields.
- Optional fields for non-critical additions.
- Field deprecation strategies instead of immediate removal.
- Data transformation layers for handling multiple versions.

With a solid understanding of format requirements and evolution strategies, we can now examine how different format choices impact two critical aspects of data platforms: performance and cost. These considerations directly influence the success of the cloud-native architectures we discussed in *Chapter 1, Modern Data Engineering Landscape*.

Performance and cost optimization

The choice of data format significantly impacts both performance and costs. These impacts manifest in several ways:

- **Storage efficiency:** Different formats offer varying levels of storage efficiency such as:
  - Row-based formats (CSV, JSON) excel at record-level operations.
  - Columnar formats (Parquet, ORC) provide better compression and query performance.
  - Binary formats offer compact storage but may require specialized processing.
- **Processing requirements:** Format choice affects processing efficiency in the following ways:
  - Text-based formats require parsing overhead but are human-readable.
  - Binary formats offer faster processing but require specialized tools.
  - Compressed formats reduce storage costs but increase CPU usage during processing.
- **Query performance:** Format selection influences query performance:
  - Columnar formats excel at analytical queries reading specific columns.
  - Row formats perform better for retrieving complete records.
  - Partitioning and indexing capabilities vary by format.
- **Real-world optimization:** A practical example comes from log analytics systems. Daily logs might arrive as JSON, but for long-term storage and analysis, converting to Parquet format offers several benefits:
  - Reduced storage costs through better compression.
  - Improved query performance through columnar storage.
  - Efficient filtering through predicate pushdown.

The key lies in selecting formats that balance these factors based on specific use cases and requirements.

Having established fundamental performance and cost considerations, let us explore how these principles apply to specialized data types that require unique handling approaches. Building upon the storage patterns from *Chapter 2, Building Data Lake Foundations,* we will see how different formats address specific use cases.

Specialized data formats

Modern data platforms must handle diverse types of data, each with its own specialized formats. Understanding these formats and their characteristics is crucial for building efficient and effective data pipelines. Before exploring specific formats, let us understand some fundamental concepts that appear across different data types.

Core concepts in data compression

Data compression plays a vital role in managing specialized data formats. There are two main approaches to compression:

- **Lossless compression** preserves data exactly as in the original. Think of it like carefully folding a paper document, you can unfold it to recover the exact original. This compression works by finding and eliminating statistical redundancy in data without losing any information. While it ensures perfect data fidelity, it typically achieves lower compression ratios.
- **Lossy compression** achieves better compression ratios by selectively discarding less important data. It is like summarizing a document instead of keeping every word. The trick lies in discarding information

that humans are less likely to notice or care about. For instance, in images, subtle color variations that human eyes cannot distinguish might be simplified to a single color.

Video data engineering

Video formats package multiple elements: visual data, audio tracks, and metadata. The efficiency of video storage and processing depends heavily on specialized software that compresses and decompresses video data:

- **Common video formats and characteristics:** The following table compares popular video formats and their key specifications including compression methods, file sizes, and optimal use cases:

Format/Codec	Compression type	Compression ratio	Processing overhead	File size (1 hour 1080p)	Best use case
H.264	Lossy	Up to 50:1	Moderate	1-2 GB	General streaming, storage
HEVC (H.265)	Lossy	Up to 75:1	High	0.5 to 1 GB	4K/8K content
ProRes	Low Lossy	5:1 to 10:1	Low	80 to 100 GB	Professional editing
Motion JPEG	Lossy	10:1 to 20:1	Very Low	4 to 5 GB	Real-time processing
Raw Video	None	1:1	None	400 to 500 GB	Professional production

Table 3.1: Common video format and use cases

- **Video format selection guide:** This comprehensive guide helps you choose the most suitable video format based on storage needs, processing requirements, and quality expectations:

Consideration	Requirements	Recommended format	Alternative format
Storage optimization			
High volume (>1TB/day)	Maximum compression	HEVC	H.264 high profile
Medium volume	Balance of quality/size	H.264 main profile	HEVC
Low volume	Quick processing	Motion JPEG	H.264 baseline
Processing speed			
Real-time analytics	Low latency	Motion JPEG	H.264 baseline
Batch processing	High compression	HEVC	H.264 high profile
Live streaming	Network efficient	H.264 main profile	HEVC
Quality requirements			
Archival	Maximum quality	ProRes	Raw
Production	High quality	ProRes	H.264 high profile
Distribution	Balanced	H.264 main profile	HEVC

Table 3.2: Video format selection guidelines

Audio engineering

Audio formats vary in their approach to storing sound data, from raw uncompressed formats to highly compressed streaming formats:

- **Common audio formats and characteristics:** This table outlines the main audio formats used in digital recording and distribution, comparing their compression methods, file sizes, and primary applications:

Format	Compression type	Bit rate	File size (1 hour)	Quality loss	Best for
WAV	None	1411 kbps	~635 MB	None	Professional work
FLAC	Lossless	~1000 kbps	~450 MB	None	Archival
MP3	Lossy	128-320 kbps	60-145 MB	Yes	Distribution
AAC	Lossy	128-256 kbps	60-120 MB	Yes	Streaming
PCM	None	Variable	~600 MB	None	Processing

Table 3.3: Audio format and use cases

- **Audio format selection guide:** This guide provides recommendations for choosing the optimal audio format based on quality requirements and specific use cases, with suitable alternatives:

Consideration	Requirements	Recommended format	Alternative format
Quality level			
Professional audio	Perfect reproduction	WAV	PCM
Archival storage	No quality loss	FLAC	ALAC
Streaming	Bandwidth efficient	AAC	MP3
Usage pattern			
Audio analysis	Raw data access	WAV	PCM
Content delivery	Size optimized	MP3 (320kbps)	AAC
Mobile apps	Efficient streaming	AAC	

Table 3.4: Audio format selection guideline

While specialized formats handle specific data types, row-based formats form the backbone of many data operations. Understanding these fundamental formats is crucial before we explore more advanced options.

Row-based formats

Row-based formats organize data by records, where each row contains all fields for a single entry. These formats have become fundamental in data engineering due to their simplicity, widespread support, and ease of human readability. Understanding their characteristics and optimal use cases is crucial for effective data platform design.

- **Common row-based formats:** This table compares popular row-based data formats, highlighting their structure, readability, schema requirements, and optimal use cases:

Format	Structure	Human readable	Schema required	Size efficiency	Best for
CSV	Delimited text	Yes	No	Moderate	Simple tabular data
TSV	Tab delimited	Yes	No	Moderate	Export compatibility
JSON	Key-value pairs	Yes	No	Low	Nested structures
JSONL	Line-delimited JSON	Yes	No	Low	Streaming data
XML	Hierarchical tags	Yes	Optional (XSD)	Very low	Legacy systems

Table 3.5: Row based format and use cases

- **Format selection guide:** This guide helps you select the most appropriate data format based on specific requirements, providing primary and alternative recommendations for different use cases:

Requirement	Recommended format	Alternative
Simple data exchange	CSV	TSV
Complex nested data	JSON	XML
Streaming processing	JSONL	CSV
Legacy system integration	XML	JSON
Large-scale processing	JSONL	CSV
Human readability	JSON	CSV

Table 3.6: Format selection guidance

Best practices

Following these key guidelines will help you make the most effective use of row-based formats while ensuring data reliability and performance:

- Use CSV for simple, tabular data requiring broad compatibility.
- Choose JSON for complex, nested structures.
- Implement JSONL for streaming and large-scale processing.
- Reserve XML for specific requirements or legacy systems.
- Consider compression for storage optimization.
- Implement robust error handling for all formats.
- Validate data structure and content during processing.

While row-based formats excel at record-level operations, they present limitations for analytical workloads, particularly in cloud environments. Recalling our discussion of analytical patterns in *Chapter 1, Modern Data Engineering Landscape*. To address these analytical requirements and optimize the cloud storage patterns we studied in *Chapter 2, Building Data Lake Foundations*, many organizations are shifting toward columnar formats.

Columnar formats

The transition from row-based to columnar storage formats represents one of the most significant advancements in data engineering. While traditional row-based formats store complete records together, columnar formats take a fundamentally different approach by organizing data by columns. This seemingly simple change in organization has profound implications for analytical workloads and big data processing.

Understanding columnar storage

To grasp the significance of columnar formats, consider how data is physically stored on disk. In a traditional row-based format, like CSV, a customer record containing ID, name, age, and city would be stored as a complete unit: *1, John, 25, NYC*. When you have millions of records, they are stored sequentially, one after another. This works well when you need to read complete records but becomes inefficient for analytical queries that typically focus on specific columns.

Columnar storage revolutionizes this approach by grouping all values from each column together. Instead of storing complete customer records sequentially, it stores all customer IDs together, all names together, all ages together, and all cities together. This reorganization enables powerful optimization. When similar values are stored together, they can be compressed more efficiently. When analyzing age demographics, for example, you only need to read the age column, not the entire dataset.

Traditional row-based storage:

```
1. id,name,age,city
2. 1,John,25,NYC  -> Stored as: 1,John,25,NYC|2,Mary,30,LA|3,Bob,28,CHI
3. 2,Mary,30,LA
4. 3,Bob,28,CHI
```

Columnar storage:

```
1. id:   [1,2,3]        -> Stored together
2. name: [John,Mary,Bob]-> Stored together
3. age:  [25,30,28]     -> Stored together
4. city: [NYC,LA,CHI]   -> Stored together
```

This organization provides several key advantages:

- Better compression (similar values stored together).
- Efficient column pruning (read only needed columns).
- Improved query performance for analytical workloads.
- Optimized for cloud storage access patterns.

Apache Parquet

Apache Parquet has emerged as the dominant columnar format in modern data lakes, and understanding its architecture reveals why. Parquet organizes data into row groups, typically 128MB in size, with each row group containing column chunks. These chunks are further divided into pages, creating a hierarchical structure that enables efficient data access and compression.

The magic of Parquet lies in its intelligent handling of different data types. For text data, it employs dictionary encoding, where repeated values are replaced with integer references to a dictionary. For numeric data, it can use various encoding schemes optimized for different patterns. When storing timestamps, Parquet might use delta encoding to store the differences between consecutive values rather than the full timestamps.

Consider a dataset of retail transactions. For a column storing product categories, which typically contains many repeated values, dictionary encoding might reduce storage requirements by 90%. For a column storing transaction amounts, delta encoding combined with appropriate compression could achieve significant space savings while maintaining quick access for analytical queries.

Apache Optimized Row Columnar optimization

While Parquet and ORC share many conceptual similarities, **Optimized Row Columnar** (**ORC**) takes a slightly different approach to optimization. ORC organizes data into stripes, typically 256MB, each containing index data, row data, and a stripe footer. This structure, combined with built-in indexing, makes ORC particularly efficient for certain types of queries.

ORC's indexing capabilities set it apart. It maintains statistics about the data in each stripe, including minimum and maximum values, and can even include Bloom filters for specific columns. These features allow ORC to skip entire sections of data that are not relevant to a query. For instance, when querying transactions from a specific date range, ORC can immediately skip stripes that do not contain data from that period.

Performance and practical considerations

The choice between columnar formats often comes down to specific use cases and ecosystem compatibility. In real-world scenarios with large datasets, both Parquet and ORC demonstrate remarkable improvements over traditional formats. A 100GB data set stored in CSV might compress to 20GB in Parquet and 25GB in ORC, while providing dramatically faster query performance.

When scanning a single column to compute averages or find patterns, columnar formats might complete in seconds what would take minutes with row-based storage. This performance difference becomes even more pronounced in cloud environments, where reducing data transfer and optimizing storage can significantly impact costs.

For modern data lakes, Parquet has become the default choice due to its excellent cloud storage optimization and broad ecosystem support. Its handling of nested structures and compatibility with services like AWS Athena and Redshift Spectrum makes it particularly attractive for cloud-native architectures. ORC, with its strong integration with the Hive ecosystem and efficient indexing, remains a compelling choice for Hadoop-based systems and scenarios requiring frequent updates.

The decision ultimately depends on your specific needs. When building a cloud-native analytics platform, Parquet's optimization for object storage and broad tool support makes it an excellent choice. For systems heavily invested in the Hadoop ecosystem or requiring sophisticated indexing, ORC might be more appropriate. Many organizations adopt a hybrid approach, using simpler formats like CSV for data ingestion and converting to columnar formats for analytical processing.

The evolution of these columnar formats continues to shape how we build modern data platforms, enabling increasingly sophisticated analytics while optimizing for both performance and cost. Their impact extends beyond mere storage efficiency, fundamentally changing how we design and implement data processing systems.

The optimization techniques we've discussed through binary formats and compression provide a foundation for data efficiency. However, modern data lakes, like the one we designed in *Chapter 2, Building Data Lake Foundations,* often require additional capabilities beyond simple storage optimization. This is where specialized table formats come into play, building upon basic compression while adding features crucial for cloud-native data management.

While columnar formats optimize data organization, binary and compression formats focus on efficient data serialization and storage. These formats build upon our previous optimization discussions while adding powerful capabilities for data management.

Binary and compression formats

In modern data engineering, efficient serialization and compression of data play a crucial role in building scalable and cost-effective data platforms. Binary formats offer superior performance and storage efficiency compared to text-based formats, while compression strategies help optimize data storage and transmission costs.

Apache Avro

Apache Avro has revolutionized how we handle schema evolution in data systems. Unlike traditional formats that struggle with changing data structures, Avro embraces change through its sophisticated schema management system. At its core, Avro uses a schema defined in JSON to serialize data into a compact binary format. This separation of schema from data enables powerful evolution capabilities while maintaining backwards compatibility.

When Avro serializes data, it includes the schema version but not the full schema with each record. Instead, schemas are typically stored in a central registry. During deserialization, Avro uses both the writer's schema (used to serialize the data) and the reader's schema (used to interpret the data) to seamlessly handle differences between versions. This approach allows for the natural evolution of data structures over time.

Consider a simple user profile schema that evolves over time:

```
1.  # Initial version of our customer tracking system
2.  initial_schema = {
3.      "type": "record",
```

```
4.        "name": "Customer",
5.        "fields": [
6.            {"name": "customer_id", "type": "string"},
7.            {"name": "email", "type": "string"}
8.        ]
9.  }
10.
11. # Initial data writing
12. original_customer = {
13.     "customer_id": "C001",
14.     "email": "customer@example.com"
15. }
16.
17. with avro.DataFileWriter(initial_schema) as writer:
18.     writer.append(original_customer)
19.
20. # Six months later, we need to add customer preferences
21. evolved_schema = {
22.     "type": "record",
23.     "name": "Customer",
24.     "fields": [
25.         {"name": "customer_id", "type": "string"},
26.         {"name": "email", "type": "string"},
27.         {"name": "preferences", "type": ["null", "map"],
    "default": null}
28.     ]
29. }
30.
31. # Reading old records with new schema
32. with avro.DataFileReader(evolved_schema) as reader:
33.     old_customer = reader.read()
34.     # Results in:
35.     # {
36.     #     "customer_id": "C001",
37.     #     "email": "customer@example.com",
38.     #     "preferences": null  # Default value applied
39.     # }
40.
41. # Writing new records with new schema
42. new_customer = {
43.     "customer_id": "C002",
44.     "email": "new@example.com",
45.     "preferences": {"newsletter": "weekly", "theme": "dark"}
46. }
```

The beauty of Avro lies in its ability to handle both old and new data formats seamlessly. Old records are automatically upgraded with default values for new fields, while new records can take advantage of the expanded schema.

Protocol Buffers

Protocol Buffers (**Protobuf**) takes a different approach to binary serialization. Developed by *Google*, Protobuf focuses on providing high-performance, cross-platform data serialization. Unlike Avro, Protobuf requires explicit schema definitions in its own **interface definition language** (**IDL**), which are then compiled into language-specific code.

What makes Protobuf particularly powerful is its strong typing system and efficient binary encoding. Each field in a Protobuf message is assigned a unique number, which is used in the binary format instead of field names, resulting in extremely compact serialization. This approach makes Protobuf an excellent choice for systems requiring high performance and minimal data size.

A notable aspect of Protobuf is its handling of schema evolution through field numbers. Once assigned, a field number should never be reused or deleted, ensuring backward compatibility. This constraint creates a clear contract for how data structures can evolve over time as you can see the following code:

```
1.  // Customer.proto
2.  message Customer {
3.      string customer_id = 1;  // Field numbers are crucial for evolution
4.      string email = 2;
5.
6.      // Adding new fields maintains compatibility
7.      CustomerPreferences preferences = 3;  // Added later
8.  }
9.
10. message CustomerPreferences {
11.     string newsletter_frequency = 1;
12.     string theme = 2;
13. }
```

When this schema evolves, Protobuf maintains compatibility through careful field numbering:

```
1.  # Original code still works with old messages
2.  old_message = read_customer_message()
3.  print(old_message.customer_id)  # Works
4.  print(old_message.email)         # Works
5.  print(old_message.preferences)   # Returns default empty preference object
6.
7.  # New code can use all fields
8.  new_message = Customer()
9.  new_message.customer_id = "C003"
10. new_message.email = "new@example.com"
11. new_message.preferences.newsletter_frequency = "weekly"
```

Compression strategies

The choice of compression algorithm can significantly impact both storage costs and processing performance. Different compression algorithms offer various trade-offs between compression ratio, compression speed, and decompression speed.

Gzip represents the traditional workhorse of data compression. It provides excellent compression ratios but at the cost of higher CPU usage during compression and decompression. Gzip is particularly effective for text-based data, making it a popular choice for log files and text-heavy datasets. However, its relatively slow compression and decompression speeds can become a bottleneck in high-throughput systems.

Snappy, developed by Google, takes a different approach. It deliberately sacrifices compression ratio in favor of speed, typically achieving compression ratios of 20-100% while maintaining extremely fast compression and decompression speeds. This makes Snappy particularly well-suited for systems where processing speed is crucial, such as real-time data pipelines.

Zstandard (**ZSTD**) represents a modern approach to compression, offering an impressive balance of compression ratio and speed. Developed by *Facebook*, ZSTD provides compression ratios comparable to Gzip while offering significantly faster compression and decompression speeds. It achieves this through sophisticated algorithms and the ability to train compression dictionaries on specific data types.

The real-world impact of these compression strategies becomes clear when we look at practical examples. Consider a dataset of 100GB of JSON logs:

- Gzip might compress this to 12GB but requires significant CPU resources.

- Snappy might achieve 25GB but process the data 5 times faster.

- ZSTD might compress to 15GB while maintaining processing speeds close to Snappy.

The choice of compression strategy should be guided by your specific requirements. For archival storage where access is infrequent, Gzip's superior compression ratio makes it an excellent choice. For real-time processing systems, Snappy's speed advantages often outweigh its lower compression ratio. ZSTD offers an attractive middle ground, making it increasingly popular in modern data platforms.

Understanding these formats and compression strategies enables data engineers to make informed decisions about data storage and processing architectures. The combination of appropriate binary formats and compression algorithms can lead to significant improvements in both performance and cost efficiency. As data volumes continue to grow, these optimizations become increasingly crucial for building scalable data platforms.

The optimization techniques we have discussed through binary formats and compression provide a foundation for data efficiency. However, modern data lakes, like those we designed in *Chapter 2, Building Data Lake Foundations*, often require additional capabilities beyond simple storage optimization. This is where specialized table formats come into play.

Specialized table formats

Modern data lakes built on cloud storage systems like Amazon S3 face a fundamental challenge. While S3 excels at storing vast amounts of data cost-effectively, it lacks the sophisticated data management capabilities that enterprises require. Simple file storage cannot handle concurrent updates, ensure data consistency, or track changes effectively. These limitations led to the development of specialized table formats that add a management layer on top of cloud storage, bringing database-like features to data lakes while maintaining their scalability and flexibility.

Understanding modern table formats

Traditional data lake implementations store data directly in files using formats like Parquet or ORC. This approach, while simple, creates significant challenges in real-world scenarios. Consider updating a single customer record in a large dataset; you would need to rewrite entire files, and if multiple processes attempt this simultaneously, you risk data corruption or lost updates. Modern table formats solve these challenges by introducing sophisticated record-keeping systems that track data changes and maintain consistency.

Each format takes a distinct approach to this challenge. Delta Lake, created by Databricks, implements a transaction log system that serves as a detailed ledger of every change. Apache Iceberg, developed at Netflix, uses a metadata tree architecture that enables efficient querying and schema evolution. Apache **Hadoop Upsert Delete and Incremental** (**Hudi**) focuses on real-time data ingestion with flexible storage options.

Architectural approaches and file organization

Delta Lake's transaction log approach tracks every change made to the dataset through a series of JSON files stored alongside the data in S3:

```
s3://your-data-lake/
├── customer_data/
    ├── _delta_log/
    │   ├── 00000.json          # Initial table creation
    │   ├── 00001.json          # Data additions or updates
    │   └── 00002.json          # Schema changes, optimizations
    └── part-00000.parquet      # Actual data files
        part-00001.parquet
        part-00002.parquet
```

This organization enables Delta Lake to maintain a complete history of changes, provide time travel capabilities, and ensure ACID transactions. When a query runs, Delta Lake consults the transaction log to determine the current valid state of the table, ensuring consistency even during concurrent operations.

Apache Iceberg takes a different approach with its metadata tree architecture:

```
s3://your-data-lake/
├── warehouse/
    └── customer_table/
        ├── metadata/
        │   ├── version-manifest.json   # Table versions
        │   ├── snap-9876543.avro        # Current snapshot
        │   └── manifest-lists/          # File tracking
        └── data/
            ├── 2024/01/01/
            │   └── data-0001.parquet
            └── 2024/01/02/
                └── data-0002.parquet
```

Iceberg's metadata tree enables sophisticated query optimization and schema evolution without data rewrites. The format maintains detailed statistics and file listings that allow query engines to skip irrelevant data files, significantly improving performance for large-scale analytics.

Apache Hudi introduces a unique approach focusing on real-time data updates:

```
s3://your-data-lake/
├── customer_records/
    ├── .hoodie/
    │   ├── .commits/           # Tracks all commits
    │   ├── .temp/              # In-progress operations
    │   └── .compaction/        # Background optimization
    └── year=2024/
        └── month=01/
            ├── base-files/
            │   └── file1.parquet
            └── delta-files/     # For Merge-on-Read tables
                └── file1.log
```

AWS integration and implementation

Implementing these formats on AWS requires understanding how they interact with various AWS services. Each format offers different integration patterns that influence architectural decisions and operational practices.

Apache Iceberg's integration with AWS services stands out through its native support in Amazon Athena. This integration enables direct SQL access to Iceberg tables without additional infrastructure:

```
1.  -- Creating an Iceberg table in Athena
2.  CREATE TABLE customer_events
3.  WITH (
4.    format = 'ICEBERG',
5.    location = 's3://analytics/customer_events/'
6.  ) AS
7.  SELECT * FROM source_table;
8.  sletter_frequency = "weekly"
```

When implementing Iceberg on AWS, the AWS Glue Data Catalogue serves as the central metadata repository, yet Iceberg maintains its own metadata tree in S3. This dual approach provides both compatibility with AWS services and Iceberg's advanced features like schema evolution and partition evolution.

Delta Lake's implementation primarily centres around Amazon EMR, reflecting its tight integration with Apache Spark:

```
1.  # Using Delta Lake on EMR
2.  from delta.tables import DeltaTable
3.
4.  DeltaTable.createOrReplace(spark) \
5.      .tableName("customer_profiles") \
6.      .addColumn("customer_id", "STRING") \
7.      .addColumn("profile", "STRUCT<name:STRING,
    preferences:MAP<STRING,STRING>>") \
8.      .addColumn("last_updated", "TIMESTAMP") \
9.      .partitionedBy("date") \
10.     .location("s3://analytics/customer_profiles") \
11.     .execute()
12. cy = "weekly"
```

Apache Hudi provides flexible integration options on AWS. While it works excellently with EMR for write operations, Hudi tables can be queried through Amazon Athena and Redshift Spectrum, offering a balance between write and read optimization:

```
1.  # Example of writing data to a Hudi table using PySpark on EMR
2.
3.  # Import required libraries
4.  from pyspark.sql import SparkSession
5.  import pyspark.sql.functions as F
6.
7.  # Initialize Spark with Hudi configurations
8.  spark = SparkSession.builder \
9.      .appName("HudiExample") \
10.     .config('spark.serializer', 'org.apache.spark.serializer.
    KryoSerializer') \
```

```
11.     .config('spark.sql.extensions', 'org.apache.spark.sql.hudi.
   HoodieSparkSessionExtension') \
12.     .getOrCreate()
13.
14. # Define Hudi configurations
15. hudi_options = {
16.     'hoodie.table.name': 'customer_events',
17.
18.     # Key configuration
19.     'hoodie.datasource.write.recordkey.field': 'customer_id',
      # Primary key
20.     'hoodie.datasource.write.partitionpath.field': 'date',
      # Partition field
21.     'hoodie.datasource.write.precombine.field': 'timestamp',
      # Field for de-duplication
22.
23.     # Table type configuration
24.     'hoodie.datasource.write.table.type': 'MERGE_ON_
   READ',        # MOR for frequent updates
25.     # Alternative: 'COPY_ON_WRITE' for read-optimized tables
26.
27.     # Index configuration
28.     'hoodie.index.type': 'BLO
   OM',                          # Use Bloom filter for lookups
29.     'hoodie.bloom.index.update.partition.path': 'true',
30.
31.     # Performance tuning
32.     'hoodie.upsert.shuffle.parallelism': 200,
33.     'hoodie.insert.shuffle.parallelism': 200,
34.     'hoodie.bulkinsert.shuffle.parallelism': 200,
35.
36.     # Compaction configuration
37.     'hoodie.compact.inline': 'true',                        # Enable inline compaction
38.     'hoodie.compact.inline.max.delta.commits': 20,
39.
40.     # Cleaning configuration
41.     'hoodie.clean.automatic': 'true',
42.     'hoodie.clean.async': 'true',
43.     'hoodie.cleaner.commits.retained': 10
44. }
45.
46. # Example data
47. data = [
48.     (1, "2024-01-01", "purchase", 100.0, "2024-01-01T10:00:00"),
49.     (2, "2024-01-01", "view", 0.0, "2024-01-01T10:05:00")
50. ]
51. columns = ["customer_id", "date", "event_type", "amount", "timestamp"]
52. df = spark.createDataFrame(data, columns)
```

```
53.
54. # Write to Hudi table
55. df.write \
56.     .format("hudi") \
57.     .options(**hudi_options) \
58.     .mode("append") \
59.     .save("s3://analytics/customer_events")
60.
61. # Reading from Hudi table
62. # Snapshot query (latest data)
63. snapshot_df = spark.read \
64.     .format("hudi") \
65.     .load("s3://analytics/customer_events")
```

Real-world performance and capabilities

In production environments, these formats demonstrate different strengths and trade-offs. Consider a real-time customer data platform handling millions of updates daily:

- Delta Lake excels in scenarios requiring strict transactional consistency. Its transaction log approach ensures that concurrent updates remain consistent, making it ideal for financial data or other scenarios where data accuracy is paramount. However, this comes with increased storage overhead for maintaining the transaction log.

- Iceberg shows its strength in analytical workloads where query performance is crucial. Its metadata tree enables efficient data pruning, particularly beneficial when querying specific time ranges or partitions. A query looking for specific customer segments might scan only relevant files:

```
1. SELECT customer_segment, COUNT(*)
2. FROM customer_profiles
3. WHERE date_partition >= '2024-01-01'
4.   AND date_partition < '2024-02-01'
5.   AND region = 'EMEA'
6. GROUP BY customer_segment;
```

- Hudi demonstrates particular efficiency in real-time data ingestion scenarios. Its merge-on-read strategy allows quick ingestion of updates while maintaining query performance:

```
1. -- Iceberg efficiently prunes irrelevant data files
2. SELECT customer_segment, COUNT(*)
3. FROM customer_profiles
4. WHERE date_partition >= '2024-01-01'
5.   AND date_partition < '2024-02-01'
6.   AND region = 'EMEA'
7. GROUP BY customer_segment;
```

Feature comparison in production environments

Real-world implementation reveals distinct characteristics of each format:

- Iceberg exhibits superior schema evolution capabilities, allowing changes to partition schemes without data reorganization. This becomes particularly valuable in long-lived data platforms where data models frequently evolve.

- Delta Lake's transactional guarantees provide strong consistency but may require more careful planning for large-scale operations. Its time travel feature proves invaluable for audit requirements and disaster recovery scenarios.

- Hudi's dual storage options offer flexibility for different workload patterns. Copy-on-write tables optimize read performance for analytical queries, while merge-on-read tables handle frequent updates efficiently.

Operational considerations

Managing these formats in production requires attention to several factors. Storage costs extend beyond raw data to include metadata management. Delta Lake's transaction logs, Iceberg's metadata trees, and Hudi's auxiliary files all contribute to overall storage costs.

Query performance varies based on access patterns. Iceberg typically offers better performance for selective queries due to its efficient metadata handling. Delta Lake provides consistent performance across different query types, while Hudi's performance depends on the chosen storage strategy.

The choice between these formats often depends on specific use case requirements, existing technology stack, and operational patterns. Organizations heavily invested in Spark might lean toward Delta Lake, while those requiring flexible query engines might prefer Iceberg. Teams dealing with real-time data ingestion often find Hudi's capabilities particularly attractive.

Having explored the theoretical foundations of various data formats, let us put this knowledge into practice. Through a hands-on implementation, we will demonstrate how these concepts come together in a real-world migration scenario.

Hands-on: Data format migration

Building upon our data lake foundation from *Chapter 2, Building Data Lake Foundations*, and applying the format considerations we have discussed, let us implement a practical data format migration. We will use the same retail analytics scenario from our previous examples, demonstrating how to evolve from simple storage to optimized formats while maintaining the security and governance principles established earlier.

In today's data landscape, companies often start simple, storing customer interactions as Parquet files in S3. But as data volumes grow and requirements evolve, they face new challenges: maintaining consistency during updates, adapting to schema changes, and ensuring query performance at scale. Let us walk through a practical example of modernizing such a data platform.

Consider a customer analytics platform tracking user interactions across an e-commerce website. Every page view, purchase, and support interaction generate data that various teams need to analyse. While simple file storage worked initially, growing complexity demands a more sophisticated approach.

The complete implementation is available on GitHub.

Setup and initialization

First, let us import required libraries and setup our environment:

```
1. import os
2. import sys
3. sys.path.append('../src')
4.
5. from utils import (
6.     AWSManager,
7.     DataGenerator,
```

```
 8.    PerformanceAnalyzer,
 9.    load_config,
10.    setup_spark_session
11. )
12.
13. import pandas as pd
14. import numpy as np
15. import matplotlib.pyplot as plt
16. import seaborn as sns
17.
18. # Set plotting style
19. plt.style.use('seaborn')
20. sns.set_p
```

Next, initialize AWS resources and Spark session:

```
 1.  # Load configuration
 2.  config = load_config()
 3.
 4.  # Initialize AWS Manager
 5.  aws_manager = AWSManager()
 6.
 7.  # Create required buckets
 8.  aws_manager.create_buckets(config)
 9.
10.  # Initialize Spark session
11.  spark = setup_spark_session()
```

Data generation

Generate realistic retail data for migration testing:

```
 1.  # Initialize data generator
 2.  data_generator = DataGenerator(config)
 3.
 4.  # Generate transaction data
 5.  transactions_df = data_generator.generate_transactions()
 6.  print("\nTransaction Data Sample:")
 7.  display(transactions_df.head())
 8.
 9.  # Generate customer data
10.  customers_df = data_generator.generate_customers()
11.  print("\nCustomer Data Sample:")
12.  display(customers_df.head())
```

Format migration

Perform the migration to optimized formats:

```
 1.  # Convert transactions to Delta format
 2.  spark_df = spark.createDataFrame(transactions_df)
 3.  delta_path = f"s3://{config['aws']['target_bucket']}/transactions_delta"
 4.
```

```
5.  # Write as Delta format with partitioning
6.  spark_df.write \
7.      .format("delta") \
8.      .partitionBy("category") \
9.      .mode("overwrite") \
10.     .save(delta_path)
11.
12. # Convert customers to Parquet format
13. parquet_path = f"s3://{config['aws']['target_bucket']}/customers_parquet"
14. customers_df.to_parquet(
15.     parquet_path,
16.     partition_cols=['country'],
17.     compression='snappy'
18. )
```

Performance analysis

Compare performance between original and optimized formats:

```
1.  # Measure storage after migration
2.  optimized_metrics = {
3.      'transactions_delta': performance_analyzer.analyze_storage_metrics(
4.          config['aws']['target_bucket'], 'transactions_delta/'
5.      ),
6.      'customers_parquet': performance_analyzer.analyze_storage_metrics(
7.          config['aws']['target_bucket'], 'customers_parquet/'
8.      )
9.  }
10.
11. # Compare query performance
12. test_query = """
13.     SELECT category,
14.            COUNT(*) as transaction_count,
15.            SUM(amount) as total_amount
16.     FROM delta.`{}`
17.     GROUP BY category
18. """.format(delta_path)
19.
20. query_metrics = performance_analyzer.measure_query_performance(test_query)
21.
22. # Display results
23. print("\nStorage Comparison:")
24. display(pd.DataFrame({
25.     'Original': initial_metrics,
26.     'Optimized': optimized_metrics
27. }))
28.
29. print("\nQuery Performance:")
30. display(pd.DataFrame(query_metrics, index=[0]))
```

Results visualization

Visualize the performance improvements:

```
# Create comparison visualizations
fig, (ax1, ax2) = plt.subplots(1, 2, figsize=(15, 5))

# Storage comparison
storage_data = pd.DataFrame({
    'Original': [initial_metrics['transactions']['total_size_gb'],
                 initial_metrics['customers']['total_size_gb']],
    'Optimized': [optimized_metrics['transactions_delta']['total_size_gb'],
                  optimized_metrics['customers_parquet']['total_size_gb']]
}, index=['Transactions', 'Customers'])

storage_data.plot(kind='bar', ax=ax1)
ax1.set_title('Storage Size Comparison (GB)')
ax1.set_ylabel('Size (GB)')

# Add percentage improvements
for i in range(len(storage_data)):
    pct_change = ((storage_data['Original'][i] - storage_data['Optimized'][i])
                  / storage_data['Original'][i] * 100)
    ax1.text(i, storage_data['Optimized'][i],
             f'{pct_change:.1f}% reduction',
             ha='center', va='bottom')

plt.tight_layout()
plt.show()
display(pd.DataFrame(query_metrics, index=[0]))
```

Finally, clean up resources:

```
1. # Clean up buckets
2. aws_manager.clean_up_buckets(config)
3.
4. # Stop Spark session
5. spark.stop()
```

Running this implementation demonstrates the practical benefits of format optimization:

- Storage efficiency improvements through compression and optimized formats.
- Query performance enhancements via partitioning and columnar storage.
- Simplified data management using modern table formats.

The complete code, including utility functions and configuration files, is available in the accompanying GitHub repository.

Conclusion

In this chapter, we studied the foundational aspects of data formats and storage optimization in modern data lakes. We examined how different formats serve distinct needs, from handling raw, unstructured data to optimizing analytical queries through columnar formats. The journey through specialized formats like Delta Lake, Apache Iceberg, and Apache Hudi demonstrated how modern table formats solve critical challenges in data management, particularly in cloud environments like AWS. Through hands-on examples, we saw how choosing the right format and implementing proper optimization strategies can significantly impact both performance and cost.

Looking ahead to the next chapter, we will explore the real-time data ingestion and streaming, a crucial capability in modern data platforms. We will explore how Amazon Kinesis services handle various streaming data types from video streams to IoT sensor data, and examine architectural patterns like Lambda and Kappa for stream processing. The chapter will demonstrate these concepts through real-world examples like connected vehicle data processing and smart city sensor networks, providing practical insights into building robust streaming pipelines.

Join our Discord space

Join our Discord workspace for latest updates, offers, tech happenings around the world, new releases, and sessions with the authors:

https://discord.bpbonline.com

CHAPTER 4
Real-time Data Ingestion and Streaming

Introduction

In today's data-driven world, the ability to process and analyze data in real-time has become a critical competitive advantage for organizations across industries. As we have explored in previous chapters, building robust data lake foundations and optimizing storage formats provides the backbone for effective data management. However, many modern use cases from fraud detection and personalized recommendations to IoT analytics and real-time dashboards require data processing at the moment events occur, rather than in periodic batches.

Streaming data represents a paradigm shift from traditional batch processing models. Instead of collecting, storing, and then processing data, streaming architectures enable continuous processing of data as it arrives. This fundamental shift brings unique challenges and opportunities in how we design, implement, and operate data systems.

In this chapter, we will explore the foundational concepts of stream processing, examine AWS's comprehensive suite of streaming services, and dive into specialized streaming data types. We will also cover implementation strategies, operational best practices, and real-world use cases that illustrate how these technologies solve complex business problems. By the end, you will understand how to architect and implement streaming solutions that can process high-volume, high-velocity data with low latency using AWS services.

Structure

This chapter will cover the following topics:

- Fundamentals of streaming data
- AWS streaming services ecosystem
- Amazon MSK for streaming pipelines
- Comparing Kinesis and MSK approaches
- Specialized streaming data types
- Stream processing implementation
- Operational excellence
- Real-world use cases
- Hands-on: Building multi-format streaming pipeline

Objectives

This chapter aims to provide a comprehensive understanding of streaming data fundamentals and AWS streaming services. By the end, you will be able to distinguish between different streaming architectures, select appropriate AWS services for specific streaming use cases, and implement resilient, high-performance streaming solutions. You will learn how to handle specialized data types like video streams and IoT sensor data, and apply operational best practices to ensure reliability, security, and efficiency. Through exploring real-world examples and a hands-on implementation, you will gain practical experience in building streaming pipelines that integrate with the broader AWS data ecosystem.

Fundamentals of streaming data

Stream processing represents a fundamental shift from traditional batch processing to real-time data handling. This section explores the fundamental concept and also the architectural patterns (Lambda and Kappa) which help organizations balance the need for real-time insights with requirements for data completeness, historical analysis, and system reliability.

Stream processing concepts

Stream processing represents a significant departure from traditional batch processing approaches. To understand this paradigm effectively, we must examine its core concepts, event-driven patterns, and how it compares with traditional batch processing approaches.

Event-driven patterns

At the heart of stream processing lies the concept of events. An event is a discrete record of something that happened at a specific point in time, a customer purchase, a temperature reading from a sensor, a click on a website, or a log entry from a system.

In event-driven architectures, these events become the primary drivers of application behaviour. Rather than executing processes on a predefined schedule, systems react to events as they occur. This reactive approach offers several advantages:

- **Responsiveness**: Systems can take immediate action when relevant events occur.

- **Loose coupling**: Components that produce events do not need to know which components consume them.

- **Scalability**: Event producers and consumers can scale independently.

Consider a retail e-commerce platform. In a traditional architecture, you might run a batch job every hour to process new orders. In an event-driven approach, each order becomes an event that triggers immediate processing:

```
1.  # Traditional batch approach
2.  def batch_process_orders():
3.      orders = database.query("SELECT * FROM orders WHERE processed = false")
4.      for order in orders:
5.          process_order(order)
6.          update_inventory(order)
7.          send_confirmation_email(order)
8.      database.execute("UPDATE orders SET processed = true WHERE processed = false")
9.
10. # Event-driven approach
```

```
11. def on_order_received(order_event):
12.     order = parse_order(order_event)
13.     process_order(order)
14.     update_inventory(order)
15.     send_confirmation_email(order)
```

The event-driven pattern eliminates the delay between order placement and processing, providing customers with immediate confirmation and updating inventory in real-time.

Real-time vs. batch processing

Understanding the differences between real-time and batch processing helps in selecting the appropriate approach for specific use cases.

Batch processing aggregates data over a period and processes it all at once. This approach has been the traditional backbone of data processing for decades and excels in scenarios where completeness and throughput are more important than immediacy.

Real-time processing, on the other hand, handles data as it arrives, typically with processing latencies measured in seconds or milliseconds. This approach shines in scenarios requiring immediate insights or actions.

The following table compares these two paradigms across key dimensions:

Characteristic	Batch processing	Real-time processing
Latency	Minutes to hours	Milliseconds to seconds
Throughput	Typically higher	Typically lower per node
Data completeness	Complete view at processing time	Potentially incomplete views
Processing complexity	Can handle complex algorithms	May need simplified algorithms
Fault tolerance	Generally easier to implement	More challenging
Cost efficiency	Often more cost-effective	Can be more resource-intensive
Example use cases	Daily reports, model training	Fraud detection, monitoring

Table 4.1: Comparison between batch and real-time processing approaches

Many modern architectures employ both approaches, creating a hybrid processing model. For instance, a financial services company might use:

- Real-time processing to detect and prevent fraudulent transactions as they happen.
- Batch processing to run complex risk models that require historical context.

Stream-table duality

As we transition from batch to real-time processing, we need to reconsider how we conceptualize data. In traditional batch systems, we primarily think about data as static tables or files. In streaming systems, however, we must embrace a more dynamic view—this leads us to the concept of stream-table duality.

Stream-table duality recognizes that streams and tables are complementary representations of the same underlying data:

- A **stream** represents a sequence of immutable events ordered by time, capturing the history of changes.
- A **table** represents the current state derived from processing all events up to a point in time, capturing the latest view.

Consider how this duality applies to our previous e-commerce example. Each customer order is an event in a stream, but the current inventory levels form a table that reflects the accumulated effect of all order events:

```
1.  Order Stream (events):
2.  Timestamp            | OrderID | ProductID | Quantity
3.  --------------------|---------|-----------|----------
4.  2023-08-01T10:15:00 | ORD-001 | PROD-A    | 2
5.  2023-08-01T14:30:00 | ORD-002 | PROD-B    | 1
6.  2023-08-01T16:45:00 | ORD-003 | PROD-A    | 3
7.
8.  Inventory Table (current state):
9.  ProductID | Available Quantity
10. ----------|-------------------
11. PROD-A    | 45  (Started with 50, sold 5)
12. PROD-B    | 29  (Started with 30, sold 1)
13. )
```

The relationship between streams and tables works in both directions:

- **Stream | Table**: By applying all events from the order stream, we can compute the current inventory table (event sourcing).

- **Table | Stream**: Each update to the inventory table can be captured as an event in a change stream (change data capture).

This duality enables powerful processing paradigms that combine the benefits of both models. With streams, we capture the complete history and can reprocess data if needed. With tables, we maintain the current state for efficient lookups and updates.

Understanding this relationship helps us design systems that can answer both temporal queries *(What orders were placed yesterday?)* and state queries *(How many items of Product A are in stock right now?)* without maintaining separate systems.

As we move forward to explore stream processing architectures, we will see how this duality influences the design of scalable, resilient streaming platforms.

Stream processing architectures

Building upon our understanding of stream processing concepts, let us examine the architectural patterns that have emerged to implement streaming solutions at scale. These architectures help organizations balance the need for real-time insights with requirements for historical analysis, data completeness, and system reliability.

Lambda architecture

The Lambda architecture, introduced by *Nathan Marz* in 2011, addresses a fundamental challenge in real-time data processing: how to provide both low-latency real-time views and accurate complete views of the same data.

It accomplishes this by splitting the data flow into three layers:

- **Batch layer**: Processes all historical data periodically to produce comprehensive, accurate views.

- **Speed layer**: Processes recent data in real-time to provide low-latency, approximate views.

- **Serving layer**: Combines results from both layers to serve queries.

This architecture acknowledges the trade-offs between completeness and timeliness by essentially running two parallel processing systems, one optimized for completeness (batch) and one for speed (real-time). The following figure illustrates the different building blocks of the architecture:

Lambda Architecture

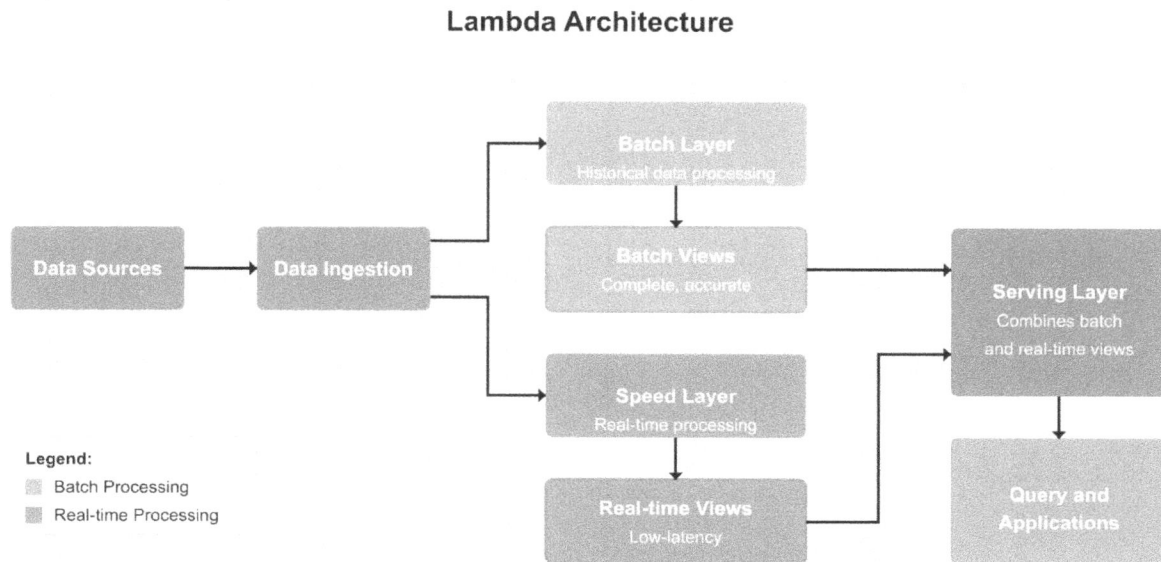

Figure 4.1: Lambda architecture showing batch, speed, and serving layers

In an AWS implementation, a Lambda architecture might look like:

Incoming events | Kinesis Data Streams:

- **Speed layer:** Kinesis Data Analytics | DynamoDB (real-time views)
- **Batch layer:** S3 | EMR/Athena/Redshift (batch processing)
- **Serving layer:** Application combining both views

This architecture excels in scenarios where both historical completeness and real-time insights are critical. For example, an advertising analytics platform might use the batch layer for accurate daily reporting and billing, while using the speed layer for real-time campaign optimization.

However, the Lambda architecture introduces significant complexity, as teams must:

- Implement and maintain two separate processing systems.
- Ensure both systems produce compatible outputs.
- Determine how to merge results from both systems accurately.

Kappa architecture

The Kappa architecture, proposed by *Jay Kreps* in 2014, offers a simplified alternative to Lambda by treating all data processing, both real-time and historical, as stream processing. Instead of maintaining separate batch and speed layers, Kappa uses a single stream processing engine capable of reprocessing historical data when needed.

The key components of the Kappa architecture are:

- **Stream layer:** A scalable streaming platform that durably stores all events.
- **Processing layer:** Stream processing applications that transform data.
- **Serving layer:** Datastores that hold the processed results.

The unique aspect of Kappa is how it handles historical reprocessing. Rather than maintaining a separate batch system, historical processing is accomplished by replaying events from the stream storage, effectively treating historical data as a very fast stream. The following figure illustrate different building blocks of the Kappa architecture:

Kappa Architecture

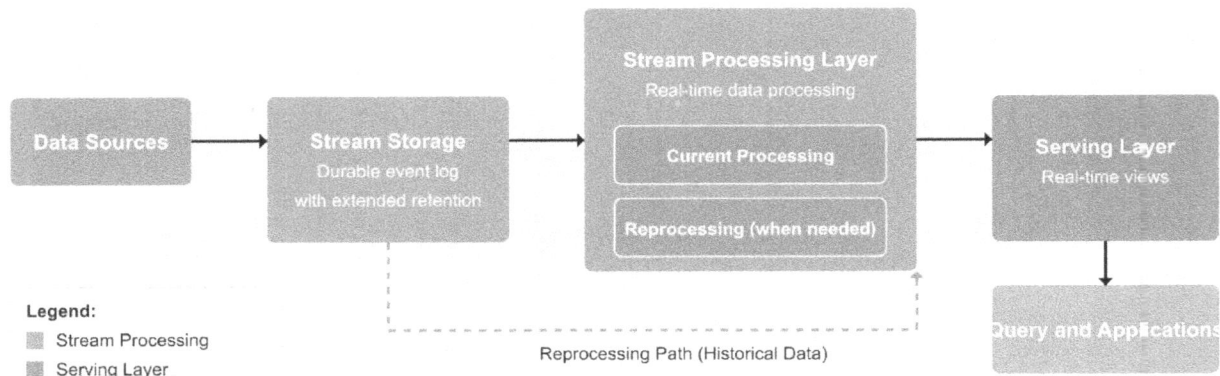

Figure 4.2: *Kappa architecture with stream storage and processing layers*

In AWS, a Kappa architecture implementation might use:

Incoming events |Kinesis Data Streams (with extended retention)

- **Processing layer:** Kinesis Data Analytics or Lambda

- **Serving layer:** DynamoDB or Aurora

- **For reprocessing**: Replay events from Kinesis (or from S3 backup)

The Kappa architecture shines in use cases where:

- Stream processing logic is relatively stable.

- The need for historical reprocessing is infrequent.

- Maintaining a single processing codebase is a priority.

For example, a real-time recommendation system might use Kappa to process user behaviour streams and update recommendation models, occasionally replaying historical data when algorithms improve.

Guidelines to use each architecture

Selecting between Lambda and Kappa architectures involves evaluating your specific requirements and constraints:

Consideration	Lambda architecture	Kappa architecture
Processing complexity	Can use different algorithms for batch and streaming	Must use same algorithm for both
Data completeness needs	Provides extremely accurate batch views	Accuracy depends on stream processing reliability
Development resources	Requires maintaining two codebases	Single codebase for all processing
Reprocessing frequency	Efficient for regular reprocessing	Better for occasional reprocessing
Infrastructure complexity	More complex (two systems)	Simpler (one system)
Storage requirements	Typically higher (duplicate storage)	More efficient (single storage)

Table 4.2: *Comparison of Lambda and Kappa architectures*

Many modern implementations take a hybrid approach, using elements from both architectures. For instance, you might:

- Follow Kappa's single-codebase philosophy but maintain a Lambda-like batch processing capability for efficiency.

- Use Lambda initially, then migrate toward Kappa as stream processing technologies mature.

As we transition to examining AWS's streaming services, keep these architectural patterns in mind. The services we will explore can be assembled to implement either architecture, giving you the flexibility to choose the approach that best fits your requirements.

AWS streaming services ecosystem

Building on our understanding of stream processing concepts and architectures, let us examine the comprehensive suite of streaming services that AWS offers. These services provide blocks for implementing real-time data processing platforms that can scale from simple applications to complex enterprise architectures.

Kinesis family overview

The AWS Kinesis family forms the backbone of AWS's streaming data capabilities, offering specialized services that work together to enable end-to-end stream processing. Building upon our discussion of data formats and storage optimization in *Chapter 3, Data Format and Storage Optimization*, these services allow organizations to process data continuously as it is generated rather than in batches.

Kinesis Data Streams

Kinesis Data Streams (**KDS**) serves as the foundational service for real-time data streaming in AWS, enabling the collection and storage of data records from multiple sources for processing. The service provides durability across three availability zones with configurable data retention from 24 hours to 365 days. KDS uses a shard-based architecture where each shard delivers one MB per second input capacity and two MB per second output capacity, allowing the service to scale from megabytes to terabytes per hour while maintaining strict ordering of records within each shard. This predictable performance model supports multiple simultaneous consumers per stream, making KDS a versatile backbone for diverse streaming applications.

Architecturally, KDS functions as a crucial decoupling layer between data producers and consumers, creating a resilient buffer that ensures no data is lost during processing peaks or downstream system failures. Unlike simple message queues that typically delete data after consumption, KDS's extended retention capability enables an architectural pattern where historical data can be replayed for new analyses or recovery scenarios. This makes KDS ideal for use cases requiring custom processing logic, strict ordering guarantees, or multiple independent applications processing the same data stream. In financial services, for example, KDS might capture market data feeds that simultaneously feed real-time trading algorithms, risk analysis systems, and historical pattern detection applications, all working with the same stream but at different paces.

Kinesis Data Firehose

Kinesis Data Firehose provides a fully managed service that reliably delivers streaming data to destinations such as S3, Redshift, OpenSearch, and third-party services without requiring custom consumer applications. Firehose handles the complex tasks of scaling, buffering, and retry logic automatically, relieving developers of operational burden. The service supports transformation of data in-flight through Lambda functions, enabling format conversion to analytics-optimized formats like Parquet or ORC before data reaches its destination. Additionally, Firehose offers compression options and configurable buffering based on time or size to optimize both storage efficiency and delivery latency.

From an architectural perspective, Firehose bridges the fundamental impedance mismatch between continuous data streams and destination systems that typically expect batched data. By eliminating the need to build and maintain custom delivery mechanisms, Firehose allows architects to focus on data flows rather than delivery infrastructure. This architectural simplification particularly benefits organizations implementing log delivery, IoT data ingestion, or clickstream analysis where operational simplicity is valued. For example, a retail analytics platform might use Firehose to reliably deliver customer interaction events from websites and mobile applications directly to S3 in Parquet format, optimized for subsequent analysis without building custom delivery pipelines.

Kinesis Data Analytics

Kinesis Data Analytics enables real-time processing of streaming data using SQL or Apache Flink without managing infrastructure. The service offers two distinct runtime options: SQL applications for straightforward stream processing using standard SQL, and Flink applications for complex event processing with Java or Scala. Kinesis Data Analytics provides sub-second processing latency with automatic scaling to match changing data volumes. The service includes built-in functions for time-based windows, aggregations, and joins, and supports integration with reference data to enrich streaming information with contextual data. For reliability, it offers dead-letter streams to capture and handle records that fail processing.

Architecturally, Kinesis Data Analytics serves as the real-time computational engine in streaming architectures. Its significance lies in enabling stateful operations over unbounded data streams, a fundamental capability that distinguishes streaming from batch processing. Maintaining application state, performing time-based operations, and detecting patterns across event sequences enables architectures that respond to data changes within seconds rather than hours. This makes the service particularly valuable for real-time dashboards, anomaly detection systems, time-series analytics, and complex event processing applications where immediate insights drive business value. For instance, a telecommunications provider might use Kinesis Data Analytics to continuously analyze network performance metrics, detecting service degradation patterns and triggering remediation before customers experience significant issues.

Kinesis Video Streams

Kinesis Video Streams (KVS) addresses the specialized requirements of video data, which fundamentally differs from standard data streams in volume, format, and processing needs. The service provides durable storage for video with configurable retention periods from hours to years, alongside capabilities for both real-time and historical playback. KVS integrates with media processing and computer vision services, supports time-synchronized metadata alongside video frames, and organizes video into time-indexed fragments for efficient access. These capabilities make KVS a purpose-built solution for the unique challenges of streaming video within cloud architectures.

Architecturally, KVS abstracts away the complexity of video ingestion and storage, providing infrastructure specifically designed for time-series video data while enabling integration with artificial intelligence services for real-time analysis. This specialized design allows architects to focus on video analytics rather than managing the video transport and storage layers. KVS typically serves applications in security monitoring, machine vision, smart home systems, and media production workflows where video is the primary data source. For example, a manufacturing company might deploy KVS to capture video feeds from production lines, using integrated machine learning services to detect quality issues in real-time while maintaining a searchable archive of production history.

Service selection guide

The following decision tree can help navigate the selection process:

- **Do you need to process video streams?**

    o   Yes | KVS

    o   No | Continue

- **Do you need custom processing logic?**
  - o No, just want to deliver data to destinations | Kinesis Data Firehose
  - o Yes | Continue
- **What type of processing is required?**
  - o Simple SQL-based analytics | Kinesis Data Analytics (SQL)
  - o Complex stateful processing | Kinesis Data Analytics (Flink)
  - o Custom application logic | Kinesis Data Streams with custom consumers
- **What is your data retention requirement?**
  - o Short-term (hours/days) | Kinesis Data Streams may be sufficient
  - o Long-term (months/years) | Consider Kinesis to S3 via Firehose
- **What is your latency requirement?**
  - o Sub-second | Kinesis Data Streams with direct consumers
  - o Seconds or minutes | Kinesis Data Firehose may be acceptable

Amazon MSK for streaming pipelines

Amazon **Managed Streaming for Apache Kafka (MSK)** provides an alternative approach to building streaming data pipelines using the popular open-source Apache Kafka platform. While the Kinesis family offers specialized services for different aspects of streaming, MSK delivers a comprehensive, topic-based messaging system that handles ingestion, storage, and delivery in a unified infrastructure. The following figure illustrates the different building blocks of the architecture:

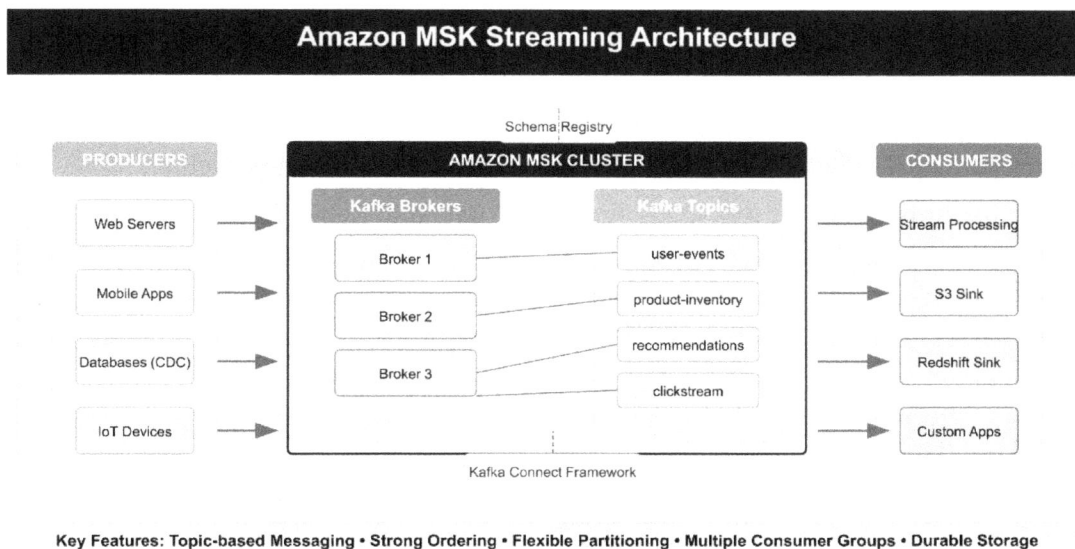

Figure 4.3: Amazon MSK streaming architecture

MSK streaming architecture

A typical MSK-based streaming pipeline consists of several core components working together:

- **Producer applications** connect to an MSK cluster and publish data to specific topics. These producers can include application servers, IoT devices, database change data capture systems, or any source generating real-time data. Producers benefit from Kafka's flexible partitioning schemes, allowing data distribution based on custom logic.

- **MSK cluster** serves as the central nervous system of the streaming architecture. The cluster comprises broker nodes that store data in topics, which are further divided into partitions for parallelism. MSK handles the complex infrastructure management, including high availability, node replacement, and security patching, while providing the full capabilities of Apache Kafka.

- **Consumer applications** subscribe to topics and process data as it arrives. These might include real-time analytics applications, data transformation services, or systems that load data into downstream destinations. Kafka's consumer group mechanism enables multiple applications to process the same data independently, with automatic workload balancing across consumer instances.

- **Schema registry** (typically implemented using AWS Glue Schema registry or third-party solutions) maintains schema definitions for data serialization formats like Avro or Protobuf, ensuring compatibility as data structures evolve over time.

- **Connect framework** extends the pipeline through pre-built connectors that integrate with external systems. Using Kafka Connect, developers can implement source connectors that pull data into MSK and sink connectors that export data to destinations like S3, DynamoDB, or Elasticsearch without writing custom consumer applications.

Implementation example

An e-commerce platform might implement an MSK-based streaming pipeline as follows:

- **Data ingestion**: Web servers and mobile applications publish user activity events (page views, searches, purchases) to an MSK topic named user-events. Database changes from the inventory system flow through Debezium (a change data capture connector) to a product-inventory topic.

- **Stream processing**: A Kafka Streams application joins the user-events and product-inventory streams to create personalized product recommendations in real-time, publishing results to a recommendations topic.

- **Data delivery**: Multiple consumer applications process this streaming data simultaneously:

  o A Kafka Connect S3 sink connector archives all raw events to S3 for long-term storage.

  o A custom application updates real-time dashboard through WebSockets.

  o Another Kafka Connect sink loads aggregated data into Redshift for business intelligence.

- **Scalability and management**: As traffic grows, the MSK cluster can be expanded by adding brokers, and topic partitions can be increased to allow greater parallelism in both producing and consuming applications.

This architecture provides significant flexibility, as new consumers can be added without affecting existing components. The platform's strong ordering guarantees and exactly-once processing capabilities ensure data integrity throughout the pipeline.

Comparing Kinesis and MSK approaches

While both Kinesis and MSK enable real-time data processing, they represent different architectural philosophies best suited to different scenarios. Kinesis takes a service-oriented approach with purpose-built components that are simple to implement but have more defined boundaries; MSK offers a unified platform with greater flexibility but requires more expertise to design and operate effectively. Kinesis excels in AWS-native architectures where operational simplicity is paramount, specialized workloads like video streaming, or serverless applications with variable throughput requirements. MSK is typically preferable when organizations need a centralized, persistent messaging backbone with strong ordering guarantees, require advanced Kafka-specific features like compacted topics or transactions, have existing Kafka expertise, or anticipate extensive integration with external systems through the broader Kafka ecosystem. The decision often comes down to balancing operational overhead against flexibility, Kinesis minimizes management complexity while potentially requiring multiple services for end-to-end pipelines, whereas MSK provides a more cohesive platform but demands a deeper understanding of Kafka's architecture and operational characteristics. Many sophisticated organizations strategically employ both technologies, using Kinesis for straightforward streaming needs and MSK for complex messaging requirements or as part of a broader data platform strategy that extends beyond AWS.

Specialized streaming data types

While architectural patterns for streaming data apply broadly across use cases, certain data types present unique challenges requiring specialized approaches. This section explores four specialized streaming data types: video, audio, IoT sensor data, and geospatial data—examining how AWS services can be leveraged to build robust streaming solutions.

Video streaming solutions

Video data fundamentally differs from other streaming types due to its substantial volume, complex structure, and temporal characteristics. A single high-definition video stream can consume several megabytes per second, requiring specialized techniques for efficient transmission, storage, and analysis.

Kinesis Video Streams architecture

KVS addresses these challenges through a purpose-built architecture designed specifically for time-indexed media. Unlike general-purpose streaming services that treat data as discrete records, KVS understands the continuous nature of video, organizing it into fragments that maintain temporal relationships.

The producer side utilizes specialized SDKs implementing adaptive buffering algorithms that adjust to network conditions, maintaining stream continuity even when connectivity fluctuates. For example, when a security camera experiences bandwidth constraints, the SDK can dynamically adjust compression ratios to ensure continuous streaming while preserving critical visual information.

Inside the service, KVS organizes video into time-indexed fragments stored across multiple availability zones, enabling both real-time access for live monitoring and time-based retrieval for historical analysis through timestamp-based queries. It supports both real-time and batch ingestion:

```
1.  # Real-time video streaming pattern
2.  video_stream = create_kinesis_video_stream(
3.      stream_name="SecurityCamera1",
4.      data_retention_in_hours=24,
5.      media_type="video/h264",
6.      kms_key_id=encryption_key
7.  )
8.
9.  # Initialize producer with adaptive bandwidth
10. kvs_producer = KinesisVideoProducer(
11.     stream_name="SecurityCamera1",
12.     retention_period=24*60*60,  # seconds
13.     bandwidth_mode="ADAPTIVE"
14. )
15.
16. # Continuous frame ingestion with timestamp correlation
17. while camera_active:
18.     frame = camera.get_next_frame()
```

```
19.     timestamp = get_current_timestamp()
20.     kvs_producer.put_frame(frame, timestamp)
```

The timestamp correlation creates a crucial foundation for subsequent analysis, enabling applications to precisely locate events within the video timeline.

Integration with ML services

KVS's architectural distinction becomes particularly valuable when integrating with machine learning services. Maintaining the temporal structure of video data, it enables frame-accurate analysis without requiring full video downloads.

Amazon Rekognition Video integrates with KVS through a connector architecture that processes video in near real-time. As fragments arrive, they can be automatically forwarded for analysis, enabling continuous monitoring without manual intervention, with results flowing back into application logic through notification services.

For sophisticated analysis, the architecture often employs a multi-stage approach: initial detection on the raw stream identifies frames of interest, which then undergo more detailed analysis through specialized ML models. This integrated architecture significantly reduces both processing costs and analysis latency, identifying critical situations in seconds rather than minutes or hours.

Real-time video processing patterns

Several architectural patterns have emerged as particularly effective for video stream processing:

- The **monitoring and alerting pattern** establishes continuous video analysis with defined trigger conditions. In retail security implementations, this pattern processes store camera feeds to detect unusual behaviours, sending immediate notifications to security personnel. The architecture includes buffer management to handle multiple simultaneous streams, prioritization logic for high-risk areas, and notification throttling to prevent alert fatigue.

- The **video transformation pattern** focuses on modifying video characteristics in transit. Content delivery networks employ this pattern to adapt streaming quality based on device capabilities and network conditions, dynamically adjusting resolution, frame rate, and compression levels to ensure optimal viewing experiences across diverse devices.

- The **video storage and replay pattern** extends beyond simple recording to create intelligent archives with rich metadata. Smart city implementations use this pattern to maintain searchable video histories that correlate with other sensor data, transforming passive video storage into an active, queryable data source.

Audio processing pipelines

Audio streaming presents distinct architectural challenges compared to video. While typically smaller in data volume, audio requires more sophisticated temporal analysis to extract meaning, particularly for human speech or environmental sounds.

Streaming audio processing

Without a dedicated service like KVS, audio streaming architectures typically leverage KDS with specialized processing layers addressing several audio-specific considerations.

Buffer management becomes critical for maintaining audio continuity. Unlike text data where each record stands independently, audio fragments must be precisely sequenced to avoid perceptible gaps or overlaps. Effective architectures implement adaptive buffering that adjusts based on network conditions while maintaining exact timing relationships.

Compression selection significantly impacts both transmission efficiency and audio quality. The architectural decision depends on the specific use case—medical audio analysis might require lossless formats to preserve diagnostic information, while consumer applications can use aggressive compression while remaining perceptually acceptable. The following code creates an AWS KDS for audio with five shards, then implements a function that dynamically adjusts audio compression based on network quality before sending the compressed audio chunks to the stream. When network quality is poor, it applies higher compression to maintain transmission continuity at the expense of some audio quality:

```
1.  # Audio streaming pattern with KDS
2.  audio_stream = boto3.client('kinesis').create_stream(
3.      StreamName='AudioStream',
4.      ShardCount=5  # Calculated based on expected volume
5.  )
6.
7.  # Producer with adaptive quality based on network conditions
8.  def stream_audio_chunk(audio_data, network_quality, partition_key):
9.      # Dynamically select compression level based on network
10.     if network_quality < THRESHOLD_POOR:
11.         compression = HIGH_COMPRESSION
12.     else:
13.         compression = NORMAL_COMPRESSION
14.
15.     compressed_data = compress_audio(audio_data, compression)
16.
17.     response = kinesis_client.put_record(
18.         StreamName='AudioStream',
19.         Data=compressed_data,
20.         PartitionKey=partition_key
21.     )
22.     return response['SequenceNumber']
```

Voice analytics

Voice analytics architectures transform unstructured audio streams into structured, actionable data through multiple processing stages that progressively extract higher-level meaning from raw signals.

The initial stage converts speech to text through services like Amazon Transcribe, handling challenges such as speaker separation, background noise filtering, and domain-specific terminology. For medical dictation systems, this incorporates specialized medical vocabularies and context-aware correction algorithms.

Once converted to text, the next stage applies natural language processing through services like Amazon Comprehend, identifying entities, extracting key phrases, and determining sentiment through both statistical and machine learning approaches.

For multi-speaker environments like call centers, the architecture incorporates speaker diarization—determining who spoke when—enabling attribution of statements to specific individuals for proper context in customer-agent interaction analysis.

Integration patterns

Audio processing architectures frequently integrate with other AWS services to create comprehensive domain-specific solutions:

- **Call center analytics** combine real-time transcription with historical context from customer relationship systems. As agents interact with customers, the streaming pipeline captures and analyzes conversations, providing immediate guidance based on detected sentiment or identified issues.

- **Media monitoring** architectures process broadcast audio for content analysis, scanning multiple channels simultaneously to detect specific topics, brand mentions, or competitive intelligence, alerting stakeholders when relevant content appears.

- **IoT voice control** implements lightweight speech recognition at the edge with more comprehensive processing in the cloud. This distributed architecture balances responsiveness (local processing provides immediate feedback) with sophisticated language understanding (cloud processing).

IoT sensor data processing

IoT sensor data introduces extreme scale and diversity to streaming architectures. With potentially millions of connected devices generating data simultaneously, solutions must address unique challenges in device connectivity, data normalization, and analytical processing.

IoT Core integration

AWS IoT Core serves as the entry point for device data, managing connectivity, security, and initial message routing. Its integration with Kinesis creates a comprehensive architecture for handling diverse device data at scale.

The message routing layer within IoT Core uses a rules engine that evaluates incoming messages against SQL-like statements. Based on message content, topic patterns, or metadata, it directs data to appropriate destinations. This AWS IoT rule filters sensor data for temperatures above 90 degrees, then simultaneously routes these readings to a Kinesis stream for processing and an SNS topic for immediate notifications:

```
1.  # IoT Rule to route sensor data to Kinesis
2.  {
3.      "sql": "SELECT temperature, humidity, device_id, timestamp FROM 'devices/+/
    sensors' WHERE temperature > 90",
4.      "actions": [
5.          {
6.              "kinesis": {
7.                  "streamName": "HighTemperatureAlerts",
8.                  "partitionKey": "${device_id}",
9.                  "roleArn": "arn:aws:iam::123456789012:role/kinesis-access"
10.             }
11.         },
12.         {
13.             "sns": {
14.                 "targetArn": "arn:aws:sns:us-east-1:123456789012:high-temp-
    notification",
15.                 "roleArn": "arn:aws:iam::123456789012:role/sns-access"
16.             }
17.         }
18.     ]
19. }
```

Device data streaming

IoT sensor data presents unique streaming challenges that the architecture must address for reliable, scalable operations:

- The **high cardinality** of data sources, potentially millions of individual devices generating data simultaneously, requires careful partitioning strategies. Sophisticated architectures implement dynamic partition mapping that distributes traffic evenly while maintaining logical grouping (such as keeping all sensors from a single facility in related partitions).

- **Intermittent connectivity** represents another challenge. Edge devices frequently experience network disruptions due to environmental factors, power constraints, or mobility. Robust architectures implement store-and-forward mechanisms that buffer data during disconnections, then synchronize when connectivity returns, preventing data loss while maintaining temporal accuracy.

- **Device diversity** introduces format and protocol variations requiring normalization for consistent processing. IoT Core's protocol adapter layer converts between device-native protocols (MQTT, HTTP, WebSockets) and standardized internal formats, while schema validation and transformation components ensure downstream processes receive consistently structured data.

Real-time sensor analytics

Real-time analysis of sensor data enables immediate insights and actions based on device conditions, transforming raw telemetry into operational intelligence. The commonly used algorithms are as follows:

- **Anomaly detection** identifies unusual patterns that might indicate equipment failure, security breaches, or other critical conditions. Rather than using simple thresholds, sophisticated implementations employ statistical and machine learning approaches establishing dynamic baselines for normal behaviour, adapting to seasonal variations, usage patterns, and equipment aging.

- **Predictive maintenance** extends anomaly detection by identifying patterns preceding failures. By analysing historical failure data alongside current telemetry, these systems forecast potential issues before operational disruptions. The architecture combines domain-specific models with adaptive learning capturing the unique characteristics of individual assets.

- **Real-time dashboarding** provides operational visibility across distributed device fleets, aggregating metrics across multiple dimensions and calculating derived metrics indicating system health. The architecture balances data freshness against system load, often implementing hierarchical aggregation rolling up detailed metrics into actionable summaries.

These analytical approaches typically operate on multiple time horizons simultaneously—immediate detection of critical conditions, short-term trend analysis, and longer-term pattern recognition, creating comprehensive operational awareness from distributed sensor networks.

Real-time geospatial data

Location-based data streams add spatial dimensions to temporal analysis, requiring specialized techniques for indexing, querying, and visualization. From vehicle fleet tracking to mobile application location services, geospatial streaming enables powerful location-aware applications. AWS provides several services that can be combined to build comprehensive geospatial streaming solutions.

Location-based processing

Processing geospatial data efficiently requires specialized techniques addressing the unique characteristics of coordinate-based information. AWS provides multiple services that can be combined into a comprehensive geospatial streaming architecture:

- **Geohashing** converts geographical coordinates into compact string representations that preserve spatial locality, enabling efficient partitioning and indexing of location data for both storage optimization and analytical efficiency.

```
1.  # Geohashing for location data partitioning
2.  def get_partition_key(lat, lng, precision=5):
3.      import geohash2
4.      return geohash2.encode(lat, lng, precision)
5.
6.  # Using geohash as partition key for Kinesis
7.  kinesis_client.put_record(
8.      StreamName='LocationStream',
9.      Data=json.dumps(location_event),
10.     PartitionKey=get_partition_key(event['latitude'], event['longitude'])
11. )
```

This approach naturally clusters related locations (points close to each other geographically share similar geohash prefixes), improving both storage locality and query performance. Within AWS, this partitioning strategy can be implemented in KDS for ingestion and carried through to Amazon OpenSearch Service or Amazon DynamoDB for persistence and querying.

- **Spatial indexing** organizes data for efficient proximity operations like *find all points within 500 meters of this location*. AWS-based streaming architectures typically implement these spatial indexes through:

  o **Amazon OpenSearch Service** with its dedicated geospatial field types and query operations supporting geo_point, geo_shape types, and distance-based queries.

  o **Amazon DynamoDB** with geohashing implemented at the application layer.

  o **Amazon Aurora PostgreSQL** with PostGIS extension for more complex geospatial operations.

The indexing strategy significantly impacts both ingestion performance and query latency, making service selection critical based on specific use case requirements.

Geospatial stream processing architecture

A complete AWS architecture for real-time geospatial data processing typically includes multiple layers working together seamlessly:

- **Data ingestion layer:**

  o **AWS IoT Core** for ingesting location updates from mobile devices and IoT sensors.

  o **Amazon KDS** as the primary streaming backbone, using geohash-based partitioning

  o **AWS SDK** for enabling mobile applications to send location updates (no specialized producer SDK is required, unlike video streaming).

- **Processing layer:**

  o **AWS Lambda** for event-based processing of location updates.

  o **Amazon Kinesis Data Analytics** for SQL-based or Apache Flink processing of spatial operations.

  o **Amazon Location Service** for geocoding, routing, and geofence evaluation.

- **Storage layer:**

  o **Amazon DynamoDB** for current device state and geofence definitions.

  o **Amazon OpenSearch Service** for spatial queries and visualization.

  o **Amazon Timestream** for time-series analysis of historical location data.

- **Notification layer**:

  o **Amazon SNS/SQS** for event notifications and action queuing.

  o **Amazon EventBridge** for orchestrating responses to spatial events.

This architecture enables real-time spatial analytics while maintaining scalability for thousands or millions of simultaneous device connections.

Specialized streaming data types require tailored architectural approaches addressing their unique characteristics. Video, audio, IoT sensor data, and geospatial information each present distinct challenges influencing streaming solution design.

By leveraging specialized services like Kinesis Video Streams and IoT Core alongside core streaming services, we can build robust pipelines handling these complex data types effectively. The key insight across all specialized types is the importance of understanding their fundamental characteristics rather than treating them as generic data streams. By designing architectures embracing these unique properties, the temporal nature of video, the semantic richness of audio, the massive scale of IoT, or the spatial dimensions of location data, we create solutions deriving maximum value from these specialized data sources.

Stream processing implementation

Building robust stream processing systems requires more than just connecting producers to consumers. The real challenges emerge when confronting the messiness of real-world data, handling inevitable failures, and maintaining contextual awareness across millions of discrete events. This section explores the implementation strategies that transform theoretical streaming architectures into resilient, production-ready systems.

Multi-format data integration

The idealized vision of streaming clean, standardized data flowing smoothly through processing stages rarely matches reality. Instead, stream processors must contend with heterogeneous formats, evolving schemas, and varying data qualities.

Data transformation patterns

Consider a retail analytics platform ingesting data from point-of-sale systems, inventory management, and online storefronts. Each source speaks its own language: legacy POS systems generate fixed-width text files, inventory systems produce XML, and e-commerce platforms emit JSON.

In-flight transformation converts data immediately upon ingestion, adapting source formats to processing requirements. In AWS, Lambda functions excel at this pattern:

```
1.  def normalize_transaction(event):
2.      source = event.get('source_system')
3.
4.      if source == 'store_pos':
5.          # Convert fixed-width text to structured data
6.          return transform_pos_data(event['data'])
7.      elif source == 'ecommerce':
8.          # Transform JSON e-commerce data
9.          return transform_ecommerce_data(json.loads(event['data']))
10.     else:
11.         logger.error(f"Unknown source system: {source}»")
12.         return minimal_transaction_structure(event)
```

The key implementation challenge is balancing transformation complexity against Lambda execution time limits. Simple transformations work well in Lambda, but complex operations may require Kinesis Data Analytics or EMR.

Stream-to-stream transformation creates new data streams optimized for specific consumption patterns. Kinesis Data Analytics with SQL provides a declarative approach where you can transform raw POS data into standardized transactions using SQL commands. This approach shines for complex transformations with time-based operations or joins across multiple streams.

Enrichment patterns augment stream data with additional context. A transaction event with just a product ID becomes more valuable when enriched with product category, price tier, and margin information. AWS Step Functions can orchestrate this enrichment process, calling multiple services to gather context and combine it with the original event.

Schema evolution

As business requirements change, data schemas inevitably evolve. New attributes are added, field types change, and structures are reorganized. Stream processing architectures must handle this evolution gracefully.

Schema versioning embeds evolution directly into the data, tagging each record with its schema version:

```
1. {
2.    "schemaVersion": "2.1",
3.    "payload": {
4.      "device_id": "sensor-123",
5.      "readings": { "temperature": 24.5, "humidity": 65 }
6.    }
7. }
```

Processors examine the schema version to apply appropriate parsing logic. This approach provides clarity but requires explicit version management in processing code.

Schema registry centralizes schema management through external services. AWS Glue Schema registry stores and validates schemas, with serializers and deserializers that handle schema resolution automatically. The registry approach excels in environments with multiple producers and consumers, providing centralized governance and compatibility checking.

Compatible evolution designs schemas to accommodate changes without breaking existing consumers. Best practices include making new fields optional, providing default values, using extensible structures like maps for dynamic attributes, and avoiding field repurposing or type changes. These practices allow schema extension without requiring all consumers to update simultaneously.

Format conversion strategies

Beyond schema variations, stream processing often requires handling entirely different data formats. Selecting the right conversion approach significantly impacts performance and compatibility.

Canonical format pattern establishes a standard internal representation, converting all data to this format regardless of source. AWS Glue provides built-in conversions between formats in streaming ETL jobs. Apache Avro and Parquet often serve as canonical formats due to their schema support and performance characteristics.

Format-preserving processing maintains the original format throughout processing when possible, converting only when specifically required. This approach minimizes transformation overhead but requires format-aware processors.

The optimal strategy depends on your ecosystem:

- For analytics-focused pipelines, adopt a columnar canonical format like Parquet.

- For service integration, use a serialization format like Avro or Protocol Buffers.
- For human-readable debugging, JSON provides the best visibility despite size overhead.

Error handling

In the world of continuous data streams, errors are not just possibilities but inevitabilities. A robust error-handling strategy is the key differentiator between systems that gracefully handle failures and those that collapse under real-world conditions. Let us explore comprehensive approaches to managing errors in stream processing systems, ensuring resilience and reliability in production environments.

Dead letter queues

In stream processing, some messages will inevitably fail processing due to data corruption, unexpected formats, or temporary service issues. **Dead letter queues (DLQs)** preserve these problematic messages while allowing processing to continue.

With AWS Lambda processing Kinesis streams, you can configure an SQS queue as a DLQ:

```
1.  StreamProcessor:
2.    Type: AWS::Lambda::Function
3.    Properties:
4.      DeadLetterConfig:
5.        TargetArn: !GetAtt DeadLetterQueue.Arn
6.      Events:
7.        Stream:
8.          Type: Kinesis
9.          Properties:
10.            Stream: !GetAtt DataStream.Arn
11.            BatchSize: 100
12.            MaximumRetryAttempts: 3
```

This configuration sends failed messages to SQS after three processing attempts, allowing investigation and reprocessing.

Effective DLQ messages include comprehensive context about the failure (error type, message, stack trace), the original message content, and processing metadata (timestamp, function name, attempt count). This structured information enables both automated analysis and manual diagnosis.

A complete DLQ implementation requires monitoring (CloudWatch alarms on queue depth) and reprocessing capabilities. Reprocessing may be automated for known, correctable errors or manual for complex issues requiring investigation.

Retry patterns

Not all processing errors are permanent. Network issues, service unavailability, or resource constraints often resolve independently. Effective retry strategies distinguish between temporary and permanent failures.

Exponential backoff increases the delay between retry attempts, typically doubling the delay after each failure. Adding jitter (small random variations) prevents retry storms where multiple failed operations retry simultaneously.

Error classification is crucial for effective retry policies. Common categories include:

- **Transient errors** (network timeouts, throttling), retry with backoff.
- **Resource errors** (out of memory, CPU limits), retry after scaling.

- **Data errors** (invalid formats, schema violations), send to DLQ immediately.

- **Dependency errors** (downstream service failures), implement a circuit breaker.

AWS Step Functions implements comprehensive retry policies based on error types:

```
1.  "Retry": [
2.    {
3.      "ErrorEquals": ["ServiceUnavailable", "TooManyRequestsException"],
4.      "IntervalSeconds": 1,
5.      "MaxAttempts": 5,
6.      "BackoffRate": 2.0
7.    }
8.  ]
```

Circuit breaker pattern prevents overwhelming downstream services during failure scenarios. It temporarily suspends operations after detecting systemic issues, transitioning through three states:

- **Closed**: Normal operation, all requests proceed.

- **Open**: Failure threshold exceeded, all requests fail fast.

- **Half-open**: Testing recovery, allowing limited requests.

This pattern is particularly valuable for protecting downstream services and providing faster failure detection during outages.

Error recovery strategies

Beyond individual message handling, stream processing systems need strategies for broader recovery after deployment errors, bugs, or infrastructure failures.

Replay capabilities serve as the foundation for many recovery approaches. Kinesis Data Streams retains records for up to 365 days, enabling reprocessing from any point within that window using shard iterators with the AT_TIMESTAMP type. This capability allows operations teams to recover from processing errors by rewinding to specific points in time.

Self-healing systems automatically recover from certain error conditions:

- Auto-scaling to address capacity-related failures.

- Automatic failover to alternate regions or components.

- Dynamic configuration adjustments based on error patterns.

AWS CloudWatch alarms linked to auto scaling policies implement this pattern by increasing capacity when processing backlogs exceed thresholds.

State management

The event-driven nature of streaming creates a fundamental challenge: individual events often have limited meaning without context. Effective state management creates this contextual awareness across event boundaries.

Stateful processing

Many streaming analytics require maintaining information beyond individual messages, such as running aggregates, time-based windows, or event correlations.

Windowed aggregation groups data within time boundaries for analysis. Kinesis Data Analytics implements this pattern using SQL:

```
1.  -- Calculate 5-minute average temperature by device
2.  SELECT STREAM
3.      device_id,
4.      FLOOR(ROWTIME TO MINUTE) / 300 AS window_start,
5.      AVG(temperature) AS avg_temperature,
6.      COUNT(*) AS reading_count
7.  FROM temperature_stream
8.  GROUP BY device_id, FLOOR(ROWTIME TO MINUTE) / 300
```

This SQL statement groups readings by device ID and five-minute time windows, calculating statistics across all readings in each window, and emitting a result record when the window closes.

Session tracking groups related events by activity periods rather than fixed time intervals. This approach adapts to user behaviour, with sessions defined by gaps in activity. Apache Flink (available through Kinesis Data Analytics) provides sophisticated session windowing that automatically detects session boundaries based on inactivity periods.

Pattern matching detects complex event sequences by tracking partial matches across multiple messages. Flink's MATCH_RECOGNIZE syntax enables declarative pattern matching to identify sequences like equipment startup-operation-shutdown cycles, returning timing information for each phase.

Checkpointing

Stream processors must track their processing position to ensure exactly-once or at-least-once semantics, particularly during scaling events or after failures.

Explicit checkpointing with **Kinesis Client Library** (**KCL**) records processing progress at the application level. After successfully processing a batch of records, the application explicitly calls **checkpoint()** to record its position. This approach provides fine-grained control but requires careful implementation.

Managed checkpointing with Kinesis Data Analytics enables automatic state preservation. The system automatically creates consistent checkpoints across all processing nodes, persisting both position information and application state to durable storage.

Effective checkpointing strategies must balance:

- **Frequency**: More frequent checkpoints reduce potential data loss but increase overhead.
- **Scope**: Fine-grained checkpoints provide precision but increase state management complexity.
- **Storage**: Durable storage prevents checkpoint loss but introduces latency.

Recovery patterns

When failures occur, recovery patterns leverage checkpoints and state management to resume processing with minimal disruption. The following list refers to the class of recovery patterns:

- **Exactly-once processing** ensures each message affects the system state precisely once despite failures or retries. This requires both careful checkpoint management and transactional state updates. AWS Step Functions implements this pattern for complex workflows through its built-in state persistence and error handling.
- **Idempotent processing** designs operations to produce the same result regardless of repetition. A payment processing function might first check if a payment ID already exists in a database before processing, ensuring that duplicate messages do not cause double charges. This approach simplifies recovery by making message reprocessing safe.

- **State rehydration** restores application state from persistent storage when restarting stream processing. A Lambda function processing user session might load previously saved session state from S3 or DynamoDB upon initialization, allowing it to resume tracking user activity as if no interruption occurred.

Building robust stream processing implementations requires carefully addressing multi-format data integration, error handling, and state management challenges. These patterns transform theoretical architectures into resilient, production-ready systems.

AWS provides specialized services that implement these patterns at scale:

- Schema registries for data governance and evolution.
- Dead letter queues and retry policies for error resilience.
- Stateful processing frameworks for contextual awareness.
- Checkpointing mechanisms for reliable recovery.

The most effective streaming architectures combine these techniques strategically based on specific business requirements, creating systems that operate continuously despite the messiness of real-world data and environments.

Operational excellence

Building a streaming pipeline is only the beginning. Operating it reliably, efficiently, and securely in production requires consistent attention to monitoring, performance, and security practices. This section examines essential operational considerations for streaming architectures.

Monitoring and alerting

Effective streaming operations depend on comprehensive visibility into system behavior. AWS provides several layers of monitoring capabilities for streaming systems.

CloudWatch metrics

AWS streaming services emit important built-in metrics automatically captured by CloudWatch:

- For Kinesis Data Streams:
    - **GetRecords.IteratorAgeMilliseconds**: Age of the oldest unprocessed record
    - **ReadProvisionedThroughputExceeded**: Throttled read requests
    - **WriteProvisionedThroughputExceeded**: Throttled write requests
- For Lambda functions processing streams:
    - **Invocations and errors**: Success and failure counts
    - **Duration**: Execution time
    - **IteratorAge**: For stream-based invocations, the age of the last record processed

Create CloudWatch dashboards combining related metrics across your streaming pipeline to establish a unified view.

Custom metrics

While built-in metrics cover service health, application-specific metrics illuminate business-relevant behaviors. Create custom metrics to track:

- Message processing rates by category
- Business event frequencies
- Data quality indicators
- End-to-end latency across multiple stages

Implement custom metrics using CloudWatch **embedded metrics format (EMF)** in your processing code. The most valuable custom metrics often combine technical and business dimensions, such as tracking processing latency by customer tier or transaction type.

Alert patterns

Implement a tiered approach to alerting:

- **Critical alerts**: Immediate human response required
  - Complete processing stoppage or data loss risk
  - **Methods**: PagerDuty, SMS
- **Warning alerts**: Investigation needed during business hours
  - Elevated error rates or increased latency
  - **Methods**: Email, Slack notifications
- **Informational alerts**: No immediate action required
  - Deployment completions or auto-scaling events
  - **Methods**: Dashboard updates, digest emails

Configure alert routing based on both severity and domain using AWS EventBridge. Implement correlations between related alerts to reduce noise—when identifying the root cause, generate a single consolidated notification rather than separate alerts for each symptom.

Performance optimization

In modern streaming architectures, achieving optimal performance requires a careful balance of throughput, latency, and scaling capabilities. As data volumes grow exponentially and real-time processing becomes increasingly critical, organizations must implement sophisticated optimization strategies to meet these demanding requirements. The difference between a good and great streaming system often lies in how well these performance aspects are tuned and maintained.

Successful optimization requires understanding both the technical capabilities of your streaming platform and the specific characteristics of your workload. Whether you're processing IoT sensor data, financial transactions, or user interactions, each use case presents unique challenges that demand tailored optimization approaches.

Throughput optimization

Three key approaches significantly impact stream throughput:

- **Efficient serialization formats** reduce message size and processing overhead. Binary formats like Avro and Protocol Buffers typically reduce message size by 30-60% compared to JSON, directly increasing effective throughput. Kinesis Data Firehose and Glue streaming jobs provide built-in support for format conversion.
- **Batching** amortizes per-request overhead across multiple records. Instead of sending individual messages, group them into appropriately sized batches (under 1MB for Kinesis). Optimal batch sizes balance throughput against latency, larger batches improve throughput but increase the delay before processing begins.

- **Partition strategy** determines throughput distribution across shards. Design partition keys to distribute traffic evenly:
  - o Avoid high-cardinality fields like timestamps
  - o Use fields with good distribution (user IDs, session IDs)
  - o For time-series data, combine time buckets with entity IDs

Skewed partitioning concentrates traffic in specific shards, causing throttling while leaving others underutilized.

Latency reduction

For real-time applications, end-to-end latency often becomes critical.

Key optimization approaches include:

- **Parallelization** distributes processing across multiple units. Kinesis enables parallelism through shards, while Lambda scales concurrency automatically based on stream activity.

- **Optimized record processing** minimizes per-record latency through techniques like:
  - o Caching reference data to avoid repeated lookups
  - o Minimizing external service calls
  - o Using connection pooling for database operations

- **Enhanced polling** reduces the delay between record production and consumption. For Lambda consumers, configure smaller batch windows to reduce wait times:

```
1. StreamProcessor:
2.   Type: AWS::Lambda::Function
3.   Properties:
4.     Events:
5.       Stream:
6.         Type: Kinesis
7.         Properties:
8.           BatchSize: 100
9.           MaximumBatchingWindowInSeconds: 1  # Process within 1 second 300
```

For latency-sensitive applications, consider direct integration patterns like API Gateway with Lambda that bypass intermediate queuing while asynchronously writing to streams for durability.

Scaling strategies

Streaming workloads rarely maintain consistent volume.

Effective scaling adjusts capacity to match changing workloads while controlling costs. Refer to the following list for more details:

- **Auto scaling** with Kinesis adjusts the shard count based on metrics like iterator age or shard utilization. Application auto scaling can implement rules like *increasing capacity when the iterator age exceeds one minute.*

- **Enhanced fan-out** provides dedicated throughput for high-priority consumers, eliminating contention among multiple readers. This approach works well for scenarios with many consumers or latency-sensitive applications.

- **Adaptive batching** dynamically adjusts batch sizes based on current conditions, larger batches during peak periods to maximize throughput, smaller batches during quieter periods to reduce latency.

Operational excellence in streaming systems requires disciplined attention to monitoring, performance, and security. By implementing comprehensive observability, optimizing for your specific workload characteristics, and applying defense-in-depth security practices, you can build streaming platforms that operate reliably and securely at scale.

Real-world use cases

The streaming patterns and practices explored throughout this book come together in real-world implementations that solve complex business challenges. This section examines four diverse use cases with architecture diagrams and focused implementation insights.

Connected vehicle data processing

Modern vehicles generate massive data volumes from hundreds of sensors and onboard systems, typically 25GB per hour per vehicle. This creates unique streaming requirements spanning from edge processing to cloud analytics.

Architecture diagram showing vehicle edge | cloud ingestion | processing | analytics tiers with AWS services labelled:

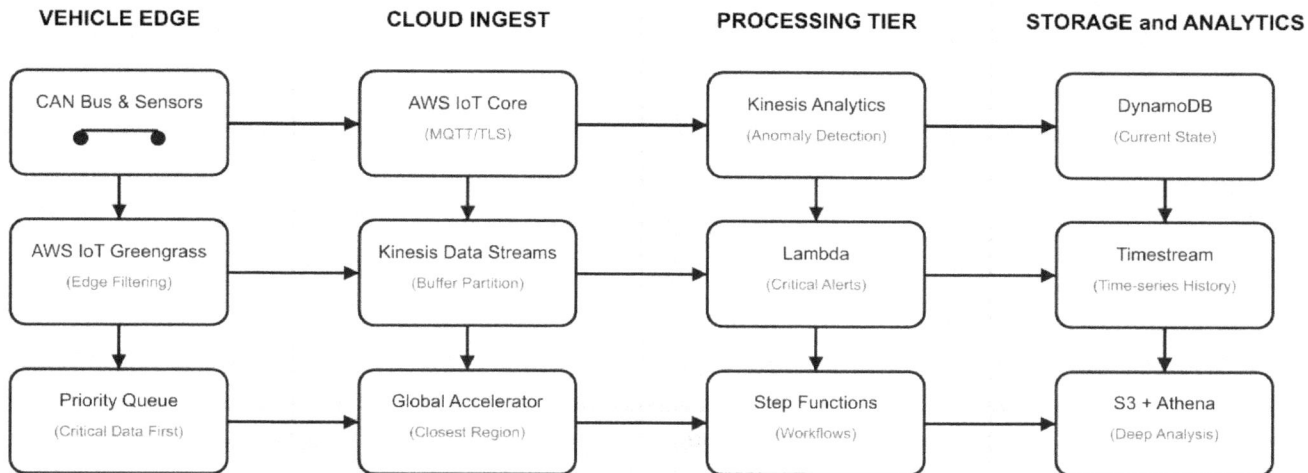

Figure 4.4: Connected vehicle data processing architecture

The connected vehicle architecture employs a multi-tier approach where AWS IoT Greengrass performs initial filtering in the vehicle to reduce transmission volumes, while implementing priority queuing for critical data. AWS IoT Core receives vehicle telemetry through secure MQTT connections, feeding into Kinesis Data Streams partitioned by vehicle ID. Processing occurs through Kinesis Analytics for anomaly detection and Lambda functions for critical alerts, while Step Functions orchestrate more complex diagnostic workflows.

Intermittent connectivity challenges are addressed through IoT Core's persistent sessions and edge buffering with Greengrass, ensuring critical safety data transmits first when connections resume. For global fleets, Global Accelerator routes to the nearest regional endpoint while DynamoDB global tables synchronize vehicle state across regions. The architecture implements dual-path processing, routing safety events directly to Lambda while channelling routine telemetry through Kinesis, enabling automotive companies to maintain real-time fleet awareness while meeting stringent safety requirements.

Smart city sensor networks

Smart cities deploy diverse sensor types across urban environments to monitor everything from traffic flow to infrastructure health, creating complex integration and analysis challenges.

The architecture figure, showing sensor network | integration layer | stream processing | analytics with AWS services labelled:

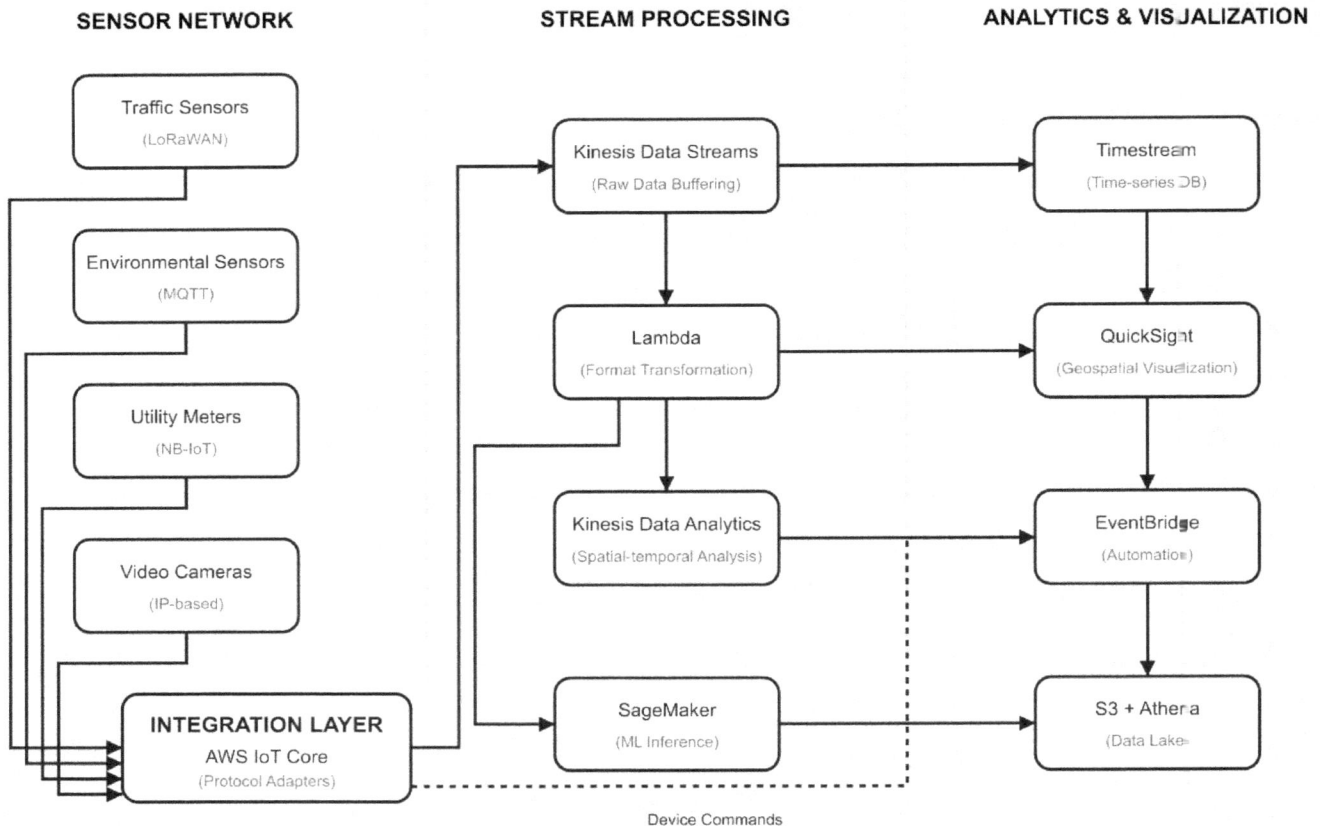

Figure 4.5: Smart city sensor data ingestion architecture

The smart city architecture integrates heterogeneous sensors—traffic monitors using LoRaWAN, environmental sensors on MQTT, utility meters via NB-IoT, and IP-based cameras—through AWS IoT Core's protocol adapters. This normalized data flows through Kinesis Streams to Kinesis Analytics for spatial-temporal analysis and Lambda for format transformation. The analytics tier leverages Timestream for time-series storage, QuickSight for geospatial visualization, and EventBridge for automated responses.

AWS IoT Core solves the fundamental challenge of integrating diverse data sources through protocol adaptation and format normalization, while IoT SiteWise creates consistent asset models across different infrastructure components. Geohash-based partitioning in Kinesis ensures spatially related data processes together enabling neighborhood-level analysis. For multi-stakeholder access, IAM with attribute-based control limits departments to relevant data while Kinesis Enhanced Fan-Out provides dedicated throughput to critical services. This approach enables municipal governments to gain comprehensive urban awareness through integrated sensor analysis.

Financial market data processing

Financial institutions require real-time market data processing with pull-based API integration for trading decisions, combining ultra-low latency requirements with complex acquisition patterns.

Architecture diagram showing data acquisition | processing | state management | distribution with AWS services labelled:

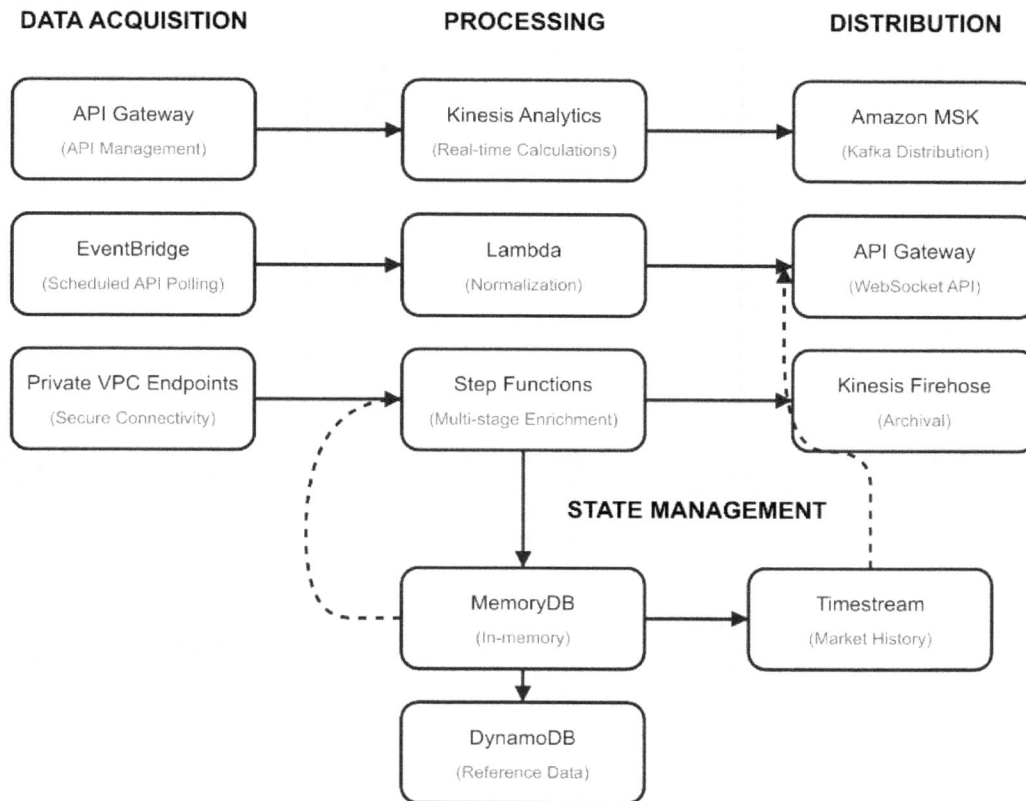

Figure 4.6: Financial market data processing architecture

The financial data architecture begins with API Gateway managing connections to external market data providers, while EventBridge schedules regular polling for API-based sources. Private VPC endpoints secure this acquisition process. The processing tier employs Kinesis Analytics for real-time metrics calculation and Lambda for data normalization, while Step Functions orchestrate multi-stage enrichment. For state management, MemoryDB provides sub-millisecond access to current market conditions, with DynamoDB for reference data and Timestream for historical analysis. The distribution tier leverages Amazon MSK for delivery to trading systems and WebSocket APIs for user interfaces.

EventBridge scheduled rules with Step Functions' sophisticated retry logic address the challenges of API-based market data acquisition, implementing backoff strategies for rate limits. Data consistency across sources is maintained through DynamoDB global tables for reference data and Lambda-based validation to detect discrepancies. For the critical requirement of ultra-low latency, direct VPC endpoints minimize network delays while enhanced fan-out consumers reduce processing latency for time-sensitive trading applications. This architecture enables financial institutions to process market data in real time with the reliability required for algorithmic trading and regulatory compliance.

Real-time video analytics

Video analytics transforms surveillance systems into intelligence tools by extracting actionable insights from video streams in real time, creating unique streaming challenges due to high data volumes and computational demands.

The architecture figure showing video ingestion | processing | analytics with AWS services labelled:

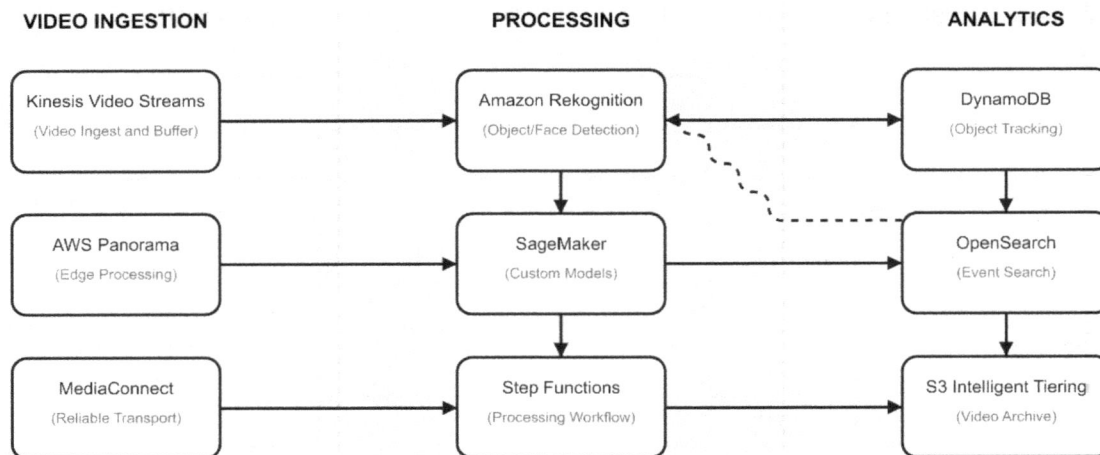

Figure 4.7: *Real-time video analytics architecture*

The video analytics architecture ingests feeds through Kinesis Video Streams with AWS Panorama performing edge processing for initial content filtering. The processing tier applies progressive analysis where Amazon Rekognition Video handles common detection tasks while SageMaker endpoints run specialized models for domain-specific detection. Step Functions coordinate multi-stage workflows ensuring efficient resource utilization. The analytics tier uses DynamoDB for object tracking, OpenSearch for complex event queries, and S3 with Intelligent-Tiering for long-term archiving.

Computational efficiency is achieved through AWS Panorama's edge processing to filter non-essential content, multi-stage pipelines that apply expensive analysis only when needed, and Lambda with GPU acceleration for inference. Bandwidth challenges are addressed through dynamic compression in Kinesis Video Streams, edge-based filtering, and region-of-interest encoding that prioritizes critical image areas. For contextual understanding, Step Functions maintain processing context across video segments while EventBridge correlates video analytics with other sensor inputs. This architecture enables organizations to transform passive video feeds into active intelligence sources for applications from retail analytics to public safety.

These real-world use cases demonstrate how AWS streaming services address diverse business challenges across industries. While each implementation solves unique requirements, several common patterns emerge: multi-tier architectures balance edge and cloud processing; service combinations leverage complementary AWS capabilities; and domain-specific optimizations tailor generic streaming patterns to address unique challenges in vehicles, cities, financial markets, and video analytics. As streaming technologies mature, these patterns will continue to evolve, enabling increasingly sophisticated real-time data processing that extracts unprecedented value from streaming data sources.

Hands-on: Building multi-format streaming pipeline

Real-world streaming applications often need to process data from different sources in varying formats. This section demonstrates how to build a unified streaming pipeline that handles multiple formats (JSON, CSV, and binary) using AWS services.

Implementation overview

The complete implementation is available as a Jupyter Notebook in our GitHub repository.

This notebook creates a fully functional AWS streaming pipeline with:

- **Kinesis Data Stream** for ingesting multi-format data.
- **Lambda function** that detects and processes each format appropriately.
- **S3 bucket** for storing standardized results with logical partitioning.

- **CloudWatch metrics** for monitoring pipeline performance.

Key implementation patterns

In the following, we will describe the key logic and code snippet used in the hands-on example:

- **Format detection logic:** The Lambda function automatically identifies the format of incoming data:

```
1. def detect_format(data):
2.      # Check for JSON format
3.      if data.startswith(b'{') and data.endswith(b'}'):
4.          return 'json'
5.
6.      # Check for CSV format
7.      if data.startswith(b'format,csv'):
8.          return 'csv'
9.
10.     # Check for binary format (BIN\0 signature)
11.     if data.startswith(b'BIN\0'):
12.         return 'binary'
13.
14.     return 'unknown'
```

Once detected, each format is processed by specialized handlers that extract the relevant information and convert it to a standardized structure.

- **Format-specific processing:** Each format requires different parsing approaches:

  o **JSON**: Parsed using standard JSON libraries

  o **CSV**: Processed with CSV parsing and row aggregation

  o **Binary**: Decoded using struct unpacking with format-specific logic

- **Standardized output structure:** All formats are converted to a consistent structure for downstream processing:

```
1. {
2.   "device_id": "device-001",
3.   "timestamp": "2023-04-15T14:30:42Z",
4.   "readings": {
5.     "temperature": 72.5,
6.     "humidity": 45.2
7.   },
8.   "original_format": "json|csv|binary",
9.   "processed_timestamp": "2023-04-15T14:30:45Z"
10. }
```

This standardization enables unified analytics across all data sources regardless of their original format.

Scalable AWS architecture

The implementation leverages key AWS services:

- **Kinesis Data Streams** provides ordering and replay capabilities.
- **Lambda** offers serverless processing that scales automatically.

- **S3** with time-based partitioning enables efficient storage and querying.
- **CloudWatch** provides operational visibility through metrics and logs.

Running the demonstration

The Jupyter Notebook allows you to create the complete infrastructure in your AWS account and observe the pipeline in action. It provides interactive visualization of the multi-format processing results and includes cleanup functions to remove all resources.

Key features you can explore:

- Generating and sending data in different formats.
- Watching the Lambda function process each format.
- Examining the standardized results in S3.
- Visualizing data across all formats.
- Monitoring performance with CloudWatch metrics.

Expanding the implementation

This foundation can be extended in several ways:

- **Additional formats**: Add support for XML, Avro, or Parquet
- **Schema validation**: Integrate AWS Glue Schema Registry
- **Enhanced processing**: Add Kinesis Data Analytics for stream aggregation
- **Visualization**: Create real-time dashboards with QuickSight

The pattern of format detection, specialized processing, and standardized output remains consistent regardless of the specific formats involved or the scale of the implementation.

For complete code, step-by-step instructions, and educational commentary, run the Jupyter Notebook from our GitHub repository.

Conclusion

This chapter helped us know the paradigm shift from batch to real-time data processing, introducing fundamental concepts of stream processing and event-driven architectures. We examined the dual architectural approaches, Lambda and Kappa, that address different streaming needs and thoroughly investigated AWS's comprehensive streaming ecosystem, including Kinesis services and Amazon MSK. The chapter discussed specialized streaming data types, covering video, audio, IoT sensor data, and geospatial information, each with unique processing requirements. We outlined practical implementation strategies for multi-format data integration, robust error handling, and effective state management, critical components of resilient production systems. The operational excellence section emphasized monitoring, performance optimization, and scaling strategies essential for maintaining high-performing streaming pipelines. Through real-world use cases spanning connected vehicles, smart cities, financial markets, and video analytics, we demonstrated how these technologies solve complex business challenges across industries.

In the next chapter, we will learn about batch data processing as a complementary approach to the streaming architectures discussed here. While streaming enables real-time insights, batch processing continues to be a fundamental workhorse of data engineering, handling everything from nightly ETL operations to complex transformations. The next chapter will examine AWS's comprehensive ecosystem for batch data processing, from fully managed services like AWS Glue to customizable frameworks on Amazon EMR and sophisticated job orchestration with AWS Step Functions.

## CHAPTER 5

Batch Data Processing

Introduction

In the data engineering landscape that we have studied so far, we have established data lake foundations, examined various data formats, and learned about real-time data ingestion. While streaming architectures enable real-time insights, batch processing remains a fundamental and essential component of modern data platforms. Batch processing, the practice of collecting data over time and processing it in scheduled, discrete job, continues to be the workhorse of data engineering, handling everything from nightly ETL operations to complex data transformations that would be impractical in streaming contexts.

The modern data landscape encompasses a rich ecosystem of tools, services, and architectural patterns for batch data processing. From fully managed services like AWS Glue to customizable frameworks on Amazon EMR, and sophisticated job orchestration with AWS Step Functions, organizations have multiple options for implementing batch workflows. This chapter explores how these components work together to create resilient, efficient processing pipelines that complement the streaming architectures we examined in *Chapter 4, Real-time Data Ingestion and Streaming*. We will learn how to select and implement the right combination of services for specific business requirements while maintaining operational excellence and cost efficiency.

Structure

This chapter will cover the following topics:

- Batch processing patterns
- Exploring AWS Glue
- Performance optimization techniques
- Custom ETL with EMR
- Job orchestration with Step Functions
- Error recovery strategies
- Hands-on: Implementing batch ETL workflows

Objectives

In this chapter, we will discuss how the strategic implementation of batch data processing serves as a foundational element of modern data engineering workflows. We will examine core batch processing patterns and their evolution in cloud environments, dive deep into AWS Glue's serverless ETL capabilities, explore custom processing frameworks with Amazon EMR, implement sophisticated workflow orchestration using AWS Step Functions, and develop robust error-handling strategies. Through practical code examples and a comprehensive hands-on implementation, you will learn to design and deploy efficient, resilient batch processing pipelines that effectively balance performance requirements with cost considerations while maintaining the flexibility needed for evolving business needs. This knowledge will enable you to integrate batch processing seamlessly with the data lake foundations, storage optimizations, and streaming architectures covered in previous chapters.

Batch processing patterns

The evolution of batch processing architectures closely parallels the broader evolution of data engineering, which we discussed in *Chapter 1, Modern Data Engineering Landscape*. Understanding these patterns provides the foundation for implementing effective batch workflows in AWS.

Evolution of batch processing

The journey of batch processing mirrors the broader evolution of enterprise computing, from monolithic systems running in isolation to distributed, cloud-native architectures that scale dynamically with business needs.

Refer to the following figure:

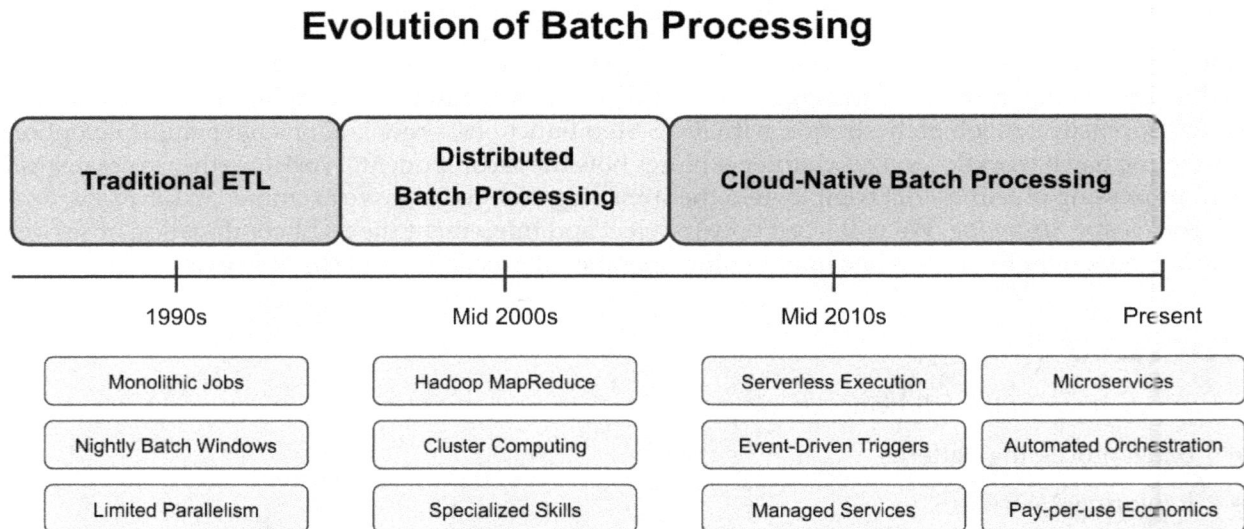

Figure 5.1: Evolution of batch processing from traditional ETL to cloud-native approaches

Traditional batch ETL 1990s to early 2000s

Early data warehousing relied on monolithic ETL jobs running on dedicated servers during nightly batch windows. These jobs used specialized tools like Informatica PowerCenter and Oracle Data Integrator, operating as tightly coupled processes: extracting from source systems, transforming on dedicated servers, and loading to data warehouses. The following code shows ETL implementation:

```
1.  -- Traditional ETL example
2.  INSERT INTO staging.orders SELECT * FROM source_system.orders WHERE order_
    date = TRUNC(SYSDATE) - 1;
3.  UPDATE staging.orders SET total_amount = total_amount * exchange_
    rate WHERE currency <> 'USD';
4.  INSERT INTO dwh.fact_orders
```

This approach worked for predictable data volumes but struggled with scale and flexibility as data complexity grew.

Distributed batch processing mid-2000s to early 2010s

The big data revolution introduced distributed processing frameworks like Hadoop MapReduce, enabling organizations to process vastly larger datasets by splitting work across clusters of commodity hardware. This approach solved scaling challenges but required specialized skills and complex cluster management. The following code shows a MapReduce implementation example:

```
1.  // MapReduce example
2.  public class SalesMapper extends Mapper<LongWritable, Text, Text, DoubleWritable> {
3.      public void map(LongWritable key, Text value, Context context) throws IOException,
    InterruptedException {
4.          String[] fields = value.toString().split(",");
5.          context.write(new Text(fields[3]), new DoubleWritable
    (Double.parseDouble(fields[5])));
6.      }
7.  }
```

Higher-level abstractions like Apache Hive and Pig emerged to simplify development, but operational complexity remained high.

Cloud-native batch processing mid-2010s to present

Modern batch processing leverages cloud services that abstract away infrastructure management. This approach combines serverless execution, microservices, orchestration layers, and event-driven patterns. The following code shows a modern cloud-native approach:

```
1.  def trigger_batch_workflow(event, context):
2.      """Lambda function triggered by data arrival"""
3.      step_functions_client.start_execution(
4.          stateMachineArn="arn:aws:states:region:account:stateMachine:DataProcessing",
5.          input=json.dumps({"dataLocation": event['Records'][0]['s3']['object']['key']})
6.      )
```

This evolution reflects a shift from managing infrastructure to focusing on data transformation logic and business value.

Core batch processing patterns

Extract, load, transform (**ELT**) and ETL are two core batch processing patterns. The following figure summarizes two approaches to batch processing architecture patterns:

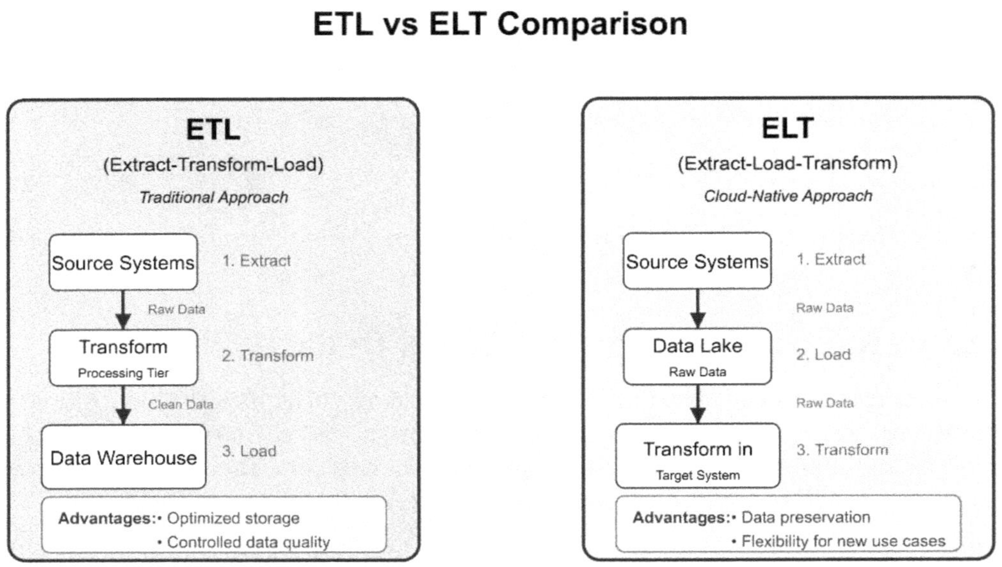

ETL vs ELT Comparison

Figure 5.2: Comparison of ETL and ELT approaches

ETL transforms data before loading to the destination system, optimizing for target system performance when compute resources and storage were expensive. It ensures data quality before entering warehouses but requires a separate processing tier.

ELT loads raw data directly into the destination system before transformation. This modern approach capitalizes on cloud economics where storage is inexpensive, and compute can be elastically applied. Advantages include preserving complete original data for reprocessing, leveraging destination system's processing power, enabling multiple transformations on the same source data, and accelerating development through immediate data availability. The shift toward ELT reflects both cloud architectural capabilities and economic realities where storage cost is rarely the primary constraint.

Medallion architecture in batch processing

The medallion architecture is shown in the following figure with three data zones:

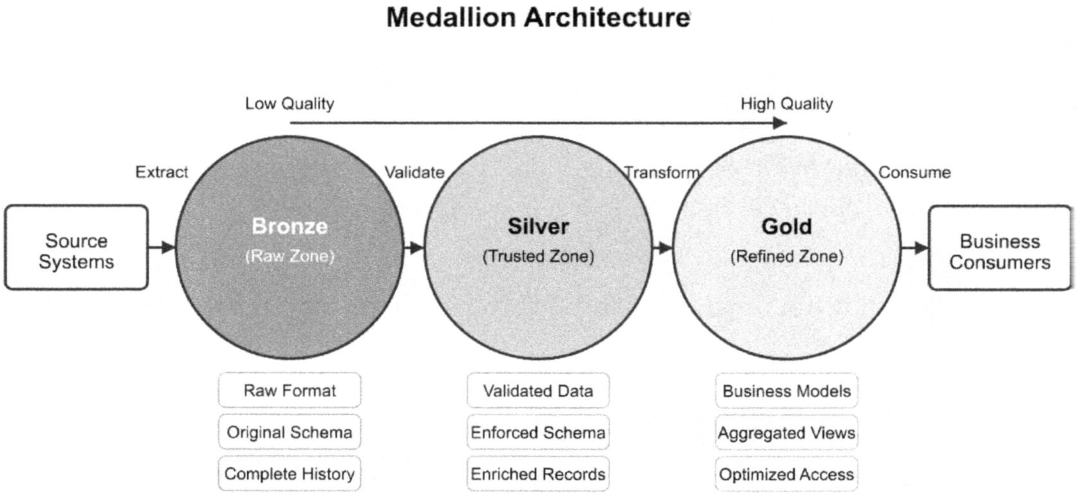

Medallion Architecture

Figure 5.3: Medallion architecture showing progression from raw to refined data

The medallion architecture organizes data processing into progressive refinement stages. The bronze/raw zone captures data in its original form with minimal modification, focusing on reliable ingestion, preservation of source data, and basic metadata addition. This immutable foundation enables reprocessing when requirements change or errors are discovered. The silver/trusted zone transforms raw data into validated, consistently structured datasets through data validation, schema standardization, entity resolution, and initial enrichment. It creates a single version of truth for downstream consumers. The gold/refined zone creates business-specific datasets optimized for particular use cases, focusing on domain-specific aggregations, analytical models, feature engineering, and performance optimization. This architecture elegantly separates concerns, enabling specialized optimization at each stage and creating clear boundaries between raw data preservation and business-specific transformations.

Incremental processing patterns

Incremental processing focuses on handling only new or changed data since the previous execution, significantly improving efficiency as data volumes grow.

Time-based windows process data based on creation or modification time:

```
1.  def process_daily_window():
2.      yesterday = (datetime.now() - timedelta(days=1)).strftime("%Y-%m-%d")
3.      process_data(f"s3://data-lake/events/date={yesterday}/")
```

This straightforward approach works well with regularly partitioned data but struggles with late arrivals.

Watermark-based processing tracks the last successfully processed record:

```
1.  def process_with_watermark():
2.      watermark = get_watermark("customer_processing")
3.      new_data = query_data(f"created_at > ‹{watermark}›»")
4.      process_data(new_data)
5.      set_watermark("customer_processing", get_max_timestamp(new_data))
```

This adaptive approach handles varying ingestion rates but requires careful state management.

Change data capture (**CDC**) processes only specific records changed in source systems, capturing database operations (inserts, updates, deletes) as events. This precise approach is valuable for dimensional data synchronization but requires source systems with change tracking capabilities.

Partitioning strategies for batch jobs

Effective partitioning improves both processing performance and query efficiency while enabling targeted lifecycle management:

- **Time-based partitioning** organizes data by temporal dimensions (year/month/day):

  `s3://data-lake/sales/year=2024/month=02/day=07/sales-data.parqueta`

  This aligns naturally with data creation patterns, enables efficient time-range queries, and simplifies lifecycle management.

- **Business domain partitioning** is organized by business entities (region/category/department):

  `s3://data-lake/customers/region=EMEA/segment=enterprise/customers.parquet`

  This approach optimizes for analytical queries that filter on business dimensions.

- **Hybrid partitioning** combines multiple strategies in a hierarchy:

  `s3://data-lake/sales/year=2024/month=02/region=EMEA/sales.parquet`

  Hybrid approaches offer greater flexibility but increase complexity. Dimensions used more frequently for filtering should appear higher in the hierarchy.

AWS Batch processing architectures

AWS offers multiple approaches to batch processing, each optimized for different requirements:

- **Serverless ETL with AWS Glue:** AWS Glue provides a fully managed, serverless approach using automatically provisioned Apache Spark environments:

```
1.  # AWS Glue job (simplified)
2.  def process_data_glue(glueContext):
3.      datasource = glueContext.create_dynamic_frame.from_catalog(
4.          database="sales_db", table_name="raw_transactions"
5.      )
6.      transformed = apply_transformations(datasource)
7.      glueContext.write_dynamic_frame.from_options(
8.          frame=transformed,
9.          connection_type="s3",
10.         connection_options={"path": "s3://data-lake/processed/"},
11.         format="parquet"
12.     )
```

Glue excels for variable workloads, standard ETL patterns, and scenarios where operational simplicity is prioritized over customization.

- **Cluster-based processing with Amazon EMR:** Amazon EMR provides managed clusters running open-source frameworks like Spark, Hive, and Presto:

```
1.  # EMR Spark job (simplified)
2.  def process_with_emr():
3.      spark = SparkSession.builder.appName("CustomerAnalytics").getOrCreate()
4.      transactions = spark.read.parquet("s3://data-lake/raw/transactions/")
5.      customers = spark.read.parquet("s3://data-lake/raw/customers/")
6.      result = transactions.join(customers, "customer_id").groupBy("segmert").
    agg(...)
7.      result.write.partitionBy("segment").parquet("s3://data-lake/analytics/")
```

EMR offers greater control and customization, making it ideal for compute-intensive transformations, specialized frameworks, and performance-critical workloads.

- **Orchestrated multi-service workflows:** AWS Step Functions coordinates complex workflows across multiple services:

```
1.  {
2.      "StartAt": "ExtractData",
3.      "States": {
4.          "ExtractData": {
5.              "Type": "Task",
6.              "Resource": "arn:aws:states:::glue:startJobRun.sync",
7.              "Parameters": { "JobName": "extract-data" },
8.              "Next": "ValidateData"
9.          },
10.         "ValidateData": {
11.             "Type": "Task",
12.             "Resource": "arn:aws:lambda:region:account:function:validate-data",
13.             "Next": "ChoiceState"
```

```
14.          },
15.          "ChoiceState": {
16.              "Type": "Choice",
17.              "Choices": [
18.                  {
19.                      "Variable": "$.validationPassed",
20.                      "BooleanEquals": false,
21.                      "Next": "HandleFailure"
22.                  }
23.              ],
24.              "Default": "ProcessData"
25.          }
26.          // Additional states omitted for brevity
27.      }
28. }
```

This approach excels for complex multi-step workflows with conditional logic, error handling, and hybrid processing requirements.

The evolution of batch processing patterns reflects the broader transformation of data engineering from infrastructure-focused to data-focused disciplines. Modern batch processing embraces cloud-native principles while incorporating proven patterns from decades of data processing experience. These patterns form the foundation for implementing effective batch processing solutions on AWS.

Exploring AWS Glue

AWS Glue provides a fully managed, serverless platform for ETL operations in batch processing workflows. This section explores how AWS Glue works, implementation approaches both through code and console, and optimization strategies.

Architecture and core components

AWS Glue architecture components and interactions:

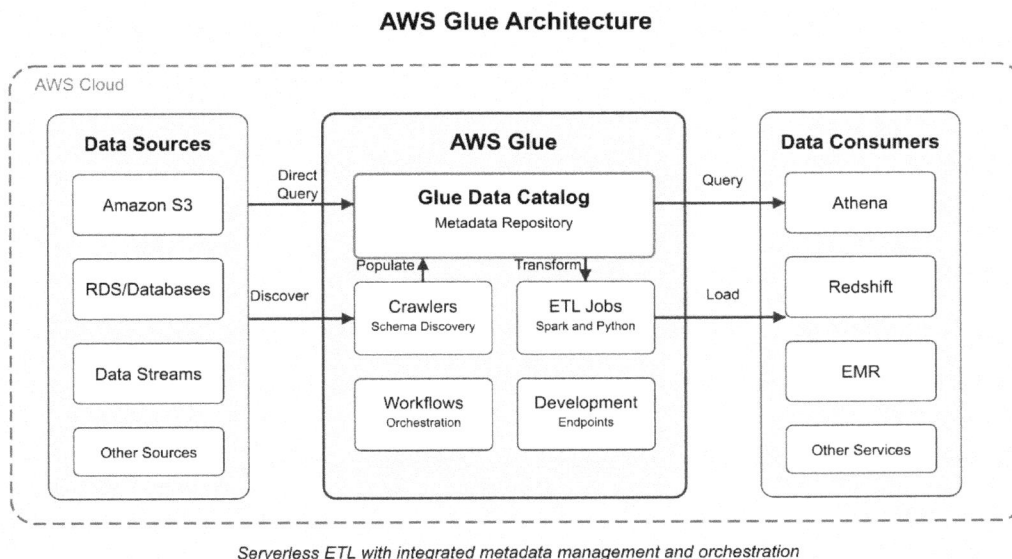

Serverless ETL with integrated metadata management and orchestration

Figure 5.4: *AWS Glue architecture showing key components interaction*

AWS Glue operates through three core components that work together to enable serverless data processing:

Data catalogue and schema discovery

The AWS Glue Data Catalogue functions as a centralized metadata repository. Here is how it works:

- **Crawlers** connect to data sources (S3 buckets, databases, streaming sources) and automatically discover their schema and structure.
- Each crawler scans your data, samples file contents, and infers the schema (column names, data types).
- The crawler populates the Data Catalogue with this metadata, creating table definitions that other AWS services can use.
- On subsequent runs, crawlers detect schema changes and update the catalogue accordingly.

The following are the steps to creating crawlers via the console:

1. Navigate to AWS Glue console | Crawlers | Create crawler.
2. Provide a name (e.g., **sales-data-crawler**).
3. Select the IAM role with required permissions.
4. Add data sources (e.g., S3 bucket path: **s3://retail-data/sales/**).
5. Choose the target database (e.g., **retail**).
6. Configure the crawler schedule (e.g., run daily at midnight).
7. Configure schema change handling (typically **Update the table definition in the data catalog**).
8. Review and create the crawler.

Creating crawlers via code:

```
1.  # Creating and running a crawler
2.  crawler = glue_client.create_crawler(
3.      Name='sales-data-crawler',
4.      Role='GlueServiceRole',   # IAM role with required permissions
5.      DatabaseName='retail',    # Target database in the catalog
6.      Targets={'S3Targets': [{'Path': 's3://retail-data/sales/'}]},
7.      # Configure schema evolution behavior
8.      SchemaChangePolicy={
9.          'UpdateBehavior': 'UPDATE_IN_DATABASE',   # Update schema when changes detected
10.         'DeleteBehavior': 'LOG'                    # Log if tables/partitions disappear
11.     }
12. )
13. glue_client.start_crawler(Name='sales-data-crawler')
```

ETL job's implementation options

AWS Glue supports multiple job types, each with distinct characteristics and use cases:

- **Spark ETL jobs:** Spark ETL jobs run on managed Apache Spark clusters and excel at processing large datasets.

  The following are the steps to creating Spark jobs via the console:

  1. Navigate to AWS Glue console | Jobs | Create job.
  2. Select Spark as the job type.
  3. Choose the authoring mode (Visual ETL, Jupyter Notebook, or Script editor).

4. Provide a name (e.g., **transform-sales-data**).

5. Select IAM role, Glue version (e.g., Glue 3.0).

6. Configure worker type (e.g., G.2X) and number of workers.

7. Add the script or develop it in the visual builder.

8. Configure job parameters, job bookmarks, and advanced properties.

9. Save and run the job.

- **Spark job script location:**

  o Scripts are stored in S3 (e.g., **s3://aws-glue-scripts/username/transform-sales-data.py**)

  o AWS Glue automatically uploads scripts from the console to this location

  o You can also provide your own S3 path for custom scripts

  o Local development is possible using the AWS Glue local development environment

- **Python shell jobs:** Python shell jobs execute Python scripts without Spark overhead, ideal for lightweight transformations and data movement.

  Creating Python shell jobs via console:

  1. Navigate to AWS Glue console | Jobs | Create job.

  2. Select Python Shell as the job type.

  3. Provide a name (e.g., **process-config-files**).

  4. Select IAM role and Python version (e.g., Python 3.9).

  5. Add the script directly in the editor.

  6. Configure job parameters and advanced properties.

  7. Save and run the job.

- Python Shell script location:

  o Similar to Spark jobs, scripts are stored in S3

  o Default location: **s3://aws-glue-scripts/username/process-config-files.py**

  o Scripts can access libraries pre-installed in the Glue Python environment

  o Custom libraries can be included via egg or wheel files in S3

Job orchestration and workflow management

AWS Glue provides built-in tools to coordinate job execution through triggers:

- **Creating triggers via console**:

  1. Navigate to AWS Glue console | Triggers | Add trigger.

  2. Select trigger type (Schedule, Event, or Conditional).

  3. Configure the trigger details:

     a. **For schedule triggers**: Define cron expression.

     b. **For conditional triggers**: Select job dependencies.

  4. Select the actions (jobs to run).

  5. Review and create.

- **Creating triggers via code**:

```
1.  # Create a workflow where job B runs after job A succeeds
2.  glue_client.create_trigger(
3.      Name='Run-After-Ingestion',
4.      Type='CONDITIONAL',  # Run when conditions are met
5.      Actions=[{'JobName': 'transform-sales-data'}],  # Job to run
6.      Predicate={
7.          'Conditions': [{
8.              'LogicalOperator': 'EQUALS',
9.              'JobName': 'ingest-sales-data',
10.             'State': 'SUCCEEDED'  # Only run if ingestion succeeds
11.         }]
12.     }
13. )
```

For complex workflows with error handling and branching logic, Step Functions provide a more powerful alternative.

- **Step functions for ETL orchestration**:

```
1.  {
2.    "Comment": "ETL Pipeline with Data Validation",
3.    "StartAt": "ExtractSalesData",
4.    "States": {
5.      "ExtractSalesData": {
6.        "Type": "Task",
7.        "Resource": "arn:aws:states:::glue:startJobRun.sync",
8.        "Parameters": {
9.          "JobName": "extract-sales-data"
10.       },
11.       "Next": "ValidateData"
12.     },
13.     "ValidateData": {
14.       "Type": "Task",
15.       "Resource": "arn:aws:lambda:region:account:function:validate-sales-data",
16.       "Next": "CheckValidation"
17.     },
18.     "CheckValidation": {
19.       "Type": "Choice",
20.       "Choices": [
21.         {
22.           "Variable": "$.validationPassed",
23.           "BooleanEquals": false,
24.           "Next": "NotifyFailure"
25.         }
26.       ],
27.       "Default": "ProcessSalesData"
28.     },
29.     "ProcessSalesData": {
30.       "Type": "Task",
```

```
31.        "Resource": "arn:aws:states:::glue:startJobRun.sync",
32.        "Parameters": {
33.          "JobName": "transform-sales-data"
34.        },
35.        "End": true
36.      },
37.      "NotifyFailure": {
38.        "Type": "Task",
39.        "Resource": "arn:aws:states:::sns:publish",
40.        "Parameters": {
41.          "TopicArn": "arn:aws:sns:region:account:validation-failures",
42.          "Message": "Sales data failed validation"
43.        },
44.        "End": true
45.      }
46.    }
47. }
```

Performance optimization techniques

This section covers various performance optimization techniques like worker configuration, data partitioning strategies, memory/compute settings, and incremental processing with bookmarks.

Worker configuration

Glue allows you to select worker types that match your workload requirements, as shown in the following table:

Worker type	DPUs	vCPU	Memory	Best for
G.1X	1	4	16GB	Basic transformations, small datasets
G.2X	2	8	32GB	Standard workloads, the most common choice
G.4X	4	16	64GB	Memory-intensive operations (joins, aggregations)
G.8X	8	32	128GB	Very large in-memory processing
Z.1X/Z.2X	1/2	4/8	16/32GB	Ray jobs (machine learning workloads)

Table 5.1: Glue worker type and use cases

Selecting the optimal configuration:

1. Start with G.2X and 10 workers for most workloads

2. Monitor CloudWatch metrics for:

    a. `glue.driver.aggregate.bytesRead` (data volume processed)

    b. `glue.driver.aggregate.numExecutors` (executor utilization)

    c. `glue.driver.BlockManager.memory.memUsed_MB` (memory usage)

3. Adjust based on observations:

    a. **If memory errors occur**: Increase to G.4X/G.8X

    b. **If processing is CPU-bound**: Add more workers

    c. **If small datasets**: Reduce to G.1X or fewer workers

Data partitioning and file optimizations

Proper partitioning significantly impacts performance and cost:

```
1.  # Reading with partition pruning - only scans relevant data
2.  sales = glueContext.create_dynamic_frame.from_catalog(
3.      database="retail",
4.      table_name="sales",
5.      push_down_predicate="year='2024' AND month='02'"  # Only process February data
6.  )
7.
8.  # Writing with appropriate partitioning
9.  sales_df.write \
10.     .partitionBy("year", "month", "store_id") \
11.     .option("maxRecordsPerFile", 100000)  # Control file size
12.     .parquet(output_path)
```

Partitioning best practices are as follows:

- **Partition cardinality**: Choose columns with 10s-100s of distinct values (not 1000s).

- **Partition order**: Most selective dimensions first (typically time-based, then business dimensions).

- **File size management**:

  o Avoid small files (<64MB) by controlling records per file.

  o Use **maxRecordsPerFile** option to prevent file explosion.

  o Consider running periodic compaction jobs for small files.

Common partitioning anti-patterns to avoid are as follows:

- Partitioning by high-cardinality fields (e.g., customer_id with millions of values).

- Using too many partition levels (3-4 levels maximum).

- Inconsistent partitioning schemes between input and output datasets.

Memory and compute optimizations

Several Glue-specific settings can dramatically improve job performance:

Setting	Description	Recommendation
--conf spark.sql.shuffle.partitions	Controls parallelism during joins/aggregations	Set to 2-3× the number of worker cores
--conf spark.sql.adaptive.enabled	Adjusts execution plans during runtime	Set to **true** for most workloads
--conf spark.dynamicAllocation.enabled	Dynamically adjusts executor allocation	Set to **true** for variable workloads
--conf spark.sql.broadcastTimeout	Timeout for broadcast joins	Increase for larger broadcast joins
--enable-s3-parquet-optimized-committer	Optimizes S3 Parquet writes	Enable for better write performance

Table 5.2: Glue optimization configurations

Console configuration: Add these in the *Job parameters* section when creating or editing a job.

Code configuration:

```
1.  # Setting job parameters programmatically
2.  glue_client.create_job(
3.      Name='optimized-sales-transform',
4.      Role='GlueServiceRole',
5.      Command={
6.          'Name': 'glueetl',
7.          'ScriptLocation': 's3://scripts/transform_sales.py'
8.      },
9.      DefaultArguments={
10.         '--job-language': 'python',
11.         '--conf': 'spark.sql.adaptive.enabled=true',
12.         '--enable-s3-parquet-optimized-committer': 'true',
13.         '--enable-metrics': 'true'
14.     },
15.     GlueVersion='3.0',
16.     WorkerType='G.2X',
17.     NumberOfWorkers=10
18. )
```

Bookmarks for incremental processing

Glue job bookmarks track processed data to enable efficient incremental processing:

Enabling bookmarks via console: Follow these steps:

1. Edit your Glue job.
2. Under Job details | Advanced properties.
3. Set Job bookmark to Enable.
4. Optionally modify Bookmark options for specific behavior.

Enabling bookmarks via code:

```
1.  # Enable job bookmarks to track processed data
2.  glue_client.create_job(
3.      Name='incremental-customer-process',
4.      Role='GlueServiceRole',
5.      Command={
6.          'Name': 'glueetl',
7.          'ScriptLocation': 's3://scripts/process_customers.py'
8.      },
9.      DefaultArguments={
10.         '--job-bookmark-option': 'job-bookmark-enable',
11.         '--job-bookmark-from': 'last-successful-run'
12.     },
13.     # Other job parameters...
14. )
15.
16. # Using bookmarks in job script
```

```
17. job = Job(glueContext)
18. job.init(args['JOB_NAME'], args)
19.
20. # Configure JDBC source with bookmark keys
21. jdbc_options = {
22.     "url": jdbc_url,
23.     "dbtable": "customers",
24.     "user": username,
25.     "password": password,
26.     "jobBookmarkKeys": ["id"],        # Track based on ID column
27.     "jobBookmarkKeysSortOrder": "asc" # Process in ascending order
28. }
29.
30. # Only process new records since last run
31. customers = glueContext.create_dynamic_frame.from_options(
32.     connection_type="mysql",
33.     connection_options=jdbc_options
34. )
```

AWS Glue's combination of automated schema discovery, flexible job types, and powerful optimization options makes it an excellent choice for batch processing workloads. By understanding its components and tuning options, you can build efficient ETL pipelines that scale with your data needs.

Custom ETL with EMR

While AWS Glue provides a fully managed serverless ETL solution, many organizations require greater customization and control over their batch processing environments. Amazon **Elastic MapReduce** (**EMR**) fills this need by providing managed clusters running popular open-source frameworks like Apache Spark, Apache Hive, and Presto. This section explores how to implement custom ETL solutions with EMR that complement or extend the capabilities of fully managed services.

Architecture and core components

Amazon EMR provides a flexible architecture that balances managed services with customization options. The following figure shows master, core and task nodes with their respective functions:

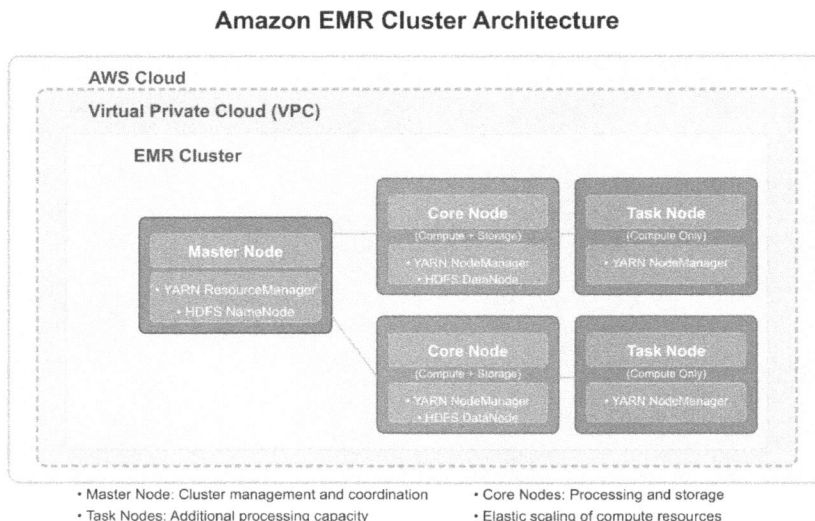

Figure 5.5: *Amazon EMR cluster architecture*

Cluster components and node types

An EMR cluster consists of three types of nodes, each with distinct responsibilities:

- **Master node** orchestrates the cluster and manages job distribution. It runs the primary components of distributed frameworks (like the YARN ResourceManager and HDFS NameNode) and tracks job execution. The master node is the entry point for job submission and monitoring.

- **Core nodes** provide both compute capacity and distributed storage. They run YARN NodeManager for processing and HDFS DataNode for storage. Core nodes form the backbone of your processing capacity while maintaining data reliability through replication.

- **Task nodes** provide additional compute capacity without participating in HDFS storage. These nodes are ideal for handling processing spikes and can be added or removed without affecting data storage. They offer cost-effective scaling for compute-intensive workloads.

Implementation approaches

When implementing batch processing workflows on Amazon EMR, one of the key architectural decisions is choosing between transient and long-running clusters. This choice significantly impacts resource utilization, cost management, and operational workflows. Understanding the characteristics and use cases for each model is crucial for optimizing your EMR deployments. Let's explore these two primary cluster deployment models and how to implement them using both the AWS Console and CLI approaches.

Transient vs. long-running clusters

EMR supports two primary cluster deployment models, each suited for different workload patterns:

The steps for console approach to create EMR clusters are as follows:

1. Navigate to Amazon EMR in the AWS Console.
2. Click Create cluster.
3. Choose Advanced configuration for more options.
4. Configure software:
    a. Select EMR release (e.g., emr-6.6.0).
    b. Choose applications (Spark, Hadoop, etc.).
5. Configure hardware:
    a. Select instance types for master, core, and task nodes.
    b. Set instance counts for each node type.
6. Configure general cluster settings:
    a. Name your cluster (e.g., Daily-Sales-Processing or Analytics-Platform).
    b. Select security configurations and IAM roles.
7. For transient clusters:
    a. Under Steps, add your processing steps (Spark, Hive, etc.).
    b. Enable Auto-termination or set Steps fail: terminate the cluster.
8. For long-running clusters:
    a. Enable Auto-termination to No.
    b. Configure auto-scaling for task node groups.
    c. Configure additional security settings.
9. Review and create.

AWS CLI approach

For both transient and long-running clusters, the core configuration is similar. The key differences are highlighted in the sample code:

```
1.  # Run this command from AWS CLI to create a cluster
2.  aws emr create-cluster \
3.      --name "Retail-Data-Processing" \
4.      --release-label "emr-6.6.0" \
5.      --applications Name=Spark Name=Hadoop Name=Hive \
6.      --ec2-attributes KeyName=my-key-pair,SubnetId=subnet-1234567890abcdef0 \
7.      --instance-groups \
8.          InstanceGroupType=MASTER,InstanceCount=1,InstanceType=m5.xlarge \
9.          InstanceGroupType=CORE,InstanceCount=4,InstanceType=r5.2xlarge \
10.         InstanceGroupType=TASK,InstanceCount=4,InstanceType=r5.2xlarge \
11.     --configurations file://./configurations.json \
12.     --use-default-roles \
13.     --log-uri "s3://my-emr-logs/" \
14.     --bootstrap-actions Path="s3://my-bootstrap-bucket/bootstrap.sh" \
15.     --steps file://./steps.json \
16.     --keep-job-flow-alive-when-no-steps=false \  # For transient clusters
17.     # --keep-job-flow-alive-when-no-steps=true \  # For long-
    running clusters (uncomment)
18.     # --auto-scaling-role EMR_AutoScaling_DefaultRole \  # For auto-
    scaling (uncomment)
```

The following are the key differences between transient and long-running clusters:

- **Transient clusters**: Set **--keep-job-flow-alive-when-no-steps=false** and include steps at creation time.

- **Long-running clusters**: Set **--keep-job-flow-alive-when-no-steps=true**, configure auto-scaling, and submit steps separately as needed.

Optimizing EMR for custom ETL

Unlike fully managed services, EMR requires more hands-on optimization but rewards this effort with superior performance for specialized workloads:

- **Instance selection and sizing:** EMR performance heavily depends on matching instance types to workload characteristics:

Workload type	Recommended instance types	Considerations
Memory-intensive transformations	R5 or R6g family	For large joins, aggregations, and window functions
Compute-intensive processing	C5 or C6g family	For complex calculations and UDFs
Balanced workloads	M5 or M6g family	Good general-purpose option
I/O-intensive operations	I3 or I3en family	For operations requiring high disk throughput

Table 5.3: Instance selection for EMR jobs

- **Storage optimization strategies:** EMR offers multiple storage options that significantly impact ETL performance:

o **HDFS** provides high throughput for intermediate processing stages. Configure with an appropriate replication factor (typically 2 for transient clusters) and consider HDFS encryption for sensitive data.

o **Instance store** volumes deliver maximum I/O performance. Choose instance types with local SSDs (like r5d, m5d) for shuffle-intensive workloads.

o **EMR File System** (**EMRFS**) connects to S3 with EMR-specific optimizations. Enable EMRFS consistent view for workloads that both read and write to the same S3 paths.

- **Custom ETL implementation patterns:** When implementing ETL on EMR, several patterns have emerged as particularly effective:

  o **Metadata-driven processing**: Configure jobs to read task definitions from a metadata store, enabling dynamic workflow adjustments without code changes.

  o **Direct integration with AWS services**: EMR jobs can directly interact with services like DynamoDB for lookup tables, SQS for job queuing, and CloudWatch for monitoring.

  o **Framework-specific optimizations**: Leverage EMR's support for advanced framework features:

    ▪ **Spark**: Dynamic allocation, adaptive query execution, custom serializers.

    ▪ **Hive**: Cost-based optimizer, vectorized execution, LLAP acceleration.

    ▪ **Presto**: Query federation across multiple data sources.

By leveraging Amazon EMR's flexibility and customization options, organizations can implement specialized ETL processes that complement the serverless approach of AWS Glue. The choice between these services is not binary, many modern data platforms use both in tandem, with EMR handling complex, performance-critical transformations and AWS Glue managing straightforward, serverless ETL workflows.

Job orchestration with Step Functions

While AWS Glue and EMR handle core processing tasks in batch workflows, complex data pipelines require sophisticated orchestration to coordinate multiple steps, manage dependencies, and handle failures gracefully. AWS Step Functions addresses this need by providing a serverless workflow service that visually connects AWS services into structured, resilient pipelines.

Architecture and core components

Step Functions uses a state machine model where workflows are defined as a series of states that determine the execution flow. In the following figure, each state represents a specific step in your workflow and controls what happens next:

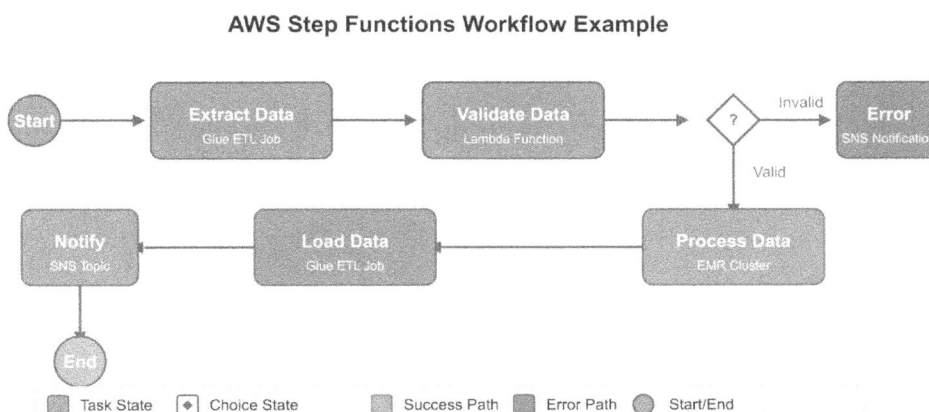

Figure 5.6: AWS Step Functions workflow example

Implementation approaches

This section explains how to create AWS Step Functions workflows using the visual designer in the AWS Console and presents three core orchestration patterns: sequential ETL pipelines, dynamic resource selection, and parallel domain processing.

Console-based visual development

The AWS Console provides a visual workflow designer that simplifies Step Functions development:

1. Navigate to AWS Step Functions | Create a state machine.

2. Select Design your workflow visually.

3. Drag and drop states from the panel on the right.

4. Configure each state through form-based inputs.

5. The JSON definition is auto-generated as you build.

6. Test executions directly from the console.

This visual approach is ideal for building and understanding complex workflows without writing JSON by hand.

Core orchestration patterns

An effective batch processing architecture relies on well-established patterns that address common challenges in data pipeline design. These patterns provide proven blueprints for handling everything from simple sequential workflows to complex, multi-domain processing scenarios:

- **Sequential ETL pipeline**: The classic pattern connects extract, transform, and load operations in sequence:

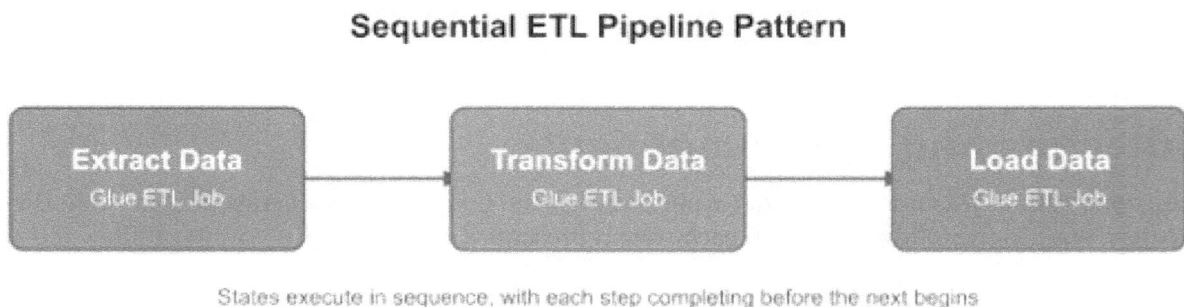

Figure 5.7: Sequential ETL pipeline pattern

This approach suits predictable, linear processing needs such as daily reconciliation jobs.

- **Dynamic resource selection**: This pattern chooses processing resources based on data characteristics, as shown in *Figure 5.8*:

Conditional Processing Pattern

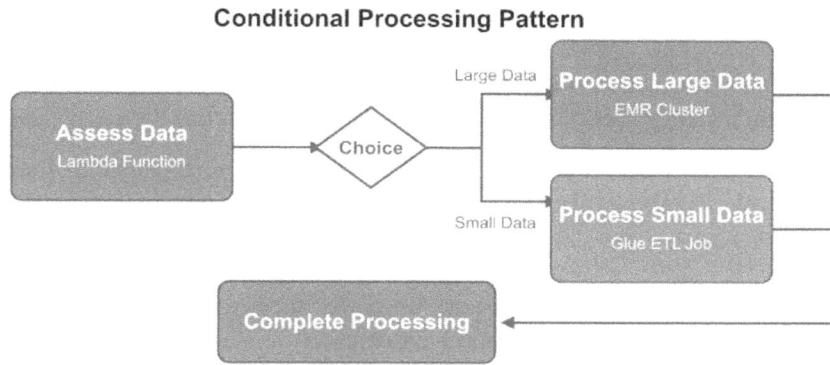

Figure 5.8: Conditional processing pattern

Implementation via console:

o   Add a Lambda Task to assess data volume

o   Add a Choice state with conditions based on size

o   Configure separate paths for small (Glue) and large (EMR) datasets

This optimizes cost and performance by matching processing resources to requirements.

*   **Parallel domain processing**: For domain data that can be processed independently, refer to the following figure:

Parallel Processing Pattern

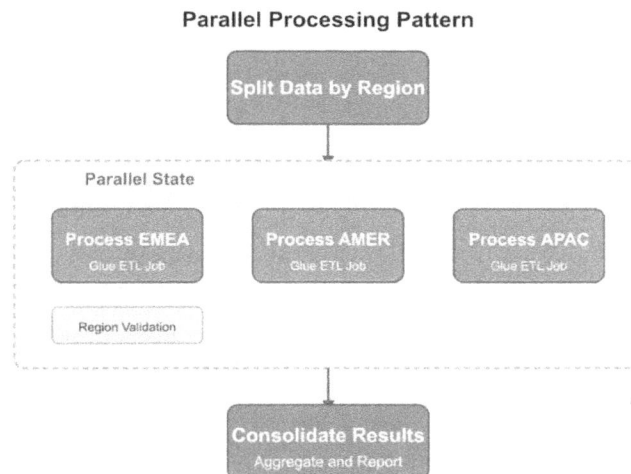

Figure 5.9: Parallel processing pattern

The following are the implementations:

o   Start with a parallel state

o   Create branches for each domain/region

o   Configure each branch with appropriate Glue or EMR tasks

o   Set up a subsequent aggregation state

This accelerates processing by handling non-dependent work concurrently.

Step Functions provides the crucial orchestration layer that ties together the various batch processing components. By implementing these patterns, organizations can create sophisticated, resilient batch processing pipelines that handle complex data processing requirements while maintaining operational excellence.

Error recovery strategies

Effective batch data processing requires robust error handling and recovery mechanisms. Even well-designed pipelines encounter failures, making recovery strategies crucial for reliable data engineering systems:

- **Understanding failure modes in batch processing:** Batch processing systems face primarily four types of failures. The following table summarizes the failure types, examples, and recovery approaches:

Failure type	Description	Examples	Basic recovery approach
Transient failures	Temporary conditions that resolve naturally over time	Network timeouts, service throttling, resource contention	Implement retries with backoff
Deterministic failures	Predictable failures with specific inputs that won't resolve through retries	Malformed records, schema violations, business rule contradictions	Isolate bad data, use error routing
Resource exhaustion	Processing demands exceed available resources	Memory errors during joins, CPU constraints during transformations	Scale resources or partition workload
Infrastructure failures	Issues with the underlying computing environment	Instance terminations, availability zone outages, and service disruptions	Implement redundancy and failover mechanisms

Table 5.4: Batch processing system failure type

- **Core error recovery patterns:** The table outlines four essential error recovery patterns for data processing systems and use cases:

Pattern	Purpose	Key components	Best for
Retry pattern	Attempts failed multiple times	• Backoff strategy • Jitter • Retry quotas • Idempotency controls	Transient failures
Circuit breaker	Prevents cascade failures during systemic issues	• Failure counting • Threshold monitoring • State transitions (closed | open | half-open)	Protecting dependent systems
Dead letter pattern	Isolates problematic data while the workflow continues	• Error detection • Separate storage for failed items • Error context preservation • Reprocessing capability	Deterministic data failures
Checkpoint/Restart	Enables recovery for long-running processes	• Work chunking • Progress tracking • Restart capability • State persistence	Long-running batch jobs

Table 5.5: Core error recovery patterns for resilient systems

Hands-on: Implementing batch ETL workflows

Building on the principles, patterns, and services we have explored in this chapter, let us implement a complete batch ETL workflow that brings these concepts together in a practical solution. We will develop a retail analytics pipeline that processes daily sales data, enriches it with product and store information, and produces aggregated reports.

Solution architecture

Our implementation follows the medallion architecture pattern with clear progression from raw to trusted to curated data. The workflow includes data ingestion, validation, transformation, and analytics generation with comprehensive error handling throughout.

The complete solution is available in the GitHub repository accompanying the book.

Core implementation components

Our batch ETL workflow consists of these essential elements:

- **Data storage zones**: S3 buckets for raw, processed, and analytics data

- **Data catalog**: Glue database and tables for metadata management

- **Processing jobs**: Glue ETL jobs with error handling capabilities

- **Orchestration workflow**: Step Functions state machine

- **Monitoring system**: SNS topics and CloudWatch alarms

Here is a glimpse of the infrastructure definition:

```
1.  # Key infrastructure components (abbreviated)
2.  class RetailETLStack(Stack):
3.      def __init__(self, scope, id, **kwargs):
4.          super().__init__(scope, id, **kwargs)
5.
6.          # Create data lake storage with zone structure
7.          self.raw_bucket = s3.Bucket(self, "RawDataBucket")
8.          self.processed_bucket = s3.Bucket(self, "ProcessedDataBucket")
9.          self.analytics_bucket = s3.Bucket(self, "AnalyticsBucket")
10.
11.         # Create Glue database for data catalog
12.         self.catalog_db = glue.CfnDatabase(self, "RetailAnalyticsDB")
13.
14.         # Create Glue jobs for each processing stage
15.         self.validate_job = self.create_glue_job("ValidateSales", "validate_sales.
    py")
16.         self.transform_job = self.create_glue_job("TransformSales", "transform_sales.
    py")
17.         self.analytics_job = self.create_glue_job("GenerateAnalytics", "generate_
    analytics.py")
18.
19.         # Create Step Functions workflow
20.         self.create_state_machine()
```

Error handling implementation highlights

The validation script demonstrates our error handling patterns:

```
1.  # Implement Dead Letter Pattern for invalid records (abbreviated)
2.  try:
3.      # Validate data and identify problematic records
4.      invalid_records = sales_df.filter(data_quality_conditions)
5.
6.      if invalid_records.count() > 0:
7.          # Route to error storage with context information
8.          invalid_records.write.mode("append").parquet(error_path)
9.
10.         # Continue with valid records only
11.         valid_records = sales_df.filter(~data_quality_conditions)
12. except Exception as e:
13.     # Send notification and preserve error context
14.     send_error_notification(e, context)
15.     Raise
```

The Step Functions workflow orchestrates the process with robust error handling:

```
1.  # Step Functions definition with error handling (abbreviated)
2.  validate_task.add_catch(
3.      errors=["States.ALL"],
4.      handler=notify_error_task,
5.      result_path="$.error"
6.  ).next(
7.      transform_task.add_catch(
8.          errors=["States.ALL"],
9.          handler=notify_error_task,
10.         result_path="$.error"
11.     )
12. )
```

This implementation demonstrates a practical application of the batch processing patterns discussed throughout this chapter. By reviewing the complete code in our GitHub repository, you will see how these components work together to create a resilient pipeline that gracefully handles various failure scenarios while maintaining data quality and operational visibility.

Conclusion

In this chapter, we explored the enduring importance of batch data processing in modern data architectures. We examined the evolution from traditional ETL to cloud-native approaches, core batch processing patterns including the medallion architecture, and AWS's comprehensive ecosystem for implementation AWS Glue provides serverless ETL capabilities, while Amazon EMR offers customizable cluster-based processing for specialized needs. We demonstrated how AWS Step Functions orchestrates complex workflows with robust error handling through retry, circuit breaker, dead letter, and checkpoint/restart patterns. Our hands-on implementation brought these concepts together in a production-ready retail analytics pipeline.

In the next chapter, we will build on these foundations to focus specifically on data transformation quality, covering frameworks, validation techniques, schema evolution, and monitoring systems that ensure the reliability of our processed data.

## CHAPTER 6

Data Transformation and Quality

Introduction

As data engineering architectures grow in complexity, organizations face an ongoing challenge: ensuring that data remains reliable, accurate, and useful throughout its lifecycle. In previous chapters, we established the foundation of modern data engineering with AWS—from data lake architectures and optimized storage formats to real-time streaming and batch processing systems. While these capabilities enable us to ingest, store, and process vast quantities of data, they do not inherently guarantee the quality of the resulting datasets. Every transformation introduces potential for quality degradation, whether through schema inconsistencies, semantic errors, duplicate records, or violations of business rules. Recent industry studies reveal that poor data quality costs organizations an average of $12.9 million annually, with data scientists reporting up to 80% of their time spent cleaning and preparing data rather than deriving insights. In this chapter, we will explore systematic approaches to ensuring data quality throughout transformation processes in AWS environments.

Structure

This chapter will cover the following topics:

- Data quality frameworks
- AWS Glue DataBrew for data preparation
- Data validation techniques
- Validation integration pattern
- Schema evolution management
- Evolution-friendly data formats
- Managing breaking schema changes
- Testing schema evolution
- Hands-on: Building data quality pipelines

Objectives

This chapter aims to provide a comprehensive understanding and practical guidance on maintaining data quality throughout transformation processes within AWS data platforms. You will learn to apply established data quality frameworks, leverage AWS Glue DataBrew for visual data preparation, implement robust validation techniques, design schema evolution strategies, create monitoring systems, and build end-to-end quality pipelines that integrate validation, monitoring, and remediation into cohesive workflows. These capabilities will enable you to design data transformation processes that are not only efficient and scalable but also reliable and trustworthy—essential qualities for data-driven decision making in modern organizations seeking to derive maximum value from their information assets.

Data quality frameworks

Ensuring high-quality data requires a systematic approach rather than isolated validation rules. Data quality frameworks provide structured methodologies for defining, measuring, and improving data quality across transformations where issues frequently emerge. These frameworks build upon key dimensions that characterize different aspects of quality. Accuracy measures how well data represents real-world entities, completeness assesses whether all required data is present, consistency examines alignment across datasets, timeliness evaluates availability when needed, validity confirms adherence to defined formats, and uniqueness identifies duplicate records. By understanding these dimensions, engineers can design targeted controls for the aspects most critical to their business context. The following figure represents the quality dimensions and their relations:

Figure 6.1: Core dimensions of data quality in modern data frameworks

Industry standard frameworks have evolved to provide comprehensive approaches to quality management. The **Data Management Association (DAMA)** framework, documented in the **Data Management Body of Knowledge (DMBOK)**, positions data quality as one of ten essential knowledge areas within the broader data management discipline. DAMA emphasizes that quality cannot exist in isolation—it must be integrated with data governance, metadata management, and data architecture to be effective. The framework defines specific roles like data stewards who establish quality standards and data custodians who implement technical controls, creating clear accountability for quality outcomes across the organization. MIT's **Total Data Quality Management (TDQM)** methodology, pioneered by *Richard Wang* and *Stuart Madnick*, takes a manufacturing-inspired approach by treating data as a product moving through a production cycle. TDQM implements a continuous improvement loop of define-measure-analyse-improve where quality requirements are explicitly defined, objective measurements are established, root causes of quality issues are systematically analysed, and improvements are implemented and verified. This process-oriented view aligns particularly well with pipeline-based data engineering on AWS, where each transformation stage can incorporate specific quality measures and controls. ISO 8000, the international standard for data quality, offers formalized measurement methodologies for cross-organizational consistency. While these frameworks originated in traditional environments, they remain relevant in cloud-native architectures with adaptation for AWS-specific characteristics like data transit integrity, consistency across distributed storage, and quality preservation during elastic scaling.

Implementing quality frameworks in AWS leverages specific services while maintaining core principles. AWS Glue Data Catalogue serves as the central repository for quality metadata, Lake Formation adds governance controls preventing unauthorized modifications, and quality rules can be implemented using SparkSQL expressions in Glue jobs or visual checks in DataBrew. Continuous monitoring essential to frameworks like TDQM is enabled through CloudWatch metrics and dashboards, with alarms triggering SNS notifications when thresholds are breached. Effective implementation requires establishing a Data Quality Council with cross-functional representation, documenting quality thresholds in the Data Catalogue, automating checks at critical pipeline points, and visualizing metrics over time. The following code shows the data quality integration in Glue:

```
1.  # Example: Implementing data quality dimensions in AWS Glue
2.  def assess_quality_dimensions(glueContext, input_frame, primary_keys=None):
3.      # Convert to Spark DataFrame for analysis
4.      df = input_frame.toDF()
5.      total_records = df.count()
6.
7.      # Completeness check
8.      completeness_metrics = {}
9.      for column in df.columns:
10.         null_count = df.filter(col(column).isNull() | isnan(col(column))).count()
11.         completeness_metrics[column] = (total_records - null_count) / total_records
12.
13.     # Uniqueness check (if primary keys provided)
14.     uniqueness_metric = 1.0
15.     if primary_keys:
16.         distinct_count = df.select(primary_keys).distinct().count()
17.         uniqueness_metric = distinct_count / total_records
18.
19.     # Return metrics package
20.     return {
21.         «record_count": total_records,
22.         "completeness": completeness_metrics,
23.         "uniqueness": uniqueness_metric
24.     }
```

Modern approaches integrate these frameworks directly into data pipelines rather than treating quality as a separate activity. This shift-left philosophy embeds checks early in the data lifecycle. Using AWS Step Functions, quality validation jobs become required nodes in pipelines, ensuring data progresses only after passing thresholds. Failed checks trigger remediation workflows ranging from alerts to correction mechanisms implemented through Lambda functions. Quality results themselves become valuable metadata stored in the Glue Data Catalog and visualized through QuickSight. Organizations increasingly adopt *Data Quality as Code*, where rules are defined, versioned, and deployed using infrastructure-as-code practices, enabling quality criteria to evolve alongside schema changes and business requirements. By treating quality frameworks as concrete, implementable systems within AWS, organizations establish the foundation for the validation techniques and monitoring systems we will explore in the next sections.

AWS Glue DataBrew for data preparation

AWS Glue DataBrew is a visual data preparation tool that integrates with the broader AWS analytics ecosystem to enable no-code data transformation and quality management. As shown in *Figure 6.2*, DataBrew fits into the AWS data processing architecture between data sources and downstream analytics or machine learning services, providing a dedicated layer for data cleansing and preparation without requiring custom code.

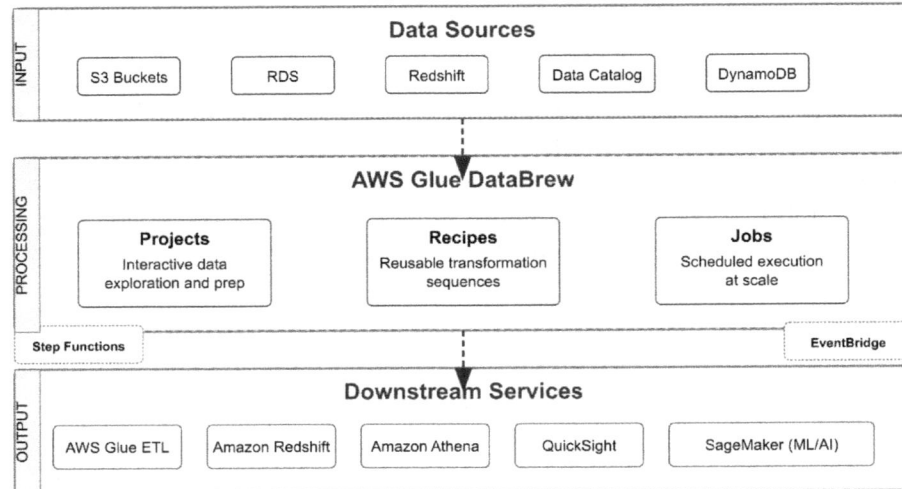

Figure 6.2: AWS Glue DataBrew architecture and integration with AWS services

DataBrew project through the AWS Console

To create a data preparation workflow in DataBrew, follow these specific steps in the AWS Console:

1. Navigate to AWS Glue DataBrew in the AWS Console and select "Projects" from the left navigation.

2. Click Create project and provide a name (e.g., `CustomerDataPrep`).

3. Under Dataset connection, select your source data:

    o   **For S3**: Choose Amazon S3 and browse to your data file.

    o   **For relational databases**: Select JDBC and configure connection parameters.

    o   **For Glue Catalog**: Choose AWS Glue Data Catalog and select database and table.

4. Configure sample settings (typically 5,000-10,000 rows provides a good balance).

5. Select an IAM role with appropriate permissions for accessing source data.

6. Click Create project to launch the visual interface.

Once in the project interface, you can interactively develop your data preparation recipe through the following workflow:

1. Examine data profile statistics for each column to identify quality issues.

2. Select columns requiring transformation and choose appropriate actions from the menu.

3. Configure parameters for each transformation (e.g., setting replacement values for nulls).

4. Preview results to verify the transformation works as expected.

5. Add steps incrementally to build a complete recipe.

6. Save the recipe for reuse across multiple datasets or jobs.

Implementing common data preparation patterns

Once your DataBrew project is created, you will work in the grid view interface to build your data preparation recipe. Here is how to access and use the grid view:

1. After creating your project, you will be automatically taken to the grid view.

2. If returning to an existing project, select it from the Projects list and click Open project.

3. The grid view displays your sample data in a spreadsheet-like interface with column headers at the top.

4. The transformation menu bar appears above the data grid.

5. To work with any column, click its header to select it (it will highlight when selected).

With this interface understanding, let us explore how to implement common data preparation steps:

Cleaning missing values

The steps are as follows:

1. Click the column header containing missing values (e.g., customer_address).

2. From the menu bar, click Clean | Handle missing values.

3. In the dialog that appears, select your desired action:

    a. Remove rows to filter out rows with missing values.

    b. Impute values to replace with statistical measures (mean, median, mode).

    c. Replace with custom value to set a specific replacement.

4. If choosing replacement, enter your value (e.g., Unknown for text fields).

5. Click Apply to add this step to your recipe.

Standardizing categorical values

The steps are as follows:

1. Click the column header with inconsistent values (e.g., state_code).

2. From the menu bar, click Format | Replace values using pattern.

3. In the dialog that appears, create mapping pairs:

    o Enter NY in Find value and NY in Replace with field.

    o Click Add another value and enter N.Y. | NY.

    o Add another for New York | NY.

4. Click Apply to add this transformation to your recipe.

Validating formats

The steps are as follows:

1. Click the column header needing validation (e.g., phone_number).

2. From the menu bar, click Validate | Pattern match.

3. In the dialog, enter a regex pattern (e.g., **\d{3}-\d{3}-\d{4}** for US phone numbers).

4. Check Create a new column with results to preserve original data.

5. Enter a name for the new column (e.g., valid_phone_flag).

6. Click Apply to add this validation to your recipe.

Removing duplicate records

The steps are as follows:

1. From the menu bar (without selecting any specific column), click Manage rows.

2. Select Remove duplicate rows.

3. In the dialog, check the boxes for columns that define uniqueness (e.g., customer_id)

4. Choose whether to keep the first or last occurrence when duplicates are found.

5. Click Apply to add this step to your recipe.

Converting data types

1. Click the column header requiring type conversion (e.g., purchase_date).

2. From the menu bar, click Data types | select target type (e.g., Date).

3. For dates, specify the format pattern (e.g., yyyy-MM-dd).

4. Choose whether to create a new column or replace the existing one.

5. Click Apply to add this conversion to your recipe.

After building your recipe step by step, you can:

- Click Recipe in the top menu to view all steps in sequence.

- Rearrange steps by dragging them in the recipe panel.

- Delete steps by clicking the trash icon next to them.

- Save the recipe by clicking Save and giving it a descriptive name.

This recipe can then be used to create a job that processes the full dataset as described in the next section.

Once you have built your recipe, you can create a job to process the full dataset:

1. Navigate to Jobs in the DataBrew console.

2. Click Create job and select Recipe job.

3. Choose your saved recipe.

4. Configure the input dataset (can be different from development dataset).

5. Specify output location (S3 bucket) and format (CSV, Parquet, etc.).

6. Set job scheduling (on-demand or recurring schedule).

7. Configure additional options like job sample size and retry behaviour.

8. Click Create job to finalize configuration.

Production implementation and monitoring

For production deployment, DataBrew jobs can be monitored and integrated as follows:

1. **Monitoring execution**: DataBrew automatically publishes execution metrics to CloudWatch:

    1. `AWS/Glue/DataBrew/Jobs/JobRunTime`

    2. `AWS/Glue/DataBrew/Jobs/RecordsProcessed`

    3. `AWS/Glue/DataBrew/Jobs/ValidationErrors`

Create CloudWatch dashboards displaying these metrics to track preparation job performance.

2. **Automated workflows**: Integrate DataBrew with AWS Step Functions for end-to-end orchestration:

```
1.  {
2.    "StartAt": "PrepareData",
3.    "States": {
4.      "PrepareData": {
5.        "Type": "Task",
6.        "Resource": "arn:aws:states:::databrew:startJobRun.sync",
7.        "Parameters": {
8.          "Name": "customer-data-preparation-job"
9.        },
10.       "Next": "LoadToWarehouse"
11.     },
12.     "LoadToWarehouse": {
13.       "Type": "Task",
14.       "Resource": "arn:aws:states:::glue:startJobRun.sync",
15.       "Parameters": {
16.         "JobName": "load-to-redshift"
17.       },
18.       "End": true
19.     }
20.   }
21. }
```

3. **Event-driven processing**: To automatically trigger DataBrew jobs when new data arrives, set up an EventBridge rule following these steps:

   a. Navigate to Amazon EventBridge in the AWS Console.

   b. Select Rules from the left navigation and click Create rule.

   c. Provide a name (e.g., **TriggerDataBrewOnNewCustomerData**).

   d. For event pattern, select AWS events or EventBridge partner events.

   e. Choose Pre-defined pattern by service and select:

      i. **Service provider**: AWS

      ii. **Service name**: S3

      iii. **Event type**: Amazon S3 Object Created

   f. Customize the pattern to specify your bucket and prefix:

```
1.  {
2.    "source": ["aws.s3"],
3.    "detail-type": ["Object Created"],
4.    "detail": {
5.      "bucket": {
6.        "name": ["raw-data-bucket"]
7.      },
8.      "object": {
9.        "key": [{
10.         "prefix": "incoming/customer/"
```

```
11.        }]
12.      }
13.    }
14. }
```

   g. For targets, click Add target and select AWS Glue DataBrew job.

   h. Select your DataBrew job from the dropdown.

   i. Create or select an execution role with sufficient permissions.

   j. Click Create to activate the rule. When a new file is uploaded to the specified S3 location, EventBridge will automatically detect it and trigger your DataBrew job to process the new data.

Integration with Glue Data Catalogue

DataBrew integrates with the AWS Glue Data Catalogue to maintain metadata consistency:

- When creating a job, select Publish to AWS Glue Data Catalogue in output settings.
- Specify a database name and table name for the processed dataset.
- DataBrew automatically registers the output dataset in the catalogue with inferred schema.
- This registration enables seamless querying from Athena, Redshift Spectrum, and other AWS analytics services.

Real-world implementation example

Consider a data quality pipeline for customer data with these requirements:

- Validate email and phone formats
- Standardize address information
- Remove duplicate customer records
- Generate data quality metrics

The implementation architecture involves:

1. Raw data lands in S3 from source systems.
2. EventBridge rule detects new files and triggers DataBrew job.
3. DataBrew executes quality recipe with these key steps:
   a. EMAIL format validation with regex.
   b. ADDRESS standardization using pattern replacement.
   c. PHONE number formatting to consistent pattern.
   d. DUPLICATE removal based on customer ID.
4. Prepared data writes to processed S3 bucket and registers in Glue Catalog.
5. Lambda function analyzes job results and publishes quality metrics to CloudWatch.
6. Dashboard displays quality trends and alerts on threshold violations.

This architecture delivers consistent, high-quality data with minimal coding while maintaining full integration with the AWS analytics ecosystem. Organizations typically implement DataBrew as the preparation layer between raw data ingestion and analytics processing, establishing a clear separation of concerns where DataBrew handles quality management before downstream transformation and analysis.

By focusing on practical configuration through the AWS Console and providing clear integration patterns, DataBrew enables both technical and business users to implement data quality frameworks effectively. In the next section, we will explore more advanced data validation techniques that complement the visual preparation capabilities of DataBrew.

Data validation techniques

Effective data validation is a cornerstone of trustworthy data pipelines. While tools like DataBrew provide visual interfaces for basic validation, more complex data transformations often require programmatic validation techniques integrated directly into ETL processes. In this section, we explore advanced validation approaches that can be implemented across AWS services to ensure data quality throughout transformations.

Schema validation fundamentals

Schema validation ensures that data adheres to expected structural requirements. In AWS environments, this can be implemented using several approaches depending on the complexity and scale of your validation requirements.

Using AWS Glue Schema registry

AWS Glue Schema registry provides centralized schema management for both streaming and batch data. To implement schema validation using this service:

1. **Create a schema registry**:

```
aws glue create-registry --registry-name customer-data-registry --description
"Registry for customer data schemas"
```

2. **Define schema with validation rules**:

```
1. aws glue create-schema \
2.   --registry-id RegistryName=customer-data-registry \
3.   --schema-name customer-profile \
4.   --compatibility BACKWARD \
5.   --data-format AVRO \
6.   --schema-definition <{
7.     "type": "record",
8.     "name": "CustomerProfile",
9.     "namespace": "com.example.customers",
10.    "fields": [
11.      {"name": "customer_id", "type": "string"},
12.      {"name": "email", "type": ["string", "null"],
13.       "default": null},
14.      {"name": "age", "type": ["int", "null"],
15.       "default": null},
16.      {"name": "subscription_tier", "type": {
17.        "type": "enum",
18.        "name": "SubscriptionTier",
19.        "symbols": ["FREE", "BASIC", "PREMIUM", "ENTERPRISE"]
20.      }}
21.    ]
22. }>
```

3. **Use in Glue ETL jobs:**

```
1. from awsglue.transforms import *
2. from pyspark.context import SparkContext
3. from awsglue.context import GlueContext
4. from awsglue.job import Job
5. from pyspark.sql import SparkSession
6. from awsglue.dynamicframe import DynamicFrame
7. import boto3
8.
9. # Initialize Glue context
10. sc = SparkContext()
11. glueContext = GlueContext(sc)
12. spark = glueContext.spark_session
13. job = Job(glueContext)
14.
15. # Read data
16. customers_dyf = glueContext.create_dynamic_frame.from_catalog(
17.     database="customers_db",
18.     table_name="raw_customers"
19. )
20.
21. # Get schema from Schema Registry
22. glue_client = boto3.client(‹glue›)
23. schema_response = glue_client.get_schema(
24.     SchemaId={
25.         ‹RegistryName': 'customer-data-registry',
26.         ‹SchemaName': 'customer-profile'
27.     }
28. )
29.
30. # Convert to schema object usable by Spark
31. from pyspark.sql.types import StructType
32. import json
33. from pyspark.sql.avro.functions import from_avro
34.
35. schema_definition = schema_response['SchemaDefinition']
36.
37. # Validate data against schema
38. try:
39.     # Convert to DataFrame for schema validation
40.     customers_df = customers_dyf.toDF()
41.
42.     # Apply schema validation using Spark›s schema enforcement
43.     validated_df = spark.createDataFrame(
44.         customers_df.rdd,
45.         schema_definition
46.     )
```

```
47.
48.    # Records that pass validation continue to processing
49.    # Convert back to DynamicFrame for further processing
50.    validated_dyf = DynamicFrame.fromDF(validated_df, glueContext, "validated_
   customers")
51.
52.    # Process valid records
53.    # ...
54.
55. except Exception as e:
56.    # Handle validation errors
57.    print(f"Schema validation failed: {str(e)}»)
58.    # Log error details or send to error handling workflow
```

This approach provides centralized schema management and evolution control, which is particularly valuable for data with changing requirements.

Deequ for data validation

Amazon Deequ is an open-source library built on top of Apache Spark that enables data validation at scale. Originally developed by Amazon Research, it is particularly well-suited for AWS Glue jobs handling large datasets. Here is how to implement it:

1. **Add Deequ as a dependency in your Glue job**:

   ```
   1. # In your AWS Glue job parameters, add:
   2. # --additional-jars s3://your-bucket/jars/deequ-1.2.2-with-dependencies.jar
   ```

2. **Implement validation in the Glue job**:

   ```
   1. from pyspark.context import SparkContext
   2. from awsglue.context import GlueContext
   3. from awsglue.dynamicframe import DynamicFrame
   4. from pyspark.sql import SparkSession
   5.
   6. # Initialize contexts
   7. sc = SparkContext()
   8. glueContext = GlueContext(sc)
   9. spark = glueContext.spark_session
   10.
   11. # Import Deequ classes
   12. from com.amazon.deequ.constraints import ConstraintResult
   13. from com.amazon.deequ.constraints.
      ConstraintStatus import Success, Warning, Failure
   14. from com.amazon.deequ.VerificationSuite import VerificationSuite
   15. from com.amazon.deequ.VerificationResult import VerificationResult
   16. from com.amazon.deequ.checks import Check
   17. from com.amazon.deequ.constraints.
      ConstrainableDataTypes import Integral, Fractional, Boolean, String
   18. from pyspark.sql.functions import col
   19.
   20. # Load data
   21. customers_dyf = glueContext.create_dynamic_frame.from_catalog(
   ```

```
22.        database="customers_db",
23.        table_name="raw_customers"
24. )
25.
26. # Convert to DataFrame for Deequ
27. customers_df = customers_dyf.toDF()
28.
29. # Define validation checks
30. verification_result = VerificationSuite() \
31.    .onData(customers_df) \
32.    .addCheck(
33.        Check().hasSize(lambda x: x >= 1000) \
34.            .hasMin("age", lambda x: x >= 18) \
35.            .hasMax("age", lambda x: x <= 120) \
36.            .isComplete("customer_id") \
37.            .isUnique("customer_id") \
38.            .isComplete("email") \
39.            .containsEmail("email", lambda x: x >= 0.95) \
40.            .isContainedIn("subscription_
    tier", ["FREE", "BASIC", "PREMIUM", "ENTERPRISE"])
41.    ) \
42.    .run()
43.
44. # Process verification results
45. verification_status = verification_result.status
46.
47. if verification_status == Success():
48.    print("Data validation passed!")
49.    # Continue processing
50.    valid_dyf = customers_dyf
51.    # ... further transformation steps
52. else:
53.    # Extract failed constraints
54.    check_results = verification_result.checkResults
55.    for check_result in check_results.values():
56.        constraint_results = check_result.constraintResults
57.        for constraint_result in constraint_results:
58.            if constraint_result.status != Success():
59.                constraint_message = constraint_result.message().get()
60.                print(f"Validation failed: {constraint_message}")
61.
62.    # Route data to error handling
63.    print("Data validation failed, sending to error handling workflow")
64.    # ... error handling steps
```

Deequ provides a powerful framework for defining complex validation rules and metrics. It's particularly valuable for statistical validation like distribution and correlation checks that go beyond simple schema enforcement.

Custom validation with Lambda functions

For lightweight validation tasks, AWS Lambda functions offer a serverless approach that can be integrated with various data processing pipelines:

1. **Define a validation Lambda function**:

```
1.  import json
2.  import boto3
3.  import re
4.
5.  def lambda_handler(event, context):
6.      """
7.      Validates customer data against business rules
8.      «"""
9.      # Get data from event
10.     if ‹s3› in event[‹Records›][0]:
11.         # Handle S3 events
12.         s3_client = boto3.client(‹s3›)
13.         bucket = event[‹Records›][0]['s3']['bucket']['name']
14.         key = event[‹Records›][0]['s3']['object']['key']
15.
16.         # Download file for validation
17.         response = s3_client.get_object(Bucket=bucket, Key=key)
18.         content = response[‹Body›].read().decode(‹utf-8')
19.
20.         # Parse data (assuming JSON)
21.         customers = json.loads(content)
22.     else:
23.         # Direct data validation
24.         customers = event[‹customers›]
25.
26.     # Initialize validation results
27.     valid_records = []
28.     invalid_records = []
29.
30.     # Email validation regex
31.     email_pattern = r›^[a-zA-Z0-9._%+-]+@[a-zA-Z0-9.-]+\.[a-zA-Z]{2,}$'
32.
33.     # Validate each record
34.     for customer in customers:
35.         validation_errors = []
36.
37.         # Required fields check
38.         for field in [‹customer_id', 'email']:
39.             if field not in customer or not customer[field]:
40.                 validation_errors.append(f"Missing required field: {field}")
41.
42.         # Data type checks
```

```
43.         if ‹age› in customer and customer[‹age›]:
44.             try:
45.                 age = int(customer[‹age›])
46.                 if age < 18 or age > 120:
47.                     validation_errors.append("Age must be between 18 and 120")
48.             except ValueError:
49.                 validation_errors.append("Age must be a number")
50.
51.         # Format checks
52.         if ‹email› in customer and customer[‹email›]:
53.             if not re.match(email_pattern, customer['email']):
54.                 validation_errors.append("Invalid email format")
55.
56.         # Business rule checks
57.         if ‹subscription_tier' in customer:
58.             valid_tiers = ["FREE", "BASIC", "PREMIUM", "ENTERPRISE"]
59.             if customer[‹subscription_tier'] not in valid_tiers:
60.                 validation_errors.
   append(f"Invalid subscription tier. Must be one of: {', '.join(valid_tiers)}")
61.
62.         # Store result
63.         if validation_errors:
64.             customer[‹validation_errors'] = validation_errors
65.             invalid_records.append(customer)
66.         else:
67.             valid_records.append(customer)
68.
69.     # Determine overall validation status
70.     validation_passed = len(invalid_records) == 0
71.
72.     # Prepare result
73.     result = {
74.         ‹validation_passed': validation_passed,
75.         ‹total_records': len(customers),
76.         ‹valid_count': len(valid_records),
77.         ‹invalid_count': len(invalid_records),
78.         ‹valid_records': valid_records,
79.         ‹invalid_records': invalid_records
80.     }
81.
82.     return result
```

2. **Integrate with Step Functions for orchestration:**

```
1. {
2.   "Comment": "Data validation workflow",
3.   "StartAt": "ValidateCustomerData",
4.   "States": {
5.     "ValidateCustomerData": {
```

```
6.        "Type": "Task",
7.        "Resource": "arn:aws:states:::lambda:invoke",
8.        "Parameters": {
9.          "FunctionName": "arn:aws:lambda:region:account:function:validate-
   customer-data",
10.         "Payload.$": "$"
11.       },
12.       "ResultPath": "$.validationResult",
13.       "Next": "CheckValidationResult"
14.     },
15.     "CheckValidationResult": {
16.       "Type": "Choice",
17.       "Choices": [
18.         {
19.           "Variable": "$.validationResult.validation_passed",
20.           "BooleanEquals": true,
21.           "Next": "ProcessValidData"
22.         }
23.       ],
24.       "Default": "HandleInvalidData"
25.     },
26.     "ProcessValidData": {
27.       "Type": "Task",
28.       "Resource": "arn:aws:states:::glue:startJobRun.sync",
29.       "Parameters": {
30.         "JobName": "process-customer-data",
31.         "Arguments": {
32.           "--data": "$.validationResult.valid_records"
33.         }
34.       },
35.       "End": true
36.     },
37.     "HandleInvalidData": {
38.       "Type": "Parallel",
39.       "Branches": [
40.         {
41.           "StartAt": "SaveInvalidRecords",
42.           "States": {
43.             "SaveInvalidRecords": {
44.               "Type": "Task",
45.               "Resource": "arn:aws:states:::s3:putObject",
46.               "Parameters": {
47.                 "Bucket": "error-records-bucket",
48.                 "Key.$": "$$.Execution.Name/invalid-customer-records.json",
49.                 "Body.$": "States.JsonToString($.validationResult.invalid_
   records)"
50.               },
51.               "End": true
```

```
52.                }
53.              }
54.          },
55.          {
56.            "StartAt": "NotifyValidationFailure",
57.              "States": {
58.                "NotifyValidationFailure": {
59.                  "Type": "Task",
60.                    "Resource": "arn:aws:states:::sns:publish",
61.                    "Parameters": {
62.                      "TopicArn": "arn:aws:sns:region:account:validation-failures",
63.                      "Message.$": "States.
      Format('Validation failed for {} of {} records. See: s3://error-records-
      bucket/{}/invalid-customer-records.json', $.validationResult.invalid_ccunt, $.
      validationResult.total_records, $$.Execution.Name)"
64.                  },
65.                  "End": true
66.                }
67.              }
68.            }
69.          ],
70.          "End": true
71.        }
72.    }
73. }
```

This Lambda-based approach is ideal for complex business rule validation that might be difficult to express in schema definitions. The Step Functions workflow provides robust error handling and branching logic based on validation results.

Validation integration patterns

Beyond individual validation techniques, organizations need consistent patterns for integrating validation into their data pipelines. Three effective patterns have emerged:

- **Pattern 1: Pre-load validation:**

    The following figure displays an architecture pattern showing a data validation step before loading:

Pre-load Validation Pattern

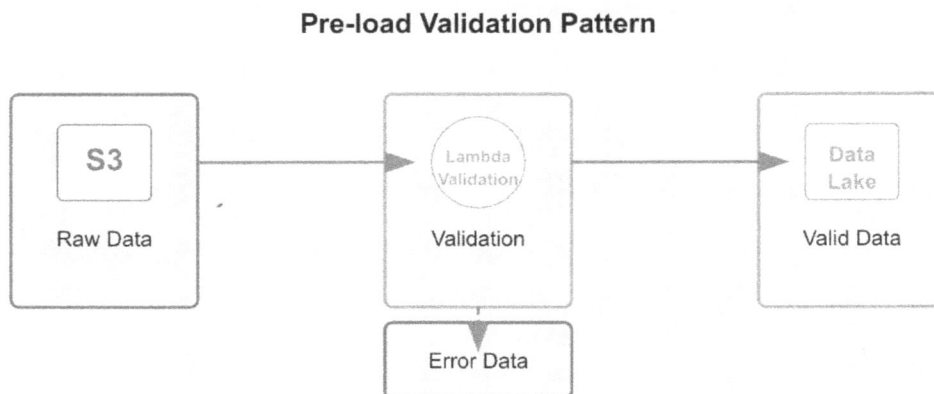

Figure 6.3: Pre-load validation pattern

This pattern validates data before it enters core data storage. Typically implemented using Lambda or Glue jobs triggered by S3 events, pre-load validation prevents invalid data from entering your data lake or warehouse. This pattern is ideal for critical datasets where quality is paramount or regulated data requiring strict governance.

- **Pattern 2: In-flight validation:**

The following figure displays an architecture pattern showing data validation on the data flow pipeline:

In-flight Validation Pattern

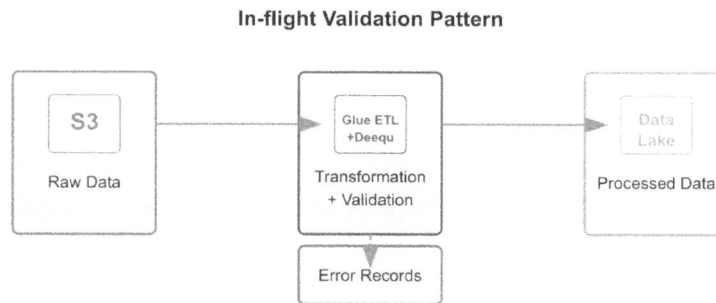

Figure 6.4: In-flight validation pattern

In-flight validation embeds validation directly within transformation processes, typically implemented within Glue ETL jobs. This pattern balances performance with quality control by allowing partial success when some records fail validation. It is particularly valuable for large-scale batch processing where a complete reload is expensive or when different validation rules apply to different transformation stages.

- **Pattern 3: Post-load validation:**

The following figure displays an architecture pattern showing data validation after data is loaded:

Post-load Validation Pattern

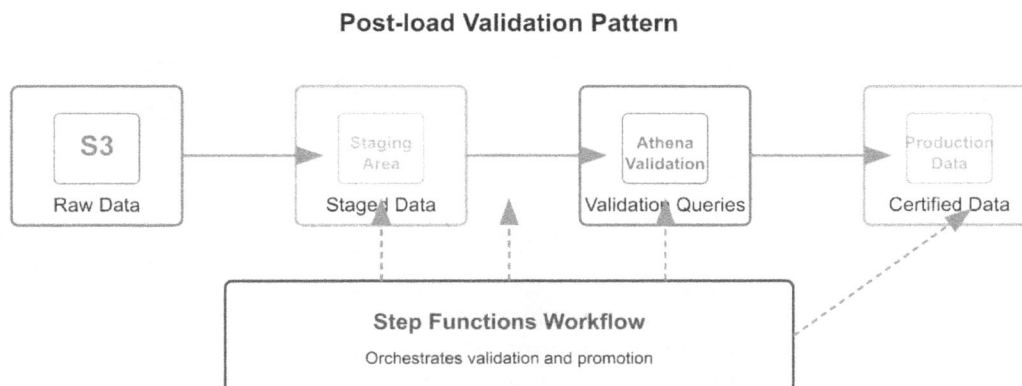

Figure 6.5: Post-load validation pattern

Post-load validation checks data after it is loaded but before it is certified for use. This pattern enables complex validation using SQL queries through Athena or Redshift, supporting cross-dataset validation rules and comparisons against historical data patterns. Organizations often implement this when validation requires comparing against existing data or in data warehouse environments with robust staging areas.

Building a validation framework

For organizations processing many datasets, building a reusable validation framework provides consistency and efficiency. An effective approach defines validation rules as configuration:

```
1. # Example validation configuration (abbreviated)
2. dataset: customer_profiles
3. rules:
4.   - type: not_null
5.     columns: [customer_id, email]
6.   - type: unique
7.     columns: [customer_id]
8.   - type: regex
9.     column: email
10.     pattern: "^[a-zA-Z0-9._%+-]+@[a-zA-Z0-9.-]+\\.[a-zA-Z]{2,}$"
11. thresholds:
12.   min_valid_percentage: 95
```

A validation engine then interprets these configurations and applies them to datasets. This configuration-as-code approach enables teams to version-control validation rules alongside other infrastructure, supporting quality-as-code principles while maintaining consistent validation practices across the organization.

Data validation techniques form a critical component of data quality management, ensuring that transformations maintain data integrity. Whether implementing schema validation with AWS Glue Schema registry, statistical validation with Deequ, custom business rule validation with Lambda, or comprehensive validation frameworks, these approaches help organizations detect and address quality issues before they impact downstream systems. In the next section, we will explore how to manage schema evolution while maintaining backward compatibility with existing data consumers.

Schema evolution management

In data systems, change is inevitable. Business requirements evolve, new data elements emerge, and formats shift over time. Schema evolution management addresses a critical challenge: how to adapt your data structures to changing requirements without breaking existing processes or losing historical information. Particularly in modern data platforms that serve multiple consumers with different release cycles, a strategic approach to schema evolution is essential.

Understanding schema compatibility types

Schema evolution follows several compatibility models that define how changes relate to existing data and consumers:

- **Backward compatibility** ensures that new schema versions can read data written with older schemas. This is the most common requirement, allowing schema fields to be added but restricting removal or type changes of existing fields. For example, adding a customer segment field to a customer record maintains backward compatibility because new processes can still read older records (treating the missing field as null).

- **Forward compatibility** means that data written with a new schema can be read by processes using older schema versions. This typically requires any new fields to be optional, allowing older readers to ignore them. In systems supporting both backward and forward compatibility, consumers can be upgraded independently from producers.

- **Full compatibility** combines both backward and forward compatibility. Changes must be non-destructive, typically limited to adding optional fields or extending enumerations with new values.

- **Breaking changes** modify schemas in ways incompatible with existing data or consumers. Examples include removing fields, changing field types, or making optional fields required. These changes necessitate coordinated upgrades of producers, storage systems, and consumers.

Implementing schema evolution in AWS Glue

AWS Glue provides several mechanisms for managing schema evolution throughout your data platform:

- **Glue Schema registry:** Glue Schema registry serves as a centralized repository for schema definitions with built-in evolution controls. When registering a schema, you specify a compatibility mode that enforces evolution rules:

```
1. aws glue create-schema \
2.    --registry-id RegistryName=retail-data-registry \
3.    --schema-name customer-profile \
4.    --compatibility BACKWARD \
5.    --data-format AVRO \
6.    --schema-definition ‹...›
```

Available compatibility modes include:

- o **NONE**: No compatibility checking (allows breaking changes).

- o **BACKWARD**: The new schema can read data written with the previous schema.

- o **BACKWARD_ALL**: The new schema can read data from all the previous schemas.

- o **FORWARD**: Old schema can read data written with the new schema.

- o **FORWARD_ALL**: All previous schemas can read data written with the new schema.

- o **FULL**: Both backward and forward compatibility with the immediate previous version.

- o **FULL_ALL**: Both backward and forward compatibility with all previous versions.

When attempting to register a schema version that violates the compatibility policy, Glue rejects the update with an error message explaining the violation.

- **Glue Data Catalog and table evolution:** For data stored in S3 and registered in the Glue Data Catalog, schema evolution happens through crawler updates or manual table modifications. When a crawler detects schema changes in underlying data, it updates the table definition according to the configured update behaviour.

The key configuration is **SchemaChangePolicy**, which can be set to:

- o **UPDATE_IN_DATABASE**: Automatically update the table schema when changes are detected.

- o **LOG**: Record changes but do not alter the schema (requiring manual updates).

For partitioned tables, you can also control how new partitions are integrated:

- o **InheritFromTable**: New partitions use the table's schema.

- o **InheritFromPartition**: Each partition maintains its own schema.

Evolution-friendly data formats

The choice of data format significantly impacts schema evolution capabilities. AWS supports several formats with different evolution characteristics:

Apache Parquet stores schema with each file, supporting column addition but requiring careful handling for other changes. Using the AWS Glue **enableUpdateCatalog** option with dynamic frames automatically reconciles schema differences:

```
1. glueContext.write_dynamic_frame.from_options(
2.     frame=transformed_dyf,
3.     connection_type="s3",
4.     connection_options={
```

```
5.         "path": "s3://processed-data/customers/",
6.         "partitionKeys": ["year", "month"]
7.     },
8.     format="parquet",
9.     format_options={"enableUpdateCatalog": True}
10. )
```

Apache Avro excels at schema evolution by storing the full schema with each file and supporting both reader and writer schemas. AWS Glue can process Avro data with evolving schemas through the **resolveChoice** transform for handling ambiguous types during schema changes:

```
1.  # Reading Avro data with schema evolution
2.  avro_dyf = glueContext.create_dynamic_frame.from_options(
3.      connection_type="s3",
4.      connection_options={"paths": ["s3://raw-data/customers/"]},
5.      format="avro"
6.  )
7.
8.  # Handle schema evolution with resolveChoice
9.  resolved_dyf = avro_dyf.resolveChoice(
10.     specs=[
11.         ("customer_value", "cast:double"),
12.         ("address", "make_struct")
13.     ]
14. )
```

JSON offers flexibility but lacks schema enforcement unless combined with services like Glue Schema registry. For self-describing data without strict schemas, JSON can accommodate changes without migration:

```
1.  # Reading various JSON versions with different schemas
2.  json_dyf = glueContext.create_dynamic_frame.from_options(
3.      connection_type="s3",
4.      connection_options={"paths": ["s3://raw-data/customers/"]},
5.      format="json"
6.  )
```

Managing breaking schema changes

Despite best practices, breaking changes sometimes become necessary. These situations require careful planning and coordination across your data platform:

1. **Dual-write pattern**: During migration, write to both old and new schemas simultaneously to ensure continuity. The following code demonstrate this pattern, it writes in first version then apply transform and write to new schema:

```
1.  # Write to both schemas during transition
2.  glueContext.write_dynamic_frame.from_options(
3.      frame=data_frame,
4.      connection_type="s3",
5.      connection_options={"path": "s3://data/customers-v1/"},
6.      format="parquet"
7.  )
8.
9.  # Transform to new schema and write
10. new_schema = apply_schema_changes(data_frame)
```

```
11. glueContext.write_dynamic_frame.from_options(
12.     frame=new_schema,
13.     connection_type="s3",
14.     connection_options={"path": "s3://data/customers-v2/"},
15.     format="parquet"
16. )
```

2. **Version-specific paths**: Store different schema versions in separate locations:

```
1. s3://data-lake/customers/v1/year=2023/month=06/...
2. s3://data-lake/customers/v2/year=2023/month=06/...
```

3. **Schema transformation jobs**: Create Glue jobs that convert between schema versions:

```
1.  def convert_schema_v1_to_v2(glueContext, source_path, target_path):
2.      # Read with v1 schema
3.      source_dyf = glueContext.create_dynamic_frame.from_options(
4.          connection_type="s3",
5.          connection_options={"paths": [source_path]},
6.          format="parquet"
7.      )
8.
9.      # Transform to v2 schema
10.     transformed_dyf = source_dyf.apply_mapping([
11.         ("id", "string", "customer_id", "string"),
12.         ("name", "string", "full_name", "string"),
13.         ("address", "string", "address", "string")
14.     ])
15.
16.     # Write with v2 schema
17.     glueContext.write_dynamic_frame.from_options(
18.         frame=transformed_dyf,
19.         connection_type="s3",
20.         connection_options={"path": target_path},
21.         format="parquet"
22.     )
```

Testing schema evolution

Robust testing is essential for successful schema evolution. AWS provides several approaches for validating schema changes before production deployment:

1. **Schema compatibility validation using Glue Schema registry**:

```
1.  # Check if proposed schema is compatible
2.  compatibility_response = glue_client.check_schema_version_validity(
3.      SchemaId={
4.          'SchemaName': 'customer-profile',
5.          'RegistryName': 'retail-data-registry'
6.      },
7.      SchemaDefinition='...new schema definition...'
8.  )
9.
10. if compatibility_response['Valid']:
```

```
11.    print("Schema is compatible!")
12. else:
13.    print("Compatibility issues:", compatibility_response['Error'])
```

2. **Sample data validation with test datasets**:

```
1. # Test reading existing data with new schema
2. try:
3.     test_df = spark.read.schema(new_schema).parquet("s3://test-data/sample-files/")
4.     print(f"Successfully read {test_df.count()} records with new schema")
5. except Exception as e:
6.     print(f"Schema compatibility issue: {str(e)}")
```

3. **Consumer simulation to verify downstream impact**:

```
1. # Simulate each consumer with the new schema
2. for consumer in consumers:
3.     test_compatibility(consumer, new_schema)
```

Effective schema evolution management ensures your data platform can adapt to changing requirements while maintaining backward compatibility. By leveraging AWS Glue Schema Registry, selecting appropriate data formats, and implementing careful testing procedures, you can evolve your data structures without disrupting existing processes. In the next section, we will explore how to monitor data quality across these evolving schemas with comprehensive metrics and alerting systems.

Hands-on: Building data quality pipelines

In this hands-on section, we will implement a serverless data quality pipeline that automatically validates data as it arrives, publishes metrics, and alerts stakeholders when quality thresholds are not met. The complete implementation is available in our GitHub repository.

Solution architecture

Our implementation demonstrates the pre-load validation pattern with a simple architecture:

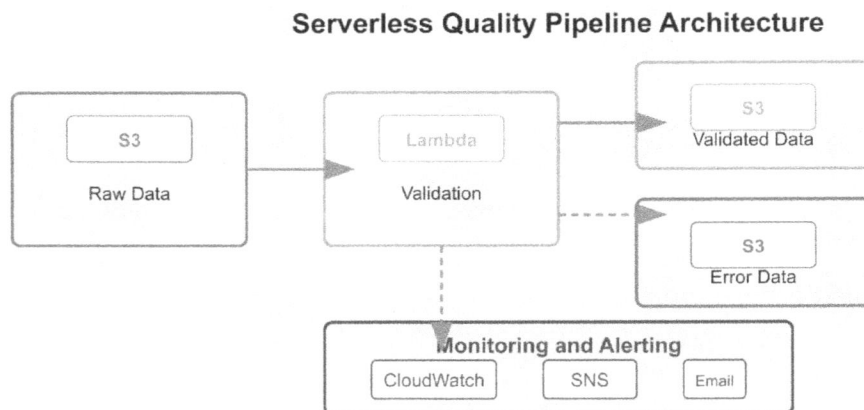

Figure 6.6: Serverless quality pipeline architecture

Modern data architectures require robust quality controls to ensure data reliability and trustworthiness. Implementing automated data quality checks using AWS services provides a scalable approach to detecting and responding to quality issues in real-time. By combining S3, Lambda, CloudWatch, and SNS, we can create a comprehensive data quality monitoring framework that validates data as it arrives and alerts stakeholders to potential problems. Let us examine how these services work together to implement automated quality controls:

1. **S3 buckets** store raw and validated data.

2. **Lambda function** validates data when triggered by S3 events.

3. **CloudWatch** tracks quality metrics and provides dashboards.

4. **SNS topic** delivers alerts when quality issues are detected.

Key implementation components

The Lambda validation function checks for issues including missing required fields, invalid values, and violations of business rules:

```
1.  # Check for quality issues in each transaction
2.  for transaction in transactions:
3.      errors = []
4.
5.      # Required field validation
6.      if 'customer_id' not in transaction or not transaction['customer_id']:
7.          errors.append('missing_customer_id')
8.          validation_metrics['missing_customer_id'] += 1
9.
10.     # Business rule validation
11.     if 'amount' in transaction and float(transaction['amount']) < 0:
12.         errors.append('negative_amount')
13.         validation_metrics['negative_amount'] += 1
14.
15.     # Store record in appropriate list
16.     if errors:
17.         transaction['validation_errors'] = errors
18.         invalid_records.append(transaction)
19.     else:
20.         valid_records.append(transaction)
```

After validation, metrics are published to CloudWatch and alerts triggered when necessary:

```
1.  # Calculate overall quality score
2.  quality_score = 100 - sum([
3.      (validation_metrics[m] / total_records) * 100
4.      for m in validation_metrics
5.  ]) / len(validation_metrics)
6.
7.  # Publish metrics to CloudWatch
8.  cloudwatch.put_metric_data(
9.      Namespace='DataQuality',
10.     MetricData=[
11.         {
12.             'MetricName': 'QualityScore',
13.             'Value': quality_score,
14.             'Unit': 'None',
15.             'Dimensions': [{'Name': 'Dataset', 'Value': 'Transactions'}]
16.         }
17.     ]
18. )
```

```
19.
20. # Alert if quality is poor
21. if quality_score < 85:
22.     sns.publish(
23.         TopicArn=alert_topic,
24.         Subject=f"Low data quality score: {quality_score:.2f}",
25.         Message=json.dumps({
26.             'quality_score': quality_score,
27.             'file': f"s3://{bucket}/{key}",
28.             'timestamp': datetime.datetime.now().isoformat()
29.         })
30.     )
```

Monitoring in the AWS Console

To view quality metrics in the AWS Console:

1. Navigate to CloudWatch service.

2. Select Dashboards in the left navigation and click DataQualityDashboard.

3. View graphs showing quality score and error percentages.

4. Check Alarms to see if any quality thresholds have been breached.

Extending the implementation

This foundation can be extended in several ways:

- **Add statistical validation** to detect anomalies in data distributions.

- **Implement schema evolution** by integrating with Glue Schema Registry.

- **Create multi-channel alerts** through AWS Chatbot for Slack or Teams.

- **Add automated remediation** workflows for common quality issues.

The GitHub repository contains the complete AWS CDK code for deploying this pipeline, along with a Jupyter Notebook that walks through testing it with sample data. This serverless approach ensures your data quality controls scale automatically with your data volume while keeping infrastructure management to a minimum.

Conclusion

Throughout this chapter, we have explored how to ensure data quality and implement robust data transformation processes within AWS environments. We examined data quality frameworks, leveraged AWS Glue DataBrew for visual data preparation, implemented various validation techniques, and addressed schema evolution management. Our hands-on implementation demonstrated building a serverless data quality pipeline that automatically validates data, publishes metrics, and alerts stakeholders when quality thresholds are not met. By integrating these practices into your transformation workflows, you can significantly reduce time spent on data cleaning and increase confidence in your data assets, ultimately enabling more effective data-driven decision making.

In the next chapter, we will explore data warehouse engineering with Amazon Redshift. We will dive into Redshift's architecture, examine table design and distribution strategies that optimize performance, investigate query optimization techniques, and explore automation and operational best practices. Through a hands-on implementation, you will learn how to build an enterprise data warehouse that delivers fast, reliable insights while effectively integrating with your data lake to create a comprehensive analytics platform.

## CHAPTER 7

Data Warehouse Engineering with Redshift

Introduction

Data warehousing emerged as a specialized discipline in response to the fundamental limitations of using transactional databases for analytics. While transactional systems excel at processing individual records with high concurrency and maintaining data integrity through normalization, they struggle with complex analytical queries that scan millions of rows and perform extensive aggregations. Data warehouses invert these priorities, optimizing read performance at scale while accepting trade-offs in write latency and normalization. This architectural divergence is not arbitrary but reflects the different workload characteristics: transactional systems handle many small, precise operations while analytical systems process fewer, more complex operations across vast datasets.

The business value of dedicated analytical systems comes from their ability to transform raw data into decision-making insights without disrupting operational systems. Organizations implement data warehouses to consolidate disparate data sources, establish a single version of truth, enable complex cross-functional analysis, and deliver consistent performance as data volumes grow. Recent McKinsey research indicates that companies with mature data warehouse implementations report 20-30% higher productivity among data analysts and business intelligence users compared to those without optimized analytical infrastructure. As data-driven decision making expands beyond specialists to frontline employees, a robust data warehouse becomes essential infrastructure for organizational agility.

Within the AWS ecosystem, Amazon Redshift serves as the centerpiece of the analytics portfolio, purposely designed for data warehouse workloads. Unlike general-purpose databases like RDS, Redshift's architecture makes fundamental trade-offs that optimize analytical performance. It integrates with upstream data sources through services like **Data Migration Service** (**DMS**) and Glue, offers direct connectivity to business intelligence tools through JDBC/ODBC drivers, and extends into data lake environments through Redshift Spectrum. For organizations building comprehensive data platforms on AWS, Redshift typically serves as the performance layer handling curated, structured data while complementary services like S3 and Athena manage raw or semi-structured data at larger scale.

Structure

- Amazon Redshift architecture
- Redshift Serverless architecture

- VPC networking and endpoint access

- Cluster scaling and elasticity

- Table design and distribution strategies

- Query optimization techniques

- Zero-ETL integration

- Automation and operations

- Integration with data lake

- Hands-on: Data warehouse with Redshift

Objectives

This chapter aims to provide a comprehensive understanding of data warehouse engineering principles using Amazon Redshift, balancing architectural concepts with practical implementation guidance. You will learn to leverage Redshift's unique architecture to design efficient table structures, optimize query performance, implement automation for operational efficiency, and integrate with data lakes to create unified analytical environments. The chapter explores emerging capabilities like zero-ETL integration that fundamentally change data integration approaches. Through a structured hands-on implementation, you will apply these concepts to build an enterprise-grade data warehouse that delivers both performance and scalability. These capabilities will enable you to architect analytical systems that process complex queries across vast datasets while maintaining the responsiveness needed for data-driven decision making in modern organizations.

Amazon Redshift architecture

Massively parallel processing (MPP) architecture represents a fundamental shift from traditional database design, addressing the core challenge of analytical workloads: how to process enormous datasets faster than a single server could manage. Unlike vertical scaling approaches that rely on increasingly powerful individual machines, MPP distributes both data and processing across multiple nodes working in parallel. This architectural approach enables near-linear scalability as more nodes are added, allowing analytical queries to complete in minutes that would take hours on single-server systems. For data warehouse workloads where queries often scan billions of rows, this parallelism is not merely a performance enhancement—it is a prerequisite for viability at enterprise scale.

Redshift implements MPP through a cluster architecture consisting of a leader node that coordinates query execution and multiple compute nodes that store data and perform processing in parallel. The leader node serves as the client-facing interface, handling connection management, query parsing, planning, and result aggregation, while compute nodes form the distributed storage and processing layer of the system. This division of responsibilities creates a scalable architecture where most data-intensive operations happen in parallel across all compute nodes, with the leader node handling only the operations that must be centralized. Understanding this architectural model explains many Redshift performance characteristics—queries that distribute efficiently across nodes scale almost linearly with cluster size, while operations that concentrate on the leader node become bottlenecks as data volumes grow.

In the following figure, you will find the building blocks of the redshift cluster:

Amazon Redshift Cluster Architecture

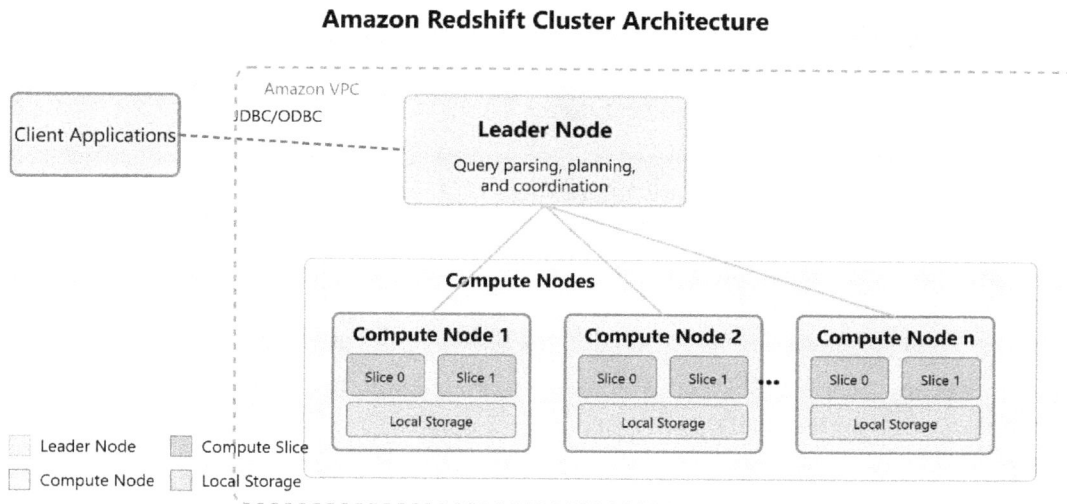

Figure 7.1: *Redshift cluster architecture showing leader and compute nodes*

Node types and sizing considerations

Redshift offers several node types optimized for different workload requirements, with the choice significantly impacting both performance and cost.

The primary node families include:

- **RA3 nodes (latest generation)**: Feature high-performance local SSD cache with separate managed storage in S3, allowing independent scaling of compute and storage.

- **DC2 nodes (previous generation)**: Combine compute and local storage with SSD drives, suitable for compute-intensive workloads under 1TB.

- **DS2 nodes (legacy)**: Pair compute with HDD storage, generally not recommended for new deployments.

When selecting node types for your cluster, consider the following key factors:

- **Query complexity and concurrency**: More complex queries and higher concurrency require more CPU and memory. RA3 nodes provide the highest per-node computing power with 12-96 vCPUs and 96-768 GB of memory depending on the specific node size.

- **Data volume**: For datasets over 1TB, RA3 nodes generally provide better price-performance due to their separate managed storage architecture.

- **Growth projections**: For environments expecting significant data growth, RA3 nodes allow scaling compute independent from storage, avoiding cluster rebuilds as data volumes increase.

- **Cost model preferences**: RA3 separates compute (paid hourly) from storage (paid per GB-month), allowing independent optimization of each resource.

For production environments, AWS recommends starting with at least two nodes to ensure high availability, as single-node clusters have no data redundancy. Pilot implementations can use a single-node configuration for cost efficiency during the development and testing phases.

Columnar storage engine

Redshift's columnar storage engine represents a fundamental architectural divergence from traditional row-based databases, designed specifically for analytical query patterns. Where transactional databases store complete records together on disk (optimizing for retrieving entire rows), columnar storage organizes data by storing all values from a single column contiguously. This architectural choice aligns with analytical queries that typically scan large numbers of rows but only a subset of columns.

The columnar approach provides three key advantages:

- **I/O efficiency**: When a query references only 3 columns from a 100-column table, Redshift reads only 3% of the data from disk. This dramatically reduces I/O requirements compared to row-based systems that must read entire rows.

- **Compression effectiveness**: Similar data values stored together enable much higher compression ratios. For example, customer state/province columns might contain only 50-60 unique values repeating millions of times—ideal for dictionary-based compression.

- **Vector processing**: Modern CPUs support **Single Instruction, Multiple Data (SIMD)** operations that can process multiple values simultaneously when they're stored contiguously—a perfect match for columnar storage.

The following image illustrates the difference between the row-based storage and columnar storage:

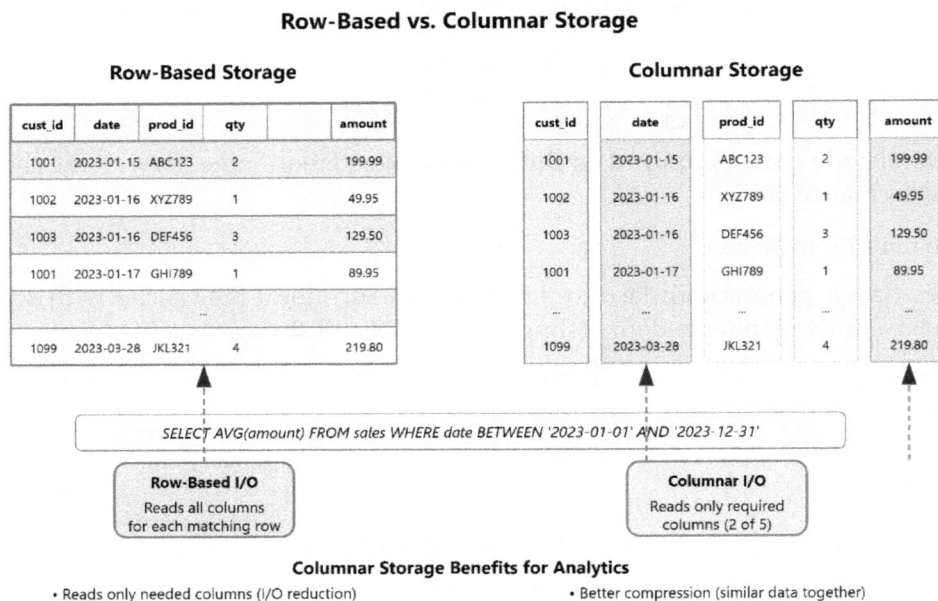

Row-Based vs. Columnar Storage

Row-Based Storage					
cust_id	date	prod_id	qty		amount
1001	2023-01-15	ABC123	2		199.99
1002	2023-01-16	XYZ789	1		49.95
1003	2023-01-16	DEF456	3		129.50
1001	2023-01-17	GHI789	1		89.95
...					
1099	2023-03-28	JKL321	4		219.80

Columnar Storage				
cust_id	date	prod_id	qty	amount
1001	2023-01-15	ABC123	2	199.99
1002	2023-01-16	XYZ789	1	49.95
1003	2023-01-16	DEF456	3	129.50
1001	2023-01-17	GHI789	1	89.95
...	...	...	...	...
1099	2023-03-28	JKL321	4	219.80

SELECT AVG(amount) FROM sales WHERE date BETWEEN '2023-01-01' AND '2023-12-31'

Row-Based I/O
Reads all columns for each matching row

Columnar I/O
Reads only required columns (2 of 5)

Columnar Storage Benefits for Analytics
- Reads only needed columns (I/O reduction)
- Better compression (similar data together)

Figure 7.2: Columnar vs. row storage organization and query pattern impact

The following query illustrates columnar storage's advantage:

```
1. SELECT AVG(amount)
2. FROM sales
3. WHERE sdate BETWEEN '2023-01-01' AND '2023-12-31';
```

In a row-based system, this query requires reading every column in each sales row, even though it only needs two columns (amount and date). On a 50-column table, approximately 96% of the data read would be irrelevant to the query. Redshift's columnar architecture reads only the necessary columns, dramatically reducing I/O for typical analytical patterns.

Data block architecture and compression

Redshift organizes columnar data into 1MB blocks, applying different compression algorithms based on data characteristics. This block-level organization delivers two important benefits:

- **Zone maps**: Each block maintains metadata about its value ranges (min/max), allowing Redshift to skip entire blocks that cannot match query predicates.

- **Parallel reads**: Multiple blocks can be read simultaneously by different slices within a compute node.

Redshift automatically selects appropriate compression encodings for each column during the COPY operation, analyzing data patterns to determine optimal encodings:

```
1. -- Example of COPY with automatic compression analysis
2. COPY sales
3. FROM 's3://mybucket/sales_data/'
4. IAM_ROLE 'arn:aws:iam::123456789012:role/RedshiftCopyRole'
5. FORMAT AS CSV
6. COMPUPDATE ON; -- Analyzes and applies optimal compression
```

For production environments, explicitly specifying compression after testing can yield better results:

```
1. -- Table with explicit compression encodings based on data analysis
2. CREATE TABLE customer_sales (
3.     customer_id INTEGER ENCODE DELTA,
4.     sale_date DATE ENCODE AZ64,
5.     product_id INTEGER ENCODE BYTEDICT,
6.     quantity INTEGER ENCODE MOSTLY8,
7.     sale_amount DECIMAL(12,2) ENCODE AZ64
8. );
```

Common compression types include:

- **AZ64**: High-performance encoding for numeric/date types.
- **BYTEDICT**: Dictionary encoding for columns with limited unique values.
- **DELTA/DELTA32K**: Differential encoding for sequential values.
- **LZO/ZSTD**: General-purpose compression for text columns.
- **RUNLENGTH**: Optimized for columns with repeated values.

Effective compression can reduce storage requirements by 60-80% while simultaneously improving query performance through reduced I/O.

Redshift Serverless architecture

For organizations seeking to eliminate infrastructure management or needing elastic capacity, Redshift Serverless provides an alternative deployment model that maintains compatibility with provisioned Redshift. This architecture abstracts away the traditional cluster and node concepts, replacing them with workgroup and namespace constructs:

- **Workgroup**: The compute resources that process queries against your data.
- **Namespace**: The logical container for database objects and users.

The key differences in Redshift Serverless architecture include:

- **Resource measurement**: Capacity is measured in **Redshift Processing Units (RPUs)** rather than node types.
- **Automatic scaling**: Compute resources scale up/down automatically based on workload.
- **Simplified management**: No need to choose node types, size clusters, or manage distribution styles.
- **Usage-based billing**: Pay only for the actual compute resources used when processing queries.

To set up Redshift Serverless through the console:

1. Navigate to the Amazon Redshift console.
2. Select Redshift Serverless from the left navigation.

3. Click Create workgroup.

4. Configure base capacity (minimum RPUs) and maximum RPUs for scaling.

5. Set up networking, security, and monitoring options.

6. Create or select a namespace to store your database objects.

Redshift Serverless is particularly well-suited for:

- Development or test environments with intermittent usage.

- Production workloads with highly variable demand.

- Organizations with limited database administration resources.

- Use cases requiring immediate setup without capacity planning.

For practical implementation, Redshift Serverless requires the same data design principles as provisioned Redshift but eliminates many operational considerations around sizing and management.

VPC networking and endpoint access

Redshift's network architecture significantly impacts both security and performance. Modern Redshift deployments operate within **Virtual Private Clouds** (**VPCs**), which are isolated network environments within AWS that allow you to define your own private network space with complete control over IP addressing, routing, and security.

Key networking concepts for Redshift include:

- **Subnet placement**: Subnets are subdivisions of your VPC network. Deploying Redshift clusters in private subnets (subnets without direct internet access) provides an additional security layer by preventing direct exposure to the internet. This means your data warehouse remains accessible only through controlled network paths.

- **Security groups**: These act as virtual firewalls controlling inbound and outbound traffic to your Redshift cluster. Security groups operate at the instance level and allow you to specify exactly which protocols, ports, and IP ranges can communicate with your cluster.

- **Enhanced VPC routing**: When enabled, this feature forces all COPY (data loading) and UNLOAD (data exporting) traffic to flow through your VPC networking infrastructure rather than through the public internet. This provides:

  o Greater network traffic control through your existing security and monitoring tools.

  o Ability to use network access control lists to further restrict traffic.

  o Compliance with regulations requiring controlled data paths.

- **VPC endpoints**: These are virtual devices that allow you to privately connect your VPC to supported AWS services without requiring an internet gateway or NAT device. For Redshift, VPC endpoints provide several important advantages:

  o **Security**: Data traffic to services like S3 never leaves the Amazon network.

  o **Reduced costs**: Eliminates need for NAT gateways and associated data processing charges.

  o **Simplified network architecture**: Removes the need to configure internet gateways.

  o **Consistent performance**: Avoids potential internet congestion and bandwidth constraints.

A typical secure configuration might include:

```
1.  # Terraform example of Redshift VPC configuration
2.  resource "aws_security_group" "redshift_sg" {
3.    name        = "redshift-security-group"
```

```
4.    description = "Security group for Redshift cluster"
5.    vpc_id      = aws_vpc.main.id
6.
7.    # Inbound rule for SQL client access
8.    ingress {
9.      from_port   = 5439
10.     to_port     = 5439
11.     protocol    = "tcp"
12.     cidr_blocks = ["10.0.0.0/16"]  # Internal VPC CIDR
13.    }
14.
15.    # Outbound rule for S3 access
16.    egress {
17.      from_port   = 0
18.      to_port     = 0
19.      protocol    = "-1"
20.      cidr_blocks = ["0.0.0.0/0"]
21.    }
22. }
```

For organizations requiring the highest level of security, Redshift supports several advanced security features:

- **VPC endpoints for S3**: Allows Redshift to interact with S3 (for COPY/UNLOAD operations) through a direct private connection within the AWS network. This provides several advantages:
  o Eliminates all S3 data transfer traffic from traversing the public internet.
  o Removes the need to configure internet gateways, NAT devices, or firewall rules.
  o Provides a consistent and reliable network path with potentially improved throughput.
  o Applies granular access policies at the endpoint level for additional security.

- **AWS PrivateLink**: Enables you to connect your on-premises data centers directly to Redshift through private connections, without exposing your traffic to the public internet. Benefits include:
  o Direct secure access from corporate networks without VPN configuration.
  o Simplified network architecture by avoiding complex routing.
  o Reduced exposure to external threats.
  o Potentially lower and more predictable network latency.

- **Encryption in transit**: All data moving to and from Redshift can be encrypted using **Secure Sockets Layer/Transport Layer Security** (**SSL/TLS**) protocols. This ensures that:
  o All client-to-cluster communication is encrypted.
  o Data remains protected from eavesdropping during network transmission.
  o Cryptographic verification of server identity prevents man-in-the-middle attacks.
  o Compliance requirements for data protection during transmission are met.

- **VPC flow logs**: This feature captures information about all IP traffic going to and from network interfaces in your VPC. For Redshift environments, VPC Flow Logs provide:
  o Comprehensive visibility into all network traffic patterns.
  o Ability to monitor for suspicious access attempts or unauthorized connections.

o   Detailed audit trail for compliance and security investigations.

o   Network troubleshooting capabilities for connectivity issues.

By combining these network security features, organizations can create highly secure Redshift environments that maintain strict control over data access while still providing the necessary connectivity for data loading, querying, and integration with other services.

Cluster scaling and elasticity

Redshift provides several mechanisms for adapting capacity to changing requirements:

- **Elastic resize**: Quickly changes the number of nodes while maintaining the same node type, typically completing in minutes.

- **Classic resize**: Changes both node count and/or node type, requiring hours or days to complete but enabling more significant configuration changes.

- **Concurrency scaling**: Automatically adds transient capacity for read workloads during high concurrency periods.

- **Serverless**: Eliminates manual scaling by automatically adjusting capacity based on workload.

For provisioned clusters, elastic resize provides the fastest adaptation:

```
1.  -- Elastic resize example: Scale from 2 to 4 nodes
2.  ALTER CLUSTER mycluster RESIZE
3.     NODES 4
4.     ELASTIC;
```

For longer-term capacity planning, monitoring CloudWatch metrics provides the data needed to determine appropriate cluster size:

- **CPUUtilization**: Sustained values over 70% indicate compute constraint.

- **PercentageDiskSpaceUsed**: Values over 75% suggest storage constraint.

- **WLMQueueLength**: Values consistently above 0 indicate concurrency constraint.

By understanding Redshift's core architectural principles and practical implementation considerations, you can make informed decisions about cluster configuration that align with your analytical requirements. In the next section, we will explore how to optimize table design to leverage this architecture effectively.

Table design and distribution strategies

Effective table design represents one of the most consequential decisions in Redshift data warehouse engineering. While query tuning can improve performance incrementally, proper table design can yield order-of-magnitude performance differences by aligning with Redshift's architectural principles. Unlike traditional databases where physical design has limited impact on well-indexed tables, Redshift's MPP architecture makes data distribution and organization fundamental to performance outcomes. Industry benchmarks consistently show that well-designed tables outperform poorly designed ones by 10-100x for complex analytical queries, even when all other configuration parameters remain identical.

Distribution styles

In traditional single-node databases, all data resides on the same server, making data location irrelevant to query performance. Redshift's distributed architecture fundamentally changes this paradigm; data must be physically divided across multiple compute nodes, and the way you distribute this data directly impacts query performance, particularly for joins and aggregations.

Distribution styles determine how data is physically allocated across compute nodes in a Redshift cluster. This distribution directly impacts performance by influencing data locality during join operations, whether the data needed for a join is already on the same node (requiring no network transfer) or must be redistributed across the network (potentially moving large amounts of data).

Redshift offers four distribution strategies, each addressing specific data patterns:

KEY distribution

When using KEY distribution, Redshift hashes the specified column values and assigns rows with the same values to the same compute node. This ensures that all rows sharing a particular key value will be stored together, which is crucial for optimizing join performance. The following SQL shows how to create a table with key distribution:

```
1.  -- Example of KEY distribution for a fact table
2.  CREATE TABLE sales_fact (
3.      sale_id BIGINT,
4.      product_id INTEGER,
5.      customer_id INTEGER,
6.      sale_date DATE,
7.      quantity INTEGER,
8.      sale_amount DECIMAL(12,2),
9.      PRIMARY KEY (sale_id)
10. )
11. DISTKEY(product_id);
```

In this example, all rows with the same **product_id** will reside on the same compute node. When joined with a product dimension table distributed on the same key, the join operation can execute locally within each node without moving data between nodes:

```
1.  -- Dimension table distributed on the same key
2.  CREATE TABLE product_dim (
3.      product_id INTEGER,
4.      product_name VARCHAR(100),
5.      category VARCHAR(50),
6.      price DECIMAL(10,2),
7.      PRIMARY KEY (product_id)
8.  )
9.  DISTKEY(product_id);
```

KEY distribution is used:

- For large fact tables that join with dimension tables on specific columns.

- When the distribution column has high cardinality (many unique values) to ensure balanced data distribution.

- To optimize frequently executed joins that would otherwise require data redistribution.

Key concept: The performance impact of distribution is most significant during joins. When tables share the same distribution key and are joined on that key, Redshift can execute co-located joins where no data movement is required between nodes.

EVEN distribution

EVEN distribution allocates rows to nodes in a round-robin fashion, ensuring approximately equal data volume on each node without regard to any particular column values:

```
1.  -- Example of EVEN distribution for a balanced table
2.  CREATE TABLE customer_survey (
3.      survey_id BIGINT,
4.      customer_id INTEGER,
5.      response_date DATE,
6.      satisfaction_score INTEGER,
7.      comments VARCHAR(1000)
8.  )
9.  DISTSTYLE EVEN;
```

EVEN distribution is used:

- When no clear join pattern exists (the table is joined in different ways with various tables).
- For tables that are not typically joined with other tables.
- When the table is used primarily for scanning operations.
- When no suitable distribution key exists (all columns have low cardinality or highly skewed values).

EVEN distribution provides balanced compute utilization across the cluster and prevents data skew, but typically requires redistribution during join operations.

ALL distribution

ALL distribution (also called broadcast) replicates the entire table on each compute node:

```
1.  -- Example of ALL distribution for a small dimension table
2.  CREATE TABLE calendar_dim (
3.      date_key DATE,
4.      day_of_week VARCHAR(10),
5.      month VARCHAR(10),
6.      quarter VARCHAR(2),
7.      year INTEGER,
8.      is_holiday BOOLEAN,
9.      PRIMARY KEY (date_key)
10. )
11. DISTSTYLE ALL;
```

This distribution style is particularly valuable for dimension tables that:

- Are relatively small (typically less than 10 million rows).
- Do not change frequently.
- Join with large fact tables distributed on different keys.

ALL distribution eliminates data movement during joins but increases storage requirements and load times. For small dimension tables, these tradeoffs are typically favorable as storage impact is minimal while join performance improves dramatically.

AUTO distribution

AUTO distribution allows Redshift to determine the optimal distribution style based on table size and structure:

```
1.  -- Example of AUTO distribution letting Redshift choose
2.  CREATE TABLE web_events (
3.      event_id BIGINT,
```

```
4.      session_id VARCHAR(50),
5.      event_timestamp TIMESTAMP,
6.      page_url VARCHAR(200),
7.      event_type VARCHAR(50)
8.  )
9.  DISTSTYLE AUTO;
```

Initially, Redshift will assign ALL distribution to small tables and convert to EVEN distribution as tables grow beyond thresholds. With automatic table optimization enabled, Redshift may even convert to KEY distribution if it identifies beneficial join patterns. It is beneficial to use this when you are uncertain about the optimal distribution style.

Sort keys

While distribution styles address data locality across nodes, sort keys optimize how data is organized within each node. Sort keys leverage Redshift's columnar architecture to improve scan efficiency through zone maps—metadata structures that track min/max values for blocks of data.

When data is physically sorted by a column, Redshift creates zone maps that allow it to skip entire blocks of data during scanning operations, as illustrated in the following diagram:

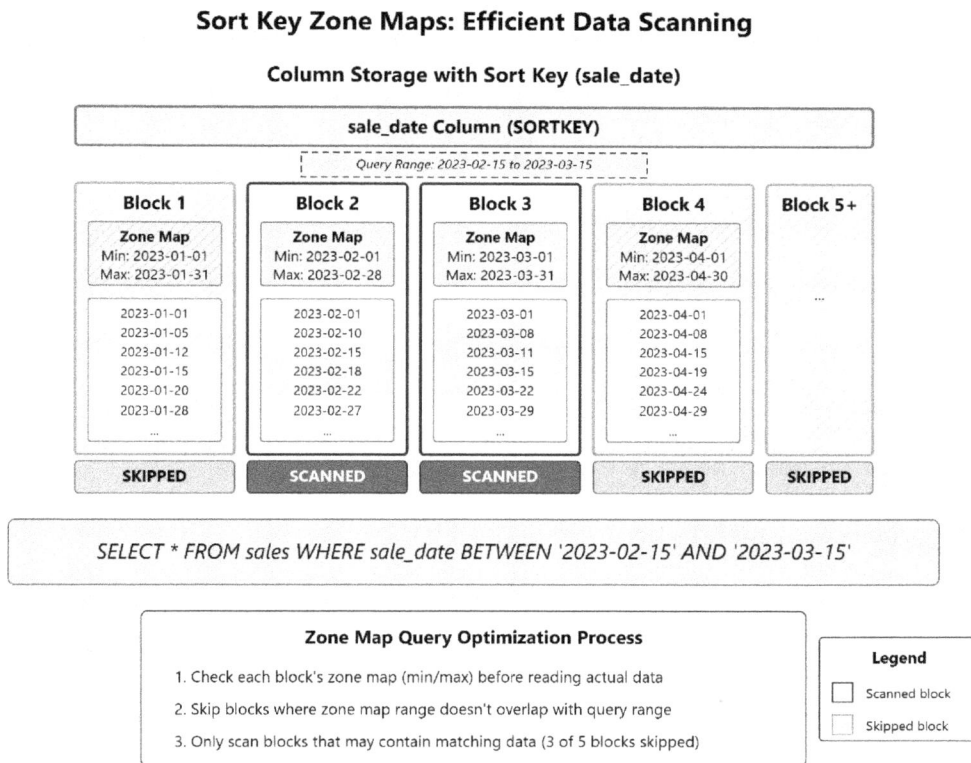

Sort Key Zone Maps: Efficient Data Scanning

Column Storage with Sort Key (sale_date)

sale_date Column (SORTKEY)				

Query Range: 2023-02-15 to 2023-03-15

Block 1	**Block 2**	**Block 3**	**Block 4**	**Block 5+**
Zone Map Min: 2023-01-01 Max: 2023-01-31	**Zone Map** Min: 2023-02-01 Max: 2023-02-28	**Zone Map** Min: 2023-03-01 Max: 2023-03-31	**Zone Map** Min: 2023-04-01 Max: 2023-04-30	...
2023-01-01 2023-01-05 2023-01-12 2023-01-15 2023-01-20 2023-01-28 ...	2023-02-01 2023-02-10 2023-02-15 2023-02-18 2023-02-22 2023-02-27 ...	2023-03-01 2023-03-08 2023-03-11 2023-03-15 2023-03-22 2023-03-29 ...	2023-04-01 2023-04-08 2023-04-15 2023-04-19 2023-04-24 2023-04-29 ...	
SKIPPED	**SCANNED**	**SCANNED**	**SKIPPED**	**SKIPPED**

SELECT * FROM sales WHERE sale_date BETWEEN '2023-02-15' AND '2023-03-15'

Zone Map Query Optimization Process

1. Check each block's zone map (min/max) before reading actual data

2. Skip blocks where zone map range doesn't overlap with query range

3. Only scan blocks that may contain matching data (3 of 5 blocks skipped)

Legend
☐ Scanned block
☐ Skipped block

Figure 7.3: Sort key zone map operation allowing blocks to be skipped

Redshift offers two types of sort keys, each with distinct advantages.

Compound sort keys

Compound sort keys order data sequentially based on the specified columns in the order listed:

```
1.  -- Example of compound sort key for time-series data
2.  CREATE TABLE customer_transactions (
```

```
 3.     transaction_id BIGINT,
 4.     customer_id INTEGER,
 5.     transaction_date DATE,
 6.     transaction_time TIME,
 7.     amount DECIMAL(12,2),
 8.     category VARCHAR(50),
 9.     PRIMARY KEY (transaction_id)
10. )
11. DISTKEY(customer_id)
12. SORTKEY(transaction_date, customer_id);
```

The order of columns in a compound sort key matters significantly. The leading column provides the greatest benefit for zone map pruning, with diminishing returns for subsequent columns.

Interleaved sort keys

Interleaved sort keys give equal weight to each specified column, making them suitable for queries that filter on different columns independently:

```
 1. -- Example of interleaved sort key for multi-dimensional filtering
 2. CREATE TABLE marketing_events (
 3.     event_id BIGINT,
 4.     event_date DATE,
 5.     region VARCHAR(50),
 6.     campaign_id INTEGER,
 7.     channel VARCHAR(50),
 8.     impressions INTEGER,
 9.     clicks INTEGER
10. )
11. DISTSTYLE EVEN
12. INTERLEAVED SORTKEY(event_date, region, channel);
```

Interleaved sort keys typically require more maintenance overhead and are less predictable than compound sort keys but offer more flexibility for diverse query patterns.

Compression encodings

Compression in Redshift serves a dual purpose: reducing storage requirements while simultaneously improving query performance by reducing I/O. Unlike traditional databases, where compression primarily saves space, Redshift's columnar architecture makes compression a key performance optimization technique.

Compression works particularly well in columnar storage because:

- Similar data is stored together, increasing compression efficiency.
- Different data types benefit from specialized compression algorithms.
- Reduced I/O directly translates to faster query execution.

Redshift supports multiple encoding types optimized for different data patterns:

```
 1. -- Example of explicit compression encodings
 2. CREATE TABLE customer_profile (
 3.     customer_id INTEGER ENCODE DELTA,
 4.     name VARCHAR(100) ENCODE LZO,
```

```
5.      email VARCHAR(100) ENCODE LZO,
6.      zip_code VARCHAR(10) ENCODE BYTEDICT,
7.      registration_date DATE ENCODE DELTA,
8.      last_login_timestamp TIMESTAMP ENCODE AZ64,
9.      customer_status VARCHAR(20) ENCODE BYTEDICT,
10.     lifetime_value DECIMAL(12,2) ENCODE AZ64
11. );
```

While Redshift can automatically assign compression encodings using ANALYZE COMPRESSION, understanding the principles behind each encoding type helps validate these assignments:

- **Raw**: No compression, used for small or random data.
- **AZ64**: High-performance encoding for numeric types.
- **Bytedict**: Dictionary encoding for columns with limited unique values.
- **Delta/Delta32K**: Effective for sequential values or dates.
- **LZO/Zstd**: General-purpose compression for large text or binary data.
- **RunLength**: Optimized for columns with many repeated values.

Automatic table optimization

Redshift provides automatic table optimization capabilities that can adjust distribution and sort keys based on observed query patterns:

```
1. -- Enable automatic table optimization
2. ALTER TABLE sales_fact ALTER DISTKEY AUTO;
3. ALTER TABLE sales_fact ALTER SORTKEY AUTO;
```

While automatic optimization can improve performance incrementally, intentional design based on understanding data patterns and query requirements typically yields better results for critical tables. Automatic optimization works best when:

- Query patterns are unpredictable or changing.
- You lack the expertise to make optimal design decisions.
- Tables serve multiple, competing query patterns.

Design process for table optimization

The following process provides a structured approach to table design decisions:

1. **Identify large fact tables** where distribution and sort decisions have the greatest impact.
2. **Analyze join patterns** to determine distribution key candidates.
3. **Evaluate filter patterns** to identify sort key candidates.
4. **Consider table sizes** to determine which tables should use ALL distribution.
5. **Test alternatives** using representative queries and data volumes.
6. **Monitor performance** after implementation and refine as needed.

This methodical approach ensures table design decisions align with actual workload requirements rather than theoretical best practices that may not apply to your specific scenario.

Table design in Redshift represents a critical foundation upon which all other optimizations build. By understanding the why behind distribution and sort strategies, you can make informed decisions that align with Redshift's architecture and your specific analytical requirements. In the next section, we will explore how to optimize query performance on top of this well-designed table foundation.

Query optimization techniques

Even with optimal table design, query performance can vary dramatically based on how SQL statements are structured and executed. Query optimization in Redshift requires understanding how the MPP architecture processes different SQL constructs. This section explores essential techniques for optimizing query performance in Amazon Redshift.

Understanding query execution plans

The query execution plan reveals how Redshift will process a query, providing the foundation for optimization efforts. Unlike traditional databases, Redshift plans expose distributed processing decisions that directly impact performance.

Using EXPLAIN and EXPLAIN ANALYZE

The **EXPLAIN** command provides insights into how a query will be processed:

```
1. EXPLAIN
2. SELECT c.customer_name, SUM(s.sale_amount) AS total_sales
3. FROM sales s
4. JOIN customers c ON s.customer_id = c.customer_id
5. WHERE s.sale_date BETWEEN '2023-01-01' AND '2023-12-31'
6. GROUP BY c.customer_name
7. ORDER BY total_sales DESC
8. LIMIT 10;
```

Key components to examine in execution plans:

1. **Join types and redistribution operations**: Look for DS_DIST_NONE (no redistribution), DS_DIST_ALL_NONE (tables using ALL distribution), DS_DIST_INNER or DS_DIST_OUTER (data redistribution required).

2. **Expensive operations**: Sort, hash aggregate, and broadcast operations often indicate potential bottlenecks.

3. **Filter application**: Early filter application (near the bottom of the plan) is generally more efficient than late filtering.

For actual runtime metrics, use EXPLAIN ANALYZE, which executes the query and returns detailed performance statistics.

Common query anti-patterns and solutions

The following table list the anti-pattern and its remedials:

Anti-pattern	Problem	Solution
Inappropriate JOINs	Tables distributed on different keys require data redistribution	Design tables with matching distribution keys for frequently joined columns
SELECT *	Reads all columns in columnar storage, wasting I/O	Select only required columns: SELECT col1, col2, col3 FROM...
Non-selective filtering	Functions prevent zone map usage:` WHERE EXTRACT(year FROM date) = 2023`	Use direct comparisons:` WHERE date BETWEEN '2023-01-01' AND '2023-12-31'`
Expensive DISTINCTs	Forces data redistribution	Use GROUP BY instead of DISTINCT where possible

Anti-pattern	Problem	Solution
Correlated subqueries	Executes subquery for each outer row	Replace with window functions or JOIN operations
Inefficient JOINs	Large-to-large table joins without distribution alignment	Consider pre-aggregating large tables before joining

Table 7.1: Redshift query anti-pattern solutions

Materialized views for performance

Materialized views are pre-computed query results that are stored physically and updated periodically, making them fundamentally different from regular views, which compute results on-demand. For data warehouse workloads with repetitive analytical queries, materialized views can deliver dramatic performance improvements.

```
1.  -- Create materialized view for common aggregation
2.  CREATE MATERIALIZED VIEW sales_by_month AS
3.  SELECT
4.      DATE_TRUNC('month', sale_date) AS month,
5.      product_category,
6.      SUM(sale_amount) AS monthly_sales,
7.      COUNT(DISTINCT customer_id) AS unique_customers
8.  FROM sales
9.  JOIN products ON sales.product_id = products.product_id
10. GROUP BY DATE_TRUNC('month', sale_date), product_category;
```

Best practices for materialized views:

- Create materialized views for queries that are executed frequently and perform expensive operations.

- Consider refresh timing based on data change frequency (after ETL processes complete).

- Monitor storage usage as materialized views consume physical space.

Workload management optimization

Workload management (WLM) in Redshift allows administrators to manage resource allocation and query prioritization, ensuring that critical queries get resources when needed without allowing any single workload to monopolize the cluster.

Key configuration parameters include:

Parameter	Description	Typical values
Query groups	Labels for classifying similar queries	`etl_jobs, dashboard_queries`
User groups	Database user groups for access control	`analysts, data_engineers`
Concurrency	Maximum concurrent queries in a queue	5 to 15 for standard queues
Memory %	Percentage of memory allocated to a queue	10 to 50% depending on query complexity
Timeout (ms)	Maximum execution time before cancellation	60000-3600000 (1min-1hr)
Priority	Relative importance of queries	HIGHEST, HIGH, NORMAL, LOW, LOWEST

Table 7.2: Workload management configuration parameters

Systematic query optimization process

Effective query optimization in Amazon Redshift begins with identifying and understanding performance bottlenecks through systematic analysis. By leveraging Redshift's system tables and diagnostic tools, we can pinpoint problematic queries and methodically improve their performance through a data-driven approach:

1. Identify slow queries using system tables:

```
1.  -- Find slow queries from past week
2.  SELECT
3.      query,
4.      TRIM(querytxt) AS query_text,
5.      starttime,
6.      DATEDIFF(seconds, starttime, endtime) AS duration_seconds
7.  FROM STL_QUERY
8.  WHERE starttime > DATEADD(day, -7, CURRENT_DATE)
9.  ORDER BY duration_seconds DESC
10. LIMIT 20;
```

2. Analyze execution plans to identify bottlenecks.

3. Examine table design focusing on distribution and sort keys.

4. Test alternative query formulations using EXPLAIN ANALYZE.

5. Implement and verify improvements by comparing performance metrics.

This systematic approach focuses optimization efforts on queries with the greatest potential for improvement, delivering maximum business value from your Redshift environment.

Zero-ETL integration

Traditional data integration processes require explicit ETL operations that introduce latency, require maintenance, and increase operational complexity. Zero-ETL integration represents a paradigm shift in how data flows from operational systems to analytical environments, eliminating the need for custom pipelines while enabling near real-time analytics. This section explores how Amazon Redshift's zero-ETL capabilities transform data integration patterns.

Understanding zero-ETL integration

Zero-ETL integration automates the movement of data between source systems and Redshift without requiring custom extract, transform, and load processes. Instead of building and managing data pipelines, you simply configure a connection between compatible source systems and Redshift, and AWS automatically handles the continuous replication and schema conversion behind the scenes.

The key principles behind zero-ETL include:

- **Automated replication**: Changes in source systems automatically propagate to Redshift without manual intervention or custom code.

- **Schema synchronization**: Source schema changes are detected and applied to destination tables.

- **Change data capture (CDC)**: Only modified data is transferred, minimizing latency and resource usage.

- **Transactional consistency**: Maintains transactional integrity between source and destination.

This approach fundamentally changes how data engineers think about the analytical data pipeline, shifting focus from pipeline development to data usage and governance.

Zero-ETL from Amazon Aurora to Redshift

One of the primary zero-ETL integration patterns connects Amazon Aurora (PostgreSQL or MySQL compatible) databases with Amazon Redshift, enabling transactional data to flow continuously into the data warehouse. The following diagram illustrates how Zero-ETL integration automatically synchronizes data between Aurora and Redshift without requiring custom ETL pipelines or code:

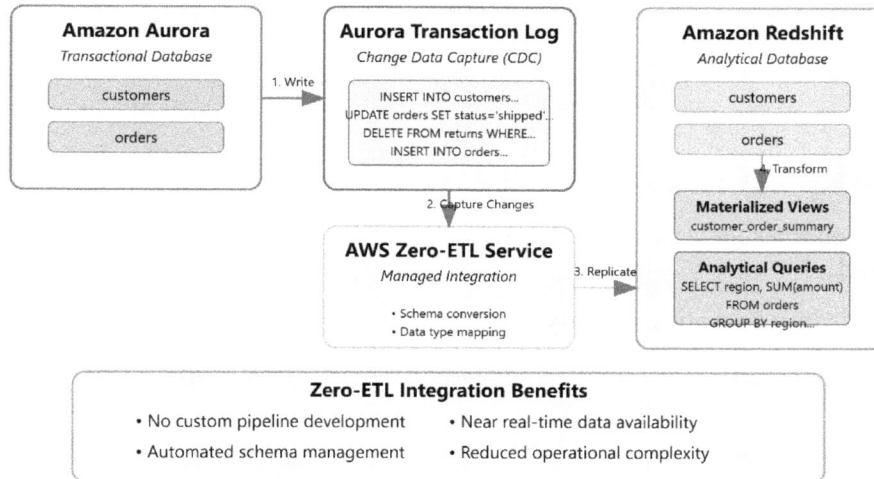

Figure 7.4: Aurora-Redshift zero-ETL automated integration flow

Setting up Aurora-to-Redshift integration

The setup process involves a few straightforward steps:

1. **Create or identify source Aurora cluster**: Ensure it is running a compatible engine version.
2. **Create or identify target Redshift cluster/namespace**: This will receive the replicated data.
3. **Configure integration through AWS console**:
   a. Navigate to the Amazon Redshift console.
   b. Select Zero-ETL integrations from the navigation pane.
   c. Click Create integration and follow the wizard.
4. **Monitor replication progress**: Track initial and ongoing replication through the console.

Behind the scenes, AWS creates and manages the necessary infrastructure to capture changes from the Aurora transaction logs, transfer this data securely, and apply changes to properly structured tables in Redshift.

Integration capabilities and limitations

Tables 7.3 and *7.4* summaries the capabilities and the limitations of zero-ETL integrations:

Capability	Description
Full table replication	Entire tables are replicated from source to destination
Incremental updates	After initial load, only changed data is transferred
Schema changes	Most schema alterations in source propagate automatically
Data type conversion	Automatic mapping between Aurora and Redshift data types
Transaction consistency	Data in Redshift represents a transactionally consistent view

Table 7.3: Aurora to Redshift integration capabilities

While zero-ETL replication offers powerful database integration, implementers must recognize its current technical constraints, from all-or-nothing table selection to limited transformation options. The following table illustrates integration limitations:

Limitation	Description
Table selection	Currently replicates all tables; selective replication coming soon
Schema modifications	Some complex schema changes require manual intervention
Custom transformations	Limited transformation capabilities beyond type conversion
Initial load time	Large databases require significant time for initial replication

Table 7.4: Aurora-Redshift integration limitations

Architectural patterns with zero-ETL

Zero-ETL integration enables several powerful architectural patterns that change how data platforms are designed and operated:

- **Pattern 1: Real-time operational analytics:**

  By connecting transactional databases directly to Redshift, organizations can analyse operational data in near real-time without building separate ETL processes:

```
1.  -- Query showing real-time sales analytics from replicated data
2.  SELECT
3.      EXTRACT(HOUR FROM transaction_timestamp) AS hour_of_day,
4.      store_id,
5.      SUM(sale_amount) AS hourly_sales,
6.      COUNT(*) AS transaction_count
7.  FROM aurora_sales_transactions -- Zero-ETL replicated table
8.  WHERE transaction_date = CURRENT_DATE
9.  GROUP BY 1, 2
10. ORDER BY 1, 2;
```

  This pattern enables operational dashboards that reflect current business conditions rather than yesterday's data, supporting more responsive decision making.

- **Pattern 2: Hybrid transactional or analytical processing:**

  Zero-ETL integration enables a hybrid OLTP/OLAP architecture where:
  o Transactional workloads run on appropriately sized Aurora/RDS databases.
  o Data automatically replicates to Redshift without custom pipelines.
  o Analytical workloads run on Redshift without impacting operational systems.
  o Both environments contain up-to-date data, but each is optimized for its purpose.

  This separation of concerns allows each system to be optimized for its specific workload characteristics while maintaining data consistency between environments.

- **Pattern 3: Progressive data transformation:**

  Rather than building complex transformation pipelines upfront, zero-ETL enables a pattern where:
  o Raw operational data is automatically replicated to Redshift.
  o Views or materialized views transform this data for specific analytical needs.
  o Additional transformations happen in Redshift rather than in ETL processes.

```
1.  -- Example of transformation view on top of raw replicated data
2.  CREATE MATERIALIZED VIEW customer_sales_summary AS
3.  SELECT
4.      c.customer_id,
5.      c.customer_name,
6.      c.segment,
7.      c.region,
8.      COUNT(DISTINCT s.order_id) AS order_count,
9.      SUM(s.amount) AS total_spent,
10.     AVG(s.amount) AS average_order_value,
11.     MAX(s.transaction_date) AS last_purchase_date
12. FROM rds_customers c -- Zero-ETL replicated table
13. JOIN rds_sales s -- Zero-ETL replicated table
14. ON c.customer_id = s.customer_id
15. GROUP BY 1, 2, 3, 4;
```

This approach simplifies the overall data architecture while providing flexibility to adapt transformations as business requirements evolve.

Performance considerations

While zero-ETL integration eliminates custom pipeline development, several performance factors should be considered:

- **Source database impact**: Change data capture processes place additional load on source databases, potentially requiring configuration tuning or capacity adjustments.

- **Initial load performance**: The initial replication can take significant time for large databases; plan accordingly and consider scheduling during low-usage periods.

- **Replication latency**: While much faster than traditional daily batch ETL, zero-ETL still has some latency (typically seconds to minutes) depending on transaction volume and network conditions.

- **Storage implications**: Replicating all tables requires additional storage in Redshift; monitor and manage this growth.

Monitoring zero-ETL integrations

AWS provides several tools for monitoring zero-ETL integrations:

```
1.  -- Query to check replication status
2.  SELECT
3.      integration_name,
4.      source_database_name,
5.      source_schema_name,
6.      source_table_name,
7.      destination_database_name,
8.      destination_schema_name,
9.      destination_table_name,
10.     status,
11.     last_cdc_timestamp,
12.     last_refresh_timestamp
13. FROM SVV_INTEGRATION_TABLE_STATE
14. ORDER BY source_schema_name, source_table_name;
```

Additionally, CloudWatch metrics provide insights into replication performance and health:

- **ReplicationLatency**: Time between a change in the source and its appearance in Redshift.
- **RecordsInserted, RecordsUpdated, RecordsDeleted**: Volume of change operations.
- **BytesTransferred**: Amount of data moved between source and destination.
- **ErrorCount**: Number of errors encountered during replication.

Setting up CloudWatch alarms on these metrics helps ensure prompt notification if replication experiences issues.

Use cases and decision factors

While zero-ETL offers significant advantages, it is not appropriate for every scenario. Consider these factors when evaluating its applicability:

Favourable factors for zero-ETL	Factors favouring traditional ETL
Need for near-real-time data	Complex transformations required
Direct replication of operational structures	Aggregation of multiple disparate sources
Limited transformation requirements	Significant data cleansing needed
Resources are constrained for ETL development	Selective replication required
Consistent source schemas	Frequent, complex schema changes

Table 7.5: Decision factors to decide between zero-ETL and traditional ETL

Zero-ETL integration represents a significant advancement in simplifying the data integration landscape, reducing the effort required to make operational data available for analytics while enabling near-real-time insights. By understanding its capabilities and limitations, you can effectively incorporate this technology into your data architecture and reduce the complexity of your data pipelines.

Automation and operations

Effective operation of a Redshift data warehouse requires implementing robust automated processes for scaling, maintenance, monitoring, and security. This section explores key operational practices to ensure consistent performance, reliability, and cost efficiency.

Cluster scaling and resizing

Redshift provides several mechanisms for adapting capacity to changing requirements:

Scaling	When to use	Characteristics	Example command
Elastic resize	For quick scaling within the same node type	<ul><li>Completes in minutes (10 to 30)</li><li>Minimal query disruption</li><li>Same node type</li><li>Limited to doubling/halving nodes</li><li>Read queries continue</li></ul>	`ALTER CLUSTER mycluster` `RESIZE NODES 4 ELASTIC;`
Classic resize	For changing node types or substantial resizing	<ul><li>Takes hours or days</li><li>Complete flexibility</li><li>Read-only during migration</li><li>Full data redistribution</li><li>Can change node types</li></ul>	`ALTER CLUSTER mycluster` `RESIZE NODES 4 TYPE ra3.4xlarge;`

Scaling	When to use	Characteristics	Example command
Concurrency scaling	For unpredictable query concurrency peaks	• Automatic operation • Pay for what you use • Transparent to users • Ideal for dashboards • Queue-specific enablement	`ALTER WLM_QUEUE_ CONFIG SET concurrency_scaling = 'auto'` `FOR queue = 'dashboard_ queries';`
Redshift Serverless	For fully managed elastic capacity	• No cluster management • Automatic scaling • Pay for RPU-seconds used • Simpler operations • Lower administrative overhead	Configure through AWS Console or with AWS CLI

Table 7.6: Cluster scaling and resizing mechanism

Automated maintenance

Regular maintenance is essential for optimal performance. The following table outlines key maintenance tasks and implementation approaches:

Maintenance	Purpose	Implementation options	Key considerations
VACUUM	Reclaim space and restore sort order	• **Automatic:** `ALTER DATABASE your_db SET auto_vacuum = true;` • **Scheduled:** Lambda with EventBridge • **Selective:** SQL queries targeting specific tables	• Run after bulk deletes • Prioritize large tables • Monitor with SVV_VACUUM_PROGRESS • Consider SORT ONLY for faster operation
ANALYZE	Update table statistics for query optimization	• **Automatic:** Triggered on significant changes • **Scheduled:** EventBridge with Lambda • **Selective:** `ANALYZE table_name(column1, column2);`	• Monitor with svv_table_info.stats_off • Prioritize tables with stats_off > 20 • Run after significant data changes
Table optimization	Maintain optimal sort and distribution	• **Automatic table optimization:** `ALTER TABLE sales_fact ALTER SORTKEY AUTO; ` • **Manual:** Based on query patterns	• Enable automatic optimization • Review Advisor recommendations • Apply recommendations from query monitoring

Table 7.7: Automated maintenance approaches

Monitoring framework

A comprehensive monitoring strategy enables proactive management of your Redshift environment:

Monitoring	Key metrics	Alert thresholds	Visualization tool
Cluster performance	• CPUUtilization • ReadIOPS, WriteIOPS • ReadLatency, WriteLatency	• CPU > 75% sustained • Latency > 10ms sustained • IOPS trend changes	CloudWatch dashboards
Storage	• PercentageDiskSpaceUsed • SnapshotStorageUsed	• Disk usage > 80% • Rapid growth trends	CloudWatch and cost explorer
Queries	• WLMQueueLength • QueryDuration • QueryRuntimeBreakdown	• Queue length consistently > 0 • Queries exceeding baselines	CloudWatch and Redshift console
Query-level metrics	• Long-running queries • Memory spills • Table scans	• Context-dependent	stl_query, svl_query_summary, custom dashboards

Table 7.8: Cluster monitoring frameworks and strategies

Query performance can be monitored with the following SQL:

```
1.  -- Find longest running queries
2.  SELECT
3.      q.query,
4.      q.elapsed/1000000 as elapsed_sec,
5.      SUBSTRING(q.querytxt, 1, 100) AS query_text
6.  FROM stl_query q
7.  WHERE q.starttime > DATEADD(day, -7, CURRENT_DATE)
8.  ORDER BY elapsed_sec DESC
9.  LIMIT 10;
```

Backup and disaster recovery

Data protection strategies balance recovery capabilities with operational overhead:

Protection	Recovery capabilities	Implementation	Best practices

Automated snapshots	• Point-in-time recovery
	• Complete cluster recovery
	• New cluster creation
		`aws redshift modify-cluster-snapshot-schedule`
		`--cluster-identifier mycluster`
		`--schedule-identifier daily-schedule`
			• Retain 3 to 35 day history
			• Test recovery quarterly
			• Document restoration procedures

Manual snapshots	• Long-term retention
	• Pre-change protection
	• Cross-account copying
		`aws redshift create-cluster-snapshot`
		`--cluster-identifier mycluster`
		`--snapshot-identifier manual-snap-20230315`
			• Create before major changes
			• Tag with purpose/owner
			• Establish retention policies

Protection	Recovery capabilities	Implementation	Best practices

Cross-region copy	• Regional disaster recovery
	• Geographic redundancy
	• Compliance requirements
		`aws redshift enable-snapshot-copy`
		`--cluster-identifier mycluster`
		`--destination-region us-west-2`
		`--retention-period 7`
			• Choose an appropriate region
			• Consider latency
			• Document cross-region procedures

Table 7.9: Backup and restore strategies

Security implementation

Security practices must address multiple protection layers:

Security area	Implementation approach	Example	Key considerations

Encryption	• At-rest encryption
	• In-transit encryption
	• KMS integration
		`aws redshift create-cluster`
		`--cluster-identifier mycluster`
		`--encrypted`
		`--kms-key-id arn:aws:kms:region:id:key/id`
			• Use customer-managed keys
			• Rotate keys periodically
			• Document key management

Authentication	• Database users
	• IAM integration
	• Identity provider federation
		`CREATE USER analyst_user PASSWORD '***';`
		
		`ALTER GROUP data_analysts ADD USER analyst_user;`
			• Use strong password policies
			• Implement least privilege
			• Consider IAM for enterprise

Authorization	• Schema-level permissions
	• Role-based access
	• Row-level security
		`CREATE RLS POLICY customer_data_access`
		
		`USING (current_user = 'admin' OR region_id IN (SELECT region FROM user_permissions`
		
		`WHERE username = current_user));`
			• Grant minimum required access
			• Use groups for management
			• Implement row-level security

Audit logging	• Connection logging • User activity tracking • Query history	`aws redshift modify-cluster` `--cluster-identifier mycluster` `--logging-properties '{"EnableLogging": true, "S3KeyPrefix": "logs"}'`	• Retain logs appropriately • Set up log analysis • Create anomaly alerts

Table 7.10: Multilayer security practices

Cost optimization strategies

Balance performance and cost with these optimization approaches:

Strategy	Implementation	Benefits	Considerations

Workload management	Configure WLM with prioritized queues:
	
	`CREATE WORKLOAD QUEUE ad_hoc_queries WITH (query_timeout = 3600000,`
	
	`query_memory_percent = 20);`
		• Controls resource allocation
		• Prioritizes critical workloads
		• Prevents runaway queries
			• Requires workload analysis
			• Monitor queue waits
			• Adjust based on usage patterns

Scheduled scaling	Lambda function triggered by EventBridge to resize the cluster on schedule	• Aligns capacity with demand • Reduces off-hours costs • Automated operation	• Plan for resize duration • Set appropriate triggers • Test thoroughly
Storage management	• Lifecycle policies • Aggregation of historical data • Cold data archiving	• Reduces active storage costs • Maintains query performance • Balances detail and history	• Define data retention policies • Consider query patterns • Validate archived data access
Reserved instances	Reserve capacity appropriate to baseline usage	• Up to 75% cost reduction • Predictable pricing • Budget certainty	• Analyse usage patterns • Use for stable capacity • Mix with on-demand

Table 7.11: Cost optimization strategies

By implementing these automation and operational practices, you transform your Redshift environment into a resilient, scalable, and cost-effective enterprise data warehouse that requires minimal manual intervention while delivering consistent performance.

Integration with data lake

Modern analytics environments often combine the performance of data warehouses with the flexibility and scale of data lakes. Amazon Redshift offers several integration capabilities that create a unified analytics platform across these environments, enabling organizations to query and analyse data regardless of where it resides.

Redshift Spectrum for querying S3 data

Redshift Spectrum extends query capabilities beyond the data warehouse to files stored in S3, eliminating the need to load data before analysing it. This capability fundamentally changes how organizations think about data architecture, allowing a clear separation between storage and compute while maintaining a unified query experience.

The following diagram illustrates the architectural relationship between Redshift, Redshift Spectrum, AWS Glue Data Catalog, and S3 for unified data lake querying:

Redshift Spectrum Architecture

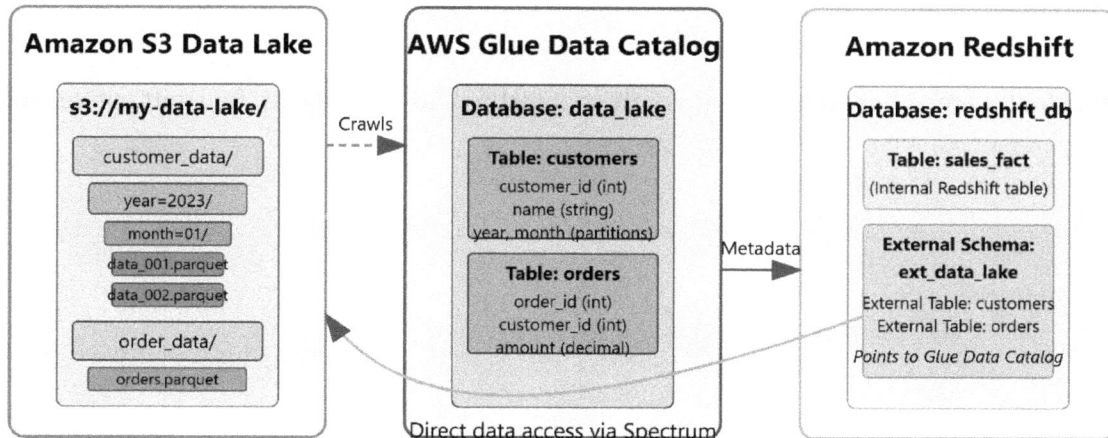

Figure 7.5: *Redshift Spectrum data lake integration architecture*

To implement Redshift Spectrum, you first define external tables that point to S3 data:

```
1.  -- Create external schema referencing AWS Glue Data Catalog and S3 data lake
2.  -- This schema acts as the bridge between Redshift and external S3 data
3.  CREATE EXTERNAL SCHEMA ext_data_lake
4.  FROM DATA CATALOG
        -- Uses AWS Glue Data Catalog
5.  DATABASE 'data_lake'
        -- Database name in Glue Catalog
6.  IAM_ROLE 'arn:aws:iam::account-id:role/RedshiftSpectrumRole'
        -- Role with S3 and Glue permissions
7.  CREATE EXTERNAL DATABASE IF NOT EXISTS;
        -- Creates database in Glue if needed
8.
9.  -- Create external table pointing to Parquet files in S3 data lake
10. -- This table definition maps S3 data to a queryable SQL structure
11. CREATE EXTERNAL TABLE ext_data_lake.customer_activity (
12.     customer_id INTEGER,                -- Maps to corresponding column in Parquet files
13.     activity_date DATE,                 -- Will be converted from Parquet date format
14.     activity_type VARCHAR(50),          -- Character data in Parquet files
15.     activity_value DOUBLE PRECISION     -- Floating-point numeric values in Parquet
16. )
17. PARTITIONED BY (year INTEGER, month INTEGER)
        -- Partition columns for filtering
18. ROW FORMAT SERDE 'org.apache.hadoop.hive.ql.io.parquet.serde.
    ParquetHiveSerDe'   -- Parquet serializer/deserializer
19. STORED AS PARQUET
        -- Files stored in Parquet format
20. LOCATION 's3://my-data-lake/customer_activity/';
        -- Base S3 path for all data files
21.
```

```
22. -- Add partition metadata to enable partition pruning
23. -- This helps Spectrum skip irrelevant S3 files during queries
24. ALTER TABLE ext_data_lake.customer_activity ADD PARTITION (year=2023, month=1)
25. LOCATION 's3://my-data-lake/customer_activity/year=2023/
    month=1'; -- Specific S3 path for this partition
```

Once external tables are defined, you can query them directly or join them with Redshift native tables:

```
1.  -- Join data warehouse and data lake data in a single query
2.  -- This query demonstrates seamless integration between environments
3.  SELECT
4.      c.customer_name,                              -- From Redshift native table
5.      c.customer_segment,                           -- From Redshift native table
6.      SUM(ca.activity_value) AS total_activity_value -- From S3 data lake via Spectrum
7.  FROM
8.      redshift_
    db.customers c                                    -- Native Redshift table (fast access)
9.  JOIN
10.     ext_data_lake.customer_activity ca            -- External S3 table (via Spectrum)
11. ON
12.     c.customer_id = ca.customer_id                -- Join between warehouse and lake
13. WHERE
14.     ca.
    year = 2023                                       -- Partition pruning (pushdown to S3)
15. GROUP BY
16.     c.customer_name, c.customer_segment
17. ORDER BY
18.     total_activity_value DESC
19. LIMIT 100;
```

This integration pattern delivers several key advantages. First, it allows querying massive datasets without loading them into Redshift, ideal for historical data, semi-structured data, or information accessed infrequently. Second, it enables a clear data lifecycle where frequently accessed data can reside in Redshift while less frequently accessed data remains in the data lake. Finally, it provides query flexibility while maintaining performance through features like partition pruning and predicate pushdown.

Federated queries to other data sources

Redshift federated query capability extends analytics beyond the data warehouse and data lake to include operational databases. This feature allows direct queries against Amazon RDS and Aurora databases without moving or copying data:

```
1.  -- Create external schema for federated queries to operational PostgreSQL database
2.  -- This schema enables Redshift to query RDS/Aurora directly
3.  CREATE EXTERNAL SCHEMA ext_postgres
4.  FROM POSTGRES                                     -- Specifies PostgreSQL source
5.  DATABASE 'operational_db'                         -- Database name in RDS/Aurora
6.  SCHEMA 'public'
    -- Schema within source database
7.  URI 'postgres-instance-endpoint:5432'
    -- RDS/Aurora endpoint with port
8.  IAM_ROLE 'arn:aws:iam::account-id:role/
```

```
        RedshiftFederationRole'   -- Role with permission to query RDS
9.  SECRET_ARN 'arn:aws:secretsmanager:region:account-id:secret:federation-
        credentials';   -- Database credentials
10.
11. -- Query recent orders directly from operational database
12. -- This query runs against live operational data without ETL
13. SELECT
14.     order_id,                           -- Live operational data
15.     customer_id,                        -- No data movement required
16.     order_date,                         -- Data remains in source system
17.     status
18. FROM
19.     ext_postgres.orders
        -- References RDS/Aurora table directly
20. WHERE
21.     order_date >= CURRENT_DATE - INTERVAL '7 days';
        -- Predicate pushdown to source database
```

Federated queries enable several powerful use cases, including real-time analytics against operational data without ETL, enriching warehouse data with operational context, and creating a unified query layer across the organization's data assets. This capability is particularly valuable when analysis requires current operational data that has not yet been loaded into the data warehouse.

Lakehouse architecture patterns

The integration capabilities between Redshift and S3 enable a lakehouse architecture that combines the best aspects of data warehouses (performance, consistency, transactions) with the best aspects of data lakes (flexibility, scale, diversity). Several key patterns emerge in successful implementations:

The first pattern involves data tiering, where data moves through distinct stages based on business value, access frequency, and performance requirements. Hot data with frequent access remains in Redshift for maximum performance, while warm or cold data migrates to the data lake for cost-effective storage while remaining queryable through Spectrum.

The second pattern leverages materialized views to accelerate queries across both environments:

```
1.  -- Create materialized view combining warehouse and lake data
2.  -- This powerful pattern pre-computes results across multiple data sources
3.  CREATE MATERIALIZED VIEW customer_360 AS
4.  SELECT
5.      c.customer_id,                          -- From Redshift native table
6.      c.customer_name,                        -- From Redshift native table
7.      c.email,                                -- From Redshift native table
8.      c.signup_date,                          -- From Redshift native table
9.      SUM(s.sale_amount) AS total_purchases,  -- Aggregated from Redshift table
10.     COUNT(DISTINCT s.order_id) AS order_count,   -- Aggregated from Redshift table
11.     MAX(s.sale_date) AS last_purchase_date,  -- Aggregated from Redshift table
12.     AVG(ca.activity_value) AS avg_site_activity   -- Aggregated from S3 data lake
13. FROM
14.     redshift_
    db.customers c                          -- Native Redshift table (primary data)
15. LEFT JOIN
```

```
16.     redshift_db.sales s ON c.customer_id = s.customer_
   id  -- Join to native Redshift table
17. LEFT JOIN
18.     ext_data_lake.customer_activity ca ON c.customer_id = ca.customer_
   id  -- Join to external S3 data
19. GROUP BY
20.     c.customer_id, c.customer_name, c.email, c.signup_date;
```

A third pattern involves using Redshift ML to train machine learning models using data from both environments, seamlessly integrating predictive capabilities with analytical processes.

Data movement strategies

Effectively managing data movement between data warehouse and data lake requires clear strategies. The **UNLOAD** command efficiently moves data from Redshift to S3:

```
1. -- Unload historical data from Redshift to data lake in Parquet format
2. -- This offloads cold data to S3 while keeping it queryable via Spectrum
3. UNLOAD ('SELECT * FROM sales WHERE sale_date < DATEADD(month, -12, CURRENT_DATE)')
4. TO 's3://my-data-lake/sales/archived/'               -- Destination S3 path
5. IAM_ROLE 'arn:aws:iam::account-id:role/RedshiftS3Role'  -- Role with S3 write permis-
   sions
6. FORMAT PARQUET                                       -- Optimized columnar for-
   mat for analytics
7. PARTITIONED BY (sale_year, sale_month)              -- Creates partition fold-
   ers in S3
8. ALLOWOVERWRITE                                      -- Allows rerunning if needed
9. PARALLEL ON;                                        -- Uses multiple slic-
   es for performance
```

Conversely, the **COPY** command loads data from S3 into Redshift when higher performance is needed:

```
1. -- Load recent data from data lake into Redshift for faster analytics
2. -- This brings frequently accessed data into Redshift for performance
3. COPY sales_current
4. FROM 's3://my-data-lake/sales/recent/'              -- Source S3 path
5. IAM_ROLE 'arn:aws:iam::account-id:role/RedshiftS3Role'  -- Role with S3 read permis-
   sions
6. FORMAT PARQUET                                      -- Reading from Parquet files
7. COMPUPDATE OFF                                      -- Skip compression analy-
   sis for speed
8. STATUPDATE ON                                       -- Update statistics af-
   ter load
9. MAXERROR 10;                                        -- Continue if < 10 er-
   rors occur-- Uses multiple slices for performance
```

The most effective lakehouse architectures establish automated data movement based on clearly defined lifecycle policies. These policies typically consider factors like data age, access frequency, and business criticality to determine where data should reside at each stage of its lifecycle.

Integration best practices

Several best practices ensure successful Redshift and data lake integration. First, optimize file formats and partitioning in S3, with columnar formats like Parquet or ORC generally providing the best performance.

Second, align partitioning strategies with query patterns to enable partition pruning. Third, use appropriate compression to reduce I/O and transfer costs. Fourth, maintain statistics on external tables to help the query optimizer make good decisions. Finally, optimize table design with judicious use of sorting and distribution keys for frequently joined data.

Through thoughtful integration between Redshift and data lake environments, organizations can build a unified analytics platform that balances performance, cost, and flexibility while enabling a consistent query experience across all their data assets.

Hands-on: Data warehouse with Redshift

This hands-on workshop guides you through the complete process of building, configuring, and using an Amazon Redshift cluster for enterprise data warehousing. The accompanying Jupyter Notebook on GitHub provides a step-by-step implementation that reinforces the core concepts covered in this chapter.

Workshop overview

The workshop is structured to provide practical experience across the full lifecycle of a data warehouse implementation:

- **Environment setup**: Configure AWS resources and dependencies required for the workshop.
- **Resource creation**: Establish IAM roles, S3 buckets, and the Redshift cluster.
- **Data modelling and loading**: Create optimized tables and load sample e-commerce data.
- **Performance optimization**: Implement materialized views and analyze query performance.
- **Query execution**: Run analytical queries that demonstrate Redshift's capabilities.
- **Execution analysis**: Examine query plans to understand performance characteristics.
- **Resource cleanup**: Properly decommission all created resources.

Sample dataset

The workshop uses a simulated e-commerce dataset that includes:

- Customer dimension data (100 records).
- Product dimension data (50 records).
- Sales transaction data (1,000 records).

This dataset demonstrates common data warehouse patterns with fact and dimension tables, creating realistic analytical scenarios that showcase Redshift's capabilities for handling star schema designs efficiently.

Implementation highlights

The notebook demonstrates several important Redshift features:

- Table distribution using both ALL and KEY methods to optimize join performance.
- Compound sort keys to enhance time-series query efficiency.
- Materialized views for aggregation acceleration.
- Query execution plan analysis to understand performance characteristics.
- Proper IAM role configuration for secure data access.

Getting started

To begin the workshop, clone the GitHub repository containing the Jupyter Notebook and follow the instructions in the Prerequisites section. The notebook is designed to be executed in sequence, with each cell building upon previous steps. For the best experience, ensure you have AWS credentials with appropriate permissions to create and manage Redshift resources.

The complete hands-on content provides approximately two hours of guided implementation experience, reinforcing the theoretical concepts covered throughout this chapter with practical application.

Conclusion

Throughout this chapter, we have explored the fundamental principles and practical implementations of data warehouse engineering with Amazon Redshift. From understanding the MPP architecture that powers analytical performance to designing optimized table structures, implementing query optimization techniques, and integrating with data lakes, we have covered the essential components needed to build and operate an enterprise-grade data warehouse. We have seen how advancements like zero-ETL integration are transforming data pipelines and simplifying architectures, while operational automation ensures consistent performance and reliability. As organizations continue to evolve their data strategies, these foundational data warehouse capabilities provide a crucial performance layer within broader analytical ecosystems.

In the next chapter, we will expand our perspective to examine modern data architecture patterns that complement and extend traditional data warehousing approaches. We will explore emerging paradigms like data mesh that reimagine organizational data ownership, investigate transactional data lakes that blur the lines between operational and analytical systems, and compare Lambda and Kappa architectures for stream and batch processing integration. These architectural patterns, combined with polyglot persistence strategies and change data capture mechanisms, represent the next evolution in enterprise data platforms.

Join our Discord space

Join our Discord workspace for latest updates, offers, tech happenings around the world, new releases, and sessions with the authors:

https://discord.bpbonline.com

CHAPTER 8
Modern Data Architecture Patterns

Introduction

Traditional data architectures evolved in an era where data volumes were moderate, sources were limited, and analytical requirements were relatively stable. Such architectures typically featured centralized data warehouses with tightly coupled ingestion, storage, and consumption layers, a model that served organizations well for decades. However, the exponential growth in data volume, variety, and velocity has revealed fundamental limitations in these monolithic approaches. Modern enterprises now manage petabytes of diverse data from thousands of sources while supporting dynamic analytical needs across hundreds of use cases. This explosion in scale and complexity has driven the emergence of new architectural patterns that reimagine how data platforms are designed, operated, and governed.

The business imperative for adopting modern data architectures stems from the need for greater organizational agility, technological flexibility, and operational efficiency. Research from *McKinsey* indicates that organizations with modern, decentralized data architectures respond to market changes 60% faster than those with traditional centralized designs. These architectures provide critical capabilities for leveraging data as a strategic asset. They enable rapid innovation through domain-specific data products, reduce time-to-insight through streamlined pipelines, and manage complexity through clear separation of concerns. For organizations seeking competitive advantage from their data assets, modern architectural patterns offer a foundation for sustainable differentiation.

Within the AWS ecosystem, these patterns are realized through combinations of purpose-built services that enable specialized implementations while maintaining integration across the data landscape. Data mesh architectures leverage services like Lake Formation and **identity and access management (IAM)** for decentralized governance, while transactional data lakes combine S3 with technologies like Apache Iceberg and Apache Hudi. Lambda architecture utilizes both batch and streaming services, such as Glue and Kinesis, while polyglot persistence strategies integrate purpose-built databases like DynamoDB, Neptune, and Timestream. Rather than presenting a one-size-fits-all solution, AWS provides the building blocks that organizations can assemble to implement the patterns best suited to their specific needs.

Structure

This chapter covers the following topics:

- Data mesh implementation

- Transactional data lakes
- Lambda and Kappa architectures
- Polyglot persistence strategies
- Change data capture patterns
- Hands-on: Implementing a data mesh

Objectives

This chapter aims to provide a comprehensive understanding of emerging data architecture patterns that address the scale, complexity, and dynamism of modern data landscapes. You will learn how data mesh reimagines organizational structures and governance models to enable domain-oriented data ownership, how transactional data lakes unify analytical and operational capabilities, and how Lambda and Kappa architectures integrate batch and stream processing. The chapter also explores polyglot persistence strategies that leverage specialized storage technologies and change data capture mechanisms that enable real-time data synchronization. Through practical implementation examples, you will understand how these patterns are realized on AWS and develop the ability to assess which patterns best address your organization's specific requirements. These capabilities will enable you to design data platforms that balance flexibility, scalability, and governance while adapting to evolving business needs.

Data mesh implementation

Data mesh represents a paradigm shift from centralized, monolithic data architectures toward a distributed, domain-oriented approach that fundamentally changes how organization's structure, manage, and govern their data assets. Unlike previous architectural evolutions that primarily addressed technical concerns, data mesh reconceptualizes the organizational and operational aspects of data management, treating data as a product managed by domain experts rather than as an infrastructure concern managed by centralized teams. This shift addresses a critical limitation of traditional approaches: the disconnect between domain knowledge and data management that often results in data assets that do not effectively serve business needs.

The four fundamental principles of data mesh provide a framework for implementation:

- **Domain ownership**: Domain teams own and manage the data they produce, taking responsibility for quality, documentation, and accessibility.

- **Data as a product**: Each data set is treated as a product with clear documentation, quality guarantees, and access patterns designed for consumers.

- **Self-serve infrastructure**: A common platform provides the tools and capabilities that domain teams need to create and manage their data products.

- **Federated governance**: Standards, policies, and practices ensure interoperability and compliance across distributed domain data products.

When properly implemented, these principles create a virtuous cycle where domain expertise drives higher-quality data products, which in turn enable better business outcomes. A 2023 *Gartner* survey of organizations implementing data mesh found that 78% reported improved time-to-market for new data-driven capabilities, with median delivery times decreasing from 6-8 months to 4-6 weeks.

The following figure shows data mesh implementation on AWS showing domain data products, self-serve platforms, and federated governance:

Data Mesh Architecture on AWS

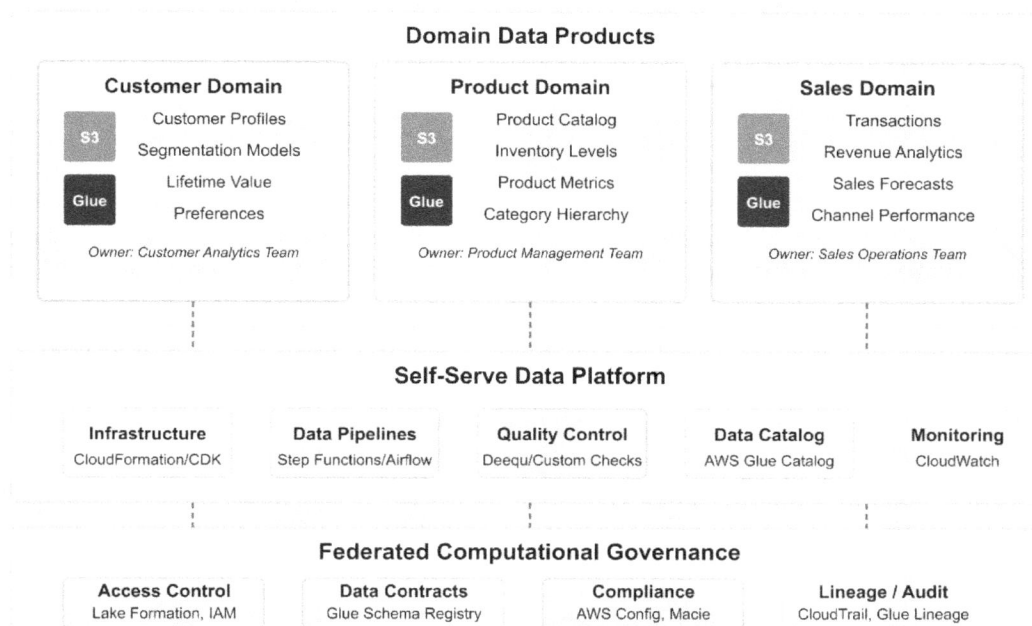

Domain Data Products

Customer Domain
S3 — Customer Profiles
Segmentation Models
Glue — Lifetime Value
Preferences
Owner: Customer Analytics Team

Product Domain
S3 — Product Catalog
Inventory Levels
Glue — Product Metrics
Category Hierarchy
Owner: Product Management Team

Sales Domain
S3 — Transactions
Revenue Analytics
Glue — Sales Forecasts
Channel Performance
Owner: Sales Operations Team

Self-Serve Data Platform

Infrastructure	Data Pipelines	Quality Control	Data Catalog	Monitoring
CloudFormation/CDK	Step Functions/Airflow	Deequ/Custom Checks	AWS Glue Catalog	CloudWatch

Federated Computational Governance

Access Control	Data Contracts	Compliance	Lineage / Audit
Lake Formation, IAM	Glue Schema Registry	AWS Config, Macie	CloudTrail, Glue Lineage

Figure 8.1: Data mesh implementation on AWS

Domain data products

The core unit in a data mesh architecture is the domain data product. It is a cohesive collection of data assets owned by a specific business domain and designed to meet the needs of data consumers. Unlike traditional dataset definitions that focus primarily on storage formats or schemas, data products encompass comprehensive information about the data's business context, quality characteristics, update frequency, and access patterns.

On AWS, domain data products typically integrate S3 storage with metadata management through AWS Glue Data Catalogue. What distinguishes these implementations from conventional data lake tables is the additional metadata that transforms them from simple datasets to managed products as you can see in the following code:

```
1.  -- Example of registering a domain data product in AWS Glue Data Catalog
2.  CREATE DATABASE customer_domain_db
3.  COMMENT 'Customer domain data products for marketing and analytics';
4.
5.  CREATE EXTERNAL TABLE customer_domain_db.customer_profiles (
6.      customer_id STRING,
7.      segment STRING,
8.      lifetime_value DECIMAL(12,2),
9.      acquisition_date DATE,
10.     last_purchase_date DATE
11. )
12. COMMENT 'Customer profile data owned by the Customer Domain team'
13. PARTITIONED BY (region STRING, year STRING, month STRING)
14. STORED AS PARQUET
15. LOCATION 's3://customer-domain-data-products/profiles/'
```

```
16. TBLPROPERTIES (
17.   'owner' = 'customer_domain_team',
18.   'data_product_version' = 'v2.3',
19.   'quality.completeness' = '99.5%',
20.   'data_update_frequency' = 'daily',
21.   'documentation_url' = 'https://wiki.example.com/customer_profiles'
22. );
```

This SQL illustrates how metadata transforms a simple dataset into a managed product with clear ownership, versioning, quality metrics, and documentation. The same technical foundation serves a fundamentally different organizational purpose: instead of IT-managed datasets, these become domain-owned products with clear accountability and service commitments.

Successful domain data products typically exhibit several key characteristics that differentiate them from traditional datasets. First, they prioritize usability through comprehensive documentation and consistent schemas that make the data immediately understandable to potential consumers. Second, they establish clear quality expectations and measure performance against those metrics, treating data quality as a product feature rather than an afterthought. Third, they provide well-defined access patterns optimized for common usage scenarios, reducing the implementation burden on consumers. Finally, they evolve based on consumer feedback, with domain teams actively soliciting and incorporating input to improve subsequent versions.

Domain data product lifecycle

Understanding how domain data products evolve throughout their lifecycle is essential for successful data mesh implementation. Rather than static entities, data products are living assets that mature and transform in response to business needs and consumer feedback. Let us explore each phase of this lifecycle in detail.

Discovery and definition phase

The journey of a data product begins with discovery, where domain teams identify specific data needs within their business context. During this critical foundation-setting phase, teams engage with stakeholders across the organization to understand use cases, establish requirements, and define success metrics. Domain experts collaborate with potential consumers to articulate the business problems the data product will solve, ensuring it delivers genuine value rather than merely serving as a technical exercise. The team documents initial metadata requirements, quality expectations, and service level objectives that will guide development. This phase culminates in a clear charter for the data product that defines its scope, purpose, and expected business impact.

Development phase

As the data product enters development, domain teams focus on building the technical foundation that will support their defined requirements. Engineers implement the necessary data pipelines, design schemas that balance flexibility with consistency, and establish quality validation mechanisms to ensure the product meets its defined standards. This phase involves continuous collaboration with potential consumers, with early versions shared for feedback to validate that the emerging product will meet analytical needs. Development is not merely a technical process—it involves parallel creation and refinement of documentation, sample queries, and comprehensive metadata that will make the product discoverable and usable. The team conducts thorough quality assessments, comparing integrated data against source systems to ensure accuracy before proceeding to publication.

Publication phase

Publication transforms the data product from an internal domain asset to an organizational resource. During this phase, the product is formally registered in the data catalogue with comprehensive metadata that describes its contents, update frequency, quality guarantees, and appropriate use cases. The domain team implements access controls based on organizational governance policies, ensuring appropriate data protection while enabling authorized use. They announce the product's availability through organizational channels, often conducting demonstration sessions to help potential consumers understand its capabilities and access patterns. This phase establishes the data product's official presence in the organization's data ecosystem, making it discoverable and accessible to authorized users across domains.

Operational phase

Once published, the data product enters its operational phase—a continuous cycle of monitoring, feedback collection, and iterative improvement. The domain team implements regular quality checks that monitor the product against its defined metrics, with alerts for any anomalies or degradation. They track usage patterns to understand which aspects of the product provide the most value and identify opportunities for enhancement. Regular engagement with consumers provides qualitative feedback that complements quantitative metrics. During this phase, the team makes incremental improvements to address emerging needs and quality issues, careful to maintain backward compatibility for existing consumers. This ongoing stewardship distinguishes the data mesh approach from traditional methods where datasets often stagnate after initial creation.

Evolution phase

As business requirements change and the data product matures, it enters an evolution phase where more substantial enhancements are implemented. Based on accumulated consumer feedback and evolving business needs, the domain team may add new attributes, implement additional derived views, or create specialized access patterns to support emerging use cases. They might optimize storage formats or partitioning strategies to improve performance for common query patterns. Throughout this evolution, careful versioning ensures that existing consumers aren't disrupted by changes. Major enhancements are often released as new versions with well-documented migration paths, allowing consumers to transition at their own pace. This phase may occur multiple times throughout a data product's life, representing significant leaps in its capabilities and value.

Retirement phase

Eventually, some data products reach the end of their useful life as business needs change or superior alternatives emerge. The retirement phase involves thoughtful sunsetting of the product to minimize disruption to consumers. The domain team communicates deprecation plans well in advance, providing clear timelines and supporting documentation. They work with consumers to establish transition paths to alternative data products or newer versions. When the retirement date arrives, the product is archived according to organizational data retention policies, with essential metadata preserved to maintain institutional knowledge. Even in retirement, proper documentation ensures that the organization retains understanding of this data and its historical context, which may prove valuable for future initiatives.

Self-serve data infrastructure

A critical enabler of the data mesh approach is a self-serve infrastructure platform that provides domain teams with the capabilities they need to create, manage, and share their data products without requiring specialized data engineering expertise. This platform abstracts away the complexity of underlying infrastructure while enforcing organizational standards and best practices.

The most successful self-serve platforms strike a careful balance between standardization and flexibility. They provide opinionated defaults that ensure consistency and compliance while allowing domain-specific customization where needed. For instance, AWS CloudFormation or **Cloud Development Kit (CDK)** templates can establish standardized S3 bucket configurations that enforce encryption, access control, and lifecycle policies, while still allowing domains to customize aspects relevant to their specific data characteristics.

The evolution of self-serve infrastructure platforms typically follows a predictable maturity curve. Early implementations focus on infrastructure provisioning, providing templates for creating storage, databases, and access controls. As the platform matures, it expands to include data pipeline orchestration, quality monitoring, and discovery mechanisms. Advanced implementations eventually incorporate automated governance enforcement, cross-domain integration capabilities, and operational monitoring. Organizations should recognize this evolutionary path and plan for incremental development rather than attempting to build a complete platform from the outset.

The transition from centralized to self-serve infrastructure represents a fundamental shift in how data capabilities are provisioned and managed within organizations. In the traditional centralized model, a specialized data engineering team owns and operates all data infrastructure, resulting in lengthy provisioning cycles where domain teams submit requests, wait for approvals, and then queue for implementation—often taking weeks to acquire needed resources. While this approach ensures high standardization, it creates significant bottlenecks as the organization scales, with the central team becoming overwhelmed by mounting requests across diverse business domains. In contrast, self-serve infrastructure empowers domain teams to provision their own resources through standardized, automated templates that embed governance controls and best practices. This distributed approach dramatically reduces provisioning time from weeks to hours, eliminates the central bottleneck, and enables each domain to customize within established guardrails to meet their specific needs. Rather than concentrating deep infrastructure expertise in a single team, self-serve models distribute basic infrastructure knowledge across domains while maintaining a platform team that focuses on improving the self-serve capabilities themselves. The result is an architecture that scales naturally with organizational growth, provides clearer cost attribution to promote efficiency, and accelerates innovation by removing approval gates while still maintaining consistent governance through code rather than processes.

Federated computational governance

Traditional centralized governance models struggle to scale in complex, distributed environments where thousands of datasets are managed by dozens of teams. Data mesh introduces federated computational governance—a model where governance policies are expressed as code and automatically enforced across distributed data products. This approach maintains organizational standards while accommodating domain-specific requirements.

On AWS, federated governance leverages services like Lake Formation for access control, CloudWatch for monitoring, and AWS Config for compliance. The key innovation in this approach is the shift from manually enforced policies to computational governance, where rules are codified and automatically applied. Lake Formation's tag-based access control provides a particularly powerful mechanism for implementing this pattern, as demonstrated by Terraform code:

```
1.  # Example of tag-based governance in Lake Formation
2.  resource "aws_lakeformation_resource_lf_tags" "data_domain" {
3.    catalog_id = data.aws_caller_identity.current.account_id
4.
5.    lf_tag {
6.      key   = «data_domain"
7.      values = [«customer», «product», «finance», «marketing», «operations»]
8.    }
9.  }
10.
11. # Define permissions based on tags rather than specific resources
12. resource "aws_lakeformation_permissions" "marketing_team_access" {
13.   principal  = «arn:aws:iam::${data.aws_caller_identity.current.account_id}:role/
      marketing-analysts»
14.   permissions = [«SELECT»]
```

```
15.
16.    lf_tag_policy {
17.      resource_type = «TABLE»
18.
19.      expression {
20.        key     = «data_domain"
21.        values = [«customer», «marketing»]
22.      }
23.    }
24. }
```

This configuration demonstrates how governance in a data mesh environment shifts from managing permissions on individual data assets to policy-based governance that can scale across thousands of datasets from different domains. This abstraction enables consistent policy enforcement even as the data landscape evolves.

The tension between centralized control and domain autonomy represents one of the most significant challenges in data mesh implementation. Organizations that lean too heavily toward centralization risk recreating the bottlenecks of traditional approaches, while those that prioritize autonomy without adequate guardrails risk governance inconsistency and compliance issues. Successful implementations establish clear boundaries: centralized governance defines non-negotiable standards for security, privacy, and compliance, while domains maintain autonomy over implementation details, data models, and quality thresholds specific to their business context.

Cross-domain integration patterns

While domain autonomy is a core principle of data mesh, enterprises must still support cross-domain analytics and insights that span multiple business areas. Several patterns facilitate this integration without undermining domain independence.

Denormalized data products represent one common approach, where domain teams create purpose-built composite views that combine their domain data with relevant information from other domains. These products optimize for specific cross-domain use cases, such as customer 360 views or product performance analysis. The key distinction from traditional integration approaches is ownership. These cross-domain assets remain owned by specific domains rather than centralized teams, maintaining clear accountability even for integrated data.

Data contracts provide another essential integration mechanism, formalizing agreements between data producers and consumers. These contracts define expectations for data structure, quality, and delivery, serving both as documentation and as enforceable standards. Effective contracts specify not just schemas but also service level objectives for freshness, completeness, and accuracy, treating data exchange as a service relationship rather than a static asset transfer. Organizations implementing data mesh should invest in standardized contract templates and automated validation mechanisms to ensure these agreements remain current and enforced as data products evolve.

Implementation challenges and solutions

Organizations implementing data mesh face several common challenges. Skills distribution often becomes an immediate obstacle, as domain teams typically lack data engineering expertise. Successful organizations address this through a combination of self-service platforms with simplified interfaces, embedded data engineers within domain teams during transition periods, and targeted upskilling programs that build necessary capabilities over time.

Data duplication presents another challenge, as domain autonomy can lead to inefficient replication. This typically manifests as multiple domains ingesting and transforming the same source data, creating infrastructure overhead and potential inconsistencies. The most effective solution combines clear policies on authoritative sources with technological approaches like virtualization and query federation that reduce physical duplication.

Governance consistency represents perhaps the most persistent challenge, requiring organizations to balance domain autonomy with enterprise standards. Leading organizations address this through computational governance that automatically enforces organizational policies while allowing domain-specific flexibility. This approach treats governance as code rather than documentation, embedding compliance checks into the self-serve platform and making it easier to do the right thing than to circumvent standards.

Cultural resistance often proves more challenging than technical implementation, as data mesh represents a fundamental shift in responsibilities and accountabilities. Organizations should recognize this as a change management initiative rather than merely a technical one, investing in executive sponsorship, clearly articulated success metrics, and phased implementation that demonstrates value incrementally rather than attempting a big bang transformation. The most successful implementations start with early-adopter domains that have both high business value and leadership supportive of the new approach, using their success to build momentum for broader adoption.

Data mesh implementation readiness checklist

Before embarking on a data mesh implementation, organizations should assess their preparedness across key dimensions. This checklist identifies the most critical readiness factors that significantly impact implementation success. Use it to quickly evaluate your organization's strengths and address gaps before proceeding.

Category	Key readiness factors	Status
Leadership and organization	Executive sponsorship with a clear mandate for transformation	
	Current state assessment with identified pain points	
	Success metrics defined for implementation and outcomes	
Domain structure	Business domains clearly mapped and prioritized	
	Domain data ownership assigned with accountable leaders	
	Skills development plan for upskilling domain teams	
Technical foundation	Self-serve infrastructure platform with templates	
	Data Catalog deployed for product discovery	
	Common data formats and interoperability standards	
Governance	Federated governance model with clear responsibilities	
	Tag-based access control strategy	
	Cross-domain data contracts template	
Implementation approach	Pilot domains selected based on value and readiness	
	Incremental plan with clear milestones	
	Lighthouse data products identified for early value	
Culture and process	Data product ownership mindset across domain teams	
	Agile approach adapted for data product development	
	Communities of practice for sharing best practices	

Table 8.1: Core implementation readiness checklist for data mesh

Transactional data lakes

The traditional separation between operational and analytical systems has long been a fundamental principle of enterprise data architecture. This bifurcation emerged from technical constraints: transactional databases optimized for high concurrency **online transaction processing** (**OLTP**) workloads struggled with analytical queries, while data warehouses designed for complex analytics performed poorly for transaction processing. Organizations accepted this division despite its significant drawbacks, primarily data latency, integration complexity, and duplicate storage costs. Transactional data lakes represent a fundamental rethinking of this architectural division, seeking to provide **atomicity, consistency, isolation, durability** (**ACID**) guarantees and transactional capabilities within data lake environments that have traditionally excelled at analytics but lacked transaction support.

The business value of transactional data lakes stems from their ability to unify operational and analytical workloads. Organizations implementing these architectures report 30-50% reductions in end-to-end data latency and 20-40% decreases in total data platform costs through storage consolidation and simplified architectures. More importantly, they enable new capabilities that were previously impractical, such as real-time operational analytics, consistent point-in-time analysis across multiple systems, and simplified compliance through unified data lineage. For organizations struggling with the growing complexity of managing separate operational and analytical systems, transactional data lakes offer a compelling path toward architectural simplification.

Transactional table formats

The foundation of transactional data lakes rests on specialized table formats that extend traditional files with additional capabilities: schema enforcement, transaction support, and time travel (point-in-time query capabilities).

Three formats have emerged as leaders in this space. They are as follows:

- **Apache Iceberg**: Developed initially by *Netflix* and now an Apache project, Iceberg provides atomicity, isolation, and consistency guarantees through a table metadata approach. It offers schema evolution, partition evolution, and time travel capabilities.

- **Apache Hudi**: Created by *Uber*, Hudi focuses on incremental data processing and upsert capabilities. It provides fine-grained control over how data is stored and accessed, with specialized optimizations for update-heavy workloads.

- **Delta Lake**: Originating from *Databricks*, Delta Lake offers ACID transactions, schema enforcement, and time travel, with particular emphasis on performance optimizations for Spark workloads.

While all three formats enable transactional capabilities, they exhibit important architectural differences that influence their suitability for specific use cases. Iceberg's separation of concerns between file format and table format creates an abstraction that supports multiple query engines effectively. Hudi's focus on incremental processing makes it particularly well-suited for CDC and streaming integration scenarios. Delta Lake's tight integration with the Spark ecosystem provides performance advantages for organizations heavily invested in that technology.

The implementation of these formats on AWS typically leverages Amazon S3 for storage, with metadata either in a dedicated store or within the S3 environment itself. The sample code is as follows:

```
1.  -- Example of creating an Iceberg table in AWS Glue Data Catalog
2.  CREATE TABLE iceberg_db.customer_transactions (
3.    transaction_id string,
4.    customer_id string,
5.    product_id string,
6.    transaction_time timestamp,
7.    amount decimal(10,2),
8.    store_id string
9.  )
```

```
10. PARTITIONED BY (year(transaction_time), month(transaction_time), day(transaction_
    time))
11. LOCATION 's3://transaction-datalake/customer_transactions/'
12. TBLPROPERTIES (
13.   'table_type'='ICEBERG',
14.   'format'='parquet',
15.   'write_compression'='zstd'
16. );
```

The key innovation in transactional table formats is not just the syntax, which resembles traditional database operations, but rather the underlying infrastructure that enables operations like INSERT, UPDATE, and DELETE on cloud object storage while maintaining consistency and performance at scale.

Architecture patterns

Transactional data lakes can be implemented in several patterns, each addressing different organizational requirements and technical constraints. Three primary patterns have emerged:

- **Pattern 1: Lakehouse architecture:**

    The lakehouse architecture combines data lake storage with database-like capabilities, creating a hybrid environment that serves both operational and analytical workloads. In this pattern, the transactional table format provides a performance layer on top of the data lake, enabling both SQL operations and machine learning workloads against the same dataset.

    The following figure shows the lakehouse architecture on AWS:

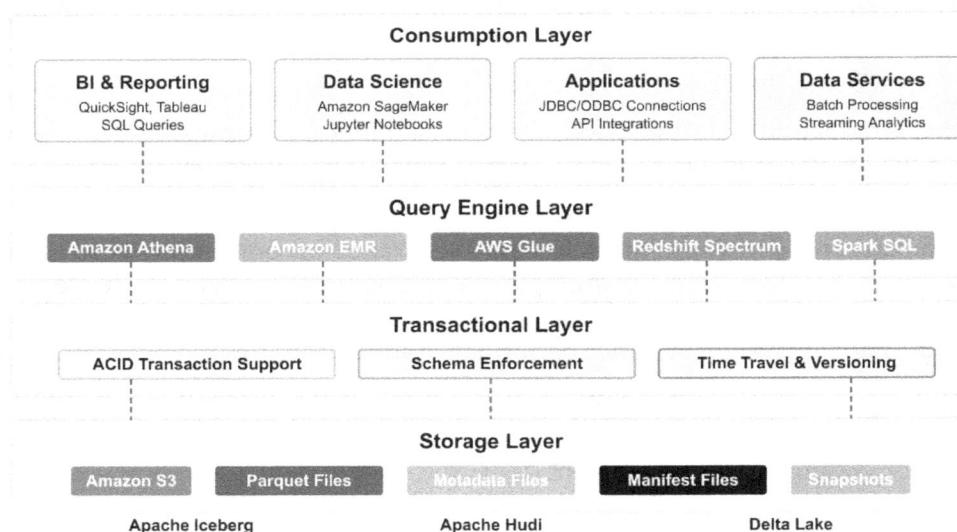

Figure 8.2: Lakehouse architecture combining transactional capabilities with data lake storage

A typical lakehouse implementation on AWS includes:

- o   Amazon S3 as the storage foundation.

- o   AWS Glue Data Catalog as the metadata repository.

- o   Amazon Athena for interactive SQL queries.

- o   Amazon EMR for batch processing.

- o   AWS Glue for ETL operations.

- o   Amazon SageMaker for machine learning.

The key advantage of this pattern is its ability to support diverse processing engines against a consistent dataset. Analytics teams can use Athena for ad-hoc SQL, data scientists can use SageMaker for model training, and application developers can use EMR Serverless for record-level operations. All against the same underlying data without copies or synchronization issues.

- •   **Pattern 2: Operational data store:**

The **operational data store (ODS)** pattern uses transactional table formats to create an environment optimized for low-latency operational analytics while maintaining historical data for deeper analysis. This pattern typically features real-time ingestion from source systems, with immediate availability for operational queries.

Key characteristics of an ODS implementation include:

- o   Streaming ingestion using Amazon Kinesis or MSK.

- o   Optimized small-file handling for performance.

- o   Denormalized data structures for query efficiency.

- o   Time-based partitioning for recency filters.

- o   Automated compaction processes to maintain performance.

This pattern serves organizations that need near-real-time analytics on operational data, such as retail inventory management, logistics optimization, or fraud detection systems, while maintaining the ability to perform historical trend analysis without separate systems.

Implementation considerations

Implementing a transactional data lake requires careful attention to several key factors that influence performance, reliability, and maintainability.

Small file management

The small file problem is a critical performance challenge for transactional data lakes. S3 is optimized for larger objects (100MB-1GB), but transactional workloads generate frequent small files, creating a fundamental mismatch that degrades performance and increases costs. Each small file requires a separate API call, leading to higher latency and S3 request charges.

Refer to the following list to effectively manage this challenge:

1. **Target optimal file sizes**: Aim for 100MB-1GB per file. For tables under 10GB, target approximately 10 files total.

2. **Configure auto-compaction**: Set table properties to enforce file size targets as shown in the following code:

```
1. ALTER TABLE iceberg_db.customer_transactions SET PROPERTIES (
2.   'write.target-file-size-bytes'='134217728',  -- 128MB target
3.   'write.distribution-mode'='hash'
4. )
```

3. **Implement regular compaction jobs**: Schedule AWS Glue jobs to identify and compact small files in high-churn partitions first.

4. **Buffer frequent transactions**: For high-frequency workloads, use Kinesis or DynamoDB as a buffer layer to accumulate changes before writing larger batches to S3.

5. **Optimize partition granularity**: Ensure each partition contains at least 100MB of data after compaction. Adjust time-based partitioning based on data volume.

Organizations that successfully manage the small file problem typically combine automated compaction with continuous monitoring of file size metrics. Without this active management, even well-designed transactional data lakes will experience significant performance degradation as transaction volumes grow.

Partition evolution

Unlike traditional databases where schema changes often require downtime or complex migrations, transactional data lakes support partition evolution. It is the ability to change how data is organized physically without interrupting operations. This capability is particularly valuable as query patterns evolve or as data volumes grow.

Iceberg provides native support for changing partition schemes through simple DDL statements such as:

```
1.  -- Change partitioning scheme from daily to hourly
2.  ALTER TABLE iceberg_db.customer_transactions
3.  SET PARTITION SPEC (
4.    hour(transaction_time),
5.    store_id
6.  );
```

After such a change, new data follows the updated partition scheme while existing data remains in the original scheme. Iceberg's query planning automatically handles the mixed partitioning, eliminating the need for immediate data migration. Organizations can then migrate historical data incrementally through background processes if desired.

Time travel capabilities

One of the most powerful features of transactional data lakes is time travel. It is the ability to query data as it existed at a specific point in time. This capability enables several valuable use cases:

- Audit and compliance investigations.

- Error recovery after incorrect updates.

- Point-in-time reporting consistency.

- A/B testing of analytical models against historical states.

Time travel is implemented through metadata that tracks the evolution of tables over time, allowing queries to specify a timestamp or snapshot ID:

```
1.  -- Query data as it existed at a specific point in time
2.  SELECT * FROM iceberg_db.customer_transactions FOR TIMESTAMP AS OF '2023-03-
    15 08:00:00';
3.
4.  -- Query data as it existed at a specific snapshot
5.  SELECT * FROM iceberg_db.customer_transactions FOR VERSION AS OF 3421;
```

Organizations implementing transactional data lakes should establish retention policies that balance analytical needs with storage costs. Most implementations retain snapshot history for 7-30 days by default, with options to extend retention for critical tables.

Performance optimization

Transactional data lakes face unique performance challenges due to their hybrid nature. Several optimization strategies have proven effective such as:

- **Z-order clustering**: Organizing data physically based on frequently joined or filtered columns improves read performance dramatically.

- **Statistics collection**: Maintaining detailed statistics on table contents enables query optimizers to generate efficient execution plans.

- **Caching layers**: Implementing caching mechanisms like Amazon ElastiCache or Amazon DynamoDB Accelerator for frequently accessed data.

- **Query routing**: Directing different query types to appropriate engines (e.g., point lookups to DynamoDB, complex aggregations to Athena).

- **Strategic denormalization**: Balancing normalization principles with query performance through targeted denormalization.

Organizations with existing data warehouses can implement transactional data lakes incrementally, beginning with specific domains or use cases before expanding to enterprise-wide adoption. This approach allows for validation of performance characteristics and operational processes with limited risk.

Security and governance

Transactional data lakes bring both opportunities and challenges for data governance. By unifying operational and analytical data, they enable consistent policy enforcement and simplified lineage tracking. However, they also require more sophisticated security models that accommodate both transactional and analytical access patterns.

Effective governance implementations for transactional data lakes typically leverage the following:

- **Column-level security**: Restricting access to sensitive columns while allowing broader access to non-sensitive data.

- **Row-level filtering**: Implementing dynamic filters based on user attributes to control record-level visibility.

- **Version-level permissions**: Restricting time travel capabilities to appropriate users.

- **Attribute-based access control**: Using user and data attributes to determine access permissions dynamically.

AWS Lake Formation provides native support for many of these capabilities, allowing organizations to implement sophisticated governance models without custom code. By combining Lake Formation's fine-grained access controls with CloudTrail's audit capabilities, organizations can maintain robust governance while still benefiting from the simplified architecture of transactional data lakes.

Transactional data lakes represent a significant architectural evolution, breaking down the traditional boundary between operational and analytical systems. While not appropriate for all workloads, they offer compelling advantages for organizations seeking to reduce data movement, improve latency, and simplify their data landscape. By understanding the capabilities, implementation patterns, and optimization strategies of these platforms, data engineers can effectively incorporate them into modern data architectures.

Lambda and Kappa architectures

Data processing architectures must balance several competing objectives: processing latency, query performance, implementation complexity, and maintenance overhead. The volume and velocity of data have increased dramatically in recent years, driving organizations to seek architectures that can efficiently handle both real-time and historical analysis. Lambda and Kappa architectures represent two influential patterns that address these requirements through different approaches to integrating batch and stream processing.

These architectures matter because they directly impact an organization's ability to derive timely insights from data. According to a 2023 Gartner survey, organizations implementing modern streaming architectures report 70% faster time-to-insight for operational analytics compared to traditional batch-only approaches. Meanwhile, batch processing remains essential for complex, resource-intensive transformations that optimize analytical performance. Lambda and Kappa architectures offer frameworks for balancing these capabilities based on specific requirements and constraints.

Lambda architecture

The Lambda architecture, introduced by *Nathan Marz* in 2011, addresses the challenge of balancing processing latency and query performance by creating parallel batch and speed layers that are eventually merged to create a complete view. This approach recognizes that batch processing excels at handling large volumes efficiently but introduces latency, while stream processing provides immediacy but often with higher resource costs and implementation complexity. The Lambda architecture is shown in the following figure:

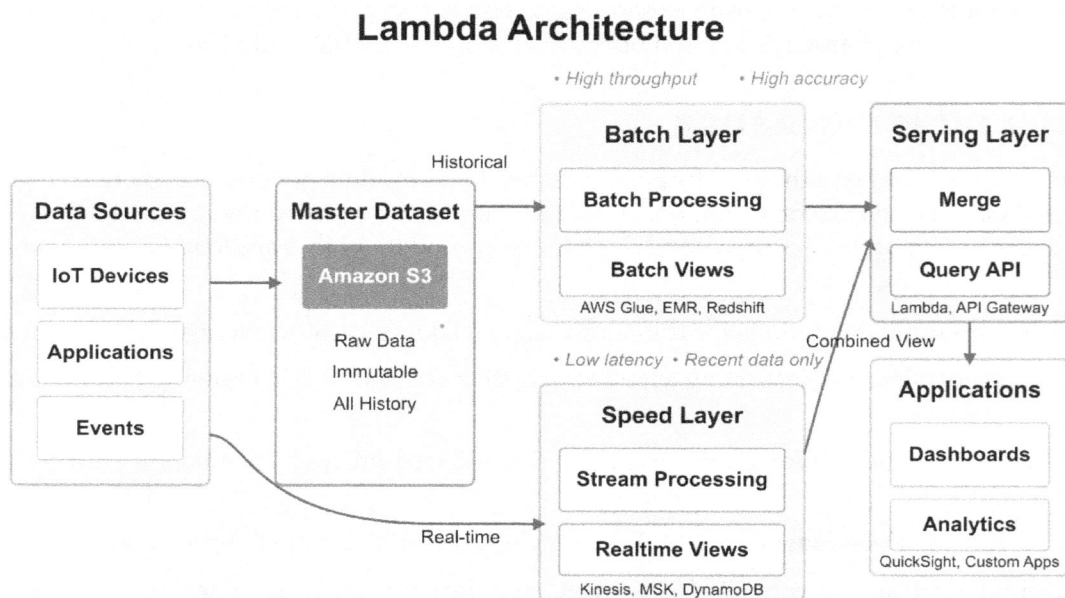

Figure 8.3: Lambda architecture with batch, speed, and serving layers

Core components

The Lambda architecture consists of three primary layers, each serving a distinct purpose:

- **Batch layer**: Processes large volumes of historical data periodically, typically using frameworks designed for high throughput rather than low latency. This layer:
  - o Stores the master dataset, typically in its raw form.
  - o Runs comprehensive transformations that may be resource intensive.
  - o Creates pre-computed views optimized for specific query patterns.
  - o Prioritizes correctness and completeness over processing speed.

- **Speed layer**: Processes real-time data streams as they arrive, compensating for the latency of the batch layer. This layer:

o Handles only recent data that has not yet been processed by the batch layer.

o Uses stream processing frameworks that optimize for low latency.

o Creates real-time views that may be approximate or less comprehensive.

o Prioritizes processing speed over completeness.

- **Serving layer**: Combines results from batch and speed layers to provide a complete view for queries. This layer:

o Integrates batch views (historical data) with real-time views (recent data).

o Provides query interfaces optimized for low-latency retrieval.

o Handles the complexity of merging potentially overlapping datasets.

o Presents a unified interface to consuming applications.

The defining characteristic of the Lambda architecture is this parallel processing approach, where the same data flows through both batch and stream paths before being combined for analysis.

AWS implementation

On AWS, a typical Lambda architecture implementation leverages several services. The batch layer typically uses S3 for raw data storage, with AWS Glue for ETL processing and Amazon Redshift for the batch views. The speed layer uses Kinesis for data ingestion, Amazon **Managed Streaming for Kafka** (**MSK**) for stream processing, and DynamoDB for storing real-time views. The serving layer often combines Lambda functions with API Gateway to merge results from both layers.

Advantages and challenges

The Lambda architecture offers several key advantages:

- **Fault tolerance**: The batch layer can reprocess data to correct errors or handle processing failures.
- **Processing flexibility**: Different technologies can be used for batch and stream processing based on their strengths.
- **Query efficiency**: Pre-computed batch views enable highly optimized query performance.
- **Scalability**: Each layer can scale independently based on its specific requirements.

However, it also presents significant challenges:

- **Implementation complexity**: Maintaining parallel processing paths and merging results adds substantial complexity.
- **Code duplication**: Processing logic often needs to be implemented twice, once for each layer.
- **Resource overhead**: Running parallel processing systems increases infrastructure costs.
- **Data reconciliation**: Ensuring consistency between batch and speed results can be difficult.

The Lambda architecture is most appropriate for organizations with complex analytical requirements that benefit from comprehensive batch processing, while also needing real-time insights for operational decision-making. It is particularly well-suited for scenarios where the cost and complexity of maintaining parallel systems is justified by the business value of both real-time and highly optimized historical analytics.

Kappa architecture

The Kappa architecture, introduced by *Jay Kreps* in 2014, presents a simplified alternative to Lambda by treating all data processing as streaming. Instead of maintaining parallel batch and speed layers, Kappa uses a single stream processing engine to handle both real-time and historical data processing, eliminating the complexity of maintaining and reconciling dual pipelines.

The following figure shows the Kappa architecture:

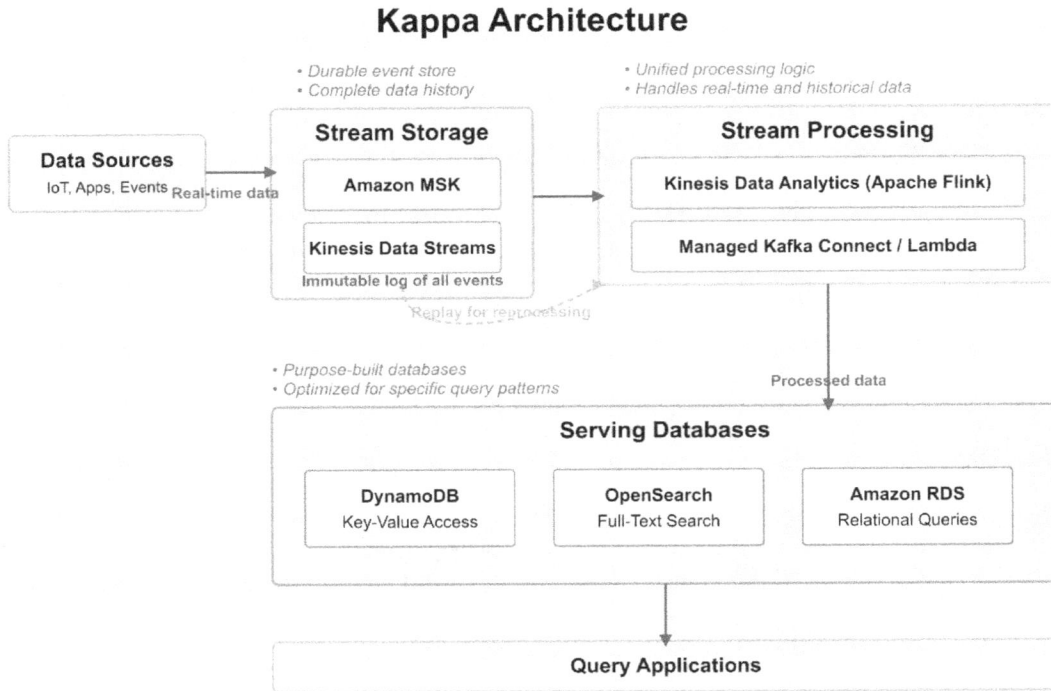

Figure 8.4: Kappa architecture with unified stream processing

Core components

The Kappa architecture consists of two primary components:

- **Stream processing system**: Handles all data processing, whether real-time or historical. This component:
    - Processes data as it arrives in real-time.
    - Reprocesses historical data when needed (by replaying from stored streams).
    - Uses the same processing logic for all data, regardless of age.
    - Maintains the complete event history in a durable, replayable stream store.
- **Serving database**: Stores the processed results for querying. This component:
    - Provides efficient query access to processed data.
    - May include multiple specialized stores for different query patterns.
    - Updates continuously as new processed data becomes available.

The key insight of the Kappa architecture is that batch processing can be viewed as a special case of stream processing where the stream consists of historical data being processed at high throughput. By unifying the processing model, Kappa eliminates the need for separate code paths and simplifies the overall architecture.

AWS implementation

On AWS, a Kappa architecture typically leverages Amazon MSK or Amazon Kinesis as the streaming backbone, with stateful stream processing handled by Amazon Kinesis Data Analytics for Apache Flink. The processed results are then stored in purpose-built databases like DynamoDB, Amazon OpenSearch Service, or RDS, depending on the query requirements.

This implementation pattern allows all data to flow through the same processing pipeline, with the stream serving as both the real-time transport and the historical record. When reprocessing is needed, applications can reset their consumer offsets and replay the stream from an earlier point.

Advantages and challenges

The Kappa architecture offers several compelling advantages:

- **Simplified implementation**: A single processing pipeline reduces code duplication and maintenance overhead.
- **Consistency**: The same processing logic handles all data, ensuring consistent results.
- **Reduced complexity**: No need to build systems for merging batch and real-time results.
- **Streamlined operations**: Fewer components to monitor, troubleshoot, and scale.

However, it also faces limitations such as:

- **Stream storage requirements**: Maintaining complete historical data in streams can be challenging for very large datasets.
- **Processing efficiency**: Stream processing may be less efficient than specialized batch systems for certain workloads.
- **Complex state management**: Stateful stream processing requires careful management of processing guarantees.
- **Reprocessing overhead**: Replaying large volumes of historical data through stream processors can be time-consuming.

The Kappa architecture is most appropriate for systems where real-time processing is the primary requirement and where the volume of historical data is manageable within a streaming context. It is particularly well-suited for event-driven systems, real-time analytics, and applications where processing simplicity outweighs raw batch processing efficiency.

Lambda vs. Kappa, the decision factors

The choice between Lambda and Kappa architecture depends on specific requirements and constraints. Key decision factors have been mentioned in *Table 8.1*:

Factors	Lambda architecture	Kappa architecture
Data volume	Better for extremely large historical datasets	Better for moderate-sized datasets
Processing latency	Can optimize batch for throughput, streams for latency	All processing has stream latency characteristics
Query complexity	Supports complex, resource-intensive batch transformations	Limited by stream processing capabilities
Implementation complexity	Higher (dual pipelines, reconciliation)	Lower (single pipeline, unified logic)
System resilience	High (batch can recompute from raw data)	Moderate (depends on stream retention policies)
Operational overhead	Higher (multiple systems to maintain)	Lower (fewer components, simplified monitoring)

Table 8.2: Architecture model selection factors

Lambda and Kappa architectures provide valuable frameworks for designing modern data processing systems. By understanding the strengths, limitations, and appropriate use cases for each approach, you can design architectures that effectively balance the competing demands of processing latency, query performance, and implementation complexity.

Polyglot persistence strategies

Traditional data architectures often relied on a single database technology to handle all data management needs. This monolithic approach emerged from practical constraints like the complexity of managing multiple technologies, the scarcity of specialized database skills, and the high cost of diverse infrastructure. However, the explosion of specialized database technologies over the past decade has driven a fundamental shift toward polyglot persistence which is the strategic use of multiple database technologies within a single application or organization. This approach recognizes that different data workloads have distinct access patterns, consistency requirements, and performance characteristics that are best served by purpose-built technologies

The business case for polyglot persistence stems from the recognition that forcing diverse workloads into a single database technology creates both technical and operational inefficiencies. Research from *Forrester* indicates that organizations implementing polyglot strategies report 40 to 60% improvements in application performance and 30-50% reductions in development cycle times for data-intensive applications. By matching each data workload to the most appropriate technology, organizations can optimize performance, reduce costs, and accelerate innovation. However, this approach also introduces complexity in data integration, consistency management, and operational overhead that must be carefully addressed.

Database categories and use cases

Modern database technologies can be categorized based on their data models, consistency guarantees, and performance characteristics. Understanding these categories helps in selecting the most appropriate technology for specific workloads.

The categories are as follows:

- **Document databases**: Document databases store semi-structured data as self-describing documents, typically in JSON or BSON format. This model enables schema flexibility, making it well-suited for content management, user profiles, and situations where data structures evolve frequently. Amazon DocumentDB and MongoDB are prominent examples of document databases, offering:

    o Schema flexibility without migration overhead.

    o Rich query capabilities against nested document structures.

    o Horizontal scaling through sharding.

    o Index support for diverse query patterns.

  Document databases excel in scenarios like content management, user profile storage, and product catalogues where the ability to evolve schemas without downtime provides significant advantages. Consider the following product catalogue that needs to accommodate varying attributes across product categories:

```
1.  // Electronics product document
2.  {
3.     "product_id": "P123456",
4.     "name": "Ultra HD Smart TV",
5.     "category": "Electronics",
6.     "price": 799.99,
7.     "technical_specs": {
```

```
8.      "resolution": "3840 x 2160",
9.      "refresh_rate": "120Hz",
10.     "hdmi_ports": 4
11.   }
12. }
13.
14. // Clothing product document
15. {
16.   "product_id": "P789012",
17.   "name": "Wool Overcoat",
18.   "category": "Clothing",
19.   "price": 249.99,
20.   "available_sizes": ["S", "M", "L", "XL"],
21.   "materials": {
22.     "shell": "80% wool, 20% polyester",
23.     "lining": "100% polyester"
24.   }
25. }
```

In a traditional relational database, this would require either a complex schema with many nullable columns or a less efficient entity-attribute-value pattern. Document databases handle this heterogeneity naturally, while still providing indexing and query capabilities.

- **Key-value stores**: Key-value stores offer high-throughput, low-latency access to data through simple key-based operations. Their simplicity enables extreme scalability and performance, making them ideal for caching, session management, and high-volume data collection. Amazon DynamoDB exemplifies this category, providing:

  o   Single-digit millisecond response times at any scale.

  o   Automatic partitioning for horizontal scalability.

  o   Secondary indexing for flexible access patterns.

  o   Provisioned or on-demand capacity modes for different workload patterns.

Key-value stores are particularly valuable in scenarios like session management, shopping carts, and real-time analytics where access patterns are simple but volume and velocity are high. For instance, in an IoT application tracking millions of devices:

```
1. // Key: deviceId:timestamp
2. // Value: Device reading
3.
4. "device_12345:2023-04-15T10:30:15Z" → {
5.     "temperature": 72.3,
6.     "humidity": 38.7,
7.     "battery": 91
8. }
```

This pattern enables efficient time-series queries by device ID while supporting enormous write volumes through distributed partitioning.

- **Graph databases**: Graph databases optimize storage and querying of highly connected data, focusing on relationships between entities. They excel at traversing complex networks of relationships, making them suitable for social networks, recommendation engines, and knowledge graphs. Amazon Neptune supports both property graph and **Resource Description Framework (RDF)** models, offering:

- o Specialized query languages (Gremlin, SPARQL) for relationship traversal.

- o High-performance for multi-hop queries.

- o Built-in algorithms for pathfinding, centrality, and community detection.

Graph databases provide particular value when relationship analysis is central to the application. For example, in a fraud detection system analysing financial transactions:

```
1. // Cypher query to find potentially fraudulent payment paths
2. MATCH (sender:Account)-[:TRANSFERRED_TO]->(intermediate:Account)
3.                         -[:TRANSFERRED_TO]->(receiver:Account)
4. WHERE sender.owner = receiver.owner
5.   AND intermediate.country != sender.country
6.   AND intermediate.country != receiver.country
7.   AND sender.flagged = false
8. RETURN sender, intermediate, receiver
```

This query, which would require multiple complex joins in a relational database, becomes a natural pattern match in a graph database, enabling detection of sophisticated money laundering patterns.

- **Time-series databases**: Time-series databases optimize for the storage and analysis of time-indexed data points, providing high-throughput ingestion and efficient time-based queries. They are ideal for monitoring metrics, IoT sensor data, and financial trading information. Amazon Timestream exemplifies this specialization, offering:

- o Automatic partitioning by time periods.

- o Optimized storage of recent vs. historical data.

- o Built-in time-based functions and aggregations.

- o SQL-compatible query interface.

Time-series databases shine in operational monitoring and IoT scenarios where data is naturally organized by time and retention policies vary based on data age. For instance, in an application monitoring system:

```
1. SELECT
2.     service_name,
3.     region,
4.     AVG(cpu_utilization) AS current_avg,
5.     (
6.         SELECT AVG(cpu_utilization)
7.         FROM metrics
8.         WHERE time BETWEEN NOW() - INTERVAL '7 days' AND NOW() - INTER-
   VAL '1 day'
9.             AND service_name = m.service_name
10.            AND region = m.region
11.            AND hour_of_day(time) = hour_of_day(m.time)
12.     ) AS historical_avg
13. FROM metrics m
14. WHERE time BETWEEN NOW() - INTERVAL '1 hour' AND NOW()
15. GROUP BY service_name, region
16. HAVING current_avg > historical_avg * 1.5
17. ORDER BY (current_avg - historical_avg) / historical_avg DESC;
```

This query naturally exploits the time-partitioning and time-function capabilities of time-series databases, delivering performance that would be difficult to achieve in general-purpose databases.

- **Relational databases**: Despite the proliferation of specialized databases, relational databases remain essential for transaction processing and complex analytical queries requiring strong consistency guarantees. They excel at enforcing complex constraints and supporting standardized SQL access. Amazon RDS and Amazon Aurora provide managed relational database services with:

    o ACID transaction guarantees.

    o Complex query optimization.

    o Schema enforcement and referential integrity.

    o Mature tooling and broad ecosystem support.

Relational databases remain the technology of choice for financial systems, inventory management, and other applications where transactional integrity is paramount. Modern offerings like Aurora combine traditional relational capabilities with cloud-native scalability features, delivering performance improvements without sacrificing the familiar model. The following code shows how the transaction integrity is enforced in a relational database using demarcating transactions:

```
1.  -- Complex transaction maintaining multiple integrity constraints
2.  BEGIN TRANSACTION;
3.
4.  -- Update inventory
5.  UPDATE product_inventory
6.  SET quantity_available = quantity_available - 3
7.  WHERE product_id = 'P123456'
8.  AND quantity_available >= 3;
9.
10. -- Verify inventory update was successful
11. IF @@ROWCOUNT = 0 THEN
12.     ROLLBACK;
13.     THROW 50000, 'Insufficient inventory', 1;
14. END
15.
16. -- Create order
17. INSERT INTO orders (order_id, customer_id, order_date, status)
18. VALUES ('O987654', 'C123456', CURRENT_TIMESTAMP, 'PENDING');
19.
20. -- Add order items
21. INSERT INTO order_items (order_id, product_id, quantity, unit_price)
22. VALUES ('O987654', 'P123456', 3, 799.99);
23.
24. -- Update customer statistics
25. UPDATE customers
26. SET lifetime_order_count = lifetime_order_count + 1,
27.     lifetime_order_value = lifetime_order_value + 2399.97
28. WHERE customer_id = 'C123456';
29.
30. COMMIT TRANSACTION;
```

Implementing polyglot persistence on AWS

Effective polyglot persistence requires more than simply deploying different database technologies. It demands a thoughtful strategy for workload segregation, data integration, and operational management.

On AWS, several patterns have emerged for implementing polyglot persistence effectively such as:

- **Command query responsibility segregation (CQRS)**: It separates read and write operations, allowing each to use database technologies optimized for their respective patterns. This pattern is particularly valuable when write patterns are transactional but read patterns are diverse and high-volume.

  A typical CQRS implementation on AWS might include:

  o **Write path**: Amazon Aurora for transactional write operations with ACID guarantees.

  o **Read path**: Amazon DynamoDB for high-throughput, low-latency read access.

  o **Synchronization**: AWS Lambda functions to propagate changes from the write store to the read store.

  The following figure shows the CQRS pattern and separation of read and write path to the datastores:

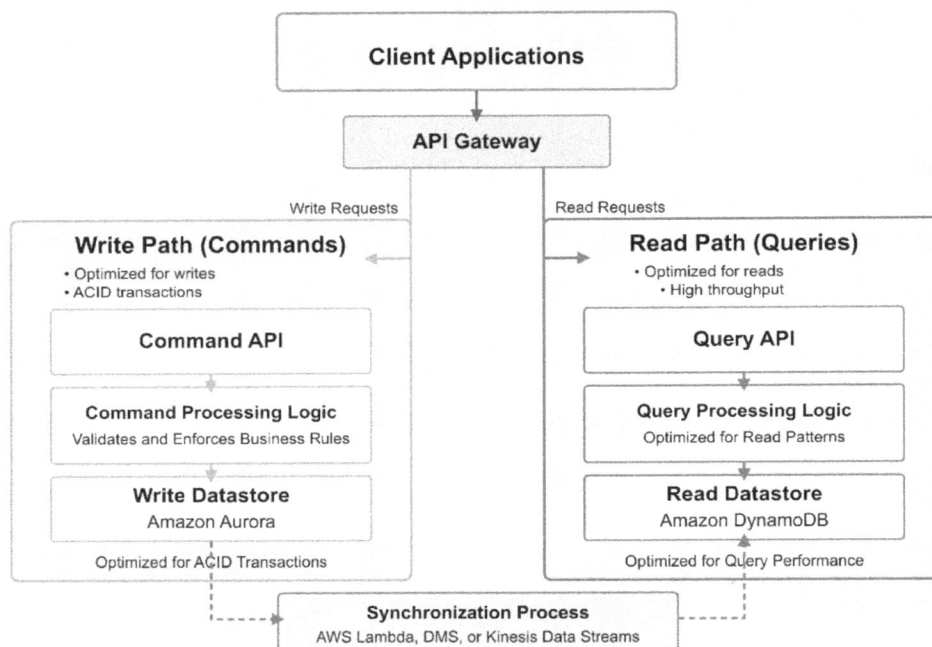

Figure 8.5: CQRS pattern with separate write and read datastores

  This pattern enables each path to scale independently according to its requirements, avoiding the common challenge where read workloads impact write performance or vice versa.

- **Decomposition by bounded context**: Bounded context decomposition, a concept from domain-driven design, identifies natural boundaries within an application domain and allows each context to use the most appropriate database technology. This approach aligns database choices with business capabilities rather than technical requirements.

  For example, an e-commerce system might decompose into:

  o **Product catalogue**: Amazon DocumentDB for flexible product attributes.

  o **Inventory management**: Amazon Aurora for transactional consistency.

o **Customer recommendations**: Amazon Neptune for relationship analysis.

o **Order history**: Amazon DynamoDB for high-throughput access.

o **Operational metrics**: Amazon Timestream for time-series analytics.

This decomposition enables teams to make independent technology decisions based on their specific domain requirements while maintaining clear integration points between contexts.

- **Cache-aside pattern**: The cache-aside pattern augments a primary database with a high-performance cache, improving read performance for frequently accessed data without changing the primary storage technology. This pattern offers a pragmatic first step toward polyglot persistence with minimal architectural complexity.

A typical implementation includes:

o **Primary database**: Amazon RDS or Aurora storing authoritative data.

o **Cache layer**: Amazon ElastiCache providing high-speed access to frequently read data.

o **Application logic**: Managing cache population, invalidation, and fallback to the primary database.

```
1.  // Example cache-aside pattern in application code
2.  async function getProductById(productId) {
3.    // Try to get from cache first
4.    const cachedProduct = await cache.get(`product:${productId}`);
5.    if (cachedProduct) {
6.      return JSON.parse(cachedProduct);
7.    }
8.
9.    // If not in cache, get from database
10.   const product = await database.query(
11.     'SELECT * FROM products WHERE product_id = ?',
12.     [productId]
13.   );
14.
15.   // Store in cache for future requests with TTL
16.   if (product) {
17.     await cache.set(`product:${productId}`, JSON.
    stringify(product), 'EX', 3600);
18.   }
19.
20.   return product;
21. }
```

This pattern can dramatically improve read performance without requiring significant architectural changes, making it an excellent starting point for polyglot adoption.

- **Event sourcing with specialized views**: Event sourcing captures all changes to application state as a sequence of events, enabling the creation of specialized views optimized for different query patterns. This pattern works particularly well with event-driven architectures on AWS.

A typical implementation includes:

o **Event store**: Amazon Kinesis or MSK capturing all domain events.

o **Processing logic**: AWS Lambda functions transforming events into specialized views.

o **Specialized stores**: Different database technologies for different query requirements.

This approach enables extreme flexibility in supporting diverse query patterns while maintaining a single source of truth in the event stream.

Data consistency challenges and solutions

Polyglot persistence introduces significant data consistency challenges. Without the atomic transactions provided by a single database system, maintaining consistency across multiple data stores requires explicit architectural patterns.

Eventually consistent integration

Many polyglot implementations embrace eventual consistency, where temporary inconsistencies are acceptable provided the system converges to a consistent state over time. This approach often uses event-driven integration to propagate changes between systems.

Key implementation patterns include:

- **CDC**: Using AWS **Database Migration Service** (**DMS**) or Debezium to capture and stream changes from source databases.

- **Event-driven propagation**: Processing change events through Amazon SNS, SQS, or EventBridge to update related data stores.

- **Conflict resolution strategies**: Implementing mechanisms to resolve conflicts when they occur, such as *last writer wins* or more sophisticated merge algorithms.

This approach prioritizes availability and partition tolerance over immediate consistency, aligning with the CAP theorem's constraints for distributed systems.

Distributed transactions

For scenarios requiring stronger consistency guarantees, distributed transaction patterns can coordinate operations across multiple data stores, though with increased complexity and potential performance impacts.

Approaches include:

- **Two-phase commit**: Implementing a prepare-and-commit protocol across participating systems.

- **Saga pattern**: Breaking long-running transactions into a sequence of smaller, compensating transactions.

- **Outbox pattern**: Atomically updating both data and an outbox table within a single database, then asynchronously processing the outbox to propagate changes.

The saga pattern, in particular, has gained popularity for maintaining consistency across polyglot systems:

```javascript
// Example saga implementation for an order process
async function createOrderSaga(orderData) {
  try {
    // Step 1: Reserve inventory
    const inventoryReservation = await inventoryService.reserveItems(orderData.items);

    try {
      // Step 2: Process payment
      const paymentResult = await paymentService.processPayment(orderData.payment);
```

```
11.
12.        try {
13.          // Step 3: Create order record
14.          const order = await orderService.createOrder({
15.            ...orderData,
16.            inventoryReservationId: inventoryReservation.id,
17.            paymentTransactionId: paymentResult.transactionId
18.          });
19.
20.          // Step 4: Finalize inventory deduction
21.          await inventoryService.commitReservation(inventoryReservation.id);
22.
23.          return order;
24.        } catch (orderError) {
25.          // Compensating transaction for payment
26.          await paymentService.refundPayment(paymentResult.transactionId);
27.          // Compensating transaction for inventory
28.          await inventoryService.cancelReservation(inventoryReservation.id);
29.          throw orderError;
30.        }
31.      } catch (paymentError) {
32.        // Compensating transaction for inventory
33.        await inventoryService.cancelReservation(inventoryReservation.id);
34.        throw paymentError;
35.      }
36.    } catch (inventoryError) {
37.      throw inventoryError;
38.    }
39. }
```

This pattern maintains consistency through compensating transactions rather than distributed locking, improving resilience at the cost of increased implementation complexity.

Consistency boundaries

A pragmatic approach to managing consistency in polyglot environments involves identifying natural consistency boundaries—groups of data that must be kept strongly consistent with each other. By aligning these boundaries with database choices, many consistency challenges can be avoided.

Best practices for defining consistency boundaries include:

- **Domain analysis**: Identifying data elements that must change together to maintain business rules.

- **Access pattern mapping**: Understanding which elements are frequently accessed together.

- **Update frequency assessment**: Determining how often different data elements change.

- **Consistency requirement definition**: Specifying the acceptable lag between updates for different relationships.

Organizations that carefully define consistency boundaries can often minimize cross-database consistency challenges while still leveraging specialized technologies for each workload.

By following these practices, organizations can implement polyglot persistence strategically, leveraging specialized technologies where they provide the most value while maintaining a manageable operational footprint.

Change data capture patterns

Modern data architectures often require near real-time data synchronization between different systems from operational databases to data warehouses, from on-premises systems to cloud platforms, and between specialized data stores in polyglot environments. Traditionally, this synchronization relied on periodic batch extraction processes that introduced significant latency and processing overhead. CDC represents a fundamental shift in this approach, focusing on identifying and capturing incremental changes in source systems as they occur, then processing and propagating only these changes rather than entire datasets. This shift enables much lower latency, reduced processing overhead, and more efficient resource utilization.

The business value of CDC stems from its ability to enable near real-time decision making while maintaining system reliability and performance. Organizations implementing CDC report 70-90% reductions in data transfer volumes and 50-80% decreases in end-to-end latency compared to traditional batch extraction. These improvements directly translate to business benefits: retailers can maintain near real-time inventory visibility across channels, financial services firms can implement more responsive fraud detection, and manufacturers can adjust production based on current supply chain conditions rather than outdated reports. As data volumes grow and latency requirements shrink, CDC has moved from a specialized technique to a core capability for competitive data architectures.

CDC techniques and mechanisms

Several techniques exist for capturing changes in source systems, each with distinct trade-offs in terms of latency, impact on source systems, and implementation complexity.

Log-based CDC

Log-based CDC reads the transaction or commit logs of database systems to identify and extract changes. This approach is particularly powerful because it operates outside the main data path, avoiding any performance impact on the source system while still capturing every change in the exact order it occurred.

In AWS environments, several services leverage log-based CDC:

- **AWS Database Migration Service (DMS)**: It can read and process database transaction logs from sources including MySQL, PostgreSQL, Oracle, and SQL Server.

- **Amazon Aurora:** It exposes database change events through its Aurora Serverless Data API.

- **Amazon MSK**: It can be integrated with Debezium to implement log-based CDC from various database systems.

Log-based CDC is particularly valuable for capturing changes from production systems where minimizing performance impact is critical. For example, with Amazon Aurora MySQL, DMS uses **binary log (binlog)** replication to capture changes:

```
1.  // Example CDC event captured from Aurora MySQL
2.  {
3.    "eventID": "d9bf641c-8661-4db0-9df2-74904f411d8a",
4.    "sourceARN": "arn:aws:rds:us-east-1:123456789012:cluster:aurora-mysql-cluster",
5.    "eventTime": "2023-04-15T12:34:56.789Z",
6.    "operation": "UPDATE",
7.    "tableName": "customers",
8.    "columns": [
```

```
 9.     {
10.       "name": "customer_id",
11.       "type": "int",
12.       "value": "12345",
13.       "isPrimaryKey": true
14.     },
15.     {
16.       "name": "email",
17.       "type": "varchar",
18.       "oldValue": "old.email@example.com",
19.       "value": "new.email@example.com",
20.       "isPrimaryKey": false
21.     },
22.     {
23.       "name": "last_updated",
24.       "type": "timestamp",
25.       "oldValue": "2023-04-10T09:22:15.342Z",
26.       "value": "2023-04-15T12:34:56.789Z",
27.       "isPrimaryKey": false
28.     }
29.   ]
30. }
```

This event captures not just the new state of the record but also the previous values of changed fields, enabling sophisticated processing downstream.

Trigger-based CDC

Trigger-based CDC uses database triggers to capture and record changes to a separate change table within the same database. When properly implemented, this approach can capture changes with minimal latency while providing flexibility in exactly what data is captured.

A typical implementation involves:

- Creating change tracking tables for each source table being monitored.

- Implementing INSERT, UPDATE, and DELETE triggers that record changes to these tracking tables.

- Setting up a process to consume changes from the tracking tables.

While AWS does not provide a specific service for trigger-based CDC, it is commonly implemented using native database capabilities and then integrated with AWS services like Lambda or Kinesis for change propagation.

Trigger-based CDC introduces some performance overhead on the source system, as triggers execute within the same transaction context as the original operations. However, for moderate-volume systems, this overhead can be acceptable given the implementation simplicity and precise control.

Query-based CDC

Query-based CDC periodically polls source tables for changes, typically by:

- Tracking the last-modified timestamp or version number in each record.

- Querying for records where this tracking field is newer than the last extraction time.

- Processing the identified changes and updating the extraction checkpoint.

This approach is the simplest to implement but has significant limitations:

- It cannot reliably detect deletes unless soft-delete patterns are used.

- It may miss intermediate changes if a record is modified multiple times between polls.

- It introduces additional load on the source system through polling queries.

In AWS environments, query-based CDC is often implemented using AWS Glue jobs or Lambda functions scheduled through EventBridge, with extraction state managed in DynamoDB or Parameter Store.

Table differencing

Table differencing compares the current state of a table with a previously captured snapshot to identify changes. This approach:

- Takes periodic snapshots of source tables.

- Compares the new snapshot with the previous one.

- Generates change records based on differences.

While conceptually simple, this approach becomes resource-intensive for large tables and struggles with high-frequency changes. It is most appropriate for smaller datasets or scenarios where other CDC techniques are not available.

Table differencing can be implemented on AWS using Glue jobs with temporary storage in S3, but It is generally considered a last resort when more efficient CDC mechanisms are not available.

CDC implementation patterns on AWS

Several patterns have emerged for implementing CDC in AWS environments, each addressing different requirements and constraints, such as:

- **Pattern 1: DMS with Kinesis for real-time synchronization:**

  This pattern uses AWS DMS to capture changes from source databases and publishes them to Kinesis Data Streams, enabling real-time processing by multiple consumers:

  Key components of this pattern include:

  o **Source database**: Operational database such as RDS, Aurora, or on-premises database.

  o **AWS DMS**: Configured with a CDC-enabled replication task pointing to the source.

  o **Amazon Kinesis Data Stream**: Receives change events from DMS.

  o **Consumers**: Lambda functions, Kinesis Data Analytics, or custom applications that process the change stream.

  This pattern excels in scenarios requiring real-time propagation to multiple destinations, such as updating search indices, refreshing caches, and maintaining materialized views simultaneously.

- **Pattern 2: Aurora with Lambda serverless event processing:**

  For workloads using Amazon Aurora, the integrated change event capabilities enable a simplified architecture:

  o **Aurora database**: Generates change events through its data API.

  o **Lambda trigger**: Invoked automatically in response to database changes.

  o **Processing logic**: Implemented in Lambda to handle the specific change events.

  o **Destination system**: Updated by the Lambda function with the processed changes.

This pattern enables highly responsive, serverless processing of change events without additional infrastructure:

```
1.  # Example Lambda function triggered by Aurora PostgreSQL change events
2.  import json
3.  import boto3
4.  import psycopg2
5.
6.  def lambda_handler(event, context):
7.      # Parse the event from Aurora PostgreSQL
8.      for record in event['Records']:
9.          # Extract the change details
10.         change_event = json.loads(record['body'])
11.         operation = change_event['operation']
12.         schema = change_event['schema']
13.         table = change_event['table']
14.
15.         # Process different operations
16.         if operation == 'INSERT':
17.             process_insert(change_event['new_record'])
18.         elif operation == 'UPDATE':
19.             process_update(change_event['old_record'], change_event['new_record'])
20.         elif operation == 'DELETE':
21.             process_delete(change_event['old_record'])
22.
23.     return {
24.         'statusCode': 200,
25.         'body': 'Processed ' + str(len(event['Records'])) + ' changes'
26.     }
27.
28. def process_insert(new_record):
29.     # Handle insert operation
30.     # For example, update an ElasticSearch index
31.     es_client = boto3.client('es')
32.     # Implementation details...
33.
34. def process_update(old_record, new_record):
35.     # Handle update operation
36.     # For example, refresh a cache
37.     redis_client = boto3.client('elasticache')
38.     # Implementation details...
39.
40. def process_delete(old_record):
41.     # Handle delete operation
42.     # Implementation details...
```

- **Pattern 3: Debezium with MSK for open-source CDC:**

For organizations invested in open-source CDC technologies, AWS supports Debezium (a CDC connector for Kafka) through Amazon MSK:

o **Source database**: Operational database with transaction log access.

o **Debezium connector**: Deployed on EC2 or ECS, reading database transaction logs.

o **Amazon MSK**: Receives change events in Kafka topics.

o **Kafka Connect**: Distributes changes to various sinks.

o **Destination systems**: Consume changes through standard Kafka interfaces.

This pattern leverages the rich ecosystem of Kafka connectors for both sources and destinations, enabling complex integration scenarios that might be difficult with AWS-native services alone.

- **Pattern 4: Hybrid migration with CDC:**

CDC plays a crucial role in hybrid cloud migrations, enabling ongoing synchronization while applications transition:

o **On-premises database**: Continues to serve operational workloads.

o **AWS DMS**: Configured for ongoing replication to AWS.

o **AWS target database**: Maintains a synchronized copy of the data.

o **Application migration**: Gradually shifts workloads to AWS while data remains synchronized.

This pattern reduces risk in cloud migrations by enabling phased transitions with continuous data synchronization, avoiding the challenges of *big bang* cutover approaches.

CDC use cases and patterns

CDC enables several powerful use cases that would be impractical with traditional batch processing approaches:

- **Real-time data warehousing:** CDC enables near real-time updates to data warehouses without the performance impact of frequent full extractions:

o **Capture changes**: Track changes in operational databases using log-based CDC.

o **Transform incrementally**: Process changes to match the data warehouse schema.

o **Apply efficiently**: Update only the affected data in the warehouse.

o **Maintain history**: Preserve historical context through appropriate versioning.

This pattern dramatically reduces the latency between operational events and analytical visibility, enabling more responsive decision-making.

- **Cache synchronization:** CDC provides an efficient mechanism for keeping caches in sync with authoritative data sources:

o **Identify relevant changes**: Filter the CDC stream for cache-relevant updates.

o **Transform to cache format**: Prepare the data for the caching technology.

o **Apply selectively**: Update or invalidate only affected cache entries.

o **Handle special operations**: Implement logic for schema changes and bulk operations.

This approach reduces cache inconsistency windows and eliminates the need for periodic full cache refreshes.

- **Cross-region replication:** For global applications, CDC enables efficient cross-region replication:

o **Capture changes in the source region**: Implement CDC on the primary database.

o **Transfer efficiently**: Send only changes across regional boundaries.

o **Apply consistently**: Maintain transactional grouping during application.

o **Monitor lag**: Track and alert on replication delays.

AWS DMS supports cross-region replication natively, simplifying the implementation of this pattern.

- **Event sourcing integration:** CDC can bridge traditional databases with event-sourced systems:

  o **Capture database changes**: Implement CDC on relational databases.

  o **Transform to domain events**: Convert technical changes to business events.

  o **Publish to event store**: Send the derived events to an event sourcing system.

  o **Maintain bidirectional consistency**: Optionally synchronize changes from the event store back to the database.

This pattern enables gradual migration from traditional architectures to event-sourced systems without disruptive rewrites.

CDC has evolved from a specialized technique to an essential component of modern data architectures. By focusing on incremental changes rather than full data transfers, organizations can significantly reduce latency, minimize system impact, and enable near real-time data integration across diverse environments. As data volumes continue to grow and businesses demand increasingly responsive analytics, the CDC patterns described here offer proven approaches to address these challenges while leveraging AWS's rich ecosystem of data services. Organizations that master these patterns position themselves to deliver more timely insights and maintain a competitive advantage in today's data-driven landscape.

Hands-on: Implementing a data mesh

This hands-on guide will help you implement a simplified data mesh architecture on AWS to reinforce the concepts covered in this chapter. The entire implementation is available in accompanying github. In the workshop you will build:

- Domain-oriented data products for customer and sales data.
- Self-serve infrastructure templates for new data products.
- Federated governance using tags.
- Cross-domain analytics views.

Prerequisites

Before we begin implementing our data processing solution, let us ensure we have all the necessary tools and permissions in place. The following prerequisites will enable us to create and execute our AWS data processing workflows effectively:

- AWS account with permissions to create S3 buckets and Glue resources.
- Python 3.7+ with boto3 and pandas installed.
- Jupyter Notebook environment.
- AWS credentials configured.

Implementation steps

The steps are as follows:

1. **Creating domain data products:** Run the domain data product creation cell to:

   a. Create S3 buckets for customer and sales domains.

b. Generate sample customer and transaction data.

c. Create Glue databases and tables with domain metadata.

d. Tag resources with domain and classification information.

This step demonstrates how domain teams maintain ownership of their data while providing clear access patterns.

2. **Implementing self-serve infrastructure:** The self-serve infrastructure template provides domain teams with:

a. Standardized S3 bucket creation with lifecycle policies.

b. Glue database setup with consistent metadata.

c. Table creation patterns with proper documentation.

Domain teams can use this template to create new data products without needing specialized data engineering expertise.

3. **Setting up federated governance:** Federated governance is implemented using:

a. Data classification tags (public, internal, confidential).

b. Domain tags (customer, sales, marketing).

c. Tag-based access policies that span domains.

This approach enables centrally defined but locally implemented governance that scales across domains.

4. **Enabling cross-domain analytics:** Cross-domain analytics demonstrates how to:

a. Create integrated views across domain boundaries.

b. Maintain domain ownership while enabling unified analysis.

c. Implement business-oriented analytics that span domains.

The sample queries show how to build customer 360 views and campaign performance analysis across domains.

Expected outputs

Refer to the following list to know the expected outcomes:

- Functional domain data products in S3 and Glue.

- Cross-domain views that demonstrate federated analysis.

- A governance structure that balances central control with domain autonomy.

Best practices

- Keep domain boundaries aligned with organizational structure.

- Design data products with consumers in mind.

- Implement computational governance that scales.

- Balance standardization with domain-specific needs.

- Start small and expand incrementally.

The complete implementation is available in the Jupyter Notebook included with the book's companion GitHub.

Conclusion

Data architectures continue to evolve in response to the growing scale, complexity, and dynamism of modern data landscapes. The patterns explored in this chapter like data mesh, transactional data lakes, Lambda and Kappa architectures, polyglot persistence, and change data capture represent powerful approaches for addressing these challenges. Each pattern offers distinct advantages such as data mesh aligns data ownership with domain expertise, transactional data lakes bridge operational and analytical workloads, Lambda and Kappa architectures integrate batch and stream processing, polyglot persistence matches workloads to specialized technologies and change data capture enables real-time data propagation.

The most effective data platforms often combine elements from multiple patterns, adapting them to specific organizational requirements rather than applying them dogmatically. By understanding the strengths, trade-offs, and implementation considerations of each pattern, data engineers can design architectures that balance flexibility, scalability, and governance while providing the foundation for data-driven innovation.

In the next chapter, we will build on these architectural foundations by exploring data governance and security, focusing on how AWS Lake Formation can implement fine-grained access controls, column-level security, and comprehensive audit capabilities while maintaining the flexibility needed for diverse analytical workloads. We will examine how modern governance approaches can enhance rather than hinder data utilization, ensuring both compliance and innovation across the enterprise data landscape.

Join our Discord space

Join our Discord workspace for latest updates, offers, tech happenings around the world, new releases, and sessions with the authors:

https://discord.bpbonline.com

CHAPTER 9

Data Governance and Security

Introduction

As organizations build increasingly complex data ecosystems, robust governance and security have evolved from compliance checkboxes to strategic imperatives. Traditional perimeter defenses and coarse-grained controls fail in today's distributed environments where thousands of user's access petabytes of sensitive data through dozens of services. Modern architectures demand governance systems balancing protection with analytical utility, enabling maximum value while maintaining appropriate controls. The stakes have never been higher. **General Data Protection Regulation (GDPR)** penalties can reach 4% of global revenue, while data breaches cost organizations an average of $4.35 million, according to IBM's 2023 report.

Beyond financial impacts, governance failures erode trust and restrict innovation. Conversely, well-implemented governance creates a competitive advantage. *McKinsey* research shows organizations with mature practices make decisions 2.5x faster while reducing regulatory risk by 40-60%. Within AWS, Lake Formation represents a pivotal evolution in governance capabilities, providing a unified control plane integrates with S3, Glue, Athena, Redshift, and other analytics services. Rather than relying on disparate security mechanisms, it enables consistent access control, encryption management, and audit capabilities regardless of which technology accesses data assets. This centralization addresses the critical inconsistency that emerges when security is implemented independently across multiple services and access patterns.

Structure

This chapter will cover the following topics:

- AWS Lake Formation
- Column-level security
- Data encryption strategies
- Access patterns and control
- Audit and compliance
- Hands-on: Implementing enterprise-grade security

Objectives

This chapter aims to provide a comprehensive understanding of implementing enterprise-grade governance and security for modern data platforms on AWS. You will learn how Lake Formation enables fine-grained access control through its permission model, how column-level security protects sensitive data elements, and how encryption strategies can be implemented across the data lifecycle. The chapter explores how to create access patterns optimized for different user personas, implement comprehensive audit capabilities, and automate compliance monitoring. Through practical implementation examples, you will understand how these capabilities function within AWS and how they integrate with broader organizational security frameworks. These capabilities will enable you to design governance models that balance protection with utility, implementing controls that secure sensitive assets while still enabling appropriate analytical access that drives business value.

AWS Lake Formation

Traditional data lake security models centred on infrastructure protection, using IAM policies to control access to storage layers like Amazon S3. While this approach provided fundamental protection, it created significant limitations as data lakes expanded to encompass thousands of tables accessed through multiple services. AWS Lake Formation represents a paradigm shift in data lake governance, introducing a specialized service layer that abstracts security management from underlying storage infrastructure. This abstraction enables fine-grained permissions across the data lake while providing a consistent access control model regardless of which service users employ to access the data.

Lake Formation permission model

The Lake Formation permission model fundamentally differs from traditional IAM approaches through its data-centric rather than service-centric orientation. Instead of defining what actions users can perform on specific services, Lake Formation permissions define what operations users can perform on specific data assets, regardless of which service they use to access those assets.

The core components of the Lake Formation permission model include:

- **Principal**: The identity requesting access can be an IAM user, role, or another AWS account.
- **Resource**: The data asset being accessed can be a database, table, or column.
- **Permission**: The operations allowed on the resource including data access operations (SELECT, INSERT, ALTER) and metadata operations (DESCRIBE, CREATE_TABLE).
- **Grant option**: The ability to extend permissions to other principals.

Lake Formation implements these permissions through a central metadata repository (AWS Glue Data Catalogue) that maintains both the data asset definitions and the associated permissions. This centralized approach enables Lake Formation to act as a policy enforcement point across multiple services including Athena, Redshift Spectrum, EMR, and Glue.

Implementing data lake permissions

Lake Formation offers multiple approaches to implementing permissions, each addressing different governance requirements.

Named resource method

The named resource method directly grants permissions on specific databases, tables, or columns:

```
1. -- Example of granting table permissions using the named resource method
2. GRANT SELECT ON TABLE customer_domain.customer_profiles
```

```
3. TO IAM_USER 'arn:aws:iam::123456789012:user/analyst';
4.
5. -- Example of granting column permissions using the named resource method
6. GRANT SELECT ON TABLE customer_domain.customer_profiles (customer_id, segment)
7. TO IAM_USER 'arn:aws:iam::123456789012:user/data_scientist';
```

The named resource method provides fine-grained control but can become difficult to maintain as the number of data assets and principals grows.

LF-Tag based method

To address the scalability challenges of the named resource method, Lake Formation introduced LF-Tags, a tag-based permission system that enables permissions to be granted based on metadata attributes rather than specific resource names:

```
1.  -- Define LF-Tags
2.  CREATE LF-TAG 'Classification' WITH ALLOWED VALUES ('Public', 'Internal', 'Confiden-
    tial', 'Restricted');
3.  CREATE LF-TAG 'Domain' WITH ALLOWED VALUES ('Customer', 'Product', 'Finance', 'Opera-
    tions');
4.
5.  -- Assign LF-Tags to data assets
6.  ASSIGN LF-TAG 'Classification' = 'Confidential' ON TABLE customer_domain.customer_
    profiles;
7.  ASSIGN LF-TAG 'Domain' = 'Customer' ON TABLE customer_domain.customer_profiles;
8.
9.  -- Grant permissions based on LF-Tag expressions
10. GRANT SELECT ON RESOURCES WHERE Domain = 'Customer' AND Classification IN ('Pub-
    lic', 'Internal')
11. TO IAM_ROLE 'arn:aws:iam::123456789012:role/marketing_analysts';
```

This LF-Tag based approach significantly reduces permission maintenance overhead. As new tables are added to the data lake, they automatically inherit the appropriate permissions once tagged, eliminating the need for explicit permission grants.

Hybrid permission models

Most organizations implement a hybrid permission model, using LF-Tags for broad access patterns and named resource permissions for exceptions or highly sensitive assets. This approach balances governance scalability with fine-grained control where needed.

Data Catalogue security

The AWS Glue Data Catalogue sits at the centre of the Lake Formation security model, serving as both a metadata repository and a control point for enforcing permissions. Securing the Data Catalogue itself is therefore a critical component of the overall governance strategy.

Lake Formation manages Data Catalogue security through several key mechanisms:

- **Resource-level IAM policies**: Control which principals can register databases and tables in the catalogue.
- **Lake Formation permissions**: Determine which principals can view and modify metadata in the catalogue.
- **Encryption**: Protects catalogue metadata at rest using AWS KMS.

Organizations should implement a layered security approach for their Data Catalogue, starting with restrictive IAM policies that limit who can register new data assets, then adding Lake Formation permissions to control metadata access.

Cross-account access patterns

Modern organizations often implement multi-account strategies to separate environments (dev/test/prod) or to isolate different business units. Lake Formation provides native capabilities for sharing data across accounts while maintaining consistent governance controls.

Cross-account data sharing in Lake Formation follows a producer-consumer model:

- **Producer account**: Owns the data assets and defines the permissions to be granted to consumer accounts.
- **Consumer account**: Receives access to specific data assets based on permissions granted by the producer.

The implementation involves several key steps:

1. **Resource shares**: The producer creates a resource share using AWS **Resource Access Manager (RAM)**.
2. **Permission grants**: The producer grants Lake Formation permissions to the consumer account.
3. **Resource acceptance**: The consumer accepts the resource share.
4. **Local permissions**: The consumer grants permissions to local principals to access the shared data.

This process enables secure, governed data sharing while maintaining clear ownership and control boundaries.

Hybrid access mode

Organizations transitioning to Lake Formation from traditional IAM-based governance often need to manage a hybrid state. Lake Formation offers a hybrid access mode that enables both permission models to coexist, with three possible configurations:

- **Lake Formation permissions only**: Access is controlled exclusively through Lake Formation permissions.
- **IAM access control only**: Access is controlled exclusively through IAM policies.
- **Hybrid access control**: Access is granted if the principal has either Lake Formation permissions or appropriate IAM permissions.

This flexibility enables phased implementation strategies where new projects adopt Lake Formation governance while existing workloads continue to operate under the established IAM framework until they can be migrated.

Governance challenges and solutions

Organizations implementing AWS Lake Formation must address critical tension points between permission granularity, integration complexity, and performance overhead—strategic decisions that shape the effectiveness of your entire data lake security architecture.

The path to effective data governance in AWS Lake Formation requires balancing competing priorities—precision versus simplicity, integration versus standardization, and security versus performance.

Challenges

The challenges are as follows:

- **Permission granularity trade-offs**: The tension between management overhead and permission precision represents a fundamental governance challenge. Implementing a tiered governance model with LF-Tags for broad classifications and named resources for exceptions provides a balanced approach, minimizing administrative overhead while maintaining appropriate security boundaries.

- **Integration with existing security frameworks**: Most organizations have established security frameworks before implementing Lake Formation. Mapping existing security tiers to LF-Tags, aligning roles with persona-based access, and integrating with existing identity management enables Lake Formation to extend rather than replace existing security frameworks.

- **Performance impacts**: Governance controls can impact query performance, particularly with column-level security or row-level filtering at scale. Organizations should balance security requirements with performance considerations by optimizing filtering operations, using materialized views for common queries, and carefully monitoring performance impacts.

Lake Formation provides a powerful foundation for implementing comprehensive data governance in AWS data lakes. By understanding its permission models, implementation patterns, and integration capabilities, organizations can build governance frameworks that protect sensitive data without impeding legitimate analytical use cases.

Column-level security

As data assets grow in both size and sensitivity, coarse-grained access controls at the table level prove increasingly insufficient. Organizations often maintain tables containing both sensitive personal information (such as social security numbers or health data) and benign analytical attributes that could be widely used without privacy concerns. Column-level security addresses this fundamental limitation by enabling fine-grained control over individual data elements, allowing organizations to protect sensitive attributes while still enabling appropriate access to non-sensitive columns within the same table.

The business value of column-level security stems from its ability to safely expand data access without compromising compliance or privacy. Organizations implementing these controls report 30-50% increases in data usage by analytical teams while simultaneously reducing sensitive data exposure. By precisely defining which data elements specific roles can access, column-level security enables organizations to tailor data visibility based on legitimate business needs rather than applying one-size-fits-all restrictions.

Implementation patterns

When securing sensitive data in your data lake, choosing the right column-level security pattern is crucial. This guide explores three powerful implementation strategies—native Lake Formation permissions, view-based security, and dynamic masking—each with distinct advantages for different use cases.

Data governance teams must balance security, usability, and maintenance when protecting sensitive columns in AWS Lake Formation. Discover how to choose between direct permission grants and view-based approaches based on your organization's specific needs:

- **Pattern 1: Lake Formation permissions:**

  Lake Formation provides native column-level security capabilities through its permission model:

```
1. -- Grant access to specific columns for customer service role
2. GRANT SELECT ON TABLE customer_domain.customer_profiles
3. (customer_id, name, email, last_contact_date)
4. TO IAM_ROLE 'arn:aws:iam::123456789012:role/customer_service';
5.
6. -- Grant access to different columns for marketing role
7. GRANT SELECT ON TABLE customer_domain.customer_profiles
8. (customer_id, age_group, location, purchase_history)
9. TO IAM_ROLE 'arn:aws:iam::123456789012:role/marketing_analyst';
```

This approach offers integrated governance, service compatibility, and simplified administration. However, it uses static definitions and a binary access model (columns are either accessible or inaccessible).

- **Pattern 2: View-based security:**

    View-based security leverages database views to implement column-level controls:

```
1.  -- Create view for customer service team
2.  CREATE OR REPLACE VIEW customer_domain.customer_profiles_cs AS
3.  SELECT customer_id, name, email, last_contact_date
4.  FROM customer_domain.customer_profiles;
5.
6.  -- Create view for marketing team
7.  CREATE OR REPLACE VIEW customer_domain.customer_profiles_marketing AS
8.  SELECT customer_id, age_group, location, purchase_history
9.  FROM customer_domain.customer_profiles;
10.
11. -- Grant permissions to views rather than base tables
12. GRANT SELECT ON TABLE customer_domain.customer_profiles_cs
13. TO IAM_ROLE 'arn:aws:iam::123456789012:role/customer_service';
```

This pattern offers transformation capabilities, query optimization, and logical abstraction, but introduces maintenance overhead, update complexities, and potential inconsistencies.

- **Pattern 3: Dynamic masking with Lake Formation:**

    For sensitive implementations, Lake Formation offers cell-level security through data masking capabilities:

```
1.  -- Define data masking expression for SSN column
2.  CREATE DATA MASKING RULE 'SSN_masking'
3.  WITH FORMAT 'XXX-XX-${last_four}'
4.  WHERE '${last_four}' = SUBSTRING(value, -4)
5.  ON COLUMN customer_domain.customer_profiles.social_security_number;
6.
7.  -- Apply masking rule to specific roles
8.  APPLY DATA MASKING RULE 'SSN_masking'
9.  ON COLUMN customer_domain.customer_profiles.social_security_number
10. TO IAM_ROLE 'arn:aws:iam::123456789012:role/customer_service';
```

This approach provides dynamic protection, granular transformations, and consistent governance, but introduces performance impacts, implementation complexity, and limited transformation options.

LF-Tag based column security

For organizations managing large data lakes, LF-Tag based column security provides a scalable solution:

```
1.  -- Create column sensitivity LF-Tag
2.  CREATE LF-TAG 'Sensitivity' WITH ALLOWED VALUES ('Public', 'Internal', 'Confiden-
    tial', 'Restricted');
3.
4.  -- Assign tags to columns
5.  ASSIGN LF-TAG 'Sensitivity' = 'Public' ON TABLE customer_domain.customer_profiles
6.  COLUMN (customer_id, signup_date);
```

```
7.
8. ASSIGN LF-TAG 'Sensitivity' = 'Restricted' ON TABLE customer_domain.customer_profiles
9. COLUMN (social_security_number, credit_score);
10.
11. -- Grant permissions based on column sensitivity
12. GRANT SELECT ON COLUMNS WHERE Sensitivity IN ('Public', 'Internal')
13. TO IAM_ROLE 'arn:aws:iam::123456789012:role/business_analyst';
```

This approach scales effectively by simplifying administration, ensuring consistency, and adapting to changes. Organizations typically implement column-level security using a combination of these patterns based on specific use cases and data sensitivity.

Implementation challenges

Column-level security introduces several implementation challenges that organizations must address to maintain both security and usability. The challenges are discussed in the following section.

Schema evolution

As table schemas evolve with new columns or changed data types, column-level security controls must adapt accordingly. To address this:

- **Implement default restrictions**: Configure systems to restrict access to new columns by default.
- **Automate classification**: Develop processes to automatically classify new columns.
- **Review security implications**: Include security impact assessment in schema change workflows.
- **Maintain documentation**: Update data dictionaries and sensitivity mappings when schema changes occur.

Query performance

Column-level security can impact query performance, particularly with dynamic masking or complex view definitions. Mitigation strategies include:

- **Benchmark performance**: Measure query performance before and after implementing column security.
- **Optimize access patterns**: Design security controls with common query patterns in mind.
- **Consider partitioning**: For tables with many sensitive columns, consider physically separating sensitive and non-sensitive attributes.
- **Balance security and performance**: For performance-sensitive workloads, consider alternative security approaches.

User experience

Column-level security creates complexity for end users who may not understand why certain data elements are unavailable. To improve user experience:

- **Provide data dictionaries**: Create accessible documentation of available data elements.
- **Implement clear error messages**: When access is denied, provide helpful error information.
- **Create access request workflows**: Establish clear processes for requesting access.
- **Offer column-level discovery**: Enable users to explore what columns exist even if they cannot view the actual data.

Column-level security provides a critical capability for balancing data protection with analytical utility. By implementing appropriate patterns based on specific requirements, organizations can enable broader data access while still protecting their most sensitive information.

Data encryption strategies

Encryption serves as the last line of defence in a comprehensive security strategy, protecting data even when other controls fail. While access controls determine who can access data, encryption ensures that unauthorized access whether through misconfiguration, credential compromise, or system breach does not result in data exposure. In modern data architectures, where information flows through multiple services and storage layers, encryption must be implemented consistently across the entire data lifecycle.

The business imperative for robust encryption has grown as both regulatory requirements and breach costs have escalated. Regulations like GDPR, CCPA, and industry-specific frameworks such as HIPAA and PCI-DSS now mandate encryption for many data categories. Meanwhile, the average cost of a data breach reached $4.35 million in 2023, with unencrypted data breaches costing substantially more than those involving encrypted data.

Encryption fundamentals

Three primary types of encryption protect data throughout its lifecycle:

- **Encryption at rest**: Protects data when stored in persistent media.
- **Encryption in transit**: Protects data as it moves between services or networks.
- **Encryption in use**: Protects data while being processed in memory.

Effective encryption depends on robust key management concepts:

- **Key hierarchy**: Master keys protect other keys, which in turn protect data.
- **Key rotation**: Periodically replacing encryption keys to limit potential compromise.
- **Key access controls**: Policies determining which principals can use specific keys.
- **Customer vs. service managed keys**: Organization-controlled or provider-managed keys.

AWS encryption implementation patterns

Securing sensitive data requires more than perimeter defenses—learn how to implement comprehensive encryption across your entire AWS data ecosystem, from S3 storage to ETL jobs, Redshift warehouses, and end-to-end data pipelines.

Data encryption is the last line of defense against both external threats and internal misuse. Discover four proven patterns for implementing robust encryption throughout your AWS data lake architecture:

- **Pattern 1: S3 encryption for data lakes:**

  S3 supports multiple encryption options, with SSE-KMS providing the optimal balance of security and manageability:

```
1. terraform
2. resource "aws_s3_bucket" "data_lake_bucket" {
3.   bucket = "enterprise-data-lake"
4.
5.   server_side_encryption_configuration {
6.     rule {
7.       apply_server_side_encryption_by_default {
```

```
8.          kms_master_key_id = aws_kms_key.data_lake_key.arn
9.          sse_algorithm     = "aws:kms"
10.      }
11.      bucket_key_enabled = true
12.    }
13.  }
14. }
```

This implementation ensures that all data written to the data lake is automatically encrypted using a customer-controlled KMS key.

- **Pattern 2: Glue job encryption:**

  AWS Glue job encryption encompasses:

  o ETL script encryption

  o Bookmark encryption

  o Job output encryption

  o Connection password encryption

  A comprehensive Glue encryption configuration ensures all aspects of ETL jobs—from scripts to output data—are protected.

- **Pattern 3: Redshift encryption:**

  Amazon Redshift provides both cluster encryption (encrypting all data and snapshots within the cluster) and column-level encryption (providing additional protection for specific sensitive columns).

- **Pattern 4: End-to-end encryption pipelines:**

  Comprehensive security requires encryption across the entire data pipeline:

  o **Ingestion**: Data is encrypted during ingestion (Kinesis, Kafka).

  o **Storage**: All storage layers implement appropriate encryption (S3, DynamoDB).

  o **Processing**: Computation services operate on encrypted data (Glue, EMR).

  o **Analytics**: Query engines maintain encryption during analysis (Athena, Redshift).

  o **Delivery**: Results are encrypted when delivered to consumers.

  Key to this pattern is consistent key management—ensuring appropriate services have access to relevant encryption keys without creating unnecessary exposure.

Encryption challenges and solutions

While encryption is essential for data protection, organizations must navigate significant obstacles, including performance degradation, key management complexity, and application integration hurdles, and strategic approaches that balance security with operational realities.

Implementing robust encryption across your AWS data ecosystem introduces three critical challenges that must be addressed proactively: discover proven strategies to minimize performance impacts, streamline key management, and ensure seamless application integration:

- **Challenge 1: Performance impact:**

  Encryption operations introduce computational overhead, particularly for large-scale data processing. Solutions include:

- o   Use S3 bucket keys to reduce API calls to KMS.

- o   Implement encryption caching for repeated operations.

- o   Apply the strongest encryption only to the most sensitive data.

- o   Benchmark performance before production deployment.

- **Challenge 2: Key management complexity:**

  As organizations scale their encryption implementations, key management becomes increasingly complex. Implement structured key management processes by:

  - o   Creating key hierarchies based on purpose and scope.

  - o   Automating key rotation for operational keys.

  - o   Maintaining clear records of which keys protect which data.

  - o   Establishing cross-functional oversight for key management.

- **Challenge 3: Application integration:**

  Integrating encryption with existing applications can introduce compatibility challenges. Solutions include:

  - o   Starting with infrastructure encryption.

  - o   Gradually introducing field-level encryption.

  - o   Thorough testing in lower environments.

  - o   Monitoring application impacts after implementation.

Comprehensive encryption strategies protect data throughout its lifecycle, creating a foundation for secure, compliant data operations. As data volumes grow and regulatory requirements become more stringent, robust encryption will remain an essential component of data governance.

Access patterns and control

Effective data governance requires more than just implementing technical controls—it demands a nuanced understanding of how different organizational roles interact with data and how those interactions can be securely enabled. Traditional approaches to access control often created a binary paradigm where data was either fully accessible or completely restricted, resulting in either excessive access that created security risks or overly restrictive policies that impeded legitimate work. Modern access patterns recognize that different organizational roles require different types of data access, from analysts exploring patterns across broad datasets to engineers managing specific domain data to executives requiring summarized views.

The business impact of well-designed access patterns extends beyond security to encompass operational efficiency and analytical effectiveness. Organizations that implement persona-based access report 40-60% reductions in access request processing time and 30-50% decreases in inappropriate access attempts. More importantly, they enable critical business capabilities by ensuring that each role has precisely the access needed to perform its function—no more and no less.

Persona-based access patterns

The foundation of effective access control lies in understanding the different ways users interact with data. Persona-based access patterns identify common data interaction profiles and design controls specifically for each profile's legitimate needs.

Analytical personas

Analytical personas focus on deriving insights from data through exploration, visualization, and modeling. These personas typically require:

- **Query-focused permissions**: Emphasizing read access with minimal or no write capabilities.
- **Broad data visibility**: Access to datasets across multiple domains, often filtered for sensitivity.
- **Performance-optimized access**: Designed for interactive exploration and visualization.

The following table lists various common analytics persona, data access patterns and needs:

Persona	Primary need	Data access pattern	Common permissions	Implementation example
Business analyst	Operational reporting and analytics	Read access to business metrics and dimensional data	SELECT on business tables across domains	`GRANT SELECT ON TABLE customers.customer_profile TO IAM_ROLE 'business_analyst'`
Data scientist	Advanced analytics and model building	Broad access to raw and processed data with restricted sensitive fields	SELECT on most tables, restricted columns for sensitive data	`GRANT SELECT ON DATABASE raw_data TO IAM_ROLE 'data_scientist'`
Executive	KPI monitoring and strategic insights	Aggregated views of performance metrics	SELECT on pre-aggregated views and dashboards	Create performance dashboard views with restricted access
Marketing analyst	Customer behavior analysis	Customer data with limited PII visibility	SELECT on customer data with column restrictions	`GRANT SELECT ON TABLE customer_profiles (customer_id, segment, behavior) TO IAM_ROLE 'marketing_analyst'`

Table 9.1: Lake Formation analytical persona permissions

Operational personas

Operational personas focus on managing data flows, quality, and infrastructure. These personas typically require:

- **Administrative permissions**: Including both read and write capabilities.
- **Domain-specific access**: Focused on specific data domains or infrastructure components.
- **Metadata access**: Visibility into data structures and lineage.

The following table shows the different operational personas:

Persona	Primary need	Data access pattern	Common permissions	Implementation example
Data engineer	Pipeline management and quality processes	Read/write access to specific data domains	Glue, S3, Athena, and Lake Formation permissions within domain	IAM policy granting Glue and S3 access to specific resources
Data steward	Metadata and governance management	Catalog access with limited data visibility	Catalog permissions with limited data access	`GRANT ALL ON CATALOG TO IAM_ROLE 'data_steward'`

Persona	Primary need	Data access pattern	Common permissions	Implementation example
Platform administrator	Infrastructure management	Broad administrative access	Administrative permissions across data services	IAM policy with admin access and audit capabilities
Domain owner	Domain data product management	Full control within domain, limited access elsewhere	Full permissions in domain, read-only elsewhere	`GRANT ALL ON DATABASE domain_db TO IAM_ROLE 'domain_owner'`

Table 9.2: Operational personas

Specialized personas

Some organizations require additional specialized personas based on their specific needs. The following table shows the specialized personas:

Persona	Primary need	Data access pattern	Common permissions	Implementation example
Compliance officer	Regulatory validation	Read access to all data including sensitive fields	SELECT on all tables, including sensitive columns	`GRANT SELECT ON RESOURCES WHERE Classification IN ('Public', 'Internal', 'Confidential', 'Restricted')`
External partner	Collaborative analytics	Limited view of shared data	Read access to specific shared tables	Cross-account Lake Formation shares with column restrictions
Automated process	Scheduled data processing	Pipeline-specific access	Limited, task-specific permissions	Service role with least-privilege permissions

Table 9.3: Specialized personas

Implementing AWS security groups for persona access

Implementing persona-based access at scale requires a structured approach to permission management. AWS security groups provide a mechanism for grouping principals with similar access requirements and applying consistent permissions across the data environment.

The implementation process involves:

1. **Create security groups for each persona**: Establish IAM roles aligned with identified personas.

2. **Implement service-specific permissions**: Attach appropriate service policies to each role.

3. **Configure Lake Formation permissions**: Align data access with each persona's requirements.

4. **Establish role assignment process**: Create structured workflows for assigning users to roles.

This structured approach ensures consistent application of persona-based access controls while maintaining appropriate separation of duties and governance oversight.

Row-level security implementation

While column-level security protects sensitive data elements, many scenarios require more granular control at the row level. **Row-level security (RLS)** enables data access to be filtered based on attributes of the data or the requesting user, ensuring that principals can only view the subset of records relevant to their role or responsibility:

- **Pattern 1: Lake Formation row filters:**

  AWS Lake Formation provides native row-level filtering capabilities through data filter expressions:

```
1.  -- Create a data filter defining which rows are accessible
2.  CREATE DATA FILTER customer_region_filter
3.  FOR TABLE analytics.customer_data
4.  ROW FILTER (region = 'us-east-1')
5.  COLUMN WILDCARD INCLUDING (customer_id, name, email, region, purchase_history);
6.
7.  -- Apply the filter to a specific role
8.  GRANT SELECT ON TABLE analytics.customer_data
9.  TO IAM_ROLE 'arn:aws:iam::123456789012:role/RegionalAnalyst'
10. WITH DATA FILTER customer_region_filter;
```

- **Pattern 2: Context-aware filtering:**

  For more dynamic scenarios, context-aware filtering uses attributes of the requesting principal to determine which rows they can access:

```
1.  -- Create a data filter based on principal tags
2.  CREATE DATA FILTER principal_region_filter
3.  FOR TABLE analytics.customer_data
4.  ROW FILTER (region = ${aws:PrincipalTag/Region})
5.  COLUMN WILDCARD;
```

- **Pattern 3: Redshift row-level security:**

  For Amazon Redshift implementations, native row-level security policies provide similar capabilities:

```
1.  -- Create a Redshift RLS policy
2.  CREATE RLS POLICY regional_access
3.  WITH (region VARCHAR(50))
4.  USING (region = current_setting('app.current_region'));
5.
6.  -- Attach the policy to a table
7.  ALTER TABLE customer_data
8.  ROW LEVEL SECURITY ON;
9.
10. ALTER TABLE customer_data
11. ADD ROW LEVEL SECURITY FOR ROLE regional_analyst
12. USING regional_access(region);
```

Effective access control requires balancing security requirements with business needs—providing each persona with the specific access required to fulfil their function while preventing inappropriate data visibility. By implementing structured, persona-based access patterns with appropriate monitoring and governance, organizations can achieve this balance at scale, maintaining both security and analytical productivity in increasingly complex data environments.

Audit and compliance

Effective governance extends beyond implementing controls to include comprehensive auditing and monitoring capabilities that validate control effectiveness. Even the most sophisticated security frameworks can degrade over time due to configuration drift, evolving access patterns, or changing business requirements. Continuous audit and compliance monitoring ensures that governance controls remain effective in the face of these changes, providing visibility into how data is actually being accessed and used.

The business drivers for robust audit capabilities have intensified with increasing regulatory scrutiny and data protection requirements. Regulations like the **General Data Protection Regulation (GDPR)**, the **California Consumer Privacy Act (CCPA)**, the **Health Insurance Portability and Accountability Act (HIPAA)**, and the industry frameworks such as the **Payment Card Industry Data Security Standard (PCI-DSS)** and the **Service Organization Control 2 (SOC2)** all require evidence of control effectiveness, not just control implementation. Organizations face potential penalties of up to 4% of global revenue for serious compliance failures, along with operational disruption, remediation costs, and reputational damage. Beyond regulatory drivers, effective audit mechanisms also provide business value through improved operational visibility, enhanced security posture, and increased trust from customers and partners.

Comprehensive audit logging

Building robust data governance requires layered monitoring through CloudTrail configuration, service-specific audit logs, and automated compliance verification, creating an auditable trail of all data access and manipulation.

Effective governance depends on visibility; implement comprehensive logging across AWS services to maintain complete awareness of who accesses what data, when, and how.

CloudTrail configuration

AWS CloudTrail records API activity across AWS services, providing a detailed record of who did what when. A comprehensive CloudTrail implementation for data governance includes:

CloudTrail	Configuration	Purpose
Multi-region trail	Enable multi-region tracking	Ensure comprehensive coverage across all AWS regions
Management events	Track all management events	Record infrastructure and service changes
Data events	Configure for sensitive S3 buckets	Record object-level access to sensitive data
Log file validation	Enable validation	Ensure log integrity for compliance
Log encryption	Encrypt with KMS	Protect audit logs from unauthorized access
Insights events	Enable API and error insights	Detect unusual API activity and error patterns

Table 9.4: CloudTrail configuration and its purpose

Service-specific audit logs

Beyond CloudTrail, service-specific logs provide detailed information about data access as shown in the following table:

Service	Log type	Key information captured
S3	Access logs	Detailed bucket and object-level access
Athena	Query logs	SQL queries executed against data lake tables
Lake Formation	Access logs	Permission checks and data access through Lake Formation
Redshift	Audit logs	Database queries, connections, and schema changes
Glue	Job logs	ETL job executions and data transformations

Table 9.5: Service specific CloudTrail logs

Log aggregation and analysis

Effective analysis requires centralized aggregation of logs from multiple sources. CloudWatch Logs provides a central platform with:

- **Log groups**: Organizational units for different log types.

- **Log streams**: Individual log sources within groups.

- **Metric filters**: Extract metrics from log data for monitoring.

- **Log Insights**: Query and analyze log data across sources.

Compliance monitoring and verification

While audit logs provide a record of what happened, compliance monitoring focuses on verifying that activities conform to defined policies and standards.

The details are shown in the following table:

Config rule type	Example	Purpose
AWS managed rules	S3_BUCKET_SERVER_SIDE_ENCRYPTION_ ENABLED	Verify S3 buckets use encryption
Custom rules	Lambda function checking table permissions	Validate custom governance requirements
Conformance packs	PCI DSS or HIPAA packs	Group related rules for regulatory compliance
Remediation actions	Auto-enable encryption on non-compliant buckets	Automatically fix compliance violations

Table 9.6: Configuration rule type for compliance monitoring

- **Automated compliance reports**: Regular compliance reporting helps stakeholders understand the organization's governance posture. These reports should include:

  o **Compliance summary**: Overall compliance status by category.

  o **Rule compliance**: Status of individual compliance rules.

  o **Resource details**: Specific resources with compliance issues.

  o **Remediation status**: Progress on addressing compliance gaps.

  o **Trend analysis**: How compliance status has changed over time.

- **Continuous security assessment**: AWS Security Hub provides a continuous, comprehensive security assessment by aggregating findings from multiple sources

The following table lists the security hub features:

Security hub feature	Purpose	Integration
Security standards	Benchmark against established standards	CIS AWS Foundations, PCI DSS, etc.
Cross-service findings	Aggregate security issues	Config, GuardDuty, Inspector, Macie
Custom insights	Track specific security concerns	Custom queries on security findings
Automated response	React to security events	EventBridge integration for automation

Table 9.7: Security hub features and their purpose

Regulatory compliance frameworks

GDPR imposes comprehensive personal data protection requirements that demand specialized AWS configurations, from automated PII detection to granular access controls and subject rights management.

Meeting GDPR obligations requires systematic implementation of AWS security services, including Macie for data identification, Lake Formation for access management, and GuardDuty for breach detection.

GDPR compliance

The GDPR imposes strict requirements for protecting personal data. The following table lists the GDPR requirements:

GDPR requirement	AWS Implementation	Audit capability
Data identification	Macie for PII detection	Comprehensive inventory of personal data
Access controls	Lake Formation permissions	Verification of appropriate restrictions
Data subject rights	Query capability for individual data	Audit of data subject request fulfillment
Breach monitoring	GuardDuty and CloudWatch	Detection and alerting for potential breaches

Table 9.8: AWS services for implementing GDPR requirements

HIPAA compliance

Healthcare organizations must comply with HIPAA requirements for protected health information. The following table shows the HIPAA requirements:

HIPAA requirement	AWS implementation	Audit capability
PHI encryption	KMS with HIPAA-compliant keys	Verification of encryption status
Access logging	CloudTrail and service-specific logs	Comprehensive access audit trail
Integrity controls	S3 Object Lock and versioning	Verification of data immutability
Transmission security	TLS enforcement policies	Validation of secure transport

Table 9.9: AWS implementation for HIPAA compliance

Audit challenges and solutions

Effective audit infrastructures must overcome three key challenges: managing overwhelming log volumes, preventing alert fatigue that obscures critical issues, and maintaining comprehensive coverage as environments evolve.

As data governance matures, organizations face escalating complexity in their audit frameworks and discover practical solutions to scale monitoring effectively while maintaining visibility and responsiveness to genuine security concerns:

- **Challenge 1: Log volume management:**

    The volume of audit logs generated by comprehensive monitoring can become overwhelming, making effective analysis difficult. The following table lists the challenges due to log volume:

Challenge	Solution	Implementation
Storage costs	Tiered storage strategy	Move older logs to lower-cost storage classes
Query performance	Log indexing and aggregation	CloudWatch Logs Insights with optimized queries
Retention management	Automated lifecycle policies	S3 lifecycle rules for log rotation
Analysis complexity	Focused analytics	Extract key metrics rather than raw analysis

Table 9.10: Log volume management strategies

- **Challenge 2: Alert fatigue:**

  Poorly configured monitoring systems can generate excessive alerts, leading to alert fatigue where important notifications are overlooked. The following table illustrate the challenges arising because of the alert fatigue:

Challenge	Solution	Implementation
Excessive alerts	Severity-based filtering	Only alert on high-impact issues
False positives	Baseline-adaptive thresholds	Adjust thresholds based on normal patterns
Alert noise	Correlation and aggregation	Group related alerts to reduce volume
Response process	Clear escalation workflows	Define ownership and SLAs for different alert types

Table 9.11: Alert fatigue management approaches

- **Challenge 3: Audit scope gaps:**

  As data environments evolve, new services or workflows may fall outside established audit frameworks, creating visibility gaps. The following table shows the challenges because of audit scope gaps:

Challenge	Solution	Implementation
Evolving services	Regular audit coverage reviews	Periodic validation of audit scope
Shadow IT	Automated discovery	Resource tagging and inventory validation
Service integration	Standardized logging requirements	Consistent log format and delivery
Compliance evolution	Regular framework updates	Keep audit capabilities aligned with regulations

Table 9.12: Audit coverage gap mitigation approaches

Comprehensive audit and compliance capabilities provide the visibility needed to validate governance effectiveness and demonstrate regulatory compliance. By implementing robust logging, monitoring, and analytics frameworks, organizations can maintain confidence in their security posture even as their data environments grow increasingly complex.

Hands-on: Implementing enterprise-grade security

This hands-on guide provides an overview of implementing an enterprise-grade security framework for your data lake on AWS. The complete implementation with step-by-step instructions is available in the accompanying GitHub repository.

Outcome expected

The workshop guides you through building a comprehensive security solution that includes:

- A secure data lake with proper encryption and Lake Formation governance.
- Column-level security tailored to different user personas.
- LF-Tags for scalable, attribute-based access control.
- Comprehensive audit logging and monitoring capabilities.

Implementation overview

The security implementation follows a modular approach:

- **Data Lake Foundation:**
    - Create an encrypted S3 bucket

- o   Register it with Lake Formation
- o   Set up domain-specific databases in the Glue Data Catalogue
- **Security layers:**
  - o   Implement persona-based IAM roles (Analyst, Scientist, Marketing, Steward)
  - o   Apply column-level security using Lake Formation permissions
  - o   Create LF-Tags for sensitivity levels and data domains
  - o   Connect tags to columns based on data sensitivity
- **Audit and monitoring:**
  - o   Configure CloudTrail for comprehensive API logging
  - o   Set up CloudWatch metrics for sensitive data access
  - o   Create dashboards for security monitoring

Key technical components

The implementation leverages multiple AWS services in an integrated security framework:

- **AWS Lake Formation** for unified permission management.
- **AWS Glue Data Catalogue** for metadata management.
- **AWS IAM** for identity and access management.
- **AWS CloudTrail** for audit logging.
- **AWS CloudWatch** for monitoring and alerting.

Next steps

After completing the base implementation, consider these extensions:

- Implement row-level security using Lake Formation row filters.
- Add data masking for sensitive fields.
- Set up cross-account data sharing.
- Implement automated remediation for security findings.

Conclusion

Effective data governance and security serve as the foundation for any successful data platform, enabling organizations to derive maximum value from their data assets while maintaining compliance and protecting sensitive information. Throughout this chapter, we have explored how AWS Lake Formation provides a unified control plane for implementing fine-grained permissions, column-level security, encryption strategies, and comprehensive audit capabilities that span heterogeneous technologies while maintaining consistent policy enforcement. We have seen how these capabilities can be combined to create governance frameworks that balance protection with utility, implementing controls that secure sensitive assets while still enabling appropriate analytical access. By leveraging Lake Formation's permission model, LF-Tags for scalability, and integration with broader AWS security services, organizations can build data platforms that not only meet regulatory requirements but also accelerate innovation through secure, governed access to data resources.

In the next chapter, we will build on these governance capabilities by exploring cross-boundary data sharing and collaborations, examining secure patterns for sharing data across organizational boundaries, implementing cross-account access, and building data exchange platforms that enable collaboration while maintaining security and compliance. As we will see, secure data sharing represents the next frontier in data governance, allowing organizations to maximize the value of their data assets beyond traditional boundaries.

## CHAPTER 10

Cross-boundary Data Sharing and Collaborations

Introduction

Traditional data architectures were designed for internal consumption within organizational boundaries, with data sharing often implemented as an afterthought through manual extracts or brittle point-to-point integrations. This approach created significant friction that limited the value organizations could derive from collaborative data initiatives. Modern enterprises, however, operate within complex ecosystems that include suppliers, partners, customers, and regulators, all requiring secure, scalable, and governed data exchange mechanisms. The ability to effectively share data across organizational boundaries has evolved from a nice-to-have feature to a strategic imperative that directly impacts business agility, innovation capacity, and competitive positioning.

Within AWS, cross-boundary data sharing has evolved from simple cross-account access policies to sophisticated, purpose-built services that balance security, governance, and utility. AWS Lake Formation's data sharing capabilities remove the need to copy data between accounts, instead providing secure, governed access to specific datasets while maintaining a single source of truth. AWS Data Exchange facilitates the discovery, subscription, and integration of third-party data through standardized patterns and entitlement management. These capabilities, combined with fundamental security services like AWS IAM and AWS **Key Management Service** (**KMS**), enable sophisticated sharing models that were previously impractical to implement at scale.

Structure

This chapter covers the following topics:

- Data sharing patterns and use cases
- AWS services for secure data sharing
- Implementing cross-account access
- Building data exchange platforms
- Collaborative analytics and insights
- Performance optimization for data sharing
- Challenges and best practices

Objectives

This chapter aims to provide a comprehensive understanding of implementing secure, governed cross-boundary data sharing on AWS. You will learn how to establish sharing relationships across AWS accounts using Lake Formation, implement fine-grained access controls for external parties, and develop data exchange platforms that enable discovery and self-service access. The chapter explores security patterns for shared data, including encryption strategies, network configurations, and just-in-time access models that protect sensitive information while enabling collaboration. Through practical implementation examples, you will understand how to address regulatory requirements for data sharing, establish audit capabilities that verify compliance with sharing agreements, and optimize performance for cross-boundary queries. These capabilities will enable you to design sharing frameworks that balance security, compliance, and utility while creating valuable collaboration opportunities with partners, suppliers, and customers.

Data sharing patterns and use cases

Cross-boundary data sharing encompasses diverse patterns that address different business needs, technical constraints, and governance requirements. Understanding these patterns provides a framework for selecting the most appropriate approach based on specific use cases and organizational contexts.

Core sharing patterns

Modern data architectures require sophisticated sharing mechanisms that balance security, performance, and governance across organizational boundaries. AWS provides multiple patterns for data sharing, each optimized for different use cases ranging from real-time collaboration to formal data product distribution. Understanding these patterns enables organizations to select the most appropriate approach based on their specific requirements for data sovereignty, latency, and access control. The following four patterns represent the most common and effective strategies for sharing data within the AWS ecosystem.

Account-to-account sharing

Account-to-account sharing enables direct access to data between AWS accounts within the same organization or between trusted external partners. This pattern maintains data in its original location while providing secure access through AWS Lake Formation, AWS **Resource Access Manager** (**RAM**), or direct IAM policies.

This sharing model eliminates the need for data duplication, which significantly reduces storage costs and eliminates synchronization challenges that often plague copy-based approaches. Access policies are managed centrally by the data owner, providing consistent governance regardless of which service consumers use to access the data. Since data remains in its original location, consumers always see the most current information without replication latency.

Consider a multinational retail corporation with separate AWS accounts for each regional business unit. Using Lake Formation cross-account sharing, the North American division can securely share sales trend data with the European division for comparative analysis. The data remains in the North American account, but European analysts can query it directly through Athena or Redshift Spectrum without needing local copies. When North American sales data updates, European analysts immediately see the changes, enabling real-time collaborative decision-making across organizational boundaries.

Data product distribution

Data product distribution focuses on packaging and delivering curated datasets as self-contained products, typically through AWS Data Exchange or custom data portals. Unlike account-to-account sharing, this pattern often involves creating copies of data specifically designed for consumption by external parties.

Organizations implementing this pattern treat data as formal products with clear documentation, quality guarantees, and standard delivery mechanisms. This approach enables sophisticated entitlement management, including subscription models, usage tracking, and monetization options that would be difficult to implement with direct access patterns.

A financial services company demonstrates this pattern by packaging anonymized transaction datasets for market research firms. They create monthly snapshots of spending trends across demographic segments, enrich the data with classification metadata, and distribute it through AWS Data Exchange with tiered subscription models. Consumers receive not just raw data but comprehensive documentation explaining collection methodology, field definitions, and suggested analytical approaches. The producing company maintains complete control over which versions each subscriber can access, with automatic entitlement verification and revocation when subscriptions expire.

Federated query

Federated query enables analysis across distributed datasets without physically moving or consolidating the data. This pattern leverages services like Amazon Athena with federated query capabilities or Amazon Redshift with cross-database queries to access data residing in multiple locations.

This approach solves complex data sovereignty challenges by leaving source data under the control of its original owner while enabling broader analytical access. Only query results traverse boundaries, minimizing bandwidth consumption and storage duplication. Since queries execute against source data, results always reflect current information without synchronization delays.

A healthcare research consortium employs federated query patterns to analyze patient outcomes across multiple hospitals without violating data residency requirements. Each hospital maintains custody of patient records in its own AWS account, complying with local privacy regulations. Researchers submit Athena federated queries that execute across all participating hospitals, returning only aggregated, anonymized results that meet privacy thresholds. This approach enables valuable population health research while maintaining strict compliance with regulations that prohibit transferring individual patient records across institutional boundaries.

Event-based interchange

Event-based interchange focuses on real-time sharing of data changes rather than providing access to complete datasets. This pattern utilizes services like Amazon EventBridge, Amazon MSK, or Amazon Kinesis to stream data modifications as they occur.

This approach creates highly responsive data integration across organizational boundaries without requiring ongoing synchronization of complete datasets. Producers can implement selective filtering to share only relevant changes, and the loosely coupled architecture allows consumers to process events according to their own requirements and schedules. The fan-out capabilities of streaming platforms enable scalable distribution where multiple consumers receive the same event streams without increasing the load on source systems.

An automotive supply chain demonstrates this pattern by sharing production events between manufacturing partners. When a vehicle assembly plant updates its production schedule, an event streams through Amazon MSK to component suppliers, who automatically adjust their own production plans. Similarly, when suppliers encounter quality issues or shipping delays, corresponding events flow back to the assembly plant, triggering appropriate adjustments to the master schedule. This real-time interchange enables just-in-time manufacturing across organizational boundaries with significantly less coordination overhead than traditional batch-oriented data sharing approaches.

Comparison of cross-boundary data sharing patterns

The following table summarises the cross-boundary data sharing patterns as discussed in the above section:

Sharing pattern	Key characteristics	Best use cases	Advantages	Limitations	AWS services
Account-to-account sharing	Direct access to data in original location	Cross-department analytics, organizational data mesh	No data duplication, always current data, reduced storage costs, centralized governance	Requires constant network connectivity, consumer depends on producer availability, limited to AWS ecosystem	AWS Lake Formation, AWS RAM, IAM policies
Data product distribution	Packaging curated datasets as self-contained products	Commercial data sharing, regulated industries with data export requirements	Complete control over versions, formal documentation, monetization options, works across cloud providers	Creates data copies, synchronization challenges, storage duplication costs, potential data staleness	AWS Data Exchange, S3 + CloudFront, custom data portals
Federated query	Analysis across distributed datasets without moving data	Healthcare research, multi-region analysis with data sovereignty requirements	Data remains under source control, minimizes data movement, respects data residency, and provides real-time access to source data	Query performance overhead, network dependency, more complex to implement, limited to supported data sources	Amazon Athena Federated Query, Amazon Redshift cross-database queries
Event-based interchange	Real-time sharing of data changes	Supply chain coordination, operational data sharing	Near real-time updates, loose coupling, selective filtering, efficient network usage	More complex to implement, requires event-handling infrastructure, not suited for bulk historical data	Amazon EventBridge, Amazon MSK, Amazon Kinesis

Table 10.1: Comparison of data sharing patterns

Business use cases

Cross-boundary data sharing delivers transformative business value across diverse industries and organizational structures, enabling collaboration that was previously impossible due to technical and governance constraints. These real-world implementations demonstrate how modern AWS architectures can break down data silos while maintaining strict security and compliance requirements. From supply chain optimization to regulatory compliance, organizations are discovering that strategic data sharing creates competitive advantages that extend far beyond traditional analytics capabilities. The following use cases illustrate how different industries leverage cross-boundary sharing to solve complex business challenges and drive operational excellence.

Supply chain collaboration

Modern supply chains function as complex ecosystems requiring coordinated visibility and planning across multiple organizations. Effective cross-boundary data sharing can transform these traditionally fragmented processes into synchronized networks with significantly improved performance.

A global retailer with over 5,000 stores implemented an AWS-based supplier collaboration platform that reduced out-of-stock incidents by 32% through secure, real-time inventory sharing. The retailer's platform uses Lake Formation for controlled access to store-level inventory data, with fine-grained controls ensuring suppliers see only categories and regions relevant to their business. Daily sales forecasts flow through EventBridge to supplier systems, enabling proactive production adjustments based on consumption patterns. When unusual demand occurs, such as during weather events or promotional periods, real-time alerting ensures suppliers can respond rapidly to prevent stockouts. The platform maintains detailed audit trails of all data access, ensuring compliance with commercial agreements while providing the transparency needed for effective collaboration.

This implementation demonstrates how modern data sharing transforms traditional vendor relationships into strategic partnerships. Before implementing cross-boundary sharing, the retailer experienced average resupply cycles of 12 days with frequent mismatches between inventory and demand. Post-implementation, cycle times decreased to four days while inventory accuracy improved from 82% to 97%, creating a significant competitive advantage through improved product availability and reduced working capital requirements.

Cross-department analytics

Even within a single organization, data often spans multiple AWS accounts or environments that function as boundaries requiring explicit sharing mechanisms. Breaking down these internal silos enables comprehensive analytics that drive enterprise-wide optimization.

A telecommunications provider with separate AWS accounts for network operations, customer service, and marketing struggled to create unified customer experience insights. Their cross-account data mesh implementation used Lake Formation to securely connect these domains while maintaining clear ownership boundaries. Network performance data from operations combined with customer service interactions and campaign response data from marketing to create a unified customer journey view. Analysts access these integrated datasets through a centralized catalogue that enforces appropriate column-level security, technical staff see detailed network metrics but limited customer information, while marketing analysts see behavioural patterns but not sensitive account details.

This implementation reduced analytical project timelines by 65% by eliminating lengthy ETL processes previously required to consolidate data across domains. The architecture enabled the discovery of critical insights at customer journey intersection points, such as how network performance impacts support call volumes and retention campaign effectiveness. These insights drove targeted investments that increased customer satisfaction scores by 18% while reducing operational costs.

Industry data consortiums

Organizations within the same industry increasingly collaborate through data consortiums that aggregate anonymized data to generate collective insights without exposing competitive details. These consortium models generate significant value that individual participants could not achieve independently.

A consortium of nine financial institutions developed an AWS-based fraud detection system that increased fraud identification by 47% by securely sharing anonymized transaction patterns. Each institution maintains complete control of its raw transaction data within its own AWS account but contributes pattern data to a shared consortium database with row-level security, ensuring each member sees only appropriate information. Machine learning models train on this combined dataset, identifying sophisticated fraud patterns that would be invisible within any single institution's data. When potential fraud patterns emerge, real-time alerts flow to all affected institutions through Amazon SNS, enabling coordinated response to emerging threats.

The consortium architecture includes sophisticated privacy-preserving techniques such as differential privacy transforms and aggregation thresholds that prevent re-identification risks. A central governance committee establishes data standards and sharing policies, with automated compliance monitoring ensuring all participants adhere to consortium rules. This collaborative approach enables consortium members to reduce fraud losses significantly while maintaining competitive independence in other aspects of their business.

Regulatory reporting

Organizations in regulated industries must regularly share data with governmental oversight bodies. Modern implementations transform this compliance burden into an automated, efficient process that reduces costs while improving reporting accuracy.

A consortium of European banks developed a regulatory reporting platform on AWS that reduced compliance costs by 30% while improving data quality. The platform standardizes reporting data from multiple institutions into consistent formats aligned with regulatory requirements, with automated validation ensuring completeness and accuracy before submission. Submissions flow through secure API gateways to regulatory bodies, with cryptographic signatures and comprehensive audit trails documenting the entire process. Since implementing the platform, participating banks have reduced regulatory preparation time from weeks to days, while significantly reducing error rates in submissions.

The platform's architecture separates raw financial data from aggregated reporting views, enabling banks to maintain complete control of sensitive details while still meeting disclosure requirements. AWS IAM and Lake Formation permissions enforce strict access controls, ensuring that only authorized regulatory staff can access specific reporting datasets. The implementation includes comprehensive lineage tracking that document how each reported value derives from source systems, enabling rapid response to regulatory inquiries and simplified audit processes.

AWS services for secure data sharing

Implementing effective cross-boundary data sharing requires careful selection and configuration of AWS services that align with specific organizational requirements and governance constraints. Each sharing approach—from Lake Formation's fine-grained access controls to Data Exchange's commercial distribution capabilities—offers distinct advantages for different use cases and architectural patterns. The following technical implementations provide detailed guidance for establishing secure, scalable data sharing foundations using AWS's core data services. These patterns demonstrate how to configure producer-consumer relationships, manage access controls, and optimize performance across account boundaries while maintaining strict security and compliance standards.

AWS Lake Formation as a sharing foundation

AWS Lake Formation serves as the foundational service for implementing secure, governed data sharing across AWS accounts while maintaining centralized access control and data lineage. The service enables a producer-consumer model where data owners can share specific databases, tables, or tagged resources without duplicating data or compromising security boundaries. The following implementation demonstrates both traditional named resource sharing and the more scalable LF-Tag approach for enterprise-level data governance.

Producer account setup

The data owner (producer) establishes the sharing foundation through these key steps:

```
1.  # Producer account CloudFormation
2.  Resources:
3.    # 1. Create a resource share
4.    ResourceShare:
5.      Type: AWS::RAM::ResourceShare
6.      Properties:
7.        Name: CrossAccountDataShare
8.        AllowExternalPrincipals: true
```

```
9.        Principals:
10.          - !Sub 'arn:aws:iam::${ConsumerAccountId}:root'
11.        ResourceArns:
12.          - !Sub 'arn:aws:glue:${AWS::Region}:${AWS::AccountId}:database/shared_
    database'
13.
14.  # 2. Grant permissions to the consumer account
15.  CrossAccountPermissions:
16.    Type: AWS::LakeFormation::Permissions
17.    Properties:
18.      Principal:
19.        DataLakePrincipalIdentifier: !Sub 'arn:aws:iam::${ConsumerAccountId}:root'
20.      Resource:
21.        DatabaseResource:
22.          Name: shared_database
23.      Permissions:
24.        - DESCRIBE
25.        - SELECT
```

Consumer account setup

The consumer account must complete three steps to access shared data:

1. Accept the RAM resource share using either, AWS Console method:

   a. Navigate to Resource Access Manager console.

   b. Select Shared with me | Resource shares.

   c. Find the pending share and click Accept resource share.

2. Create a Lake Formation resource link to the shared database:
```
1. CREATE DATABASE shared_database_link
2. FROM RESOURCE LINK shared_database OF aws://123456789012/us-east-1;
```

3. Grant permissions to local users/roles:
```
1. -- Grant Lake Formation permissions to local users
2. GRANT SELECT ON DATABASE shared_database_link TO IAM_ROLE 'AnalyticsTeam';
```

After setup, users in the consumer account can query shared data through Athena, Redshift Spectrum, or EMR using the resource link name:
```
1. -- Example query from consumer account
2. SELECT * FROM shared_database_link.customer_table
3. WHERE region = 'Northeast'
4. LIMIT 10;
```

LF-Tag based sharing

For large-scale implementations, LF-Tag based sharing offers better scalability than named resource permissions:
```
1. -- Producer account: Define and assign tags
2. CREATE LF-TAG 'SharingBoundary' WITH ALLOWED VALUES ('Partners', 'Public');
3. ASSIGN LF-TAG 'SharingBoundary' = 'Partners' ON TABLE sales.transactions;
```

```
4.
5.  -- Grant tag-based permissions to consumer
6.  GRANT SELECT ON RESOURCES WHERE SharingBoundary = 'Partners'
7.  TO ACCOUNT '123456789012';
8.
9.  -- Consumer account: Grant access to local users based on tags
10. GRANT SELECT ON RESOURCES WHERE SharingBoundary = 'Partners'
11. TO IAM_ROLE 'arn:aws:iam::123456789012:role/AnalyticsTeam';
```

This approach allows permissions to automatically adjust as data classifications change, without manual updates. New datasets with appropriate tags automatically inherit the correct sharing permissions, enabling governance at scale.

AWS Data Exchange for commercial data sharing

AWS Data Exchange simplifies the process of finding, subscribing to, distributing, and using third-party data in the cloud. Unlike Lake Formation, which focuses on direct sharing relationships, Data Exchange addresses formalized data distribution scenarios with integrated entitlement management, discovery capabilities, and standardized delivery mechanisms.

For data providers

Organizations that want to distribute data products can use Data Exchange to package and deliver datasets with comprehensive governance controls:

```
1.  # Creating a data product using AWS SDK
2.  import boto3
3.
4.  dataexchange = boto3.client('dataexchange')
5.
6.  # Step 1: Create a data set
7.  data_set = dataexchange.create_data_set(
8.      Name='Retail Foot Traffic Analysis 2025',
9.      Description='Daily visitor metrics across 500+ retail locations',
10.     AssetType='S3_SNAPSHOT',
11.     Tags={
12.         'Industry': 'Retail',
13.         'UpdateFrequency': 'Daily',
14.         'DataCategory': 'Location'
15.     }
16. )
17.
18. # Step 2: Create a revision (version)
19. revision = dataexchange.create_revision(
20.     DataSetId=data_set['Id'],
21.     Comment='Initial release with Q1 2025 data'
22. )
23.
24. # Step 3: Add assets to the revision
25. dataexchange.create_job(
26.     Type='IMPORT_ASSETS_FROM_S3',
```

```
27.     Details={
28.         'ImportAssetsFromS3': {
29.             'DataSetId': data_set['Id'],
30.             'RevisionId': revision['Id'],
31.             'AssetSources': [
32.                 {
33.                     'Bucket': 'retail-analytics-source',
34.                     'Key': 'foot-traffic/2025-q1.parquet'
35.                 }
36.             ]
37.         }
38.     }
39. )
40.
41. # Step 4: Finalize the revision
42. dataexchange.update_revision(
43.     DataSetId=data_set['Id'],
44.     RevisionId=revision['Id'],
45.     Finalized=True
46. )
47.
48. # Step 5: Create the product
49. product = dataexchange.create_product(
50.     Name='Retail Foot Traffic Intelligence',
51.     Description='Daily visitor patterns with demographic breakdown',
52.     DataSetIds=[data_set['Id']],
53.     ProductType='DATA_EXCHANGE_PRODUCT'
54. )
```

Data providers can implement several distribution models:

- **Public listings**: Publishing products to the AWS Data Exchange catalogue for any AWS customer to discover and subscribe.

- **Private offers**: Creating custom terms for specific customers with tailored pricing and usage rights.

- **Bring-your-own-subscription**: Managing commercial relationships outside AWS while using Data Exchange for technical distribution.

The service automatically handles entitlement verification, ensuring subscribers can only access data during valid subscription periods, and provides usage metrics to track consumption patterns.

For data consumers

Organizations looking to consume third-party data will find a streamlined discovery and subscription process:

```
1. # CLI example for listing available data products
2. aws dataexchange search-data-products \
3.     --filter-criteria '{"Origins":["ENTITLED","AMAZON_MARKETPLACE"]}' \
4.     --max-results 10
5.
6. # Subscribe to a product (through console or AWS Marketplace API)
7. # After subscription is complete:
```

```
8.
9.  # List entitled data sets
10. aws dataexchange list-data-sets \
11.     --origin ENTITLED
12.
13. # Create a job to export an asset to S3
14. aws dataexchange create-job \
15.     --type EXPORT_ASSETS_TO_S3 \
16.     --details <{
17.         "ExportAssetsToS3": {
18.             "AssetDestinations": [
19.                 {
20.                     "AssetId": "asset-1234567890abcdef0",
21.                     "Bucket": "my-destination-bucket",
22.                     "Key": "retail-data/foot-traffic.parquet"
23.                 }
24.             ],
25.             "DataSetId": "dataset-1234567890abcdef0",
26.             "RevisionId": "revision-1234567890abcdef0"
27.         }
28.     }>
29.
30. # Start the export job
31. aws dataexchange start-job --job-id job-1234567890abcdef0
```

AWS Data Exchange addresses the unique requirements of commercial data sharing, providing purpose-built capabilities for secure, governed distribution. By streamlining discovery, subscription, and delivery processes, it enables data providers to reach broader markets while giving consumers efficient access to valuable third-party datasets with minimal integration overhead.

Amazon Redshift data sharing

Amazon Redshift provides native data sharing capabilities that enable real-time access to data across different clusters, accounts, and AWS regions without copying or moving the underlying data. This approach is particularly valuable for analytical workloads that require high-performance querying on large datasets.

Producer cluster configuration

The data owner (producer) creates datashares and controls which objects are accessible:

```
1.  -- Create a datashare in the producer cluster
2.  CREATE DATASHARE sales_analytics;
3.
4.  -- Add objects to the datashare
5.  ALTER DATASHARE sales_analytics ADD SCHEMA public;
6.  ALTER DATASHARE sales_analytics ADD TABLE public.sales;
7.  ALTER DATASHARE sales_analytics ADD TABLE public.customers;
8.
9.  -- Create a specialized view with pre-calculated aggregations
10. CREATE VIEW public.sales_summary AS
```

```
11. SELECT region, product_category, date_trunc('month', sale_date) as month,
12.     SUM(amount) as total_sales, COUNT(*) as transaction_count
13. FROM public.sales
14. GROUP BY 1, 2, 3;
15.
16. -- Add the view to the datashare
17. ALTER DATASHARE sales_analytics ADD TABLE public.sales_summary;
18.
19. -- Grant usage to a specific AWS account
20. GRANT USAGE ON DATASHARE sales_analytics TO ACCOUNT '123456789012';
```

The producer maintains complete control over what has been shared. They can add or remove objects at any time, and changes are immediately reflected in consumer access. Producers can also implement sophisticated access patterns through specialized views, such as pre-aggregated summaries that optimize query performance or filtered views that implement row-level security.

Consumer cluster access

Once the producer shares data, the consumer account must create a database from the datashare to access the shared objects:

```
1.  -- In the consumer cluster
2.  -- Create a database from the received datashare
3.  CREATE DATABASE sales_analytics_consumer
4.  FROM DATASHARE sales_analytics
5.  OF ACCOUNT '987654321098'
6.  REGION 'us-east-1';
7.
8.  -- Grant access to roles within the consumer account
9.  GRANT USAGE ON DATABASE sales_analytics_consumer TO data_analyst_role;
10. GRANT USAGE ON SCHEMA sales_analytics_consumer.public TO data_analyst_role;
11. GRANT SELECT ON ALL TABLES IN SCHEMA sales_analytics_consumer.public TO data_analyst_
    role;
12.
13. -- Query the shared data directly
14. SELECT
15.     region,
16.     product_category,
17.     SUM(total_sales) as quarterly_sales
18. FROM sales_analytics_consumer.public.sales_summary
19. WHERE month BETWEEN '2025-01-01' AND '2025-03-31'
20. GROUP BY 1, 2
21. ORDER BY quarterly_sales DESC
22. LIMIT 10;
```

The consumer can query shared data as if it were local but cannot modify the data or schema of shared objects. This read-only default ensures data integrity while enabling broad analytical access. For more granular access control within the consumer organization, administrators can create custom views on top of shared objects:

```
1.  -- Creating restricted access for regional teams
2.  CREATE SCHEMA regional_sales;
3.
```

```
4.  CREATE VIEW regional_sales.northeast AS
5.  SELECT * FROM sales_analytics_consumer.public.sales_summary
6.  WHERE region = 'Northeast';
7.
8.  GRANT USAGE ON SCHEMA regional_sales TO northeast_analyst_role;
9.  GRANT SELECT ON ALL TABLES IN SCHEMA regional_sales TO northeast_analyst_role;
```

Key benefits of Redshift data sharing

Redshift's sharing architecture delivers several unique advantages:

- **Zero-copy sharing**: Data remains in the producer cluster, eliminating storage duplication and synchronization overhead.

- **Real-time access**: Consumers always see current data without replication lag.

- **Performance**: Leverages Redshift's columnar storage and query optimization for high-performance analytics.

- **Simplified data operations**: Producers maintain data in a single location while enabling broad consumption.

Redshift data sharing provides an ideal solution for organizations that need to enable cross-account analytics on large datasets without the overhead of data replication. The combination of high performance, real-time access, and granular controls makes it well-suited for enterprise-scale data sharing requirements.

Implementing cross-account access

Secure cross-account data sharing in AWS relies on carefully configured trust relationships and layered permission models that establish who can access what resources under which conditions. These trust mechanisms form the security foundation for all cross-boundary interactions, combining IAM roles, resource policies, and organizational controls to create defense-in-depth architectures. Understanding and properly implementing these permission patterns is essential for maintaining security while enabling the collaborative data access that modern enterprises require.

Trust relationships and permission models

The role-based access pattern represents the gold standard for secure cross-account data sharing, providing granular control through temporary credentials and comprehensive audit capabilities. This approach establishes a four-component architecture where producer accounts create trusted roles, consumer accounts assume those roles, and permission boundaries enforce least-privilege access throughout the interaction. The following implementation demonstrates how to configure both the trust relationships and permission policies that enable secure, auditable cross-account access while maintaining strict security controls.

Role-based access pattern

The most robust implementation pattern for cross-account data sharing leverages IAM roles:

- **Producer account**: Creates a role with appropriate permissions to access specific data resources.

- **Trust policy**: Configures the role to trust specific consumer accounts or principals.

- **Consumer account**: Contains users or roles that can assume the producer's role.

- **Permission boundary**: Limits the actions allowed when assuming the cross-account role.

This approach offers several security advantages. Access is granted through short-lived session tokens rather than permanent credentials, minimizing exposure risk. Roles can be scoped to the minimum required permissions following the principle of least privilege. Access can be immediately revoked by modifying the trust relationship if needed. Additionally, role assumption actions create comprehensive audit trails in CloudTrail for compliance and monitoring:

```
1.  // Producer account role definition
2.  {
3.    "Version": "2012-10-17",
4.    "Statement": [
5.      {
6.        "Effect": "Allow",
7.        "Principal": {
8.          "AWS": "arn:aws:iam::CONSUMER_ACCOUNT_ID:root"
9.        },
10.       "Action": "sts:AssumeRole",
11.       "Condition": {
12.         "StringEquals": {
13.           "aws:PrincipalOrgID": "o-xxxxxxxxxxx"
14.         }
15.       }
16.     }
17.   ]
18. }
19.
20. // Producer account permission policy
21. {
22.   "Version": "2012-10-17",
23.   "Statement": [
24.     {
25.       "Effect": "Allow",
26.       "Action": [
27.         "glue:GetTable",
28.         "glue:GetPartition*",
29.         "glue:GetDatabase*",
30.         "athena:GetQueryExecution",
31.         "athena:GetQueryResults",
32.         "athena:StartQueryExecution"
33.       ],
34.       "Resource": [
35.         "arn:aws:glue:us-east-1:PRODUCER_ACCOUNT_ID:catalog",
36.         "arn:aws:glue:us-east-1:PRODUCER_ACCOUNT_ID:database/shared_data",
37.         "arn:aws:glue:us-east-1:PRODUCER_ACCOUNT_ID:table/shared_data/*",
38.         "arn:aws:athena:us-east-1:PRODUCER_ACCOUNT_ID:workgroup/primary"
39.       ]
40.     },
41.     {
42.       "Effect": "Allow",
43.       "Action": [
44.         "s3:GetObject",
45.         "s3:ListBucket"
46.       ],
47.       "Resource": [
```

```
48.              "arn:aws:s3:::data-lake-bucket",
49.              "arn:aws:s3:::data-lake-bucket/shared-data/*"
50.          ]
51.      }
52.  ]
53. }
```

On the consumer side, IAM policies determine which users or roles can assume the cross-account role. This two-step permission model creates defense-in-depth, requiring authorization in both accounts for successful access.

Cross-account resource policies

Resource-based policies provide an alternative approach to cross-account sharing by attaching permissions directly to AWS resources rather than requiring role assumption. This method works particularly well for straightforward sharing scenarios where the overhead of IAM role management is not warranted, offering simpler configuration for trusted partnerships. The following examples demonstrate how S3 bucket policies and KMS key policies can be combined to create secure, direct access patterns for encrypted data lakes.

S3 bucket policies

For data lakes built on Amazon S3, bucket policies provide a direct mechanism for cross-account sharing:

```
1.  {
2.    "Version": "2012-10-17",
3.    "Statement": [
4.      {
5.        "Effect": "Allow",
6.        "Principal": {
7.          "AWS": "arn:aws:iam::CONSUMER_ACCOUNT_ID:role/AnalyticsTeam"
8.        },
9.        "Action": [
10.          "s3:GetObject",
11.          "s3:ListBucket"
12.        ],
13.        "Resource": [
14.          "arn:aws:s3:::data-lake-bucket",
15.          "arn:aws:s3:::data-lake-bucket/shared-data/*"
16.        ],
17.        "Condition": {
18.          "StringEquals": {
19.            "aws:PrincipalOrgID": "o-xxxxxxxxxxx"
20.          }
21.        }
22.      }
23.    ]
24. }
```

This approach works well for use cases where data sharing is primarily S3-based and does not require the governance capabilities of Lake Formation. It is particularly suitable for simple sharing scenarios with trusted partners where the overhead of setting up Lake Formation may not be justified.

KMS key policies

For encrypted data, KMS key policies must be configured to allow cross-account access to decrypt the data:

```
1.  {
2.    "Version": "2012-10-17",
3.    "Statement": [
4.      {
5.        "Effect": "Allow",
6.        "Principal": {
7.          "AWS": "arn:aws:iam::CONSUMER_ACCOUNT_ID:role/AnalyticsTeam"
8.        },
9.        "Action": [
10.         "kms:Decrypt",
11.         "kms:DescribeKey"
12.       ],
13.       "Resource": "*",
14.       "Condition": {
15.         "StringEquals": {
16.           "kms:ViaService": "s3.us-east-1.amazonaws.com",
17.           "aws:PrincipalOrgID": "o-xxxxxxxxxxx"
18.         }
19.       }
20.     }
21.   ]
22. }
```

This policy grants a role in the consumer account permission to decrypt data, but only when the request comes through Amazon S3 in the specified region. This limits the scope of the permission, ensuring the consumer can only decrypt data in the intended context.

Combined approach

The most robust implementations use a combination of IAM roles and resource policies, creating defence-in-depth:

- **IAM roles**: Define who can access resources across accounts.
- **Resource policies**: Specify which resources can be accessed and what actions are permitted.
- **Service controls**: Add service-specific permissions and restrictions.
- **Encryption policies**: Control access to encrypted content.

This layered approach ensures that access requires satisfaction of multiple conditions, reducing the risk of misconfiguration or unintended exposure.

AWS Organizations integration

AWS Organizations transforms cross-account data sharing from a point-to-point configuration challenge into a scalable, hierarchy-based governance model that aligns with enterprise organizational structures. By leveraging organizational units and conditional policies, enterprises can create dynamic sharing permissions that automatically adapt as accounts move between organizational units or new accounts join the organization. This approach is particularly powerful for large enterprises managing dozens or hundreds of AWS accounts, where individual account-based sharing would become administratively unmanageable.

Understanding Organization-based sharing

AWS Organizations provides a hierarchical structure where:

- The **Organization** is the top-level entity containing all your accounts.
- **Organizational Units (OUs)** group accounts by function, team, or environment.
- **Accounts** are individual AWS accounts within your organization.

This structure enables efficient sharing based on organizational hierarchy rather than individual accounts.

Policy example explained

The following is a resource policy that grants access based on organizational structure:

```
1.  {
2.    "Version": "2012-10-17",
3.    "Statement": [
4.      {
5.        "Effect": "Allow",                   // Permits the specified actions
6.        "Principal": "*",                    // Applies to any IAM entity
7.        "Action": [
8.          "s3:GetObject",                    // Permission to read objects
9.          "s3:ListBucket"
     // Permission to list bucket contents
10.       ],
11.       "Resource": [
12.         "arn:aws:s3:::data-lake-bucket",          // The bucket itself
13.         "arn:aws:s3:::data-lake-bucket/shared-data/*"
      // All objects in shared-data prefix
14.       ],
15.       "Condition": {
16.         "StringEquals": {
17.           "aws:PrincipalOrgID": "o-xxxxxxxxxxx"    // Require membership in this or-
     ganization
18.         },
19.         "StringLike": {
20.           "aws:PrincipalOrgPaths": [              // Require membership in specif-
     ic OU
21.             "o-xxxxxxxxxxx/r-xxxx/ou-xxxx-analyticsou"
22.           ]
23.         }
24.       }
25.     }
26.   ]
27. }
```

Example use case:

Consider a company with separate accounts for finance, marketing, and sales departments, all contained within a business OU. They can create a resource policy that grants access to their quarterly reports' S3 bucket to all accounts in this OU:

```
1.  {
2.    "Version": "2012-10-17",
3.    "Statement": [
```

```
4.     {
5.       "Effect": "Allow",
6.       "Principal": "*",
7.       "Action": ["s3:GetObject"],
8.       "Resource": ["arn:aws:s3:::quarterly-reports/*"],
9.       "Condition": {
10.        "StringEquals": {
11.          "aws:PrincipalOrgID": "o-a1b2c3d4e5"
12.        },
13.        "StringLike": {
14.          "aws:PrincipalOrgPaths": ["o-a1b2c3d4e5/r-f6g7/ou-h8i9-businessou"]
15.        }
16.      }
17.    }
18.  ]
19.}
```

With this policy, any user or role in the business OU can access the quarterly reports, while IT, development, and other departments outside this OU cannot.

Organizational integration is particularly valuable for enterprises implementing data mesh architectures, where each domain owns an AWS account but needs to share data products across organizational boundaries.

Building data exchange platforms

Data exchange platforms create the infrastructure and processes needed for secure, efficient sharing across organizational boundaries. While individual data sharing mechanisms like Lake Formation and Redshift data sharing provide the technical foundation, comprehensive platforms add the discovery, governance, and user experience layers that make cross-boundary sharing truly useful at enterprise scale. The following figure illustrates how these components work together to create a cohesive platform rather than disconnected technical capabilities:

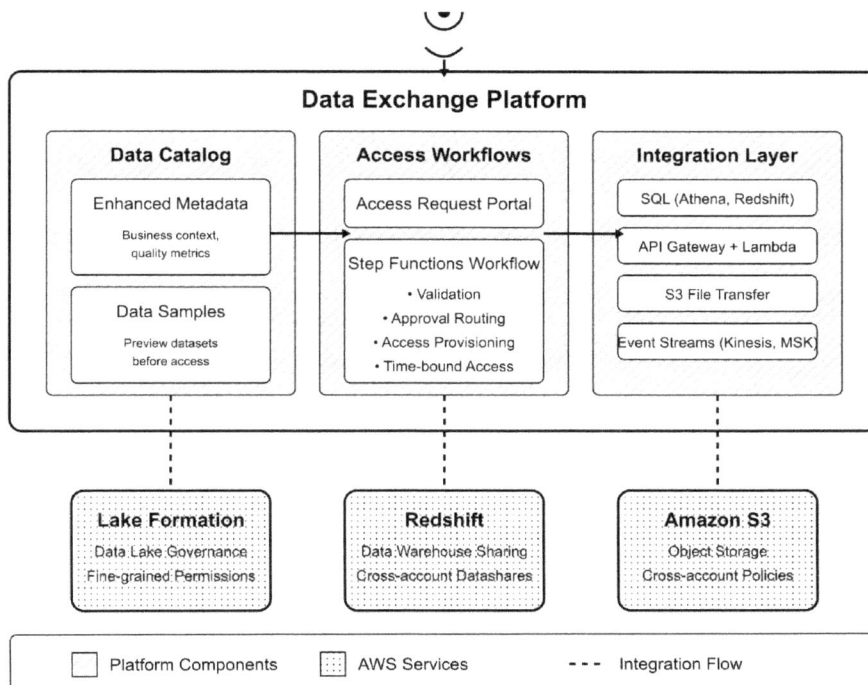

Figure 10.1: Data Exchange reference architecture

Architectural components

Effective data sharing platforms require sophisticated discovery mechanisms that transform technical data assets into business-relevant resources that stakeholders can easily find, understand, and evaluate. A comprehensive data catalogue serves as both inventory and storefront, providing not just metadata but business context, lineage information, and usage patterns that enable informed decision-making about data consumption. The following components demonstrate how to build discovery and access infrastructure that reduces friction for consumers while maintaining governance and security controls throughout the data sharing lifecycle.

Data catalogue and discovery

A robust catalogue forms the foundation of any data exchange platform, making datasets findable and understandable for potential consumers. Beyond basic technical metadata, effective catalogues provide business context, quality metrics, and usage patterns.

Many organizations extend AWS Glue Data Catalogue with additional metadata layers that transform raw technical information into business-relevant descriptions. This enhanced catalogue becomes the storefront of your data exchange, where users can browse, search, and evaluate available datasets before requesting access.

Companies implementing enhanced catalogues frequently reduce time-to-insight by 40-60%, as analysts spend less time hunting for and deciphering datasets. The most effective catalogues include not just what the data contains, but where it came from, who maintains it, how frequently it updates, and how others are using it.

Access request workflows

Every data exchange platform must balance convenient access with appropriate governance. Access request workflows create structured processes that replace ad-hoc emails or tickets with consistent evaluation and provisioning.

The workflow process typically follows these steps:

1. **Request capture**: Users submit structured requests specifying which datasets they need, why they need them, and for how long.

2. **Sensitivity classification**: The system determines the sensitivity level of requested data, which drives approval requirements.

3. **Approval routing**: Requests are automatically directed to the appropriate approvers based on data classification.

4. **Access provisioning**: Upon approval, permissions are automatically configured in Lake Formation or other sharing mechanisms.

5. **Time-bound access**: Permissions include expiration dates aligned with the approved duration.

When implemented through Step Functions, these workflows provide consistent governance while dramatically reducing access provisioning times, often from weeks to hours. The structured nature creates clear audit trails showing who requested access, why, and who approved it.

Integration layer

Different consumers need different ways to access shared data. A flexible platform provides multiple integration options:

- **SQL interfaces**: Enable analysts to query shared data directly through Athena or Redshift.

- **API access**: Allow applications to integrate shared data through REST or GraphQL interfaces.

- **File transfers**: Support traditional ETL processes with scheduled or on-demand file exports.

- **Event streams**: Enable real-time consumption through Kinesis or MSK for operational use cases.

This flexibility ensures that consumers can integrate shared data into their existing workflows and systems with minimal friction. Rather than forcing all consumers into a single access pattern, the platform accommodates diverse needs while maintaining consistent governance.

Implementation patterns

Choosing the right implementation pattern for your data exchange platform is critical for long-term success. The approach you select must align with your organizational structure, security requirements, and collaboration goals. When evaluating patterns, consider not just current needs but how your sharing relationships will evolve over time. The most successful implementations start with clear business objectives and then select technical patterns that enable those objectives, rather than being driven solely by technological considerations.

Internal data marketplace

Many organizations start with an internal marketplace focused on cross-department sharing. This model treats data as products, with clear ownership, documentation, and service commitments.

The most successful internal marketplaces take cues from consumer digital experiences. They offer intuitive search and browsing interfaces for dataset discovery. They provide one-click access requests for permitted datasets. They include ratings and reviews to help users identify the most valuable assets.

This approach solves the classic problem where valuable datasets exist but remain unknown to potential users in other departments. Marketing analysts might never discover that the product team maintains a dataset perfectly suited for their campaign effectiveness analysis, or finance might recreate datasets that operations already maintain.

By implementing a unified catalogue with standardized metadata and consistent access processes, these platforms significantly increase data reuse and reduce duplicate work. Organizations with mature internal marketplaces commonly report 30-40% reductions in redundant dataset creation as teams discover and leverage existing assets.

Trusted partner exchange

As data sharing extends beyond organizational boundaries, trusted partner exchanges create secure channels for business collaboration. This pattern addresses the significant governance challenges of external sharing by creating structured onboarding processes tied to formal agreements.

The partner onboarding process typically includes:

- Creating secure cross-account roles with appropriate permissions.

- Establishing unique external IDs for additional security.

- Configuring fine-grained permissions based on agreement terms.

- Implementing time-bound access aligned with agreement duration.

- Generating access credentials and instructions for the partner.

This approach replaces the traditional pattern of ad-hoc data sharing implementations that create security risks and governance headaches. Each sharing relationship follows a consistent pattern with appropriate controls, documentation, and expiration handling.

The technical implementation directly reflects contractual terms, creating precise permission boundaries with automatic enforcement of agreement durations. Organizations implementing structured partner exchanges often reduce data sharing implementation time by 60-70% while significantly improving security posture.

Operational considerations

Successful data sharing platforms require continuous monitoring and optimization capabilities that transform usage data into actionable insights for platform improvement and strategic decision-making. By analyzing access patterns, consumption trends, and governance metrics, organizations can evolve their sharing strategies from assumption-based to evidence-driven approaches that maximize value while minimizing risk. The following capabilities demonstrate how analytics and automation can scale governance processes while providing the insights needed to optimize data sharing investments and identify new collaboration opportunities.

Usage insights and optimization

Understanding how data is used provides critical information for platform optimization. Monitoring access patterns reveals:

- Which datasets provide the most value, helping prioritize quality improvements.
- Inactive sharing relationships that may need re-evaluation or retirement.
- Changing access patterns that might indicate evolving needs.
- Potential new sharing opportunities based on query patterns.

Many organizations discover that actual data usage differs significantly from anticipated patterns, allowing them to refine their sharing strategies based on real evidence rather than assumptions. Platforms with mature analytics capabilities enable data-driven decisions about which assets to improve, which to deprecate, and where to focus development efforts.

Governance automation

As data sharing scales, manual governance becomes impossible. Automated checks maintain compliance without creating bottlenecks:

- Validating sharing relationships against current agreements.
- Verifying that technical permissions match governance policies.
- Checking for data classification compliance.
- Detecting abnormal access patterns that might indicate security issues.
- Managing the lifecycle of sharing relationships, including expiration.

These automated checks ensure that technical implementations accurately reflect current agreements, detect potential issues before they become incidents, and manage routine governance tasks without manual intervention.

Organizations implementing governance automation report significantly fewer security and compliance incidents related to data sharing, while maintaining governance overhead at manageable levels even as sharing relationships multiply.

As data sharing becomes increasingly central to business strategy, these platforms will evolve from operational infrastructure to strategic assets that enable new business models, unlock partnership opportunities, and create competitive advantage through data-driven collaboration.

Collaborative analytics and insights

Cross-boundary data sharing creates new opportunities for collaborative analytics that generate insights impossible to achieve with siloed data. When organizations effectively combine data across boundaries, they can develop richer analyses, identify patterns invisible within isolated datasets, and create shared intelligence that benefits all participants. However, realizing these benefits requires more than just technical data access—it demands collaborative analytical tools, shared semantic understanding, and governance models that enable joint exploration while maintaining appropriate boundaries.

Joint analytical workspaces

Collaborative analytics often requires shared environments where analysts from different organizations or departments can work together on common datasets. These shared workspaces create neutral territory for joint analysis without requiring data movement across organizational boundaries.

Amazon SageMaker Studio features prominently in these implementations, providing notebook-based collaborative environments where analysts can combine code, visualization, and documentation:

```python
1.  # Example of collaborative notebook implementing cross-boundary analysis
2.  import boto3
3.  import pandas as pd
4.  import matplotlib.pyplot as plt
5.
6.  # Access shared data using cross-account role
7.  sts_client = boto3.client('sts')
8.  assumed_role = sts_client.assume_role(
9.      RoleArn='arn:aws:iam::PARTNER_ACCOUNT:role/AnalyticsCollaboration',
10.     RoleSessionName='CollaborativeAnalysis'
11. )
12.
13. # Create session with temporary credentials
14. session = boto3.Session(
15.     aws_access_key_id=assumed_role['Credentials']['AccessKeyId'],
16.     aws_secret_access_key=assumed_role['Credentials']['SecretAccessKey'],
17.     aws_session_token=assumed_role['Credentials']['SessionToken']
18. )
19.
20. # Query partner data using Athena
21. athena_client = session.client('athena')
22. query_execution = athena_client.start_query_execution(
23.     QueryString='SELECT region, product_category, SUM(sales_amount) as total_
    sales FROM partner_data.sales WHERE sale_date >= DATE_ADD(\'day\', -90, CURRENT_
    DATE) GROUP BY region, product_category ORDER BY total_sales DESC LIMIT 10',
24.     QueryExecutionContext={'Database': 'partner_data'},
25.     ResultConfiguration={'OutputLocation': 's3://collaborative-analysis-results/'}
26. )
27.
28. # Query our internal data
29. internal_athena = boto3.client('athena')
30. internal_query = internal_athena.start_query_execution(
31.     QueryString='SELECT region, product_category, SUM(marketing_spend) as total_
    spend FROM marketing.campaigns WHERE campaign_date >= DATE_ADD(\'day\', -90, CURRENT_
    DATE) GROUP BY region, product_category ORDER BY total_spend DESC LIMIT 10',
32.     QueryExecutionContext={'Database': 'marketing'},
33.     ResultConfiguration={'OutputLocation': 's3://collaborative-analysis-results/'}
```

```
34. )
35.
36. # Combine and analyze the datasets
37. partner_data = get_query_results(athena_client, query_execution['QueryExecutionId'])
38. internal_data = get_query_results(internal_athena, internal_
    query['QueryExecutionId'])
39.
40. # Join datasets on region and product_category
41. combined_data = pd.merge(
42.     partner_data,
43.     internal_data,
44.     on=['region', 'product_category']
45. )
46.
47. # Calculate ROI
48. combined_data['roi'] = combined_data['total_sales'] / combined_data['total_spend']
49.
50. # Visualize results
51. plt.figure(figsize=(12, 8))
52. plt.bar(combined_data['product_category'], combined_data['roi'])
53. plt.title('Marketing ROI by Product Category')
54. plt.xlabel('Product Category')
55. plt.ylabel('ROI (Sales/Spend)')
56. plt.xticks(rotation=45)
57. plt.tight_layout()
58. plt.savefig('collaborative_analysis_results.png')
```

For organizations with strict data residency requirements, federated approaches keep data in place while enabling joint analysis. Amazon Redshift's federated query capabilities allow analysts to query data across database boundaries without data movement, while Athena's federated query connectors provide similar capabilities for diverse data sources.

Semantic interoperability

Collaborative analytics requires more than just technical data access; it demands a shared understanding of what the data means. Semantic interoperability addresses this challenge by establishing common definitions, taxonomies, and metrics across organizational boundaries.

Many cross-boundary analytics initiatives fail not because of technical limitations but because participants have different definitions of seemingly basic concepts. Consider a simple metric like active customer, one organization might define this as having made a purchase in the last 30 days, while another uses having logged in within the last 90 days. Without alignment on these fundamental definitions, collaborative analysis produces misleading or contradictory results.

Successful cross-boundary initiatives establish semantic layers that translate between different data models and definitions:

```
1. -- Example of semantic views providing consistent definitions
2. CREATE OR REPLACE VIEW shared_semantic.active_customers AS
3. -- Organization A definition: Purchased in last 30 days
4. SELECT
5.     customer_id,
```

```
 6.      first_name,
 7.      last_name,
 8.      email,
 9.      'Purchase Activity' as activity_type,
10.      most_recent_purchase as last_activity_date
11. FROM
12.      org_a.customers
13. WHERE
14.      most_recent_purchase >= CURRENT_DATE - INTERVAL '30' DAY
15.
16. UNION ALL
17.
18. -- Organization B definition: Logged in within last 90 days
19. SELECT
20.      customer_id,
21.      first_name,
22.      last_name,
23.      email,
24.      'Login Activity' as activity_type,
25.      last_login_date as last_activity_date
26. FROM
27.      org_b.customers
28. WHERE
29.      last_login_date >= CURRENT_DATE - INTERVAL '90' DAY;
```

Technologies like AWS Glue DataBrew help implement semantic interoperability by providing visual data preparation capabilities that transform diverse datasets into consistent formats with shared definitions. For more complex scenarios, custom semantic mappings implemented through views or transformation layers bridge the differences between organizational data models.

Collaborative data science

When organizations share not just data but analytical expertise, they unlock powerful new insights. Collaborative data science extends beyond shared access to include joint model development, federated learning, and collective interpretation of results.

Amazon SageMaker provides several capabilities that enable collaborative machine learning across organizational boundaries:

- **SageMaker Studio**: Shared development environments for collaborative model building.

- **SageMaker Feature Store**: Cross-account feature sharing for model development.

- **SageMaker Model Registry**: Version control and governance for shared models.

- **SageMaker Pipelines**: Reproducible workflows across organizational boundaries.

A particularly powerful pattern for cross-boundary data science is federated learning, where models are trained collaboratively without sharing raw data:

```
1. # Simplified federated learning implementation
2. def train_federated_model(organization_ids, model_base, iterations=5):
3.     """
4.     Train a model across multiple organizations without sharing raw data
```

```
5.
6.     Args:
7.         organization_ids: List of organization IDs participating in federation
8.         model_base: Initial model parameters
9.         iterations: Number of training rounds
10.
11.    Returns:
12.        Trained global model
13.    «»»
14.    global_model = model_base
15.
16.    for i in range(iterations):
17.        # For each iteration, train on each organization's data
18.        local_models = []
19.
20.        for org_id in organization_ids:
21.            # Create temporary credentials for the organization
22.            sts_client = boto3.client('sts')
23.            assumed_role = sts_client.assume_role(
24.                RoleArn=f'arn:aws:iam::{org_id}:role/FederatedLearning',
25.                RoleSessionName=f'FedLearning-Iteration-{i}'
26.            )
27.
28.            # Train on local data without exposing raw data
29.            local_model = train_on_local_data(
30.                global_model,
31.                org_id,
32.                assumed_role['Credentials']
33.            )
34.
35.            local_models.append(local_model)
36.
37.        # Aggregate results (e.g., weighted averaging of model parameters)
38.        global_model = aggregate_models(local_models)
39.
40.        # Evaluate global model performance
41.        performance = evaluate_global_model(global_model, organization_ids)
42.        print(f"Iteration {i}: Global model performance = {performance}")
43.
44.    return global_model
```

This approach enables organizations to benefit from collective intelligence without exposing sensitive underlying data. For example, financial institutions can collaborate on fraud detection models while keeping customer transaction data private, or healthcare providers can develop improved diagnostic models without sharing protected patient information.

Insights, visualization, and sharing

The ultimate value of collaborative analytics comes from the insights it generates and the decisions it informs. Effective cross-boundary programs include mechanisms for visualizing and sharing these insights in forms accessible to diverse stakeholders.

Amazon QuickSight serves as a central platform for sharing visualizations across organizational boundaries. Its embedding capabilities allow insights to be integrated into partner portals and applications, while row-level security ensures participants see only the results they are authorized to access.

For more sophisticated visualization needs, custom dashboards built with tools like Plotly or D3.js can be deployed through Amazon CloudFront with appropriate authentication mechanisms:

```python
1.  # Example of implementing cross-boundary dashboard with row-level security
2.  def generate_dashboard_embed_url(user_id, partner_id):
3.      """Generate a QuickSight dashboard URL with appropriate permissions"""
4.      quicksight = boto3.client('quicksight')
5.
6.      # Get user's identity groups to determine access scope
7.      user_groups = get_user_groups(user_id)
8.
9.      # Set namespace based on partner relationship
10.     namespace = f"partner-{partner_id}"
11.
12.     # Generate dashboard URL with appropriate RLS
13.     response = quicksight.generate_embed_url_for_registered_user(
14.         AwsAccountId=ACCOUNT_ID,
15.         ExperienceConfiguration={
16.             'Dashboard': {
17.                 'InitialDashboardId': DASHBOARD_ID
18.             }
19.         },
20.         UserArn=f"arn:aws:quicksight:{REGION}:{ACCOUNT_ID}:user/{namespace}/{user_
    id}",
21.         AllowedDomains=[f"https://{partner_id}.example.com"],
22.         Namespace=namespace,
23.         AdditionalDashboardIds=[DASHBOARD_ID]
24.     )
25.
26.     return response['EmbedUrl']
```

Organizations implementing effective visualization strategies report significantly higher adoption of collaborative insights, with executive stakeholders 3-4x more likely to incorporate findings into decision-making when presented with well-designed visualizations compared to raw analytical results.

Collaborative analytics transforms data sharing from a technical capability into a strategic business asset. By enabling joint analysis across organizational boundaries, companies generate insights impossible to achieve with isolated data, creating a competitive advantage through collective intelligence while maintaining appropriate governance and security boundaries.

Summarizing the collaborative analytics tools and governance for each layer:

Collaboration layer	Key AWS tools	Purpose	Governance ownership	Governance considerations
Joint analytical workspaces	Amazon SageMaker Studio, AWS IAM, AWS STS	Shared environments where analysts from different organizations/ departments work together	Data owner (producer account)	Producer maintains control over data access through IAM roles and time-bound credentials, while consumers maintain control over workspace configuration

Collaboration layer	Key AWS tools	Purpose	Governance ownership	Governance considerations
Semantic interoperability	AWS Glue DataBrew, Custom semantic views, Lake Formation	Establishes common definitions and taxonomies across organizational boundaries	Jointly owned with formal governance committee	Requires explicit agreement on business term definitions, usually formalized in business glossaries maintained by cross-organizational data stewards
Collaborative data science	SageMaker Feature Store, SageMaker Model Registry, SageMaker Pipelines	Joint model development without sharing raw data	Federated ownership with clear domain boundaries	Each organization maintains sovereignty over their data while sharing model artifacts and insights, with centralized model registry for versioning
Federated learning	SageMaker, AWS Lambda, Amazon S3	Training models collaboratively without sharing raw data	Distributed ownership with centralized coordination	Each organization maintains control of local training, central authority manages model aggregation and distribution protocol
Insights visualization	Amazon QuickSight, CloudFront, Amazon CloudWatch	Sharing analysis results in accessible formats	Content producer with consumer-specific views	Dashboard creators own visualization layer while respecting row-level security defined by data owners, with cross-account embedding permissions

Table 10.2: Summary of collaborative analytic tools and governance

Performance optimization for data sharing

As data volumes grow and sharing relationships become more complex, performance optimization becomes essential to ensure that cross-boundary data sharing remains both responsive and cost-effective. Without careful attention to performance, data sharing initiatives can suffer from excessive latency, resource contention, and spiralling costs, issues that ultimately undermine adoption and value realization.

Query optimization techniques

Cross-boundary data sharing performance depends heavily on how data is structured, stored, and accessed, with optimization strategies that benefit both data providers and consumers. Effective performance tuning requires understanding consumer query patterns and implementing storage optimizations that reduce latency, minimize costs, and improve the overall user experience for shared datasets. The following techniques demonstrate how partitioning strategies, columnar storage formats, and query optimization can dramatically improve performance in cross-account and cross-organizational data sharing scenarios.

Partitioning strategies

Partition design significantly impacts query performance in cross-boundary scenarios. The most effective partitioning aligns with common filtering patterns used by data consumers:

```
1.  -- Creating an optimized table structure for shared data
2.  CREATE EXTERNAL TABLE shared_sales.transactions (
3.      transaction_id STRING,
4.      customer_id STRING,
5.      product_id STRING,
6.      amount DECIMAL(10,2),
7.      store_id STRING,
8.      transaction_time TIMESTAMP
9.  )
10. PARTITIONED BY (
11.     year INT,
12.     month INT,
13.     day INT,
14.     region STRING
15. )
16. STORED AS PARQUET
17. LOCATION 's3://shared-data/sales/transactions/';
```

Organizations sharing data should analyze consumer query patterns to identify optimal partition keys. Time-based partitioning (year/month/day) benefits time-series analysis, while business dimensions like region, product category, or customer segment can dramatically improve performance for business-oriented queries.

Columnar storage optimization

For sharing analytical datasets, columnar storage formats like Parquet and **Optimzed Row Columnar (ORC)** provide significant performance advantages:

```
1.  # Optimizing Parquet files for shared access
2.  import pyarrow as pa
3.  import pyarrow.parquet as pq
4.
5.  def optimize_parquet_for_sharing(input_path, output_path, row_group_size=1000000):
6.      """
7.      Create optimized Parquet files for shared access
8.
9.      Args:
10.         input_path: Path to the original data
11.         output_path: Path to write optimized Parquet
12.         row_group_size: Number of rows per row group (tune based on query patterns)
13.     «»»
14.     # Read the original data
15.     data = pq.read_table(input_path)
16.
17.     # Write with optimized settings
18.     pq.write_table(
19.         data,
20.         output_path,
21.         row_group_size=row_group_size,
22.         compression='snappy',  # Balance of compression and decode speed
23.         use_dictionary=True,   # Enable dictionary encoding
24.         write_statistics=True  # Include column statistics for predicate pushdown
```

```
25.    )
26.
27.    # Verify the optimization
28.    optimized = pq.read_metadata(output_path)
29.    print(f"Original size: {os.path.getsize(input_path)}")
30.    print(f"Optimized size: {os.path.getsize(output_path)}")
31.    print(f"Number of row groups: {optimized.num_row_groups}")
32.    print(f"Number of columns: {optimized.num_columns}")
```

For cross-boundary sharing, these optimizations are particularly valuable as they reduce both the storage costs for providers and the query costs for consumers. Organizations frequently report 40-60% reductions in query execution time after implementing these optimizations on shared datasets.

Predicate pushdown and projection

Predicate pushdown is the concept of sending filtering conditions (**WHERE** clauses) directly to the storage layer so only matching data is read and transferred, rather than filtering after retrieving all data. Projection retrieves only the specific columns needed (**SELECT column1, column2**) instead of all columns (**SELECT ***), significantly reducing the amount of data that must be read, transferred, and processed.

Educating data consumers about leveraging predicate pushdown and projection can dramatically improve query performance:

```
1.  -- Inefficient query without leveraging pushdown/projection
2.  SELECT * FROM shared_finance.transactions
3.  WHERE transaction_date BETWEEN '2025-01-01' AND '2025-03-31';
4.
5.  -- Optimized query leveraging pushdown/projection
6.  SELECT
7.      transaction_id,
8.      customer_id,
9.      amount,
10.     transaction_date
11. FROM shared_finance.transactions
12. WHERE transaction_date BETWEEN '2025-01-01' AND '2025-03-31'
13. AND region = 'NORTHEAST';
```

For organizations sharing data across boundaries, providing query pattern guidance and examples can significantly improve the consumer experience while reducing system load and costs.

Caching strategies

Query result caching and data materialization strategies can dramatically reduce compute costs and improve response times for shared datasets, particularly when multiple consumers access similar data with predictable patterns. These optimization techniques shift processing overhead from query time to preparation time, creating better user experiences while reducing system load on source data. The following approaches demonstrate how to implement intelligent caching and pre-computation strategies that scale efficiently across cross-boundary sharing scenarios.

Result caching

For queries that run frequently against relatively static datasets, result caching provides significant benefits:

```
1.  -- Configuring Athena workgroup with result caching
2.  CREATE WORKGROUP partner_analytics
3.  WITH (
```

```
4.      DESCRIPTION = 'Workgroup for partner analytics with query result caching',
5.      QUERY_RESULTS_S3_PATH = 's3://partner-analytics/query-results/',
6.      ENFORCE_WORKGROUP_CONFIGURATION = true,
7.      PUBLISH_CLOUDWATCH_METRICS = true,
8.      BYTES_SCANNED_CUTOFF_PER_QUERY = 10737418240, -- 10GB
9.      REQUESTER_PAYS_ENABLED = false,
10.     RESULT_REUSE_ENABLED = true,   -- Enable query result reuse
11.     RESULT_REUSE_MINUTES = 60      -- Cache results for 1 hour
12. );
```

Result caching is particularly valuable for shared dashboards and reports that multiple users access with similar query patterns. Organizations implementing result caching often see 30% to 50% reductions in overall query volume against source data.

Data materialization

For complex transformations or aggregations that consumers frequently need, pre-materialization improves performance and reduces compute costs:

```
1.  -- Creating a materialized view for commonly accessed aggregations
2.  CREATE MATERIALIZED VIEW shared_sales.monthly_product_performance AS
3.  SELECT
4.      year,
5.      month,
6.      product_category,
7.      region,
8.      SUM(sales_amount) AS total_sales,
9.      COUNT(DISTINCT customer_id) AS unique_customers,
10.     SUM(sales_amount) / COUNT(DISTINCT customer_id) AS avg_customer_spend
11. FROM
12.     shared_sales.transactions
13. GROUP BY
14.     year,
15.     month,
16.     product_category,
17.     region;
18.
19. -- Schedule regular refreshes
20. -- This would typically be implemented through AWS Glue workflows or Step Functions
```

When implementing materialized views for shared data, organizations should balance freshness requirements against performance benefits. Daily or weekly refreshes may be sufficient for strategic analytics, while operational use cases might require more frequent updates.

Network optimization

Strategic data placement and transfer optimization are critical for maintaining performance and controlling costs in cross-boundary data sharing, especially when consumers are geographically distributed or operate across multiple AWS regions. By implementing intelligent data locality strategies and leveraging AWS's global infrastructure for transfer acceleration, organizations can significantly reduce latency and bandwidth costs while improving the user experience for distributed data consumers.

Data locality

Placing data physically close to where it will be processed improves performance by reducing network latency and transfer costs.

Effective data locality strategies include:

- **Regional replicas**: Maintaining copies in regions where major partners operate.
- **Edge caching**: Using CloudFront to cache frequently accessed objects.
- **Query location**: Executing queries close to the data rather than transferring data.
- **Materialized views**: Creating regional views for cross-region analytics.

These approaches reduce both latency and data transfer costs, which can be substantial for large cross-region data movements. Organizations with global sharing relationships have reported 50% to 70% improvements in query response times after implementing regional replicas.

Transfer acceleration

For data that must move across regions or between organizations, transfer acceleration technologies improve performance:

- **S3 Transfer Acceleration**: Leverages the AWS edge network for faster uploads/downloads.
- **CloudFront**: Caches and distributes frequently accessed content.
- **DataSync**: Optimizes large-scale data transfers with bandwidth throttling and parallelism.
- **Global accelerator**: Provides static IP addresses that route to the optimal endpoint.

These technologies are particularly valuable for initial data loads or periodic bulk updates in cross-boundary sharing relationships, where large volumes of data need to move efficiently across organizational boundaries.

Scaling considerations

Effective concurrency management and scaling strategies ensure that cross-boundary data sharing platforms maintain consistent performance as usage grows and consumer demands intensify. By implementing intelligent workload management, auto-scaling capabilities, and federated query architectures, organizations can support increasing numbers of concurrent users while maintaining responsive query performance across distributed data sources.

Query concurrency management

Managing query concurrency ensures consistent performance even during peak usage periods:

```
1.  -- Setting concurrency scaling for Redshift shared data
2.  ALTER WORKGROUP partner_workgroup
3.  SET CONCURRENCY_SCALING = AUTO;
4.
5.  -- Configure query priority based on workload
6.  CREATE WORKLOAD_MANAGEMENT 'partner_wlm'
7.  WITH (
8.      'service_class_name' = 'partner_queries',
9.      'service_class_max_concurrency' = 8,      -- Up to 8 concurrent queries
10.     'service_class_priority' = 'HIGHEST',     -- Priority for partner queries
11.     'concurrency_scaling_enabled' = true      -- Enable auto-scaling
12. );
```

Effective concurrency management includes:

- **Workload classification**: Identifying different query types and their performance needs.
- **Resource allocation**: Assigning appropriate compute resources to different workloads.
- **Auto-scaling**: Dynamically adjusting resources based on demand.
- **Query queuing**: Implementing priority-based queuing during peak periods.

These strategies ensure that critical workloads maintain performance even as sharing relationships scale to support more consumers and use cases.

Federated scaling

For advanced sharing scenarios, federated query engines allow scaling across distributed data sources. Federated query approaches offer several scaling advantages:

- **Distributed processing**: Queries execute where the data resides.
- **Reduced data movement**: Only results traverse network boundaries.
- **Specialized optimization**: Each data store can leverage its native performance capabilities.
- **Independent scaling**: Different data sources can scale according to their specific needs.

These approaches are particularly valuable for complex sharing relationships involving diverse data stores across organizational boundaries.

Performance optimization transforms data sharing from a technical capability into a business-friendly service. By focusing on query efficiency, caching strategies, network optimization, cost management, and scaling considerations, organizations can ensure that cross-boundary data sharing delivers a responsive, cost-effective experience that encourages adoption and maximizes business value.

Challenges and best practices

Cross-boundary data sharing presents unique challenges that extend beyond technical implementation. Organizations that succeed in this space understand both the common pitfalls and proven approaches that lead to sustainable sharing relationships.

Schema evolution represents one of the most persistent challenges. As data models inevitably change, maintaining compatibility across organizational boundaries becomes complex. A simple field addition that works seamlessly internally might break downstream consumer applications. Successful organizations address this through semantic versioning of data products, formalized change notification processes, and transition periods that support both old and new schemas during migrations.

Establishing a shared understanding of data presents equally significant hurdles. Different organizations often define common business terms differently. An active customer might mean made a purchase in 30 days to one team, but logged in within 90 days to another. This semantic gap leads to misinterpretation and flawed analysis. Business glossaries, rich data dictionaries, and example analyzes help bridge this divide by creating a common language for collaboration.

Data quality assurance becomes more challenging when crossing organizational lines. Quality issues may not be visible to consumers who lack context, while feedback loops to producers often break down across boundaries. Leading organizations establish explicit quality **service level agreements** (**SLAs**), implement automated validation before sharing, and create dedicated feedback channels to maintain high-quality data products.

Operational coordination, aligning on maintenance windows, managing incidents, and coordinating change, requires deliberate attention. Formalized operational agreements, dedicated communication channels, and clear escalation paths ensure day-to-day management continues smoothly even as systems evolve.

Beyond addressing these challenges, effective implementation frameworks provide structure for successful sharing initiatives. Comprehensive data sharing agreements document expectations and responsibilities. Robust onboarding programs with documentation, sample queries, and training significantly accelerate time-to-value while reducing support overhead.

Organizations increasingly apply product thinking to data sharing, treating datasets as products with defined features, roadmaps, and user experiences. This shift transforms sharing from technical integration into managed capabilities that evolve based on business value. Similarly, data mesh principles around domain ownership and federated governance provide valuable patterns for establishing clear accountability while maintaining enterprise standards.

As sharing scales, automation becomes essential across the lifecycle from onboarding to quality validation to access provisioning. Organizations with mature automation typically manage 3-5x more sharing relationships with the same resources compared to those relying on manual processes.

The most sustainable initiatives embrace continuous improvement rather than treating implementation as a one-time project. Regular reviews, systematic collection of consumer feedback, and ongoing performance monitoring create relationships that continue delivering value as business needs evolve.

By understanding these challenges and applying proven frameworks, organizations can build sharing relationships that deliver significant business value while maintaining appropriate controls. As cross-boundary sharing evolves from tactical integration to strategic capability, organizations with mature practices gain a competitive advantage through enhanced collaboration and insights.

Conclusion

Cross-boundary data sharing has evolved from a technical capability into a strategic business imperative. As organizations increasingly operate within complex ecosystems of partners, suppliers, and customers, the ability to securely share and collaborate on data directly impacts competitive advantage. AWS provides a comprehensive suite of services—from Lake Formation and Redshift data sharing to AWS Data Exchange—that enable sophisticated sharing models while maintaining governance and security. By implementing proper trust relationships, access controls, and purpose-built exchange platforms, organizations can transform data from an isolated asset into a catalyst for innovation and collective intelligence.

The journey from data sharing to collaborative insights forms a natural bridge to our next chapter on analytics and visualization. While this chapter focused on making data accessible across boundaries, the next chapter will explore how to transform that shared data into actionable intelligence through interactive dashboards, embedded analytics, and ML-powered insights using services like Amazon QuickSight. These capabilities complete the value chain, from secure data sharing to compelling visualizations that drive decision-making.

Join our Discord space

Join our Discord workspace for latest updates, offers, tech happenings around the world, new releases, and sessions with the authors:

https://discord.bpbonline.com

CHAPTER 11
Analytics and Visualization

Introduction

Data collection and processing create valuable assets, but these assets remain untapped without effective analytics and visualization. This chapter focuses on transforming raw data into actionable insights through Amazon QuickSight, AWS's powerful cloud-native business intelligence service. Today's tools empower business users with interactive, self-service capabilities that allow them to explore data independently, without requiring specialized technical expertise.

QuickSight has evolved from simple charts to a comprehensive platform supporting embedded analytics, machine learning insights, and direct connections to data lakes, warehouses, and databases. Modern organizations need more than just pretty dashboards; they need secure, scalable analytics that perform well with massive datasets while balancing governance with self-service. This chapter shows you how to build enterprise-grade analytics solutions that deliver insights, driving real business value.

Structure

In this chapter, we will be discussing the following topics:

- Amazon QuickSight architecture and capabilities
- Building interactive dashboards
- Embedding analytics in applications
- Performance optimization techniques
- ML-powered insights
- Framework for creating analytics solutions

Objectives

This chapter aims to provide a comprehensive understanding of implementing enterprise-grade analytics and visualization solutions on AWS. You will learn how to design and deploy scalable QuickSight implementations that connect to diverse data sources, create compelling interactive dashboards that drive business decisions, and embed analytics directly into applications and portals. The chapter explores performance optimization techniques for handling large-scale datasets, including **Super-fast, Parallel, In-memory Calculation Engine (SPICE)** optimization and direct query configurations. Through practical implementation examples, you will understand how to leverage QuickSight's machine learning capabilities to automatically discover insights, anomalies, and forecasts without requiring data science expertise. These capabilities will enable you to create analytics solutions that balance self-service exploration with governance, scalability, and performance, transforming raw data into valuable business intelligence that drives organizational decision-making.

Amazon QuickSight architecture and capabilities

QuickSight's architectural design addresses the key challenges that have historically limited business intelligence adoption: performance bottlenecks, complex infrastructure management, and inflexible security models. The platform's serverless nature automatically handles scaling and resource allocation, while the SPICE engine delivers sub-second query performance for interactive analytics. Built-in security features and comprehensive APIs enable both self-service analytics and custom embedded solutions. Together, these components create a foundation for analytics that grows with business requirements.

Core architectural components

Amazon QuickSight's serverless architecture connects diverse data sources, processes through SPICE or direct query, and delivers insights via multiple channels, as shown in the following figure:

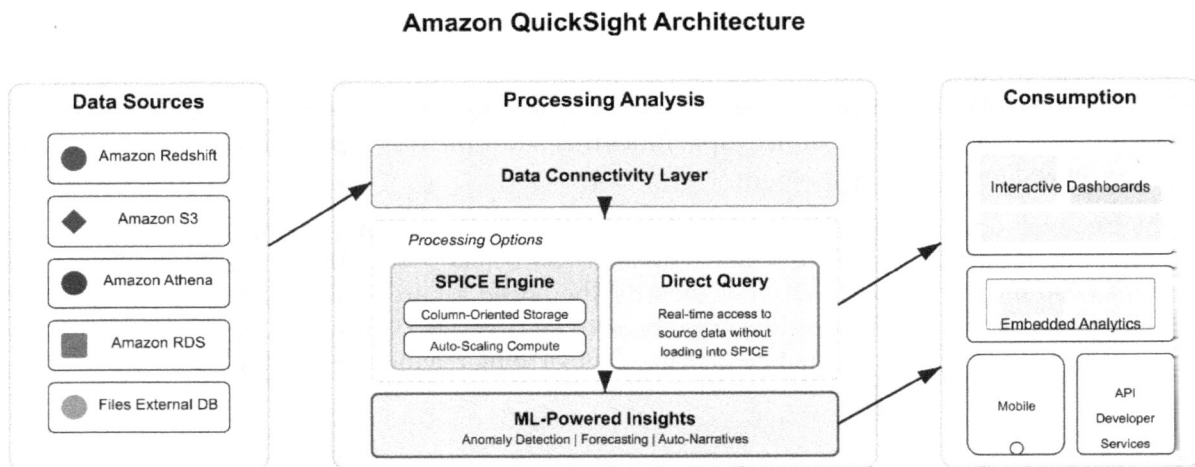

Figure 11.1: Amazon QuickSight architecture

QuickSight's architecture consists of several integrated components, as we have seen earlier, that work together to deliver analytics at scale.

SPICE engine

At the heart of QuickSight's performance capabilities sits the SPICE. This proprietary in-memory technology provides several key advantages:

- **Column-oriented storage**: Data is organized by columns rather than rows, dramatically improving analytical query performance.

- **In-memory processing**: Queries execute directly in memory, eliminating disk I/O bottlenecks.

- **Compression algorithms**: Specialized encoding reduces storage requirements while maintaining query performance.

- **Automatic scaling**: Capacity expands and contracts based on usage patterns without manual intervention.

SPICE represents an important architectural consideration when implementing QuickSight. Data loaded into SPICE benefits from dramatically faster query response times compared to direct queries, particularly for frequently accessed datasets. However, this improved performance comes with trade-offs in data freshness, as SPICE datasets represent point-in-time snapshots rather than real-time views.

For time-sensitive operational analytics where absolute data freshness is critical, QuickSight also supports direct query mode, which bypasses SPICE to query source systems directly. This flexibility enables architects to make appropriate trade-offs between performance and freshness based on specific use case requirements.

Serverless compute layer

QuickSight's compute layer scales automatically based on usage patterns, eliminating the capacity planning challenges associated with traditional BI platforms:

- **Concurrent user scaling**: Automatically adjusts resources as user numbers increase.

- **Query parallelization**: Distributes complex analytical workloads across multiple compute nodes.

- **Workload isolation**: Prevents resource contention between different dashboards and users.

- **Pay-per-session pricing**: Aligns costs directly with actual usage rather than provisioned capacity.

This serverless approach enables QuickSight to handle both steady-state analytics needs and unpredictable usage spikes without performance degradation. The serverless architecture proves particularly valuable for embedded analytics scenarios, where usage patterns may vary dramatically based on factors outside the organization's direct control.

Data connectivity layer

QuickSight connects to AWS data services and external sources through a flexible connectivity layer:

```
1.  // Example AWS CloudFormation template for QuickSight data source
2.  Resources:
3.    RedshiftDataSource:
4.      Type: AWS::QuickSight::DataSource
5.      Properties:
6.        AwsAccountId: !Ref AWS::AccountId
7.        DataSourceId: sales-analytics-redshift
8.        Name: Sales Analytics Warehouse
9.        Type: REDSHIFT
10.       DataSourceParameters:
11.         RedshiftParameters:
12.           Database: sales_analytics
13.           Host: !GetAtt RedshiftCluster.Endpoint.Address
14.           Port: 5439
15.       Credentials:
16.         CredentialPair:
17.           Username: quicksight_user
18.           Password: !Ref RedshiftPassword
19.       VpcConnectionProperties:
20.         VpcConnectionArn: !GetAtt QuickSightVPCConnection.Arn
21.       SslProperties:
22.         DisableSsl: false
```

This connectivity layer supports a wide range of sources:

- **AWS analytics services**: Native integration with Redshift, Athena, and OpenSearch.
- **AWS databases**: Direct connections to RDS, Aurora, and DynamoDB.
- **SaaS applications**: Pre-built connectors for Salesforce, ServiceNow, and other business applications.
- **Custom sources**: JDBC/ODBC connectivity to specialized data repositories.
- **Flat files**: Direct upload of Excel, CSV, and JSON files for rapid analysis.

The architecture includes VPC connectivity options that enable QuickSight to securely access data sources within private networks, a critical capability for enterprises with strict security requirements. This flexibility in data connectivity enables QuickSight to function as a unified analytics layer across diverse data sources, preventing the analytical silos that often emerge with disconnected BI tools.

Security model

QuickSight's security architecture implements a comprehensive, multi-layered approach that addresses enterprise requirements:

- **IAM**: User authentication and authorization leverage several integration points:
  - **Native IAM integration**: For AWS-centric organizations, QuickSight integrates directly with IAM for permission management.
  - **Enterprise identity federation**: Support for SAML 2.0 enables integration with enterprise identity providers like Okta, Azure AD, and AWS IAM Identity Center.
  - **Row-level security**: Fine-grained data access control based on user attributes or group membership.
  - **Column-level restrictions**: Control access to sensitive data elements based on user roles.

Row-level security (RLS) proves particularly powerful for implementing complex security requirements where different users need to see different subsets of the same dataset:

```
1.
    -- Example RLS rules for sales data
2.  -- Sales representatives see only their own territories
3. SELECT * FROM sales
4. WHERE territory_id IN (
5.     SELECT territory_id
6.     FROM user_territories
7.     WHERE username = ${useremail}
8. )
9.
10. -- Regional managers see all territories in their region
11. SELECT * FROM sales
12. WHERE region = (
13.     SELECT user_region
14.     FROM user_attributes
15.     WHERE username = ${useremail}
16. )
17.
18. -- Executives see all data
19. SELECT * FROM sales
```

These rules can be implemented either through direct **structured query language** (**SQL**) rules or through calculated fields in QuickSight's semantic layer, providing flexibility for different security scenarios.

Data protection

For data in transit and at rest, QuickSight implements industry-standard encryption practices:

- **SPICE encryption**: All data imported into SPICE is automatically encrypted.

- **TLS for data in transit**: Communications between QuickSight and data sources use TLS 1.2+.

- **AWS KMS integration**: SPICE datasets can be encrypted with customer-managed keys for additional control.

- **VPC connectivity**: Private connections to data sources prevent exposure to public networks.

Developer capabilities

Beyond its end-user features, QuickSight provides robust APIs and development frameworks for custom analytics implementations:

- **QuickSight API** The comprehensive API enables programmatic control of all QuickSight components:

  o **Python**:

```python
# Example: Automated dashboard deployment with Python
import boto3

quicksight = boto3.client('quicksight')

# Create a dataset
response = quicksight.create_data_set(
    AwsAccountId='123456789012',
    DataSetId='sales_analysis',
    Name='Sales Analysis Dataset',
    PhysicalTableMap={
        'sales_table': {
            'RelationalTable': {
                'DataSourceArn': 'arn:aws:quicksight:us-east-1:123456789012:datasource/redshift-sales',
                'Schema': 'public',
                'Name': 'sales',
                'InputColumns': [
                    {'Name': 'sale_date', 'Type': 'DATETIME'},
                    {'Name': 'product_id', 'Type': 'STRING'},
                    {'Name': 'region', 'Type': 'STRING'},
                    {'Name': 'amount', 'Type': 'DECIMAL'}
                ]
            }
        }
    },
    LogicalTableMap={
        'sales_analysis': {
```

```
28.                    'Alias': 'Sales Analysis',
29.                  'Source': {
30.                      'PhysicalTableId': 'sales_table'
31.                  }
32.              }
33.          },
34.      ImportMode='SPICE'
35. )
36.
37. # Create a dashboard using the dataset
38. dashboard_response = quicksight.create_dashboard(
39.      # Dashboard configuration parameters
40. )
```

These APIs enable DevOps approaches to analytics, including infrastructure-as-code patterns, CI/CD pipelines for dashboard deployment, and automated testing workflows. Organizations with mature DevOps practices often implement dashboard deployment pipelines that promote changes through development, testing, and production environments, maintaining consistency and quality throughout the analytics lifecycle.

Embedding SDK

For integrating analytics directly into applications, QuickSight provides a JavaScript SDK that enables seamless embedding:

- **Javascript**:

```javascript
1.  // Example: Embedding a QuickSight dashboard
2.  const embedDashboard = async () => {
3.      // Step 1: Get the dashboard embedding URL from your backend
4.      const response = await fetch('/api/get-quicksight-embed-url', {
5.          method: 'POST',
6.          headers: {
7.              'Content-Type': 'application/json'
8.          },
9.          body: JSON.stringify({
10.             dashboardId: 'your-dashboard-id',
11.             userArn: 'user-or-anonymous-arn'
12.         })
13.     });
14.
15.     const { embedUrl } = await response.json();
16.
17.     // Step 2: Use QuickSight Embedding SDK to render the dashboard
18.     const dashboard = QuickSightEmbedding.createDashboard({
19.         container: '#dashboard-container',
20.         url: embedUrl,
21.         width: '100%',
22.         height: '700px',
23.         locale: 'en-US',
24.         footerPaddingEnabled: true,
```

```
25.        onMessage: (event) => {
26.            // Handle events from the embedded dashboard
27.            console.log('Message received', event);
28.        }
29.    });
30.
31.    dashboard.render();
32. };
```

This embedding capability enables the integration of interactive analytics directly into business applications, portals, and custom interfaces, bringing insights to users in their existing workflows rather than requiring them to switch to separate analytics tools.

Understanding QuickSight's architecture provides the foundation for implementing effective analytics solutions on AWS. The combination of the high-performance SPICE engine, flexible data connectivity, comprehensive security model, and robust development capabilities creates a platform capable of addressing diverse analytics requirements from simple departmental dashboards to sophisticated embedded analytics applications.

Building interactive dashboards

The most successful dashboards anticipate how users think, scan, and process information, then design the interface to support these natural patterns. When executives open a dashboard, they need to grasp the overall situation within seconds, while analysts require the ability to drill into details without losing context. Understanding these different user needs and cognitive behaviors enables you to create dashboard layouts that feel intuitive rather than overwhelming. The design principles that follow show how to structure information hierarchically, guide attention strategically, and provide interactive elements that enhance rather than complicate the analytical experience.

Dashboard design principles

Effective dashboard design leverages fundamental principles of human visual perception to create interfaces that feel intuitive and reduce cognitive burden. The strategic placement of visual elements can dramatically improve how quickly users extract insights and make decisions.

Visual hierarchy and layout

When users first view a dashboard, they should immediately understand what matters most. In QuickSight, you can achieve this through intentional layout choices:

- Position critical metrics in the top-left quadrant. This is where Western users naturally begin scanning, making it ideal for your most important **key performance indicators** (**KPI**). To implement this strategic positioning in QuickSight's visual interface:

```
1. // In the QuickSight interface:
2. Drag your most critical KPI visual to the top-left position
3. Set its size larger than supporting visuals (typically 6x4 grid units)
4. Use a complementary color to draw attention
```

- Create a Z-pattern flow through your dashboard. Users typically scan from top-left to top-right, then diagonally down to bottom-left, and finally to bottom-right. Place visuals in this sequence to guide users from summary metrics to detailed analysis.

  The Z-pattern layout aligns with natural reading habits, reducing cognitive load and helping users absorb information in logical progression without feeling overwhelmed.

Practical visualization selection

Choosing the right visualization dramatically impacts how quickly users grasp insights:

- **For time-series data**: Always start with line charts rather than tables. The human brain processes visual patterns faster than numbers.

  Here is how to configure an effective time-series visualization in QuickSight:

```
1. // When implementing a time-based analysis in QuickSight:
2. Select your measure (e.g., «Revenue»)
3. Add your time field to the «X-axis» field well
4. Set appropriate time grain (day/week/month) based on patterns you want to reveal
5. Add a trend line by selecting «Add insight» > «Add trendline
```

- **For comparisons across categories**: Use horizontal bar charts when you have more than 6-7 categories, never pie charts. Sort bars by value (not alphabetically) to highlight the relative importance.

- **For detailed metrics with context**: Use KPI visuals with comparison indicators rather than just numbers.

  To create a comprehensive KPI visual that provides both current values and performance context:

```
1. // Creating an effective KPI visual:
2. Drag the "KPI" visual from the visualization panel
3. Add your primary metric (e.g., «Current Month Revenue»)
4. Add comparison field (e.g., «Previous Month Revenue»)
5. Set comparison method to «Difference» or «Percentage»
6. Configure conditional format-
   ting for the comparison (red for negative, green for positive)
```

Interactive elements that drive adoption

Static dashboards quickly become obsolete. Interactive elements transform dashboards into exploration tools:

- **Action-oriented filters**: Do not just add filters, design a filtering strategy:

  o **Use filter cascades** where selections in one filter dynamically update available options in related filters. To set up this intelligent filtering relationship in QuickSight:

```
1. // Implementing cascading filters:
2. Create a filter for «Region»
3. Create a second filter for «Store»
4. Add a filter action from the Region visual:
5.    Actions > Add filter action > Target: Store filter >
6.    Scope: "Selected fields only" >
7.    Fields: Connect Region to Store's region field
```

- **Cross-visual interactions**: Enable discoveries through connected visualizations:

  o **Implement cross-filtering** between related charts to create coordinated views. Here is how to configure coordinated visual interactions in QuickSight:

```
1. // Setting up cross-filtering between visuals:
2. Select source visual
3. Choose Actions > Create filter action
4. Target: All visuals (or specific visuals)
5. Set activation: «Select» (triggers on click)
6. Configure which fields should filter which target fields
```

This technique transformed how a manufacturing client analyzed production issues. Clicking on a specific product in their defect chart automatically filters all other charts to show related suppliers, production lines, and quality metrics, reducing root cause analysis time from hours to minutes.

- **Actionable insights with drilling:** Enable users to move from summary to detail naturally:

  o **Configure drill-down paths** that follow analytical reasoning:

```
1.  // Creating effective drill paths:
2.  Add multiple hierarchy levels to a field well (e.g., Year > Quarter > Month
    > Day)
3.  Enable "Drill down to next level by double-click" in visual menu
4.  Add tooltip actions that jump to detailed dashboards
```

A financial services firm implemented drill-down from customer segments to individual customers, then added a tooltip action linking to a customer detail dashboard. This reduced the need for separate reports by 60% and accelerated their quarterly review process significantly.

Practical dashboard implementation

Let us discuss creating a sales performance dashboard that demonstrates these principles:

- Start with a clear business question around sales performance and driving factors.

- Build the top section with critical KPIs:
  o Current month sales with year-over-year comparison.
  o Sales vs. target with percentage variance.
  o Average order value trend.

- Add the middle section with dimension analysis:
  o Product category performance (horizontal bar chart, sorted by value).
  o Regional performance (map visual with conditional coloring).

- Include detailed tables in the bottom section:
  o Top performing products (table with sparklines).
  o Underperforming regions (table with conditional formatting).

- Implement interactive elements:
  o Date range control affecting all visuals.
  o Product category filter with the Select all option.
  o Cross-filtering is enabled between product and region visuals.
  o Drill down from region to store to individual transaction.

The resulting dashboard balances strategic overview with detailed analysis capabilities, allowing executives to spot trends while giving analysts the ability to investigate drivers behind those trends.

A manufacturing client implemented this exact pattern and discovered that while overall sales were only 2% below target, a single product line was masking serious underperformance across multiple regions. The interactive nature of the dashboard allowed them to identify and address the issue within days rather than waiting for the next monthly report cycle.

Building effective dashboards is both an art and a science. The technical implementation in QuickSight must serve the analytical purpose, not just display data. By following these practical design patterns and understanding why they work, you will create dashboards that drive decisions rather than just presenting information.

Embedding analytics in applications

The true power of analytics emerges when insights are delivered within the context of business workflows rather than isolated in dedicated dashboard interfaces. Embedded analytics integrates visualizations directly into applications, portals, and operational systems, bringing data to users where they already work. Amazon QuickSight offers robust embedding capabilities that enable this contextual analytics approach without requiring extensive development effort.

Embedding approaches

QuickSight provides multiple embedding options to address different integration requirements and user experiences:

- **Dashboard embedding**: The most straightforward approach embeds complete dashboards into applications:

```
1.  // Backend code (Node.js) to generate embedding URL
2.  const AWS = require('aws-sdk');
3.  const quicksight = new AWS.QuickSight({ region: 'us-east-1' });
4.
5.  async function getDashboardEmbedUrl(dashboardId, userArn, identityType) {
6.    const params = {
7.      AwsAccountId: process.env.AWS_ACCOUNT_ID,
8.      DashboardId: dashboardId,
9.      IdentityType: identityType, // QUICKSIGHT or IAM or ANONYMOUS
10.     UserArn: userArn,
11.     SessionLifetimeInMinutes: 600,
12.     UndoRedoDisabled: false,
13.     ResetDisabled: false
14.   };
15.
16.   try {
17.     const response = await quicksight.getDashboardEmbedUrl(params).promise();
18.     return response.EmbedUrl;
19.   } catch (error) {
20.     console.error('Error generating QuickSight embed URL:', error);
21.     throw error;
22.   }
23. }
24.
25. // Frontend code (React) to render embedded dashboard
26. import React, { useEffect, useState } from 'react';
27.
28. function EmbeddedDashboard({ dashboardId }) {
29.   const [embedUrl, setEmbedUrl] = useState(null);
30.
31.   useEffect(() => {
```

```
32.     // Call your backend API to get the embed URL
33.     fetch('/api/quicksight/dashboard-url', {
34.       method: 'POST',
35.       headers: { 'Content-Type': 'application/json' },
36.       body: JSON.stringify({ dashboardId })
37.     })
38.     .then(response => response.json())
39.     .then(data => setEmbedUrl(data.embedUrl));
40.   }, [dashboardId]);
41.
42.   useEffect(() => {
43.     if (!embedUrl) return;
44.
45.     const dashboard = QuickSightEmbedding.createDashboard({
46.       container: '#dashboard-container',
47.       url: embedUrl,
48.       height: '700px',
49.       width: '100%',
50.       footerPaddingEnabled: true,
51.       onMessage: handleDashboardMessage
52.     });
53.
54.     dashboard.render();
55.   }, [embedUrl]);
56.
57.   function handleDashboardMessage(event) {
58.     // Handle events from the embedded dashboard
59.     console.log('Message from QuickSight:', event);
60.   }
61.
62.   return (
63.     <div id="dashboard-container"></div>
64.   );
65. }
```

This approach works well when you need to provide complete analytical functionality with minimal development effort. A financial services company implemented this pattern in their advisor portal, embedding client portfolio analysis dashboards that advisors could explore during client meetings. The embedded dashboards maintained all interactive capabilities, allowing advisors to answer client questions in real-time without switching applications.

- **Visual embedding**: For more granular integration, QuickSight allows embedding individual visualizations:

```
1.  // Backend code for generating visual embed URL
2.  async function getVisualEmbedUrl(dashboardId, sheetId, visualId, userArn) {
3.    const params = {
4.      AwsAccountId: process.env.AWS_ACCOUNT_ID,
5.      DashboardId: dashboardId,
6.      SheetId: sheetId,
```

```
7.      VisualId: visualId,
8.      IdentityType: 'IAM',
9.      UserArn: userArn,
10.     SessionLifetimeInMinutes: 600
11.   };
12.
13.   try {
14.     const response = await quicksight.getSessionEmbedUrl(params).promise();
15.     return response.EmbedUrl;
16.   } catch (error) {
17.     console.error('Error generating QuickSight visual embed URL:', error);
18.     throw error;
19.   }
20. }
```

Visual embedding enables more seamless integration with application interfaces. A healthcare provider used this approach to embed specific metrics within their patient management system, showing readmission risk scores and treatment compliance visualizations directly in the patient record screen. This contextual embedding increased data usage by healthcare providers by over 200% compared to their previous separate analytics portal.

- **Q&A embedding**: For more exploratory use cases, QuickSight's natural language Q&A capabilities can be embedded:

```
1.  // Frontend code for embedding QuickSight Q
2.  useEffect(() => {
3.    if (!embedUrl) return;
4.
5.    const qSearchBar = QuickSightEmbedding.createQSearchBar({
6.      container: '#q-search-container',
7.      url: embedUrl,
8.      contentOptions: {
9.        title: 'Ask a question about your data',
10.       theme: 'LIGHT'
11.     },
12.     onMessage: handleQMessage
13.   });
14.
15.   qSearchBar.render();
16. }, [embedUrl]);
```

This approach enables users to ask ad-hoc questions in natural language, receiving instant visualized answers without predefined dashboards. A retail organization embedded QuickSight Q in their merchandise planning application, allowing buyers to ask questions like *How are denim sales trending in the Northeast?* directly in their workflow. This capability reduced the need for custom dashboard development by 40% while increasing analytical adoption among business users.

Customization and branding

Effective embedding requires visual integration with host applications to create a seamless experience:

- **Theme customization**: QuickSight's theme capabilities enable visual alignment with application branding:

```
1.  // Custom theme definition
2.  {
3.    «Name»: "CorporateTheme",
4.    "Configuration": {
5.      «DataColorPalette": {
6.        «Colors": [
7.          "#1B95D9", "#4CB5F5", "#45B2B8", "#94CF8A",
8.          "#EFC26A", "#EB9943", "#D64946", "#A2D0F2"
9.        ],
10.       "MinMaxGradient": {
11.         «Colors": ["#D64946", "#FFFFFF", "#4CB5F5"]
12.       }
13.     },
14.     «Sheet»: {
15.       «TileLayout": {
16.         «BackgroundColor": "#FFFFFF",
17.         "Border": {
18.           «Color": "#E0E0E0",
19.           "Show": true,
20.           "Thickness": 1
21.         },
22.         «Margin": {
23.           «Top": 8,
24.           "Bottom": 8,
25.           "Left": 8,
26.           "Right": 8
27.         }
28.       },
29.       «TileStyle": {
30.         «Border": {
31.           «Color": "#E0E0E0",
32.           "Show": true,
33.           "Thickness": 1
34.         }
35.       }
36.     },
37.     «Typography»: {
38.       «FontFamilies": [
39.         {
40.           «FontFamily": "Open Sans, sans-serif"
41.         }
42.       ]
43.     }
44.   }
45. }
```

Custom themes ensure embedded analytics visually match your application's design language. A healthcare software provider applied their existing color scheme, typography, and visual styling to embedded QuickSight dashboards, creating such a seamless experience that users couldn't distinguish between native application screens and embedded analytics.

- **Programmatic customization**: Beyond themes, QuickSight's embedding SDK enables runtime customization:

```
1.  // Frontend code for runtime customization
2.  const dashboard = QuickSightEmbedding.createDashboard({
3.    container: '#dashboard-container',
4.    url: embedUrl,
5.    width: '100%',
6.    height: '700px',
7.    parameters: {
8.      country: 'United States',
9.      timeframe: 'Current Quarter'
10.   },
11.   hooks: {
12.     onLoad: () => {
13.       console.log('Dashboard loaded');
14.     },
15.     onError: (error) => {
16.       console.error('Dashboard error:', error);
17.     }
18.   },
19.   className: 'embedded-dashboard',
20.   locale: 'en-US',
21.   layoutOptions: {
22.     managementOptions: {
23.       disablePrint: true,
24.       disableRefresh: false,
25.       disableExport: true
26.     },
27.     hideSheet: true,
28.     hideSheetSelector: true,
29.     hideParameterControls: false,
30.     hideFilterBar: true
31.   }
32. });
```

These configuration options allow precise control over the embedded experience, including hiding QuickSight **user interface (UI)** elements, controlling available actions, and customizing the initial view.

Embedded analytics transforms how organizations deliver insights to users, moving from isolated dashboards to contextual, integrated experiences. By implementing these patterns, you can bring analytics directly into the applications where users already work, dramatically increasing adoption and the business impact of your data investments. The most successful implementations create such seamless integration that users don't even perceive they are using a separate analytics tool; they simply have the insights they need, when and where they need them.

Performance optimization techniques

As analytics implementations scale to handle larger datasets, more users, and complex visualizations, performance optimization becomes critical to user satisfaction and adoption. Even the most insightful dashboard will be abandoned if it loads too slowly or responds sluggishly to user interactions. Amazon QuickSight provides several levers for optimizing performance across the analytics stack, from data storage to query execution to dashboard rendering.

SPICE optimization

SPICE's in-memory architecture delivers exceptional query performance, but realizing these benefits requires strategic data modeling and proactive management that aligns with how the engine processes and stores data. The difference between fast and slow QuickSight dashboards often comes down to how thoughtfully data is structured for SPICE ingestion rather than the complexity of the visualizations themselves. By implementing proven optimization techniques for data types, refresh strategies, and capacity management, you can ensure consistent sub-second query performance even as data volumes grow.

Data modelling for SPICE

The way data is structured in SPICE significantly impacts query performance:

```python
1.  # Python example for optimizing SPICE ingestion
2.  import boto3
3.  import json
4.
5.  def optimize_spice_dataset(dataset_id, account_id, region="us-east-1"):
6.      """
7.      Optimize an existing SPICE dataset by configuring data types
8.      and appropriate aggregations
9.      """
10.     quicksight = boto3.client('quicksight', region_name=region)
11.
12.     # First, get current dataset definition
13.     response = quicksight.describe_data_set(
14.         AwsAccountId=account_id,
15.         DataSetId=dataset_id
16.     )
17.
18.     dataset_definition = response['DataSet']
19.
20.     # Modify column data types for optimal performance
21.     logical_table_map = dataset_definition['LogicalTableMap']
22.     for table_id, table in logical_table_map.items():
23.         for column in table.get('Columns', []):
24.             # Convert high-cardinality string fields to categorical type
25.             if column['Type'] == 'STRING' and is_high_cardinality(column['Name']):
26.                 column['Type'] = 'CATEGORICAL'
27.
28.             # Ensure date fields use appropriate type
29.             if is_date_field(column['Name']) and column['Type'] != 'DATETIME':
```

```
30.                      column['Type'] = 'DATETIME'
31.
32.        # Update dataset with optimized definition
33.        update_response = quicksight.update_data_set(
34.            AwsAccountId=account_id,
35.            DataSetId=dataset_id,
36.            Name=dataset_definition['Name'],
37.            PhysicalTableMap=dataset_definition['PhysicalTableMap'],
38.            LogicalTableMap=logical_table_map,
39.            ImportMode='SPICE'
40.            # Include other required properties from the original definition
41.        )
42.
43.        return update_response
```

Several key practices optimize SPICE performance:

- **Appropriate data types**: Ensure each column uses the most efficient data type. For high-cardinality string fields with repeating values (like product categories or regions), use the CATEGORICAL type rather than STRING.

- **Pre-aggregation**: For large fact tables, pre-aggregate to the most used grain rather than loading row-level detail when detailed analysis is not required.

- **Calculated field placement**: Create calculated fields in the dataset definition rather than in individual analyses when possible, allowing SPICE to optimize these calculations during ingestion.

Incremental refreshes

For large datasets that update frequently, incremental refreshes maintain performance while reducing refresh time and SPICE capacity consumption:

```
1.  # Python function for managing incremental refresh
2.  def configure_incremental_refresh(dataset_id, account_id,
3.                                     incremental_columns, region="us-east-1"):
4.      """
5.      Configure a dataset for incremental refresh
6.      «»»
7.      quicksight = boto3.client('quicksight', region_name=region)
8.
9.      # Update dataset to enable incremental refresh
10.     response = quicksight.update_data_set(
11.         AwsAccountId=account_id,
12.         DataSetId=dataset_id,
13.         IngestionWaitPolicy={
14.             'IngestionWaitTimeInHours': 1,
15.             'WaitForSpiceIngestion': True
16.         },
17.         RefreshProperties={
18.             'RefreshConfiguration': {
19.                 'IncrementalRefresh': {
20.                     'LookbackWindow': {
```

```
21.                          'ColumnName': incremental_columns['timestamp_column'],
22.                          'Size': 7,
23.                          'SizeUnit': 'DAY'
24.                      }
25.                   }
26.               }
27.            }
28.         # Include other required properties
29.      )
30.
31.    return response
```

Incremental refresh strategies include:

- **Timestamp-based refresh**: Update only records with timestamps newer than the last refresh, ideal for append-only data patterns.

- **Changed-record detection**: Use hash values or change tracking columns to identify and refresh only modified records.

- **Partition-based refresh**: Refresh only specific partitions (e.g., the current month's data) while keeping historical partitions static.

SPICE monitoring and management

Proactive monitoring helps identify and address SPICE performance issues before they impact users:

```python
1.  # Python function for SPICE usage monitoring
2.  def monitor_spice_usage(account_id, region="us-east-1"):
3.      """
4.      Monitor SPICE usage across datasets
5.      """
6.      quicksight = boto3.client('quicksight', region_name=region)
7.
8.      # Get SPICE capacity information
9.      capacity_response = quicksight.describe_account_subscription(
10.         AwsAccountId=account_id
11.     )
12.
13.     spice_capacity = capacity_response['AccountSubscription']['ActiveCapacityUnit']
14.
15.     # Get list of all datasets
16.     dataset_response = quicksight.list_data_sets(
17.         AwsAccountId=account_id,
18.         MaxResults=100
19.     )
20.
21.     total_spice_used = 0
22.     dataset_sizes = []
23.
24.     # Calculate size of each SPICE dataset
25.     for dataset in dataset_response['DataSetSummaries']:
```

```
26.          if dataset['ImportMode'] == 'SPICE':
27.              dataset_info = quicksight.describe_data_set(
28.                  AwsAccountId=account_id,
29.                  DataSetId=dataset['DataSetId']
30.              )
31.
32.              if 'ConsumedSpiceCapacityInBytes' in dataset_info['DataSet']:
33.                  spice_size = dataset_info['DataSet']['ConsumedSpiceCapacityInBytes']
34.                  total_spice_used += spice_size
35.
36.                  dataset_sizes.append({
37.                      'DataSetId': dataset['DataSetId'],
38.                      'Name': dataset['Name'],
39.                      'SpiceSize': spice_size,
40.                      'SpiceSizeGB': spice_size / (1024 * 1024 * 1024)
41.                  })
42.
43.      return {
44.          'TotalCapacity': spice_capacity,
45.          'UsedCapacity': total_spice_used / (1024 * 1024 * 1024),
46.          'UtilizationPercentage': (total_spice_used / (spice_
    capacity * 500 * 1024 * 1024 * 1024)) * 100,
47.          'DatasetSizes': sorted(dataset_
    sizes, key=lambda x: x['SpiceSize'], reverse=True)
48.      }
```

Key monitoring practices include:

- **Utilization tracking**: Monitor SPICE consumption relative to provisioned capacity to avoid hitting limits during refreshes.

- **Dataset size analysis**: Identify oversized datasets that may benefit from optimization or aggregation.

- **Refresh performance**: Track refresh duration trends to identify degrading performance that may require optimization.

Query optimization

Query optimization represents the most direct path to improving dashboard performance, often delivering 5 to 10x speed improvements through strategic SQL design and database configuration. The difference between a responsive dashboard and one that frustrates users frequently lies in how efficiently QuickSight can retrieve and process the underlying data.

Query tuning strategies

Optimizing how QuickSight generates and executes queries dramatically impacts performance:

```
1. -- Example of implementing a custom SQL query with optimizations
2. -- Instead of using automatic joins, use a custom optimized query
3. SELECT
4.     c.customer_id,
5.     c.name,
```

```
6.        c.segment,
7.        c.region,
8.        -- Pre-aggregate metrics at required grain
9.        COUNT(DISTINCT o.order_id) AS order_count,
10.       SUM(o.amount) AS total_sales,
11.       AVG(o.amount) AS avg_order_value
12. FROM
13.       customers c
14. LEFT JOIN
15.       orders o ON c.customer_id = o.customer_id
16. WHERE
17.       -- Use partition pruning for large datasets
18.       o.order_date BETWEEN '2025-01-01' AND '2025-03-31'
19.       -- Add frequently used filter columns to WHERE clause for push-down
20.       AND c.region IN ('East', 'West')
21. GROUP BY
22.       c.customer_id,
23.       c.name,
24.       c.segment,
25.       c.region
```

Effective query optimization techniques include:

1. **Custom SQL**: Replace automatic join generation with custom SQL that includes performance optimizations specific to your data model and database engine.

2. **Pre-aggregation**: Aggregate data in the query to the required grain rather than retrieving row-level detail that will be aggregated in QuickSight.

3. **Selective columns**: Request only the specific columns needed for analysis rather than **SELECT ***.

4. **Filter push-down**: Place filters in the SQL query to leverage database indexes and reduce data transfer.

Database optimization

Performance tuning of source databases complements QuickSight's query optimization:

```
1.  -- Example Redshift-specific optimizations
2.  -- Create distribution keys for commonly joined tables
3.  ALTER TABLE customers
4.  ALTER DISTSTYLE KEY DISTKEY (customer_id);
5.
6.  ALTER TABLE orders
7.  ALTER DISTSTYLE KEY DISTKEY (customer_id);
8.
9.  -- Create sort keys for frequently filtered columns
10. ALTER TABLE orders
11. ALTER SORTKEY (order_date, status);
12.
13. -- Create materialized views for common analytical patterns
14. CREATE MATERIALIZED VIEW customer_order_summary AS
15. SELECT
```

```
16.     c.customer_id,
17.     c.region,
18.     c.segment,
19.     DATE_TRUNC('month', o.order_date) AS month,
20.     COUNT(DISTINCT o.order_id) AS order_count,
21.     SUM(o.amount) AS total_sales
22. FROM
23.     customers c
24. JOIN
25.     orders o ON c.customer_id = o.customer_id
26. GROUP BY
27.     c.customer_id,
28.     c.region,
29.     c.segment,
30.     DATE_TRUNC('month', o.order_date);
```

Database-specific optimizations include:

- **Appropriate indexes**: Create indexes on commonly filtered and joined columns.
- **Distribution keys**: For MPP databases like Redshift, align distribution keys with join patterns.
- **Materialized views**: Create database materialized views for frequently accessed analytical patterns.
- **Query monitoring**: Identify and tune slow queries using database performance tools.

Dashboard performance tuning

Dashboard performance is not just about data processing speed—the visual rendering and interaction responsiveness directly determine whether users engage with your analytics or abandon them in frustration. Even perfectly optimized queries can result in poor user experience if the dashboard design creates unnecessary rendering bottlenecks or overwhelming visual complexity.

Visual optimization

Thoughtful visual design significantly impacts dashboard performance:

```
1.  // JavaScript function to monitor dashboard load performance
2.  function monitorDashboardPerformance(dashboard) {
3.    const startTime = performance.now();
4.
5.    // Add event listener for dashboard load complete
6.    dashboard.addEventListener('loaded', () => {
7.      const loadTime = performance.now() - startTime;
8.      console.log(`Dashboard load time: ${loadTime}ms`);
9.
10.     // Record metrics for analysis
11.     recordDashboardMetric('loadTime', loadTime);
12.   });
13.
14.   // Monitor individual visual render times
15.   dashboard.addEventListener('rendered', (event) => {
16.     // event.detail includes information about the specific visual
```

```
17.    recordVisualMetric(event.detail.visualId, 'renderTime', event.detail.renderTime);
18.  });
19.}
```

Effective visual optimization techniques include:

- **Appropriate visualization types**: Choose visualizations appropriate for the data volume. Tables with thousands of rows perform worse than aggregated visuals like bar charts.

- **Progressive loading**: Configure dashboards to load visuals progressively rather than waiting for all queries to complete.

- **Visual count reduction**: Limit dashboards to eight to ten visuals per sheet for optimal performance, using drill-throughs for detailed analysis.

- **Pagination**: For table visuals with many rows, enable pagination rather than scrolling to improve render performance.

Parameter and filter optimization

How parameters and filters are implemented significantly impacts performance:

```
1.  -- Performance-optimized filter implementation
2.  -- Create a dedicated lookup table for filter values
3.  CREATE TABLE region_lookup AS
4.  SELECT DISTINCT region_id, region_name
5.  FROM customer_data
6.  ORDER BY region_name;
7.
8.  -- Use the lookup table for filter dropdowns
9.  SELECT region_id, region_name
10. FROM region_lookup;
```

Parameter and filter best practices include:

- **Cascading filters**: Implement cascading filter dependencies to reduce the number of values in each dropdown.

- **Filter lookup tables**: For high-cardinality filters, use dedicated lookup tables rather than scanning fact tables.

- **Default filter values**: Set reasonable default filter values to limit initial data volume.

- **Control types**: Choose appropriate control types (dropdowns vs. text fields) based on cardinality and user requirements.

Dashboard design patterns

Certain design patterns inherently perform better than others:

```
1.  // JavaScript example of implementing progressive dashboard loading
2.  function implementProgressiveLoading(dashboardId) {
3.    // Get the dashboard configuration
4.    const dashboardConfig = getDashboardConfig(dashboardId);
5.
6.    // Reorder visuals for progressive loading
7.    dashboardConfig.sheets.forEach(sheet => {
8.      // Prioritize KPI visuals
```

```
9.      const kpiVisuals = sheet.visuals.filter(v => v.type === 'KPI');
10.     const otherVisuals = sheet.visuals.filter(v => v.type !== 'KPI');
11.
12.     // Reorder to load KPIs first
13.     sheet.visuals = [...kpiVisuals, ...otherVisuals];
14.
15.     // Apply staggered loading
16.     otherVisuals.forEach((visual, index) => {
17.       visual.loadDelay = index * 200; // Stagger loading by 200ms per visual
18.     });
19.   });
20.
21.   // Update dashboard configuration
22.   updateDashboardConfig(dashboardId, dashboardConfig);
23. }
```

Performance-oriented design patterns include:

- **Overview-then-detail**: Present high-level metrics initially, with drill-down paths to detailed data.

- **Progressive disclosure**: Use actions and drill-downs to reveal detailed information only when requested.

- **Logical grouping**: Organize related analyses in separate sheets to reduce initial load requirements.

- **KPI prioritization**: Load key performance indicators first, then supporting visualizations.

Performance optimization represents a critical yet often overlooked aspect of analytics implementations. Even the most insightful dashboard will be abandoned if it loads too slowly or responds sluggishly to user interactions. By systematically applying these optimization techniques across the analytics stack, from SPICE configuration to query tuning to dashboard design. You can create QuickSight implementations that deliver both powerful insights and exceptional user experiences.

ML-powered insights

Traditional business intelligence requires users to actively search for patterns, anomalies, and trends. Machine learning capabilities in Amazon QuickSight fundamentally change this paradigm by automatically discovering insights that might otherwise remain hidden. These capabilities transform static dashboards into intelligent analytical tools that proactively surface meaningful patterns and predictions without requiring specialized data science expertise.

Automated anomaly detection

QuickSight's anomaly detection capabilities transform reactive monitoring into proactive intelligence, automatically identifying unusual patterns that might indicate opportunities or problems requiring immediate attention. The following table demonstrates how to configure and integrate anomaly detection across your dashboards for maximum business impact:

Feature	Implementing in the console	Best practices
Setting up anomaly detection	• Navigate to Anomaly Detection in the left menu • Click on New anomaly detection • Select dataset • Choose metric and aggregation method • Add dimensions for granular analysis • Set the time field and granularity • Adjust the sensitivity slider • Configure schedule and alerts	• Choose metrics with clear business significance • Include relevant dimensions to detect localized anomalies • Adjust sensitivity based on metric volatility • Consider seasonal patterns in your data

Incorporating anomalies in dashboards	• While editing the dashboard, click Add in the toolbar
	• Select Add insight | Anomaly detection
	• Choose metrics to monitor
	• Configure display options
	• Position prominently
	    For existing charts:
	      o Select chart | Format visual
	      o Navigate to the Analytics section
	      o Enable Anomaly detection
	      o Configure settings
		• Place anomaly insights at the dashboard top
		• Add anomaly markers to time series charts
		• Configure drill-downs for investigation
		• Connect critical anomalies to alerts

Table 11.1: Anomaly detection setup and implementation guide

Automated narrative insights

Narrative insights bridge the gap between data visualization and business understanding by automatically generating contextual explanations that help users interpret complex patterns and trends. These AI-powered narratives transform dashboards from passive displays into active storytelling tools that guide decision-making through clear, business-focused explanations.

Feature	Implementing in the console	Best practices
Adding narrative insights	• Click Add | Add insight in the toolbar • Select Auto-narrative • Choose fields to include • Select analysis types (time comparisons, rankings, etc.) • Choose between a comprehensive or a summary style • Customize language templates • Format appearance	• Include contextual comparisons (YoY, MoM) • Focus on exceptions rather than obvious patterns • Use your organization's terminology • Keep narratives concise and action-oriented

Feature	Implementing in the console	Best practices
Strategic placement	• Add dashboard-level narrative at top • Create section-specific narratives • Place focused narratives next to complex visuals • Connect narratives to dashboard filters	• Use dashboard intro placement for executive summary • Create consistent section summaries • Focus adjacent narratives on a specific visualization context • Ensure narratives are updated with filter changes

Table 11.2: Narrative insights configuration and placement strategy

Forecasting and what-if analysis

Predictive analytics capabilities in QuickSight enable organizations to move beyond historical reporting to forward-looking insights that support strategic planning and scenario analysis. These features transform dashboards into decision-support systems that help users understand not just what happened, but what might happen under different conditions.

Feature	Implementing in the console	Best practices
Time-series forecasting	• Create or select a line chart with a time dimension • Click the Visual | Analytics menu • Select the Forecast and toggle on • Set forecast length and confidence bounds • Configure seasonality options • Choose algorithm (ARIMA or ETS) • Customize visual appearance	• Match forecast granularity to business needs • Ensure sufficient historical data (three to five cycles) • Keep forecast periods reasonable • Clearly distinguish historical vs. forecast data
Parameter-driven what-if	• Create parameters (Analysis menu | Parameters) • Create calculated fields using parameters • Add parameter controls to the dashboard • Create visuals using calculated fields • Show actual vs. projected values together	• Create multiple scenario parameter sets • Set realistic parameter bounds • Link related parameters when appropriate • Use visual indicators for thresholds

Table 11.3: Forecasting and what-if analysis implementation

ML pattern discovery

Advanced analytics insights help transform correlation into causation by identifying which factors most significantly drive business outcomes and performance changes. These analytical features enable data-driven root cause analysis that moves beyond surface-level observations to actionable intelligence about what truly impacts your key metrics.

Feature	Implementing in the console	Best practices
Key driver analysis	• Click on Add | Add insight in the toolbar • Select Key drivers • Choose the target metric and aggregation • Select dimensions to evaluate • Configure the maximum drivers to display • Choose an analysis method • Set significance threshold	• Start broad, then refine dimensions • Focus on actionable factors • Refresh analysis periodically • Validate against business knowledge
Contribution analysis	• Click Add | Add insight in the toolbar • Select Contribution analysis • Choose metric, time field, and granularity • Select dimensions to analyze • Set comparison method • Configure display options • Position near related visualizations	• Focus on material contributors (5%+ impact) • Configure multiple time comparisons • Enable drill-down exploration • Combine with anomaly detection

Table 11.4: Driver and contribution analysis setup guide

These ML-powered capabilities democratize advanced analytics, allowing business users without technical expertise to benefit from sophisticated techniques. The most successful implementations integrate these capabilities seamlessly into dashboards and workflows, making insight discovery a natural extension of everyday analysis rather than a separate, specialized activity.

Framework for creating analytics solutions

Analytics success begins by understanding the decisions that need to be made, not the data that's available. The AWS working backward methodology offers a proven framework for this decision-first approach, helping organizations move beyond creating dashboards to enabling meaningful business outcomes. By starting with the end user's needs and working backward to implementation, teams can ensure their QuickSight solutions drive tangible value through better, faster decision-making.

Working backward approach to analytics

At AWS, the working backward methodology starts with the customer and their desired outcomes, then develops solutions that fulfil these needs. For analytics, this means beginning with the decisions users need to make, then building dashboards that enable those decisions. This framework applies this philosophy to QuickSight implementations.

Start with a press release

Begin your analytics project by writing a future press release announcing its successful completion:

- **Headline**: A clear statement of the analytics solution's impact.
- **Problem statement**: The business challenge being addressed.
- **Solution**: How analytics solves this problem.
- **Customer quote**: How users will benefit from these insights.
- **Getting started**: How users will access and use the solution.

This exercise forces clarity on what success looks like before technical implementation begins. A healthcare provider used this approach for their patient outcomes dashboard, defining specific decisions the solution would enable before designing a single visualization.

Define the customer experience

Document how users will interact with the analytics through experience narratives. Refer to the following table:

User persona	Key decisions	Analytics requirements
Executive	• Strategic resource allocation • Performance evaluation	• High-level KPIs with exception highlighting • YoY trend visualization
Manager	• Operational adjustments • Team performance coaching	• Detailed operational metrics • Comparative benchmarks
Analyst	• Root cause analysis • Opportunity identification	• Drill-down capabilities • Data exploration flexibility

Table 11.5: Decision roles and analytics needs matrix

Four-phase implementation framework

Effective analytics implementation requires a systematic approach focused on business decisions, user needs, and continuous improvement. This framework outlines four key phases:

- **Define: Decision-first requirements:**

  Start with clear business decisions that need support, rather than available data. Map specific decisions, assess data readiness, and design user experiences that enable decision-making:

Activity	Description	Outcome
Decision mapping	Identify three to five specific decisions the analytics should enable	Prioritized decision list with clear success criteria
Data assessment	Evaluate data availability and quality for decision support	Data gap analysis and remediation plan
Experience design	Create simple wireframes showing analytical flow	User-validated design concepts

Table 11.6: Analytics implementation planning and design workflow

- **Build: Outcome-oriented implementation:**

  Develop analytics solutions iteratively, beginning with core datasets and essential KPIs. Progress to more sophisticated features like ML-driven insights once foundations are solid:

Activity	Description	Outcome
Dataset creation	Connect to data sources and create an appropriate data model	Optimized QuickSight datasets with calculated fields
Progressive development	Build a dashboard in phases, starting with core KPIs	Functioning dashboard with key visualizations
Insight enhancement	Add ML features to automatically surface patterns	Anomaly detection and narrative insights

Table 11.7: QuickSight dashboard development implementation process

- **Validate: User-focused testing:**

  Ensure the solution effectively supports decision-making through rigorous testing of functionality, performance, and usability with actual users:

Activity	Description	Outcome
Decision testing	Validate that analytics enables target decisions	Confirmation of decision support capability
Performance verification	Ensure acceptable response times under load	Optimized dashboard performance
User acceptance	Gather feedback on usability and utility	Refinement priorities based on user input

Table 11.8: Analytics solution testing and validation framework

- **Evolve: Continuous improvement:**

  Monitor real usage patterns, document business impact, and continuously enhance the solution based on decision-making effectiveness and user feedback.

Activity	Description	Outcome
Usage monitoring	Track which visualizations drive decisions	Insight into actual usage patterns
Value assessment	Document-specific decisions influenced	ROI validation and success stories
Enhancement cycle	Prioritize improvements based on decision impact	Roadmap for continual dashboard evolution

Table 11.9: Analytics value monitoring and evolution process

Five core best practices

The following are the five core principles for effective analytics solution development.

- **Simplify relentlessly**: Start with minimally viable analytics that address core decisions, then expand based on validated needs.

- **Embed ML insights contextually**: Place machine learning insights where they enhance human decision-making rather than as separate analyses.

- **Create analytical pathways**: Design clear navigation from high-level insights to detailed exploration.

- **Measure what matters**: Establish metrics tied to business outcomes, not just dashboard usage.

- **Iterate based on decision value**: Prioritize enhancements by focusing on their impact on target decisions.

This decision-first, working backward approach ensures QuickSight implementations deliver meaningful business value rather than just attractive visualizations. By focusing relentlessly on enabling better decisions, your analytics solution will become an indispensable business tool rather than just another dashboard.

Conclusion

Analytics and visualization represent the culmination of the data engineering journey, transforming raw data into actionable insights that drive business decisions. Throughout this chapter, we have explored how Amazon QuickSight provides a robust foundation for building enterprise-grade analytics solutions, from understanding its architecture and capabilities to implementing interactive dashboards, embedding analytics into applications, optimizing performance, and leveraging ML-powered insights. The working backward framework we have outlined emphasizes starting with business decisions rather than available data, ensuring analytics solutions deliver meaningful value rather than just attractive visuals. By following these structured approaches and best practices, organizations can create analytics experiences that democratize data insights while maintaining appropriate governance and performance. As data volumes continue to grow and business environments become increasingly dynamic, the ability to quickly analyze information and surface meaningful patterns becomes not just advantageous but essential for competitive success.

In the next chapter, we will explore how machine learning can be integrated into your data platforms through Amazon SageMaker. We will examine how to build ML pipelines that leverage the data foundations established in previous chapters, implement feature engineering at scale, and deploy models that transform predictive insights into operational actions. From automated model development to production deployment and monitoring, *Chapter 12, Machine Learning Integration,* will provide a comprehensive guide to extending your data platform with machine learning capabilities that unlock the full predictive potential of your data assets.

Join our Discord space

Join our Discord workspace for latest updates, offers, tech happenings around the world, new releases, and sessions with the authors:

https://discord.bpbonline.com

Machine Learning Integration

Introduction

The convergence of data engineering and machine learning represents one of the most transformative developments in modern data platforms. While previous chapters focused on ingesting, storing, and analyzing data, this chapter explores how to extend your data infrastructure to support the complete machine learning lifecycle from feature engineering through model deployment and monitoring. Amazon SageMaker, AWS's comprehensive machine learning platform, provides the tools needed to integrate ML capabilities seamlessly into your existing data architecture.

Modern ML implementations require more than just model training; they demand sophisticated data pipelines that can handle feature engineering at scale, automated model deployment workflows, and continuous monitoring systems that ensure model performance over time. The integration between your data lake, warehouse, and ML platforms must be seamless, enabling data scientists to focus on model development while data engineers ensure the underlying infrastructure scales reliably and cost-effectively.

This chapter demonstrates how to build production-ready ML platforms that leverage the data foundations established in earlier chapters. You will learn to create systems that transform raw data into business value through machine learning while maintaining the governance, security, and operational excellence standards essential for enterprise deployments.

Structure

This chapter covers the following topics:

- Amazon SageMaker architecture
- Feature engineering at scale
- ML pipeline architecture and orchestration
- Model deployment and serving patterns
- Performance optimization for ML workloads
- ML architecture pattern

Objectives

This chapter aims to provide a comprehensive understanding of integrating machine learning capabilities into AWS data platforms. You will learn how to design and implement scalable feature engineering pipelines that transform raw data into ML-ready features, architect end-to-end ML workflows using SageMaker and related services, and establish robust model deployment patterns that support both batch and real-time inference scenarios. The chapter is explained through practical implementation examples, you will understand how to optimize ML workloads for cost and performance while maintaining the governance and security standards required for enterprise ML deployments. These capabilities will enable you to create ML platforms that seamlessly integrate with your existing data infrastructure, transforming your data platform from a repository of information into an engine for predictive insights and automated decision-making.

Amazon SageMaker architecture

Amazon SageMaker provides a comprehensive machine learning platform that integrates seamlessly with AWS data services, enabling end-to-end ML workflows from data preparation through model deployment and monitoring. Understanding SageMaker's architecture and how it connects to your existing data infrastructure is essential for building effective ML platforms.

Core SageMaker components

SageMaker's architecture consists of several integrated services that work together to support the complete ML lifecycle. The platform follows a modular design where each component addresses specific aspects of the machine learning workflow while maintaining seamless integration with the broader AWS ecosystem. Architecture components and interactions is given in the following figure:

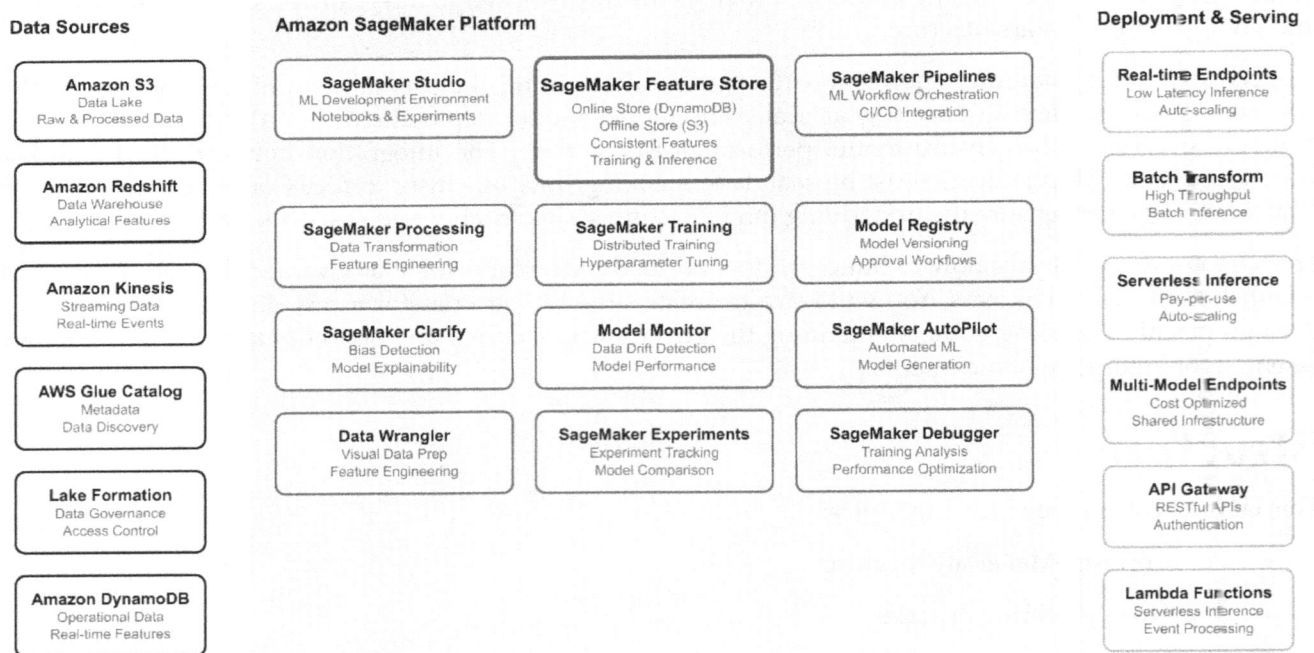

Figure 12.1: Amazon SageMaker ML platform architecture

SageMaker Studio and development environment

SageMaker Studio serves as the integrated development environment for machine learning, providing a unified interface for data scientists and ML engineers. When you create a SageMaker Domain, it establishes the foundational infrastructure that connects to your existing AWS data services through VPC endpoints and IAM roles.

The Studio environment connects directly to your data lake through the same Lake Formation permissions established in *Chapter 9, Data Governance and Security*. This means data scientists can access governed datasets without requiring separate permission management. When a user launches a Studio notebook, it automatically inherits the appropriate IAM role that provides access to S3 buckets, Redshift clusters, and other data sources based on their organizational role.

Studio automatically connects to your data lake with governance. To demonstrate SageMaker Studio's seamless integration with Lake Formation, let us query customer transaction data directly from our governed data lake:

```
1.  import sagemaker
2.  import pandas as pd
3.
4.  # Session inherits IAM permissions from Studio domain
5.  session = sagemaker.Session()
6.
7.  # Direct access to Lake Formation governed tables
8.  df = pd.read_sql("""
9.      SELECT customer_id, purchase_amount, product_category
10.     FROM «data_lake».»customer_transactions»
11.     WHERE purchase_date >= current_date - interval ‹30› day
12. """, session.get_glue_connection('data-lake-connection'))
```

Studio's integration with AWS CodeCommit and GitHub enables version control of notebooks and ML code, while integration with SageMaker Projects provides CI/CD templates specifically designed for ML workflows. This creates a development environment that follows enterprise development practices while accommodating the unique requirements of ML experimentation.

SageMaker Feature Store

The **Feature Store** addresses one of production ML's most persistent challenges: ensuring that features computed during model training exactly match those computed during inference, a problem known as training-serving skew that can silently degrade model performance in production. Feature Store provides a centralized repository that maintains feature consistency across the entire ML lifecycle while integrating seamlessly with your existing data architecture patterns.

When you create a **Feature Group** in SageMaker, AWS automatically provisions two integrated storage systems: an online store built on DynamoDB for real-time serving with sub-second latency, and an offline store using S3 with automatic Glue Catalog integration for historical analysis and model training. This dual-store architecture enables consistent feature definitions while optimizing for different access patterns, including real-time inference requirements and batch training workflows.

The offline store leverages S3 optimization strategies, automatically storing features in Apache Iceberg format with time-based partitioning that aligns with standard data lake organization patterns. Features appear as regular tables in your Glue Catalog, meaning data analysts can query features using the same Athena queries they use for other datasets, while the automatic partitioning ensures cost-effective storage with lifecycle policies that move older feature versions to less expensive storage tiers.

For real-time serving, the online store provides single-digit millisecond latency through DynamoDB with automatic scaling based on request patterns. The architecture handles the complexity of keeping online and offline stores synchronized, ensuring training-serving consistency without manual intervention. Feature ingestion can occur through direct API calls, streaming through Kinesis integration, or batch processing through SageMaker Processing jobs, providing flexibility for different data freshness requirements. SageMaker Feature Store automatically provisions both online and offline storage infrastructure, eliminating the operational complexity of managing separate systems for real-time serving and batch analytics:

```python
1.  # Creating a Feature Group with automatic dual-store provisioning
2.  from sagemaker.feature_store.feature_group import FeatureGroup
3.  from sagemaker.feature_store.inputs import FeatureDefinition
4.
5.  def create_customer_feature_group():
6.      """
7.      Create a comprehensive feature group for customer behavioral features
8.      with both online and offline storage automatically configured
9.      """
10.
11.     # Define feature schema
12.     feature_definitions = [
13.         FeatureDefinition(feature_name='customer_id', feature_type='String'),
14.         FeatureDefinition(feature_name='avg_purchase_amount_30d', feature_
    type='Fractional'),
15.         FeatureDefinition(feature_name='purchase_frequency_30d', feature_
    type='Integral'),
16.         FeatureDefinition(feature_name='days_since_last_purchase', feature_
    type='Integral'),
17.         FeatureDefinition(feature_name='preferred_category', feature_type='String'),
18.         FeatureDefinition(feature_name='lifetime_value', feature_type='Fractional'),
19.         FeatureDefinition(feature_name='churn_risk_score', feature_type='Fractional'),
20.         FeatureDefinition(feature_name='event_time', feature_type='String')
21.     ]
22.
23.     # Create feature group with automatic infrastructure provisioning
24.     feature_group = FeatureGroup(
25.         name='customer-behavioral-features',
26.         sagemaker_session=sagemaker_session
27.     )
28.
29.     feature_group.create(
30.         s3_uri='s3://ml-feature-store/customer-features/',
31.         record_identifier_name='customer_id',
32.         event_time_feature_name='event_time',
33.         role_arn=execution_role_arn,
34.         feature_definitions=feature_definitions,
35.         enable_online_store=True,  # DynamoDB for real-time serving
36.         offline_store_config={
37.             'S3StorageConfig': {
38.                 'S3Uri': 's3://ml-feature-store/customer-features/',
```

```
39.                    'KmsKeyId': 'arn:aws:kms:region:account:key/feature-store-key'
40.              },
41.              'DisableGlueTableCreation': False,  # Automatic Glue Catalog integration
42.              'TableFormat': 'Iceberg'  # Optimized columnar format
43.          }
44.     )
45.
46.     return feature_group
```

The architectural decision to implement Feature Store depends on your ML maturity and specific requirements:

- **Implement Feature Store when**: You have multiple models sharing common features, need sub-second inference latency, require consistent training-serving patterns, or have complex feature engineering that benefits from centralized management.

- **Use direct data lake access when**: You have isolated models with unique features, only batch inference requirements, or simple feature engineering that does not justify the additional infrastructure complexity.

Feature Store's integration with your existing data governance extends security and access control policies to ML features, ensuring that sensitive customer data remains protected while enabling feature sharing across appropriate teams and applications. The service automatically inherits IAM policies and Lake Formation permissions, maintaining consistent data protection without requiring separate ML-specific security frameworks.

Processing and training infrastructure

SageMaker Processing and training provide managed infrastructure that extends standard data processing capabilities to include ML-specific workloads with automatic scaling, fault tolerance, and integration with ML-optimized libraries and frameworks. Unlike generic compute services, these capabilities are specifically designed for the unique characteristics of ML workloads from the I/O-intensive nature of feature engineering to the GPU requirements of deep learning training.

SageMaker Processing jobs integrate seamlessly with your existing data processing architecture. They can read directly from S3 partitioned structures, automatically leveraging partition pruning to optimize data access and reduce both processing time and costs. When processing customer behavioural data, for example, SageMaker automatically reads only the relevant date partitions, respecting the same optimization strategies used by your Glue ETL jobs and Athena queries.

The processing infrastructure maintains your existing data governance through Lake Formation integration. ML processing jobs inherit the same column-level and row-level security policies applied to other data consumers, ensuring that sensitive customer data remains protected while enabling ML feature engineering at scale. This governance extends to output data, where processed features automatically inherit appropriate classifications and access controls based on their source data sensitivity. For large-scale feature engineering that exceeds notebook capabilities, SageMaker Processing provides managed compute clusters that automatically handle resource provisioning, scaling, and cleanup:

```
1. # SageMaker Processing job with automatic resource management
2. from sagemaker.processing import ProcessingInput, ProcessingOutput
3. from sagemaker.sklearn.processing import SKLearnProcessor
4.
5. def create_feature_processing_job():
6.     """
7.     Create a scalable feature engineering job that integrates with
8.     existing data lake structure and governance policies
```

```
9.       «»»
10.
11.      # Processor with automatic scaling and ML-optimized environment
12.      sklearn_processor = SKLearnProcessor(
13.          framework_version='0.23-1',
14.          instance_type='ml.m5.2xlarge',
15.          instance_count=2,   # Automatic parallel processing
16.          base_job_name='customer-feature-engineering',
17.          role=sagemaker_execution_role,
18.          max_runtime_in_seconds=7200,
19.          volume_size_in_gb=100,
20.          volume_kms_key='arn:aws:kms:region:account:key/processing-key',
21.          network_config={
22.              'EnableNetworkIsolation': True,
23.              'SecurityGroupIds': ['sg-ml-processing'],
24.              'Subnets': ['subnet-private-a', 'subnet-private-b']
25.          }
26.      )
27.
28.      # Input from partitioned S3 data with automatic optimization
29.      processing_inputs = [
30.          ProcessingInput(
31.              source='s3://data-lake/customer-events/year=2025/month=05/',
32.              destination='/opt/ml/processing/input/events',
33.              input_name='customer_events'
34.          ),
35.          ProcessingInput(
36.              source='s3://data-lake/product-catalog/current/',
37.              destination='/opt/ml/processing/input/products',
38.              input_name='product_data'
39.          )
40.      ]
41.
42.      # Output to Feature Store and S3 with governance inheritance
43.      processing_outputs = [
44.          ProcessingOutput(
45.              source='/opt/ml/processing/output/features',
46.              destination='s3://ml-feature-store/processed-features/',
47.              output_name='ml_features'
48.          ),
49.          ProcessingOutput(
50.              source='/opt/ml/processing/output/quality',
51.              destination='s3://ml-pipeline/quality-reports/',
52.              output_name='quality_metrics'
53.          )
54.      ]
55.
```

```
56.    # Launch processing with automatic monitoring
57.    sklearn_processor.run(
58.        code='feature_engineering_script.py',
59.        inputs=processing_inputs,
60.        outputs=processing_outputs,
61.        arguments=[
62.            '--feature-window', '30',
63.            '--quality-threshold', '0.95'
64.        ]
65.    )
66.
67.    return sklearn_processor.latest_job_name
```

Training infrastructure follows similar integration patterns while adding ML-specific optimizations. SageMaker automatically provisions the appropriate instance types for your algorithm requirements: CPU instances for traditional ML algorithms, GPU instances for deep learning, or distributed clusters for large-scale training. The service integrates with existing cost optimization strategies through support for Spot Instances, which can reduce training costs by up to 90% for workloads that can tolerate interruptions, while automatic checkpointing ensures training progress is preserved when spot instances are reclaimed.

The training environment automatically handles the complexity of distributed training across multiple instances while managing data distribution and gradient synchronization. Integration with Amazon FSx for Lustre provides high-performance shared storage for very large datasets, while S3 Transfer Acceleration minimizes data loading bottlenecks through optimized network configurations and parallel data loading patterns. As datasets grow beyond single-machine capabilities, SageMaker's distributed training automatically scales compute resources while optimizing costs through spot instances and checkpoint management:

```
1.  # Distributed training with automatic resource optimization
2.  from sagemaker.tensorflow import TensorFlow
3.
4.  def create_distributed_training_job():
5.      """
6.      Set up distributed training with automatic scaling and cost optimization
7.      """
8.
9.      # Training estimator with distributed configuration
10.     tf_estimator = TensorFlow(
11.         entry_point='training_Script.py',
12.         framework_version='2.8',
13.         py_version='py39',
14.         instance_type='ml.p3.2xlarge',
15.         instance_count=4,    # Distributed across 4 GPU instances
16.         use_spot_instances=True,   # 90% cost reduction
17.         max_wait=7200,    # Wait time for spot instances
18.         checkpoint_s3_uri='s3://ml-training/checkpoints/',
19.         role=sagemaker_execution_role,
20.
21.         # Distributed training configuration
22.         distribution={
23.             'parameter_server': {
24.                 'enabled': True
```

```
25.                    }
26.               },
27.
28.          # Hyperparameter optimization
29.          hyperparameters={
30.              'epochs': 100,
31.              'batch_size': 32,
32.              'learning_rate': 0.001
33.          }
34.      )
35.
36.      # Training data from optimized S3 structure
37.      training_data = 's3://ml-datasets/training/customer-churn/'
38.      validation_data = 's3://ml-datasets/validation/customer-churn/'
39.
40.      # Launch training with automatic monitoring
41.      tf_estimator.fit({
42.          'training': training_data,
43.          'validation': validation_data
44.      })
45.
46.      return tf_estimator
```

Both processing and training jobs integrate with comprehensive monitoring and alerting infrastructure, providing detailed execution metrics through CloudWatch and comprehensive logging for debugging and optimization. This observability extends to resource utilization metrics that help optimize instance selection and cost management for different workload patterns, enabling data-driven decisions about infrastructure scaling and cost optimization strategies.

Integration with existing data architecture

The true power of SageMaker emerges when it seamlessly extends your existing data platform rather than creating a separate ML silo. This integration leverages the investments you have made in data lake architecture, warehouse optimization, and streaming infrastructure, transforming them into the foundation for intelligent, predictive systems. Understanding these integration patterns ensures that your ML initiatives build upon existing data engineering work while maintaining the governance, security, and performance standards you have established across your data platform.

Data lake integration patterns

Your S3-based data lake from *Chapter 2, Building Data Lake Foundations,* becomes the primary data source for ML feature engineering, with SageMaker Processing jobs designed to work directly with the partitioned structures and optimization strategies you have already implemented. This integration goes beyond simple data access—SageMaker automatically leverages the partition pruning strategies that optimize your Athena queries and Glue ETL jobs, ensuring that ML workloads benefit from the same performance optimizations without requiring separate data preparation processes. In the following you can see data flow from the S3 data lake through SageMaker to the Feature Store.

When processing customer behavioral data for churn prediction, SageMaker Processing jobs read only the relevant date partitions from your data lake, automatically applying the same filtering logic that optimizes costs for your analytical workloads. This partition-aware processing reduces both processing time and costs while ensuring that ML feature engineering operates on the same high-quality, validated datasets used by your business intelligence and reporting systems.

```
1.  # SageMaker Processing leveraging existing data Lake partitioning
2.  def process_partitioned_customer_data():
3.      """
4.      Efficiently process customer data using existing S3 partitioning
5.      for optimal performance and cost management
6.      """
7.
8.      # Automatic partition pruning based on date filters
9.      input_data_path = "s3://enterprise-data-lake/customer-events/year=2025/month=05/"
10.
11.     processing_code = """
12. import pandas as pd
13. import boto3
14. from datetime import datetime, timedelta
15.
16. def main():
17.     # Read partitioned data with automatic optimization
18.     s3_client = boto3.client(‹s3›)
19.
20.     # Process only relevant partitions for feature engineering
21.     recent_data = pd.read_parquet(‹/opt/ml/processing/input/events/›)
22.
23.     # Feature engineering leveraging existing data structure
24.     customer_features = recent_data.groupby(‹customer_id›).agg({
25.         ‹purchase_amount›: [‹sum›, ‹mean›, ‹count›],
26.         ‹session_duration›: ‹mean›,
27.         ‹page_views›: ‹sum›
28.     }).round(2)
29.
30.     # Flatten column names for Feature Store compatibility
31.     customer_features.columns = [‹_›.join(col).strip() for col in customer_features.
    columns]
32.     customer_features[‹event_time›] = datetime.now().isoformat()
33.
34.     # Output follows same partitioning strategy as source data
35.     output_path = f›/opt/ml/processing/output/features/year=2025/month=05/›
36.     customer_features.to_parquet(output_path, index=False)
37.
38. if __name__ == '__main__':
39.     main()
40.     """
41.
42.     return processing_code
```

The integration maintains your existing data governance through Lake Formation, with ML processing jobs inheriting the same column-level and row-level security policies applied to other data consumers.

This governance extends seamlessly to ML workflows; if a data scientist does not have access to personally identifiable information through Athena, they automatically lack access to the same data through SageMaker Processing. This consistency eliminates the need for separate ML-specific governance frameworks while ensuring that sensitive data protection extends naturally to ML applications.

SageMaker's integration with AWS Glue enables sophisticated workflows that combine traditional data processing with ML-specific transformations. You can extend your existing Glue jobs to include feature engineering steps or create dedicated ML feature pipelines that consume the processed datasets from your regular ETL workflows. This flexibility enables organizations to choose the integration approach that best fits their existing data processing patterns and team responsibilities.

The data lake integration also extends to cost optimization strategies. SageMaker Processing jobs automatically work with compressed Parquet files, columnar storage formats, and intelligent tiering configurations, ensuring that ML workloads benefit from the storage optimizations you have implemented while maintaining the performance characteristics needed for feature engineering at scale.

SageMaker's integration with AWS Glue enables sophisticated ETL workflows that combine traditional data processing with ML-specific transformations. You can extend your existing Glue jobs to include feature engineering steps or create dedicated ML feature pipelines that consume the processed datasets from your regular ETL workflows.

Data warehouse integration

The analytical capabilities you have built in *Chapter 7, Data Warehouse Engineering with Redshift,* become powerful feature engineering engines when integrated with SageMaker, enabling sophisticated ML features that leverage the complex aggregations, window functions, and cross-table joins that would be inefficient to recreate in Python or Spark. This integration transforms your data warehouse from a reporting system into an active component of your ML pipeline, where pre-computed analytical views and materialized views become the foundation for ML features.

SageMaker Data Wrangler provides a visual interface for connecting to Redshift, exploring data relationships, and creating feature engineering workflows that can be exported as SageMaker Processing jobs or Glue ETL scripts. This visual approach enables business analysts familiar with SQL to contribute to feature engineering while automatically generating production-ready code that data engineers can integrate into ML pipelines. The generated code maintains the same connection patterns and security models established for other analytical workloads.

For complex analytical features requiring advanced SQL operations, SageMaker Processing jobs can query Redshift directly through JDBC connections managed by AWS Glue connections. This approach enables feature engineering that leverages sophisticated analytical functions, such as customer segmentation based on **recency frequency monetory (RFM)** analysis, seasonal trend calculations, or cohort analysis metrics, while maintaining the security and connection management patterns you have established for other data warehouse consumers.

```
1.  # SageMaker Processing connecting to Redshift for analytical features
2.  def process_redshift_features():
3.      """
4.      Generate complex analytical features from Redshift data warehouse
5.      leveraging existing analytical views and materialized views
6.      «»»
7.      feature_query = """
8.      WITH customer_segments AS (
9.          SELECT
10.             customer_id,
```

```
11.              -- Leverage existing RFM materialized view
12.              rfm_score,
13.              customer_lifetime_value,
14.              -- Complex analytical features from data warehouse
15.              seasonal_purchase_pattern,
16.              category_affinity_score
17.          FROM analytics.customer_analytics_mv  -- Existing materialized view
18.          WHERE last_updated >= current_date - interval <1> day
19.      )
20.      SELECT * FROM customer_segments
21.      «»»
22.      return feature_query
```

The integration respects your existing Redshift security models and performance optimizations. ML processing jobs connect using the same database users and permissions established for other analytical workloads, ensuring consistent access control across your data platform. Query performance benefits from the same distribution keys, sort keys, and materialized views you have optimized for analytical workloads, ensuring that ML feature engineering does not compromise data warehouse performance.

This integration pattern is particularly valuable for features that require complex temporal analysis or sophisticated business logic that is already encoded in your data warehouse views and stored procedures. Rather than recreating this analytical logic in ML-specific code, you can leverage existing warehouse investments while extending their value to ML applications.

Real-time integration with streaming data

The streaming architecture established in *Chapter 4, Real-time Data Ingestion and Streaming*, extends naturally to support real-time ML features, enabling models that respond to current events while maintaining historical context through your data lake and warehouse integrations. This real-time capability transforms static ML models into dynamic systems that adapt to changing conditions, supporting use cases like fraud detection, real-time personalization, and dynamic pricing that require immediate response to streaming events.

Kinesis Data Firehose can deliver streaming data directly to SageMaker Feature Store's online store, enabling real-time feature updates that support low-latency inference scenarios. This integration maintains the same data quality and transformation patterns you have established for streaming analytics, with the added capability of serving features for ML inference with sub-second latency. The streaming data flows through the same validation and enrichment processes used for operational dashboards while simultaneously updating ML features.

For more complex real-time processing, Kinesis Data Analytics performs streaming aggregations and transformations before delivering results to the Feature Store. This enables sophisticated real-time features like transaction velocity in the last hour, click-through rate trends, or inventory depletion rate that update continuously as new events arrive. These streaming features complement historical features stored in your data lake, providing models with both immediate context and long-term patterns.

Lambda functions provide lightweight feature engineering for simple transformations, handling real-time events that require immediate processing before storage in the Feature Store. This serverless pattern enables event-driven feature updates that scale automatically with streaming volume while maintaining cost efficiency for variable workloads.

The hybrid approach of combining real-time streaming features with batch-processed historical features creates comprehensive customer profiles that capture both immediate behavior and long-term patterns. This integration enables ML models that can detect anomalies based on recent activity while understanding those anomalies in the context of historical customer behavior patterns, providing both responsiveness and accuracy in ML predictions.

Feature engineering at scale

Feature engineering represents the critical bridge between raw data and effective machine learning models, transforming business events and operational data into the numerical representations that algorithms can understand and learn from. At enterprise scale, this transformation must be automated, reproducible, and capable of handling diverse data types while maintaining consistency across training and inference workflows. The feature engineering architecture you build determines whether your ML initiatives will scale successfully or become bottlenecked by data preparation complexity, making the design decisions in this section fundamental to your overall ML platform success.

Feature engineering architecture on AWS

Effective feature engineering at scale requires an architecture that separates concerns appropriately while leveraging AWS services to balance flexibility, performance, and maintainability. The most successful implementations treat feature engineering as an extension of existing data processing patterns, using AWS Glue for large-scale ETL operations and SageMaker Processing for ML-specific transformations that require specialized libraries or computational patterns.

AWS-native separation of concerns

The most successful feature engineering architectures use AWS Glue for raw data processing and SageMaker Processing for ML-specific transformations. Your existing Glue ETL jobs from *Chapter 5, Batch Data Processing*, continue processing raw data into analytical datasets stored in S3. SageMaker Processing jobs then consume these datasets, applying ML-specific transformations without disrupting upstream data processing.

This separation leverages AWS service strengths. Glue excels at large-scale ETL with automatic scaling and built-in data catalog integration. SageMaker Processing provides ML-optimized environments with pre-installed libraries and frameworks. The result is a clear separation between data engineering and ML engineering responsibilities.

AWS Step Functions orchestrates the handoff between Glue and SageMaker, ensuring that ML feature processing waits for upstream data processing completion. CloudWatch Events can trigger feature engineering when new data arrives in S3, creating event-driven pipelines that maintain data freshness.

AWS service integration for feature patterns

Different types of features require different AWS services based on their computational requirements and access patterns, with the architecture routing feature engineering workloads to the most appropriate service for optimal performance and cost efficiency. Understanding these patterns enables you to make architectural decisions that optimize both development velocity and operational efficiency while leveraging the full capabilities of the AWS ML ecosystem:

- **Historical aggregation features** that require complex analytical operations across large datasets leverage Amazon Redshift Serverless or EMR for computational power while maintaining integration with your existing data warehouse architecture. When you need customer lifetime value calculations, seasonal trend analysis, or cohort-based features, these services provide the analytical capabilities for sophisticated aggregations across historical datasets. SageMaker Processing then consumes results from Redshift through JDBC connections managed by AWS Glue connections, maintaining security and connection management consistency.

- **Real-time features** integrate with streaming architecture through Amazon Kinesis Data Analytics for streaming aggregations and Lambda functions for simple transformations. These services handle features like purchases in the last hour, session activity metrics, or real-time inventory levels that must update continuously as new events arrive. Results flow directly to SageMaker Feature Store's online store, enabling sub-second feature retrieval for real-time inference while maintaining the same data quality and governance standards applied to other streaming data consumers.

- **Cross-entity features** that require complex joins across multiple datasets leverage Amazon Athena's serverless query engine for efficient processing without requiring dedicated compute resources. Athena excels at queries that span multiple data lake tables, enabling features like customer-product affinity analysis, supplier-category performance metrics, or geographic correlation features. The serverless nature of Athena makes it cost-effective for periodic feature computation, while its integration with the Glue Catalog ensures consistent metadata management across your feature engineering workflows.

Feature Store integration strategy on AWS

SageMaker Feature Store provides centralized feature management with automatic integration to AWS data services. When you create a Feature Group, AWS automatically provisions DynamoDB tables for online serving and S3 buckets for offline storage, with Glue Catalogue entries that make features discoverable through existing data discovery tools.

The offline store uses the same S3 storage optimizations from *Chapter 3, Data Formats and Storage Optimization*. Features are automatically compressed using Snappy compression and stored in columnar formats for efficient querying. S3 Intelligent-Tiering moves infrequently accessed features to lower-cost storage tiers, while S3 lifecycle policies can archive old feature versions to Glacier for compliance requirements.

For online serving, DynamoDB automatically scales based on read patterns, with built-in monitoring through CloudWatch. Point-in-time recovery ensures feature consistency, while global tables can replicate features across regions for low-latency global applications.

The decision to use Feature Store depends on your scale and integration requirements:

- **Use Feature Store when**: You have multiple models sharing features, need consistent training-serving patterns, or require sub-second inference latency.
- **Use direct S3 access when**: You have isolated models, batch-only inference, or simple feature engineering that does not benefit from centralized management.

Advanced feature engineering with AWS Services

Moving beyond basic transformations, advanced feature engineering leverages specialized AWS capabilities to create sophisticated features that capture complex patterns, temporal relationships, and cross-domain insights that often provide the most predictive power for business problems. These advanced techniques require careful architectural consideration to balance computational complexity with operational efficiency while maintaining the scalability and cost-effectiveness that enterprise ML platforms demand.

Time-series feature engineering using AWS

Time-series features capture temporal patterns, trends, and seasonality that enable models to understand how behaviors and conditions change over time, often providing critical predictive signals for business forecasting, anomaly detection, and behavioral analysis. The complexity of time-series features engineering increases significantly at enterprise scale, requiring specialized AWS services and architectural patterns that can efficiently process temporal data while maintaining the performance characteristics needed for both batch training and real-time inference.

Amazon Timestream provides purpose-built time-series storage with automatic data retention policies, down-sampling capabilities, and optimized query performance for temporal analytics. For customer behavioral features, you can store interaction events in Timestream with automatic down sampling, maintaining granular data for recent periods while aggregating to hourly summaries after 30 days and daily summaries after 90 days. This automated lifecycle management reduces storage costs while maintaining the temporal resolution needed for different features of engineering requirements.

SageMaker Processing jobs integrate with Timestream to compute complex temporal features using specialized time-series libraries and frameworks. These jobs can efficiently calculate rolling averages across multiple time windows, detect trend changes and seasonal patterns, and identify temporal anomalies that indicate significant behavior changes. The integration handles the complexity of temporal data processing while providing the scalability needed for enterprise-scale feature engineering.

AWS Glue can orchestrate multi-window feature engineering by launching parallel SageMaker Processing jobs for different temporal horizons, enabling efficient computation of features that require different time scales. One processing job computes short-term features like seven-day rolling averages and recent trend changes, while another handles longer-term features like seasonal patterns and customer lifecycle analysis. Results are combined and ingested into Feature Store as comprehensive temporal feature vectors that capture both immediate and historical patterns.

Cross-domain feature engineering with AWS data services

Modern enterprises generate data across multiple domains, customer interactions, product catalogs, supply chain events, market conditions, and operational metrics, with the most predictive features often emerging from relationships between these different data sources. Cross-domain feature engineering captures these relationships but requires architectural patterns that can handle different data update frequencies, storage systems, and processing requirements while maintaining consistency and performance across the integrated feature pipeline.

AWS Glue DataBrew provides visual feature engineering capabilities that can connect to multiple data sources simultaneously, enabling data engineers to create transformation flows that join customer transaction data from S3, support interaction data from RDS, product catalog updates from DynamoDB, and market condition data from third-party APIs. The visual interface generates production-ready PySpark code that can be deployed as Glue ETL jobs, providing a bridge between exploratory feature engineering and scalable production processing.

For more complex cross-domain transformations, SageMaker Processing jobs orchestrate multi-source feature engineering using the AWS SDK to access different services within the same processing environment. The managed processing environment automatically includes AWS credentials and network access to other services, enabling seamless integration across data stores without manual configuration or complex permission management.

```
1.  # Cross-domain feature engineering spanning multiple AWS services
2.  def create_cross_domain_features():
3.      """
4.      Combine features from S3 data lake, DynamoDB product catalog,
5.      and RDS customer support data for comprehensive feature engineering
6.      """
7.
8.      # Customer transaction features from S3 data lake
9.      s3_features = pd.read_parquet('s3://data-lake/customer-transactions/')
10.
11.     # Product catalog features from DynamoDB
12.     dynamodb = boto3.resource('dynamodb')
13.     product_table = dynamodb.Table('product-catalog')
14.     product_features = pd.DataFrame([
15.         item for item in product_table.scan()['Items']
16.     ])
17.
18.     # Support interaction features from RDS
```

```
19.     rds_connection = create_connection('customer-support-db')
20.     support_features = pd.read_sql("""
21.         SELECT customer_id,
22.                COUNT(*) as support_cases_30d,
23.                AVG(satisfaction_score) as avg_satisfaction
24.         FROM support_cases
25.         WHERE created_date >= current_date - interval ‹30› day
26.         GROUP BY customer_id
27.     «»», rds_connection)
28.
29.     # Cross-domain feature engineering
30.     combined_features = (s3_features
31.                          .merge(product_features, on='product_id', how='left')
32.                          .merge(support_features, on='customer_id', how='left')
33.                          .fillna(0))  # Handle missing values appropriately
34.
35.     # Create interaction features across domains
36.     combined_features['support_to_purchase_ratio'] = (
37.         combined_features['support_cases_30d'] /
38.         combined_features['purchases_30d'].clip(lower=1)
39.     )
40.
41.     return combined_features
```

The architectural challenge of cross-domain features lies in managing different data update frequencies and consistency requirements. Customer features might update daily through batch processing, while product catalog features change multiple times per hour, and market condition features update in real-time. SageMaker Processing jobs handle these different cadences by implementing staged feature computation where domain-specific features are computed independently and then combined through join operations, enabling parallel processing while managing the complexity of cross-domain dependencies.

Feature quality and monitoring with AWS

At enterprise scale, manual feature quality validation becomes impossible, requiring automated quality checks that validate feature distributions, detect anomalies, and ensure consistency across different computation paths and time periods. AWS provides comprehensive monitoring capabilities through CloudWatch custom metrics, AWS Config rules for governance compliance, and SageMaker Data Quality for ML-specific validation that extends beyond traditional data quality to include ML-relevant checks like feature drift and correlation analysis.

SageMaker Data Wrangler includes built-in data quality analysis that identifies data quality issues, suggests appropriate transformations, and generates comprehensive quality reports that integrate with CloudWatch dashboards for ongoing visibility into feature health. These reports track feature completeness, distribution consistency over time, and correlation stability between features, providing early warning when feature engineering processes may be producing inconsistent results.

Amazon SNS notifications provide automated alerting when feature quality degrades below acceptable thresholds, while AWS Lambda functions can automatically trigger data quality investigations or feature recomputation when issues are detected. This automated quality management extends the monitoring and alerting patterns from *Chapter 13, DataOps and Automation,* to feature engineering workflows, ensuring that ML pipelines maintain data quality standards without requiring manual oversight of every feature engineering process.

ML Pipeline architecture and orchestration

Production machine learning requires sophisticated orchestration that coordinates data processing, feature engineering, model training, validation, and deployment across distributed systems. Unlike traditional application pipelines that follow predictable execution patterns, ML pipelines must handle the inherent uncertainty of model performance, dynamic resource requirements, and complex dependencies between data quality and model accuracy. This orchestration becomes the nervous system of your ML platform, determining whether your organization can reliably transform data insights into business value.

The architectural complexity emerges from ML workflows' unique characteristics: they consume massive datasets requiring specialized compute resources, they produce models whose performance can degrade over time, and they must balance exploration with production stability. Understanding how to design orchestration systems that handle these challenges while integrating seamlessly with existing data infrastructure determines the success of enterprise ML initiatives.

Pipeline design principles

Building production-ready ML pipelines requires more than connecting data processing steps—it demands architectural principles that address the unique challenges of machine learning workflows at enterprise scale.

Modularity and reusability

Effective ML pipeline architecture decomposes complex workflows into discrete, reusable components that can be independently developed, tested, and deployed. This modularity differs from traditional application architectures because ML components must handle both deterministic data processing and probabilistic model behavior. The most successful implementations create clear boundaries between data engineering components that ensure data quality and ML engineering components that handle model development and deployment.

The separation of concerns becomes critical when multiple teams collaborate on ML initiatives. Data engineers focus on scalable, reliable data processing using services like AWS Glue and EMR, while data scientists concentrate on feature engineering and model development using SageMaker Processing and Training. This division enables parallel development while ensuring that each team can leverage its specialized expertise without interfering with other components.

SageMaker Pipelines provides the framework for implementing this modularity through pipeline steps that encapsulate specific functionality:

```
1.  # Modular pipeline components with clear interfaces
2.  feature_step = ProcessingStep(
3.      name='FeatureEngineering',
4.      processor=sklearn_processor,
5.      inputs=[ProcessingInput(source=raw_data_uri)],
6.      outputs=[ProcessingOutput(output_name='features')],
7.      code='feature_engineering.py'
8.  )
9.
10. training_step = TrainingStep(
11.     name='ModelTraining',
12.     estimator=xgboost_estimator,
13.     inputs={'training': TrainingInput(
14.         s3_data=feature_step.properties.ProcessingOutputConfig.Outputs['features'].
    S3Output.S3Uri
15.     )}
```

```
16.)
```

This architectural approach enables feature engineering components to be shared across multiple models, training components to support different algorithms, and deployment components to handle various serving patterns. Organizations report a 40-60% reduction in development time when implementing modular ML pipelines compared to monolithic approaches, while significantly improving consistency and reliability across ML workflows.

Error handling and recovery

ML pipelines must address failure modes that do not exist in traditional applications: data quality degradation, model convergence failures, resource capacity constraints, and performance regression in production models. The architecture must provide graceful degradation and recovery mechanisms that maintain system stability while enabling rapid problem resolution.

The challenge lies in distinguishing between failures that require immediate intervention and those that can be automatically resolved. Data quality issues might trigger alternative processing paths, while resource constraints might initiate automatic retries with different instance types. Model performance regression might trigger retraining workflows, while infrastructure failures require notification and manual intervention.

Effective error handling implements multiple recovery strategies:

- **Circuit breaker patterns** prevent cascade failures by isolating problematic components while maintaining overall pipeline functionality. If feature engineering fails for a specific data source, the pipeline continues with alternative data sources rather than failing completely.

- **Checkpoint mechanisms** enable pipeline restart from intermediate states without reprocessing earlier stages. This becomes critical for long-running training jobs that might face spot instance interruptions or temporary resource constraints.

- **Quality gates** prevent downstream processing of invalid data through automated validation steps that verify data quality, completeness, and consistency before triggering expensive training operations.

Organizations implementing comprehensive error handling report 70-80% reduction in pipeline failures and significantly faster recovery times when failures do occur. The investment in robust error handling pays dividends in improved reliability and reduced operational overhead.

Scalability and resource management

ML workloads exhibit unique scaling characteristics that require sophisticated resource management strategies. Feature engineering might require hundreds of CPU instances for parallel processing, while training might need specialized GPU instances that cost $10+ per hour. The pipeline architecture must dynamically allocate appropriate resources while optimizing for both performance and cost.

The complexity increases when considering the interdependencies between different scaling requirements. Large-scale feature engineering jobs might produce massive datasets that overwhelm downstream training jobs unless resource allocation is coordinated appropriately. Real-time inference endpoints require consistent resource availability, while batch processing can leverage spot instances for significant cost savings.

AWS Step Functions enables sophisticated resource orchestration by analyzing workload characteristics and dynamically selecting appropriate compute configurations:

```
1.  # Dynamic resource allocation based on data volume
2.  def determine_processing_resources(data_size_gb):
3.      if data_size_gb > 100:
4.          return {'instance_count': 10, 'instance_type': 'ml.m5.2xlarge'}
5.      elif data_size_gb > 10:
```

```
6.            return {'instance_count': 2, 'instance_type': 'ml.m5.xlarge'}
7.      else:
8.            return {'instance_count': 1, 'instance_type': 'ml.t3.medium'}
```

Orchestration patterns

Moving beyond simple scheduled batch jobs, modern ML pipelines require sophisticated orchestration strategies that respond intelligently to data changes, model performance, and business conditions.

Event-driven orchestration

Event-driven ML pipelines transform reactive data processing into intelligent, responsive systems that adapt to changing business conditions. This pattern extends the event-driven architectures from *Chapter 4, Real-time Data Ingestion and Streaming,* to include ML-specific triggers that respond to data arrival, model performance degradation, and business metric changes.

The architectural power emerges from creating feedback loops between business outcomes and ML model updates. When customer behavior patterns change, event-driven systems can automatically trigger feature engineering and model retraining without manual intervention. When model accuracy degrades below acceptable thresholds, automated workflows can initiate investigation and remediation processes.

EventBridge provides the integration layer that connects data lake events to ML workflows. New data arriving in S3 triggers feature engineering, completed training jobs automatically evaluate model performance, and detected model drift initiates retraining workflows. This creates responsive ML systems that continuously adapt to changing conditions while maintaining stability and governance.

The challenge lies in intelligent event filtering to prevent unnecessary processing. Not every data update requires model retraining, and not every performance fluctuation indicates model degradation. Successful implementations use sophisticated trigger evaluation that considers data volume changes, business impact metrics, and model performance trends to determine appropriate responses.

Organizations implementing event-driven ML report significant improvements in model freshness and business relevance. Models stay current with changing patterns rather than becoming stale between scheduled updates, while automation reduces the operational overhead required to maintain model performance.

Scheduled orchestration

Scheduled ML workflows provide predictability and alignment with business cycles, enabling organizations to plan resource usage and integrate ML updates with operational processes. Customer segmentation models might retrain weekly to capture behavioural changes, demand forecasting models might update daily to incorporate new sales data, and financial risk models might refresh monthly to align with reporting cycles.

The architectural benefit of scheduled orchestration extends beyond simple automation. Predictable execution patterns enable better resource planning, cost optimization through reserved instance usage, and integration with business processes that depend on consistent model updates. Teams can plan model validation activities around known update schedules, and business users can expect fresh insights according to established cadences.

EventBridge scheduled rules coordinate different ML workflows based on their update requirements:

```
1. # Multiple scheduling patterns for different model types
2. schedule_patterns = {
3.     'real_time_features': 'cron(0 2 * * ? *)',      # Daily at 2 AM
4.     'customer_segmentation': 'cron(0 4 ? * SUN *)',  # Weekly on Sunday
5.     'financial_models': 'cron(0 6 1 * ? *)'          # Monthly on 1st
6. }
```

The key architectural decision involves balancing update frequency with computational costs and business value. More frequent updates provide fresher insights but increase infrastructure costs and complexity. The optimal schedule depends on how quickly underlying patterns change and how sensitive business decisions are to model freshness.

Successful implementations establish different scheduling patterns for different model types while maintaining the flexibility to trigger ad-hoc updates when business conditions change significantly. This hybrid approach provides predictability while preserving responsiveness to exceptional circumstances.

Hybrid orchestration

Production ML platforms typically require hybrid approaches that combine event-driven responsiveness with scheduled predictability. Core business models might follow scheduled retraining cycles to ensure consistent performance, while operational models respond to real-time events to maintain relevance for immediate decision-making.

The architectural complexity lies in coordinating different orchestration patterns without creating conflicts or resource contention. A customer churn model might follow weekly scheduled retraining while also responding to significant customer behavior changes detected in real-time streams. The orchestration system must intelligently manage these overlapping requirements.

Step Functions provides the coordination layer that manages hybrid orchestration through state machines that can be triggered by both scheduled events and real-time conditions. The same pipeline definition can execute on different schedules while responding to exceptional events that require immediate attention.

Resource coordination becomes critical in hybrid systems where scheduled and event-driven workflows might compete for the same compute resources. Effective implementations use priority queuing and resource reservation to ensure that critical business processes maintain access to required resources while opportunistic workloads utilize available capacity.

Organizations implementing hybrid orchestration report improved balance between operational stability and business responsiveness. Critical business processes maintain predictable execution while the system adapts dynamically to changing conditions and emerging opportunities.

Pipeline monitoring and observability

The transition from experimental models to production systems represents one of the most critical phases in the ML lifecycle, where theoretical accuracy transforms into real business value through comprehensive monitoring and deployment strategies.

Execution monitoring

ML pipeline monitoring extends far beyond traditional application observability to include ML-specific metrics that indicate model health, data quality, and prediction accuracy. The monitoring architecture must provide visibility into pipeline execution while tracking the statistical properties that determine ML system effectiveness.

Effective monitoring creates layered visibility: infrastructure metrics show resource utilization and execution status, data quality metrics track input validation and feature consistency, and model performance metrics indicate prediction accuracy and business impact. This comprehensive view enables rapid problem identification and resolution across the entire ML stack.

CloudWatch provides the foundational monitoring infrastructure, while custom metrics track ML-specific indicators:

- **Pipeline execution metrics**: Success rates, execution duration, and resource utilization.

- **Data quality metrics**: Schema compliance, missing value percentages, and distribution shifts.
- **Model performance metrics**: Accuracy, precision, recall, and business **key performance indicator (KPI)** impact.
- **Feature Store metrics**: Feature serving latency, consistency checks, and update frequencies.

The architectural challenge involves establishing appropriate alerting thresholds that balance sensitivity with noise reduction. ML metrics often exhibit natural variation that would trigger false alarms in traditional systems, requiring more sophisticated anomaly detection approaches.

Lineage tracking

Data lineage becomes critical in ML pipelines where model predictions depend on complex feature engineering and data transformation processes spanning multiple systems and time periods. The architecture must track data flow from source systems through feature engineering to model training and inference, enabling comprehensive impact analysis and debugging capabilities.

ML lineage extends beyond traditional data lineage to include model versioning, experiment tracking, and feature provenance. When model performance degrades, teams need to understand which data sources contributed to the issue, which feature engineering steps might have introduced problems, and how changes propagate through the entire ML system.

SageMaker automatically captures certain lineage information, while AWS DataBrew and Glue provide lineage tracking for feature engineering processes. The integrated lineage view enables rapid root cause analysis when model performance issues emerge and supports compliance requirements for regulated industries.

Model deployment and serving patterns

The transition from experimental models to production systems represents one of the most critical phases in the ML lifecycle, where theoretical accuracy transforms into real business value. Model deployment and serving patterns determine whether your ML investments deliver consistent, reliable predictions that drive business decisions or become expensive experiments that never impact operations. Understanding the architectural implications of different serving patterns, from real-time inference to batch predictions, enables you to design deployment strategies that balance performance, cost, and operational complexity while maintaining the governance and security standards established across your data platform.

The complexity of production ML serving extends far beyond simply hosting a trained model. Modern deployment patterns must handle model versioning, A/B testing, traffic routing, auto-scaling, and performance monitoring while integrating seamlessly with existing application architectures. The serving infrastructure becomes a critical component of your overall data platform, requiring the same attention to reliability, security, and operational excellence applied to your data lake and warehouse implementations.

Real-time inference patterns

Production ML deployment encompasses three distinct serving patterns—real-time endpoints for immediate predictions, serverless inference for variable demand, and edge deployment for distributed processing—each optimized for specific business requirements and operational constraints.

SageMaker endpoints for low-latency serving

Real-time inference represents the most demanding deployment pattern, requiring sub-second response times while maintaining high availability and automatic scaling capabilities. SageMaker endpoints provide managed infrastructure that handles the operational complexity of real-time serving while integrating with your existing AWS security and monitoring frameworks.

The architectural foundation of SageMaker endpoints leverages the same security models established for your data infrastructure. Endpoints inherit IAM policies, integrate with VPC configurations, and support the same encryption standards used across your data platform. This consistency ensures that ML serving maintains your established security posture without requiring separate governance frameworks.

Auto-scaling capabilities address the variable demand patterns typical of business applications. Customer-facing applications might experience significant traffic fluctuations throughout the day, while internal analytics tools might have predictable usage patterns. SageMaker endpoints automatically adjust capacity based on request volume and response latency, ensuring consistent performance while optimizing costs:

```
1.  # Endpoint configuration with auto-scaling and monitoring
2.  endpoint_config = {
3.      'EndpointConfigName': 'customer-churn-endpoint-config',
4.      'ProductionVariants': [{
5.          'VariantName': 'primary',
6.          'ModelName': 'customer-churn-model-v2',
7.          'InitialInstanceCount': 2,
8.          'InstanceType': 'ml.m5.large',
9.          'InitialVariantWeight': 100
10.     }]
11. }
```

Serverless inference with Lambda integration

For applications with unpredictable or intermittent inference requirements, serverless patterns eliminate the cost of maintaining always-on infrastructure while providing automatic scaling from zero to thousands of concurrent requests. This pattern proves particularly effective for event-driven ML applications where predictions are triggered by specific business events rather than constant user requests.

Lambda functions can host lightweight models directly for simple inference requirements or coordinate with SageMaker endpoints for more complex models. The serverless approach handles traffic spikes automatically while minimizing costs during periods of low demand. Integration with API Gateway provides additional capabilities, including authentication, throttling, and caching that complement the serverless inference pattern.

The architectural trade-off involves cold start latency versus infrastructure costs. Lambda functions experience initialization delays when scaling from zero, which might be acceptable for batch-oriented workflows but problematic for user-facing applications. Understanding your latency requirements and traffic patterns determines whether serverless inference provides appropriate performance characteristics.

Edge deployment considerations

Edge deployment extends ML capabilities to locations with limited connectivity or strict latency requirements, bringing inference capabilities closer to data sources and decision points. IoT applications, mobile devices, and remote locations benefit from local inference that does not depend on network connectivity while reducing bandwidth costs and improving response times.

SageMaker Edge provides device management and model deployment capabilities that extend your centralized ML platform to distributed edge locations. Models trained in SageMaker can be optimized for edge deployment through compilation and quantization that reduces model size and computational requirements while maintaining prediction accuracy.

The architectural challenge involves managing model consistency across distributed edge locations while handling device constraints and connectivity limitations. Edge devices might have limited computational resources, storage capacity, and intermittent network connectivity that require specialized deployment strategies.

Model synchronization becomes critical for maintaining consistency across edge deployments. Updates must be coordinated carefully to prevent version conflicts while handling devices that might be offline during update windows. Effective edge deployment strategies implement gradual rollout patterns and fallback mechanisms that maintain service availability during updates.

Batch inference patterns

When real-time responses are not required, batch inference patterns optimize for throughput and cost efficiency, processing entire datasets to generate predictions that support strategic decision-making and operational planning.

Scheduled batch processing

Batch inference patterns optimize for throughput and cost efficiency when real-time responses are not required, processing large datasets to generate predictions that support strategic decision-making and operational planning. Customer segmentation, demand forecasting, and risk analysis often benefit from batch processing that can leverage cost-optimized compute resources and process entire datasets comprehensively.

SageMaker Batch Transform provides managed infrastructure for large-scale batch inference that integrates seamlessly with your data lake architecture. Batch jobs can process data directly from S3 using the same partitioned structures established for analytical workloads, leveraging partition pruning and columnar storage optimizations to minimize processing time and costs.

The integration with existing data processing patterns enables batch inference to consume the same high-quality, validated datasets used for business intelligence and reporting. This consistency ensures that ML predictions use the same data governance and quality standards applied across your data platform, reducing the risk of inconsistencies between analytical and predictive insights.

Distributed processing for large-scale inference

Large-scale batch inference requires distributed processing strategies that can handle datasets too large for single-instance processing while maintaining cost efficiency and reasonable processing times. The architecture must coordinate data distribution, result aggregation, and error handling across multiple processing instances.

EMR provides distributed processing capabilities that can handle massive inference workloads using Spark or other distributed computing frameworks. This approach proves effective when inference logic is complex or when pre-processing and post-processing operations require distributed computation beyond simple model evaluation.

The integration between SageMaker and EMR enables hybrid approaches where complex data preparation occurs on EMR clusters while model inference leverages SageMaker's optimized serving infrastructure. This division of responsibilities optimizes resource utilization while leveraging the strengths of different AWS services.

A/B testing and canary deployments

Production model deployment requires systematic validation approaches that verify model performance with real business data before full rollout, using A/B testing and canary deployment patterns to minimize business risk while enabling rapid rollback when issues emerge.

Production validation patterns

Production model deployment requires systematic validation approaches that verify model performance with real business data before full rollout. A/B testing and canary deployment patterns provide controlled mechanisms for evaluating model changes while minimizing business risk and enabling rapid rollback when issues emerge.

SageMaker endpoints support traffic splitting that enables sophisticated A/B testing patterns without requiring application-level routing logic. Production traffic can be distributed between model versions based on configurable weights, enabling controlled evaluation of model performance with real user interactions and business outcomes.

The architectural benefit extends beyond simple model comparison to include comprehensive business impact analysis. A/B testing enables measurement of how model changes affect business KPIs, customer satisfaction, and operational metrics rather than relying solely on offline model accuracy metrics:

```
1.  # A/B testing configuration with traffic splitting
2.  production_variants = [
3.      {
4.          'VariantName': 'model-v1',
5.          'ModelName': 'recommendation-model-v1',
6.          'InitialInstanceCount': 2,
7.          'InstanceType': 'ml.m5.large',
8.          'InitialVariantWeight': 70  # 70% of traffic
9.      },
10.     {
11.         'VariantName': 'model-v2',
12.         'ModelName': 'recommendation-model-v2',
13.         'InitialInstanceCount': 1,
14.         'InstanceType': 'ml.m5.large',
15.         'InitialVariantWeight': 30  # 30% of traffic
16.     }
17. ]
```

Canary deployments provide an alternative approach that gradually increases exposure to new models based on performance validation. Initial deployment might serve new models to a small percentage of traffic, expanding coverage as confidence in model performance increases. This pattern minimizes risk while enabling systematic validation of model improvements.

Success metrics for production validation extend beyond traditional ML metrics to include business impact indicators. Revenue per user, conversion rates, customer satisfaction scores, and operational efficiency metrics provide a comprehensive evaluation of model effectiveness in real business contexts.

Performance optimization for ML workloads

Performance optimization for machine learning workloads requires understanding the unique computational characteristics that distinguish ML processing from traditional application workloads. While conventional applications typically exhibit predictable CPU and memory usage patterns, ML workloads involve complex mathematical operations on large datasets that create distinctive bottlenecks in data I/O, memory bandwidth, and computational throughput. The optimization strategies must address these characteristics while leveraging AWS service capabilities to achieve optimal performance at acceptable costs.

The complexity of ML performance optimization emerges from the diverse nature of different ML phases, each with unique resource requirements and scaling characteristics. Feature engineering might be I/O-bound, requiring optimization of data transfer and storage access patterns. Model training might be compute-bound, benefiting from specialized hardware like GPUs or distributed processing. Inference might be latency-bound, requiring optimization of model serving and caching strategies. Understanding these different optimization domains enables targeted performance improvements that address the actual bottlenecks rather than applying generic optimization approaches.

Compute optimization strategies

Performance optimization for machine learning workloads requires understanding the unique computational characteristics that distinguish ML processing from traditional application workloads, where predictable patterns give way to complex mathematical operations on large datasets.

Instance type selection and sizing

The foundation of ML performance optimization lies in matching compute resources to workload characteristics, a decision that significantly impacts both performance and cost efficiency. Unlike traditional web applications that can often standardize on general-purpose instances, ML workloads benefit from specialized instance types designed for specific computational patterns and data access requirements.

Feature engineering workloads typically benefit from compute-optimized instances with high CPU performance and substantial memory capacity for in-memory data processing. These workloads often involve complex transformations across large datasets where memory bandwidth becomes the limiting factor rather than raw computational power. The C5 instance family provides optimized performance for these CPU-intensive operations while offering cost efficiency for sustained processing workloads.

Training workloads exhibit more diverse requirements depending on algorithm complexity and dataset characteristics. Traditional machine learning algorithms like XGBoost or Random Forest perform well on CPU-optimized instances with large memory configurations, while deep learning models require GPU acceleration for acceptable training times. The P4 and P3 instance families provide high-performance GPU capabilities, while G4 instances offer cost-effective GPU resources for less demanding deep learning workloads:

```
1.  # Instance selection matrix based on workload characteristics
2.  instance_selection_guide = {
3.      'feature_engineering': {
4.          'small_datasets': 'ml.c5.xlarge',       # CPU-optimized for <10GB data
5.          'large_datasets': 'ml.c5.4xlarge',      # High memory for 10-100GB data
6.          'massive_datasets': 'ml.c5.18xlarge'    # Distributed processing >100GB
7.      },
8.      'training': {
9.          'traditional_ml': 'ml.c5.2xlarge',      # CPU for XGBoost, Random Forest
10.         'deep_learning': 'ml.p3.2xlarge',       # Single GPU for standard models
11.         'large_models': 'ml.p3.8xlarge',        # Multi-GPU for complex models
12.         'distributed_training': 'ml.p3.16xlarge' # Maximum GPU for distributed jobs
13.     },
14.     'inference': {
15.         'low_latency': 'ml.c5.large',           # Fast CPU for real-time serving
16.         'high_throughput': 'ml.c5.4xlarge',     # More CPU cores for batch processing
17.         'gpu_inference': 'ml.g4dn.xlarge'       # Cost-effective GPU serving
18.     }
19. }
```

The selection process must consider not only current performance requirements but also cost optimization opportunities through spot instances, which can provide 50-90% cost savings for fault-tolerant workloads. Training jobs can leverage spot instances effectively when combined with checkpointing strategies that preserve progress when instances are reclaimed.

Memory optimization becomes particularly critical for ML workloads that process large datasets or complex models. Insufficient memory forces disk-based processing that dramatically increases execution time, while excessive memory increases costs without providing performance benefits. The optimal memory configuration depends on dataset size, processing algorithms, and parallelization strategies.

GPU utilization and optimization

GPU acceleration provides dramatic performance improvements for deep learning workloads, but realizing these benefits requires careful optimization of data pipelines, model architectures, and memory management. Poor GPU utilization often stems from data loading bottlenecks, inefficient memory management, or suboptimal batch sizing that prevents GPUs from operating at full capacity.

Data pipeline optimization ensures that GPUs receive data at rates that match their processing capabilities. Slow data loading creates GPU idle time that wastes expensive compute resources, while inefficient data formats require excessive preprocessing that limits training throughput. The data pipeline must be optimized holistically from storage access through preprocessing to model feeding.

SageMaker provides optimized data loading capabilities through Pipe mode, which streams data directly from S3 to training instances without requiring local storage for complete datasets. This approach reduces training startup time while enabling processing of datasets larger than available instance storage. For maximum GPU utilization, data preprocessing should be parallelized and occur on CPU cores while GPU cores focus on model computation.

Memory management optimization addresses the limited memory capacity of GPU instances while maximizing the utilization of available memory. Gradient accumulation enables training with larger effective batch sizes than GPU memory would normally allow, while mixed precision training reduces memory requirements while maintaining model accuracy. These techniques enable the training of larger models or the processing of larger batches within GPU memory constraints.

Batch size optimization balances GPU utilization with memory constraints and training stability. Larger batch sizes typically improve GPU utilization and training speed but require more memory and may impact model convergence. The optimal batch size depends on model architecture, available GPU memory, and training objectives.

Multi-GPU optimization extends performance improvements through data parallelism or model parallelism strategies. Data parallelism distributes training examples across multiple GPUs while maintaining model replicas, while model parallelism distributes model components across GPUs when models are too large for a single GPU's memory. SageMaker automatically handles the complexity of distributed training coordination while optimizing communication patterns between GPUs.

Distributed processing patterns

Large-scale ML workloads often require distributed processing to achieve acceptable performance and handle datasets that exceed single-instance capabilities. The distributed processing architecture must coordinate data distribution, computation parallelization, and result aggregation while minimizing communication overhead and handling potential instance failures.

Feature engineering benefits from embarrassingly parallel distribution, where different instances process independent data partitions. This approach scales linearly with the number of instances while minimizing coordination overhead. AWS Glue and EMR provide managed distributed processing that automatically handles resource allocation, fault tolerance, and data coordination for large-scale feature engineering workloads.

Training workload distribution depends on model characteristics and dataset size. Data parallelism replicates models across multiple instances while distributing training examples, requiring gradient synchronization between instances. Model parallelism distributes model components across instances when models are too large for a single instance of memory. Hybrid approaches combine both strategies for very large models and datasets.

SageMaker distributed training libraries optimize communication patterns and synchronization strategies for different distributed training scenarios. The libraries handle the complexity of efficient gradient aggregation, parameter synchronization, and fault tolerance while providing simple APIs that do not require distributed systems expertise.

Communication optimization becomes critical for distributed training performance. Gradient synchronization can become a bottleneck when communication bandwidth is insufficient or when synchronization frequency is suboptimal. Gradient compression, asynchronous communication, and optimized network topologies can significantly improve distributed training performance.

Data pipeline optimization

ML workloads often exhibit I/O-intensive characteristics that can create significant performance bottlenecks if not properly optimized, requiring targeted strategies that address the actual data access patterns rather than applying generic performance improvements.

I/O performance tuning

ML workloads often exhibit I/O-intensive characteristics that can create significant performance bottlenecks if not properly optimized. The data pipeline must efficiently move large datasets from storage systems through preprocessing stages to computational resources while minimizing latency and maximizing throughput. Understanding the I/O patterns of different ML phases enables targeted optimizations that address actual bottlenecks rather than applying generic performance improvements.

Storage access patterns vary significantly between ML workload types. Feature engineering typically involves sequential reads of large datasets, benefiting from high-throughput storage configurations and prefetching strategies. Training workloads might exhibit random access patterns when sampling training examples, requiring optimization for **input/output operations per second (IOPS)** rather than sequential throughput. Inference workloads typically access smaller, frequently-used datasets that benefit from caching and low-latency storage.

S3 optimization strategies address the unique characteristics of object storage for ML workloads. Transfer acceleration can significantly improve data loading performance for geographically distributed teams or when transferring large datasets across regions. Multipart uploads and parallel downloads maximize bandwidth utilization for large files, while intelligent request patterns minimize request overhead for many small files.

The integration between S3 and processing instances benefits from optimization of request patterns, data formats, and network configurations. S3 Select enables server-side filtering that reduces data transfer volumes, while optimized data formats like Parquet provide better compression and faster parsing compared to CSV or JSON formats:

```
1.  # S3 optimization configuration for ML workloads
2.  s3_optimization_config = {
3.      'data_loading': {
4.          'transfer_acceleration': True,
5.          'multipart_threshold': '64MB',        # Parallel uploads for large files
6.          'multipart_chunksize': '16MB',        # Balance parallelism with overhead
7.          'max_concurrency': 10,                # Concurrent transfer operations
8.          'use_accelerate_endpoint': True       # Global acceleration for cross-region
9.      },
10.     'preprocessing': {
11.         'enable_s3_select': True,             # Server-side filtering
12.         'preferred_formats': ['parquet', 'orc'],  # Columnar formats
13.         'compression': 'snappy',              # Balance compression and speed
14.         'partition_strategy': 'date_based'    # Optimize for access patterns
15.     }
```

```
16. }
```

Local storage optimization addresses the performance characteristics of instance storage for ML workloads. **Non-Volatile Memory Express (NVMe)** SSD storage provides high IOPS and low latency for random access patterns, while network-attached storage might be more cost-effective for sequential access workloads. The storage configuration must balance performance requirements with cost considerations and data durability needs.

EBS optimization ensures that storage performance matches instance capabilities while providing appropriate durability and backup capabilities. **General purpose (GP3)** volumes provide configurable IOPS and throughput that can be tuned for specific workload requirements, while IO2 volumes provide higher performance for demanding workloads. The storage configuration should align with workload characteristics rather than using default configurations.

Caching and data locality

Intelligent caching strategies can dramatically improve ML workload performance by reducing redundant data access and computation while optimizing for the access patterns exhibited by different ML phases. The caching architecture must balance memory utilization with performance improvements while considering the cost implications of different caching strategies.

Feature caching addresses the common pattern where multiple models or experiments use similar feature sets, enabling reuse of expensive feature engineering computations. SageMaker Feature Store provides managed caching capabilities that maintain feature consistency while optimizing access performance. The online store provides sub-second feature retrieval for real-time inference, while the offline store enables efficient batch access for training workloads.

Model artifact caching optimizes the deployment and serving performance by maintaining frequently accessed models in high-performance storage. Container image caching reduces startup time for training and inference jobs by maintaining pre-built environments with required dependencies. This optimization becomes particularly valuable for short-running jobs where startup time represents a significant portion of total execution time.

Data locality optimization ensures that computational resources have efficient access to required datasets while minimizing network transfer overhead. EMR clusters can leverage HDFS for high-performance distributed storage, while SageMaker Processing jobs can use FSx for Lustre when shared high-performance storage is required across multiple instances.

The caching strategy must consider data freshness requirements and cache invalidation policies that maintain consistency while optimizing performance. Feature caches must be updated when underlying data changes, while model caches must be refreshed when new versions are deployed. The invalidation strategy should balance freshness with performance benefits.

Model serving performance

Production ML inference demands a sophisticated optimization strategy that transforms raw model capabilities into responsive, cost-effective services capable of meeting enterprise-scale performance requirements.

Inference optimization techniques

Model serving performance optimization addresses the unique requirements of production inference workloads where response latency, throughput, and resource utilization directly impact user experience and operational costs. The optimization strategy must consider model complexity, traffic patterns, and business requirements while maintaining prediction accuracy and system reliability.

Model optimization techniques reduce computational requirements without significantly impacting prediction accuracy. Quantization reduces model precision from 32-bit to 8-bit or 16-bit representations, significantly reducing memory requirements and computation time while maintaining acceptable accuracy for most applications. Pruning removes unnecessary model parameters, reducing model size and inference time with minimal accuracy impact.

SageMaker Neo provides automated model optimization that compiles models for specific hardware targets, optimizing performance for CPU, GPU, or specialized inference chips. The optimization process analyzes model architectures and generates optimized code that leverages hardware-specific capabilities while maintaining prediction accuracy.

Batching strategies optimize inference throughput by processing multiple requests simultaneously, amortizing model loading and initialization costs across multiple predictions. Dynamic batching adjusts batch sizes based on request patterns and latency requirements, while static batching provides predictable performance characteristics for steady workload patterns. A comprehensive optimization configuration demonstrates how multiple techniques can be coordinated to maximize inference performance while maintaining operational flexibility:

```
1.  # Model serving optimization configuration
2.  serving_optimization_config = {
3.      'model_optimization': {
4.          'quantization': '8bit',            # Reduce precision for speed
5.          'pruning_threshold': 0.01,         # Remove small weights
6.          'compilation_target': 'cpu',       # Hardware-specific optimization
7.          'batch_size': 'dynamic'            # Adaptive batching
8.      },
9.      'caching': {
10.         'enable_response_cache': True,     # Cache frequent predictions
11.         'cache_ttl': 300,                  # 5-minute cache lifetime
12.         'cache_size': '1GB',               # Memory allocation for cache
13.         'cache_strategy': 'lru'            # Least-recently-used eviction
14.     }
15. }
```

Memory management optimization addresses the limited memory resources available for model serving while maximizing concurrent request handling. Model loading strategies determine whether models are loaded on-demand or kept resident in memory, balancing memory utilization with response latency. Memory pooling and garbage collection optimization ensure efficient memory utilization patterns.

Auto-scaling and load balancing

Auto-scaling optimization ensures that inference endpoints can handle variable traffic patterns while minimizing resource costs and maintaining acceptable response latency. The scaling strategy must balance responsiveness to traffic changes with stability and cost efficiency, considering both horizontal scaling (adding instances) and vertical scaling (changing instance types).

SageMaker endpoint auto-scaling provides configurable policies that respond to different metrics including request rate, CPU utilization, and custom business metrics. The scaling policies should be tuned based on actual traffic patterns and business requirements rather than using default configurations that might be suboptimal for specific use cases.

Scaling policies must consider the cold start characteristics of different instance types and model loading times. GPU instances might have longer startup times but provide better performance for complex models, while CPU instances might start faster but provide lower throughput. The scaling configuration should align with business requirements for response time and cost efficiency.

Load balancing optimization distributes requests across available instances while considering instance health, response time, and resource utilization. Application Load Balancer provides sophisticated routing capabilities that can distribute traffic based on request characteristics, geographic location, or custom headers.

Target tracking policies provide automatic scaling based on predefined metrics, while step scaling enables more complex policies that respond differently to various load levels. Predictive scaling can anticipate traffic patterns based on historical data, enabling proactive scaling that avoids performance degradation during traffic spikes.

Caching and CDN integration

Caching strategies for ML inference can dramatically improve response times and reduce computational costs by storing frequently requested predictions or intermediate results. The caching architecture must balance cache hit rates with memory utilization while ensuring that cached predictions remain relevant and accurate.

Response caching stores complete prediction results for requests that are likely to be repeated, eliminating the need for model inference when identical requests are received. This approach works well for applications with predictable request patterns or when prediction inputs have high reuse rates. The cache management must consider prediction freshness requirements and storage costs.

Feature caching stores pre-processed input features that are expensive to compute, enabling reuse across multiple model invocations or different models that share common features. This optimization is particularly valuable when feature engineering involves complex computations or external data access that would otherwise impact inference latency.

CloudFront integration provides global caching and content delivery capabilities that can cache model predictions or pre-processed data closer to end users. This geographic distribution reduces latency for global applications while providing additional capacity for handling traffic spikes.

Performance optimization for ML workloads requires systematic analysis of computational bottlenecks, data access patterns, and resource utilization characteristics that distinguish ML processing from traditional application workloads. By implementing targeted optimizations that address the unique requirements of feature engineering, model training, and inference serving, organizations can achieve significant improvements in both performance and cost efficiency while maintaining the quality and reliability standards required for production ML systems. The investment in performance optimization pays dividends through reduced infrastructure costs, improved user experience, and faster time-to-value for ML initiatives that drive business outcomes.

ML architecture pattern

Selecting the appropriate ML architecture pattern represents one of the most critical decisions in platform design, directly impacting development velocity, operational complexity, and business value delivery. The three fundamental patterns, batch-first with real-time extension, event-driven real-time, and hybrid batch-stream architecture, each address different organizational contexts and business requirements. Understanding when and how to implement each pattern enables organizations to build ML platforms that align with their technical capabilities, business objectives, and operational constraints while establishing foundations for future evolution.

Pattern 1: Batch-first with real-time extension

The batch-first pattern represents a pragmatic approach to ML architecture that builds upon proven data warehouse foundations, delivering enterprise-grade stability and governance while selectively incorporating real-time capabilities where business impact justifies the additional complexity.

Architecture overview

The batch-first pattern prioritizes stability, auditability, and cost efficiency by building upon established data warehouse architectures while selectively adding real-time capabilities where business value justifies the additional complexity. This approach leverages existing ETL investments and data governance frameworks, making it the optimal choice for organizations with mature data operations and regulatory requirements that mandate comprehensive audit trails and data lineage. The batch-first architecture systematically balances operational stability with ML capabilities, as demonstrated by the strategic trade-offs across each system component:

Component	Implementation	Rationale	Trade-offs
Data processing	Glue ETL | Redshift | SageMaker	Leverage existing infrastructure investments	Higher latency, lower operational cost
Feature engineering	Scheduled batch jobs with validation	Consistent, auditable processing workflows	Less responsive to rapid business changes
Model training	Weekly or monthly retraining cycles	Stable, well-tested model performance	Slower adaptation to emerging trends
Inference	Batch scoring with intelligent caching	Cost-effective for most business use cases	Limited real-time capability

Table 12.1: Batch architecture components and strategic trade-offs

Implementation strategy

Organizations implementing this pattern typically begin with existing Redshift data warehouses containing high-quality, validated business data. AWS Glue ETL jobs extend existing data processing workflows to include feature engineering specifically designed for ML consumption, while maintaining the same data quality and governance standards applied to traditional analytics. This approach ensures that ML initiatives benefit from years of investment in data quality, validation, and business logic without requiring parallel infrastructure development.

The feature engineering pipeline operates on predictable schedules that align with business reporting cycles, enabling thorough validation and quality assurance that would be difficult to achieve in real-time systems. Features undergo comprehensive statistical validation, business rule verification, and historical consistency checks before being made available for model training. This thorough validation process significantly reduces the risk of data quality issues impacting model performance while providing the audit trails required for regulatory compliance.

Model training follows similarly disciplined schedules, typically weekly or monthly, that enable comprehensive evaluation of model performance against business objectives. The extended training cycles allow for sophisticated hyperparameter tuning, ensemble model evaluation, and thorough A/B testing that would be impractical with more frequent update cycles. This approach produces highly stable, well-validated models that provide consistent business value with minimal operational overhead.

Business value and use cases

The batch-first pattern excels in scenarios where business decisions operate on predictable cycles and where stability and auditability take precedence over immediate responsiveness:

- **Customer segmentation** initiatives benefit from this approach because customer behavior patterns evolve gradually, and marketing campaigns typically plan weeks or months in advance. The stable, thoroughly validated customer segments enable confident strategic decisions, while the batch processing approach keeps operational costs manageable.

- **Demand forecasting** represents another ideal use case where the pattern's strengths align perfectly with business requirements. Retail and manufacturing organizations need highly accurate forecasts for strategic planning, but they can typically tolerate forecast updates on weekly or monthly cycles. The batch processing approach enables sophisticated seasonal modeling, economic indicator integration, and comprehensive validation that produces forecasts with confidence intervals and detailed explanations of underlying assumptions.

- **Risk assessment** applications in financial services leverage this pattern's emphasis on auditability and stability. Credit scoring, insurance underwriting, and compliance monitoring all require models that can be thoroughly documented, validated, and explained to regulators. The batch processing approach provides comprehensive model lineage, detailed performance tracking, and the stability required for regulatory approval processes.

Pattern 2: Event-driven real-time

Event-driven real-time architecture transforms business responsiveness by processing data and adapting models as events occur, enabling organizations to capitalize on fleeting opportunities and respond to threats within milliseconds of their emergence.

Architecture overview

Event-driven real-time architecture prioritizes immediate responsiveness and adaptability, processing data and updating models as business events occur. This pattern proves essential for applications where competitive advantage depends on split-second decision making and where user experiences require immediate personalization based on current behavior patterns. Real-time architecture components are optimized for immediate responsiveness, creating a system design that prioritizes speed and adaptability over operational simplicity:

Component	Implementation	Rationale	Trade-offs
Data processing	Kinesis | Lambda | Feature Store	Real-time responsiveness to business events	Higher complexity and operational cost
Feature engineering	Streaming analytics with immediate updates	Captures temporal patterns and immediate signals	Requires specialized stream processing expertise
Model training	Continuous or online learning approaches	Adapts quickly to changing business conditions	Model stability and reproducibility challenges
Inference	Real-time endpoints with auto-scaling	Sub-second response times for user-facing applications	Higher infrastructure costs and complexity

Table 12.2: Real-time components: Speed over operational simplicity

Implementation strategy

Real-time architecture implementations centre around event streaming platforms that capture business events as they occur and immediately route them to multiple processing pipelines. Kinesis Data Streams provides the foundational event backbone, while Lambda functions and Kinesis Analytics enable lightweight, serverless processing that scales automatically with event volume. This serverless approach minimizes operational overhead while providing the elasticity required to handle unpredictable event patterns.

Feature engineering in real-time systems requires fundamentally different approaches compared to batch processing. Streaming analytics must maintain state across time windows while processing events in the order they arrive, requiring sophisticated handling of late-arriving data, duplicate events, and processing failures. SageMaker Feature Store's online store provides the high-performance feature serving required for real-time inference while maintaining consistency with offline feature engineering processes.

Continuous learning approaches enable models to adapt immediately to changing patterns, but they require careful implementation to maintain model stability and business predictability. Online learning algorithms update model parameters incrementally as new data arrives, while careful monitoring ensures that rapid model changes do not degrade performance or create unexpected business impacts. This balance between adaptability and stability represents one of the most challenging aspects of real-time ML systems.

Business value and use cases

Fraud detection represents the canonical use case for real-time ML architecture because fraudulent transactions must be identified within milliseconds to prevent financial loss while minimizing false positives that frustrate legitimate customers. The real-time architecture enables sophisticated behavioral analysis that considers immediate transaction context, recent customer activity patterns, and network effects that indicate coordinated fraudulent activity. The ability to process transactions in real-time while maintaining sub-second response times provides direct, measurable business value through reduced fraud losses and improved customer experience.

Real-time recommendations demonstrate how event-driven architecture transforms user experiences by providing immediate personalization based on current browsing behavior, purchase history, and contextual signals like time of day or device type. E-commerce platforms using real-time recommendation systems typically see 10-25% increases in conversion rates and user engagement because recommendations remain relevant to users' immediate interests rather than reflecting historical behavior patterns that may no longer be relevant.

Dynamic pricing applications in travel, hospitality, and ride-sharing industries leverage real-time architecture to adjust prices based on immediate supply and demand conditions, competitor pricing changes, and external factors like weather or events. The ability to respond immediately to changing market conditions provides a competitive advantage through optimized revenue capture while maintaining customer satisfaction through fair, market-responsive pricing.

Pattern 3: Hybrid batch-stream architecture

Hybrid batch-stream architecture eliminates the false choice between stability and responsiveness, creating sophisticated ML platforms that harness the complementary strengths of both processing paradigms to deliver comprehensive business solutions.

Architecture overview

Hybrid architecture combines the stability and cost efficiency of batch processing with the responsiveness of real-time systems, creating comprehensive ML platforms that can address diverse business requirements without forcing organizations to choose between competing approaches. This pattern enables organizations to optimize different aspects of their ML systems independently while maintaining integration and consistency across the entire platform. Hybrid architecture components are designed to leverage the optimal characteristics of both batch and streaming approaches, creating a sophisticated balance between stability and responsiveness:

Component	Implementation	Rationale	Trade-offs
Data processing	Batch for historical and stream for real-time	Leverages the strengths of both approaches	Increased architectural complexity
Feature engineering	Dual pipeline (batch and streaming)	Comprehensive feature coverage across time horizons	Feature consistency and synchronization challenges
Model training	Batch training and online updates	Stable foundation with adaptive responsiveness	Complex model versioning and validation
Inference	Multi-modal serving (batch and real-time)	Flexible response to different business needs	Operational complexity and cost management

Table 12.3: Dual processing: Stability meets real-time responsiveness

Implementation strategy

Hybrid implementations require sophisticated orchestration that coordinates batch and streaming components while maintaining data consistency and feature alignment across both processing modes. AWS Step Functions provide the orchestration backbone that manages dependencies between batch and streaming workflows, ensuring that real-time processing can access the most recent batch-processed features while maintaining consistency during batch update cycles.

The dual feature engineering pipeline represents the most complex aspect of hybrid architecture, requiring careful design to ensure that features computed in batch mode remain consistent with those computed in streaming mode. Feature Store integration becomes critical for maintaining this consistency, providing a unified interface that abstracts the underlying processing mode while ensuring that downstream consumers receive consistent feature values regardless of how they were computed.

Model training in hybrid systems typically follows a foundation-plus-adaptation approach where stable, batch-trained models provide the foundational intelligence while online learning mechanisms adapt to immediate patterns and changes. This approach requires sophisticated model versioning that can track both batch model updates and incremental online learning adjustments while maintaining the ability to rollback to previous stable states when adaptation produces unexpected results.

Business value and use cases

Customer churn prediction exemplifies hybrid architecture benefits by combining comprehensive historical analysis of customer behavior patterns with real-time responsiveness to immediate risk signals. The batch processing component analyzes years of customer data to identify subtle behavioral patterns and lifecycle stages that predict churn risk, while the real-time component responds immediately to signals like support case creation, billing failures, or usage pattern changes that indicate immediate churn risk. This combination enables both strategic retention planning and tactical intervention capabilities.

Personalization platforms leverage a hybrid architecture to provide comprehensive user understanding that spans from long-term preference modeling to immediate behavioral adaptation. Batch processing analyzes purchasing history, demographic patterns, and seasonal behaviors to build stable user preference profiles, while real-time processing adapts recommendations based on current browsing session, immediate search queries, and contextual signals. This comprehensive approach typically produces 30-50% better engagement metrics compared to systems using only batch or only real-time processing.

Financial trading systems demonstrate a hybrid architecture in high-stakes environments where both historical analysis and immediate responsiveness determine success. Batch processing analyzes market patterns, economic indicators, and historical price movements to identify strategic trading opportunities and risk factors, while real-time processing responds to immediate market movements, news events, and order flow patterns. The combination enables both strategic position management and tactical execution optimization, providing a competitive advantage in markets where millisecond response times can determine profitability.

Conclusion

Machine learning integration represents the culmination of modern data platform evolution, transforming information repositories into intelligent systems that drive automated decision-making and measurable business value. This chapter demonstrated how Amazon SageMaker and AWS ML services seamlessly extend existing data lake and warehouse architectures, enabling organizations to implement sophisticated ML capabilities while leveraging established data governance and operational frameworks. The architectural patterns explored provide proven blueprints for implementing ML platforms that balance technical sophistication with operational pragmatism, enabling organizations to transform their data platforms from passive analytical tools into active business intelligence systems that continuously adapt to changing conditions and drive competitive advantage through automated, data-driven decision-making.

The next chapter explores *DataOps and Automation*, focusing on operationalizing the sophisticated data and ML platforms we have built through systematic CI/CD pipelines for data workflows, infrastructure-as-code patterns, comprehensive monitoring and observability, cost management strategies, and disaster recovery approaches that ensure business continuity and operational excellence.

Join our Discord space

Join our Discord workspace for latest updates, offers, tech happenings around the world, new releases, and sessions with the authors:

https://discord.bpbonline.com

CHAPTER 13

DataOps and Automation

Introduction

The sophisticated data platforms explored in previous chapters, from data lakes and warehouses to streaming architectures and machine learning systems, deliver value only when they operate reliably, efficiently, and securely in production environments. DataOps represents the evolutionary convergence of DevOps practices with data engineering, creating a disciplined approach to building, deploying, and operating data platforms that balance innovation with stability. As organizations scale their data infrastructure across hundreds of pipelines, dozens of data stores, and multiple environments, manual processes become unsustainable, making automation not just beneficial but essential.

This chapter explores how to implement comprehensive DataOps practices on AWS, transforming brittle, manually-managed data systems into resilient, self-healing platforms that enable both operational excellence and rapid innovation. We will examine how to apply infrastructure as code principles to data workloads, implement CI/CD pipelines specifically designed for data workflows, establish observability frameworks that provide actionable insights, optimize costs through automation, and ensure business continuity through robust disaster recovery strategies.

The challenge extends beyond simply adopting individual automation tools; it requires creating integrated systems where infrastructure provisioning, pipeline deployment, monitoring, and remediation work together seamlessly. Organizations that successfully implement DataOps practices report 70-80% reductions in data pipeline incidents, 40-60% faster time-to-market for new data products, and significant improvements in data quality and trust. These outcomes directly impact business value, transforming data teams from reactive firefighters into proactive innovators who can focus on creating new capabilities rather than maintaining existing ones.

Structure

This chapter covers the following topics:

- CI/CD for data pipelines
- Infrastructure as code for data platforms
- Monitoring and observability
- Cost management automation

- Disaster recovery strategies
- DataOps implementation framework

Objectives

This chapter aims to provide a comprehensive understanding of implementing DataOps practices and automation for AWS data platforms. You will learn how to design and implement CI/CD pipelines specifically tailored for data workflows, leveraging AWS CodePipeline, CodeBuild, and related services to automate testing and deployment of data infrastructure and pipelines. The chapter explores infrastructure as code patterns using AWS CloudFormation and CDK, enabling consistent, version-controlled deployment of complex data platforms across multiple environments. Through practical implementation examples, you will understand how to establish comprehensive monitoring and observability frameworks that provide actionable insights into data platform health, quality, and performance. The chapter details cost management automation strategies that optimize resource utilization and implement intelligent scaling based on workload patterns. These capabilities will enable you to create self-healing, efficient data platforms that maintain reliability and performance while reducing operational overhead and enabling rapid innovation.

CI/CD for data pipelines

In the world of data engineering, reliable and efficient deployment of data pipelines is essential for maintaining business continuity and competitive advantage. **Continuous integration and continuous deployment (CI/CD)** practices that automate the testing and deployment of code changes have transformed software development by enabling faster, more reliable releases. When applied to data pipelines, these practices require specialized approaches to address the unique challenges of data workloads.

While traditional CI/CD focuses primarily on application functionality, data pipeline CI/CD must address additional complexities: processing massive datasets, managing intricate data dependencies, and ensuring data quality throughout the pipeline. A successful implementation must balance agility with the stability and governance requirements essential for enterprise data platforms.

CI/CD architecture for data pipelines

As illustrated in *Figure 13.1,* an effective CI/CD architecture for data pipelines on AWS spans three distinct environments: development, testing, and production, with specialized components in each environment that work together to ensure reliable, governed deployments:

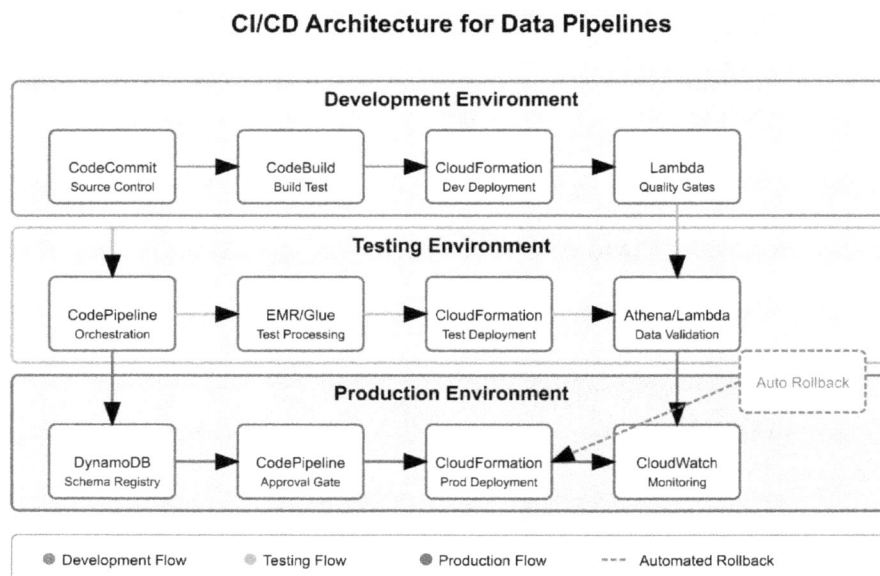

Figure 13.1: CI/CD architecture for data pipelines

Development environment

The development environment provides the foundation for pipeline creation and initial validation:

- **Source control (AWS CodeCommit)**: On the left side of the development environment, we see CodeCommit serving as the version control system for data pipeline code. Unlike application repositories, data pipeline repositories contain diverse artifacts, including pipeline definitions (AWS Glue scripts, Step Functions workflows), infrastructure templates, schema definitions, and test specifications. This centralized source control ensures that all pipeline components are versioned, tracked, and reviewable.

- **Build and test (AWS CodeBuild)**: Moving right in the diagram, CodeBuild automatically executes initial validation when changes are committed. For data pipelines, this includes unit testing transformation logic, linting infrastructure templates, and validating schema compatibility. These fast-running tests provide immediate feedback to developers before changes progress further.

- **Development deployment (AWS CloudFormation)**: The next component deploys the pipeline into an isolated development environment. CloudFormation provisions the necessary infrastructure: S3 buckets, Glue jobs, and Lambda functions, allowing developers to test with small datasets before advancing to more comprehensive testing.

- **Quality gates (AWS Lambda)**: On the right side of the development environment, Lambda functions implement automated quality checks that validate data transformations, schema compliance, and basic performance metrics. These gates ensure that only changes meeting baseline quality standards progress to the testing environment.

Testing environment

The middle section of *Figure 13.1* shows the testing environment, where more comprehensive validation occurs:

- **Orchestration (AWS CodePipeline)**: On the left, CodePipeline coordinates the entire workflow, ensuring that changes progress through environments only after passing appropriate validations. This orchestration maintains consistency and provides visibility into the deployment process.

- **Test processing (AWS EMR/Glue)**: For data pipelines, testing requires processing representative datasets to validate both functionality and performance. EMR clusters or Glue jobs execute pipeline code against larger datasets, capturing metrics about processing time, resource utilization, and data quality.

- **Test deployment (AWS CloudFormation)**: Like the development environment, CloudFormation deploys the pipeline infrastructure, but with configurations that more closely resemble production. This environment often includes connections to anonymized production data or production-scale test datasets.

- **Data validation (AWS Athena/Lambda)**: The right side shows comprehensive data validation using Athena for SQL-based analysis of processed data and Lambda for custom validation rules. This validation ensures that pipelines maintain data quality, schema compliance, and referential integrity before proceeding to production.

The arrows between development and testing environments illustrate how quality gates control progression between environments, ensuring that only validated changes advance to more critical environments.

Production environment

The last section of the *Figure 13.1* shows the production environment with additional controls:

- **Schema registry (Amazon DynamoDB)**: On the left, DynamoDB implements a schema registry that tracks and governs schema evolution, ensuring backward compatibility and preventing breaking changes. This registry becomes increasingly important as data platforms grow in complexity and support multiple consumers.

- **Approval gate (AWS CodePipeline)**: Before production deployment, human approval provides a final checkpoint for changes with potential business impact. For critical data pipelines, this approval might involve data stewards, business stakeholders, or compliance officers, depending on data sensitivity.

- **Production deployment (AWS CloudFormation)**: Once approved, CloudFormation deploys the pipeline to production using parameters optimized for production workloads. For critical pipelines, this often implements blue-green deployment patterns where new pipeline versions run in parallel with existing versions before traffic cutover.

- **Monitoring (Amazon CloudWatch)**: The right side shows CloudWatch, which provides comprehensive monitoring of deployed pipelines. Dashboards track processing time, data volumes, error rates, and quality metrics, while alarms detect anomalies that might indicate problems.

Automated rollback

The dashed arrow in *Figure 13.1* illustrates the automated rollback mechanism that activates when monitoring detects issues with a newly deployed pipeline. This self-healing capability immediately reverts to the previous stable version, maintaining business continuity while teams investigate the root cause. CloudWatch alarms trigger Lambda functions that execute the rollback, often completing the process before human intervention would be possible.

Specialized patterns for data pipelines

CI/CD architecture in *Figure 13.1* incorporates several specialized patterns designed specifically for data workloads:

- **Data quality gates**: The quality gates component in the development environment and the data validation component in the testing environment implement increasingly comprehensive quality checks as changes progress toward production:

  o **Development quality gates** perform basic validation with small datasets, checking transformation correctness, schema compliance, and simple quality rules. These fast-running checks provide immediate feedback to developers.

  o **Testing data validation** performs more extensive quality assessment with production-scale datasets, validating data relationships, aggregate metrics, and performance characteristics. This validation often includes comparative analysis between current and previous pipeline versions.

  o **Production monitoring** continuously evaluates data quality in production, detecting gradual degradation or sudden changes that might indicate pipeline issues. This monitoring connects directly to the automated rollback mechanism, enabling immediate response to quality problems.

- **Schema governance**: The schema registry shown in the production environment maintains the history and evolution rules for data structures:

  o **Compatibility validation** ensures that schema changes maintain backward compatibility, preventing breaking changes from disrupting downstream consumers. This validation happens early in the development environment and continues through all deployment stages.

  o **Version management** tracks the lineage of schema changes, enabling precise identification of when specific fields or structures were introduced or modified. This tracking supports both troubleshooting and compliance requirements.

  o **Access control** governs which teams can modify schemas for different data domains, implementing organizational data governance policies through technical controls. This governance becomes increasingly important as data platforms scale across multiple teams and domains.

- **Environment progression**: The arrows connecting components across environments illustrate the controlled progression of changes:

  o **Development to testing** transition occurs only after passing initial quality gates, ensuring that obvious issues are addressed before more comprehensive testing.

  o **Testing to production** progression requires successful data validation and explicit approval, preventing problematic changes from affecting business operations.

  o **Automated rollback** provides protection when issues escape pre-production validation, creating a safety net that maintains system stability.

Implementation considerations

When implementing the CI/CD architecture shown in *Figure 13.1*, several key considerations ensure successful adoption:

- **Security integration**: The architecture must integrate with enterprise security frameworks:

  o **IAM roles** implement least-privilege access for each component, ensuring that deployment automation can't bypass governance controls. Development environments use more restricted permissions than production pipelines.

  o **Secrets management** securely handles credentials for data sources and destinations, using AWS Secrets Manager to avoid embedding sensitive information in pipeline code.

  o **Audit trails** capture all changes, approvals, and deployments through CloudTrail and custom logging, supporting compliance requirements and security investigations.

- **Progressive implementation**: For organizations new to CI/CD for data pipelines, a phased implementation approach works best:

  o **Start with source control** by migrating existing pipeline definitions to CodeCommit, establishing versioning before adding automation.

  o **Implement basic testing** focused on pipeline functionality before adding more sophisticated data quality validation.

  o **Automate development deployment** to gain experience with deployment automation in lower-risk environments.

  o **Gradually add quality gates** with increasingly comprehensive validation as confidence in the process grows.

  o **Extend to production** only after establishing reliability in pre-production environments.

  This progressive approach builds confidence while delivering incremental benefits throughout the implementation process.

By implementing the comprehensive CI/CD architecture illustrated in *Figure 13.1*, organizations can transform brittle, manually deployed data pipelines into reliable, self-healing systems that continuously evolve to meet changing business requirements while maintaining the stability and governance controls essential for enterprise data platforms.

Infrastructure as code for data platforms

In today's data-driven enterprise, data platforms have evolved from simple databases into complex ecosystems comprising dozens of specialized services: storage layers, compute engines, **extract transform load** (ETL) tools, orchestration systems, and monitoring components. Traditionally, teams would configure these services manually through console interfaces, a process that was time-consuming, error-prone, and difficult to replicate consistently across environments. **Infrastructure as code (IaC)** transforms this approach by defining infrastructure through machine-readable definition files, enabling automated provisioning that ensures consistency while providing the governance essential for enterprise data platforms.

Advantages of infrastructure as code

For data engineering teams, IaC offers several transformative benefits that directly address the unique challenges of building and maintaining data platforms:

- **Consistency across environments**: Data pipelines must perform identically across development, testing, and production environments to prevent the *work in development but fail in production* syndrome. IaC ensures that all environments share identical configurations except for deliberately different parameters like resource sizing or connection strings. This consistency significantly reduces environment-specific bugs that plague manually configured systems.

  A financial services organization implementing IaC for their data platform reported a 65% reduction in environment-related failures after moving from manual configuration to infrastructure code. Their data quality team noted that test results became dramatically more reliable predictors of production behaviour, enabling faster release cycles with greater confidence.

- **Version control and history**: Data platforms evolve continuously as business requirements change and new technologies emerge. IaC enables teams to maintain a complete history of infrastructure changes through the same version control systems used for application code. This history provides crucial context when troubleshooting issues and supports compliance requirements by documenting exactly when and why configuration changes occurred.

  This versioning capability becomes particularly valuable when diagnosing data quality issues. When analysts identify data anomalies, engineers can correlate them with infrastructure changes by examining the version history, dramatically reducing investigation time compared to manually configured systems, where changes often go undocumented.

- **Automated testing and validation**: Data infrastructure contains complex interdependencies where seemingly small changes can have significant downstream impacts. IaC enables automated validation of infrastructure changes before deployment, catching potential issues early in the development cycle. These validations range from simple syntax checking to sophisticated tests that verify security configurations, network access patterns, and compliance requirements.

  A healthcare analytics team implemented automated validation for their data platform infrastructure, including **Health Insurance Portability and Accountability Act (HIPAA)** compliance checks that verified appropriate encryption, access controls, and audit logging. This automation caught several potential compliance issues during development that would have created significant regulatory risk if deployed to production.

- **Self-documenting infrastructure**: Well-written infrastructure code serves as living documentation that clearly articulates how the data platform is constructed and configured. Unlike traditional documentation that quickly becomes outdated, infrastructure code always reflects the actual state of the system. This self-documenting nature improves knowledge sharing across teams and reduces onboarding time for new team members.

- **Disaster recovery and business continuity**: When infrastructure exists as code, recovering from catastrophic failures becomes dramatically simpler. Rather than manually reconstructing complex configurations from backup documentation (which is often incomplete or outdated), teams can simply redeploy their infrastructure code to rebuild the entire platform consistently and completely.

AWS implementation approaches

AWS offers several complementary approaches for implementing IaC for data platforms, each with distinct advantages for different scenarios:

- **AWS CloudFormation (declarative templates)**: CloudFormation provides a declarative approach where you specify the desired end state of your infrastructure using JSON or YAML templates. AWS then determines and executes the steps required to achieve that state. This template-based approach works well for standardized infrastructure patterns:

```
1.  Resources:
2.    # S3 Data Lake Storage
3.    DataLakeBucket:
4.      Type: AWS::S3::Bucket
5.      Properties:
6.        BucketName: !Sub 'data-lake-${AWS::AccountId}-${Environment}'
7.        VersioningConfiguration:
8.          Status: Enabled
9.        LifecycleConfiguration:
10.         Rules:
11.           - Status: Enabled
12.             Transitions:
13.               - StorageClass: INTELLIGENT_TIERING
14.                 TransitionInDays: 90
15.
16.    # Glue Catalog Database
17.    DataCatalog:
18.      Type: AWS::Glue::Database
19.      Properties:
20.        CatalogId: !Ref AWS::AccountId
21.        DatabaseInput:
22.          Name: !Sub 'data_catalog_${Environment}'
23.          Description: 'Data catalog for analytics datasets'
```

CloudFormation's key strengths include:

- o **Native integration** with all AWS services, ensuring complete coverage of data platform components from storage to processing to analytics.

- o **Drift detection** capability that identifies unauthorized changes made outside the IaC process, helping maintain governance and prevent shadow IT configurations.

- o **Change sets** that preview modifications before deployment, enabling teams to understand the impact of infrastructure changes before applying them.

CloudFormation works particularly well for organizations that prefer a declarative approach and need to maintain strict governance over infrastructure changes. The template-based approach enforces consistency and makes it straightforward to implement organizational standards.

- **AWS CDK (programmatic infrastructure)**: The AWS **Cloud Development Kit (CDK)** enables teams to define infrastructure using familiar programming languages like Python and TypeScript rather than markup languages. This programmatic approach offers additional flexibility and abstraction capabilities:

```python
1. from aws_cdk import (
2.     aws_s3 as s3,
3.     aws_glue as glue,
4.     Stack
5. )
6.
7. class DataLakeStack(Stack):
8.     def __init__(self, scope, id, environment, **kwargs):
9.         super().__init__(scope, id, **kwargs)
10.
11.         # Create data lake bucket with optimized configuration
12.         data_lake = s3.Bucket(
13.             self, "DataLakeBucket",
14.             bucket_name=f"data-lake-{self.account}-{environment}",
15.             versioned=True,
16.             lifecycle_rules=[
17.                 s3.LifecycleRule(
18.                     transitions=[
19.                         s3.Transition(
20.                             storage_class=s3.StorageClass.INTELLIGENT_TIERING,
21.                             transition_after=Duration.days(90)
22.                         )
23.                     ]
24.                 )
25.             ]
26.         )
27.
28.         # Create Glue catalog database
29.         glue_db = glue.CfnDatabase(
30.             self, "GlueDatabase",
31.             catalog_id=self.account,
32.             database_input=glue.CfnDatabase.DatabaseInputProperty(
33.                 name=f"data_catalog_{environment}",
34.                 description="Data catalog for analytics datasets"
35.             )
36.         )
```

CDK's advantages include:

- o **Abstraction capabilities** that enable creation of reusable infrastructure components that encapsulate best practices and organizational standards.

- o **Programming constructs** like loops, conditionals, and functions that simplify the creation of complex or repetitive infrastructure patterns.

- o **Type safety** that catches errors during development rather than deployment, improving reliability and reducing failed deployments.

CDK proves particularly valuable for data engineering teams already proficient in Python or TypeScript, as it allows them to leverage existing programming skills for infrastructure definition. The ability to create reusable constructs also benefits large organizations looking to standardize infrastructure patterns across multiple teams.

- **AWS SAM (serverless specialization)**: For data platforms leveraging serverless components like Lambda functions, Step Functions, and API Gateway, AWS **Serverless Application Model (SAM)** provides specialized capabilities focused on serverless architecture:

```
1.  Resources:
2.    # Lambda function for data transformation
3.    TransformFunction:
4.      Type: AWS::Serverless::Function
5.      Properties:
6.        CodeUri: ./transform/
7.        Handler: app.lambda_handler
8.        Runtime: python3.9
9.        MemorySize: 1024
10.       Timeout: 300
11.       Environment:
12.         Variables:
13.           SOURCE_BUCKET: !Ref SourceBucket
14.           TARGET_BUCKET: !Ref TargetBucket
15.       Policies:
16.         - S3ReadPolicy:
17.             BucketName: !Ref SourceBucket
18.         - S3WritePolicy:
19.             BucketName: !Ref TargetBucket
```

SAM's benefits include:

o **Simplified syntax** is specifically designed for serverless applications, reducing boilerplate compared to raw CloudFormation.

o **Local testing** capabilities that enable developers to validate serverless functions before deployment.

o **Integrated deployment pipeline** that streamlines the process of packaging and deploying serverless applications.

SAM works best for data platforms heavily leveraging serverless components, particularly those building real-time data processing pipelines or API-driven data services.

- **Choosing the right approach**: The optimal IaC approach depends on your team's skills and your data platform's requirements:

o **CloudFormation** is ideal when you need maximum governance, prefer declarative configuration, and want native AWS integration without additional abstractions. It works well for teams new to IaC or those with strict change control requirements.

o **CDK** excels when your team has programming experience, you need to create reusable infrastructure patterns, or you're building complex data platforms with many interdependent components. Data engineering teams often find CDK's approach natural as it aligns with their existing coding practices.

o **SAM** fits best when your data platform leverages serverless architecture extensively, particularly for real-time data processing or event-driven pipelines.

Many organizations adopt a hybrid approach, using CloudFormation for stable foundation components like networking and security, while leveraging CDK for data-specific infrastructure that changes more frequently and benefits from programmatic definition.

Implementation best practices

Regardless of the approach chosen, several best practices ensure successful IaC implementation for data platforms:

- **Modular organization** divides infrastructure into logical components (storage, processing, security, etc.) that can evolve independently, improving maintainability and enabling parallel development.

- **Environment parameterization** uses variables to define environment-specific settings rather than hardcoding values, ensuring consistency while accommodating necessary differences between development, testing, and production.

- **Pipeline integration** connects infrastructure deployment with the same CI/CD pipelines used for data processing code, ensuring synchronized deployment of interdependent components.

- **Automated testing** validates infrastructure changes before deployment, verifying security configurations, access patterns, and compliance requirements to prevent issues in production.

By adopting IaC practices, data engineering teams transform infrastructure from a bottleneck into an enabler, delivering more reliable data platforms with greater agility while maintaining the governance and security essential for enterprise data environments.

Monitoring and observability

In data platforms, where processing might span hours and involve terabytes of information, traditional application monitoring approaches fall short. Data workloads require specialized observability frameworks that provide visibility into data quality, pipeline performance, and resource utilization across distributed systems. Effective monitoring transforms reactive firefighting into proactive management, enabling teams to detect and address issues before they impact business operations or decision-making.

Observability imperative

Traditional monitoring focuses on known failure modes, checking predefined metrics against thresholds. For data platforms, this approach proves insufficient due to the complex, distributed nature of data processing and the unpredictable ways data quality issues can manifest. Observability extends monitoring by creating systems that enable investigation of unknown failure modes, providing context that helps engineers understand not just that something went wrong, but why it went wrong.

Three pillars of data platform observability

Comprehensive observability for data platforms rests on three foundational elements:

- **Metrics** provide quantitative measurements of system behavior: processing time, record counts, error rates, and resource utilization. These time-series data points enable trend analysis, anomaly detection, and alerting on known conditions.

- **Logs** capture detailed information about specific events and transactions, providing context essential for troubleshooting. For data platforms, logs must capture not just system events but also data-specific information like schema violations, transformation errors, and integration failures.

- **Traces** track requests as they flow through distributed systems, showing the complete journey of data from ingestion through processing to consumption. These traces help identify bottlenecks, understand dependencies, and diagnose latency issues across complex data architectures.

Data-Specific observability requirements

Data platforms require specialized observability beyond traditional application monitoring:

- **Data quality metrics** measure completeness, accuracy, consistency, and timeliness of data, providing early warning of potential issues. Quality degradation often precedes outright failures and can significantly impact business decisions even when systems appear operational.

- **Lineage tracking** records the origin and transformation history of data, enabling impact analysis when issues occur. When data quality problems emerge, lineage information helps identify affected downstream systems and trace issues back to their source.

- **Processing metadata** captures information about execution context: partition sizes, processing rates, transformation counts, which helps identify performance bottlenecks and scaling limitations.

AWS implementation approaches

AWS provides several complementary services for implementing comprehensive observability for data platforms, each addressing different aspects of the monitoring challenge:

- **CloudWatch provides foundational monitoring**: Amazon CloudWatch provides the core monitoring infrastructure for AWS-based data platforms, collecting and visualizing metrics, logs, and alarms:

```
1.  # Collect processing metrics
2.  processing_metrics = cloudwatch.get_metric_data(
3.      MetricDataQueries=[
4.          {
5.              'Id': 'processing_time',
6.              'MetricStat': {
7.                  'Metric': {
8.                      'Namespace': 'DataPipelines',
9.                      'MetricName': 'ProcessingTime',
10.                     'Dimensions': [
11.                         {'Name': 'PipelineId', 'Value': pipeline_id}
12.                     ]
13.                 },
14.                 'Period': 60,
15.                 'Stat': 'Sum'
16.             }
17.         }
18.     ],
19.     StartTime=start_time,
20.     EndTime=end_time
21. )
```

CloudWatch offers several features particularly valuable for data platforms:

- o **Composite alarms** combine multiple metrics to detect complex conditions like *processing time increasing while record count decreasing*, which might indicate data quality issues or processing inefficiencies.

- o **Metric math** enables derived metrics like *records processed per second* or *error rate as percentage of total records*, providing more meaningful indicators than raw measurements.

- o **Dashboard integration** with AWS services like Glue, EMR, and Redshift provides unified visibility across the entire data platform from a single interface.

- **CloudWatch Logs Insights (Advanced Log Analysis)**: CloudWatch Logs Insights enables SQL-like queries against log data, helping engineers identify patterns and anomalies across distributed systems:

```
1.  # Find pipeline executions with high error rates
2.  filter @logStream like /data-pipeline/
3.  | parse @message «Pipeline * completed with status * Records: *, Errors:
    *» as pipeline, status, records, errors
4.  | calculate (errors * 100) / records as error_rate
5.  | filter error_rate > 5
6.  | sort by error_rate desc
```

This query demonstrates the analytical capabilities essential for data platform troubleshooting:

o **Structured extraction** parses semi-structured log data into queryable fields, enabling sophisticated analysis without preprocessing.

o **Calculated fields** derive meaningful metrics like error rates from raw log data, helping identify problematic pipeline executions.

For data platforms processing billions of records across hundreds of pipelines, these analytical capabilities transform overwhelming log volumes into actionable insights.

- **AWS X-ray (Distributed tracing)**: X-ray provides distributed tracing that tracks requests as they flow through microservices and serverless functions, essential for understanding complex data processing flows:

```
1.  @xray_recorder.capture('data_transformation')
2.  def lambda_handler(event, context):
3.      """Process data transformation with tracing"""
4.
5.      # Create subsegment for input validation
6.      subsegment = xray_recorder.begin_subsegment('input_validation')
7.      try:
8.          # Validation logic here
9.          subsegment.put_annotation('source_bucket', event['source_bucket'])
10.     finally:
11.         xray_recorder.end_subsegment()
12.
13.     # Additional processing segments...
```

X-ray provides several capabilities essential for data platform observability:

o **End-to-end tracing** connects distributed components, showing how data flows through complex processing pipelines spanning multiple services.

o **Performance analysis** identifies bottlenecks by measuring time spent in each processing step, helping engineers focus optimization efforts where they'll have greatest impact.

o **Error context** captures detailed information about failures, including which processing stage failed and what conditions preceded the failure.

- **AWS CloudTrail (Governance and security monitoring)**: CloudTrail records API calls across AWS services, providing an audit trail essential for security monitoring and compliance:

```
1.  # Look up data access events
2.  response = cloudtrail.lookup_events(
3.      LookupAttributes=[
```

```
4.          {
5.              'AttributeKey': 'EventName',
6.              'AttributeValue': 'GetObject'
7.          }
8.      ],
9.      StartTime=start_time,
10.     EndTime=end_time
11. )
```

For enterprises with strict governance requirements, CloudTrail provides the detailed audit capabilities essential for demonstrating regulatory compliance and maintaining data security.

By implementing comprehensive observability across metrics, logs, and traces, data engineering teams transform reactive firefighting into proactive management, addressing issues before they impact business operations or decision-making. This visibility enables faster troubleshooting, better capacity planning, and continuous optimization of data platform performance.

Cost management automation

In the world of modern data platforms, where workloads can span petabytes of storage and thousands of compute hours, cloud costs can quickly escalate without proper management. While the cloud offers tremendous flexibility and scalability, this very elasticity creates the risk of unexpected expenses if left unmanaged. Effective cost management for data platforms requires automated approaches that continuously optimize resource utilization, implement appropriate scaling strategies, and enforce financial governance while maintaining performance and reliability.

Traditional cost management often relies on periodic reviews and manual adjustments, an approach that proves insufficient for the dynamic nature of data workloads. Data processing requirements can fluctuate dramatically based on business cycles, data growth, and changing analytical needs. Automated cost management transforms reactive expense control into proactive financial optimization, ensuring that data platforms deliver maximum business value at minimum cost.

Three dimensions of data platform cost optimization

Effective cost optimization requires a multi-dimensional approach that addresses the three primary cost drivers for data platforms. Each dimension offers distinct strategies that together create comprehensive cost management while maintaining performance and reliability. Refer to the following table:

Dimension	Key strategies	Implementation analysis
Storage optimization	• **Intelligent-Tiering**: Automatically moves data between storage classes based on access patterns • **Compression and format Optimization**: Converts data to columnar formats like Parquet, reducing storage by 40-60% • **Duplication management**: Identifies and eliminates redundant data across storage systems	• **Implementation complexity**: Medium; requires access pattern analysis and data classification • **Cost impact**: High; typically 30-60% reduction in storage costs • **Performance trade-offs**: Minimal; properly implemented tiering maintains performance for active data • **Use case fit**: Ideal for data lakes with varied access patterns and long retention requirements

Dimension	Key strategies	Implementation analysis
Compute optimization	• **Right-sizing**: Aligns resource allocation with actual requirements based on workload characteristics • **Spot instance utilization**: Leverages discounted pricing for interruptible workloads • •**Serverless adoption**: Eliminates idle capacity costs for intermittent workloads	• **Implementation complexity**: High; requires workload analysis and potential code changes • **Cost impact**: High; typically 40-70% reduction in compute costs • **Performance trade-offs**: Potential for increased latency or job failures if implemented improperly • **Use case fit**: Spot instances work best for batch processing; serverless for event-driven pipelines
Usage optimization	• **Idle resource detection**: Identifies and terminates unused or underutilized resources • **Usage-based chargeback**: Creates accountability by allocating costs to consuming business units • **Query optimization**: Reduces processing costs by improving analytical workload efficiency	• **Implementation complexity**: Medium; requires tagging strategy and usage monitoring • **Cost impact**: Medium; typically 15-30% reduction in overall costs • **Performance trade-offs**: None when implemented correctly • **Use case fit**: Essential for multi-team platforms with diverse workloads

Table 13.1: Optimizing costs across platform dimensions

AWS implementation approaches

AWS provides a comprehensive suite of services for implementing cost management automation. These services work together to create a multi-layered approach to cost optimization that addresses visibility, control, and automated management of data platform resources. Refer to the following table:

AWS service	Key capabilities	Practical considerations
AWS Cost Explorer and Budgets	• Provides visibility into cloud spending patterns • Enables proactive cost control through budgets and alerts • Supports detailed analysis by service, account, and tags	• **Required setup**: Consistent tagging strategy across all resources • **Integration**: Connect to SNS for notifications and Lambda for automated responses • **Limitations**: 24-hour delay in cost data availability • **Best practice**: Combine with CloudWatch metrics for near real-time monitoring
AWS Cost Anomaly Detection	• Automatically identifies unusual spending patterns • Detects potential misconfigurations or inefficient usage • Provides immediate alerts when anomalies are detected	• **Required setup**: Historical baseline data (minimum 10 days) • **Integration**: SNS topics for alerts, Lambda for remediation • **Limitations**: May miss gradual cost increases • **Best practice**: Combine with custom monitoring for service-specific metrics

AWS service	Key capabilities	Practical considerations
S3 Intelligent-Tiering and Lifecycle Management	• Automates storage class transitions based on access patterns • Implements zone-specific storage policies • Applies appropriate retention and expiration rules	• **Required setup**: Clear data organization strategy with defined prefixes • **Integration**: Works with S3 Event Notifications for tracking • **Limitations**: Small objects (<128KB) can incur more overhead than savings • **Best practice**: Combine with S3 Analytics to identify optimization opportunities
AWS Compute Optimizer	• Analyzes resource utilization patterns • Provides automated right-sizing recommendations • Quantifies potential savings for each recommendation	• **Required setup**: CloudWatch detailed monitoring for accurate data • **Integration**: Works with Systems Manager for implementation • **Limitations**: Requires at least 14 days of utilization data • **Best practice**: Verify recommendations in the test environment before production

Table 13.2: AWS services for cost management

Data platform-specific optimization strategies

Data platforms have unique characteristics that require specialized optimization approaches beyond general cloud cost management. These strategies address the specific cost drivers and usage patterns common to data processing workloads. Refer to the following table:

Platform component	Optimization strategy	Implementation method	Cost-benefit analysis
Data Lake Storage	• Implement zone-based lifecycle policies • Optimize file formats and partitioning • Implement data archiving workflows	• Use S3 lifecycle policies with different rules for raw, processed, and curated zones • Convert text formats to Parquet or ORC with appropriate compression • Create automated archiving workflows with Glue and Step Functions	• **Potential savings**: 40-70% reduction in storage costs • **Implementation cost**: Low to medium; primarily configuration changes • **ROI timeline**: Immediate for format conversion; 3-6 months for lifecycle policies • **Risk level**: Low; minimal impact on data accessibility
ETL processing	• Right-size Glue/EMR resources • Implement job-specific scaling strategies • Use spot instances for batch workloads	• Configure appropriate DPU/executor settings based on data volume • Set different autoscaling for different job types • Use instance fleets with spot instances for non-critical jobs	• **Potential savings**: 50-80% reduction in processing costs • **Implementation cost**: Medium; requires workload analysis and testing • **ROI timeline**: one to three months, depending on processing volume • **Risk level**: Medium; may impact job reliability if misconfigured

Platform component	Optimization strategy	Implementation method	Cost-benefit analysis
Data warehousing	• Implement automated scaling • Use concurrency scaling selectively • Optimize query patterns with materialized views	• Schedule scaling based on usage patterns • Apply concurrency scaling only to critical workloads • Create materialized views for common query patterns	• **Potential savings**: 30-60% reduction in warehouse costs • **Implementation cost**: Medium to high; requires query analysis • **ROI timeline**: Two to four months to realize full benefits • **Risk level**: Medium; query performance may be affected
Real-time processing	• Implement buffering for variable workloads • Use provisioned capacity efficiently • Scale services based on throughput needs	• Use Kinesis with appropriate shard counts • Optimize batch sizes and processing intervals • Implement dynamic scaling based on stream metrics	• **Potential savings**: 20-40% reduction in streaming costs • **Implementation cost**: High; requires sophisticated monitoring • **ROI timeline**: Three to six months due to implementation complexity • **Risk level**: High; may impact data processing latency

Table 13.3: Data platform cost optimization analysis

By implementing comprehensive cost management automation across storage, compute, and usage dimensions, data engineering teams transform cloud spending from an unpredictable expense to a controllable, optimized investment. This financial discipline enables organizations to scale their data platforms to meet growing business needs while maintaining predictable costs aligned with actual value delivery.

Disaster recovery strategies

In data platforms, where critical business information flows through interconnected systems, disruptions can have far-reaching consequences beyond simple downtime. A comprehensive disaster recovery strategy transforms reactive crisis management into a structured approach for maintaining business continuity in the face of system failures, data corruption, or catastrophic events. Effective disaster recovery planning balances protection against potential risks with the practical realities of implementation cost and recovery time objectives.

Traditional backup approaches often prove insufficient for modern data platforms due to their scale, complexity, and the business-critical nature of the data they manage. Contemporary disaster recovery strategies must address not just data preservation but also the rapid restoration of processing capabilities, maintaining data consistency across interconnected systems, and ensuring appropriate prioritization of recovery efforts based on business impact.

Core principles of data platform disaster recovery

Effective disaster recovery strategies for data platforms rest on four foundational principles that guide implementation decisions:

Principle	Description	Implementation considerations	Business impact
Recovery time objective (RTO)	Maximum acceptable time between service disruption and restoration	• Varies by system component and business criticality • Typically ranges from minutes for critical pipelines to hours for analytical systems • Directly impacts required infrastructure investment	• Shorter RTOs require more sophisticated (and expensive) recovery mechanisms • Business stakeholders must balance cost against acceptable downtime • Critical data pipelines often require RTOs measured in minutes
Recovery point objective (RPO)	Maximum acceptable data loss measured in time	• Determines frequency of backups or replication • Ranges from near-zero (continuous replication) to hours/days • Must consider data value depreciation over time	• Near-zero RPO requires continuous replication techniques • Data value varies dramatically by type and recency • Legal and compliance requirements often dictate minimum RPOs
Recovery consistency objective (RCO)	Degree of consistency required across interdependent systems	• Addresses dependencies between data stores • Requires understanding of business process boundaries • Prevents partial recoveries that create logical inconsistencies	• Critical for maintaining data integrity across pipeline stages • Often overlooked in traditional DR planning • Prevents scenarios where partial recovery creates worse problems
Recovery priority objective (RPO)	The order in which systems and data should be restored	• Aligns recovery sequence with business impact • Prioritizes restoration of critical upstream dependencies • Creates a clear decision framework during recovery operations	• Ensures limited resources focus on the highest-value systems first • Prevents wasted effort on non-critical components • Provides clear guidance during high-pressure recovery scenarios

Table 13.4: Disaster recovery core principles

AWS disaster recovery patterns

AWS provides multiple implementation patterns for disaster recovery, each offering different trade-offs between recovery speed, cost, and implementation complexity. The appropriate pattern depends on your specific recovery objectives. Refer to the following table:

Pattern	Description	Implementation approach	Analysis
Backup and restore	Periodic backups with manual or automated restoration when needed	• AWS Backup for centralized management • S3 cross-region replication for data lake content • RDS automated snapshots for databases • CloudFormation for infrastructure rebuilding	• **RTO**: Hours to days • **RPO**: Hours (depends on backup frequency) • **Cost**: Low (primarily storage) • **Best for**: Non-critical components, development environments, or static reference data
Pilot light	Core infrastructure is maintained in a standby region with minimal resources	• Replicated data with minimal compute resources • Automated database replication • Infrastructure is defined as code for rapid scaling • Regular testing of scale-up procedures	• **RTO**: Tens of minutes to hours • **RPO**: Minutes (with continuous replication) • **Cost**: Low to medium • **Best for**: Batch processing systems, data warehouses, and analytics platforms
Warm standby	Scaled-down but functional copy maintained in the standby region	• Fully functional secondary environment • Continuous data replication • Reduced capacity in a standby environment • Automated failover mechanisms	• **RTO**: Minutes to tens of minutes • **RPO**: Near-zero to minutes • **Cost**: Medium to high • **Best for**: Interactive systems, operational data stores, and real-time pipelines
Multi-region active	Workloads are distributed across multiple regions with active operations	• Application designed for multi-region operation • Distributed data storage with cross-region synchronization • Global routing layer for traffic management • Independent regional capability for continued operation	• **RTO**: Near-zero (continuous operation) • **RPO**: Near-zero • **Cost**: High • **Best for**: Mission-critical systems, customer-facing applications, and revenue-generating pipelines

Table 13.5: AWS disaster recovery patterns

AWS resilience building blocks

To implement these disaster recovery patterns effectively, you need to understand the fundamental resilience building blocks available in AWS. These building blocks provide the foundation for constructing robust disaster recovery solutions. Refer to the following table:

Resilience level	Description	Key AWS features	Architectural considerations
Availability zone resilience	Independent data centers within a region with isolated power, cooling, and networking	• Multi-AZ deployments for managed services • Subnets across multiple AZs • Auto Scaling groups spanning AZs	• Entry point for resilience strategy • Protects against data center failures • Requires minimal application changes • Typically adds 10-15% to infrastructure costs
Regional resilience	Complete redundancy across geographically distant AWS regions	• Cross-region replication • Global services (Route 53, CloudFront) • Regional resource independence	• Protects against regional outages and disasters • Significantly more complex than multi-AZ • Requires data synchronization strategy • Typically adds 60-100% to infrastructure costs
Global resilience	Distributed architecture operating seamlessly across multiple global regions	• Global tables (DynamoDB) • Multi-region Active-Active • Global Accelerator • CloudFront distribution	• Highest level of resilience • Complex data consistency challenges • Requires application-level support • Typically adds 100%+ to infrastructure costs

Table 13.6: AWS resilience building blocks

Disaster recovery for data platform components

Different components of a data platform require tailored disaster recovery approaches based on their specific characteristics, recovery requirements, and architectural patterns. Refer to the following table:

Platform component	AWS service	Recovery strategy	Implementation of best practices
Data Lake Storage	Amazon S3	• Cross-region replication • Version control • Lifecycle management	• Use same-region replication for availability zone protection • Implement cross-region replication for critical data paths • Apply appropriate replication scope to control costs
Metadata Catalog	AWS Glue	• Database backup/replication • Cross-region catalog export • Infrastructure as code	• Backup Glue Data Catalog to S3 in a secondary region • Implement automated import procedures for recovery • Use CloudFormation for catalog resource definitions • Test catalog restoration quarterly

Platform component	AWS service	Recovery strategy	Implementation of best practices
Data warehouse	Amazon Redshift	• Automated snapshots • Cross-region copy • Rapid provisioning	• Configure automated snapshots with cross-region copy • Implement multi-AZ deployment for zone resilience • Use CloudFormation for infrastructure definition • Maintain schema definitions in version control
Processing engines	AWS Glue/ EMR	• Job definition replication • State management • IaC	• Store job definitions in version-controlled repositories • Implement job bookmarks for resumable processing • Use CloudFormation for infrastructure definitions • Configure appropriate retry mechanisms
Streaming infrastructure	Amazon Kinesis/ MSK	• Multi-AZ deployment • Enhanced fan-out • Replication to secondary region	• Deploy across multiple AZs by default • Implement proper partition strategy for parallel processing • Configure automated retention policies • Use enhanced fan-out for critical consumers
Orchestration	Step Functions/ EventBridge	• Cross-region workflow definitions • State persistence • Event routing	• Maintain workflow definitions in both regions • Implement idempotent actions for safe retry or replay • Configure appropriate error handling and timeouts • Test cross-region event routing regularly

Table 13.7: Component-specific recovery strategies

Testing and validation

Even the most sophisticated disaster recovery strategy is worthless if it fails when needed. AWS provides several specialized services for testing and validating DR capabilities, enabling automated verification without disrupting production systems. AWS **Fault Injection Simulator** (**FIS**) allows controlled chaos engineering through simulated infrastructure failures, while CloudWatch Synthetics continuously validates endpoint availability and functionality across regions. Route 53 **Application Recovery Controller** (**ARC**) provides readiness checks and routing controls for traffic management during recovery scenarios. Systems Manager Automation enables orchestrated testing of recovery procedures with detailed reporting of results. Organizations should implement regular testing at increasing levels of complexity, from component validation to availability zone failure simulation to complete regional failover exercises, with each test measuring actual recovery times against.

DataOps implementation framework

DataOps represents the convergence of agile development, DevOps principles, and data engineering, creating a methodology that emphasizes collaboration, automation, and continuous delivery of high-quality data products. While previous sections have explored individual automation techniques for specific platform components, a comprehensive DataOps implementation requires an integrated framework that brings these elements together into a cohesive operational model. This section outlines a practical DataOps implementation framework that organizations can adopt to transform their data engineering practices from siloed, manual processes to collaborative, automated workflows.

The successful implementation of DataOps requires more than just adopting tools: it demands cultural shifts, process changes, and new organizational structures. Organizations that effectively implement DataOps typically see 70-80% reductions in data defects, 30-50% faster time-to-market for new data products, and significantly improved cross-team collaboration. These benefits directly translate to increased business agility, higher data quality, and more efficient utilization of data engineering resources.

Core DataOps principles

Effective DataOps implementations rest on five foundational principles that guide technology choices, process designs, and organizational structures:

- **Automation first** prioritizes the automation of repetitive tasks, testing, and deployments throughout the data lifecycle. Rather than relying on manual processes that introduce human error and inconsistency, DataOps embraces infrastructure as code, CI/CD pipelines, and automated testing. This principle enables teams to move quickly, maintain consistency, and focus human effort on high-value creative work rather than repetitive operational tasks.

- **Continuous quality** builds data validation into every step of the data lifecycle, rather than treating it as a final checkpoint. By implementing automated quality checks that execute continuously, organizations detect issues early when they are less expensive and disruptive to fix. This principle creates a foundation of trust in data products while reducing downstream impacts from quality problems.

- **Collaboration culture** breaks down traditional silos between data teams, analytics professionals, and business users. By fostering cross-functional teamwork through shared tools, repositories, and transparent processes, DataOps accelerates knowledge sharing and innovation. This collaborative approach ensures technical implementations align with business needs while reducing handoff delays between specialized teams.

- **Observability by design** integrates comprehensive monitoring into data platforms from the beginning rather than adding it as an afterthought. By implementing end-to-end lineage tracking, granular performance metrics, and data quality dashboards, teams gain immediate visibility into their data operations. This principle enables rapid troubleshooting, builds confidence in data, and supports both capacity planning and compliance requirements.

- **Continuous iteration** embraces small, incremental improvements over high-risk **big bang** implementations. By adopting short release cycles, feedback-driven development, and ongoing optimization, DataOps teams deliver value faster while reducing implementation risk. This principle allows organizations to adapt quickly to changing requirements while continuously enhancing data capabilities. The following figure shows the key practices and principles of DataOps, which have revolutionized data engineering practices:

Core DataOps Principles

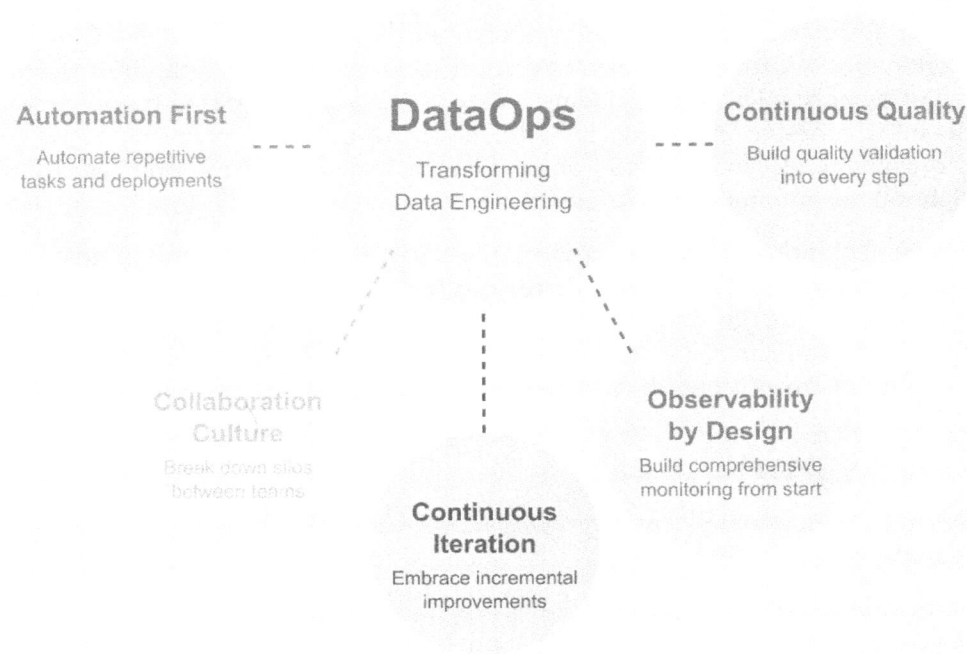

Figure 13.2: DataOps principles driving data engineering excellence

DataOps maturity model

Implementing DataOps is a journey rather than a destination. Organizations typically progress through several maturity levels as they adopt and refine DataOps practices:

Maturity level	Characteristics	Implementation focus	Transition strategies
Level 1: Manual	• Ad-hoc processes • Siloed teams • Manual deployments • Limited monitoring	• Documentation of current processes • Identifying automation opportunities • Building team awareness • Initial monitoring implementation	• Start with simple automation wins • Document tribal knowledge • Implement basic monitoring • Build cross-team relationships
Level 2: Partially automated	• Some automation • Basic CI/CD • Team-level collaboration • Reactive monitoring	• Expanding CI/CD coverage • Implementing testing • Standardizing environments • Enhancing monitoring capabilities	• Focus on repeatable processes • Implement version control for all code • Create self-service capabilities • Build monitoring dashboards

Maturity level	Characteristics	Implementation focus	Transition strategies
Level 3: Mostly automated	• Comprehensive CI/CD • Automated testing • Cross-team collaboration • Proactive monitoring	• Optimizing CI/CD pipelines • Expanding test coverage • Implementing self-service • Enhancing observability	• Standardize CI/CD across teams • Implement data quality frameworks • Create collaborative platforms • Build comprehensive observability
Level 4: Fully optimized	• Full automation • Comprehensive testing • Collaborative culture • Predictive monitoring	• Continuous optimization • Advanced testing strategies • Organizational alignment • AI-driven monitoring	• Implement feedback-driven improvement • Optimize for specific business outcomes • Measure and improve team productivity • Adopt predictive quality measures

Table 13.8: DataOps maturity progression framework

Organizations should assess their current maturity level and create a roadmap for advancing to higher levels. The most successful implementations focus on incremental progress rather than attempting to jump directly to *Level 4*, with each step delivering tangible business benefits that build momentum for continued improvement.

Practical implementation roadmap

A successful DataOps implementation follows a systematic approach that builds capabilities incrementally while delivering business value at each stage:

- **Phase 1**: Foundation building (1 to 3 months):

  The initial phase focuses on establishing the technical and cultural foundation for DataOps. Key activities include conducting a maturity assessment to identify the current state and priority improvement areas, implementing version control for all pipeline code and configurations, establishing infrastructure as code for at least one environment (typically development), implementing a basic CI/CD pipeline for a pilot data workflow, and creating initial monitoring for critical data pipelines and platform components.

  Success in this phase is measured by having 100% of new pipeline code in version control, at least one environment fully defined as code, a CI/CD pipeline successfully implementing basic testing, and monitoring dashboards providing visibility into key metrics. This foundational work creates the platform for more advanced DataOps capabilities while delivering immediate benefits through increased consistency and visibility.

- **Phase 2**: Capability expansion (3 to 6 months):

  The second phase expands automation and quality capabilities across the data platform. Organizations should focus on extending CI/CD coverage to all critical data pipelines, implementing automated testing, including data quality validation, creating self-service capabilities for common data engineering tasks, enhancing monitoring and observability with comprehensive dashboards, and establishing feedback mechanisms for continuous improvement.

Success metrics for this phase include having 80% above of data pipelines covered by CI/CD, automated quality validation for critical datasets, self-service provisioning for development environments, and end-to-end monitoring of data pipelines. These expanded capabilities significantly reduce manual effort while increasing data quality and team productivity.

- **Phase 3**: Optimization and scaling (6 to 12 months):

The final phase focuses on optimizing DataOps practices and scaling them across the organization. Key activities include implementing advanced testing strategies such as performance and regression testing, creating cross-team collaboration platforms for knowledge sharing, establishing DataOps centers of excellence to promote best practices, implementing predictive monitoring to identify issues before they impact users, and measuring and optimizing team productivity through enhanced automation.

Organizations should measure success through metrics like 95% plus reduction in production data quality issues, 50% plus reduction in time-to-market for new data products, comprehensive test coverage across the data platform, and predictive alerts successfully preventing production issues. These optimized capabilities transform how the organization delivers and operates data products, creating sustainable competitive advantages through higher quality, faster delivery, and more efficient resource utilization.

AWS implementation architecture

AWS provides a comprehensive suite of services that support DataOps implementation across the entire data lifecycle. These services create an integrated platform that enables automation, quality, collaboration, observability, and continuous improvement:

- **Version control** leverages AWS CodeCommit or integrations with GitHub/GitLab to store all code, configurations, and infrastructure definitions. Organizations should implement branch protection and review workflows while automating governance validation. These repositories integrate directly with AWS CodePipeline, connect to CloudFormation/CDK for infrastructure deployment, and provide comprehensive audit trails for compliance purposes.

- **CI/CD pipelines** use AWS CodePipeline, CodeBuild, and CodeDeploy to create automated workflows that build, test, and deploy data pipelines and infrastructure. These pipelines should include stages for each environment, with appropriate validation and approval gates. The pipelines integrate with version control systems to trigger on code changes, deploy infrastructure through CloudFormation, and connect with monitoring systems to verify successful deployments.

- **Infrastructure management** relies on AWS CloudFormation, AWS CDK, and AWS Service Catalog to define all infrastructure as code, create reusable patterns, and enable self-service provisioning. This approach ensures consistency across environments while enabling rapid, reliable infrastructure changes. These tools integrate with CI/CD pipelines for automated deployment, with CloudWatch for monitoring, and with AWS Config for governance enforcement.

- **Testing automation** leverages AWS Lambda, Step Functions, and EventBridge to implement comprehensive testing, including data quality validation, functional testing, and regression testing. These automated tests execute as part of CI/CD pipelines while also running on schedules to verify ongoing system health. Test results should be stored in S3 for historical analysis and trend identification.

- **Monitoring and observability** uses Amazon CloudWatch, AWS X-Ray, and Amazon OpenSearch to create comprehensive visibility into data platform operations. Organizations should implement dashboards that combine metrics, logs, and traces to provide a complete view of system health and performance. These tools enable both real-time alerting through SNS and historical analysis for performance optimization and capacity planning.

Organizational considerations

Successful DataOps implementation requires appropriate organizational structures and roles to support new ways of working:

- **Team structures** should evolve to support collaborative, cross-functional work rather than traditional silos. Most successful implementations include a platform team responsible for core infrastructure, CI/CD pipelines, and shared services; data product teams focused on specific data domains or business capabilities; and a DataOps center of excellence that promotes best practices, provides training, and facilitates knowledge sharing across the organization.

- **Key roles** emerge to support specialized DataOps functions:

  o **DataOps engineer**: Specializes in automation, CI/CD, and infrastructure as code for data platforms.

  o **Data quality engineer**: Focuses on testing frameworks, quality validation, and monitoring.

  o **Data product owner**: Represents business stakeholders and prioritizes data product features based on business value and user needs.

- **Cultural considerations** are critical to successful DataOps adoption:

  o **Collaboration over silos**: Encourage cross-team interaction and knowledge sharing.

  o **Blameless culture**: Focus on improving processes rather than assigning blame for issues.

  o **Continuous learning**: Promote experimentation, growth, and ongoing improvement as core values.

Implementing a comprehensive DataOps framework transforms how organizations deliver and operate data platforms, enabling faster innovation, higher quality, and more efficient resource utilization. By following a structured implementation approach that addresses both technical and organizational aspects, data engineering teams can progressively evolve from manual, siloed processes to automated, collaborative workflows.

The most successful DataOps implementations focus on delivering incremental business value while building toward a comprehensive vision. Each phase of implementation should demonstrate tangible benefits that build momentum for continued improvement. By leveraging AWS's comprehensive suite of services and following the implementation roadmap outlined in this section, organizations can accelerate their DataOps journey and unlock the full potential of their data engineering teams.

Conclusion

Throughout this chapter, we have explored how DataOps transforms data engineering from a collection of manual, siloed processes into an integrated framework that enables automation, quality, collaboration, and observability. By implementing the core principles of DataOps: automation first, continuous quality, collaboration culture, observability by design, and continuous iteration, organizations can dramatically reduce data defects, accelerate time-to-market, and improve cross-team collaboration. The AWS implementation architecture we have examined provides a proven approach for realizing these benefits, with services organized to create seamless integration while maintaining appropriate governance and isolation between environments. By following the implementation roadmap and addressing the organizational considerations outlined in this chapter, data engineering teams can progressively evolve their practices while delivering tangible business value at each stage. The most successful DataOps implementations recognize that the journey is as important as the destination, focusing on incremental improvements that build momentum for the continuous evolution of the data platform.

The next chapter explores how the GenAI revolution is fundamentally transforming the data platforms we build using DataOps principles. While DataOps provides the operational framework for reliable, automated data engineering, the emergence of AI systems as primary data consumers requires rethinking our architectural approaches entirely. We will examine how traditional human-centric data platforms must evolve into AI-native systems that serve both deterministic business intelligence and probabilistic AI workloads through enhanced medallion architectures. The chapter demonstrates how to architect platforms that leverage the automation and observability principles of DataOps while meeting the massive scale, real-time inference, and continuous learning requirements of generative AI systems.

Join our Discord space

Join our Discord workspace for latest updates, offers, tech happenings around the world, new releases, and sessions with the authors:

https://discord.bpbonline.com

## CHAPTER 14

GenAI Revolution in Data Engineering

Introduction

The sophisticated data platforms explored in previous chapters, from data lakes and warehouses to streaming architectures and DataOps frameworks, were designed for a world where humans were the primary consumers of data and deterministic rules governed data processing. Today, we stand at the threshold of a fundamental transformation that challenges these foundational assumptions. **Generative AI** (**GenAI**), autonomous agents, and machine learning models are not merely consuming data; they are becoming the dominant users of our data platforms, requiring massive training datasets, real-time inference capabilities, and probabilistic rather than deterministic processing approaches.

This paradigm shift extends far beyond simply adding AI features to existing data platforms. It represents a complete reimagining of how we architect, build, and operate data systems. Where traditional data engineering focused on extracting, transforming, and loading data with predictable outcomes, the GenAI revolution demands platforms that can handle uncertainty, adapt to changing patterns, and serve both human and machine consumers simultaneously. The volume of machine-generated data now exceeds human-generated data by orders of magnitude, while the computational requirements for training large language models and other AI systems have grown exponentially.

The implications are profound and immediate. Organizations that built their data platforms around deterministic batch processing now find themselves needing to support petabyte-scale training datasets, real-time model inference, and continuous learning pipelines. The traditional medallion architecture must evolve to include new layers optimized for AI consumption, including feature stores, vector databases, and semantic understanding capabilities. This chapter explores how to architect, implement, and operate data platforms that embrace the GenAI revolution while maintaining the reliability, governance, and cost-effectiveness that modern enterprises require.

Structure

This chapter covers the following topics:

- From human-centric to AI-native systems
- Enhanced medallion for GenAI
- Enhanced medallion architecture on AWS

- Machines as primary data consumers

- Large-scale AI training and data requirements

- GenAI-native data platform on AWS

- Challenges, solutions, and future outlook

Objectives

This chapter aims to provide a comprehensive understanding of how generative AI is transforming data engineering practices and how to architect platforms that capitalize on these changes. You will learn to identify the fundamental differences between deterministic and probabilistic data processing approaches, understand when each is appropriate, and how to design systems that support both paradigms. The chapter explores advanced architectural patterns for extending traditional data lake architectures to support AI-native workflows, including the implementation of feature stores, vector databases, and semantic layers that enable sophisticated AI applications. Through practical AWS implementation examples, you will understand how to build data platforms that serve both human and machine consumers, handling the unique requirements of AI training data, real-time inference, and continuous learning workflows. These capabilities will enable you to architect next-generation data platforms that deliver immediate business value while positioning your organization to leverage emerging AI capabilities for competitive advantage in an increasingly AI-driven marketplace.

From human-centric to AI-native data platform

The data platforms we have built over the past decades were architected with a fundamental assumption: humans would be the primary consumers of processed data. Business analysts would query data warehouses, executives would review dashboard reports, and operational teams would monitor system metrics. This human-centric design influenced every aspect of our data architecture, from how we structure databases to how we implement data quality checks; from the interfaces we build to the performance optimizations we prioritize.

Today, this foundational assumption is being challenged by a profound shift. Artificial intelligence systems, particularly large language models, machine learning algorithms, and autonomous agents, are becoming the dominant consumers of data. These AI systems do not just consume more data than humans; they consume it differently, process it probabilistically rather than deterministically, and generate vast amounts of new data in return. This transformation demands a fundamental rethinking of how we architect data platforms.

Traditional human-centric data platform

Traditional data platforms were designed around human cognitive patterns and business processes. Humans prefer structured information, consistent formats, and predictable outcomes. When a business analyst runs a quarterly sales report, they expect identical results each time the query executes against the same dataset. Financial systems must produce exact calculations for regulatory compliance. Dashboard visualizations need to display consistent metrics that business users can trust and act upon.

These human-centric requirements shaped our data architecture principles:

- **Structured data models** organize information into clearly defined schemas with fixed relationships. Relational databases enforced referential integrity, ensuring that foreign key relationships remained consistent. Data warehouses implemented dimensional modelling that aligned with how business users naturally think about their domains, facts, and dimensions, measures, and hierarchies.

- **Deterministic processing** ensured that identical inputs always produced identical outputs. ETL pipelines applied fixed transformation rules that could be audited and repeated. Data quality validation implemented binary checks; data was either correct or incorrect, complete or incomplete. Business rules were encoded as explicit logic that could be understood and modified by human data engineers.

- **Batch-oriented workflows** aligned with human decision-making cycles. Monthly reports supported quarterly planning meetings. Daily aggregations provided overnight insights for morning business reviews. The latency requirements matched human cognitive processing speeds, and minutes or hours were acceptable for most analytical workloads.

- **Human-readable interfaces** provided SQL query languages, graphical dashboards, and structured reports. Data catalogues organize information using business terminology that domain experts could understand. Documentation focused on explaining data lineage and business meaning to human consumers.

AI-native data platform paradigm

AI systems fundamentally challenge these human-centric assumptions. Machine learning models do not require data to be presented in human-readable formats. They can process raw text, images, audio, and sensor data directly. Large language models learn from vast, unstructured text corpora rather than carefully curated business datasets. Computer vision systems analyze pixel-level information that would be meaningless to human analysts.

More importantly, AI systems produce probabilistic rather than deterministic outputs. When a recommendation engine suggests products to a customer, it provides ranked lists with confidence scores rather than definitive answers. Fraud detection models assign probability scores to transactions rather than binary fraud or legitimate classifications. Natural language processing systems generate responses with varying degrees of creativity and accuracy based on statistical patterns learned from training data.

This probabilistic nature demands different data platform characteristics:

- **Confidence-based data quality** moves beyond binary pass or fail validation to implement quality scores and uncertainty measures. Instead of rejecting incomplete customer records, AI systems might process them with lower confidence scores. Data drift detection monitors statistical properties of datasets over time, alerting when distributions shift beyond acceptable thresholds rather than waiting for absolute rule violations.

- **Continuous learning workflows** enable AI systems to improve their performance by learning from new data continuously. Unlike traditional ETL pipelines that transform data once, AI-native platforms implement feedback loops where model predictions are compared against actual outcomes, and the differences are used to retrain and improve the models automatically.

- **Multi-modal data processing** handles diverse data types: text, images, audio, video, sensor data, without requiring them to be transformed into human-readable formats first. Vector databases store high-dimensional embeddings that capture semantic relationships between different data types. Feature stores provide real-time access to processed features that AI models can consume directly.

- **Real-time inference requirements** support AI systems that must make decisions in milliseconds rather than hours. Recommendation engines provide suggestions as users browse websites. Fraud detection systems evaluate transactions as they occur. Autonomous vehicles process sensor data continuously to make driving decisions.

Dual consumer challenge

Perhaps the most significant implication of the AI revolution is that modern data platforms must serve dual consumers: traditional human users who still need structured reports and dashboards, and AI systems that require massive datasets, real-time features, and continuous learning capabilities. This dual consumer requirement creates unique architectural challenges:

- **Human consumers still need**:
  - o Structured reports with consistent formatting.
  - o Dashboard visualizations that update predictably.
  - o SQL query interfaces for ad-hoc analysis.
  - o Data governance controls that ensure compliance.
  - o Audit trails that explain how business metrics were calculated.

- **AI consumers require**:
  - o Massive training datasets with billions of examples.
  - o Real-time feature access for online inference.
  - o Continuous data streams for ongoing learning.
  - o Vector embeddings for semantic similarity search.
  - o Probabilistic quality measures that reflect uncertainty.

The challenge is designing platforms that serve both sets of requirements efficiently. A customer data platform, for example, must provide clean, structured customer records for CRM systems and business reporting while simultaneously supplying rich behavioural data streams for real-time personalization engines and vast historical datasets for training recommendation models.

Characteristics of future data platforms

The evolution toward AI-native data platforms requires new architectural patterns that can handle both human and machine consumers effectively:

- **Layered architecture with AI-specific layers**: Traditional medallion architectures with bronze (raw), silver (cleaned), and gold (business-ready) layers must expand to include AI-specific layers:
  - o **Platinum layer** contains AI-ready features, embeddings, and pre-processed data optimized for machine learning consumption. This layer might include vector embeddings of text documents, pre-processed image features, and time-series data formatted for training neural networks.
  - o **Semantic layer** provides meaning and context that AI systems can leverage to understand relationships between different data elements. This layer might include knowledge graphs, ontologies, and relationship mappings that help AI systems make more informed decisions.
  - o **Feedback layer** captures AI system outputs and performance metrics, creating closed-loop learning systems that continuously improve. This layer stores model predictions, confidence scores, and actual outcomes that enable automated model retraining.

- **Hybrid processing engines**: Future platforms must support both deterministic processing for traditional business logic and probabilistic processing for AI workloads:
  - o **Deterministic processing** continues to handle financial calculations, regulatory reporting, and operational processes that require exact repeatability. These workflows use traditional ETL patterns with strict validation and error handling.
  - o **Probabilistic processing** handles AI training, inference, and continuous learning workflows. These systems embrace uncertainty, provide confidence scores, and adapt to changing data patterns automatically.
  - o **Hybrid workflows** combine both approaches, using deterministic processing for data preparation and validation while leveraging probabilistic processing for insights and predictions.

- **Real-time and batch integration**: AI systems often require both real-time inference capabilities and batch processing for model training:

  o **Stream processing** provides real-time features for online inference, handling thousands of requests per second with millisecond latency requirements.

  o **Batch processing** trains models on massive historical datasets, processing petabytes of data to learn complex patterns and relationships.

  o **Lambda architecture** combines both approaches, providing real-time views for immediate decision-making and batch views for comprehensive analysis and model training.

- **Automated quality and governance**: With AI systems generating and consuming vast amounts of data, manual quality checks and governance processes become impractical:

  o **Automated data profiling** uses AI to understand data characteristics, detect anomalies, and monitor quality continuously without human intervention.

  o **Intelligent governance** applies AI to automatically classify sensitive data, enforce access controls, and maintain compliance with evolving regulations.

  o **Explainable lineage** tracks not just where data came from but how AI systems processed it, providing transparency needed for regulatory compliance and model debugging.

- **Implementation implications**: This evolution from human-centric to AI-native data platforms has profound implications for how we design, build, and operate data systems. Organizations must:

  o **Rethink storage strategies** to handle both structured business data and unstructured AI training data efficiently. This might involve hybrid storage architectures that combine data lakes for AI workloads with data warehouses for business reporting.

  o **Redesign processing pipelines** to support both deterministic business logic and probabilistic AI processing. This requires new orchestration patterns that can handle both traditional ETL workflows and machine learning training pipelines.

  o **Implement new quality frameworks** that move beyond binary validation to embrace uncertainty and continuous improvement. Quality measures must reflect the probabilistic nature of AI outputs while maintaining the reliability needed for business decisions.

  o **Develop dual interfaces** that serve both human users through familiar SQL queries and dashboards and AI systems through APIs, feature stores, and vector databases.

The next section explores how these principles manifest in the evolution of specific architectural patterns, particularly the enhancement of traditional medallion architectures to support AI-native workflows.

Enhanced medallion for GenAI

The medallion architecture has become the de facto standard for organizing data lakes, with its intuitive bronze (raw), silver (cleaned), and gold (business-ready) layers providing a clear progression from ingestion to consumption. This pattern worked exceptionally well for traditional analytics workloads where human analysts consumed structured reports and dashboards. However, the rise of AI systems as primary data consumers exposes fundamental limitations in this three-layer approach that require architectural evolution rather than simple extension.

Traditional vs. enhanced medallion architecture

The following figure demonstrates how traditional medallion data architecture with three layers has been enhanced to a multilayer data architecture with additional AI-specific layers. We have stacked traditional medallion architecture and proposed enhanced medallion architecture for easy comparison. For AI-centric data, additional processing is required, which is represented as additional AI layers:

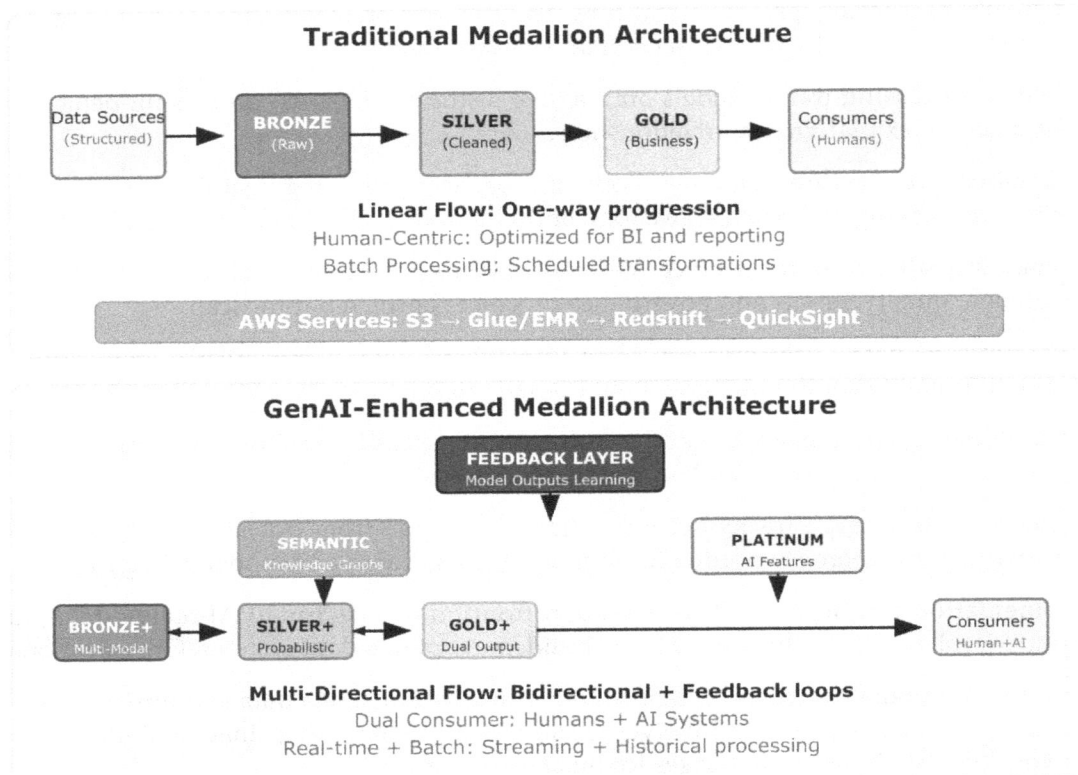

Figure 14.1: Traditional vs. enhanced medallion architecture

Limitations of medallion architecture for AI

The traditional three-layer medallion architecture faces several challenges when supporting AI-native workloads:

- **Linear processing assumptions** do not align with AI workflows that need bidirectional data flow. While traditional analytics follows a clear Bronze | Silver | Gold progression, AI systems might need raw bronze data for training, processed silver data for feature engineering, and gold data for business context, all simultaneously. Machine learning models also generate predictions and feedback that need to flow back through the layers to improve data quality and model performance.

- **Human-centric data formats** in gold layers optimize for dashboard consumption rather than machine learning. Business metrics like *quarterly revenue growth* or *customer satisfaction scores* are perfect for executive reports but provide little value for training neural networks. AI systems need access to granular behavioral data, time-series patterns, and multi-modal content that traditional gold layers often aggregate away.

- **Batch-oriented design** assumes data can be processed in scheduled intervals, but AI systems increasingly require real-time inference and continuous learning. A recommendation engine cannot wait for nightly batch jobs to update customer preferences; it needs immediate access to behavioral signals as they occur.

- **Missing semantic context** means that while traditional medallion architectures organize data by processing stage, they do not capture the semantic relationships between different data elements that AI systems need for sophisticated analysis.

Enhanced medallion architecture

To address these limitations, we propose the enhanced medallion architecture, which expands the traditional three-layer model with additional layers specifically designed for AI consumption and generation:

- **Enhanced layer structure**:
  - o **Bronze layer (raw data+)** retains its traditional role as the landing zone for all incoming data but expands to handle much larger volumes and more diverse data types. This layer now ingests not just structured business data but also unstructured content like documents, images, audio, and video that AI systems can process directly. The bronze layer also stores machine-generated data from AI systems themselves, creating feedback loops for continuous learning.

  - o **Silver layer (cleaned and standardized+)** continues to provide cleaned, validated data but implements probabilistic quality measures alongside traditional deterministic checks. Instead of rejecting incomplete records, the silver layer assigns quality scores that AI systems can use to weight their training data appropriately. This layer also implements schema evolution patterns that allow AI systems to adapt to changing data structures automatically.

  - o **Gold layer (business-ready+)** maintains its role in providing structured business metrics for traditional analytics while also generating derived features that AI systems can consume. This layer now includes feature engineering pipelines that create ML-ready datasets from business data, bridging the gap between traditional business intelligence and AI consumption.

  - o **Platinum layer (AI-ready features)** represents the first AI-specific layer, containing pre-processed features, embeddings, and model-ready datasets optimized for machine learning consumption. This layer includes vector embeddings of text and images, time-series features for temporal models, and aggregated behavioural patterns for recommendation systems.

  - o **Semantic layer (context and relationships)** captures the meaning and relationships between different data elements through knowledge graphs, ontologies, and semantic mappings. This layer helps AI systems understand that *customer complaints* and *product returns* are related concepts, enabling more sophisticated analysis and better model performance.

  - o **Feedback layer (continuous learning)** stores AI system outputs, predictions, and performance metrics to enable closed-loop learning. This layer captures model predictions alongside actual outcomes, enabling automated model retraining and performance monitoring.

- **Multi-directional data flow**: Unlike traditional medallion architectures with linear progression, the enhanced version implements multi-directional data flow:
  - o **Forward flow**: Traditional Bronze | Silver | Gold | Platinum progression
  - o **Lateral flow**: Data movement between layers at the same level
  - o **Backward flow**: AI feedback improving earlier layers
  - o **Feedback loops**: Continuous learning cycles

Enhanced medallion architecture on AWS

Amazon Web Services provides a comprehensive suite of services that enable the implementation of enhanced medallion architectures at enterprise scale. The following implementation approach leverages native AWS capabilities to create seamless integration between traditional data processing and AI-native workflows, ensuring organizations can modernize their data platforms while maintaining operational excellence and cost efficiency.

AWS services by layer

Leveraging AWS services, we can build the different layers of enhanced medallion architecture. The following table gives layer-wise AWS services that can be used:

Layer	Primary AWS services	Purpose	Key features
Bronze layer	Amazon S3 Amazon Kinesis AWS Glue Amazon Textract Amazon Rekognition	Multi-modal data ingestion and storage	• Object storage with metadata • Real-time streaming • Schema discovery • Document text extraction • Image analysis
Silver layer	AWS Glue DataBrew Amazon Glue AWS Data Quality Amazon EMR	Data cleaning with probabilistic quality	• Visual data preparation • ETL with quality scoring • Automated profiling • Distributed processing
Gold layer	Amazon Redshift Amazon SageMaker Feature Store AWS Glue Amazon Athena	Dual-output for humans and AI	• Data warehousing • Feature serving • Feature engineering • Serverless queries
Platinum layer	Amazon Bedrock Amazon OpenSearch Amazon SageMaker Amazon Timestream	AI-ready features and embeddings	• Foundation models • Vector search • ML training or inference • Time-series data
Semantic layer	Amazon Neptune AWS Glue Amazon OpenSearch Amazon Comprehend	Knowledge graphs and relationships	• Graph database • Entity resolution • Semantic search • NLP services
Feedback layer	Amazon S3 Amazon Kinesis Amazon SageMaker Amazon CloudWatch	Model outputs and performance tracking	• Output storage • Real-time monitoring • Model performance • Metrics and logs

Table 14.1: Primary AWS services for enhanced medallion layers

Integration services

While the core layers provide the foundation for GenAI-enhanced data processing, successful implementation requires additional AWS services that handle orchestration, security, and observability across the entire platform. These integration services ensure that data flows seamlessly between layers while maintaining enterprise-grade security and governance standards. Refer to the following table:

Service category	AWS services	Purpose
Orchestration	• AWS Step Functions • Amazon EventBridge • AWS Lambda	Workflow coordination and event-driven processing
Security and governance	• AWS Lake Formation • AWS IAM • AWS CloudTrail	Access control, governance, and audit trails
Monitoring and observability	• Amazon CloudWatch • AWS X-Ray • Amazon QuickSight	Performance monitoring and business intelligence

Table 14.2: Supporting AWS services for platform integration

Customer 360 platform implementation example

Consider a customer 360 platform that needs to serve both traditional business reporting and AI-powered personalization. The following code illustrates an example approach for the same:

```
1.  # Minimal example: Enhanced medallion data flow
2.  def process_customer_data():
3.      # Bronze: Ingest multi-modal customer data
4.      bronze_data = ingest_multimodal_data(['transactions', 'reviews', 'support_
    calls'])
5.
6.      # Silver: Clean with probabilistic quality
7.      silver_data = apply_quality_scoring(bronze_data)
8.
9.      # Gold: Dual output for humans and AI
10.     business_metrics = create_business_reports(silver_data)
11.     ml_features = engineer_ml_features(silver_data)
12.
13.     # Platinum: AI-ready embeddings and features
14.     embeddings = generate_embeddings(ml_features)
15.
16.     # Semantic: Build customer knowledge graph
17.     knowledge_graph = build_customer_ontology(silver_data)
18.
19.     # Feedback: Capture model outputs for improvement
20.     model_feedback = capture_prediction_feedback()
21.
22.     return {
23.         'business_reports': business_metrics,
24.         'ml_features': ml_features,
25.         'embeddings': embeddings,
26.         'knowledge_graph': knowledge_graph,
27.         'feedback': model_feedback
28.     }
```

Benefits of the enhanced architecture

The enhanced medallion architecture provides several key advantages:

- **Unified data platform** serves both traditional business intelligence and AI workloads from a single, coherent architecture. Business users can continue accessing familiar reports and dashboards while AI systems get the specialized layers they need for training and inference.

- **Flexible data flow** accommodates the complex, multi-directional data flows that AI systems require. Models can access raw data for training, processed features for inference, and feedback data for continuous learning, all within the same architectural framework.

- **Scalable AI operations** provide the infrastructure needed to scale AI operations from experimental models to production systems serving millions of users. The architecture supports both batch training on historical data and real-time inference on streaming data.

- **Continuous learning** enables AI systems to improve automatically through feedback loops built into the architecture. Model predictions flow back into the data platform, creating opportunities for automated retraining and quality improvement.

- **Governance and lineage** maintain comprehensive tracking of data flow across all layers supporting both traditional compliance requirements and emerging AI governance needs like explainable AI and bias detection.

This enhanced architecture provides the foundation for building truly AI-native data platforms that can support the full spectrum of GenAI applications while maintaining the reliability and governance that enterprises require.

Machines as primary data consumers

The most profound shift in the GenAI revolution is not just that machines can now generate human-like content, but that they have fundamentally changed who consumes data and how. For decades, data platforms were optimized for human consumption: structured reports, dashboard visualizations, and SQL queries that business analysts could understand and act upon. Today, artificial intelligence systems consume orders of magnitude more data than humans ever could, process it in entirely different ways, and generate new data at unprecedented scales.

This transformation creates a new data ecosystem where machines are not just tools that help humans analyze data; they are the primary consumers, processors, and generators of information. Understanding this shift is crucial for architecting data platforms that can serve both traditional human users and the growing population of AI systems that require fundamentally different approaches to data access, processing, and quality.

Scale of machine data consumption

The scale at which AI systems consume data dwarfs traditional human consumption patterns. A business analyst might query a few gigabytes of data per day to generate reports and insights. In contrast, a large language model training run consumes terabytes of text data, a recommendation engine processes billions of user interactions in real-time, and computer vision systems analyze millions of images continuously:

- **Training data requirements** represent the most dramatic example of this scale difference. GPT-4 was trained on approximately 13 trillion tokens of text data, equivalent to roughly 10 million books. Image generation models like DALL-E require millions of image-caption pairs. These training datasets are so large that they fundamentally change storage, processing, and transfer requirements for data platforms.

- **Real-time inference demands** create entirely different consumption patterns. While humans might access data intermittently throughout the day, AI systems often require continuous, millisecond-latency access to current information. A fraud detection system evaluates every transaction as it occurs. A recommendation engine updates suggestions with each user click. An autonomous vehicle processes sensor data continuously to make driving decisions.

- **Continuous learning cycles** mean that AI systems do not just consume static datasets; they generate new data that feeds back into their own improvement. Every prediction becomes potential training data for future model versions. User interactions with AI-generated content provide signals for refinement. This creates dynamic, self-improving data ecosystems that grow and evolve automatically.

Different data access patterns

AI systems access data in ways that fundamentally differ from human consumption patterns, requiring new approaches to data platform design:

- **Parallel processing requirements** mean that AI systems often need to access many data points simultaneously rather than sequentially. Training a neural network requires loading thousands of examples in parallel across multiple GPUs. Batch inference processes hundreds of thousands of predictions simultaneously. Traditional data platforms optimized for single-user queries struggle with these massively parallel access patterns.

- **Multi-modal data integration** enables AI systems to process different types of data: text, images, audio, video, sensor data, as part of unified workflows. A content moderation system might analyze both the text and images in a social media post simultaneously. A customer service AI might process voice recordings, chat transcripts, and account information together. This requires data platforms that can handle diverse data types without forcing them into traditional relational structures.

- **Temporal data relationships** become crucial when AI systems need to understand how data changes over time. Recommendation engines do not just need to know what products a customer bought; they need to understand the sequence and timing of purchases to predict future behavior. Fraud detection systems identify suspicious patterns by analyzing the temporal relationships between transactions. This requires specialized storage and processing approaches optimized for time-series analysis.

- **Semantic similarity search** replaces traditional exact-match queries with approximate searches based on meaning and context. Instead of searching for products with specific keywords, AI systems find items that are semantically similar to user preferences. Rather than matching exact customer demographics, they identify users with similar behavioral patterns. This requires vector databases and embedding-based search capabilities that traditional SQL databases cannot provide efficiently.

Machine-generated data characteristics

AI systems do not just consume data differently; they generate fundamentally different types of data that require new management approaches:

- **Probabilistic outputs** mean that AI systems rarely provide definitive answers. Instead, they generate predictions with associated confidence scores, probability distributions, and uncertainty measures. A sentiment analysis system does not classify text as definitively positive or negative; it provides probability scores for different emotional states. This probabilistic data requires storage and processing systems that can handle uncertainty and confidence metrics alongside traditional data values.

- **Synthetic data generation** enables AI systems to create realistic but artificial data for training, testing, and privacy protection. Language models generate synthetic customer reviews for testing sentiment analysis systems. Image generation models create training data for computer vision applications. Synthetic financial transactions help train fraud detection systems without exposing real customer data. This synthetic data often has different statistical properties from real data and requires specialized validation and quality measures.

- **Embeddings and high-dimensional data** represent how AI systems encode semantic meaning in numerical form. Text embeddings capture the meaning of words and documents in high-dimensional vectors. Image embeddings encode visual features in numerical representations. These embeddings enable semantic similarity search and transfer learning but require specialized storage and indexing systems optimized for high-dimensional data.

- **Continuous model outputs** flow from AI systems operating in production environments. Every recommendation, classification, prediction, and generation creates new data that organizations need to store, analyze, and learn from. A recommendation engine serving millions of users generates billions of prediction records daily. A content moderation system creates millions of classification decisions. This continuous output requires data platforms that can handle high-velocity data streams without overwhelming storage or processing systems.

Implications for data platform design

The shift to machines as primary data consumers has profound implications for how we design and operate data platforms:

- **Storage architecture changes**:

  o **Multi-modal storage** becomes essential when platforms need to efficiently store and retrieve text, images, audio, video, and sensor data alongside traditional structured information. Object storage systems like Amazon S3 provide the flexibility needed for diverse data types, while specialized databases handle specific requirements like vector similarity search for embeddings or time-series optimization for temporal data.

  o **Hierarchical storage management** automatically moves data between different storage tiers based on access patterns and AI workflow requirements. Frequently accessed training data stays in high-performance storage, while historical model outputs move to cost-effective archive storage. Unlike traditional approaches that focus on data age, AI-oriented hierarchical storage considers factors like model training schedules, inference frequency, and continuous learning requirements.

  o **Partitioning strategies** optimize data organization for AI access patterns rather than traditional business reporting. Instead of partitioning by geography or time periods that align with business processes, AI-oriented partitioning considers factors like data modality, training or inference splits, and semantic similarity. This might mean co-locating related embeddings, grouping training examples by difficulty, or organizing data to optimize parallel processing workflows.

- **Processing architecture evolution**:

  o **Streaming-first design** prioritizes real-time data processing over traditional batch-oriented approaches. AI systems increasingly require immediate access to new information for online learning, real-time personalization, and adaptive behavior. This requires processing architectures built around streaming platforms like Amazon Kinesis that can handle continuous data flows with millisecond latency requirements.

  o **GPU-optimized pipelines** leverage specialized hardware for AI workloads rather than relying solely on CPU-based processing. Training neural networks, generating embeddings, and performing inference operations benefit dramatically from GPU acceleration. Data platforms need to incorporate GPU clusters, optimize data transfer to minimize GPU idle time, and support distributed training across multiple GPU nodes.

  o **Elastic scaling patterns** accommodate the variable and often unpredictable resource requirements of AI workloads. Model training might require massive compute resources for hours or days, followed by periods of minimal activity. Inference workloads can spike dramatically based on user demand. Unlike traditional business applications with relatively predictable load patterns, AI workloads require platforms that can scale resources dynamically based on actual demand.

AWS services for machine-centric data platforms

AWS provides specialized services designed to support machine-centric data consumption patterns:

- **Amazon SageMaker feature store** provides managed infrastructure for storing, discovering, and serving machine learning features at scale. Unlike traditional databases optimized for business queries, Feature Store optimizes for high-throughput serving of numerical features to models with millisecond latency requirements.

- **Amazon OpenSearch with vector engine** enables semantic similarity search across high-dimensional embeddings. This allows AI systems to find semantically related content, recommend similar items, and perform approximate matching based on learned representations rather than exact keywords or attributes.

- **Amazon Bedrock** provides managed access to foundation models that can process and generate various types of content. This enables organizations to leverage pre-trained models for tasks like text generation, image analysis, and embedding creation without building and training models from scratch.

- **Amazon Kinesis** handles high-velocity data streams that support real-time AI applications. Unlike traditional batch processing systems, Kinesis can process millions of events per second with sub-second latency, enabling real-time personalization, fraud detection, and adaptive systems.

The transformation of data platforms to serve machine consumers represents one of the most significant architectural shifts in modern data engineering. Organizations that successfully navigate this transition will unlock new capabilities for automation, personalization, and intelligent decision-making while maintaining the traditional analytics capabilities that business users still require.

Large-scale AI training and data requirements

The computational and data requirements for training modern AI systems have grown exponentially, fundamentally changing how organizations approach data platform architecture. Where traditional analytics might process gigabytes of data to generate business insights, AI training operations consume terabytes or petabytes of data to create models that can understand language, recognize images, or make complex predictions. This scale transformation requires data platforms that can handle unprecedented volumes while maintaining the performance, reliability, and cost-effectiveness that enterprises demand.

Understanding these requirements is crucial for architecting data platforms that can support both current AI initiatives and future scaling needs. The challenge extends beyond simply storing large datasets to encompass efficient data preparation, high-throughput processing, distributed training coordination, and specialized data annotation workflows that can prepare raw information for machine learning consumption.

Scale of modern AI training

The data requirements for training state-of-the-art AI models have grown dramatically over the past decade, driven by the discovery that larger models trained on more data consistently deliver better performance across diverse tasks. In the following, we illustrate the scale of data required for different AI training tasks:

- **Language models** represent some of the most data-intensive training workloads. GPT-3 was trained on approximately 45 terabytes of text data, equivalent to roughly 300 billion words or 570 gigabytes of compressed text. More recent models like GPT-4 and Claude are estimated to have been trained on even larger datasets, potentially reaching 100-plus terabytes of raw text. These datasets must be deduplicated, cleaned, and tokenized before training can begin, often expanding storage requirements by multiplying them by two to three during pre-processing.

- **Computer vision models** require massive image datasets for training. ImageNet, one of the foundational computer vision datasets, contains 1.2 million labelled images totalling approximately 150 gigabytes. Modern vision models often train on datasets containing hundreds of millions of images, requiring tens of terabytes of storage. When including video data for temporal understanding, storage requirements can reach hundreds of terabytes or even petabytes.

- **Multimodal models** that process both text and images simultaneously require datasets that combine both modalities. Training datasets for models like DALL-E or GPT-4V include hundreds of millions of image-caption pairs, each requiring careful curation to ensure alignment between visual and textual content. These datasets can easily exceed 50 to 100 terabytes and require specialized storage and processing approaches to handle the correlation between different data types.

- **Domain-specific models** for specialized applications like protein folding, drug discovery or financial modelling require their own large-scale datasets. AlphaFold was trained on hundreds of thousands of protein structures, weather prediction models require decades of meteorological data, and financial models need historical market data across multiple time scales and asset classes.

Data preparation and curation challenges

The sheer volume of data required for AI training creates unprecedented challenges in data preparation and curation that traditional data platforms were not designed to handle. In the following, we look at different data preparation tasks, challenges because of scale, and possible mitigation:

- **Data quality at scale:**
  - o **Deduplication** becomes computationally intensive when applied to petabyte-scale datasets. Traditional deduplication algorithms that work well on gigabyte datasets become prohibitively expensive when applied to training corpora containing billions of documents or images. Organizations need distributed deduplication systems that can identify near-duplicates across massive datasets using techniques like locality-sensitive hashing and distributed similarity computation.

  - o **Content filtering** requires automated systems that can identify and remove inappropriate, biased, or low-quality content from training datasets. Manual review becomes impossible at the scales required for modern AI training. Instead, organizations implement multi-stage filtering pipelines that use existing AI models to classify content quality, detect harmful material, and identify potential copyright issues before data enters training pipelines.

  - o **Data validation** extends beyond traditional schema checking to include semantic validation of training data. For language models, this might involve checking that text is in the expected language, contains meaningful content, and maintains consistent formatting. For computer vision models, validation includes checking image quality, resolution, and content appropriateness. These validation processes must operate at high throughput while maintaining accuracy standards.

- **Preprocessing pipelines:**
  - o **Tokenization and encoding** for language models require processing billions of documents through computationally intensive text processing pipelines. Modern tokenization approaches like byte-pair encoding or sentence piece require multiple passes through the entire dataset to build vocabularies and encode text efficiently. These preprocessing steps can take weeks or months for large datasets and require distributed processing systems that can handle both the computational load and the I/O requirements.

  - o **Data augmentation** artificially expands training datasets by creating variations of existing examples. For images, this might involve rotation, scaling, color adjustment, or more sophisticated transformations. For text, augmentation might include paraphrasing, back-translation, or syntactic modifications. These augmentation processes can increase dataset sizes by orders of magnitude while improving model robustness.

o **Feature engineering** for structured data requires distributed processing systems that can compute complex features across billions of records. This might involve aggregating user behavior patterns, computing time-series features, or generating interaction features between different data elements. The computational requirements for feature engineering often exceed those of the actual model training.

Storage architecture for AI training

The storage requirements for AI training workloads differ significantly from traditional analytics workloads, requiring specialized approaches to achieve the performance and scale needed for modern AI systems. In the following, we look at the strategy for dealing with the large storage requirements for AI training:

- **High-performance storage systems**:

  o **Distributed file systems** provide the foundation for storing petabyte-scale training datasets with the performance characteristics needed for distributed training. Unlike traditional databases optimized for transactional workloads, training workloads require high-throughput sequential access to large files. Amazon S3 provides the scalability needed for massive datasets, while services like Amazon FSx offer high-performance parallel file systems for compute-intensive workloads.

  o **Data locality optimization** becomes crucial when training datasets are too large to transfer repeatedly between storage and compute resources. Modern training architectures co-locate data and compute resources to minimize data transfer overhead. This might involve replicating frequently accessed data across multiple availability zones, implementing intelligent caching systems, or using container-based approaches that package data and compute together.

  o **Tiered storage management** automatically manages the lifecycle of training data across different storage tiers based on access patterns and training schedules. Actively used training data stays in high-performance storage, while historical datasets or intermediate processing results move to cost-effective archive storage. This requires automated systems that can predict training schedules and optimize storage placement accordingly.

- **Data format optimization**:

  o **Columnar formats** like Parquet provide significant advantages for training workloads that need to access subsets of features across millions of records. These formats enable efficient compression, predicate pushdown, and column pruning that can dramatically reduce I/O requirements during training. For structured data, columnar formats can reduce storage requirements by 80 to 90% compared to row-based formats while improving query performance.

  o **Specialized ML formats** like TFRecord (TensorFlow) or WebDataset provide optimized storage for machine learning workloads. These formats package training examples efficiently, support streaming access patterns, and integrate seamlessly with training frameworks. They often include built-in compression, support for complex data types like images and audio, and efficient serialization or deserialization for high-throughput training.

  o **Compression strategies** become essential when dealing with petabyte-scale datasets. Modern compression algorithms like Zstandard can reduce storage requirements by 70 to 80% while maintaining decompression performance suitable for training workloads. The choice of compression algorithm requires balancing storage savings against decompression CPU overhead and throughput requirements.

AWS services for large-scale AI training

AWS provides a comprehensive suite of services specifically designed to handle the storage, processing, and training requirements of large-scale AI workloads. In the following, we look at different AWS services categories as architecture components:

- **Storage services**:

  o **Amazon S3** serves as the foundational storage layer for AI training datasets, providing virtually unlimited capacity with multiple storage classes optimized for different access patterns. S3 Intelligent-Tiering automatically moves data between storage tiers based on access patterns, while S3 Transfer Acceleration provides high-speed data transfer for global training operations.

  o **Amazon FSx** provides high-performance parallel file systems optimized for compute-intensive workloads. FSx for Lustre can deliver hundreds of GB/s of throughput for distributed training workloads, while FSx for NetApp ONTAP provides advanced data management capabilities for complex training pipelines.

  o **Amazon EFS** offers managed NFS file systems that can scale to petabyte capacity while providing consistent performance for distributed training workloads. EFS automatically scales storage capacity and can be accessed concurrently from thousands of compute instances.

- **Processing services**:

  o **Amazon SageMaker** provides managed infrastructure for training machine learning models at scale. SageMaker handles the complexity of distributed training, including cluster management, fault tolerance, and integration with storage systems. It supports popular frameworks like TensorFlow, PyTorch, and Hugging Face while providing optimization for training performance.

  o **Amazon EMR** enables distributed processing of large datasets using frameworks like Apache Spark and Hadoop. EMR can handle the data preprocessing, feature engineering, and data preparation tasks required before training while integrating seamlessly with storage systems and training platforms.

  o **AWS Batch** provides managed batch processing for data preparation workloads that can scale to thousands of concurrent jobs. Batch handles job scheduling, resource provisioning, and fault tolerance for the data preprocessing pipelines that prepare raw data for training.

- **Specialized AI services**:

  o **Amazon Bedrock** provides managed access to foundation models that can be fine-tuned on custom datasets. This allows organizations to leverage pre-trained models as starting points for domain-specific applications, reducing the data and compute requirements for achieving high performance.

  o **Amazon Rekognition** and **Amazon Textract** provide pre-trained models for image and document analysis that can be used to preprocess training data or extract features for downstream training tasks.

  o **Amazon comprehend** offers natural language processing capabilities that can be used to preprocess text data, extract entities, or generate features for training custom models.

Implementation considerations

Successfully implementing large-scale AI training on AWS requires careful consideration of several key factors:

- **Cost management**:

  o **Spot instances** can reduce training costs by 50 to 90% by using spare AWS capacity for non-time-critical training workloads. Training jobs can be designed to checkpoint progress regularly and handle interruptions gracefully, making them well-suited for spot instance usage.

o **Reserved instances** provide significant discounts for predictable training workloads while maintaining guaranteed capacity. Organizations with regular training schedules can commit to reserved capacity for their baseline training needs while using on-demand or spot instances for additional capacity.

o **Data transfer optimization** minimizes costs by reducing unnecessary data movement between regions and services. This might involve co-locating training and storage resources, implementing intelligent caching, or using compression to reduce transfer volumes.

- **Performance optimization**:

o **Distributed training strategies** enable training across multiple machines to reduce training time for large models. This requires careful consideration of data parallelism, model parallelism, and communication patterns between training nodes.

o **I/O optimization** ensures that data loading does not become a bottleneck for training performance. This might involve implementing parallel data loading, using faster storage systems, or optimizing data formats for training frameworks.

o **Resource monitoring** provides visibility into training performance and resource utilization, enabling optimization of training pipelines and identification of bottlenecks.

- **Security and compliance**:

o **Data privacy** protects sensitive training data through encryption, access controls, and audit logging. This is particularly important when training on personal data or proprietary business information.

o **Model security** prevents unauthorized access to trained models and protects intellectual property embedded in model parameters.

o **Compliance requirements** ensure that training processes meet regulatory requirements for data handling, model governance, and audit trails.

The scale and complexity of modern AI training requirements represent a fundamental shift in data platform architecture. Organizations that successfully implement these capabilities will be positioned to leverage the full potential of AI while maintaining the operational excellence and cost-effectiveness that business success demands.

GenAI-native data platform on AWS

Building a GenAI-native data platform requires more than simply adding AI services to an existing data infrastructure. It demands a fundamental reimagining of how data flows through systems, how different services integrate, and how platforms scale to meet the unique demands of AI workloads. AWS provides the comprehensive service ecosystem needed to build these next-generation platforms, but success requires understanding how to architect these services into cohesive, scalable systems that serve both traditional analytics and cutting-edge AI applications.

This section explores the architectural patterns, service integrations, and implementation strategies for building complete GenAI-native data platforms on AWS. Rather than focusing on individual services, we examine how to combine AWS capabilities into integrated platforms that can handle the full spectrum of AI workloads while maintaining the reliability, security, and cost-effectiveness that enterprises require.

Reference architecture overview

A GenAI-native data platform on AWS combines multiple service layers into an integrated system that supports the complete AI lifecycle from data ingestion through model deployment and continuous learning. The following architecture figure illustrates what a GenAI-native data platform will look like on AWS:

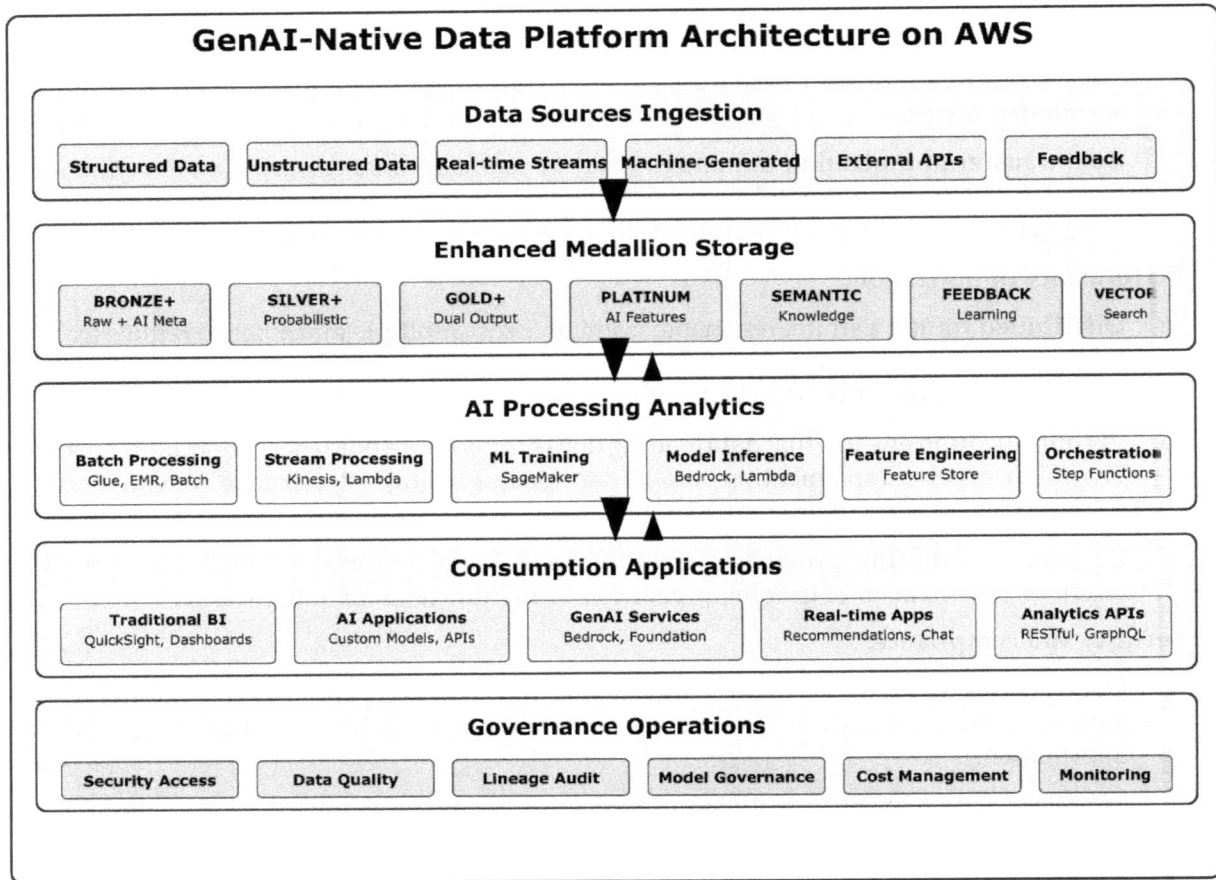

Figure 14.2: GenAI-native data platform architecture on AWS

This reference architecture demonstrates how AWS services integrate across multiple layers to create a comprehensive GenAI-native data platform. The architecture emphasizes bidirectional data flow, multi-modal processing, and integrated governance that spans both traditional analytics and AI workloads.

Core architectural principles

The GenAI-native data platform architecture is built on several core principles that differentiate it from traditional data platforms:

- **API-first design** ensures that all platform capabilities are accessible through programmatic interfaces, enabling both human users and AI systems to interact with data services seamlessly. This approach facilitates automation, integration with external systems, and the development of custom AI applications.

- **Event-driven architecture** enables real-time responsiveness to data changes, model updates, and user interactions. Rather than relying on batch processing cycles, the platform responds immediately to events, supporting real-time personalization, continuous learning, and adaptive behaviour.

- **Microservices decomposition** breaks platform functionality into specialized, independently scalable services that can evolve at different rates. This allows teams to optimize specific components for AI workloads while maintaining stability in other areas.

- **Data mesh integration** supports decentralized data ownership while maintaining platform-wide consistency and governance. Different teams can manage their domain-specific data while leveraging shared platform capabilities for AI processing and analytics.

Implementation patterns

Let us look at various implementation patterns of the GenAI-native data platform:

- **Multi-modal data ingestion**: The platform must handle diverse data types with different ingestion patterns and processing requirements:

```python
1.  # Example: Multi-modal data ingestion orchestration
2.  import boto3
3.  import json
4.  from datetime import datetime
5.
6.  class GenAIDataIngestionOrchestrator:
7.      def __init__(self):
8.          self.s3_client = boto3.client('s3')
9.          self.kinesis_client = boto3.client('kinesis')
10.         self.stepfunctions_client = boto3.client('stepfunctions')
11.         self.lambda_client = boto3.client('lambda')
12.
13.     def orchestrate_ingestion(self, data_source, content_type, metadata):
14.         """Orchestrate ingestion based on data type and requirements"""
15.
16.         ingestion_config = {
17.             'structured': self._handle_structured_data,
18.             'text': self._handle_text_data,
19.             'image': self._handle_image_data,
20.             'video': self._handle_video_data,
21.             'audio': self._handle_audio_data,
22.             'streaming': self._handle_streaming_data,
23.             'feedback': self._handle_feedback_data
24.         }
25.
26.         handler = ingestion_config.get(content_type, self._handle_generic_data)
27.         return handler(data_source, metadata)
28.
29.     def _handle_structured_data(self, data_source, metadata):
30.         """Handle structured data through traditional ETL"""
31.         workflow_input = {
32.             'data_source': data_source,
33.             'metadata': metadata,
34.             'processing_type': 'structured_etl',
35.             'target_layers': ['bronze', 'silver', 'gold']
36.         }
37.
38.         return self.stepfunctions_client.start_execution(
39.             stateMachineArn='arn:aws:states:region:account:stateMachine:StructureddDataPipeline',
40.             input=json.dumps(workflow_input)
41.         )
```

```
42.
43.    def _handle_text_data(self, data_source, metadata):
44.        """Handle text data with AI preprocessing"""
45.        workflow_input = {
46.            'data_source': data_source,
47.            'metadata': metadata,
48.            'processing_type': 'text_ai_pipeline',
49.            'target_layers': ['bronze', 'silver', 'platinum', 'semantic'],
50.            'ai_services': ['comprehend', 'bedrock_embeddings']
51.        }
52.
53.        return self.stepfunctions_client.start_execution(
54.            stateMachineArn='arn:aws:states:region:account:stateMachine:TextAIPip
    eline',
55.            input=json.dumps(workflow_input)
56.        )
57.
58.    def _handle_streaming_data(self, data_source, metadata):
59.        """Handle real-time streaming data"""
60.        # Route to appropriate Kinesis stream based on data characteristics
61.        stream_name = f"genai-stream-{metadata.get('domain', 'general')}"
62.
63.        return self.kinesis_client.put_record(
64.            StreamName=stream_name,
65.            Data=json.dumps(data_source),
66.            PartitionKey=metadata.get('partition_key', 'default')
67.        )
```

- **Unified feature store architecture**: The platform implements a unified feature store that serves both traditional ML and GenAI applications:

```
1.  class UnifiedFeatureStore:
2.      def __init__(self):
3.          self.sagemaker_client = boto3.client('sagemaker-featurestore-runtime')
4.          self.opensearch_client = boto3.client('opensearch')
5.          self.bedrock_client = boto3.client('bedrock-runtime')
6.
7.      def store_traditional_features(self, feature_group_name, features):
8.          """Store traditional ML features in SageMaker Feature Store"""
9.          records = []
10.         for feature_name, feature_value in features.items():
11.             records.append({
12.                 'FeatureName': feature_name,
13.                 'ValueAsString': str(feature_value)
14.             })
15.
16.         return self.sagemaker_client.put_record(
17.             FeatureGroupName=feature_group_name,
18.             Record=records
```

```
19.          )
20.
21.      def store_embeddings(self, index_name, document_id, content, embedding=None):
22.          """Store embeddings in OpenSearch for semantic search"""
23.          if embedding is None:
24.              embedding = self._generate_embedding(content)
25.
26.          document = {
27.              'id': document_id,
28.              'content': content,
29.              'embedding': embedding,
30.              'timestamp': datetime.utcnow().isoformat()
31.          }
32.
33.          return self.opensearch_client.index(
34.              index=index_name,
35.              body=document,
36.              id=document_id
37.          )
38.
39.      def _generate_embedding(self, content):
40.          """Generate embedding using Bedrock"""
41.          body = json.dumps({'inputText': content})
42.
43.          response = self.bedrock_client.invoke_model(
44.              body=body,
45.              modelId='amazon.titan-embed-text-v1',
46.              accept='application/json',
47.              contentType='application/json'
48.          )
49.
50.          result = json.loads(response['body'].read())
51.          return result['embedding']
```

- **Continuous learning pipeline**: The platform implements continuous learning capabilities that automatically improve models based on feedback:

```
1.  class ContinuousLearningPipeline:
2.      def __init__(self):
3.          self.sagemaker_client = boto3.client('sagemaker')
4.          self.s3_client = boto3.client('s3')
5.          self.cloudwatch_client = boto3.client('cloudwatch')
6.
7.      def monitor_model_performance(self, model_name, performance_threshold=0.85):
8.          """Monitor model performance and trigger retraining if needed"""
9.
10.         # Get current model performance metrics
11.         current_performance = self._get_model_performance(model_name)
12.
```

```python
13.          if current_performance < performance_threshold:
14.              # Trigger retraining workflow
15.              self._trigger_retraining(model_name)
16.
17.              # Update feedback layer with retraining decision
18.              self._log_retraining_decision(model_name, current_performance)
19.
20.      def _get_model_performance(self, model_name):
21.          """Get current model performance from CloudWatch"""
22.          response = self.cloudwatch_client.get_metric_statistics(
23.              Namespace='AWS/SageMaker',
24.              MetricName='ModelAccuracy',
25.              Dimensions=[{'Name': 'ModelName', 'Value': model_name}],
26.              StartTime=datetime.utcnow() - timedelta(hours=24),
27.              EndTime=datetime.utcnow(),
28.              Period=3600,
29.              Statistics=['Average']
30.          )
31.
32.          if response['Datapoints']:
33.              return response['Datapoints'][-1]['Average']
34.          return 0.0
35.
36.      def _trigger_retraining(self, model_name):
37.          """Trigger model retraining with updated data"""
38.          training_job_name = f"{model_name}-retrain-{int(datetime.utcnow().timestamp())}"
39.
40.          return self.sagemaker_client.create_training_job(
41.              TrainingJobName=training_job_name,
42.              RoleArn='arn:aws:iam::account:role/SageMakerRole',
43.              InputDataConfig=[{
44.                  'ChannelName': 'training',
45.                  'DataSource': {
46.                      'S3DataSource': {
47.                          'S3DataType': 'S3Prefix',
48.                          'S3Uri': f's3://genai-training-data/{model_name}/updated/',
49.                          'S3DataDistributionType': 'FullyReplicated'
50.                      }
51.                  }
52.              }],
53.              OutputDataConfig={
54.                  'S3OutputPath': f's3://genai-models/{model_name}/retrained/'
55.              },
56.              ResourceConfig={
57.                  'InstanceType': 'ml.p3.2xlarge',
58.                  'InstanceCount': 1,
```

```
59.                    'VolumeSizeInGB': 30
60.              },
61.              StoppingCondition={'MaxRuntimeInSeconds': 86400}
62.          )
```

Service integration patterns

For a large-scale AI system, besides data integration, we also need orchestration between the services. In the following, we illustrate approaches and patterns for service integration:

- **Cross-service communication**: The platform implements sophisticated communication patterns between AWS services to enable seamless data flow and processing coordination:

  o **EventBridge integration** coordinates events across services, enabling loose coupling and event-driven processing. When new data arrives in S3, EventBridge can trigger processing workflows, update downstream systems, and notify relevant services without tight coupling.

  o **Step Functions orchestration** manages complex workflows that span multiple services and processing steps. This is particularly important for AI workflows that might involve data preprocessing, model training, validation, and deployment steps that need to be coordinated across different services.

  o **Lambda-based microservices** provide lightweight, event-driven processing capabilities that can respond to data changes, user requests, or system events with minimal overhead. Lambda functions serve as the glue between different services, implementing custom logic that bridges service gaps.

- **Data consistency and synchronization**: Maintaining data consistency across the enhanced medallion architecture requires sophisticated synchronization patterns:

  o **Eventually consistent updates** acknowledge that some data consistency can be relaxed in favor of availability and partition tolerance. For example, embedding updates might not be immediately consistent across all systems, but eventual consistency is acceptable for many AI applications.

  o **Transactional boundaries** identify where strong consistency is required and implement appropriate coordination mechanisms. Financial calculations, audit trails, and regulatory reporting require transactional consistency even in AI-native platforms.

  o **Conflict resolution** handles cases where different systems generate conflicting updates to the same data. This might involve timestamp-based resolution, business rule-based prioritization, or manual intervention for critical conflicts.

Performance and scalability considerations

In the demanding world of AI infrastructure, performance and scalability considerations extend far beyond traditional IT optimization metrics, requiring a delicate balance between compute power, storage efficiency, and cost management. Modern AI systems must seamlessly handle massive training workloads while simultaneously serving real-time inference requests, demanding sophisticated resource management strategies that can dynamically adapt to varying demands. In the following, we illustrate a strategy for various performance and scalability considerations:

- **Compute optimization**:

  o **Auto-scaling policies** automatically adjust compute resources based on workload demands, accounting for the variable and often unpredictable nature of AI workloads. Training jobs might require significant compute resources for hours or days, while inference workloads can spike dramatically based on user demand.

o **GPU resource management** optimizes the allocation and utilization of expensive GPU resources across different workloads. This includes intelligent scheduling of training jobs, efficient sharing of GPU resources between different models, and automatic scaling of inference endpoints based on demand.

o **Serverless-first architecture** leverages serverless services where possible to minimize operational overhead and optimize costs. Lambda functions, serverless databases, and managed services reduce the infrastructure management burden while providing automatic scaling.

- **Storage performance:**

o **Multi-tier storage strategy** automatically moves data between different storage tiers based on access patterns, performance requirements, and cost considerations. Frequently accessed training data stays in high-performance storage, while archived models and historical data move to cost-effective storage tiers.

o **Caching layers** implement intelligent caching at multiple levels to reduce latency and improve performance. This includes caching of frequently accessed features, model predictions, and pre-processed data that can be reused across different applications.

o **Data locality optimization** ensures that compute and storage resources are co-located to minimize data transfer latency and costs. This is particularly important for large-scale training workloads where data movement can become a significant bottleneck.

Security and governance integration

As AI systems become increasingly central to business operations, security and governance considerations must be woven deeply into the fabric of data platform architecture, not added as an afterthought. The sensitive nature of AI training data, combined with the complex interactions between various platform components, demands a sophisticated approach to security that spans identity management, data protection, and compliance monitoring. This comprehensive security framework must balance robust protection measures with the need for efficient data access and processing that AI workloads require. In the following, we have discussed security postures:

- **Identity and access management:**

o **Fine-grained permissions** implement least-privilege access controls that account for the different access patterns of human users, AI systems, and automated processes. This includes role-based access control, attribute-based access control, and dynamic permissions based on context.

o **Service-to-service authentication** secures communication between different platform components using IAM roles, service-linked roles, and cross-service authentication mechanisms. This ensures that only authorized services can access specific data and functionality.

o **Audit and compliance** maintain comprehensive audit trails that track all data access, model training, and prediction activities. This supports regulatory compliance, security investigations, and operational troubleshooting.

- **Data protection:**

o **Encryption at rest and in transit** protects sensitive data throughout its lifecycle using AWS-managed encryption services. This includes S3 encryption, database encryption, and encrypted communication between services.

o **Data masking and anonymization** protect sensitive information in training datasets and analytics workloads. This might involve automatic detection and masking of personal information, synthetic data generation, or differential privacy techniques.

o **Backup and recovery** ensure that critical data and models can be recovered in case of failures or disasters. This includes automated backup of training data, model artifacts, and configuration information.

The GenAI-native data platform on AWS represents a comprehensive approach to building a modern data infrastructure that can support both traditional analytics and cutting-edge AI applications. By leveraging AWS's broad service ecosystem and implementing sophisticated integration patterns, organizations can create platforms that scale to meet growing AI demands while maintaining the reliability and governance standards required for enterprise operations.

Challenges, solutions, and future outlook

The transformation to GenAI-native data platforms represents one of the most significant shifts in data engineering since the advent of cloud computing. While the opportunities are immense, organizations face substantial challenges in implementing these new architectures, managing the complexity of probabilistic systems, and ensuring that AI capabilities deliver sustainable business value. Understanding these challenges and their solutions is crucial for successful adoption, while anticipating future developments enables organizations to build platforms that can evolve with the rapidly changing AI landscape.

This section examines the most significant challenges organizations encounter when building GenAI-native data platforms, provides practical solutions based on real-world implementations, and explores the future trends that will shape the next generation of data engineering practices. The goal is to help organizations navigate current obstacles while positioning themselves to capitalize on emerging opportunities.

Technical challenges and solutions

Organizations implementing GenAI-native data platforms encounter five primary technical challenges that require specialized solutions different from traditional data engineering approaches. These challenges stem from the fundamental differences between deterministic and probabilistic systems, the massive scale requirements of AI workloads, and the complexity of integrating traditional and AI-native capabilities. Refer to the following table:

Challenge	Impact	Solution approach
Data quality at scale	85% of AI projects fail due to data quality issues	Hierarchical quality assessment, ML-based anomaly detection, progressive validation
Model reliability	67% of AI models degrade within 6 months	Continuous monitoring, graceful degradation, A/B testing validation
Integration complexity	40% of development time spent on integration	Microservices architecture, service mesh, event-driven patterns
Scalability challenges	Resource waste and performance bottlenecks	Intelligent auto-scaling, workload-aware scheduling, elastic resource management
Security and privacy	Regulatory violations and reputational damage	Comprehensive AI security frameworks, privacy-preserving techniques, and robust access controls

Table 15.3: Technical challenges and solution approaches for GenAI-native data platforms

Organizational challenges and solutions

Beyond the technical complexities of implementing GenAI-native data platforms, organizations face equally significant challenges in managing the human, cultural, and procedural aspects of transformation. These organizational challenges often prove more difficult to address than technical issues, as they require fundamental changes in how teams work, make decisions, and approach data management. Successfully navigating these challenges requires systematic approaches to change management, skills development, and governance evolution.

Skills and knowledge gaps

The shift to GenAI-native platforms requires new skills that blend traditional data engineering with AI or ML expertise. Organizations struggle to find talent with the necessary combination of skills and existing teams need significant upskilling. Skills gaps lead to delayed implementations, suboptimal architectures, and increased reliance on external consultants. The shortage of qualified professionals can increase project costs by 30 to 50%. Refer to the following table:

Role	Core competencies	Learning timeline
Traditional data engineers	Probabilistic thinking, vector databases, feature engineering	three to six months of intensive, more than six months of application
AI/ML engineers	Data architecture, ETL/ELT pipelines, data governance	two to four months of architecture, more than four months of implementation
Business analysts	AI/ML concepts, model interpretation, data-driven decisions	one to two months concepts, more than an ongoing application

Table 15.4: Skills development requirements for GenAI-native data platform implementation

Change management and adoption

Moving from deterministic to probabilistic systems requires significant cultural change. Organizations struggle with the mindset shift from seeking perfect answers to embracing uncertainty and continuous learning. Resistance to change can delay implementations, reduce adoption rates, and limit business value. Studies show that 70% of AI transformations fail due to organizational resistance rather than technical challenges.

The most successful implementations follow a phased adoption strategy: Awareness phase (months one to two) focuses on education about AI capabilities and limitations, pilot phase (months three to six) implements small-scale projects with clear success metrics, expansion phase (months 7 to 12) enables broader rollout with lessons learned integration, and optimization phase (months 13 and more) drives continuous improvement and advanced capabilities.

Governance and compliance

Traditional data governance frameworks do not adequately address AI-specific requirements like model fairness, explainability, and bias detection. Organizations must develop new governance approaches while maintaining compliance with existing regulations. Inadequate governance leads to regulatory violations, ethical issues, and loss of stakeholder trust. Organizations face potential fines, legal challenges, and reputational damage from poorly governed AI systems.

Best practices include establishing AI ethics committees with diverse stakeholders, implementing automated bias detection and fairness monitoring, creating clear documentation and audit trails for all AI decisions, developing model interpretability standards and tooling, and conducting regular compliance reviews and governance framework updates.

Future outlook and emerging trends

The evolution of GenAI-native data platforms will be shaped by five major technological trends that promise to transform how organizations process, store, and analyze data. Understanding these trends and their potential timelines enables strategic planning and investment decisions that position organizations for future success. The following figure maps these trends across time horizons and impact levels, providing a framework for prioritizing preparation efforts:

Future Trends in GenAI-Native Data Platforms

| Now | 2-3 Years | 3-5 Years | 5-10 Years | 10+ Years |

Edge AI Distributed Intelligence
- Local AI processing
- Reduced latency

Autonomous Data Platforms
- Self-optimizing systems
- Predictive maintenance

Neuromorphic Computing
- Brain-inspired chips
- Ultra-low power

Federated Learning
- Privacy-preserving AI
- Distributed training
- Regulatory compliance

Quantum-Enhanced Processing
- Exponential speedup
- Optimization problems

Organizations should prioritize preparation for high-impact, near-term trends

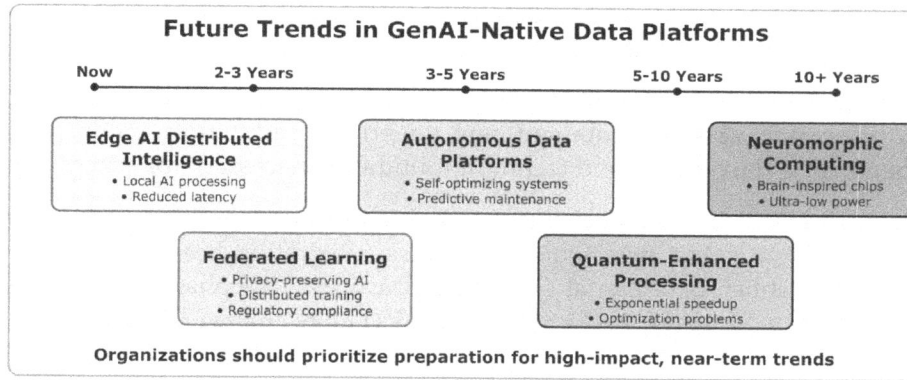

Figure 14.3: GenAI data platform evolution timeline roadmap

The future of GenAI-native data platforms will be shaped by several converging technological trends that promise to dramatically enhance capabilities while introducing new challenges. **Edge AI and distributed intelligence** represent the most immediate opportunity, with rapid adoption already occurring as organizations seek to reduce latency and enhance privacy through local processing. This trend will fundamentally change data platform architectures, requiring new approaches to distributed model management and hybrid cloud-edge data flows.

Autonomous data platforms will emerge as AI systems become sophisticated enough to manage their own infrastructure, optimize performance, and make operational decisions with minimal human intervention. This evolution will dramatically reduce operational overhead while enabling more responsive and adaptive data systems. However, it will also require new governance frameworks and oversight mechanisms to ensure autonomous systems operate within acceptable parameters and business objectives.

The longer-term prospects include **quantum-enhanced processing** and **neuromorphic computing**, which promise to revolutionize data processing capabilities. While these technologies are still in early stages, their potential impact on AI training, optimization problems, and real-time processing will require a fundamental rethinking of data platform architectures. Organizations should monitor these developments closely while focusing their immediate efforts on more mature technologies that can deliver near-term value.

Strategic recommendations

Successful transformation to GenAI-native data platforms requires a systematic, phased approach that balances innovation with operational stability. The following figure provides a strategic roadmap framework for organizations to plan and execute their GenAI transformation while managing risks and maximizing return on investment. This roadmap emphasizes incremental progress, continuous learning, and adaptability to changing requirements.

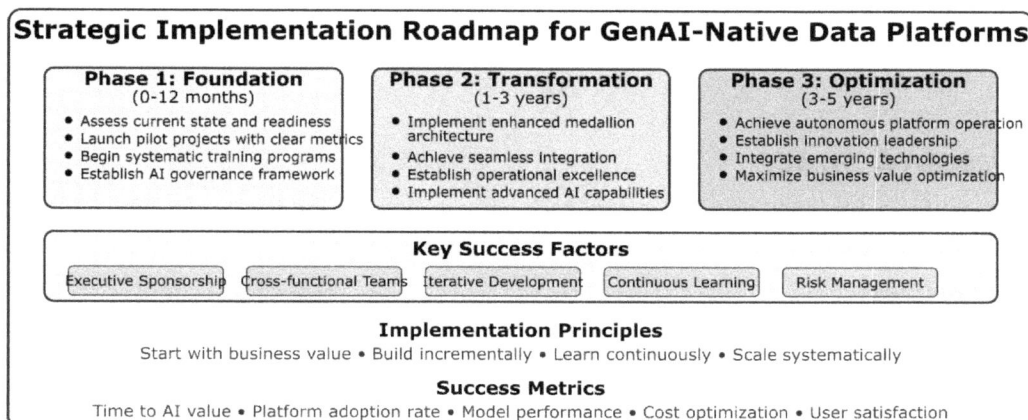

Strategic Implementation Roadmap for GenAI-Native Data Platforms

Phase 1: Foundation (0-12 months)
- Assess current state and readiness
- Launch pilot projects with clear metrics
- Begin systematic training programs
- Establish AI governance framework

Phase 2: Transformation (1-3 years)
- Implement enhanced medallion architecture
- Achieve seamless integration
- Establish operational excellence
- Implement advanced AI capabilities

Phase 3: Optimization (3-5 years)
- Achieve autonomous platform operation
- Establish innovation leadership
- Integrate emerging technologies
- Maximize business value optimization

Key Success Factors

Executive Sponsorship | Cross-functional Teams | Iterative Development | Continuous Learning | Risk Management

Implementation Principles
Start with business value • Build incrementally • Learn continuously • Scale systematically

Success Metrics
Time to AI value • Platform adoption rate • Model performance • Cost optimization • User satisfaction

Figure 14.4: GenAI platform implementation strategy and timeline

The strategic implementation of GenAI-native data platforms requires a systematic, phased approach that balances innovation with operational stability:

- **Phase 1 (Foundation)** focuses on building organizational readiness through current state assessment, pilot project execution, skill development, and governance establishment. This foundational phase is critical for creating the cultural and technical foundation necessary for successful transformation.

- **Phase 2 (Transformation)** represents the core implementation period where organizations deploy enhanced medallion architectures, achieve seamless integration between traditional and AI-native capabilities, and establish operational excellence practices. This phase requires the most significant investment in both technology and organizational change management but delivers the primary business value from GenAI capabilities.

- **Phase 3 (Optimization)** enables organizations to achieve autonomous platform operation, establish innovation leadership, and maximize business value through continuous optimization. Success in this phase depends on the strong foundation established in earlier phases and represents the full realization of GenAI-native data platform potential.

Conclusion

The GenAI revolution in data engineering represents a fundamental transformation that extends far beyond adding AI capabilities to existing data platforms. The shift from human-centric to AI-native systems requires rethinking every aspect of data architecture, from storage and processing patterns to quality management and governance frameworks. Organizations that embrace this transformation thoughtfully and systematically will position themselves to capitalize on unprecedented opportunities for innovation, efficiency, and competitive advantage through enhanced medallion architectures, probabilistic data processing, and AI-native operational practices.

The most successful path forward involves systematic planning, gradual implementation, and continuous learning from both successes and failures. Organizations that can harness the power of AI as a fundamental capability embedded throughout their data infrastructure—rather than merely as an application or tool—will shape the future of data-driven business success. As organizations embark on this transformation journey, they must also prepare for the broader evolution of data platforms beyond GenAI capabilities, ensuring their investments remain valuable as new technologies emerge and business requirements continue to evolve.

The next chapter will examine emerging trends in data engineering, serverless architectures, AI-driven operations, and sustainable practices that will shape the next generation of data platforms. It will provide practical frameworks for evaluating new technologies, managing technical evolution, and building resilient architectures that can adapt to changing requirements while maintaining operational stability.

Join our Discord space

Join our Discord workspace for latest updates, offers, tech happenings around the world, new releases, and sessions with the authors:

https://discord.bpbonline.com

CHAPTER 15

Future-Proofing Data Platforms

Introduction

The data engineering landscape continues to evolve at an unprecedented pace, driven by technological innovation, changing business requirements, and the relentless pursuit of operational efficiency. While *Chapter 14, GenAI Revolution in Data Engineering* explored how GenAI is transforming data platforms today, this chapter looks beyond the current GenAI revolution to examine the broader trends and technologies that will shape the future of data engineering. Organizations that successfully navigate this evolution will not only adapt to change but will anticipate and leverage emerging capabilities to maintain competitive advantage.

The challenge of future-proofing data platforms extends beyond simply adopting new technologies. It requires building architectures that can evolve gracefully, operational practices that embrace continuous learning, and governance frameworks that adapt to changing regulatory landscapes. Modern data platforms must be simultaneously stable enough to support critical business operations and flexible enough to incorporate breakthrough technologies as they mature. This balance between stability and adaptability defines the core challenge of contemporary data engineering.

This chapter provides practical frameworks for evaluating emerging technologies, implementing serverless architectures that scale automatically, leveraging AI for platform operations, and building sustainable data practices that optimize both cost and environmental impact. Rather than focusing on speculative future technologies, we emphasize proven approaches for building resilient, extensible platforms that can incorporate new capabilities without requiring complete rebuilds. The goal is to equip data engineering teams with the knowledge and tools needed to build platforms that remain valuable and effective as the technological landscape continues to evolve.

Through concrete implementation examples, cost-benefit analysis frameworks, and migration strategies, this chapter demonstrates how to make informed decisions about technology adoption while maintaining the operational excellence that business success demands.

Structure

This chapter covers the following topics:

- Emerging trends in data engineering
- Serverless data platforms

- AI-driven data engineering
- Sustainability in data engineering
- Building resilient architectures

Objectives

This chapter aims to provide a forward-looking perspective on data platform evolution and practical strategies for creating adaptable architectures. You will learn to identify significant emerging trends that will impact data engineering practices and evaluate their potential business value and implementation feasibility. The chapter explores architectural approaches for designing flexible data platforms that can incorporate new capabilities with minimal disruption, including patterns for modularity, abstraction, and extensibility. Through practical examples and implementation guidance, you will understand how to balance innovation with stability, ensuring your data platform can evolve continuously while maintaining reliable operations. These capabilities will enable you to build future-ready data architectures that deliver immediate business value while positioning your organization to capitalize on emerging opportunities in the rapidly evolving data landscape.

Emerging trends in data engineering

The data engineering landscape is undergoing several fundamental shifts that will redefine how we build, operate, and scale data platforms in the coming years. Understanding these trends enables architects to design platforms that anticipate future requirements rather than reacting to them after they become urgent business needs. The following figure illustrates the transition from standard data engineering practices to AI-driven data engineering practices:

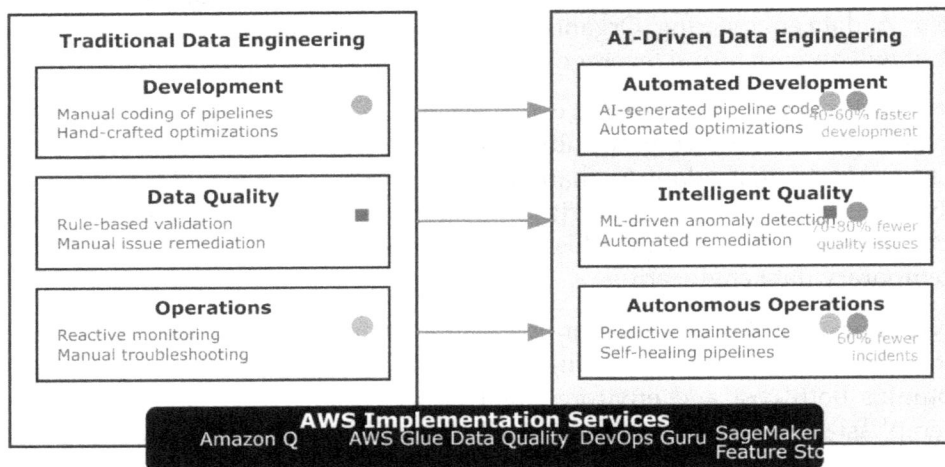

Figure 15.1: AI-driven data engineering trend

The transformation illustrated in *Figure 15.1* represents the journey from traditional, monolithic data architectures toward more flexible, resilient, and automated platforms. This evolution encompasses several key trends that collectively reshape how organizations approach data engineering:

- **Decomposition of monoliths** into modular, specialized components that can evolve independently. Unlike traditional platforms where upgrading one component often required system-wide changes, modern architectures employ clear interfaces and separation of concerns that enable targeted improvements without cascading disruption.

- **Shift from provisioned to on-demand resources** that scale automatically with workload requirements. This transition eliminates both the waste of over-provisioning and the performance risks of under-provisioning, creating more efficient and responsive data platforms.

- **Increased automation** across the entire data lifecycle, reducing manual intervention while improving consistency and reliability. Automated processes replace human-intensive activities in everything from infrastructure management to data quality validation to operational monitoring.

- **Distributed ownership models** that align data responsibility with domain expertise rather than centralizing all data functions. This organizational shift creates clearer accountability for data quality and relevance while enabling greater agility through parallel, independent development.

- **Intelligence embedding** throughout the data platform, leveraging machine learning to automate decisions previously requiring human judgment. This trend extends beyond using ML for data analysis to employing it for platform operations, optimization, and governance.

These trends do not exist in isolation but rather reinforce each other, collectively driving the evolution toward more adaptable, efficient, and resilient data platforms. The following sections explore these transformative shifts in detail, examining both their architectural implications and implementation considerations for AWS-based data platforms.

Serverless data platforms

The transition to serverless represents one of the most significant architectural shifts in data engineering, fundamentally changing how we design, deploy, and operate data platforms. Unlike traditional approaches that required provisioning and managing infrastructure for peak capacity, serverless architectures dynamically allocate resources as needed, automatically scaling to match workload demands while charging only for resources consumed. The following figure illustrates the reference architecture for a serverless data platform built on AWS:

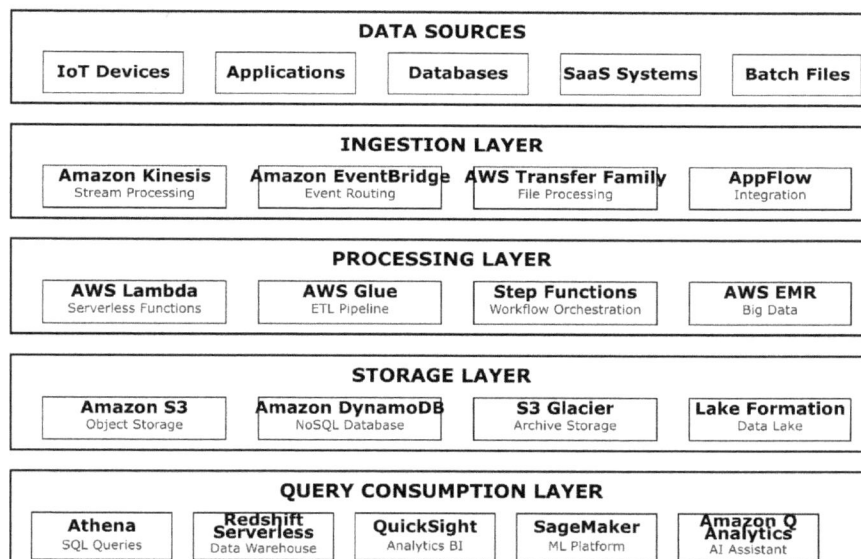

Figure 15.2: Serverless data platform architecture on AWS

Architectural components

As illustrated in *Figure 15.2*, modern serverless data platforms on AWS leverage specialized services across each layer of the data lifecycle:

- **Ingestion layer**: The ingestion layer captures data from various sources and prepares it for processing without maintaining persistent infrastructure:

  o **Amazon Kinesis Data Firehose** provides fully managed, serverless data delivery without capacity planning or management overhead. It automatically scales to handle gigabytes per second of streaming data while managing buffering, batching, and compression for optimal delivery.

- o **Amazon EventBridge** enables event-driven data ingestion through a serverless event bus that connects applications with data sources using custom or partner events. This service eliminates the need to build and maintain event-routing infrastructure while providing sophisticated filtering and transformation capabilities.

- o **AWS Transfer Family** offers fully managed file transfer services that seamlessly integrate with existing workflows using SFTP, FTPS, and FTP protocols. These services automatically scale to handle varying throughput requirements without provisioning or managing servers.

- **Processing layer**: The processing layer transforms raw data into analytics-ready formats without maintaining persistent compute resources:

  - o **AWS Lambda** executes code in response to events without provisioning or managing servers. For data platforms, Lambda excels at event-driven preprocessing, validation, and routing for small to medium-sized records, automatically scaling from a few requests per day to thousands per second.

  - o **AWS Glue** provides serverless **extract, transform, and load** (ETL) capabilities that automatically provision and scale resources based on workload requirements. Unlike traditional ETL tools that required dedicated servers or clusters, Glue allocates resources on demand and releases them when processing completes.

  - o **AWS Step Functions** coordinates multiple processing steps into sophisticated workflows without managing orchestration infrastructure. This service handles state management, error handling, and retry logic for complex data pipelines while integrating natively with other AWS services.

- **Storage layer**: The storage layer maintains data without provisioning capacity or managing storage servers:

  - o **Amazon S3** provides virtually unlimited, automatically scaling object storage with multiple storage classes optimized for different access patterns. Features like S3 Intelligent-Tiering automatically move objects between storage tiers based on usage patterns, eliminating manual data lifecycle management.

  - o **Amazon DynamoDB** offers serverless NoSQL database capabilities with automatic scaling and per-request pricing options. For data platforms, DynamoDB excels at storing metadata, processing state, and serving low-latency data access without capacity planning or cluster management.

  - o **Amazon S3 Glacier** provides automated archival storage for long-term retention of infrequently accessed data. This service integrates with S3 Lifecycle policies to automatically transition data based on age or access patterns, eliminating manual archival processes.

- **Query layer**: The query layer enables analytics without managing query infrastructure:

  - o **Amazon Athena** provides serverless SQL query capabilities against data stored in S3, automatically parallelizing queries and scaling resources based on data volume and query complexity. This service eliminates the need to load data into specialized analytical systems while providing standard SQL access.

  - o **Amazon Redshift Serverless** delivers data warehousing without cluster management, automatically scaling compute resources based on workload demands. Unlike traditional data warehouses that required careful capacity planning, Redshift Serverless adjusts resources in seconds to maintain performance as concurrency and complexity change.

  - o **Amazon QuickSight** offers serverless business intelligence with capacity that automatically scales based on user activity. This service eliminates the infrastructure typically required for visualization systems while providing pay-per-session pricing that aligns costs with actual usage.

Implementation considerations

While serverless architectures offer significant advantages, they also introduce new design considerations that architects must address:

- **State management strategies**: Without persistent infrastructure, state management requires explicit design rather than relying on local storage:

    o **Externalize state** to durable services like DynamoDB or S3 rather than maintaining state in compute environments that may terminate. For example, AWS Glue job bookmarks track processing progress in a managed service rather than within the processing environment, enabling consistent resumption even when resources change between executions.

    o **Implement checkpointing** at appropriate intervals to enable efficient recovery and partial reprocessing. Services like Kinesis Data Analytics provide automatic checkpointing capabilities that maintain processing state without developer intervention, while Step Functions maintains execution state throughout long-running workflows.

    o **Leverage managed workflow services** that handle state persistence automatically. AWS Step Functions maintains execution state throughout complex workflows, tracking exactly which steps have completed and which remain, even for processes spanning days or weeks.

- **Cost optimization approaches**: Serverless pricing models require different optimization strategies than traditional infrastructure:

    o **Optimize processing efficiency** to reduce execution time rather than increasing utilization of provisioned resources. For Lambda functions and Glue jobs, this means minimizing unnecessary processing, optimizing memory allocation, and structuring code for efficient execution rather than maximizing throughput on fixed resources.

    o **Implement appropriate batching** to balance processing efficiency with latency requirements. While processing records individually might provide lower latency, batching multiple records into a single function invocation typically reduces overall cost by amortizing the fixed costs of function initialization across multiple records.

    o **Configure resource release** to avoid idle resources that continue to accrue charges. Services like AWS Glue provide worker timeout settings that automatically terminate resources after a specified idle period, preventing unnecessary costs while maintaining availability for active workloads.

Integration patterns

Serverless architectures typically employ event-driven, loosely coupled integration patterns:

- **Design for idempotence** to handle potential duplicate processing without side effects. Since serverless architectures often use event-driven integration with at-least-once delivery guarantees, components must safely handle repeated processing of the same event without creating duplicate data or inconsistent state.

- **Implement asynchronous messaging** rather than synchronous API calls for cross-component communication. Services like SNS and SQS provide managed message delivery that decouples components while handling backpressure, retry logic, and scaling automatically, creating more resilient integration patterns.

- **Leverage event-driven architectures** that react to changes rather than polling for updates. Services like EventBridge enable sophisticated event routing without custom infrastructure, automatically invoking appropriate processing based on event patterns while maintaining loose coupling between components.

A major retail organization implemented this serverless approach for their product catalog processing, reducing operational costs by 60% compared to their previous server-based architecture. Their implementation used S3 for storage, Lambda for initial validation and routing, Step Functions to coordinate processing steps, Glue for complex transformations, and Athena for ad-hoc analysis. This architecture automatically scaled to handle seasonal demand spikes during holiday periods without capacity planning, while eliminating infrastructure management overhead that previously consumed 30% of their engineering capacity.

AI-driven data engineering

Artificial intelligence is transforming data engineering from a discipline that merely serves AI applications into one that is itself enhanced by AI capabilities. This shift represents a fundamental evolution where AI technologies are embedded throughout the data engineering lifecycle, automating routine tasks while enabling engineers to focus on higher-value activities.

This transformation is creating intelligent data platforms that can self-optimize, self-heal, and continuously adapt to changing business requirements without constant human oversight. Data engineering teams are evolving from builders and maintainers of static infrastructure to orchestrators of intelligent systems that learn and improve over time. The result is a new paradigm where data platforms become increasingly autonomous, reliable, and capable of handling complexity at unprecedented scales.

Core applications of AI in data engineering

The integration of AI into data engineering manifests across four primary dimensions:

- **Automated development** accelerates pipeline creation through AI-assisted coding and configuration. Rather than writing each transformation and pipeline component manually, AI systems generate optimized implementations from high-level specifications, reducing development time by 40-60% for common patterns.

- **Intelligent operations** transform reactive monitoring into predictive maintenance through AI systems that anticipate failures, automatically remediate issues, and continuously optimize resource utilization without human intervention.

- **Enhanced data quality** moves beyond rule-based validation to AI systems that understand data semantics, automatically detect anomalies in complex patterns, and identify quality issues that traditional approaches would miss entirely.

- **Dynamic governance** replaces static policies with adaptive systems that automatically classify sensitive data, apply appropriate controls based on context, and maintain comprehensive lineage without manual documentation effort.

Implementation approaches on AWS

AWS provides several practical services and patterns for implementing AI-driven data engineering capabilities. Refer to the following table:

AWS service	Key capabilities	Implementation considerations	Business impact
Amazon Q for developers	<ul><li>Architecture and solution design assistance</li><li>Data pipeline code generation</li><li>IaC assistance</li><li>Automated documentation generation</li></ul>	<ul><li>Start with well-defined, scoped requests</li><li>Review and validate generated code for AWS best practices</li><li>Incrementally adopt for specific pipeline components before wider implementation</li></ul>	<ul><li>40-60% reduction in development time</li><li>Decreased ramp-up time for new team members</li><li>More consistent implementation of best practices</li></ul>

AWS service	Key capabilities	Implementation considerations	Business impact
AWS Glue data quality	• ML-powered data profiling • Automated anomaly detection • Relationship intelligence across datasets • Adaptive rule generation	• Begin with a hybrid approach (rules + ML) • Train on clean datasets to establish baselines • Implement feedback loops to improve detection accuracy	• 70-80% reduction in undetected data quality issues • 50% decrease in time spent creating and maintaining quality rules • Earlier detection of data issues
Amazon DevOps Guru for data pipelines	• Predictive failure detection • Root cause analysis • Automated remediation recommendations • Workload-specific insights	• Deploy first in non-critical environments • Configure service role with appropriate permissions • Integrate alerts with existing operational tools	• 35-50% reduction in MTTR for pipeline issues • 60% decrease in pipeline failures • Shift from reactive to proactive operations
Aurora/ Redshift with ML optimization	• Adaptive query optimization • Automatic performance tuning • Resource utilization optimization • Workload-specific configuration	• Ensure monitoring is in place to verify improvements • Gradually enable advanced features • Combine with traditional performance tuning	• 30-45% query performance improvement • Reduced manual tuning effort • More consistent performance under varying loads
SageMaker Feature Store for data engineers	• Automated feature generation • Feature discovery and reuse • Drift detection and monitoring • Feature quality validation	• Define clear feature ownership boundaries • Implement feature approval workflows • Start with an offline feature store before real-time	• 60% reduction in duplicate feature creation • Improved model performance through better features • Faster time-to-market for ML products

Table 15.1: AWS AI services for data engineering

Organizations that successfully implement AI-driven data engineering transform not just their technology but their entire approach to building and operating data platforms. Rather than seeing AI as a separate tool, they integrate it as a collaborative partner throughout the data engineering lifecycle, from design to development to operations. This integration enables them to operate at scales and speeds that would be impossible with traditional approaches, creating data platforms that continuously evolve to meet changing business requirements with minimal human intervention.

Sustainability in data engineering

Data platforms have traditionally been designed with performance, cost, and reliability as primary considerations, often treating energy consumption and environmental impact as secondary concerns.

However, as data volumes grow exponentially and computing requirements increase, sustainability has emerged as a critical design consideration for modern data architectures. Organizations now recognize that environmentally responsible data engineering not only supports corporate social responsibility goals but also delivers tangible business benefits through reduced operational costs and improved resource efficiency.

Sustainable data engineering focuses on minimizing the environmental footprint of data operations while maintaining performance and reliability. This approach requires rethinking fundamental aspects of data platform design, from storage optimization and compute resource allocation to workload scheduling and retention policies. AWS has made sustainability a core pillar of its cloud infrastructure, providing services and features that enable data engineers to build more energy-efficient and environmentally responsible data platforms.

Business case for sustainable data engineering

Sustainability initiatives in data engineering deliver value across multiple dimensions:

- **Cost optimization** directly correlates with reduced energy consumption. By designing more efficient data platforms, organizations typically achieve a 20% to 40% reduction in compute costs and a 30% to 50% reduction in storage costs. These efficiency improvements translate directly to lower operational expenses, creating a clear business incentive for sustainable practices.

- **Regulatory compliance** requirements increasingly include environmental impact reporting. Organizations across industries face growing pressure to measure and reduce their carbon footprint, with data operations often representing a significant component of overall IT energy consumption. Proactively implementing sustainable practices helps organizations prepare for current and future regulatory requirements.

- **Brand reputation** benefits accrue to organizations demonstrating environmental leadership. As consumers and business partners increasingly factor environmental responsibility into their decision-making, sustainable data practices become a competitive differentiator. Organizations that can demonstrate concrete steps toward reducing the environmental impact of their data operations gain reputational advantages in the marketplace.

- **Operational resilience** improves through more efficient resource utilization. Sustainable architectures typically incorporate more granular scaling, intelligent workload distribution, and improved resource management, enhancing overall platform resilience during demand spikes or service disruptions.

Sustainable design patterns on AWS

AWS provides several architectural patterns and services that enable sustainable data engineering practices. These patterns focus on optimizing resource utilization, reducing energy consumption, and minimizing environmental impact while maintaining high performance and reliability. By implementing these sustainable approaches, organizations can significantly reduce their carbon footprint while often achieving cost savings and improved operational efficiency. The key to successful sustainable data engineering lies in understanding that environmental responsibility and business value are not competing priorities but complementary objectives that reinforce each other.

Right-sized storage hierarchy

Traditional approaches often store all data in high-performance tiers regardless of access patterns, leading to unnecessary energy consumption and costs. A more sustainable approach implements a multi-tiered storage hierarchy that aligns storage characteristics with actual access patterns. Refer to the following table:

Storage tier	AWS service	Access pattern	Sustainability benefits
Hot tier	S3 Standard	Frequently accessed data (daily or weekly)	• Minimize to only active datasets • Use columnar formats like Parquet or ORC • Implement compression (30% to 90% reduction)
Warm tier	S3 Intelligent-Tiering	Variable or unpredictable access	• Automatic migration between tiers • No performance penalty for accessed data • 30% to 40% cost/energy reduction vs Standard
Cool tier	S3 Standard-IA	Occasional access (monthly)	• 40% energy reduction vs Standard • Minimal retrieval overhead • Ideal for infrequent analytics
Cold tier	S3 Glacier Instant Retrieval	Rare access (quarterly)	• 60% energy reduction vs Standard • Millisecond retrieval • Suitable for compliance data
Archive tier	S3 Glacier Deep Archive	Almost never accessed	• 90% and above energy reduction vs Standard • Hours retrieval latency • Perfect for regulatory archives

Table 15.2: AWS storage tiers for sustainable access

Implementing this pattern requires more than simply enabling lifecycle policies. Sustainable implementations analyse data access patterns to determine optimal placement, use comprehensive metadata to maintain accessibility, and align retention policies with actual business value rather than defaulting to indefinite storage. Data engineers should establish clear transitions between tiers based on data age, access frequency, and business criticality.

Compute efficiency optimization

Compute resources typically represent the largest component of a data platform's energy footprint. Sustainable data platforms implement several key patterns to minimize unnecessary resource consumption:

- **Serverless prioritization** eliminates idle resource consumption by utilizing services that scale to zero when not in use. AWS Lambda, AWS Glue serverless, Amazon Athena, and other serverless offerings consume energy only during actual processing, reducing the overall carbon footprint compared to continuously running instances. This approach is particularly valuable for workloads with variable or unpredictable execution patterns.

- **Graviton processor adoption** delivers up to 60% better energy efficiency compared to equivalent x86-based instances. AWS's Graviton processors, built on ARM architecture, provide significant sustainability benefits while maintaining or improving performance for most data workloads. Data engineering teams should evaluate Graviton instances for their ETL processes, data processing, and analytics workloads to reduce energy consumption without sacrificing performance.

- **Spot instance utilization** for non-time-critical workloads improves overall infrastructure efficiency. By using spare capacity that would otherwise remain idle, Spot instances effectively increase the utilization rate of existing infrastructure, reducing the need for additional resource provisioning. Data pipelines for non-urgent batch processing, data preparation, and analytical workloads can be designed to utilize spot instances, incorporating appropriate checkpointing and retry logic to handle potential interruptions.

Workload scheduling optimization

When and how data processing occurs significantly impacts energy consumption. Sustainable data platforms implement intelligent scheduling patterns:

- **Carbon-aware computing** schedules non-time-sensitive workloads during periods of lower grid carbon intensity or higher renewable energy availability. By shifting flexible workloads to times when the electricity supply has a lower carbon footprint, organizations can reduce the environmental impact of their data operations without changing the actual processing performed.

  AWS provides carbon footprint monitoring tools that enable organizations to understand their emissions patterns, though the direct scheduling of workloads based on carbon intensity currently requires custom implementations using AWS native scheduling capabilities like EventBridge, Step Functions, or Managed Workflows for Apache Airflow.

- **Workload consolidation** runs multiple smaller jobs together rather than distributing them across time. This approach improves resource utilization and reduces the startup or shutdown overhead associated with independent job execution. AWS Glue supports job bookmarking and flexible scheduling that enables data engineers to design consolidated job execution strategies that maximize resource efficiency.

- **Regional selection** considerations include the carbon intensity of available AWS regions. Different AWS regions utilize varying energy mixes, with some leveraging significantly higher percentages of renewable energy. For global organizations, considering carbon intensity alongside performance, compliance, and cost factors when selecting regions for data processing can significantly reduce overall environmental impact.

Sustainable data lifecycle management

Truly sustainable data engineering extends beyond infrastructure efficiency to address the fundamental question of what data should be stored and processed in the first place:

- **Data minimization** practices identify and eliminate unnecessary data collection and retention. By implementing more selective data collection strategies and stricter retention policies, organizations can significantly reduce their storage footprint and associated processing requirements. AWS services like S3 Object Lock and Lifecycle policies enable the implementation of defensible deletion strategies that balance business needs with sustainability goals.

- **Synthetic data utilization** for testing and development environments eliminates the need to maintain multiple copies of production datasets. AWS provides capabilities through services like AWS Glue DataBrew that enable the generation of realistic synthetic datasets that maintain statistical properties and relationships without duplicating the energy footprint of full production data. This approach is particularly valuable for large datasets where maintaining multiple copies would incur significant storage and energy costs.

- **Compression and format optimization** reduce both storage requirements and data transfer energy costs. Converting data from row-based formats like CSV and JSON to columnar formats like Parquet and ORC typically reduces storage requirements by 40-90% while also improving query performance. AWS Glue provides built-in transformation capabilities that make these optimizations straightforward to implement.

Implementation considerations

When implementing sustainable data engineering practices on AWS, several key considerations ensure successful adoption:

- **Measurement and baselining** establish the foundation for sustainability improvements. AWS Cost Explorer and AWS Cost and Usage Reports provide visibility into resource consumption patterns, while the AWS Customer Carbon Footprint Tool offers insights into the associated carbon emissions. Organizations should establish baseline measurements before implementing sustainability initiatives to quantify improvements and identify priority areas.

- **Incremental implementation** focuses efforts on the highest-impact components first. Rather than attempting to transform the entire data platform simultaneously, organizations should analyze their workloads to identify the components with the highest energy consumption or inefficiency. Typical starting points include:

  o Converting frequently accessed datasets to optimized formats.

  o Implementing tiered storage for large historical datasets.

  o Migrating batch processing to serverless and Graviton-based services.

  o Optimizing retention policies for low-value data.

- **Cross-functional collaboration** aligns sustainability initiatives with business requirements. Successful implementations require cooperation between data engineering teams, business stakeholders, and sustainability specialists to ensure that environmental improvements do not compromise critical business functionality. Establishing clear sustainability KPIs alongside traditional performance and reliability metrics helps maintain this balance.

- **Automated governance** enforces sustainable practices across the organization. AWS Config Rules, Service Control Policies, and custom Lambda-based automation can implement guardrails that prevent the creation of inefficient resources and enforce sustainability best practices without requiring manual intervention.

Future directions

Sustainable data engineering continues to evolve, with several promising developments on the horizon:

- **Automated carbon optimization** will eventually enable intelligent workload scheduling based on real-time carbon intensity data. As cloud providers expand their sustainability offerings, we can expect more sophisticated tools for carbon-aware computing that automatically shift flexible workloads to times and regions with lower emissions.

- **Energy-efficient algorithms** are emerging that deliver equivalent results with significantly lower computational requirements. Research in areas like approximate query processing, progressive analytics, and efficient machine learning training promises to reduce the energy footprint of data processing while maintaining result quality.

- **Circular hardware lifecycle** initiatives aim to reduce the embodied carbon in computing infrastructure. Cloud providers, including AWS, are implementing more sustainable hardware practices, from designing for repairability and longer service life to improving recycling and materials recovery. As these practices scale, they will further reduce the environmental impact of data operations.

By adopting sustainable data engineering practices today, organizations position themselves to benefit from these future advancements while immediately reducing costs, improving efficiency, and minimizing environmental impact. The most successful implementations recognize that sustainability is not a constraint but an opportunity to build more efficient, resilient, and future-proof data platforms.

Building resilient architectures

As data platforms increasingly become critical infrastructure supporting core business operations, resilience has evolved from a desirable attribute to an essential requirement. Resilient data architectures maintain operational capabilities and data integrity despite disruptions, which may range from transient service issues to regional outages or cyberattacks. While previous chapters explored operational practices like disaster recovery, this section focuses on architectural approaches that build resilience into the fundamental design of data platforms.

Resilience goes beyond basic availability to encompass adaptability, graceful degradation, and rapid recovery. Truly resilient architectures anticipate potential failure modes and incorporate design patterns that prevent, mitigate, or rapidly recover from disruptions. They balance defensive mechanisms with proactive capabilities, creating systems that not only withstand challenges but potentially emerge stronger from them.

Principles of resilient data architectures

Building resilient data architectures requires embracing several core principles that guide design decisions across all platform components:

- **Assume failure will occur** represents the foundational mindset shift in resilient design. Rather than treating failures as exceptional cases, resilient architectures assume that components will fail and design accordingly. This principle manifests in practices like designing for partial availability, implementing graceful degradation paths, and regularly testing failure scenarios to validate recovery mechanisms.

- **Eliminate single points of failure** requires identifying and addressing potential bottlenecks throughout the data pipeline. This principle extends beyond obvious infrastructure redundancy to encompass data sources, processing logic, and even operational knowledge. Truly resilient architectures distribute functionality to ensure that no single component failure can cause system-wide disruption.

- **Implement defense in depth** creates multiple layers of protection against different failure modes. Rather than relying on a single resilience mechanism, this approach combines complementary strategies like redundancy, isolation, and degradation paths to create comprehensive protection. By implementing multiple defensive layers, architectures can withstand the failure of individual protection mechanisms.

- **Design for recoverability** focuses on minimizing **mean time to recovery** (**MTTR**) rather than solely trying to prevent failures. This principle acknowledges that despite best efforts, disruptions will occur and optimizes for rapid restoration of service. Implementations include capabilities like automated rollback, state preservation, and incremental recovery that reduce downtime duration and impact.

- **Build observability** in enables rapid detection and diagnosis of resilience issues. Comprehensive observability goes beyond basic monitoring to provide insights into system behavior, component interactions, and failure modes. This principle emphasizes that resilience requires not just robust architecture but also the ability to understand system state during both normal operation and disruption.

Resilience patterns for data platforms

AWS provides several architectural patterns that implement resilience principles across different aspects of data platforms:

- **Resilient data ingestion**: Data ingestion represents the entry point for information flowing into data platforms, making its resilience particularly critical. Several patterns ensure continued data capture even during disruptions:

  - **Multi-endpoint ingestion** enables sources to route data to alternate ingestion points when primary endpoints experience issues. This pattern is particularly valuable for critical data streams where any loss is unacceptable. Implementation on AWS typically combines regional endpoints with routing logic:

```
1.  # Example: Multi-endpoint ingestion with fallback logic
2.  def route_data_to_kinesis(data_payload, region_endpoints):
3.      """Send data to primary endpoint with automatic fallback to secondar-
    ies"""
4.      for endpoint in region_endpoints:
5.          try:
6.              # Attempt to send data to current endpoint
7.              kinesis_client = boto3.client('kinesis', region_name=end-
    point['region'])
8.              response = kinesis_client.put_record(
9.                  StreamName=endpoint['stream_name'],
10.                 Data=json.dumps(data_payload),
11.                 PartitionKey=data_payload['id']
12.             )
13.             # If successful, return without trying additional endpoints
14.             logger.info(f"Successfully sent data to {endpoint['region']}")
15.             return response
16.         except Exception as e:
17.             logger.warning(f"Failed to send data to {endpoint['re-
    gion']}: {str(e)}")
18.             continue
19.
20.     # If we reach here, all endpoints failed
21.     raise Exception("Failed to send data to any available endpoint")
```

o **Buffer-based resiliency** incorporates local caching or queuing mechanisms that retain data when downstream systems are unavailable. AWS IoT Core, for example, provides device-side buffering options that preserve data during connectivity interruptions, while Amazon Kinesis Producer Library implements configurable buffering with retry logic. These capabilities ensure that transient disruptions do not result in permanent data loss.

o **Cross-regional data mirroring** continuously replicates ingested data across geographic boundaries, protecting against regional failures. This pattern typically leverages services like Kinesis Data Streams with enhanced fan-out consumers or MSK's mirroring capabilities to maintain synchronized copies of incoming data in multiple regions. The approach provides protection against both component failures and regional outages, though it requires careful consideration of consistency requirements and failure detection mechanisms.

- **Resilient processing architectures**: Data processing resilience ensures that transformation and analysis workflows continue functioning despite disruptions. Several patterns address different aspects of processing resilience:

o **Stateless processing with idempotency** enables fault-tolerant execution by allowing operations to be safely retried without side effects. This pattern is particularly valuable for serverless processing using Lambda and Step Functions, where execution may be interrupted or retried automatically. Implementing idempotent operations requires careful design:

  ▪ Using unique identifiers for each operation to detect and prevent duplicates.

  ▪ Implementing transactional updates that can be safely repeated.

  ▪ Designing state transitions that can be reapplied without causing inconsistency.

o **Checkpointing and resume** preserve processing progress, enabling workflows to restart from intermediate points rather than beginning again after disruption. AWS Glue job bookmarks provide built-in checkpointing for ETL workloads, while Step Functions enables the creation of workflow checkpoints that persist execution state. For streaming workloads, Kinesis Enhanced Fan-Out with persistent consumer applications enables checkpointing of stream positions to support resumable processing.

o **Parallel processing paths** distribute workloads across multiple execution streams, limiting the impact of individual processing failures. This pattern can be implemented using services like AWS Batch with multiple queues, EMR with instance fleets spanning availability zones, or Lambda functions invoked through SNS topic fanout. By dividing processing across independent paths, architectures can continue partial operation even when some components fail.

o **Circuit breaker pattern** prevents cascading failures by temporarily disabling problematic components. When implemented in data processing workflows, this pattern monitors error rates and response times for downstream dependencies, automatically disabling calls to degraded components to prevent wider system impact. AWS Step Functions supports implementing circuit breakers through state machine design patterns that include fallback paths and retry limits.

- **Resilient storage strategies**: Storage resilience ensures data remains available and intact despite infrastructure failures or corruption issues. Several patterns provide protection for different storage scenarios:

o **Multi-modal persistence** stores critical data in complementary storage systems with different failure characteristics. For example, maintaining transactional data in both Amazon RDS (optimized for consistency and queries) and S3 (optimized for durability and scale) provides protection against service-specific issues while enabling different access patterns. This pattern requires careful consideration of synchronization mechanisms and potential consistency issues but provides substantial resilience benefits for critical datasets.

o **Immutable data layers** prevent corruption by implementing append-only storage models where existing data is never modified. AWS services like S3 with versioning enabled, Amazon **Quantum Ledger Database (QLDB)**, and transactional data lakes implemented with frameworks like Delta Lake or Apache Hudi support immutable storage patterns. These approaches not only enhance resilience against data corruption but also simplify recovery processes since previous consistent states remain accessible.

o **Point-in-time recovery** enables restoration to specific moments before corruption or deletion occurred. Most AWS database services, including RDS, DynamoDB, and DocumentDB, support point-in-time recovery through automated backups, while S3 provides similar capabilities through versioning and replication. For maximum resilience, these capabilities should be configured with retention periods aligned to business recovery requirements and tested regularly to validate restoration procedures.

- **Resilient access patterns**: Access resilience ensures that data consumers can continue operations during disruptions to query layers or analytical systems. Several patterns support continuous data access:

o **Read replicas with automated promotion** provide continued access when primary database instances fail. Amazon RDS and Aurora support automated failover to replicas, while Aurora Global Database enables cross-regional failover for wider-scale resilience. The most robust implementations combine automated promotion with client-side awareness through mechanisms like the Amazon RDS Proxy to minimize disruption during failover events.

o **Query federation** enables workloads to access data across multiple storage systems, providing alternative access paths when primary systems are unavailable. Amazon Athena's federated query capabilities allow queries to span S3, RDS, and other data sources, while Redshift Spectrum enables integrated access to data lake content. By implementing federated access patterns, architectures can maintain analytical capabilities even when some data stores experience disruption.

o **Client-Side Caching** maintains local copies of frequently accessed data, reducing dependency on continuous access to central data stores. Amazon ElastiCache and **DynamoDB Accelerator (DAX)** provide managed caching capabilities, while application-level caching can be implemented using services like AWS AppSync for GraphQL APIs with offline capabilities. These approaches not only enhance resilience but also often improve performance and reduce costs by decreasing load on primary data systems.

o **Multi-region access points** provide geographically distributed entry points to data platforms. S3 Multi-Region Access Points automatically route requests to the nearest available region containing the requested data, while Global Accelerator provides similar capabilities for custom endpoints. These services maintain continuous access even during regional disruptions while optimizing performance by minimizing latency.

Implementation approach

Building resilient data architectures requires a systematic approach that addresses different failure modes at appropriate architectural layers:

* **Resilience mapping**: The first step in building resilient architectures is mapping potential failure scenarios to architectural components. This process identifies resilience requirements and prioritizes implementation efforts. Refer to the following table:

Failure scenario	Impact level	Affected components	Resilience patterns
Single **availability zone (AZ)** outage	Medium	Zone-specific resources Single-zone deployments	Multi-AZ deployments Auto-scaling groups Cross-zone load balancing
Regional service disruption	High	Regional services Regional deployments	Multi-region replication Cross-region routing Service-specific resilience
Regional outage	Critical	All regional components Regional data stores	Multi-region active-active Global data replication Regional isolation
Data corruption	Critical	Databases Data lakes Metadata stores	Immutable storage Versioning Point-in-time recovery
Dependency failure	Medium	Interconnected services External integrations	Circuit breakers Fallback capabilities Graceful degradation
Capacity limitations	Medium	Processing components Storage systems	Auto-scaling Throttling Load shedding

Table 15.3: Failure scenarios and corresponding resilience patterns

For each identified scenario, architects should define acceptable RPO/RTO and design appropriate resilience mechanisms. This mapping process should be collaborative, involving both technical teams and business stakeholders to ensure alignment between resilience investments and business priorities.

- **Layered implementation**: Resilience implementation should follow a layered approach that builds protection from the foundation upward:

  o **Infrastructure resilience** forms the base layer, addressing physical and virtual resource availability. At this layer, implementations focus on redundancy across zones and regions, automated recovery mechanisms, and capacity management. For AWS data platforms, this typically includes:

    ▪ Multi-AZ deployments for services like RDS, Redshift, and ElastiCache.

    ▪ Auto-scaling groups for EC2-based components with cross-AZ distribution.

    ▪ S3 cross-region replication for critical data assets.

    ▪ Reserved capacity for essential workloads to protect against resource contention.

  o **Data resilience** builds on infrastructure protection to ensure information remains available and intact. This layer addresses data durability, consistency, and accessibility through patterns like:

    ▪ Multi-region data replication with appropriate consistency models.

    ▪ Immutable storage with versioning and point-in-time recovery.

    ▪ Backup strategies aligned with recovery objectives.

    ▪ Verification mechanisms that detect and address corruption.

  o **Application resilience** focuses on ensuring that data processing and access components continue functioning despite disruptions. This layer implements patterns like:

    ▪ Circuit breakers and bulkheads that prevent cascading failures.

    ▪ Retry mechanisms with exponential backoff and jitter.

    ▪ Graceful degradation paths that maintain core functionality.

    ▪ Stateless designs that enable flexible scaling and recovery.

  o **Operational resilience** represents the final layer, ensuring that monitoring, management, and response capabilities themselves are resilient. This includes:

    ▪ Multi-region monitoring with independent alerting paths.

    ▪ Automated remediation for common failure scenarios.

    ▪ Comprehensive playbooks for managing complex disruptions.

    ▪ Regular testing through chaos engineering and disaster recovery exercises.

- **Progressive implementation**: Most organizations implement resilience progressively, starting with critical components and expanding coverage as capabilities mature:

  o **Essential resilience** focuses on preventing catastrophic failure through basic redundancy and recovery mechanisms. This stage typically addresses single points of failure, implements fundamental backup strategies, and establishes basic monitoring.

  o **Enhanced resilience** expands protection to address more sophisticated failure scenarios and reduce recovery times. This stage implements patterns like circuit breakers, immutable storage, and regional replication for critical components.

o **Comprehensive resilience** extends protection across the entire data platform with integrated mechanisms that address multiple failure modes. This stage implements advanced patterns like active-active deployments, automated remediation, and chaos engineering practices.

Each stage should deliver meaningful resilience improvements while building toward a comprehensive architecture that addresses the full spectrum of potential disruptions.

Real-world examples

Several organizations have successfully implemented resilient data architectures on AWS that demonstrate these principles in action:

- **Financial services**: A global payment processor implemented a resilient transaction analytics platform that maintained continuous operation despite multiple disruption types. Their architecture combined active-active processing across three AWS regions with synchronized data replication and intelligent routing. When one region experienced a significant service disruption, the platform automatically redirected processing to the remaining regions while maintaining data consistency and reporting capabilities. The architecture successfully processed over two million transactions per minute with zero data loss during the disruption.

- **Healthcare**: A healthcare analytics provider built a resilient data platform that protected sensitive patient information while ensuring continuous availability for critical care applications. Their implementation used a combination of multi-region replication, immutable storage patterns, and federated access mechanisms. When a configuration error corrupted a portion of their primary database, the architecture automatically failed over to replicas while maintaining application functionality. Simultaneously, their immutable data lake enabled rapid recovery of the corrupted information, resulting in minimal impact to healthcare providers.

- **Retail**: An e-commerce company implemented a resilient customer data platform that supported peak sales events despite infrastructure challenges. Their architecture used a layered approach combining infrastructure redundancy, data replication, and application-level resilience patterns. During their largest sales event, when demand exceeded capacity in their primary region, the platform automatically balanced processing across regions while maintaining data consistency. The resilient design enabled them to process 5x normal transaction volumes despite partial infrastructure limitations.

Beyond technical resilience

Truly resilient architectures extend beyond technical mechanisms to encompass broader organizational capabilities:

- **Documentation and knowledge sharing** prevent single points of failure in operational knowledge. Comprehensive documentation, cross-training, and collaborative practices ensure that multiple team members understand system architecture and recovery procedures. AWS services like systems manager can maintain secure, accessible documentation for operational procedures.

- **Continuous resilience testing** validates that protection mechanisms function as expected. Regular testing through activities like chaos engineering experiments, failover drills, and recovery exercises builds confidence in resilience capabilities while identifying improvement opportunities. AWS Fault Injection simulator enables controlled testing of resilience mechanisms through managed fault injection.

- **Feedback loops and continuous improvement** transform incidents into resilience enhancements. Post-incident reviews, near-miss analysis, and proactive resilience assessments identify opportunities to strengthen architectures before major disruptions occur. Implementing structured processes for capturing and addressing resilience gaps creates architectures that continuously evolve to address emerging threats.

By implementing these architectural patterns and organizational practices, data engineering teams can build platforms that not only withstand disruption but potentially emerge stronger from challenges. Resilient architectures protect critical data assets, maintain business continuity, and provide competitive advantages in increasingly uncertain operating environments.

Conclusion

In our exploration of future-proofing data platforms, we have examined the transformative forces reshaping data engineering, from serverless architectures that eliminate operational overhead to AI-driven capabilities that enhance productivity and intelligence, sustainable practices that reduce environmental impact, and resilient designs that withstand disruption. These innovations represent more than incremental improvements; they fundamentally redefine how organizations approach data infrastructure and operations. As we conclude this journey through modern data engineering on AWS, successful organizations will be those that embrace adaptability as a core principle, building platforms designed not just for today's requirements but for tomorrow's possibilities. The most effective data architects recognize that futureproofing is not about predicting specific technologies but about creating flexible foundations that can evolve continuously, balancing innovation with stability, automation with control, and performance with sustainability. By implementing the architectural patterns, implementation approaches, and operational practices described throughout this book, you are now equipped to build data platforms that deliver immediate value while positioning your organization to capitalize on emerging opportunities in an increasingly data-driven world. As data continues to grow in both volume and strategic importance, your ability to architect scalable, resilient, and adaptable data platforms on AWS will become an increasingly vital competitive advantage, one that transforms data from a technical challenge into a powerful catalyst for business transformation.

Join our Discord space

Join our Discord workspace for latest updates, offers, tech happenings around the world, new releases, and sessions with the authors:

https://discord.bpbonline.com

APPENDIX: Performance Tuning Guide

Overview

This guide provides practical approaches for identifying and resolving performance issues across AWS data platform components. Rather than attempting to optimize every aspect of a data platform simultaneously, this appendix focuses on high-impact areas that typically deliver the greatest performance improvements with reasonable effort.

Optimization methodology

Effective performance tuning follows a structured approach rather than implementing random optimizations:

- **Establish baseline metrics**: Measure current performance using relevant metrics for your workload.

- **Identify bottlenecks**: Determine which components are limiting overall performance.

- **Implement targeted changes**: Apply specific optimizations to address identified bottlenecks.

- **Measure impact**: Quantify performance improvements against the baseline.

- **Iterate**: Continue the process, focusing on the next most significant bottleneck.

This methodology ensures that optimization efforts deliver meaningful improvements rather than simply shifting bottlenecks between components.

Performance optimization checklists

The following checklists address common performance issues across major components of AWS data platforms:

- **S3 data lake performance**: Optimizing S3 data lake performance requires attention to access patterns, data formats, and partitioning strategies. The following optimizations can significantly improve query performance and reduce costs:

Area	Optimization technique	Impact level
Access patterns	• Distribute objects across prefixes • Use partitioning aligned with query patterns • Implement a year/month/day hierarchy for time-series data	High
Data format	• Use Parquet for analytics workloads • Implement compression (Snappy/ZSTD) • Configure optimal file sizes (100 MB to 1 GB)	High
Partitioning	• Avoid over-partitioning (<100K partitions) • Partition on high-cardinality fields • Align with common query filters	Medium-High
Request rate	• Use random prefixes for high-throughput uploads • Implement multi-part uploads • Consider S3 Transfer Acceleration	Medium
Metadata operations	• Use manifest files • Maintain external metadata catalogs • Implement caching for repeated operations	Medium

Table Appendix 1.1: S3 Data lake performance optimization techniques

- **AWS Glue ETL optimization**: AWS Glue job performance depends heavily on proper configuration and data distribution strategies. These optimizations address the most common bottlenecks in ETL processing:

Area	Optimization technique	Impact level
Job configuration	• Start with ten DPUs and scale based on volume • Use G.1X/G.2X workers for memory-intensive jobs	High
Data distribution	• Implement repartitioning for skewed data • Match partition count to available executors	High
Memory management	• Increase driver/executor memory for large datasets • Use broadcast joins for small tables	Medium-High
Job design	• Enable job bookmarks for incremental processing • Use pushdown predicates	Medium
File operations	• Combine small files before processing • Group output files efficiently	Medium

Table Appendix 1.2: AWS Glue ETL performance optimization guide

- **Redshift query performance**: Amazon Redshift performance optimization focuses on table design, sort keys, and query patterns. Implementing these techniques can dramatically improve analytical query response times:

Area	Optimization technique	Impact level
Table design	• Use EVEN distribution for isolated tables • KEY distribution on join columns • ALL distribution for dimensions	High
Sort keys	• Use compound sort keys for AND filters • Interleaved sort keys for varied patterns • Sort on frequent filters	High
Query patterns	• Avoid SELECT * • Remove unnecessary DISTINCT • Use UNLOAD for large result sets	Medium-High
Maintenance	• Schedule VACUUM after bulk loads • Implement automatic table optimization	Medium
Workload management	• Separate ETL and analytical workloads • Set appropriate concurrency limits	Medium

Table Appendix 1.3: *Redshift query performance optimization best practices*

- **Lambda Function performance**: AWS Lambda performance optimization balances memory allocation, cold start mitigation, and code efficiency. These techniques ensure optimal function execution and cost management:

Area	Optimization technique	Impact level
Memory allocation	• Start with 1024MB and test increments • Consider CPU vs memory-bound operations	High
Cold starts	• Use provisioned concurrency for latency-sensitive functions • Minimize package size	Medium to high
Code efficiency	• Move initialization outside the handler • Implement connection pooling	Medium
Dependencies	• Remove unnecessary libraries • Use Lambda layers for common dependencies	Medium
Execution environment	• Use Node.js/Python for the fastest startup • Deploy on ARM64 architecture	Low-medium

Table Appendix 1.4: *Lambda function performance optimization configuration guide*

- **Kinesis Data Streams performance**: Kinesis Data Streams performance optimization centers on shard management and partition key design. Proper configuration ensures high throughput and low-latency data streaming:

Area	Optimization technique	Impact level
Shard count	• Plan 1MB/sec input or 2MB/sec output per shard • Use on-demand mode for variable loads	High
Partition keys	• Use high-cardinality keys • Implement strategies to avoid hot partitions	High

Area	Optimization technique	Impact level
Batch operations	• Use PutRecords for batches • Optimize batch size (up to 500 records/5MB)	Medium to high
Consumer design	• Implement enhanced fan-out for high throughput • Use parallel processing	Medium
Record size	• Keep records under 1 MB • Compress large payloads	Medium

Table Appendix 1.5: KDS performance optimization strategies

Common performance problems

Data platform performance issues often follow predictable patterns with established solutions. This reference guide helps identify symptoms and implement appropriate remediation strategies:

Problem	Key symptoms	Primary solutions	Impact
Data skew	Tasks timing out, stuck at high completion %	Explicit repartitioning, salting techniques	High
Memory pressure	OOM errors, excessive GC time	Increase executor memory, disk spill configs	High
Slow queries	Minutes vs seconds, full table scans	Optimize keys, update statistics, and use EXPLAIN	High
S3 latency	High latency, slow LIST operations	Use manifest files, implement partitioning	Medium to high
Lambda inefficiency	Timeouts, high costs, cold starts	Reuse connections, parallel processing	Medium to high
Kinesis bottlenecks	High iterator age, throttling	Increase shards, improve partition keys	Medium to high
Glue slowness	Excessive shuffles, stage failures	Optimize joins and partition data correctly	Medium
Redshift concurrency	Queue waits, timeouts	Configure WLM, use query priority	Medium

Table Appendix 1.6: Common data platform performance issues solutions

Troubleshooting guidelines

When addressing performance issues in AWS data platforms, follow these structured troubleshooting approaches:

- **Diagnostic process**:
  - **Gather performance data**: Collect CloudWatch metrics and logs for relevant services.
  - **Isolate the bottleneck**: Determine if issues are CPU, memory, I/O, or network bound.
  - **Test incremental changes**: Implement one change at a time and measure impact.
  - **Validate root cause**: Confirm that changes address the actual problem.
- **Service-specific diagnostic tools**: Effective troubleshooting requires the right diagnostic tools and metrics for each AWS service. These tools provide the visibility needed to identify and resolve performance bottlenecks:

AWS service	Diagnostic tools	Key metrics to monitor
S3	• S3 Storage Lens • CloudWatch request metrics	• 4xx/5xx error rates • First byte latency
Glue	• Spark UI • CloudWatch metrics	• ExecutorAllocationManager metrics • Job duration
Redshift	• Query monitoring • System tables (SVL/SVV/STV)	• Query execution time • Disk-based operations
Lambda	• Lambda insights • X-ray tracing	• Duration • Memory usage
Kinesis	• Enhanced monitoring • CloudWatch metrics	• getrecords latency • iterator age

Table Appendix 1.7: AWS data services diagnostic tools reference

Performance testing approach

Effective performance optimization requires a structured testing methodology:

1. **Develop realistic test scenarios**: Use representative data volumes and patterns.

2. **Establish clear success criteria**: Define specific performance targets.

3. **Implement controlled testing**: Isolate test environments and ensure consistency.

4. **Document findings and patterns**: Record optimization results and create guidelines.

By following these systematic approaches to performance optimization, data engineering teams can deliver substantial improvements to data platform efficiency, reducing costs while enhancing user experience and analytical capabilities.

Join our Discord space

Join our Discord workspace for latest updates, offers, tech happenings around the world, new releases, and sessions with the authors:

https://discord.bpbonline.com

Index

www.ingramcontent.com/pod-product-compliance
Lightning Source LLC
Chambersburg PA
CBHW061741210326

41599CB00034B/6751